F. SCOTT FITZGERALD
A to Z

F. SCOTT FITZGERALD
A to Z

The Essential Reference to
His Life and Work

Mary Jo Tate
With a Foreword by Matthew J. Bruccoli

Facts On File, Inc.

For Forrest, Andrew, and Perry

F. Scott Fitzgerald A to Z: The Essential Reference to His Life and Work

Copyright ©1998 by Mary Jo Tate

Facts On File, Inc.
11 Penn Plaza
New York NY 10001

Library of Congress Cataloging-in-Publication Data

Tate Mary Jo.
 F. Scott Fitzgerald A to Z / Mary Jo Tate.
 p. cm.
 Includes bibliographical references and index.
 ISBN 0-8160-3150-9 (alk. paper)
 1. Fitzgerald, F. Scott (Francis Scott), 1896–1940—Encyclopedias.
2. Authors, American—20th century—Biography—Encyclopedias.
I. Title
PS3511.I9Z873 1997 97–11321
831'.52—dc21

Cover design by Nora Wertz

Printed in the United States of America

VB VCS 10 9 8 7 6 5 4 3 2 1

This book is printed on acid-free paper.

CONTENTS

FOREWORD

I wish that I had written this volume, but I could not have done it better than Mary Jo Tate. It is the essential reference tool for all categories of F. Scott Fitzgerald readers: for the celebrated common reader, students, and teachers. Moreover, it is a readable reference book. Serious Fitzgerald readers will make their own connections by going from entry to entry. *Fitzgerald A to Z* replaces shelves of books.

This volume provides a reassuring reminder of the staying power of great writing. At the time of Fitzgerald's death in 1940 the anticipation of anything like *Fitzgerald A to Z* would have seemed a fantasy. The newspaper obituaries were mainly condescending. Tributes by his friends and fellow writers expressed regret that Fitzgerald had been prevented from fulfilling his genius: from writing as much or as well as he could have—should have—written. But no one publicly predicted a Fitzgerald revival, except Stephen Vincent Benét in his review of *The Last Tycoon*: "This is not a legend, this is a reputation—and seen in perspective, it may well be one of the most secure reputations of our time." This prediction was regarded as hyperbolic in 1941, and Benét was given credit for generosity toward an unfortunate writer. In 1945 the Fitzgerald revival was under way; in the fifties it resembled a resurrection; and in the sixties Fitzgerald achieved his stated ambition to "be one of the greatest writers who ever lived." Unlike many literary revivals, the posthumous Fitzgerald comeback that raised him to a stature he had not achieved during his writing life was not rigged by critics and professors. Fitzgerald's restoration was mainly reader-generated. The readers who read for pleasure were ahead of the professional reputation-makers. Nor is it the case that Charles Scribner's Sons stimulated the revival in order to sell books. Scribners reprinted Fitzgerald in cloth to meet the demand, but the firm had no paperback line and did not make *The Great Gatsby* available in a student edition until 1957. But Scribners did own a piece of Bantam, which reprinted *The Great Gatsby* in 1945. People read Fitzgerald because the people they knew were reading Fitzgerald. People kept reading Fitzgerald because they were excited by what they read. Some new readers who discovered Fitzgerald after World War II were writers or apprentice writers who have acknowledged the impact of their first encounters with his prose.

A concomitant of the rediscovery of Fitzgerald's writings was the growth of interest in the author. He became an American literary culture hero. The attention to Fitzgerald's life is inevitable. Admiration of a masterpiece triggers curiosity about the masterpiece-maker—especially when the author had a romantic or dramatic life embracing triumph and disaster. A reader who knows nothing about Fitzgerald can achieve a rewarding reading of *Gatsby* or *Tender Is the Night*, but knowledge of the connections between his life and work enriches the reader's understanding of Fitzgerald's transmuted autobiography. Unhappily, literary history tends to degenerate into literary gossip, and biography becomes slander. The belittling anecdotes about Fitzgerald—founded or unfounded—have interfered with the proper assessment of his work. Nothing else about a writer matters as much as his words.

By the end of 1996 there were more than 60 books about Fitzgerald, including collections of articles. Only fully committed specialists are familiar with most of these volumes, and only the largest research libraries hold all of them. Serious readers outside of the academic groves require a Fitzgerald vade mecum to provide the facts and details. Indeed *Fitzgerald A to Z* qualifies as a trade reference book: a work that serious Fitzgerald readers will read—not just refer to—as preparation for a lifetime relationship. This is the way to establish that commitment: read everything he wrote. *Everything* means *everything*. Some of it is uneven; but it is all Fitzgerald, and it all connects. Then reread his best works—if necessary with the help of other books to understand the data that Fitzgerald built into his fiction. All great fiction is great social history. Soon there will be proper annotated editions of Fitzgerald's writings. During his lifetime Fitzgerald's books were published in flawed texts. The serious reader will obtain the corrected or critical editions to read what Fitzgerald expected to

have published. (See the entry here for EDITING FITZGERALD'S TEXTS.)

Everything Fitzgerald wrote was personal because, as he stated, he took things hard. Fitzgerald's letters constitute a superbly readable introduction to his character, mind, and art. The most useful reference material for Fitzgerald was assembled and miraculously preserved by him. Much of the data in this reference work draws on his activities as a self-historiographer. There is nothing like his *Ledger* (published in facsimile, 1973) for any other American author. Combining autobiography, bibliography, and accounting, it establishes the record of his career as a literary artist and a professional writer. Fitzgerald's *Notebooks*—first excerpted in *The Crack-Up* (1945) and then published in full (1978)—document his working habits and the quality of his literary intelligence.

One area of Fitzgerald's career that has received exaggerated attention is his Hollywood work, a stint of three and one-half years. For a long time the distorted impression prevailed of Fitzgerald as ruined victim of Hollywood. Many critics approach Hollywood with the presuppositional bias that it was the graveyard of American literary talent. The writers who were destroyed by Hollywood embraced destruction along with their paychecks. Metro-Goldwyn-Mayer was very good to Fitzgerald during his 18 months on the payroll. Moreover, he was an undistinguished screenwriter; his unproduced screenplay for "Babylon Revisited," the only one of his works that he adapted, is disappointing. Fitzgerald was a storyteller whose style, voice, and narrative technique were developed for print; these did not translate to the silver screen—which is why all the movies made from his books have been unsatisfactory. The morbid interest in Fitzgerald's work for the studios has resulted in the overrating of the Pat Hobby stories. Ultimately, the chief importance of the Hollywood years is that they provided material for *The Love of the Last Tycoon: A Western,* the great American Hollywood novel.

While his Hollywood exile was being overexposed, Fitzgerald's short stories were neglected or disparaged until the seventies. During the fifties and sixties the notion persisted that, apart from a few brilliant stories and novellas, most of the 160 magazine contributions were hackwork and that it was a kindness to ignore them. Consequently, his "commercial" stories were denied a proper appraisal or reappraisal because they were not readily available. Malcolm Cowley's excellent one-volume story selection, the only omnibus available from 1951 to 1989,

included only 28 stories. The publication of *Afternoon of an Author* (1957), *Bits of Paradise* (1973), and *The Price Was High* (1979) facilitated a reassessment of the buried stories and an understanding of the creative relationship between Fitzgerald's magazine work and his novels. The profession-of-authorship approach to literary history provides a corrective to noncombatant misapprehensions about Fitzgerald's alleged hackery. Professional writers write for money. Money makes it possible for them to keep writing. Even if they don't need the money because of other incomes, the money earned from writing is a way of keeping score. The critics and scholars who denounced Fitzgerald's *Saturday Evening Post* bondage never had to live from story to story. Even his less-than-brilliant stories bear his brand.

Detractors who dismissed Fitzgerald and his characters for their materialism and triviality were unable to comprehend that serious writers write about the things they want to write about and have to write about. If the writer is good enough, then the "forlorn Laplander" is made to "*feel* the importance of a visit to Cartier's!" Literature—fiction—is not required to teach readers how to solve their own problems or world problems. Nor is it mandatory that it express noble sentiments or denounce injustice. It is enough that literature provide pleasure—the pleasure of the words and the pleasure of recognizing that the writer got it right. Like all great writers, Fitzgerald wrote like nobody else. He answered the profundity-seekers and the burden-of-guilt types for keeps in his 1934 introduction to *Gatsby*:

> Reading it over one can see how it could have been improved—yet without feeling guilty of any discrepancy from the truth, as far as I saw it; truth or rather the *equivalent* of the truth, the attempt at honesty of imagination. I had just re-read Conrad's preface to *The Nigger*, and I had recently been kidded half haywire by critics who felt that my material was such as to preclude all dealing with mature persons in a mature world. But, my God! it was my material, and it was all I had to deal with.

Since this introduction has became a personal statement, I will use it to acknowledge the benefactions of Fitzgerald's daughter, Scottie, who kept his papers together and gave them to Princeton University. She was endlessly generous to students, scholars, and buffs. I was the chief beneficiary of her bounty during the 16 years we worked on "Daddy projects."

Matthew J. Bruccoli
August 21, 1996

ACKNOWLEDGMENTS

My principal debt is to Matthew J. Bruccoli, who helped plan this volume, vetted the typescript, and aided me throughout the process of writing and revision; he also contributed several entries. Judith S. Baughman read the typescript, responded to endless queries, and provided crucial assistance throughout the project. Dr. Bruccoli and Mrs. Baughman also supplied illustrations and captions.

Thanks are due to the following people who contributed entries to this volume: George P. Anderson, Tracy Simmons Bitonti, Park Bucker, Marvin J. La-Hood, Roger Lathbury, Catherine Lewis, Alan Margolies, and Don C. Skemer. In addition to signed entries, Park Bucker provided all unsigned brief entries about illustrators.

I am also indebted to Robert W. Trogdon, Robert Moss, Ian Olney, and Park Bucker of the University of South Carolina for research assistance; Nancy Anderson (Auburn University at Montgomery); Joseph M. Bruccoli (photography; Columbia, S.C.); John Delaney (Princeton University Library); Harry M. Drake (volunteer archivist for St. Paul Academy and Summit School); Scott Marsh (Archival Assistant of the Alan Mason Chesney Medical Archives of the Johns Hopkins Medical Institutions); Michelle Martin (Assistant to the City Manager, Rockville, Md.); Patrick D. McQuillan (St. Paul, Minn.); Dana J. Pratt (Publishing Consultant, Bethesda, Md.); Walt Reed (Illustration House, Inc., N.Y.); Rick Ryan (Biographical Research Aide, Alumni Records Office, Princeton University Library); Paul D. Schulz (Thomas Cooper Library, University of South Carolina); and Don C. Skemer (Princeton University Library).

I could not have written this book without the encouragement and assistance of my husband Stephen. I am grateful to my parents, Jim and Rosemary Alinder, for their support in ways too numerous to mention. My children, Forrest, Andrew, and Perry, provided comic relief; and Kathy Formsma helped make this book possible by taking care of them while I was writing.

CAPITALS, except in the case of Fitzgerald himself and titles of his works.

The following abbreviations and short titles are used:

AOAA	*Afternoon of an Author*
Apprentice Fiction	*The Apprentice Fiction of F. Scott Fitzgerald*
As Ever	*As Ever, Scott Fitz—*
ASYM	*All the Sad Young Men*
B&D	*The Beautiful and Damned*
B&J	*The Basil and Josephine Stories*
Bits	*Bits of Paradise*
Correspondence	*The Correspondence of F. Scott Fitzgerald*
CU	*The Crack-Up*
F&P	*Flappers and Philosophers*
FSF	F. Scott Fitzgerald
GG	*The Great Gatsby*
In His Own Time	*F. Scott Fitzgerald In His Own Time*
Ledger	*F. Scott Fitzgerald's Ledger*
Letters	*The Letters of F. Scott Fitzgerald*
Life in Letters	*F. Scott Fitzgerald: A Life in Letters*
LOLT	*The Love of the Last Tycoon: A Western*
LT	*The Last Tycoon*
PH	*The Pat Hobby Stories*
Price	*The Price Was High*
St. Paul Plays	*F. Scott Fitzgerald's St. Paul Plays*
Scott/Max	*Dear Scott/Dear Max*
TAR	*Taps at Reveille*
TJA	*Tales of the Jazz Age*
TITN	*Tender Is the Night*
TSOP	*This Side of Paradise*
ZF	Zelda Fitzgerald

the Abbot Character in "In the Darkest Hour" and "The Kingdom in the Dark." In "In the Darkest Hour," he resists PHILIPPE's urging to fight against the Viking invaders. In "The Kingdom in the Dark" he argues with Philippe over the boundaries between their properties, claiming that the wine slopes and forest land have belonged to the monastery for 20 years.

Abbot, Charley Character in "Diamond Dick and the First Law of Woman." Injured war hero who for five years forgets his marriage to Diana DICKEY.

Abbot, Hamilton (Ham) Character in "The Love Boat." One of three young Harvard graduates who board a boat where a high-school dance is being held. He dates Mae PURLEY for a year after she breaks up with Bill FROTHINGTON.

Abby Character in "The Intimate Strangers." Friend to whom SARA reveals her concern about her second husband KILLIAN's unexplained absences.

Abercrombie Character in "Two for a Cent." Wealthy and successful man who visits his Southern hometown to see if his roots hold any significance for him. He decides that they do not and resents that he did not realize that the town was "worthless" when he was younger.

Abercrombie, Bill Character in "The Dance." Sheriff whose gun Catherine JONES used to murder Marie BANNERMAN.

Abrams, Mrs. Character in *TITN*. Woman on the beach who recognizes Rosemary HOYT as an actress. She is later part of Mary [NORTH] Minghetti's entourage on the RIVIERA.

"Absolution" Fiction. Written June 1923. *The AMERICAN MERCURY*, 2 (June 1924), 141–149; *ASYM*. Young Rudolph MILLER tells a lie in confession and is afraid to take communion. His father forces him to go to confession again, where he chooses not to confess the previous day's lie. He visits Father Adolphus SCHWARTZ to unburden himself; and, though he is frightened by the deranged priest's ravings, he senses a confirmation of his conviction that "there was something ineffably gorgeous somewhere that had nothing to do with God" (p. 131).

An event from Fitzgerald's youth provided the source for this story; he noted in his *Ledger* for September 1907: "He went to Confession about this time and lied by saying in a a shocked voice to the priest 'Oh no, I never tell a lie' " (p. 162).

There has been much speculation on the relationship between "Absolution" and *GG*. Fitzgerald described "Absolution" to Maxwell PERKINS as having been planned as the "prologue of the novel" (June 18, 1924; *Life in Letters*, p. 76; *Scott/Max*, p. 72); and he stated that it was intended to be "a picture of his [Gatsby's] early life" but that he cut it "to preserve the sense of mystery" (to John Jamieson, April 15, 1934; *Letters*, p. 509). Although these statements seem to support the general assumption that Rudolph Miller is young Jimmy Gatz (Jay GATSBY), it is not clear that they are the same character from the same work of fiction. Fitzgerald's 1922 plan for the novel that became *GG* included a "catholic element" that is absent from the published novel though central to the short story (c. June 20, 1922; *Life in Letters*, p. 60; *Scott/Max*, p. 61); and the story may have been salvaged from a version of the novel which Fitzgerald discarded before approaching it from "a new angle," by which he meant a new plot (c. April 10, 1924; *Life in Letters*, p. 67; *Scott/Max*, p. 69). It is safest to regard Rudolph Miller as an early treatment of the character who became Jay Gatsby, with whom he shares a romantic disposition.

"The Adjuster" Fiction. Written December 1924. *REDBOOK*, 45 (September 1925), 47–51, 144–148; *ASYM*. Luella HEMPLE tells her friend Ede KARR that she is bored with her baby and that she believes she and her husband are drifting toward divorce. That night Charles HEMPLE brings home Doctor MOON to talk with his wife. While Moon is informing Luella that trying to live her kind of life has been too great a strain for her husband, Charles suffers a nervous collapse; and Luella is forced to assume new responsibilities around the household. Some time later their baby dies, and after the baby's funeral Doctor Moon informs Luella

that Charles is nearly well. She sees this as an opportunity to escape to a new life, but Moon compels her to stay with her husband. The Hemples resume a normal life together and have two more children. Doctor Moon informs Luella that she has grown up and no longer needs him, and that she must be responsible for making her home happy.

"The Adolescent Marriage" Fiction. Written December 1925. *The SATURDAY EVENING POST*, 198 (March 6, 1926), 6–7, 229–230, 233–234; *The Price Was High*. George WHARTON asks Chauncey GARNETT to help with his daughter, Lucy CLARK, who ran away to marry Garnett's employee Llewellyn CLARK but left him after a month. After talking with both Lucy and Llewellyn, who refuse to be reconciled, Garnett tells the Whartons that he has arranged an annulment for the couple. Garnett urges Llewellyn Clark to enter an architectural competition, and Clark's plan for a suburban bungalow wins the prize. Garnett tells Clark that Lucy plans to marry a man named George Hemmick; but after Clark's bungalow is built, he realizes that he still loves Lucy and that he had designed the house with her in mind. Garnett brings Lucy, who is pregnant, to Clark and reveals that he had never gotten the annulment.

"Afternoon of an Author" Autobiographical essay. *ESQUIRE*, 6 (August 1936), 35, 170; *AOAA*. Description of a tired and lonely author trying to come up with an idea for a story. When the author notices a high-school girl and boy with their attention fixed on each other, he is moved by their isolation: "he knew he would get something out of it professionally, if only in contrast to the growing seclusion of his life and the increasing necessity of picking over an already well-picked past" (*AOAA*, p. 182). Fitzgerald was undecided as to whether to classify this piece as nonfiction or a story.

Afternoon of an Author: A Selection of Uncollected Stories and Essays With introduction and notes by Arthur MIZENER. Princeton, N.J.: Princeton University Library, 1957; New York: SCRIBNERS, 1958; London: Bodley Head, 1958. Contents: "A Night at the Fair," "Forging Ahead," "Basil and Cleopatra," "Princeton," "Who's Who—and Why," "How to Live on $36,000 a Year," "How to Live on Practically Nothing a Year," "How to Waste Material," "Ten Years in the Advertising Business," "One Hundred False Starts," "Outside the Cabinet-Maker's," "One Trip Abroad," " 'I Didn't Get Over,' " "Afternoon of an Author," "Author's House," "Design in Plaster," "Boil Some Water—Lots of It," "Teamed with Genius," "No Harm Trying," "News of Paris—Fifteen Years Ago."

Agents *See* Phil BERG, Leland HAYWARD, Harold OBER, Paul Revere REYNOLDS, H. N. SWANSON.

Agge, Prince Character in *LT/LOLT*. Danish prince who visits the movie studio. Based on a combination of Prince Aage of Denmark (d. 1940) and Count Sigvard Bernadotte of Sweden (b. 1907). See Gabrielle Winkel, "Fitzgerald's Agge of Denmark," *Fitzgerald/Hemingway Annual* (1975), pp. 131–132.

Ahearn, Clarence Character in "The Cut-Glass Bowl." A competitor with whom Harold PIPER plans to form a partnership.

Ahearn, Mrs. Character in "The Cut-Glass Bowl." Clarence AHEARN's socially inept wife.

"Air Raid" In March 1939 Fitzgerald worked for producer Jeff Lazarus at Paramount with Donald Ogden STEWART on "Air Raid" for Madeleine Carroll (1906–87), but the movie was not made.

"An Alcoholic Case" Fiction. Written December 1936. *ESQUIRE*, 6 [7] (February 1937), 32, 109; *Stories*. A NURSE contemplates quitting the case of an alcoholic CARTOONIST, but after her agency has difficulty locating a replacement for her, she decides to return to the job because she likes the man and feels a duty to live up to the ideals of her profession.

"Aldous Huxley's 'Crome Yellow' " Review. *St. Paul Daily News*, February 26, 1922, feature section, p. 6; *In His Own Time*. Fitzgerald designates Huxley (1894–1963) "after Beerbohm, the wittiest man now writing in English" (*In His Own Time*, p. 129). He describes this satirical novel about an English country house party as "the sort of book that will infuriate those who take anything seriously, even themselves" (p. 129).

Alix Character in "Babylon Revisited." RITZ bartender who tells Charlie WALES what has happened to all his old friends, and with whom Charlie leaves his brother-in-law's address for Duncan SCHAEFFER.

All the Sad Young Men Story collection. New York: Charles SCRIBNER's Sons, 1926. Dedication: "TO RING AND ELLIS LARDNER." Contents: "The Rich Boy," "Winter Dreams," "The Baby Party," "Absolution," "Rags Martin-Jones and the Pr-nce of W-les," "The Adjuster," "Hot and Cold Blood," "The Sensible Thing," and "Gretchen's Forty Winks." Fitzgerald originally considered calling the collection *Dear Money*. Published on February 26, 1926 in a first printing of 10,100 copies at $2.00, with a dust jacket illustrated by Cleon (Cleonikes DAMIANAKES). The volume sold well, with

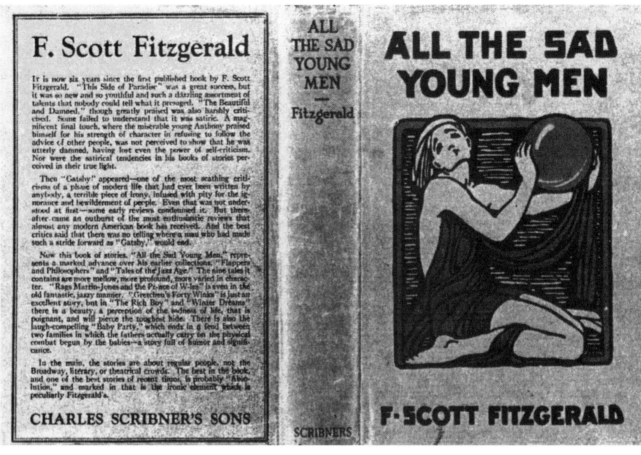

Cleon's dust jacket for Fitzgerald's third story collection, published in 1926 (Bruccoli Collection, University of South Carolina)

three printings totaling 16,170 copies in 1926. *ASYM* was Fitzgerald's strongest story collection and received favorable reviews; the unsigned review in *The Bookman* noted: "As F. Scott Fitzgerald continues to publish books, it becomes apparent that he is head and shoulders better than any writer of his generation" ("The Best of His Time," *The Bookman*, 63 [May 1926], 348–349; *FSF: The Critical Reception*, p. 272).

Allenby Character in *TSOP*. Football captain at PRINCETON. Based on Hobey Baker (1892–1918), the legendary Princeton athlete who was killed in the war. (See John Davies, *The Legend of Hobey Baker* [Boston: Little, Brown, 1966].)

Allerdyce, Mrs. Thomas *See* CAROLINE.

Allison, Parker Character in *B&D*. Acquaintance whom Anthony PATCH meets at SAMMY's bar.

Altwater, Lieutenant Percy, C.S.A. Character in *Coward*. Pompous Englishman who joined the Confederate Army and who becomes attracted to Virginia TAYLOR while visiting the home of Charley DOUGLAS. Altwater proposes to her after the war.

Ambassador Hotel Los Angeles hotel with bungalows grouped around a garden. The Fitzgeralds lived there in January and February 1927 while Fitzgerald was writing the "Lipstick" screenplay; they shared a four-apartment bungalow with Carl VAN VECHTEN, Carmel MYERS, and John Barrymore (1882–1942).

Ambler, Joe Character in "The Cut-Glass Bowl." IRENE's beau and a guest at Harold and Evylyn PIPER's dinner party.

the American (unnamed) Character in *LT/LOLT*. Man to whom Kathleen MOORE is engaged when she meets Monroe STAHR and whom she marries. Fitzgerald's notes for the unwritten episodes of the novel indicate that Pat BRADY reveals Kathleen's affair with Stahr to her husband, identified in the notes as W. Bronson Smith.

The American Mercury Magazine, founded by H. L. MENCKEN and George Jean NATHAN in 1924, which published two of Fitzgerald's stories: "Absolution" (June 1924) and "Crazy Sunday" (October 1932). In "In Literary New York" Fitzgerald describes the appearance of this magazine as "the real event of the year" (*In His Own Time*, p. 169).

Ames, Betty and Ted Sister and brother who were childhood friends of Fitzgerald in ST. PAUL; members of William BAKER's dancing class. Betty married Norris JACKSON, another of Fitzgerald's childhood friends. The Ameses lived at 501 Grand Hill in the SUMMIT AVENUE neighborhood; and Fitzgerald later recalled their yard, which had a three-story treehouse, as "one of those predestined places where young people gather in the afternoon" ("The Scandal Detectives," *TAR*, p. 5).

Ames, Ellsworth (Ellie) Character in "The Love Boat." One of three young Harvard graduates who board a boat where a high-school dance is being held.

Amy Character in "Zone of Accident." Doctor Bill TULLIVER's fiancée, who wants to go to HOLLYWOOD.

Anderson, Sherwood (1876–1941) American novelist and short-story writer; author of *Winesburg, Ohio* (1919). Fitzgerald reviewed Anderson's 1923 novel *Many Marriages; see* "Sherwood Anderson on the Marriage Question." He wrote to Maxwell PERKINS that Anderson "is one of the very best and finest writers in the English language today" (c. June 1, 1925; *Life in Letters*, pp. 119–120; *Scott/Max*, p. 111); but later, writing to Perkins about Ernest HEMINGWAY's parody of Anderson, *The Torrents of Spring* (1926), he noted: "I agree with Ernest that Anderson's last two books have let everybody down who believed in him—I think they're cheap, faked, obscurantic and awful" (c. December 30, 1925; *Life in Letters*, p. 133; *Scott/Max*, p. 127). In his analysis of the state of American literature in "How to Waste Material" (1926), Fitzgerald described Anderson as "the possessor of a brilliant and almost inimitable prose style, and of scarcely any ideas at all" (*AOAA*, p. 119). Anderson and Fitzgerald were both present at a party given by Theodore DREISER in NEW YORK CITY in spring 1923. There are conflicting accounts of Fitzgerald's behavior; one version is related in *Sherwood Anderson's Memoirs* (New York: Harcourt Brace, 1942, pp. 336–337).

Andros, Ede Character in "The Baby Party." Two-and-a-half-year-old daughter of John and Edith ANDROS. Her grabbing of Billy MARKEY's teddy bear precipitates a fight between both the children and their parents.

Andros, Edith Character in "The Baby Party." Ede ANDROS's mother, who laughs at her child's misbehavior and calls her neighbors "common."

Andros, John Character in "The Baby Party." Edith ANDROS's husband, who fights Joe MARKEY but makes his wife apologize to Mrs. MARKEY.

Andy Narrator of "The Last of the Belles." Yankee soldier stationed in TARLETON, Georgia, during World War I.

"The Ants at Princeton" Satire. ESQUIRE, 5 (June 1936), 35, 201. Account of PRINCETON UNIVERSITY admitting ants to the student body, with a focus on an unusually large ant who starred on the football team.

Appleton Character in "Basil and Cleopatra." Yale freshman quarterback whom Basil Duke LEE replaces when he is injured in the PRINCETON game.

Appleton, Lila Character in "Strange Sanctuary." Mrs. APPLETON's daughter, who resents Dolly HAINES's visit because her use of the guest room prevents Lila's friends from visiting.

Appleton, Mrs. Character in "Strange Sanctuary." Woman whose family Dolly HAINES is visiting while her father is sick.

Appleton, Warren Character in "Myra Meets His Family." Actor who poses as Knowlton WHITNEY's father, Ludlow Whitney.

The Apprentice Fiction of F. Scott Fitzgerald 1909–1917 Story collection, edited with introduction by John Kuehl. New Brunswick, N.J.: Rutgers University Press, 1965. A collection of Fitzgerald works originally published in *The ST. PAUL ACADEMY NOW AND THEN*, *The NEWMAN NEWS*, and *The NASSAU LITERARY MAGAZINE*. Contents: "The Mystery of the Raymond Mortgage," "Reade, Substitute Right Half," "A Debt of Honor," "The Room with the Green Blinds," "A Luckless Santa Claus," "The Trail of the Duke," "Pain and the Scientist," "Shadow Laurels," "The Ordeal," "The Debutante," "The Spire and the Gargoyle," "Tarquin of Cheepside," "Babes in the Woods," "Sentiment—and the Use of Rouge," "The Pierian Springs and the Last Straw," and Appendix: "The Death of My Father."

Apprenticeship With the publication of *This Side of Paradise* in 1920, F. Scott Fitzgerald became a national literary figure. While this novel does not have the depth and technical control of his later work, neither is it the lucky first effort of a complete amateur. Rather, it is the culmination of Fitzgerald's literary self-appren-

ticeship. In Fitzgerald's time, writers were largely self-taught; there were no creative writing programs where aspiring authors could nurture and develop their talents. Several of Fitzgerald's contemporaries, including Ernest HEMINGWAY and John O'HARA, served part of their apprenticeships by working for newspapers, writing under deadlines. Fitzgerald, however, learned his craft by utilizing the publications available to him at the schools he attended; and he tried his hand at a variety of genres—fiction, poetry, drama, musical comedy, parody, humor, and essay.

Fitzgerald's apprentice work is available in the following collections: *The Apprentice Fiction of F. Scott Fitzgerald, 1909–1917,* ed. John Kuehl (New Brunswick, N.J.: Rutgers University Press, 1965); *Poems 1911–1940,* ed. Matthew J. BRUCCOLI (Bloomfield Hills, Mich. & Columbia, S.C.: Bruccoli Clark, 1981); *F. Scott Fitzgerald's St. Paul Plays, 1911–1914,* ed. Alan Margolies (Princeton: Princeton University Library, 1978); *F. Scott Fitzgerald in His Own Time: A Miscellany,* ed. Bruccoli and Jackson R. Bryer (Kent, Ohio: Kent State University Press, 1971); and a facsimile edition of *Fie! Fie! Fi-Fi!* (Columbia: University of South Carolina Press for the Thomas Cooper Library, 1996).

Although Fitzgerald's first appearance in print occurred when he was 13, it was not his first writing effort. An entry for January 1907 in his *Ledger* (p. 161) indicates that he had begun writing a history, a detective story, and an essay, none of which are extant. His first surviving publication is "The Mystery of the Raymond Mortgage," printed in the October 1909 issue of *The ST. PAUL ACADEMY NOW AND THEN,* the periodical of the private school he was attending. The story, told from the point of view of an inept police chief, describes reporter/detective John SYREL's solution of a double murder case (the mortgage actually has little to do with anything). It is clumsy and implausible, yet it does contain traces of skills Fitzgerald would later develop. For example, the opening sentences indicate the writer's sense of time and place: "When I first saw John Syrel of the New York Daily News, he was standing before an open window of my house gazing out on the city. It was about six o'clock and the lights were just going on. All down Thirty-third street was a long line of gayly illuminated buildings" (*Apprentice Fiction,* p. 20). Fitzgerald wrote three more pieces for the *Now and Then.* "Reade, Substitute Right Half" (February 1910) is a vignette in which a "light haired stripling" becomes the hero of a football game. In "A Debt of Honor" (March 1910), a young Confederate soldier almost executed for falling asleep at his post regains his honor by capturing a strategically important house and dies a hero. "The Room with the Green Blinds" (June 1911) is a mystery about an inherited house in which John Wilkes BOOTH is revealed to be hiding.

During these same years, Fitzgerald was making entries in a book he titled *Thoughtbook of Francis Scott Key Fitzgerald of St. Paul Minn. U.S.A.* In the surviving 26 pages, dated from August 1910 to February 1911, Fitzgerald details the social interactions of the boys and girls with whom he was acquainted in ST. PAUL. The document reveals Fitzgerald's skill as a social observer and includes character sketches and snippets of dialogue. Fitzgerald's *Thoughtbook* was published in a facsimile edition with an introduction by John Kuehl (Princeton: Princeton University Library, 1965).

In August 1911, Fitzgerald wrote and acted in a playlet for the ELIZABETHAN DRAMATIC CLUB, an amateur group made up of his St. Paul friends and directed by Elizabeth MAGOFFIN, a local drama buff. *The Girl from Lazy J,* performed in the Magoffin home, involved a masked cowgirl capturing a blackmailing thief. It is clumsy; but Fitzgerald persisted in the genre, writing and starring in three more plays which the Club presented in more public venues to raise money for charity. In *The Captured Shadow* (performed in August 1912), Fitzgerald took the title role of a quick-witted gentleman thief; he showed much improvement in the creation of a clever plot and dialogue. *Coward* (August 1913) is a Civil War drama, and *Assorted Spirits* (September 1914) is a comedy of errors about a supposedly haunted house.

In September 1911, Fitzgerald began attending the NEWMAN SCHOOL in New Jersey and contributing to its magazine, *The NEWMAN NEWS.* In addition to news features and a poem, "Football" (Christmas 1911?), *The Newman News* published three of his stories. "A Luckless Santa Claus" (Christmas 1912) is one of the first Fitzgerald stories to explore and even criticize the world of the wealthy and the "right way" to spend money. Idle aristocrat Harry TALBOT is challenged by his girlfriend to give away $25 in an evening, but "real charity" proves to be difficult. "Pain and the Scientist" (1913) lampoons Christian Science doctrines. "The Trail of the Duke" (June 1913), like "A Luckless Santa Claus," is a prototype of one of Fitzgerald's basic plots: a man is pushed to do or become something (sometimes with destructive results) for the love of a beautiful woman. The opening paragraph of this story shows Fitzgerald's increasing skill as a writer who can strongly evoke the atmosphere of a specific time and place. He depicts "a typical, hot New York summer night" by detailing the sights, sounds, and mood "In the drug stores . . . In the flats. . . . In the tenements" (*Apprentice Fiction,* p. 54).

Fitzgerald's PRINCETON career began in September 1913, and he was actively involved in writing for the TRIANGLE CLUB (which produced an original musical show every year), *The PRINCETON TIGER* (the campus humor magazine), and *The NASSAU LITERARY MAGAZINE.* For the Triangle, he wrote the highly praised

lyrics for three of their productions: *Fie! Fie! Fi-Fi!* (for which he also wrote the book, 1914), *The Evil Eye* (1915), and *Safety First* (1916). For the *Tiger* he provided parodies, jokes, and doggerel. For the *Nassau Lit* he wrote book reviews, stories, plays, and poems. Although Fitzgerald loved poetry, his own poems are unexceptional. As James Dickey points out in his introduction to *Poems 1911–1940,* one is rather surprised to find that they are not better. But Fitzgerald did manage to carry a lyric quality into his prose.

Material in some of the early stories, plays, and poems, including "The Debutante" and "Babes in the Woods" (about the social games between the sexes) and "The Spire and the Gargoyle" (about Princeton) was revised and incorporated into *TSOP,* just as Fitzgerald later "stripped" material from his stories to use in his novels. The reviewer for *The New Republic* called his first novel "the collected works of F. Scott Fitzgerald" (R.V.A.S., *The New Republic,* 22 [May 12, 1920], 362; *FSF: The Critical Reception,* p. 22) since it recycles samples of several of the forms in which he had been teaching himself to write.

From the beginning, Fitzgerald was dedicated to his craft. He kept writing, testing himself in a variety of genres and selecting from them the elements that worked best for him: a sense of structure and effective dialogue from drama, and economy and use of imagery from poetry. By the time he left Princeton, he had decided that he wanted to be "one of the greatest writers who ever lived" (Edmund WILSON, "Thoughts on Being Bibliographed," *The Princeton University Library Chronicle,* 5 [February 1944], p. 54).

by Tracy Simmons Bitonti

Aquilla's brother Character in "On Schedule." René DU CARY'S black servant, who has never been called by his own name since replacing Du Cary's former houseman.

Aquilla's sister Character in "On Schedule." Black servant who cleans René DU CARY'S house.

Armstrong, Margaret Childhood friend and sweetheart of Fitzgerald in ST. PAUL; a member of the ELIZABETHAN DRAMATIC CLUB and William BAKER'S dancing class. She was the model for Imogene BISSEL in the Basil Duke LEE stories. Fitzgerald noted in his *Thoughtbook* for February 1911 that of his "two new crushes"—Marie HERSEY and Margaret—Margaret was the best talker (Chap. VII); and he elaborated on his relationship with Margaret in "Chap. IX"(pp. XXXV–XXXX).

Archives *See* BRUCCOLI COLLECTION and PRINCETON UNIVERSITY LIBRARY.

Army Fitzgerald was commissioned as a second lieutenant in the infantry on October 26, 1917 and reported to FORT LEAVENWORTH, Kansas, on November 20 for training. He reported to the 45th Infantry Regiment at CAMP ZACHARY TAYLOR near LOUISVILLE, Kentucky, on March 15, 1918 and served as assistant to the regimental school officer for several weeks before his regiment was transferred to CAMP GORDON in Augusta, Georgia, in April. To prepare for overseas service the regiment was combined with the 67th Infantry Regiment of the Ninth Division at CAMP SHERIDAN near MONTGOMERY, Alabama, in June; and Fitzgerald was promoted to first lieutenant. However, he was a poor soldier, and his fellow officers played pranks on him. The 67th Infantry was shipped to CAMP MILLS on Long Island on October 26 to prepare for embarkation to France, but the war ended before they were shipped overseas, and the regiment returned to Camp Sheridan in November. Fitzgerald served as aide-de-camp to Brigadier General J. A. RYAN at Camp Sheridan and was discharged from the army in February 1919.

Aronstael Character in "Two Wrongs." Bill MCCHESNEY'S best friend, with whom he had a drunken quarrel.

Asheville, North Carolina Fitzgerald lived in Asheville at the GROVE PARK INN in the summer of 1935 and July through December of 1936. Anthony BUTTITTA'S 1974 memoir *After the Good Gay Times,* based on notes of his conversations with Fitzgerald, gives an account of the summer 1935 visit, as does Laura GUTHRIE'S journal. Zelda FITZGERALD entered HIGHLAND HOSPITAL in Asheville on April 8, 1936 and was discharged around April 15, 1940. She returned to Highland in November 1947 and died in a fire there on March 10, 1948.

Ashton, Cecilia Character in *Coward.* Lindy DOUGLAS'S friend and Charley DOUGLAS'S fiancée.

Assorted Spirits Play. In *F. Scott Fitzgerald's St. Paul Plays, 1911–1914.* Performed by the ELIZABETHAN DRAMATIC CLUB on September 8, 1914 at the ST. PAUL Y.W.C.A. Auditorium and September 9 at the WHITE BEAR YACHT CLUB in DELLWOOD, raising $500 for the Baby Welfare Association. Fitzgerald played the role of Peter WETHERBY and was also listed on the program as Stage Manager. A newspaper article reported that when a fuse blew during the second performance, Fitzgerald kept the audience from panic: He "proved equal to the situation, however, and leaping to the edge of the stage quieted the audience with an improvised monologue" (scrapbook, PRINCETON UNIVERSITY LIBRARY).

Act I

Peter Wetherby, who needs $10,000 to save his business, offers to sell his house to Josephus HENDRIX, his second cousin. Hendrix, who knows that the railroad intends to buy the property, plans to dress as a devil to prove the house is haunted so that he can buy it at a low price from Wetherby. Wetherby hires fortune-teller Madame ZADA, who is his sister, to drive any spirits from the house. While Hendrix is visiting the Wetherby home, he gives his cash to Peter's son, Dickie WETHERBY, for safekeeping; and the maid, HULDA, lets in SECOND STORY SALLE to steal the money. Meanwhile William CHAPMAN, dressed as a devil for a masquerade ball, mistakenly enters the Wetherby house, thinking it is the home of his aunt, Miss SPIGOT, who has a similar address. There are various encounters between the three intruders and Dickie; his sister, Cecile WETHERBY; and Hendrix's ward, Clara KING.

Act II

The next morning Dickie tells his father that Hendrix's money has disappeared; Wetherby tells him he must marry Miss King, an heiress, to save his business. Salle returns disguised as a book agent to get the money from Hulda, and two policemen arrive to apprehend her. The missing money is found in Chapman's coat pocket, where Hulda had stashed it. Hendrix is discovered in his devil costume; Madame Zada is revealed to be his wife, Amelia, whom he had left years before, and they are reunited. Chapman, who is a railroad contractor, offers Wetherby $15,000 for his house and proposes to Cecile.

Astoria Section of the borough of Queens in NEW YORK CITY. Fitzgerald incorrectly identifies it as the place where the motorcycle policeman tries to stop Jay GATSBY in Chapter IV of *GG*. The correct location of this event is Long Island City, at the Queens end of the 59th Street Bridge between Manhattan and Queens.

"At Your Age" Fiction. Written June 1929. *The SATURDAY EVENING POST*, 202 (August 17, 1929), 6–7, 79–80; *The Price Was High*. Fifty-year-old Tom SQUIRES admires a young blonde clerk in a drugstore and is overcome with a desire to restore youth to his life before it's too late. He becomes attracted to young Annie LORRY, who is dating Randy CAMBELL, but who agrees to go out with Tom several times. When Tom realizes that Annie isn't really interested in him, he writes to her mother for permission to court Annie, knowing that her mother's refusal will be the spark that kindles Annie's interest in a forbidden beau. When Annie is asked not to participate in the Junior League show because of her defiance of her mother, Tom decides he is harming her and leaves town. However, he is unable to relinquish her and returns; and they become engaged. When Tom is forced to wait several hours for Annie's return from a car ride with Randy Cambell, and realizes that he and Annie's mother are of the same generation with the same attitude toward young Annie's behavior, he breaks off his relationship with Annie.

"At Your Age" brought a raise from the *Post* to $4,000, Fitzgerald's top story price. It was probably based on Fitzgerald's ST. PAUL friends Oscar and Xandra KALMAN; Oscar was considerably older than his wife Xandra.

"Auction—Model 1934" Autobiographical article. *ESQUIRE*, 2 (July 1934), 20, 153, 155; *CU*. By-lined "F. Scott and Zelda Fitzgerald," but credited to Zelda FITZGERALD in *Ledger;* written by Zelda and revised by Fitzgerald. Inventory of the Fitzgeralds' possessions that evokes their life during the 1920s and early 1930s.

Augustine Character in *TITN*. Drunken cook at the VILLA DIANA who threatens Dick DIVER with a butcher knife when he fires her.

Aunt Georgie Character in "That Kind of Party." She pays her nephew, Terrence R. TIPTON, a quarter for eating a raw egg; he uses the quarter to pay for a forged telegram to Joe SHOONOVER's mother to keep her away from Joe's party. Fitzgerald's Aunt Clara MCQUILLAN had paid him twenty-five cents a day for eating a raw egg during his vacation in the Catskill Mountains in July 1905 (*Ledger*, p. 159).

Aunt Gladys Character in "A Nice Quiet Place." DICK's mother; the PERRYS' hostess at Island Farms.

Aunt Mamie Character in "The Jelly-Bean." Jim POWELL's aunt, who runs a boardinghouse in his family home and is later in a sanitarium.

Aunt Rose Character in "Lo, the Poor Peacock!" Black worker who helps make sausage on Annie Lee DAVIS's family farm.

"The Author's Apology" Tipped-in leaf, signed by Fitzgerald, in about 500 copies of the third printing of *TSOP*, which were distributed at the May 1920 American Booksellers Association meeting; printed text facsimiled as a keepsake in a limited edition of 50 copies (Columbia, S.C.: Matthew J. BRUCCOLI, 1970); holograph facsimiled in a limited edition of 200 copies (Kent, Ohio: Kent State University Press, 1971); printed

text facsimiled in *In His Own Time*. Includes Fitzgerald's pronouncement: "My whole theory of writing I can sum up in one sentence: An author ought to write for the youth of his own generation, the critics of the next, and the schoolmasters of ever afterward" (*In His Own Time*, p. 164). The first two paragraphs of "The Author's Apology" were revised from "An Interview with F. Scott Fitzgerald."

"Author's House" Autobiographical essay. *ESQUIRE*, 6 (July 1936), 40, 108; *AOAA*. Allegorical tour of Fitzgerald's house, with an exploration of what influenced him to become a writer and a description of the circumstances of a writer's life.

"An Author's Mother" Fiction. *ESQUIRE*, 6 (September 1936), 36; *The Price Was High*. Mrs. JOHNSTON faints after shopping for a birthday present for her son, Hamilton T. JOHNSTON, a successful author. While in the ambulance, she says that her son will write about the incident. As she is dying at the hospital she senses the presence of her favorite sentimental poets, Alice and Phoebe Cary (1820–71 and 1824–71).

This obituary story for Fitzgerald's mother, Mollie McQuillan FITZGERALD, was written before her death in early September 1936.

Avery, Helen Character in "Magnetism." Actress who is interested in George HANNAFORD.

"Babes in Wonderland" On January 6, 1939 Fitzgerald wrote a two-page memo to M-G-M producer John Considine (b. 1898) proposing a musical about a group of aspiring actors and actresses hiding out in a movie studio (*Correspondence,* pp. 524–525). The project was not developed.

"Babes in the Woods" Fiction. *The NASSAU LITERARY MAGAZINE,* 73 (May 1917), 55–64; revised in *The SMART SET,* 60 (September 1919), 67–71; incorporated into *TSOP; Apprentice Fiction.* During a Christmas party 16-year-old ISABELLE attracts Kenneth POWERS. After dinner they are alone but are interrupted just as they are about to kiss. This story of "simply very sophisticated, very calculating and finished, young actors, each playing a part that they had played for years" (*Apprentice Fiction,* p. 136) is based on Fitzgerald's first meeting with Ginevra KING in ST. PAUL. Fitzgerald recycled it in *TSOP* as the first meeting of Isabelle BORGÉ and Amory BLAINE.

"The Baby Party" Fiction. Written February 1924. *HEARST'S INTERNATIONAL,* 47 (February 1925), 32–37; *ASYM.* Two-and-a-half-year-old Ede ANDROS grabs two-year-old Billy MARKEY's teddy bear at his birthday party and knocks Billy down twice—once accidentally and once intentionally. Ede's mother, Edith ANDROS, laughs in response to her child's laughter, which angers Mrs. MARKEY. The women exchange insults, and their husbands engage in a fistfight.

"Babylon Revisited" Fiction. Written December 1930. *The SATURDAY EVENING POST,* 203 (February 21, 1931), 3–5, 82–84; *TAR.* American businessman and recovering alcoholic Charlie WALES, who had lived in PARIS during the boom, returns there in 1930. His first stop is the RITZ BAR, where he inquires about his old companions and leaves his brother-in-law's address for Duncan SCHAEFFER. He then goes to dinner at the home of his brother- and sister-in-law, Lincoln and Marion PETERS, where his daughter, Honoria WALES, has been living; he refuses a cocktail because he now limits himself to one drink a day. After dinner he visits some of his former haunts and recalls the dissipation of his past. While at lunch with Honoria the next day, he

encounters old friends Duncan Schaeffer and Lorraine QUARRLES but declines to give them his address. Honoria tells him she wants to live with him—a change which is the purpose of his visit. When he broaches the subject with the Peterses, Marion recalls how after a drunken quarrel he had locked his wife, Helen WALES, Marion's sister, out in the snow, which contributed to her death from heart trouble. Charlie had been in a sanitarium when he consented to Marion's guardianship of Honoria. Lincoln agrees for Charlie to take Honoria, but Marion wants to retain legal guardianship for a while longer. The next evening, while Charlie is at the Peterses' apartment, Duncan and Lorraine show up drunk; Charlie sends them away, but Marion is so upset that she and Lincoln decide to delay letting Charlie have Honoria for six months. At the Ritz bar, Charlie tells the bartender he lost everything he wanted in the boom; he comforts himself with the thought that Helen wouldn't have wanted him to be so alone.

"Babylon Revisited," usually regarded as one of Fitzgerald's best stories, explores and evaluates the wealthy EXPATRIATE lifestyle in Paris in the twenties. Charlie encapsulates the attitude of the decade by reflecting that "the snow of twenty-nine wasn't real snow. If you didn't want it to be snow, you just paid some money" (*TAR,* p. 406).

See William White, "The Text of 'Babylon Revisited,' " *Fitzgerald Newsletter,* no. 28 (Winter 1965); and "Two Versions of Fitzgerald's 'Babylon Revisited,' " *Papers of the Bibliographical Society of America,* 60 (Fourth Quarter 1966), 439–452. See also Kenneth McCollum, " 'Babylon Revisited' Revisited," *Fitzgerald/Hemingway Annual* (1971), pp. 314–316.

In 1940 Fitzgerald worked on a screenplay for "Babylon Revisited," but it was never produced. *See* "Cosmopolitan."

Bach, Mr. Character in "A Man in the Way." Pat HOBBY's old friend who is in Jack BERNERS' office when Hobby enters.

Bach, Mr. Character in "Zone of Accident." Loretta BROOKE's father, who wants to keep her injury a secret to avoid scandal.

Bacon, Doctor Character in the Basil Duke LEE stories; headmaster of ST. REGIS. In "The Freshest Boy" he wonders why Basil is so unpopular and sends Mr. ROONEY with him when Basil can't get any of his fellow students to accompany him to NEW YORK. In "The Perfect Life" he congratulates Basil on his play in a football game and introduces him to alumnus John GRANBY.

Baedeker, Miss Character in *GG*. Drunk girl at Jay GATSBY's party.

Baer, Doctor Bill Character in *LT/LOLT*. Monroe STAHR's doctor.

Bailey, John Boynton Character in "A Snobbish Story." Reporter for the *Chicago Tribune* whom Josephine PERRY meets at Lake Forest. His wife, EVELYN, attempts suicide as a result of his attention to Josephine.

Baily Character in "The Camel's Back." "Bad man" who invites Perry PARKHURST to his hotel room to drink champagne.

Baird, Tudor Character in *B&D*. An old beau with whom Gloria PATCH spends time while her husband, Anthony PATCH, is away in the army. Baird is killed in a plane crash.

Baker, Dr. Benjamin May (b. 1901) Physician who treated Fitzgerald at JOHNS HOPKINS UNIVERSITY HOSPITAL and privately in BALTIMORE in the 1930s. At the recommendation of H. L. MENCKEN, Dr. Baker gave Fitzgerald special attention and succeeded in keeping him from drinking for several months by having Fitzgerald call him when he wanted a drink. Fitzgerald, who was seeking story material, asked Baker about his personal and professional life.

Baker, Ellen Character in "A Short Trip Home." Young woman who is preyed on by the spectre of Joe VARLAND.

Baker, George Character in "Discard." Dolly BORDON's nephew, a student at a military school. He wants to be in the movies, and he is impressed by the way in which Dolly handles her husband's infidelity.

Baker, Jordan Character in *GG*. Golf champion based on Edith Cummings (b. 1899), a friend of Ginevra KING's who won the 1923 women's golf championship. Jordan was a girlhood friend of Daisy Fay [BUCHANAN] in LOUISVILLE. She dates Nick CARRAWAY until they quarrel after Myrtle WILSON's death. Nick describes her as "incurably dishonest" (p. 47).

Baker, Mrs. Character in "A Short Trip Home." Ellen BAKER's mother.

Baker, William H. Instructor of a ST. PAUL dancing class, organized in December 1909, in which Fitzgerald was enrolled at age 13. The class met at Ramaley Hall on Grand Avenue on Saturday afternoons, and many of Fitzgerald's friends took part in it. Fitzgerald described the class in his *Thoughtbook* (pp. XXIX–XXX). Baker also worked as a bartender at the WHITE BEAR YACHT CLUB in the summers.

"Ballet Shoes" Movie treatment. " 'Ballet Shoes': A Movie Synopsis," *Fitzgerald/Hemingway Annual* (1976), pp. 2–7. In 1936 L. G. Braun, manager of ballerina Olga Spessivtzewa (1895–1991), was in America to arrange a movie contract with Samuel Goldwyn (1884–1974). Braun, who had met Fitzgerald during his 1930 trip to NORTH AFRICA, asked him to write a screenplay for the ballerina. Fitzgerald believed that Zelda FITZGERALD's ballet experiences provided him with material that would allow him to "deliver something entirely authentic in the matter full of invention and feeling" (February 8, 1936; *Life in Letters,* p. 295; *As Ever,* p. 248). However, the movie treatment called "Ballet Shoes," which he wrote in March and which included a benevolent rum-runner, a "little waif," and a long-lost father, was full of coincidence; and it was not accepted.

Ballion, Paul One of Fitzgerald's closest childhood friends in ST. PAUL; a member of the ELIZABETHAN DRAMATIC CLUB. He was the model for Bill KAMPF in the Basil Duke LEE stories. In his *Thoughtbook*, Fitzgerald noted that he had once been Paul's "ardent admirer" but that he liked Paul less now that Bob CLARK was Fitzgerald's close friend: "I dont dislike him. I have simply out grown him" (p. XXIII).

"The Baltimore Anti-Christ" Review of *Prejudices, Second Series* by H. L. MENCKEN. *The Bookman,* 53 (March 1921), 79–81; *In His Own Time*. Fitzgerald states that "Mencken's work is inevitably distinguished" (*In His Own Time,* p. 120). He notes Mencken's enviable literary reputation and contribution to American literature, and he wonders what Mencken will do in the next 20 years after "a success so complete" (p. 121).

Baltimore, Maryland Fitzgerald lived in or near Baltimore for most of 1932–36. Zelda FITZGERALD was a patient at the PHIPPS CLINIC of JOHNS HOPKINS UNIVERSITY HOSPITAL in Baltimore from February 12 to June 26, 1932 and again briefly in February 1934. She was a patient at SHEPPARD-PRATT HOSPITAL outside Baltimore from May 19, 1934 to April 8, 1936. F. Scott Fitzgerald was admitted to Johns Hopkins Hospital in August

1932 with a tentative diagnosis of typhoid fever and was hospitalized there eight more times between 1933 and 1937 for alcoholism and chronic inactive fibroid tuberculosis. Fitzgerald moved from MONTGOMERY to the HOTEL RENNERT in Baltimore on March 30, 1932, then rented "LA PAIX" on the Bayard TURNBULL estate at RODGERS FORGE, TOWSON, outside Baltimore, from May 20, 1932 to November 1933. While the Fitzgeralds were at "La Paix" Zelda's novel, *Save Me the Waltz,* was published in October 1932; and her play, *Scandalabra,* was produced by the VAGABOND JUNIOR PLAYERS in Baltimore June 26–July 1, 1933. After completing *TITN* Fitzgerald gave up "La Paix" in December 1933 and moved to a rented townhouse at 1307 Park Avenue, where he stayed until May 1935. After spending the summer at the GROVE PARK INN in ASHEVILLE, North Carolina, Fitzgerald returned to Baltimore in September; for a while he had two apartments—one at 3300 St. Paul Avenue and another two blocks away at the CAMBRIDGE ARMS on Charles Street, across from the Johns Hopkins University campus. He spent November and most of December at the SKYLAND HOTEL in HENDERSONVILLE, North Carolina; and when he returned to Baltimore he lived at the Cambridge Arms until his July 1936 return to the Grove Park Inn.

In September 1935 Fitzgerald wrote to Laura GUTHRIE: "Baltimore is warm but pleasant—I love it more than I thought—it is so rich with memories—it is nice to look up the street + see the statue of my great uncle, + to know Poe is buried here and that many ancestors of mine have walked in the old town by the bay. I belong here, where everything is civilized and gay and rotted and polite" (*Life in Letters,* p. 291).

Bangs, Angelina Character in *Coward.* A proud and sanctimonious visitor who annoys Judge DOUGLAS's family.

Banizon, Mr. Character in "Pat Hobby's Secret." Producer who has forgotten the movie ending which R. Parke WOLL told him and who hires Pat HOBBY to discover it.

Bannerman, Marie Character in "The Dance." Charley KINCAID's fiancée, who is murdered by Catherine JONES.

Baptiste Character in *B&D.* A Sicilian immigrant in Anthony PATCH's army company, who is assigned to learn blacksmithing despite his fear of horses, and who dies when a horse crushes his skull.

Barban, Tommy Character in *TITN.* Half-French, half-American soldier-of-fortune with whom Nicole DIVER has an affair and whom she marries after leaving her husband, Dick DIVER. Fitzgerald's notes for the novel indicate that Barban was based on a combination of Edouard JOZAN, Mario BRAGGIOTTI, Tommy HITCHCOCK, and Princetonians Percy Pyne and Denny Holden. Barban probably also has connections with Ernest HEMINGWAY, although he was not listed.

Barkis, Private Character in *Coward.* Union soldier who attempts to plunder Judge DOUGLAS's house after the war.

Barley Character in *B&D.* A man who liked Gloria Gilbert [PATCH] and fought Percy WOLCOTT.

Barlotto Character in "On Your Own." Actor whom Evelyn LOVEJOY has disliked since he got fresh with her while they were dancing.

Barlow, Mr. Character in *TSOP.* President of the advertising agency where Amory BLAINE works after his discharge from the army.

Barnes, Ed Character in "Six of One—". Man who helps six boys from his Ohio hometown through college in an experiment to match the six wealthy, privileged boys about whom his friend Jack SCHOFIELD brags.

Barnes, Rachael Jerryl Character in *B&D.* Gloria PATCH's friend, to whom Anthony PATCH is excessively attentive at the party which his grandfather, Adam PATCH, interrupts.

Barnes, Rodman Character in *B&D.* Rachael BARNES's husband, a captain in the Quartermaster Corps.

Barney, Charles Character in "On Your Own." Producer of the show in which Evelyn LOVEJOY has been acting.

Barnfield, Teddy Character in "The Captured Shadow." Little boy who has the mumps. Basil Duke LEE deliberately sends Ham BEEBE to play with Teddy so that he will get the mumps and his sister, Evelyn BEEBE, who has a leading role in Basil's play, won't be able to leave town.

Barr, Bert (Bertha Weinberg Goldstein) (1896–1973) While returning to America on the *New York* for his father's funeral in January 1931, Fitzgerald met a woman who called herself Bert Barr, but who was Bertha Weinberg Goldstein, the wife of Brooklyn judge Louis Goldstein. Barr, who was a member of Texas oilman Herman Cornell's party, convinced Fitzgerald that she was a professional cardsharp; impressed by her cleverness, he invited her to collaborate on stories with

him, but nothing came of the plan. He saw her in NEW YORK and later in PARIS and wrote to her for several years. Evelyn LOVEJOY in "On Your Own" (1931), a story Fitzgerald wrote after his return to SWITZERLAND after his father's funeral, is partly based on Barr. In 1962 Barr donated to PRINCETON UNIVERSITY LIBRARY a collection of typescripts and proofs of 39 of Fitzgerald's ESQUIRE stories. See Matthew J. BRUCCOLI, "Epilogue," *Esquire*, 91 (January 30, 1979), p. 67.

Barron, Father Joseph (1889–1939) Dean of students at St. Paul Seminary and a friend of Fitzgerald. While in ST. PAUL in summer 1919, Fitzgerald discussed his work on *TSOP* with Barron, who wrote about philosophy and religion; Donald Ogden STEWART often joined their conversations. Barron attended Scottie FITZGERALD's 1921 baptism at the Convent of the Visitation as her godfather.

Barrows, Colonel Character in "A Debt of Honor." Confederate officer who asks General JACKSON for permission to assault a house held by the enemy.

Bartholomew Character in "May Day." Fat man who works on a radical newspaper with Henry BRADIN.

Bartlett, Dolly Character in "That Kind of Party." Girl with whom Terrence R. TIPTON is in love. She invites him to supper after Joe SHOONOVER's party.

Bartney, Walter Hamilton (William) Character in "Pain and the Scientist." Law student who takes revenge on Dr. Hepezia SKIGGS, a Christian Scientist, for an earlier unpleasant encounter.

Barton, Mr. Character in *TSOP*. The BLAINE family's lawyer, who keeps Amory BLAINE apprised of the decline of his family's wealth.

"Basil and Cleopatra" Fiction—Basil Duke LEE story. Written February 1929. *The SATURDAY EVENING POST*, 201 (April 27, 1929), 14–15, 166, 170, 173; *AOAA*; *B&J*. Basil Duke Lee, age 17, and Minnie BIBBLE are both visiting friends in Mobile, Alabama, where Minnie falls in love with Littleboy LE MOYNE. Basil is discouraged because Minnie no longer prefers him, although she reluctantly kisses him and invites him to visit her at school. Basil enters Yale and plays freshman football. He insults Le Moyne during the Princeton-Yale game; and Le Moyne informs him that Minnie has left him for JUBAL, Basil's classmate. Basil tells Jobena DORSEY about his relationship with Minnie, and she advises him not to go back to her. When Minnie is once again attracted to Basil, he resists the urge to return to her, because he wishes to concentrate on his ambitions.

Fitzgerald recycled the passage from this story about Minnie and Littleboy getting into trouble in a locked train compartment as Collis CLAY's report to Dick DIVER about Rosemary HOYT and Bill HILLIS in *TITN*.

The Basil and Josephine Stories Story collection. Edited with an introduction by Jackson R. Bryer and John Kuehl. New York: Charles SCRIBNER's Sons, 1973. Contents: "That Kind of Party," "The Scandal Detectives," "A Night at the Fair," "The Freshest Boy," "He Thinks He's Wonderful," "The Captured Shadow," "The Perfect Life," "Forging Ahead," "Basil and Cleopatra," "First Blood," "A Nice Quiet Place," "A Woman with a Past," "A Snobbish Story," and "Emotional Bankruptcy." In July 1928 Fitzgerald informed Maxwell PERKINS that he planned to publish a book of his Basil Duke LEE stories, which "would make a nice light novel," after his novel in progress (*TITN*) was published (*Life in Letters*, p. 158; *Scott/Max*, p. 152). Six years later, a month after the publication of *TITN*, he proposed a volume of Basil stories, Josephine PERRY stories, and new stories bringing the characters together as one of four possible collections for publication in fall 1934. Though Perkins favored the Basil and Josephine collection, Fitzgerald decided against it because he feared that presenting it as a novel was an artistic risk at a time when he was counting on the publication of *TITN* to restore his reputation as a serious novelist, and also because too much revision would be required (May 15 and 21, 1934; *Life in Letters*, pp. 259–262; *Scott/Max*, pp. 195–200). He chose instead a volume of previously uncollected stories, *Taps at Reveille*, including five Basil stories and three Josephine stories.

Battles, Johanna Character in "I Got Shoes." Former debutante who writes for a newspaper and interviews actress Nell MARGERY.

Beach, Sylvia (1887–1962) Proprietress of Shakespeare & Co., a bookshop and lending library on the rue de l'Odéon on the Left Bank in PARIS; in 1922 she published the first edition of James JOYCE's *Ulysses*. Fitzgerald was friendly with Beach, whose shop served as a gathering place for American writers. Beach introduced Fitzgerald to French novelist André CHAMSON; and she hosted a dinner on June 27, 1928 at which Fitzgerald met James Joyce.

See Beach, *Shakespeare & Company* (New York: Harcourt, Brace, 1959).

Beacon, New York Zelda FITZGERALD was a patient at CRAIG HOUSE sanitarium in Beacon, March–May 1934.

the Beard Character in "Shaggy's Morning." One of SHAGGY's owners.

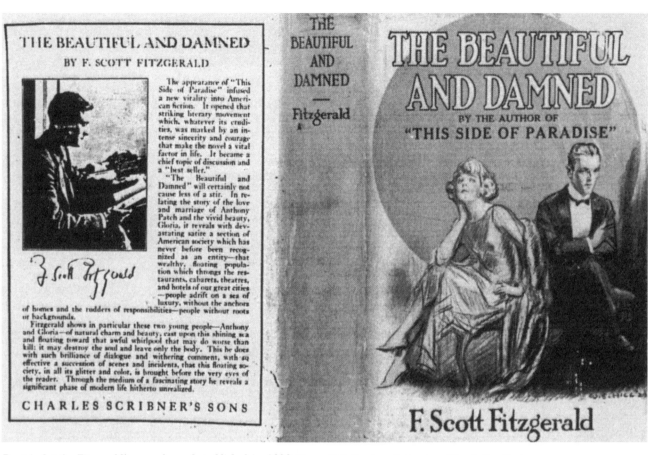

Dust jacket for Fitzgerald's second novel, published in 1922 (Bruccoli Collection, University of South Carolina)

The Beautiful and Damned Novel. New York: Charles SCRIBNER'S Sons, 1922; London: Collins, 1922. Dedication: "TO SHANE LESLIE, GEORGE JEAN NATHAN AND MAXWELL PERKINS IN APPRECIATION OF MUCH LITERARY HELP AND ENCOURAGEMENT." Serialized in *METROPOLITAN,* 54–55 (September 1921), 9–12, 55, 60–62, 65; (October 1921), 27–30, 44–49; (November 1921), 31–34, 50–52; (December 1921), 33–36, 50–54; (January 1922), 39–42, 52–55; (February 1922), 35–38, 44–47; (March 1922), 57–62, 108–109, 112–113. An excerpt from Book Two, Chapter II appeared in *The SMART SET* (February 1922) as "The Far-Seeing Skeptics."

Fitzgerald informed Scribners editor Maxwell PER-KINS on September 18, 1919 that he had begun "a very ambitious novel called 'The Demon Lover' " (*Life in Letters,* p. 32; *Scott/Max,* p. 22). By February 3, 1920 he informed Perkins that because of recent enforcement of obscenity laws he had "practically decided" to give up his new novel, now titled "Darling Heart," which involved the seduction of a girl: "I don't know what I'll do now—what in hell is the use of trying to write decent fiction if a bunch of old women refuse to let anyone hear the truth!" (*Scott/Max,* pp. 27–28).

After the March 1920 publication of *TSOP* and his marriage to Zelda Sayre [FITZGERALD] on April 3, Fitzgerald rented a house in WESTPORT, Connecticut, where he began work on a new plot. On August 12 he wrote to Charles SCRIBNER II: "My new novel, called 'The Flight of the Rocket,' concerns the life of one Anthony Patch, between his 25th and 33d years (1913–1921). He is one of those many with the tastes and weaknesses of an artist but with no actual creative inspiration. How he and his beautiful young wife are wrecked on the shoals of dissipation is told in the story. This sounds sordid but it's really a most sensational book + I hope won't dissapoint the critics who liked my first one" (*Life in Letters,* p. 41). By Christmas 1920 the title was "The Beautiful Lady Without Mercy" (to James Branch Cabell; *Letters,* p. 464); and by February 1921 Fitzgerald had changed it to "The Beautiful and Damned" (to Robert CLARK, February 9, 1921; *Life in Letters,* p. 46). Other titles on the title page of his manuscript include "The House of Pain," "Misfortune Street," "O, Beautiful," "The Broken Lute," "The Corruption of Anthony," "A Love Affair," and "Corruption." On April 22, 1921 he sent agent Harold OBER a typescript of Part I for serialization (*As Ever,* p. 23; see also

his April 22 letter to Carl Hovey, *Correspondence*, p. 82); *Metropolitan* bought the serial rights for $7,000 and published the novel in seven installments from September 1921 through March 1922. Editor Carl Hovey (1875–1956) cut the 130,000-word typescript by 40,000 words. When Fitzgerald was considering serialization of *GG*, he told Ober, "I wouldn't want it to be chopped as Hovey chopped the Beautiful + Damned" (October 25, 1924; *Life in Letters*, p. 83; *As Ever*, p. 67).

Fitzgerald revised the novel for book publication while living in ST. PAUL in summer 1921, following Zelda's advice in cutting out the didactic conclusion of the serial:

> That exquisite heavenly irony which has tabulated the demise of many generations of sparrows seems to us to be content with the moral judgments of man upon fellow man. If there is a subtler and yet more nebulous ethic somewhere in the mind, one might believe that beneath the sordid dress and near the bruised heart of this transaction there was a motive which was not weak but only futile and sad. In the search for happiness, which search is the greatest and possibly the only crime of which we in our petty misery are capable, these two people were marked as guilty chiefly by the freshness and fullness of their desire. Their disillusion was always a comparative thing—they had sought glamor and color through their respective worlds with steadfast loyalty—sought it and it alone in kisses and in wine, sought it with the same ingenuousness in the wanton moonlight as under the cold sun of inviolate chastity. Their fault was not that they had doubted but that they had believed.
>
> The exquisite perfection of their boredom, the delicacy of their inattention, the inexhaustibility of their discontent—were disastrous extremes—that was all. And if, before Gloria yielded up her gift of beauty, she shed one bright feather of light so that someone, gazing up from the grey earth, might say, "Look! There is an angel's wing!" perhaps she had given more than enough in exchange for her tinsel joys.
>
> . . . The story ends here. (*Metropolitan*, 55 [March 1922], 113)

The Beautiful and Damned was published on March 4, 1922 in a first printing of 20,600 copies at $2.00, with a dust jacket illustrated by W. E. HILL. Scribners' three 1922 printings totaled 50,000 copies, and *B&D* made the best-seller list in *Publishers Weekly* for March (10th place), April (sixth), and May (10th). The novel's reception was disappointing, however, although some critics praised it as an improvement over *TSOP*. H. L. MENCKEN wrote: "There are a hundred signs in it of serious purpose and unquestionable skill. Even in its defects there is proof of hard striving. Fitzgerald ceases to be a *Wunderkind*, and begins to come into his maturity" ("Fitzgerald and Others," *The Smart Set*, 67 [April 1922], 140–141; *FSF: The Critical Reception*, p. 107). Zelda Fitzgerald's review of *B&D*, "Friend Husband's Latest," was her first professional publication. Though the review was partly a joke, she criticized the novel's intellectual pretentiousness: "The other things I didn't like in the book—I mean the unimportant things— were the literary references and the attempt to convey a profound air of erudition. It reminds me in its more soggy moments of the essays I used to get up in school at the last minute by looking up strange names in the Encyclopaedia Britannica" (*New York Tribune*, April 2, 1922, Section 5, p. 11; *FSF: The Critical Reception*, p. 111). (*See* also CRITICAL REPUTATION AND RECEPTION OF NOVELS.)

Fitzgerald sold the film rights to *B&D* to Warner Brothers for $2,500, but he was disappointed with the 1922 movie. He wrote to Oscar KALMAN: "Its by *far* the worst movie I've ever seen in my life—cheap, vulgar, ill-constructed and shoddy. We were utterly ashamed of it" (after December 10, 1922; *Correspondence*, p. 119).

Cover for the first installment of Fitzgerald's The Beautiful and Damned *serialized from September 1921 through March 1922* (Bruccoli Collection, University of South Carolina)

BOOK ONE

Chapter I: Anthony Patch
In 1913, Anthony PATCH, age twenty-five, is living in NEW YORK. A year earlier he had returned from a trip

to ROME after his Harvard graduation because of the illness of his grandfather, millionaire reformer Adam J. PATCH. Anthony had told his grandfather that he was thinking of writing a history of the Middle Ages, but he really "did nothing." His best friends are fellow Harvard graduates Maury NOBLE and aspiring novelist Dick CARAMEL, with whom he discusses literature and philosophy.

Chapter II: Portrait of a Siren
Dick Caramel tells Anthony about his beautiful cousin, Gloria Gilbert [PATCH], whom Anthony finally meets when he invites her and Dick to tea. Gloria and Anthony have several dates.

Chapter III: The Connoisseur of Kisses
Dick tells Gloria's mother, Catherine GILBERT, that he thinks Anthony is in love with Gloria. Mrs. Gilbert tells Dick she would like to see Gloria settle down and tells him about all the boys who have always flocked around Gloria and how she has recently begun going with a different crowd. Gloria arrives with two friends, Rachael Jerryl [BARNES] and Muriel KANE, whom Dick considers rather common. Geraldine BURKE, a lower-class girl whom Anthony has dated for a few months, observes that he drinks all the time. Gloria hosts a dinner for Muriel, Rachael, Dick, Maury, Anthony, and Joseph BLOECKMAN, a filmmaker who does business with her father and who wants to marry her. Gloria and Anthony leave the party for a while, and they kiss. When they see each other again a few days later, she rebuffs him when he kisses her more passionately; they part on bad terms. Anthony desperately realizes that he is in love with her, but he decides he should wait several weeks before calling her to allow time for the unpleasant incident to fade. After five weeks they begin to go out together again, and Anthony tells her he loves her.

BOOK TWO

Chapter I: The Radiant Hour
Anthony and Gloria plan to be married in June, but they quarrel incessantly. They dream of the time when they will have more money after the death of Anthony's grandfather. Dick Caramel's novel, *The Demon Lover,* is published; and his fame almost overshadows the wedding preparations. Gloria and Anthony are married at the home of his grandfather, and they travel to California for their honeymoon. Anthony discovers that Gloria is "a girl of tremendous nervous tension and of the most high-handed selfishness," and she discovers that he is "an utter coward toward any one of a million phantasms created by his imagination" (p. 157). They settle in a gray rental house in MARIETTA in the New York countryside for the summer, returning to Anthony's New York apartment for the winter, and going

back to Marietta for the next summer. Gloria's mother dies.

Chapter II: Symposium
Gloria has "lulled Anthony's mind to sleep" (p. 191), and they have spent too much money. Anthony grows tired of Gloria's dominance of their relationship, and one night when he is drunk he grows angry when she insists they leave the home of some friends they are visiting. He determines to gain the upper hand and physically prevents Gloria from boarding the train she wants; she tells him that the incident has changed her and that she knew "what was left of me would always love you, but never in quite the same way" (p. 202). Adam Patch offers to send Anthony overseas as a war correspondent, but Anthony declines. Anthony and Gloria are living above their income and doing nothing productive, although Anthony has sold one essay to a magazine. Joseph Bloeckman offers to arrange a screen test for Gloria, but Anthony objects. Anthony and Gloria return to his New York apartment for the winter, and Anthony takes a job as a bond salesman at Wilson, Hiemer and Hardy after his grandfather gives him a letter of introduction to the company's president. After Anthony and Gloria celebrate Anthony's new job with a two-day drunken revel with Maury and Dick, a change comes over their lifestyle: "The magnificent attitude of not giving a damn altered overnight; from being a mere tenet of Gloria's it became the entire solace and justification for what they chose to do and what consequence it brought. Not to be sorry, not to loose one cry of regret, to live according to a clear code of honor toward each other, and to seek the moment's happiness as fervently and persistently as possible" (p. 226). Anthony quits his job, and they renew their lease on the Marietta house for the summer by mistake during a drunken party.

Chapter III: The Broken Lute
Gloria asks Anthony not to drink too much, not to insist on paying for everything when they're out with friends, and not to be so attentive to her friend Rachael Barnes. Adam Patch, whose telephone message Anthony has not received, arrives at their Marietta house in the middle of a drunken party and leaves in disgust. A week later Anthony goes to visit him but is turned away by his secretary, Edward SHUTTLEWORTH, who says Patch is not well. Anthony and Gloria return to New York for the winter but are unable to afford the increased rent on Anthony's old apartment. Adam Patch dies; when Anthony learns that he has been cut out of the will, he hires a lawyer to contest it. Despite their worries about money, Anthony and Gloria continue to squander money on wild parties every weekend. Anthony's attempt to write popular magazine stories fails. Gloria's father dies. America declares war on Germany; Anthony's application for officers' training

camp is denied because of his blood pressure, but he is later drafted. Adam Patch's will is upheld in court, and Gloria and Anthony file an appeal.

BOOK THREE

Chapter I: A Matter of Civilization

In October Anthony arrives at CAMP HOOKER in South Carolina to begin his military training. He has an affair with Dot RAYCROFT, a lower-class girl, and discourages Gloria from traveling South to join him. In March his brigade moves to CAMP BOONE in Mississippi, and he maintains Dot at a boardinghouse downtown. Anthony lies about his name when he is caught returning to camp late, and he is demoted from corporal and sentenced to the guard-house for three weeks. His regiment is moved to CAMP MILLS on Long Island just before the war ends, and he and Gloria are reunited at the Armistice Ball.

Chapter II: A Matter of Æsthetics

During Anthony's year in the army Gloria misses him, even though they have not gotten along well for about a year. Rachael Barnes invites her to dinner with two officers, Captain COLLINS and Captain WOLF; and Gloria is offended by Captain Collins' attentions to her. She is lonely and is discouraged by Anthony's apparent reluctance for her to travel South to join him. When Anthony is discharged after the war their relationship has changed and become empty, and their concerns about money have increased. At Gloria's insistence Anthony takes a job selling stock in a company that produces motivational pamphlets called "Heart Talks," but he is unable to interest any customers and gets drunk after one day of trying. The appellate court upholds Adam Patch's will, and Anthony and Gloria file a final appeal. As Gloria approaches her 29th birthday she determines to make some use of her beauty and asks Joseph Bloeckman, who has changed his name to Black, for a screen test. The director, Percy B. DEBRIS, decides that the part calls for a younger woman but offers Gloria a small character part, which she doesn't want; she becomes aware of tiny wrinkles in her face and the tiredness of her eyes.

Chapter III: No Matter!

Within another year Anthony and Gloria have moved to another, cheaper apartment; and they explain to Muriel Kane that they don't see their old friends because they don't go where they're not wanted. Anthony, who has resigned from all his clubs and now frequents a speakeasy called Sammy's, is drunk every day and hates to be sober. His bank closes his account because he fails to keep the required $500 balance, and he and Gloria discover one Saturday that they have only $2.50 between them. Anthony goes out to pawn his watch, but first stops to drink at Sammy's. When he discovers

the pawn shops are all closed that night, he tracks down Joseph Black at a nightclub with the intention of asking him for a loan; but instead he rebukes Black for keeping Gloria out of the movies and tells him to leave her alone. Anthony insults Black, who knocks him down and has him thrown into the street. A stranger helps Anthony into a taxi; but when he discovers that Anthony can't pay the fare, he knocks him unconscious. Three weeks later, on the day the trial is to be settled at last, Dot Raycroft appears at Anthony's door and tells him that she still loves him; he blacks out after trying to throw a chair at her. Gloria and Dick Caramel later find him going through his childhood stamp collection, and they tell him he has won the case and is worth thirty million dollars—but he only threatens to tell his grandfather if they won't leave. While sailing to EUROPE with Gloria a few months after he gets his money, Anthony, who is "a little crazy," reflects on "the hardships, the insufferable tribulations he had gone through." He rejoices that he had refused to "submit to mediocrity" despite the urging of his friends that he go to work: "I showed them. . . . It was a hard fight, but I didn't give up and I came through!" (p. 449).

B&D was influenced by Theodore DREISER'S *Sister Carrie* (1900), Frank NORRIS'S *Vandover and the Brute* (1914), and Charles NORRIS'S *Salt* (1917), all works of naturalism, a form of literary realism that emphasizes that human behavior is determined by forces beyond the control of the characters. For example, after Anthony first kisses Gloria, "It never occurred to him that he was a passive thing, acted upon by an influence above and beyond Gloria, that he was merely the sensitive plate on which the photograph was made. Some gargantuan photographer had focussed the camera on Gloria and *snap!*—the poor plate could but develop, confined like all things to its nature" (pp. 105–106). Fitzgerald's interest in naturalism was influenced by H. L. Mencken and George Jean NATHAN. (Mencken's influence on *B&D* is discussed in detail by William Goldhurst in *F. Scott Fitzgerald and His Contemporaries,* Chapter III.)

See *F. Scott Fitzgerald Manuscripts II: "B&D:* The Manuscript," and Amy J. Elias, "The Composition and Revision of Fitzgerald's *The Beautiful and Damned," The Princeton University Library Chronicle,* 51 (Spring 1990), 245–266.

Beauty Boy Character in "Dearly Beloved." Pullman car porter and black golf champion of Chicago who reads Plato and Rosicrucian literature. Fitzgerald's only black protagonist, he has connections with the black FISHERMAN in *LT/LOLT.*

Bebé Character in "Gretchen's Forty Winks." Roger and Gretchen HALSEY'S servant.

Becker, Gwen Character in "Magnetism." Girl who claims George HANNAFORD spent the night with her. Her phone call is a joke instigated by studio executive Pete SCHROEDER.

Becker, Joe Character in "Last Kiss." Agent who introduces Pamela KNIGHTON to Jim LEONARD.

Beebe, Evelyn Character in "The Captured Shadow." Basil Duke LEE asks Evelyn to be the leading lady in his play; but she drops out of the play when leading man Hubert BLAIR does, claiming she has to leave town on a family trip. When her little brother, Ham BEEBE, gets the mumps after Basil has deliberately exposed him to a sick boy, she is unable to leave town and acts in the play after all.

Beebe, Ham Character in "The Captured Shadow." Evelyn BEEBE's little brother, whom Basil Duke LEE deliberately exposes to Teddy BARNFIELD's mumps so that Evelyn will be unable to leave town and miss acting in Basil's play.

Behrer, Doctor Character in "Family in the Wind." Incompetent doctor whom Forrest JANNEY dislikes.

Belknap, Sarah *See* Sarah Belknap SUMMER.

Bellamy, Gordon Character in "The Ice Palace." Harry BELLAMY's brother.

Bellamy, Harry Character in "The Ice Palace." Sally Carrol HAPPER's Yankee fiancé.

Bellamy, Mr. Character in "The Ice Palace." Harry BELLAMY's father, whom Sally Carrol HAPPER likes.

Bellamy, Mrs. Character in "The Ice Palace." Harry BELLAMY's mother, whom Sally Carrol HAPPER dislikes.

Bellamy, Myra Character in "The Ice Palace." Gordon BELLAMY's half-Swedish, spiritless wife.

"Belly Acres" Estate of actor Edward Everett Horton (1886–1970) in ENCINO, California; Fitzgerald rented a cottage (5521 Amestoy Avenue) on the estate for $200 a month from November 1938 to May 1940. His life at "Belly Acres," where he worked on *LT/LOLT,* has been chronicled by his secretary, Frances KROLL Ring, in *Against the Current.*

Beltzman Character in "The Freshest Boy." Man who gave JERRY her part in a play and whom she has promised to marry.

Bement, Ed Character in the Josephine PERRY stories; Josephine's earliest beau, from dancing-school days. In "First Blood" he drives Josephine to and from her meetings with Anthony HARKER. He believes that anyone as beautiful as Josephine could never do anything really wrong. In "A Nice Quiet Place" he hosts a house party where Josephine wins back the affection of Ridgeway SAUNDERS, who had fallen for another girl in her absence. Ed drives Josephine to the railroad station after Constance PERRY's wedding so that she can return to Island Farms. In "A Woman with a Past" he dances with Josephine at the Yale prom. In "A Snobbish Story" he is at the dance at Lake Forest. In "Emotional Bankruptcy" he arrives at Josephine's house at the same time as Edward DICER.

Benchley, Robert (1889–1945) American drama critic, humorist, and actor; theater critic for *Life* (1920–29) and *The NEW YORKER* (1929–40); his books include *Of All Things* (1921) and *The Treasurer's Report* (1930). While in France in 1926 Fitzgerald saw a good deal of Benchley, who had come abroad with Ernest HEMINGWAY. Fitzgerald first saw Sheilah GRAHAM at a party Benchley gave in HOLLYWOOD on July 14, 1937 to celebrate Graham's engagement to the Marquess of Donegal.

See Nathaniel Benchley, *Robert Benchley: A Biography* (New York: McGraw-Hill, 1955).

"Benediction" Fiction. Written October 1919. *The SMART SET,* 61 (February 1920), 35–44; *F&P.* On her way to meet HOWARD, her lover, LOIS stops at a Jesuit seminary to visit her brother, KIETH, whom she hasn't seen since she was a little girl. They discuss their mother, who has suffered a nervous breakdown; and Kieth explains his decision to enter the priesthood. During the Benediction service which she attends with Kieth, Lois is frightened by a presence that she senses in the candle flame; and she faints. Afterwards she tells Kieth how inconvenient Catholicism is, and he reveals how he has idealized her. After leaving the seminary, Lois writes a farewell telegram to Howard, then changes her mind and tears it up.

"Benediction" incorporates material from a 1915 story, "The Ordeal," from which Fitzgerald transferred the JESUIT NOVICE's experience with the candle to Lois.

Bennett, Jim Character in "Inside the House." Boy who is helping Gwen BOWERS decorate her Christmas tree.

Benson, Leslie L. (Langille) (1885–1971) Illustrator for "The Offshore Pirate" (*The SATURDAY EVENING POST,* May 29, 1920) and *The Beautiful and Damned* serial (*METROPOLITAN,* September 1921–March 1922). During the 1920s his black-and-white wash drawings appeared regularly in the *Post, COSMOPOLITAN, REDBOOK, Good Housekeeping,* and *MCCALL'S.*

Benson, Robert Hugh (1871–1914) English novelist. The son of the Archbishop of Canterbury, Benson was ordained in 1895 but converted to Catholicism in 1903. His religious novels include *None Other Gods* (London, 1910), which Fitzgerald mentions in *TSOP* as one of the "quest" novels which influences Amory BLAINE; *None Other Gods* concerns a young English aristocrat who takes to the road as a tramp to seek spiritual fulfillment after converting to Catholicism.

Berg, Phil (1902–1983) Fitzgerald's HOLLYWOOD agent beginning in February 1940; partner in the Phil Berg–Bert Allenberg agency.

Berl Character in "Reade, Substitute Right Half." Captain of READE's football team.

Berners, Jack Character in "A Man in the Way," "Teamed with Genius," "Pat Hobby, Putative Father," "Pat Hobby Does His Bit," "Pat Hobby's Preview," "A Patriotic Short," and "On the Trail of Pat Hobby." HOLLYWOOD producer who occasionally hires Pat HOBBY.

Bernice Character in "Bernice Bobs Her Hair." Boring young girl whose cousin, Marjorie HARVEY, teaches her how to be popular.

"Bernice Bobs Her Hair" Fiction. Written January 1920. *The SATURDAY EVENING POST,* 192 (May 1, 1920), 14–15, 159, 163, 167; *F&P.* BERNICE, pretty but boring, is visiting her cousin, Marjorie HARVEY, whom she overhears discussing her unpopularity. At Bernice's request, Marjorie agrees to instruct her in the art of popularity, which she does with great success. Bernice's best-known line is her often-announced intention of bobbing her hair—a shocking thing that nice girls didn't do. When Marjorie's beau, Warren MCINTYRE, becomes interested in Bernice, Marjorie stops helping Bernice and spitefully announces that Bernice's line about bobbing her hair is a bluff. Bernice reluctantly goes through with the haircut, which spoils her beauty. When she learns that her hostess for the following evening regards bobbed hair as an abomination, she resolves to return home early. Just before leaving town, she cuts off the sleeping Marjorie's long blond braids, which she tosses into Warren McIntyre's yard.

Fitzgerald noted that a long letter of instructions to his sister, Annabel FITZGERALD, was the basis for this story (see *Life in Letters,* pp. 7–10). It was his first story to achieve national prominence, and it inspired the dust jacket illustration for *Flappers and Philosophers*. It is noteworthy as an early exploration of a characteristic Fitzgerald subject: young people's—especially young

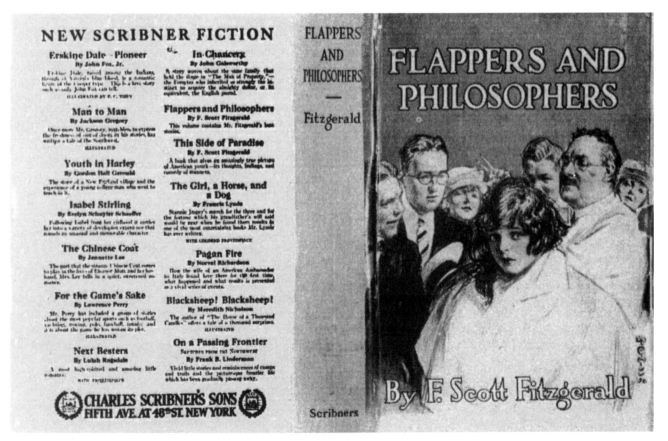

Dust jacket illustrating "Bernice Bobs Her Hair" for Fitzgerald's first short-story collection, published in 1921 (Bruccoli Collection, University of South Carolina)

women's—struggle for social success and the seriousness of their competition.

D. D. Brooke wrote a one-act play based on Fitzgerald's story (Chicago: The Dramatic Publishing Company, 1982). Joan Micklin Silver (b. 1935) adapted Fitzgerald's story for a television movie produced by Learning in Focus, 1977; her screenplay was published in *The American Short Story,* ed. Calvin Skaggs (New York: Dell, 1977).

Berry, Ralph (Rafe) Character in "The Hotel Child." Man who introduces the Marquis KINKALLOW to Fifi SCHWARTZ.

"Between Three and Four" Fiction. Written June 1931. *The SATURDAY EVENING POST,* 204 (September 5, 1931), 8–9, 69, 72; *The Price Was High.* During the Depression Sarah Belknap SUMMER asks Howard BUTLER to give her a job six months after he fired her. Butler still resents that she refused to marry him 30 years ago and doesn't want to rehire her, but he tells her to come back in a week. She says she'll probably jump out of a ninth-floor window if he doesn't have a job for her then. When she returns, he refuses to see her; and later that afternoon he hears that a woman jumped out of a ninth-story window. He believes he sees Mrs. Summer identified as the victim in the newspaper, and he convinces himself that her ghost is returning to his office every afternoon. After he jumps to his death from his own office window, it is revealed that it was not Mrs. Summer who had died and that she has twice been in his office, alive, when he thought she was a ghost.

Bibble, Ermine Gilberte Labouisse (Minnie) Character in the Basil Duke LEE stories. In "He Thinks He's Wonderful," while she is visiting her cousin, Bill KAMPF, Minnie and Basil Duke Lee fall in love. In "Forging Ahead" she is distressed by Basil's attention to Rhoda SINCLAIR. In "Basil and Cleopatra" she falls in love with Littleboy LE MOYNE, with whom she gets into trouble in a locked train compartment—an incident Fitzgerald transferred to Rosemary HOYT in *TITN.* Basil regards Minnie as "one of the immortal sirens of the world" (*AOAA,* p. 66), but he chooses his ambitions over a return to Minnie.

Bibble, Mr. and Mrs. Characters in the Basil Duke LEE stories. Minnie BIBBLE's parents. In "He Thinks He's Wonderful," Mr. Bibble is initially flattered by Basil's attentiveness to his conversation; but after Basil talks too much about himself, Mr. Bibble decides not to take him along on their family trip as he had previously planned. In "Forging Ahead" the Bibbles are visiting Bill KAMPF's family. In "Basil and Cleopatra" Minnie informs Basil that her parents are getting a divorce.

Bigelow, Alida and Donald Sister and brother who were childhood friends of Fitzgerald in ST. PAUL; members of William BAKER's dancing class. Alida, whom Fitzgerald described as "the most popular girl I know of" (*Thoughtbook,* p. XX), was one of his childhood sweethearts; but he noted in his *Thoughtbook* for February 1911 that he had deserted Alida for "two new crushes"—Margaret ARMSTRONG and Marie HERSEY (p. XXIX). Alida and Fitzgerald corresponded while they were at college, and he wrote to her on September 23, 1919 about SCRIBNERS' acceptance of *TSOP* (*Life in Letters,* pp. 33–34).

Biggs, John, Jr. (1895–1979) American novelist, lawyer, and judge; friend of Fitzgerald. A member of the PRINCETON class of 1918, Biggs was Fitzgerald's roommate at Campbell Hall when Fitzgerald returned to Princeton in September 1917. They had collaborated on the 1916 TRIANGLE CLUB musical *Safety First.* Biggs was editor of *The PRINCETON TIGER,* and Fitzgerald claimed that he and Biggs wrote an entire issue overnight. At Fitzgerald's recommendation, SCRIBNERS published Biggs's first novel, *Demigods,* in 1926; Scribners also published Biggs's novel *Seven Days Whipping* in 1928. In 1927 Biggs, then a lawyer in WILMINGTON, Delaware, helped the Fitzgeralds find "ELLERSLIE," a mansion they rented. While Fitzgerald lived at "Ellerslie," Biggs had to respond to late-night phone calls to get him out of jail for alcoholic escapades. When Fitzerald wrote his will on June 17, 1937, he appointed Biggs and Harold OBER as executors; but on November 10, 1940 he substituted Maxwell PERKINS for Ober. After Fitzgerald's death both Perkins and Ober withdrew as executors to avoid possible legal problems from Fitzgerald's alteration of his will; but they worked closely with Biggs, who was then a federal judge in Wilmington, in the administration of Fitzgerald's literary affairs. Biggs administered the estate for the benefit of Zelda FITZGERALD until her death in 1948.

See Seymour I. Toll, *A Judge Uncommon: A Life of John Biggs, Jr.* (Philadelphia: Legal Communications, 1993).

Billings, Senator Character in "One Interne." Patient whom Bill TULLIVER is examining when Tulliver collapses with stomach pain.

Biloxi, "Blocks" Character in *GG.* Man who fainted at Tom and Daisy BUCHANAN's wedding. Jordan BAKER's recollection of Biloxi's false claim that he was president of Tom's class at Yale serves as an opening for Tom to question Jay GATSBY's claim that he attended Oxford.

Bilphism Religion based on reincarnation which Fitzgerald invented as a parody of theosophy; in *B&D* Catherine GILBERT is a Bilphist. In 1922 Fitzgerald explained to Dr. Frank H. Vizetelly, editor of the Funk

and Wagnall's *Standard Dictionary:* "Bilphism is a coinage of my own. It is a euphemism for Theosophy—I wanted to take a crack at theosophy without hurting the feelings of a relative of mine. Several people have inquired about it. So I guess it will enter no dictionary" (*F. Scott Fitzgerald Collection Notes,* No. 1, September 1995).

Biographical Studies Fitzgerald wrote in his *Notebooks,* "There never was a good biography of a good novelist. There couldn't be. He is too many people if he's any good" (#1037). Certainly Fitzgerald was many people. His life and his work are closely connected, and he has inspired several biographical studies.

Arthur MIZENER was the first Fitzgerald biographer, with *The Far Side of Paradise* (Boston: Houghton Mifflin, 1951; revised edition, 1965). Mizener helped to revive interest in Fitzgerald and his works, and the book was the first to depict Fitzgerald as a serious literary figure. As John B. Chambers points out in *The Novels of F. Scott Fitzgerald* (New York: St. Martin's Press, 1989), Mizener began linking the life and the work, providing an approach used by many subsequent scholars. Andrew TURNBULL, whose family owned "LA PAIX"—the house Fitzgerald rented near BALTIMORE, and who as a child had spent time with Fitzgerald—wrote *Scott Fitzgerald* (New York: Scribners, 1962) to present more of Fitzgerald's personality as Turnbull and others had known him. André LeVot's *F. Scott Fitzgerald* (Paris: Julliard, 1979) provides a European perspective on the distinctly American writer. Nancy Milford presents a highly sympathetic biography of Zelda FITZGERALD in *Zelda* (New York: Harper & Row, 1970).

Some biographers focus on a particular aspect of Fitzgerald's life. Aaron Latham concentrates on Fitzgerald's last years in HOLLYWOOD with *Crazy Sundays* (New York: Viking, 1971). In *Fool for Love* (New York: Congdon & Weed, 1983), Scott Donaldson writes about Fitzgerald's relationships with women, his need for approval and admiration, and how these factors influenced his work. James R. Mellow's *Invented Lives* (Boston: Houghton Mifflin, 1984) focuses on the Fitzgeralds' marriage and the many roles they created for themselves within it. Interest in Fitzgerald's life continues unabated; in the most recent biography, *Scott Fitzgerald* (New York: HarperCollins, 1994), Jeffrey Meyers states that he wants to be "more analytical and interpretive" than previous chroniclers.

The standard biography of Fitzgerald is Matthew J. BRUCCOLI's *Some Sort of Epic Grandeur* (New York: Harcourt Brace Jovanovich, 1981; revised edition, New York: Carroll & Graf, 1991). Bruccoli is most concerned with the facts, and his meticulous research clarifies the distinction between the real Fitzgerald and the popular legend. He also focuses on Fitzgerald the professional writer, asserting that the author's work is what ultimately has the greatest significance. The Fitzgeralds' daughter, Scottie FITZGERALD Smith, collaborated with Bruccoli and Joan P. Kerr to edit *The Romantic Egoists: A Pictorial Autobiography from the Scrapbooks and Albums of Scott and Zelda Fitzgerald* (New York: Scribners, 1974), which reproduces material from the Fitzgeralds' scrapbooks, with photographs, letters, clippings, and autobiographical bits from their writings, to present their own portrait of their lives.

There have also been several memoirs by people who knew Fitzgerald. Foremost among these are the books by Sheilah GRAHAM, who began chronicling her love affair with Fitzgerald in *Beloved Infidel* (written with Gerold Frank; New York: Holt, Rinehart & Winston, 1958), which takes its title from a poem Fitzgerald wrote to her. She also wrote *College of One* (New York: Viking, 1967) about the educational plans Fitzgerald devised for her when he discovered her insecurity about her lack of formal schooling. She rewrote and augmented the best portions of her previous books in *The Real F. Scott Fitzgerald Thirty-five Years Later* (New York: Grossett & Dunlap, 1976). One of her motives for writing was to correct some of the misconceptions about Fitzgerald's last years in Hollywood, since he had been depicted as a broken, drunken failure. A similar motive spurred Frances KROLL Ring's *Against the Current: As I Remember F. Scott Fitzgerald* (San Francisco: Ellis/Creative Arts, 1985). As a young woman, Kroll had been Fitzgerald's secretary during the last twenty months of his life; she presents a portrait of the writer at work on *The Love of the Last Tycoon.*

Other memoirs include Anthony BUTTITTA's *After the Good Gay Times* (New York: Viking, 1974; republished as *The Lost Summer* [London: Robson, 1987]). Buttitta, a bookshop proprietor, knew Fitzgerald briefly in ASHEVILLE, North Carolina, in the summer of 1935. Sara Mayfield, a childhood friend of Zelda Fitzgerald, created a dual portrait of the Fitzgeralds as she saw them in *Exiles from Paradise* (New York: Delacorte Press, 1971); her account is very sympathetic to Zelda Fitzgerald and disapproving of Scott Fitzgerald. Canadian novelist Morley CALLAGHAN recalls his acquaintance with the Fitzgeralds and Ernest HEMINGWAY in *That Summer in Paris* (New York: Coward-McCann, 1963). Hemingway's *A Moveable Feast* (New York: Scribners, 1964), presents a devastating portrayal of Fitzgerald, which is also unreliable; a more accurate examination of the relationship between these two authors is presented in Bruccoli's *Fitzgerald and Hemingway: A Dangerous Friendship* (New York: Carroll & Graf, 1994).

For some of the best biographical material, one can go to the subject himself. Fitzgerald was an extraordinary self-chronicler; in addition to his fiction and autobiographical essays, as in the "Crack-Up" series, he saved letters and kept records and scrapbooks. *F. Scott Fitzgerald's Ledger* (introduction by Matthew J. Bruccoli;

Washington: Bruccoli Clark/NCR Microcard Books, 1973), is a facsimile edition of a document which Fitzgerald maintained from about 1920 to 1937, in which he listed his works and Zelda Fitzgerald's, indicating where they had been published, how much money they had brought in, and whether he had "stripped" them (cutting out the best parts to be reused). The *Ledger* also includes Fitzgerald's detailed "Outline Chart of My Life," a month-by-month self-summary. There are also several collections of correspondence, which illuminate personal and professional relationships (*see* LETTERS). The most recent collection, *F. Scott Fitzgerald: A Life in Letters* (ed. Bruccoli; New York: Scribners, 1994), is "the standard one-volume edition." Finally, *The Notebooks of F. Scott Fitzgerald* (ed. Bruccoli; New York: Harcourt Brace Jovanovich/Bruccoli Clark, 1978), which Fitzgerald kept in the 1930s, were his "bank" for the pieces he stripped from his stories, as well as other ideas, observations, bits of dialogue, and self-reflections.

by Tracy Simmons Bitonti

Bisby, Mrs. Caxton Character in "The Intimate Strangers." SARA's oldest sister, who is concerned over Sara's temporary disappearance with Cedric KILLIAN.

Bishop Character in "The Kingdom in the Dark." Bishop traveling with King LOUIS. He agrees with the ABBOT in the abbot's dispute with PHILIPPE over the boundaries between their properties.

Bishop, John Peale (1892–1944) American author; friend of Fitzgerald. His books include *The Collected Poems of John Peale Bishop,* ed. Allen Tate (New York & London: Scribners, 1948) and *The Collected Essays of John Peale Bishop,* ed. Edmund WILSON (New York & London: Scribners, 1948). Fitzgerald and Bishop, a member of the PRINCETON Class of 1917, became friends in April 1914. As editor of *The NASSAU LITERARY MAGAZINE* he published Fitzgerald's serious writing at Princeton. Bishop won English prizes, was class poet, and collaborated on the class ode for the 1917 graduation. He influenced the development of Fitzgerald's increasingly serious literary ambitions. Fitzgerald later acknowledged Bishop's influence in a letter to his daughter, Scottie FITZGERALD, regarding learning about poetry: "It isn't something easy to get started on by yourself. You need, at the beginning, some enthusiast who knows his way around—John Peale Bishop performed that office for me at Princeton. I had always dabbled in 'verse' but he made me see, in the course of a couple of months, the difference between poetry and non-poetry" (August 3, 1940; *Life in Letters,* p. 460). Bishop served as the model for Thomas Parke D'INVILLIERS in *TSOP;* and Fitzgerald credited the epigraph in *The Great Gatsby* to D'Invilliers.

John Peale Bishop

Bishop reviewed *B&D,* acknowledging it as an advance from *TSOP,* but criticizing it as well: "Fitzgerald is at the moment of announcing the meaninglessness of life magnificently alive. His ideas are too often treated like paper crackers, things to make a gay and pretty noise with and then be cast aside; he is frequently at the mercy of words with which he has only a nodding acquaintance; his aesthetics are faulty; his literary taste is at times extremely bad" ("Mr. Fitzgerald Sees the Flapper Through," *New York Herald,* March 5, 1922, section 8, p. 1; *FSF: The Critical Reception,* p. 74). He later wrote to Fitzgerald that he was "overcome with the magnificence" of *TITN:* "It surpasses *The Great Gatsby.* You have shown us, what we have wanted so long and impatiently to see, that you are a true, a beautiful and a tragic novelist. I have only praise for its understanding, its characterization, and its deep tenderness" (April 3, 1934; *Correspondence,* p. 339).

The Fitzgeralds saw Bishop in PARIS in May 1924, at which time he may have told Fitzgerald about Ernest HEMINGWAY, whom he had met in 1922. Fitzgerald met Bishop for literary conversations in Paris during the summer of 1928; but their friendship was no longer

intimate, for Bishop had married a wealthy woman who didn't like his friends and whom they disliked. Bishop had not published a book since *The Undertaker's Garland,* a 1922 collaboration with Edmund Wilson. Fitzgerald read Bishop's novel (never published), which he described to Maxwell PERKINS as "impossible" (c. July 15, 1928; *Scott/Max,* p. 151); but he told Perkins that Bishop's Civil War novelette was excellent. Fitzgerald urged Bishop to submit the novelette to SCRIBNER'S MAGAZINE, which rejected it as too long; the story was probably "The Cellar," later published in Bishop's 1931 volume *Many Thousands Gone* (Scribners).

While Fitzgerald was living at "LA PAIX" and working on *TITN,* he designated Bishop as his literary executor "in case of misfortune" (August 9, 1933; *Correspondence,* p. 316). Years later he was offended by an article Bishop published in the *Virginia Quarterly Review* ("The Missing All," 13 [Winter 1937], 106–121), which falsely stated that Fitzgerald flunked out of Princeton and which Fitzgerald read as an accusation of "being a suck around the rich" (to Edmund Wilson, November 25, 1940; *Life in Letters,* p. 471).

After Fitzgerald's death Bishop mourned the passing of his friend in "The Hours," a requiem published in *The New Republic* in 1941 and later collected in *CU,* including these lines:

> None had such promise then, and none
> Your scapegrace wit or your disarming grace;
> For you were bold as was Danaë's son,
> Conceived like Perseus in a dream of gold.
> And there was none when you were young, not one,
> So prompt in the reflecting shield to trace
> The glittering aspect of a Gorgon age. (*CU,* p. 345)

See Elizabeth Carroll Spindler, *John Peale Bishop: A Biography* (Morgantown: West Virginia University Library, 1980).

Bissel, Imogene Character in the Basil Duke LEE stories. Based on Fitzgerald's ST. PAUL friend Margaret ARMSTRONG. In "The Scandal Detectives" Imogene leaves Basil for Hubert BLAIR. In "He Thinks He's Wonderful," she names Basil as her favorite boy during a game of Truth. Basil believes he is in love with her, but she is no longer interested in him after word spreads that he thinks he's wonderful. However, at the end of the story she is eager to go riding with him in his grandfather's car. In "The Captured Shadow" Basil and Riply BUCKNER want her to be the leading lady in Basil's play, but she is having an appendectomy.

Bits of Paradise: 21 Uncollected Stories by F. Scott and Zelda Fitzgerald Story collection. Selected by Scottie FITZGERALD Smith and Matthew J. BRUCCOLI, with foreword by Smith and preface by Bruccoli. London: Bodley Head, 1973; New York: Charles SCRIBNER's Sons, 1974. Contents: "The Popular Girl" (FSF), "Love in the Night" (FSF), "Our Own Movie Queen" (FSF & ZF), "A Penny Spent" (FSF), "The Dance" (FSF), "Jacob's Ladder" (FSF), "The Swimmers" (FSF), "The Original Follies Girl" (ZF), "The Southern Girl" (ZF), "The Girl the Prince Liked" (ZF), "The Girl with Talent" (ZF), "A Millionaire's Girl" (ZF), "Poor Working Girl" (ZF), "The Hotel Child" (FSF), "A New Leaf" (FSF), "Miss Ella" (ZF), "The Continental Angle" (ZF), "A Couple of Nuts" (ZF), "What a Handsome Pair!" (FSF), "Last Kiss" (FSF), "Dearly Beloved" (FSF).

Black, Joseph *See* Joseph BLOECKMAN.

Blaine, Amory Character in *TSOP.* Young man who from his boyhood considers himself superior and destined for a great future and who lives by a code of "aristocratic egotism" (p. 19). He is unpopular at ST. REGIS prep school until he becomes a football hero. He becomes the protégé of Monsignor Thayer DARCY, who encourages his ambitions and introspection. Amory goes to PRINCETON, where he becomes active in the TRIANGLE CLUB, is elected to the COTTAGE CLUB, and serves on the board of the *Princetonian,* though he forfeits his chance at the editorship by failing a crucial exam. He falls in love with Isabelle BORGÉ, but they eventually break up because she thinks he is too critical. He serves in the army during the war, and he learns of the loss of his family's wealth after his mother's death. He takes a job with an advertising agency in NEW YORK. He falls in love with Princeton classmate Alec CONNAGE's sister Rosalind CONNAGE, and they talk of marriage; but she breaks up with him to marry wealthy Dawson RYDER. Amory drinks for three weeks to get over her loss and quits his advertising job. While visiting an uncle in Maryland he meets reckless, romantic Eleanor SAVAGE. He makes a "supercilious sacrifice" when Alec is caught in an Atlantic City hotel room with Jill WAYNE; Amory tells the house detective she was with him. Amory's sense of evil, which he connects with sex, is underscored by supernatural events, such as his sense of a presence in the curtains of the hotel room and his earlier hallucination of a devil figure in the apartment of two New York showgirls. Discouraged with the progress of his life and disillusioned with the inconsistencies he sees in the lives of others, Amory reflects that life is a "damned muddle" (p. 285). Finally, with the death and funeral of Darcy, Amory realizes that he wants not to be admired or loved, but to be indispensable and to give people a sense of security. Returning to Princeton at the end of the novel, he determines to continue his struggle, to "use to the utmost himself and his heritage from the personalities he had passed" (p. 305). He cries, "I know myself . . . but that is all" (p. 305).

Amory Blaine is a highly autobiographical character, sharing Fitzgerald's sense of the possibilities of life and his aspiration toward the fulfillment of his unique destiny.

Blaine, Beatrice O'Hara Character in *TSOP*. Amory BLAINE's eccentric, indulgent mother who enjoys recounting her various ailments. "Though she thought of her body as a mass of frailties, she considered her soul quite as ill," so "next to doctors, priests were her favorite sport" (p. 7). She had a romance with Monsignor DARCY before he joined the Catholic Church. She dies while Amory is in the army.

Blaine, Stephen Character in *TSOP*. Amory BLAINE's unassertive father, who passes to his son his "tendency to waver at crucial moments" (p. 3). He and Amory are never shown together in the novel, and he dies during Amory's junior year at PRINCETON.

Blair, Mr. and Mrs. George P. Characters in "The Scandal Detectives." Hubert BLAIR's parents. They are concerned about the warning notes Hubert has received, and Mr. Blair calls the police after Hubert encounters a "gang of toughs" (really Basil Duke LEE, Riply BUCKNER, and Bill KAMPF wearing disguises) in an alley. Hubert and his mother go to the shore for the summer as a result of the incident.

Blair, Hubert Character in the Basil Duke LEE stories. Based on Fitzgerald's ST. PAUL friend and rival Reuben WARNER. The boys admire Hubert's athletic prowess, and the girls find him fascinating. In "The Scandal Detectives" Basil, Riply BUCKNER, and Bill KAMPF plan to waylay him because Imogene BISSEL preferred his attention to Basil's. In "A Night at the Fair" he uses the name "Bill Jones" when making a date with a girl named OLIVE, who abandons Riply Buckner for him. Gladys VAN SCHELLINGER asks Basil to bring Hubert to visit her after she sees him cavorting at the fair. In "He Thinks He's Wonderful" he rides with Joe GORMAN to Connie DAVIES' dance. Margaret TORRENCE tells Basil that Hubert and Joe have told everyone that Basil thinks he's wonderful. In "The Captured Shadow" Hubert temporarily takes the role of the leading man in Basil's play.

Blair, William Brevoort Character in "Majesty." Emily CASTLETON's abandoned fiancé, whom Olive MERCY marries.

Bleuler, Dr. Paul Eugen (1857–1939) The leading authority on schizophrenia, which he named, Bleuler was called in for a consultation on Zelda FITZGERALD on November 22, 1930 after she suffered relapses that fall at PRANGINS. He confirmed Dr. Oscar FOREL's diagnosis

of schizophrenia but offered Fitzgerald hope for Zelda's recovery.

Bliss, Doctor Character in "Her Last Case." Ben DRAGONET's doctor.

Bloeckman, Joseph Character in *B&D*. Jewish filmmaker who does business with Gloria Gilbert PATCH's father. He wants to marry Gloria and offers to put her in the movies. He is a little more dignified and refined each time Anthony PATCH and Gloria encounter him after their marriage, and he changes his last name to Black. He arranges a screen test for Gloria at her request shortly before her 29th birthday, but the director decides the role in question requires a younger actress. When Anthony needs money he tracks down Black at a nightclub, where Anthony tells him to leave Gloria alone and insults him; Black knocks him down and has him thrown out.

Boardman, Laurence (Larry) Childhood friend of Fitzgerald in ST. PAUL; a member of the ELIZABETHAN DRAMATIC CLUB and William BAKER's dancing class. In September 1919, while Fitzgerald was waiting to learn whether SCRIBNERS would accept *TSOP*, Boardman helped him find a job at the Northern Pacific Railroad yards, which he quit after a few days.

The Bodley Head Scott Fitzgerald 6 vols. London: Bodley Head, 1958–63. Contents: I (1958): *GG*, *LT*, "May Day," "The Diamond as Big as the Ritz," "The Crack-Up," "Handle With Care," "Pasting It Together," "Crazy Sunday"; II (1959): "Echoes of the Jazz Age," "My Lost City," "Ring," "Early Success," Letters to Frances Scott Fitzgerald, *TITN* (original version), "The Last of the Belles," "A Patriotic Short," "Two Old-Timers," "An Alcoholic Case," "Financing Finnegan"; III (1960): *TSOP*, "The Cut-Glass Bowl," "The Curious Case of Benjamin Button," "The Lees of Happiness," "The Rich Boy," "The Adjuster," "Gretchen's Forty Winks"; IV (1961): *B&D*, "The Rough Crossing," "Babylon Revisited"; V & VI (1963): Adds 12 stories to Cowley's *The Stories of F. Scott Fitzgerald* (1951): "The Jelly Bean," "A Short Trip Home," "The Bowl," "Outside the Cabinet-Maker's," "Majesty," "A Night at the Fair," "He Thinks He's Wonderful," "First Blood," "One Trip Abroad," "Design in Plaster," " 'Boil Some Water—Lots of It,' " "Teamed with Genius."

" 'Boil Some Water—Lots of It' " Fiction—Pat HOBBY story. Submitted September 21, 1939. *ESQUIRE*, 13 (March 1940), 30, 145, 147; *AOAA*; *PH*. Pat Hobby is employed to polish the script for a medical movie, and he takes nurse Helen EARLE to lunch to ask her some questions. While they are in the studio commissary, writer Walter HERRICK, disguised as a Russian Cossack,

creates a commotion by attempting to join the powerful men at the Big Table. Hobby, outraged by the Cossack's impudence and by the inaction of the others, assaults the Cossack with a tray before his real identity is discovered.

Boldini, Jeff Character in "Pat Hobby and Orson Welles." Makeup artist who makes up Pat HOBBY like Orson Welles (1915–85) and drives him to the studio in a car with a sign bearing Welles's name.

"A Book of One's Own" Humor article. *The NEW YORKER,* 13 (August 21, 1937), 19; *In His Own Time.* Humorous prospectus for a "super-anthology that over a single weekend should make the conscientious reader as nearly omniscient as a man can be" (*In His Own Time,* p. 237). One sample chapter includes "Memoirs of a Statistician (Cond.), Cath. Index, Readers' Digest (Cond.), Sorrows of Grand Dukes (Compressed), Orph. Annie (Selects.), Scenario Writing, quick course, Elements of Brewing, Familiar Quots., Apostles' Creed" (p. 237).

A Book of Princeton Verse II Ed. Henry Van Dyke, Morris William Croll, Maxwell Struthers Burt, and James Creese, Jr. (Princeton: Princeton University Press/London: Humphry Milford/Oxford University Press, 1919). Fitzgerald's first appearance in a book; includes "Marching Streets," "The Pope at Confession," and "My First Love," reprinted from *The NASSAU LITERARY MAGAZINE* and signed "T. Scott Fitzgerald."

Boone, Joe Character in " 'I Didn't Get Over.' " One of three classmates to whom HIBBING tells the story of Abe DANZER.

Booth, Jacob Character in "Jacob's Ladder." Wealthy man whose singing career has been cut short by laryngitis and who helps Jenny DELEHANTY, with whom he falls in love, become an actress.

Booth, John Wilkes (1838–1865) Historical figure and character in "The Room with the Green Blinds." Assassin of President Abraham Lincoln (1809–1865). Booth was shot by Union soldiers in a burning barn near Bowling Green, Virginia. In Fitzgerald's fictional account, Booth escaped in a case of mistaken identity.

Bopes See Marquis KINKALLOW.

Bordon, Dolly (Countess de Lanclerc) Character in "Discard." Actress whose husband, Count Hennen DE LANCLERC, leaves her for Phyllis BURNS.

Borgé, Isabelle Character in *TSOP.* Amory BLAINE's first love, whom he meets during the Christmas holi

days of his sophomore year at PRINCETON when she is visiting her cousin, Sally WEATHERBY, in Minneapolis. They correspond all spring, and she comes to Princeton in June for the prom. The next day they go to her family's summer place on Long Island, and they quarrel and break up. Based on Ginevra KING.

Borgé, Mrs. Character in *TSOP.* Isabelle BORGÉ's mother, who escorts her daughter to PRINCETON to attend the prom with Amory BLAINE.

Borowki, Count Stanislas Karl Joseph Character in "The Hotel Child." Penniless man, posing as a Hungarian count, who is seeking a wealthy wife. He tries to persuade Fifi SCHWARTZ to marry him, and he runs away with Miss HOWARD.

Borzage, Frank (1893–1962) Director of *Three Comrades* (1938), for which Fitzgerald received his only screen credit. Borzage may be the source for John BROACA in *LT/LOLT.*

Bounds Character in *B&D.* Anthony PATCH's English servant.

Bourne, Mark H. Character in "More Than Just a House." Man who takes away the GUNTHERS' mortgaged possessions.

Bowers, Bryan Character in the Gwen BOWERS stories. Widower who is raising his teenaged daughter, Gwen. In "Too Cute for Words" he finds that Gwen has sneaked into the PRINCETON prom. In "Inside the House" he refuses to let Gwen go on a movie date with Jason CRAWFORD.

Bowers, Donald Character in "Three Hours Between Planes." Boy with whom Nancy Holmes [GIFFORD] used to go to a cave and whom she briefly confuses with Donald PLANT, who visits her years later.

Bowers, Gwen Character in "Too Cute for Words" and "Inside the House." Based on Scottie FITZGERALD. In "Too Cute for Words" she sneaks into the PRINCETON prom. In "Inside the House" she sneaks out to a movie with Jason CRAWFORD. Fitzgerald hoped to create a series of Gwen stories and wrote four in 1935 and 1936, but *The SATURDAY EVENING POST* declined "The Pearl and the Fur" and "Make Yourself at Home" and recommended that he discontinue the series. Harold OBER sent Fitzgerald a list of 29 improbabilities and inconsistencies requiring revision in "The Pearl and the Fur" (April 25, 1936; *As Ever,* pp. 265–267). Fitzgerald changed the names of the characters and sold the two rejected stories to *Pictorial Review,* which went out of business without publishing them. "Make Yourself at

Home" was resold to *LIBERTY,* which published it as "Strange Sanctuary" in 1939.

"The Bowl" Fiction. Written November 1927. *The SATURDAY EVENING POST,* 200 (January 21, 1928), 6–7, 93–94, 97, 100; *The Bodley Head Scott Fitzgerald; The Price Was High.* Jeff DEERING tells the story of his PRINCETON roommate, Dolly HARLAN, a good football player who hates the game but feels a moral responsibility to follow through on his commitment to play. In the Yale game Dolly feels that the Yale Bowl is closing in on him; however, he plays well, and Princeton beats Yale for the first time in three years. After the game Dolly meets and falls in love with Vienna THORNE, who doesn't mention the game because her brother was killed in a prep-school football game. When they become engaged the next year Vienna convinces Dolly not to play football that fall. Dolly breaks his ankle, which gives him an excuse not to play; but as the season progresses he feels a sense of responsibility and rejoins the team, causing Vienna to break off their relationship. After a tie game with Yale, he becomes interested in actress Daisy CARY, who shares his dedication to work despite illness or injury.

Except for two Basil Duke LEE stories with football scenes, "The Bowl" is Fitzgerald's only professionally published football story. Work on "The Bowl" rekindled his interest in Princeton football. Thomas B. COSTAIN, an editor at *The Saturday Evening Post,* reported to Harold OBER that the *Post* felt that Fitzgerald had "got the real spirit of the game as it has perhaps never been done before" (*As Ever,* p. 104).

Bowman, Tom Character in "The Popular Girl." Yanci BOWMAN's alcoholic father, who dies suddenly, leaving her destitute.

Bowman, Yanci Character in "The Popular Girl." Beautiful girl who, when her father's sudden death leaves her with little money, attempts to win wealthy Scott KIMBERLY by conveying an impression of prosperity and popularity.

Boxley, George Character in *LT/LOLT.* English novelist who struggles to adjust to writing for the movies. Based on English novelist Aldous Huxley (1894–1963), with whom Fitzgerald worked on *Madame Curie.*

"The Boy Who Killed His Mother" Verse. *Neurotica,* 9 (Winter 1952), 38–39 [unauthorized publication]; *Notebooks* #884. This poem, which Fitzgerald performed as a party stunt, provided a working title for an early version of *TITN.*

Boyd, Peggy (1898–1965) Thomas BOYD's wife; American author who wrote as Woodward Boyd. Fitzgerald

became a friend of the Boyds while living in ST. PAUL in 1921 and 1922. He recommended Peggy's novel, *The Love Legend,* to SCRIBNERS, which published it in 1922; *see* "A Rugged Novel" for his review.

Boyd, Thomas A. (1898–1935) American novelist and biographer, friend of Fitzgerald. His books include *Through the Wheat* (1923) and *Mad Anthony Wayne* (1929). As literary editor of the *St. Paul Daily News* he interviewed Fitzgerald in August 1921 when the Fitzgeralds moved to ST. PAUL to await the birth of their daughter ("Scott Fitzgerald Here on Vacation; 'Rests' by Outlining New Novels," August 28, 1921, City Life Section, 6); and his three-part interview in March 1922 provided a description of Fitzgerald's working habits ("Literary Libels—Francis Scott Key Fitzgerald," March 5, 12, 19, 1922, City Life Section, 6; shortened version in *In His Own Time,* pp. 245–254). In early 1923 Fitzgerald conferred with SCRIBNERS editor Maxwell PERKINS about the publication of Boyd's World War I novel, *Through the Wheat*; and he wrote a favorable review for the *New York Evening Post* when the novel appeared in May (*see* "Under Fire"). Boyd inscribed Fitzgerald's copy "for F. Scott Fitzgerald the most generous and engaging individual I've ever known—and without whom Saint Paul is a pretty sallow spot Thomas Boyd" (*Correspondence,* p. 129).

Boyd, Woodward *See* Peggy BOYD.

Braden, Carty Character in "The Popular Girl." Young man with whom Yanci BOWMAN dances at the country club.

Bradin, Edith Character in "May Day." Gordon STERRETT's former girlfriend, who thinks she would like to revive their relationship until she sees him drunk and pitiful at the Gamma Psi dance.

Bradin, Henry Character in "May Day." Edith BRADIN's brother, a socialist and pacifist who writes for a radical newspaper. His leg is broken when a mob invades the newspaper office.

Brady, Cecelia Narrator of *LT/LOLT.* Pat BRADY's daughter, a junior at Bennington College. She is in love with Monroe STAHR. Based on Fitzgerald's daughter, Scottie FITZGERALD, and Budd SCHULBERG, with whom Fitzgerald worked on *Winter Carnival* (1939) and whose father, B. P. Schulberg (1892–1957), was the former head of production at Paramount. Fitzgerald wrote to Kenneth LITTAUER: "Cecelia is the narrator because I think I know exactly how such a person would react to my story. She is *of* the movies but not *in* them. She probably was born the day 'The Birth of a Nation' was previewed and Rudolf Valentino came to her fifth

birthday party. So she is, all at once, intelligent, cynical but understanding and kindly toward the people, great or small, who are of Hollywood" (September 29, 1939; *Life in Letters*, p. 409). But he admitted to the editors of The SATURDAY EVENING POST, "Though she has adventures of her own she is not one of the characters I am primarily interested in" (December 6, 1939; *Life in Letters*, p. 424).

Brady, Earl Character in *TITN*. Director who wants to work with Rosemary HOYT and to whom she is physically attracted, despite her preference for Dick DIVER. Based on Irish-American movie director Rex Ingram (1893–1950), who had a studio on the RIVIERA in the 1920s; Ingram was also the model for Lew Kelly, the protagonist of an early version of *TITN*.

Brady, Pat Character in *LT/LOLT*. Movie producer and Monroe STAHR's treacherous partner. He is Cecelia BRADY's father. Based on a combination of MGM executives Louis B. Mayer (1885–1957) and Eddie Mannix (1891?–1963).

Braggiotti, Mario (b. 1909) Young American musician born in ITALY. The Fitzgeralds met him while he was staying with Gerald and Sara MURPHY on the RIVIERA, probably in 1926; he was one of several sources for Tommy BARBAN in *TITN*.

the Brain Character in "Shaggy's Morning." One of SHAGGY's owners.

Brancusi, Mr. Character in "Two Wrongs." Producer with whom Bill MCCHESNEY sometimes collaborates. He attempts to persuade McChesney to return to America from LONDON.

Bray, Mrs. Character in "First Blood." Josephine PERRY's mother's friend, who has a bad opinion of Josephine.

"Breakfast" Article by Zelda FITZGERALD. *Favorite Recipes of Famous Women*, ed. Florence Stratton. New York & London: Harper & Brothers, 1925, p. 98; *Zelda Fitzgerald: The Collected Writings*. Humorous instructions for preparing breakfast.

Brereton, Miss Character in "A Woman with a Past." Headmistress at Josephine PERRY's boarding school. She overreacts when she finds Josephine, who has fallen, in the arms of her nephew, Ernest WATERBURY; and Josephine's father removes her from the school.

Brett, Mr. Character in *B&D*. Adam PATCH's lawyer, who informs Anthony PATCH that he was cut out of his grandfather's will.

"The Bridal Party" Fiction. Written May 1930. *The SATURDAY EVENING POST*, 203 (August 9, 1930), 10–11, 109–110, 112, 114; *Stories*. Michael CURLY is shocked to hear of the engagement of Caroline DANDY, whom he had lost due to his lack of money but whom he still loves. When he encounters Caroline and her fiancé, Hamilton RUTHERFORD, in PARIS, they invite him to the wedding and several parties. Michael learns that he has inherited a quarter of a million dollars from his grandfather; and he tells Caroline one more time of his enduring love for her, as well as his inheritance; but she remains committed to Rutherford, who has just lost all his money. Despite Rutherford's financial trouble, he goes ahead with the elaborate wedding reception he had planned; and the ceremony and reception cure Michael of his longing for Caroline.

This story was based on the 1930 Paris wedding of Fitzgerald's friend Ludlow FOWLER's brother Powell.

Briggs, John DeQuedville (1885–1965) Headmaster of ST. PAUL ACADEMY from 1914 to 1950; a friend of Fitzgerald during his summer 1919 stay in ST. PAUL while working on *TSOP*. At that time Briggs lived in the same boardinghouse as Donald Ogden STEWART.

Brimmer Character in *LT/LOLT*. Communist labor organizer whom Cecelia BRADY takes to meet Monroe STAHR. When Stahr drunkenly attempts to beat him up, Brimmer knocks Stahr down.

Brinson, Marjorie Sayre *See* Marjorie SAYRE.

Broaca, John Character in *LT/LOLT*. Movie director whose picture is under discussion at the script conference. May be based on Frank BORZAGE, the director of *Three Comrades*.

"The Broadcast We Almost Heard Last September" Satire. Written in 1935. *Furioso*, 3 (Fall 1947), 8–10. Sports-style broadcast of a battle in Central EUROPE.

Bronson, Ed Character in "Hot & Cold Blood." Young man to whom Jim MATHER lends $300 to help him out of trouble with a girl.

Bronson, Edgar Character in "The Family Bus." Member of Dick HENDERSON's fraternity who calls Dick a snob and defaces his car.

Bronson, Will Character in "Pat Hobby's Christmas Wish." Recipient of Harry GOODDORF's letter about the murder of director William Desmond Taylor (1877–1922).

Brooke, Loretta Character in "Zone of Accident." Actress who is stabbed by a rejected lover and who becomes attracted to Doctor Bill TULLIVER.

Brooke, Rupert (1887–1915) Handsome young English poet whose patriotic poems brought him popularity at the beginning of World War I. When Fitzgerald's friend Shane LESLIE, who was a friend of Brooke, submitted "The Romantic Egotist"— an early version of *TSOP*—to SCRIBNERS in May 1918, he described Fitzgerald as an American prose Rupert Brooke (*Correspondence*, p. 29). Brooke's "Tiare Tahiti" provided the title and an epigraph for Fitzgerald's first novel: "Well this side of Paradise! . . . / There's little comfort in the wise."

See Christopher Hassall, *Rupert Brooke: A Biography* (London: Faber, 1972).

"Brooklyn Bridge" Fitzgerald wrote a memo on this proposed movie for Twentieth Century-Fox on August 12, 1940 (PRINCETON UNIVERSITY LIBRARY); he may have worked briefly on the movie, which was never produced.

Brooks, Van Wyck (1886–1963) Literary historian and critic, best known for *The Flowering of New England, 1815–1865* (1936). In 1920 Maxwell PERKINS gave Fitzgerald a copy of Brooks's *The Ordeal of Mark Twain* (1920), which Fitzgerald found impressive. In 1925 Fitzgerald sent Brooks an inscribed copy of *GG*, noting, "I'm taking the liberty of sending you this after having run across a copy of America's Coming of Age in a book store here and bought and read it with enormous pleasure" (*Life in Letters,* p. 102). Brooks replied on April 22 that *GG* "seems to me by far the best thing you've done—certainly a real creation and one that leaves in the mind a most haunting impression" (*Correspondence*, p. 160); he sent Fitzgerald a copy of *The Pilgrimage of Henry James* (1925), which Fitzgerald praised as "exquisitely done + entirely facinating" (postmarked June 13, 1925; *Life in Letters,* p. 122).

See Raymond Nelson, *Van Wyck Brooks: A Writer's Life* (New York: Dutton, 1981).

Brother Brian Character in the PHILIPPE stories. In "In the Darkest Hour," this Irish-born friar joins Philippe to fight the Viking invaders. In "The Count of Darkness" and "The Kingdom in the Dark," he is a leader of Philippe's band of supporters.

Brown, Arthur William (1881–1966) Popular illustrator of magazine fiction for over 40 years. He illustrated

Brown's illustration for "The Camel's Back" in the April 24, 1920 Saturday Evening Post (Bruccoli Collection, University of South Carolina)

several Fitzgerald stories, including "The Camel's Back" (April 24, 1920), "A Penny Spent" (October 10, 1925), and "Presumption" (January 9, 1926) for *The SATURDAY EVENING POST* and "The Jelly-Bean" (October 1920) and "Winter Dreams" (December 1922) for *METROPOLITAN MAGAZINE*. Fitzgerald corresponded with Brown concerning possible illustration ideas for "Winter Dreams" (Fall 1922; *Correspondence*, pp. 114–115).

<div align="right">by Park Bucker</div>

Brown, Ben Character in "A Patriotic Short." Head of the shorts department, who tells Pat HOBBY that no new angles are needed on the story about General Fitzhugh Lee (1835–1905).

Brown, Bugs Character in "The Freshest Boy." A ST. REGIS student who refuses to accompany Basil Duke LEE to NEW YORK.

Brown, Captain *See* HIBBING.

Brown, Delia Character in "Pat Hobby, Putative Father." John Brown Hobby INDORE's mother, who was married to Pat HOBBY when John was born, although Pat was not the child's father.

Brown, Orrison Character in "The Lost Decade." Young man who takes Louis TRIMBLE to lunch.

Brown, Satterly Character in "Inside the House." Boy who is helping Gwen BOWERS decorate her Christmas tree.

Bruccoli Collection The Matthew J. and Arlyn Bruccoli Collection of F. Scott Fitzgerald was acquired by the University of South Carolina, in Columbia, South Carolina, in 1994. The collection of more than 10,000 items is housed in the Fitzgerald Room at the Thomas Cooper Library; Matthew J. BRUCCOLI is curator. This is the most comprehensive Fitzgerald collection—a working research library for the use of students and scholars. It includes Fitzgerald manuscripts and revised typescripts; the only set of original unrevised galleys for *GG*; one of two existing copies of the printed acting script for *Fie! Fie! Fi-Fi!*; some of Fitzgerald's correspondence; books inscribed by and to Fitzgerald, including a copy of *For Whom the Bell Tolls* inscribed to Fitzgerald by Ernest HEMINGWAY; Bruccoli's papers, correspondence, and working drafts for the Fitzgerald books he has written and edited; Fitzgerald memorabilia, such as two engraved whiskey flasks, his briefcase, a passport, a track medal from the NEWMAN SCHOOL, and his commission as a second lieutenant in the United States ARMY; and a Zelda FITZGERALD collection, including her published writings, some manu-scripts, and some of her letters. In addition to Fitzgerald items, the collection is a resource for American literature in the time of Fitzgerald, with some 2,000 books about Fitzgerald's literary friends and the literary and social backgrounds of the 1920s and 1930s, including material about HOLLYWOOD and the EXPATRIATE writers.

The University is committed to expanding the collection, and *F. Scott Fitzgerald Collection Notes* are published occasionally. An exhibition was opened in September 1996 to commemorate Fitzgerald's 100th birthday (*see* CENTENNIAL), and a catalogue was published in conjunction with that event (*F. Scott Fitzgerald Centenary Exhibition* [Columbia: University of South Carolina Press for the Thomas Cooper Library, 1996]). A full catalogue of the collection is also available (*Catalogue of the Matthew J. and Arlyn Bruccoli F. Scott Fitzgerald Collection*. ed. Park Bucker [Columbia, S.C.: MJB, 1997]).

For more information about the collection, contact Patrick Scott, Head of Special Collections, Thomas Cooper Library, University of South Carolina, Columbia, S.C. 29208; 601–777–8154. The Fitzgerald HOME PAGE, which includes information about the collection, may be accessed at HTTP://WWW.SC.EDU/FITZGERALD/INDEX.HTML.

Bruccoli, Matthew J. (b. 1931) Leading Fitzgerald scholar, curator of the Matthew J. and Arlyn BRUCCOLI COLLECTION of F. Scott Fitzgerald at the University of South Carolina, and Jefferies Professor of English at the University of South Carolina. He has written the standard Fitzgerald biography—*Some Sort of Epic Grandeur*—as well as *F. Scott Fitzgerald: A Descriptive Bibliography*, *Reader's Companion to F. Scott Fitzgerald's Tender Is the Night* (with Judith S. Baughman), *The Composition of Tender Is the Night*, *"The Last of the Novelists": F. Scott Fitzgerald and The Last Tycoon*, and *Fitzgerald and Hemingway: A Dangerous Friendship*. He served as editor of the CAMBRIDGE EDITION OF THE WORKS OF F. SCOTT FITZGERALD (*The Great Gatsby*, 1991; *The Love of the Last Tycoon: A Western*, 1993), but resigned because of interference with his editorial judgment by Andrew Brown of Cambridge University Press and by Eleanor Lanahan and S. J. Lanahan, his fellow trustees of the Frances Scott Fitzgerald Smith TRUST. His Centennial Edition of *Tender Is the Night* was published by Everyman in England in 1996. Bruccoli has edited some 35 volumes of Fitzgerald's writings, including *F. Scott Fitzgerald Manuscripts* (18 volumes); *F. Scott Fitzgerald on Authorship* (with Judith S. Baughman), *F. Scott Fitzgerald: A Life in Letters* (with Baughman), *The Short Stories of F. Scott Fitzgerald*, *F. Scott Fitzgerald: Poems 1911–1940*, *The Price Was High*, *The Notebooks of F. Scott Fitzgerald*, *Bits of Paradise* (coedited by Scottie FITZGERALD Smith), *Correspondence of F. Scott Fitzgerald* (coedited by Margaret M.

Duggan, with Susan Walker), *As Ever, Scott Fitz*—(with Jennifer M. Atkinson), and *F. Scott Fitzgerald In His Own Time* (coedited by Jackson R. Bryer). He edited the *Fitzgerald Newsletter* and coedited the *Fitzgerald/Hemingway Annual*. Bruccoli worked with Scottie Fitzgerald Smith on volumes for which she declined to claim credit: she vetted *Some Sort of Epic Grandeur, The Price Was High*, and *Correspondence*. She appointed him one of the three original trustees of the Frances Scott Fitzgerald Smith Trust.

Buchanan, Daisy Fay Character in *GG*. Nick CARRAWAY'S cousin, a beautiful young woman from LOUISVILLE whose "thrilling voice" is "full of money" (pp. 11, 94). Jay GATSBY fell in love with her during the war, but she married wealthy Tom BUCHANAN while Gatsby was overseas. Gatsby, who is committed to her as to a quest for the Grail, unsuccessfully attempts to win her back. She becomes involved with him; but when he urges her to leave Tom, she backs down. She accidentally kills Myrtle WILSON while driving Gatsby's car, and she agrees to let Gatsby take the blame. After the accident, Nick sees her and Tom conversing as if "they were conspiring together" (p. 113); she leaves town with Tom.

Buchanan, Pammy Character in *GG*. Young daughter of Tom and Daisy BUCHANAN. Fitzgerald stipulates Pammy's age as three, but the novel's chronology indicates her age as two: Daisy married Tom in June 1919, and Jordan BAKER specifies "the next April Daisy had her little girl" (p. 61); thus, in summer 1922, the time of the novel, the child would be two years old. If Pammy were three, Daisy would have been at least nine months pregnant at the time of her marriage; but it is clear that Fitzgerald did not intend to imply illegitimacy or a forced marriage. He made a mathematical error, as he did frequently.

Buchanan, Tom Character in *GG*. Daisy BUCHANAN'S husband and Myrtle WILSON'S lover. Tom came from an extremely wealthy Chicago family and was a football star at Yale. After Myrtle's death he reveals to George WILSON that the car which killed Myrtle belongs to Jay GATSBY, thereby setting up Gatsby's murder by Wilson.

Buckner, Mrs. Character in "The Scandal Detectives." Riply BUCKNER'S mother, whom Fitzgerald uses to describe the generation gap.

Buckner, Riply Jr. Character in the Basil Duke LEE stories. Based on Fitzgerald's ST. PAUL friend Cecil READ. In "The Scandal Detectives" Riply and Basil collaborate on a "Book of Scandal" and, with Bill KAMPF, plot to waylay Hubert BLAIR. In "A Night at the Fair" Riply has been wearing long pants for a week and belittles Basil, who is still in short pants. In "He Thinks He's Wonderful," he takes Imogene BISSEL to Connie DAVIES' dance and resents Basil's attempt to persuade Imogene to have supper with him rather than Riply. In "The Captured Shadow" he serves as business manager for Basil's play and also plays the role of a policeman.

Buffalo, New York In April 1898, after the failure of his furniture factory in ST. PAUL, Minnesota, Edward FITZGERALD—F. Scott Fitzgerald's father—moved his family to Buffalo, where he worked as a wholesale grocery salesman for Procter & Gamble. They lived at the Lennox apartment hotel and then in a flat at Summer Street and Elmwood Avenue before the company transferred him to SYRACUSE, New York, in January 1901. When he was transferred back to Buffalo in September 1903, he took an apartment at 29 Irving Place; and Scott attended school half days at Holy Angels Convent. Two years later they moved to 71 Highland Avenue and Scott transferred to Miss Narden's, a private Catholic school, where he first received recognition as a writer with an essay on George Washington and Ignatius Loyola. Edward Fitzgerald lost his job in March 1908, and he and his family returned to St. Paul in July.

Bugs (Trevellion) Character in " 'Send Me In, Coach.' " Small boy at Camp Rahewawa.

Burke, Geraldine Character in *B&D*. A lower-class girl whom Anthony PATCH dates before his engagement to Gloria Gilbert [PATCH].

Burne-Dennison, Martha Character in "The Intimate Strangers." SARA'S sister, who comes from LONDON both times that Sara becomes involved with Cedric KILLIAN.

Burns, Phyllis Character in "Discard." Actress for whom Count Hennen DE LANCLERC leaves his wife, Dolly BORDON.

Busch, Arthur Character in "Magnetism." Continuity writer and director who has loved Kay HANNAFORD for years and in whom she briefly expresses interest to make her husband, George HANNAFORD, jealous.

Bushmill, Hallie Character in "A Penny Spent." Ohio belle who falls in love with CORCORAN, whom her father has hired as a tour guide.

Bushmill, Jessie Pepper Character in "A Penny Spent." Julius BUSHMILL'S wife and Hallie BUSHMILL'S mother.

Bushmill, Julius Character in "A Penny Spent." Hallie BUSHMILL's father, an Ohio manufacturer who hires CORCORAN as a tour guide for his wife and daughter.

Butler Character in "The Room with the Green Blinds." Detective who accompanies Governor CARMATLE to Robert Calvin RAYMOND's house.

Butler, Howard Character in "Between Three and Four." Man who fires and refuses to rehire Sarah Belknap SUMMER, whom he had wished to marry thirty years before.

Butler, Samuel (1835–1902) English author whose works include *Erewhon* (1872), *Erewhon Revisited* (1901), and *The Way of All Flesh* (1903). Fitzgerald wrote in his copy of *The Note-Books of Samuel Butler* (1912) "The most interesting human document ever written" (September 19, 1919; *F. Scott Fitzgerald: Inscriptions,* item 43). He wrote to Maxwell PERKINS that "every young author ought to read Samuel Butler's Note Books" (September 18, 1919; *Life in Letters,* p. 32; *Scott/Max,* p. 22), and included the volume in his 1923 list of "10 Best Books I Have Read."

See Peter Raby, *Samuel Butler: A Biography* (Iowa City: University of Iowa Press, 1991).

Butterfield, Warren Character in "The Camel's Back." NEW YORK architect who is visiting the Howard TATES and whom Betty MEDILL mistakenly believes is inside the camel costume.

Butterworth, Mr. Character in "The Rough Crossing." Fellow passenger who is interested in Eva SMITH.

Buttitta, Anthony (b. 1907) Proprietor of the bookshop in the George Vanderbilt Hotel in ASHEVILLE, North Carolina, whom Fitzgerald met while living in Asheville in the summer of 1935. Buttitta published an interview with Fitzgerald: "Fitzgerald's Six Generations," *Raleigh News and Observer* (September 1, 1935), 3 (a shortened version appears in *In His Own Time,* pp. 292–294). Fitzgerald lectured Buttitta, an aspiring writer, about literature; Buttitta's recollections of their conversations form the basis of his memoir *After the Good Gay Times* (1974; republished as *The Lost Summer,* 1987).

Button, Benjamin Character in "The Curious Case of Benjamin Button." Man who is born seventy years old and grows younger rather than older.

Button, Mrs. Roger Character in "The Curious Case of Benjamin Button." Benjamin BUTTON's mother.

Button, Roger Character in "The Curious Case of Benjamin Button." Benjamin BUTTON's father, the president of a wholesale hardware company.

Button, Roscoe Character in "The Curious Case of Benjamin Button." Benjamin BUTTON's son, who demands that his father call him "Uncle" when his father begins to look younger than Roscoe.

Cable Character in *B&D*. An usher at Anthony and Gloria PATCH's wedding.

Cable, Joe Character in "The Dance." Young man whom Catherine JONES loves and who is discovered kissing Charley KINCAID's fiancée, Marie BANNERMAN.

Cale, Mr. Character in "Lo, the Poor Peacock!" Man to whom Jason DAVIS pawns the family silver.

Calhoun, Ailie Character in "The Last of the Belles." Belle who represents "the Southern type in all its purity" (*TAR*, p. 256). She flirts with the officers stationed in TARLETON, Georgia, during World War I, including Lieutenant Earl SCHOEN, to whom she is attracted despite his lower-class qualities. Though she considers marrying a Northern man she finally plans to marry a man from Savannah.

Calkins, Mr. Character in "Porcelain and Pink." A divorced, literary man who has a date with Lois MARVIS.

Callaghan, Morley (1903–1990) Canadian novelist whose work Fitzgerald recommended to SCRIBNERS editor Maxwell PERKINS. He had worked with Ernest HEMINGWAY on the *Toronto Star,* and they boxed in PARIS. In June 1929 Fitzgerald served as timekeeper for one of their private bouts and inadvertently let the three-minute second round run a minute long, during which Callaghan knocked down Hemingway. Hemingway reacted angrily, blaming Fitzgerald, who was troubled by the accusation. Callaghan provides a detailed account of the incident in *That Summer in Paris;* Hemingway altered his versions of the incident over the years, claiming in 1951 that Fitzgerald had let the round go 13 minutes (to Arthur MIZENER, January 4, 1951; *Ernest Hemingway: Selected Letters,* pp. 716–718). On November 24, 1929 a *New York Herald Tribune* article alleged that Callaghan had knocked out Hemingway for disparaging his boxing stories. Callaghan's correction appeared in the *Tribune* on December 8, but meanwhile Fitzgerald—at Hemingway's insistence—cabled Callaghan for a correction. Callaghan was angry, and though Perkins tried to make peace among his three authors, Callaghan's friendship with Fitzgerald and Hemingway ended. Matthew J. BRUCCOLI details the incident and its repercussions in *Fitzgerald and Hemingway: A Dangerous Friendship.*

Calman, Miles Character in "Crazy Sunday." Brilliant movie director with a troubled marriage who dies in an airplane crash. Loosely based on King VIDOR.

Calman, Mrs. Character in "Crazy Sunday." Miles CALMAN's mother, who tells Joel COLES she had always expected a lot from her son and isn't surprised by his success.

Calman, Stella Walker Character in "Crazy Sunday." Miles CALMAN's wife, who becomes interested in screenwriter Joel COLES.

Cambell, Randy Character in "At Your Age." Young man whom Annie LORRY is dating when she begins to go out with Tom SQUIRES and who brings her home late after she and Squires are engaged.

Cambridge Arms Fitzgerald had an apartment at the Cambridge Arms in BALTIMORE, Maryland, September–November 1935 and from the end of December 1935 to July 1936.

The Cambridge Edition of the Works of F. Scott Fitzgerald. Cambridge: Cambridge University Press, 1991– . *The Great Gatsby,* ed. with intro. by Matthew J. BRUCCOLI, 1991; *The Love of the Last Tycoon: A Western,* ed. with intro. by Bruccoli, 1993; *This Side of Paradise,* ed. with intro. by James L. W. West III, 1995. *See* EDITING FITZGERALD'S TEXTS.

"The Camel's Back" Fiction. Written January 1920. *The SATURDAY EVENING POST,* 192 (April 24, 1920), 16–17, 157, 161, 165; *TJA*. An interfering man named WARBURTON persuades Perry PARKHURST to get a marriage license and present his girlfriend, Betty MEDILL, with the ultimatum that she must marry him at once or never. Perry and Betty quarrel, and he leaves and gets drunk. He rents a camel costume for the TOWNSENDS' circus ball and persuades a TAXI DRIVER to wear the back half of the costume. At the party, Warburton

announces that he thinks part of the camel is Warren BUTTERFIELD, a visitor in town; and Betty, interested in the prospect of a new man, flirts with the camel. Betty and the camel win prizes for the best costumes; and they are married in a mock ceremony presided over by JUMBO, a waiter at the club. Jumbo then discovers that the camel has handed him a real marriage license, and he reveals that his status as a Baptist minister makes the ceremony binding. Betty is furious, and Perry renounces his claim to her. However, when the camel's back refuses to relinquish his claim as Betty's husband, she agrees to marry Perry in a real ceremony and go West with him.

Fitzgerald wrote "The Camel's Back" in one day and used his earnings from it to buy a platinum-and-diamond wristwatch for Zelda Sayre [FITZGERALD]. It was his first story to appear in the *O. Henry Prize Stories,* an annual collection of fiction. "The Camel's Back" was made into a movie (retitled *Conductor 1492*) in 1924; see Alan Margolies, " 'The Camel's Back' and *Conductor 1492,*" *Fitzgerald/Hemingway Annual* (1974), pp. 87–88.

"The Cameo Frame" Verse. *The NASSAU LITERARY MAGAZINE,* 73 (October 1917), 169–172; *In His Own Time, Poems.* Fitzgerald incorporated portions of this poem in *TSOP* on p. 154 as "St. Cecilia" and on p. 160.

Camp Boone In *B&D,* a fictional army base in Mississippi to which Anthony PATCH's brigade is transferred from South Carolina and where he is demoted after lying when he is caught returning to camp late.

Camp Gordon ARMY camp in Augusta, Georgia, where Fitzgerald was stationed with the 45th Infantry Regiment from April to June 1918. In *TSOP* Thomas Parke D'INVILLIERS is stationed at Camp Gordon.

Camp Hooker In *B&D,* a fictional army base in South Carolina where Anthony PATCH is first stationed for training after being drafted. While stationed there he has an affair with Dot RAYCROFT, a lower-class girl.

Camp Mills ARMY camp on Long Island where Fitzgerald was sent with the 67th Infantry Regiment on October 26, 1918 to prepare for embarkation to France; the war ended before the unit was sent overseas. Fitzgerald participated in alcoholic escapades while on leave in NEW YORK CITY; despite being confined to camp to keep him from further trouble, he was AWOL in New York when the 67th was ordered back to CAMP SHERIDAN in MONTGOMERY, Alabama in November. In *TSOP* Amory BLAINE is stationed at Camp Mills. In *B&D* Anthony PATCH's regiment is transferred there to prepare for embarkation to France, but the war ends before they go overseas.

Camp Sheridan ARMY camp near MONTGOMERY, Alabama. In June 1918 the 45th Infantry Regiment was combined with the 67th Infantry Regiment of the Ninth Division at Camp Sheridan in preparation for overseas duty. At Camp Sheridan Fitzgerald was promoted to first lieutenant but was the victim of practical jokes by his fellow officers. He rescued men from drowning when a barge sank in the Talapoosa River during an exercise, an incident which he used in " 'I Didn't Get Over' " (October 1936). While stationed at Camp Sheridan, Fitzgerald met Zelda Sayre [FITZGERALD] in July 1918; and he revised "The Romantic Egotist," an early version of *TSOP,* for resubmission to SCRIBNERS. His regiment was shipped to CAMP MILLS on Long Island in October but was ordered back to Camp Sheridan in November; and Fitzgerald was made aide-de-camp to Brigadier General J. A. RYAN. Fitzgerald remained at Camp Sheridan until his discharge from the army in February 1919.

Camp Zachary Taylor ARMY camp near LOUISVILLE, Kentucky, where Fitzgerald reported to the 45th Infantry Regiment on March 15, 1918. He served as assistant to the regimental school officer for several weeks before his unit was transferred to CAMP GORDON in Augusta, Georgia. In *GG* Lieutenant Jay GATSBY is stationed at Camp Taylor when he meets Daisy Fay [BUCHANAN].

Campbell, Dizzy Character in "Too Cute for Words." Gwen BOWERS's friend, with whom she travels to PRINCETON.

Campbell, Lawton (1896–1980) Friend of Fitzgerald at PRINCETON (Class of 1916); Fitzgerald's *Fie! Fie! Fi-Fi!* won the competition over Campbell's submission for the 1914–15 TRIANGLE CLUB show. Campbell, who was from MONTGOMERY, was one of the group the newlywed Fitzgeralds partied with in NEW YORK. He wrote two Broadway plays, *Immoral Isabella* (1927) and *Solid South* (1930).

Campion, Luis Character in *TITN.* Homosexual whom Rosemary HOYT meets on the RIVIERA and who takes her to see the duel between Albert MCKISCO and Tommy BARBAN.

Canby, Carleton Character in "The Cut-Glass Bowl." Rejected suitor who gave Evylyn PIPER the bowl.

Canby, Lieutenant Horace Character in "The Last of the Belles." Aviator who is in love with Ailie CALHOUN and threatens to crash his plane if she marries Bill KNOWLES. When he does crash his plane after Knowles returns to town, Ailie doesn't want anyone to know about his threat.

Canisius, John Character in "The Guest in Room Nineteen." Mr. CASS's partner, who looked like the WATCHMAN's description of the GUEST in room nineteen.

Cannel, John Character in "The Debutante." Helen HALCYON's forlorn suitor, who climbs up to her window before her debut and complains that they are drifting apart. She rejects him because the novelty has gone out of their relationship. This character is renamed Howard GILLESPIE in *TSOP.*

Cannes, France RIVIERA city where the Fitzgeralds rented the VILLA FLEUR DES BOIS July–September 1929.

Cannon, Mr. Character in "Financing Finnegan." Literary agent who lends money to author FINNEGAN. Based on Harold OBER.

Cap d'Antibes, France Resort on the RIVIERA near Antibes. The Fitzgeralds' friends Gerald and Sara MURPHY's home here, VILLA AMERICA, was a partial model for VILLA DIANA in *TITN.* The Fitzgeralds spent a month at Cap d'Antibes in August 1925, probably staying at the Grand-Hôtel du Cap.

Capps-Karr, Lady Character in "The Hotel Child." Woman who looks down on Fifi SCHWARTZ and who inadvertently causes a fire in the hotel. Based on Bijou O'CONOR.

Capri, Italy The Fitzgeralds lived at the HOTEL TIBERIO on Capri February–April 1925, while awaiting publication of *GG.* Zelda took painting lessons, and Fitzgerald began writing "The Rich Boy" (January–February 1926).

Captain Character in "Two Old-Timers." Police captain who is unimpressed by Phil MACEDON.

"The Captured Shadow" Fiction—Basil Duke LEE story. Written September 1928. *The SATURDAY EVENING POST,* 201 (December 29, 1928), 12–13, 48, 51; *TAR*; *B&J.* Basil Duke Lee, age 15, writes a play called "The Captured Shadow" and has difficulty casting the lead roles. He asks Evelyn BEEBE to be the leading lady in his play, but she refuses until Basil says that Hubert BLAIR will be the leading man. Evelyn drops out of the play when Hubert does, claiming she has to leave town on a family trip. When her little brother, Ham BEEBE, gets the mumps, after Basil has deliberately exposed him to a sick boy, Evelyn is unable to leave town and acts in the play after all. The play is a success, but Basil feels only emptiness and sadness over what he did to Ham.

See also *The Captured Shadow,* a play which Fitzgerald wrote in 1912.

The Captured Shadow Play. In *F. Scott Fitzgerald's St. Paul Plays, 1911–1914.* Performed by the ELIZABETHAN DRAMATIC CLUB of ST. PAUL on August 23, 1912 at Mrs. Backus's School for Girls in Oak Hall. Fitzgerald wrote the play on the train back to St. Paul from the NEWMAN SCHOOL for summer vacation, and the performance earned $60 for the Baby Welfare Association. Fitzgerald played the lead role of "The SHADOW." His play was influenced by the popular crook melodramas of the time, such as *Alias Jimmy Valentine* and *Arsène Lupin.*

Act I
Dorothy CONNAGE tells housekeeper Miss SAUNDERS that she has read a "romantic" newspaper story about a burglar called "The Shadow" whom the police have been unable to catch and who always returns what he steals. Dorothy's brother, Hubert CONNAGE, comes home drunk with two crooks, Chinyman RUDD and Rabbit SIMMONS, whom he met on the street and who tell him that they spy for the Shadow. The Shadow enters the house; and detectives MCGINNESS and DUREAL, who see him, come in and warn Mr. CONNAGE that the Shadow is in his house. The Shadow persuades Hubert Connage not to reveal his presence by threatening to tell Hubert's fiancée, Helen MAYBURN, that he was in prison three days the week before. The Shadow then persuades Miss Saunders that he is a detective and directs her to tie up Mr. and Mrs. Connage, whom he claims are the real thieves. He convinces the detectives that he is Detective Johnston from the central office and tells them that Hubert Connage is the Shadow.

Act II
The Connages persuade the detectives to release Hubert, who reveals that the "detective," who has disappeared, is the Shadow. After encountering Dorothy Connage, locking Dureal into a closet, and grappling with McGinness, the Shadow is temporarily captured by Hubert but escapes. He calls the police station to withdraw the guard around the house, but Dorothy Connage discovers him. She agrees not to betray him, and when the clock strikes twelve he explains that he is really Thorton Hart Dudley and that two weeks before he had made a $5,000 bet that he could prove the NEW YORK police incompetent by committing daring robberies and not getting caught.

Sixteen years later Fitzgerald assessed his achievement through this comment about Basil Duke LEE in his story "The Captured Shadow": "It might all have been very bad and demoralizing for Basil, but it was already behind him. Even as the crowd melted away and the last few people spoke to him and went out, he felt a great vacancy come into his heart. It was over, it was done and gone—all that work, and interest and absorption. It was a hollowness like fear" (*TAR,* pp. 101–102).

Caramel, Richard (Dick) Character in *B&D*. Gloria Gilbert PATCH's cousin; one of Anthony PATCH's best friends. He works in the NEW YORK slums for a year after graduating from Harvard, where he was editor of the *Harvard Crimson*. He then works as a reporter for *The Sun* before beginning his first novel, *The Demon Lover*. After the success of his novel, he lowers his standards to turn out stories that can be made into movies.

Carhart, Peter Character in "The Four Fists." Samuel MEREDITH's employer and eventually his partner.

Carleton, Sammy Character in *B&D*. Author of motivational pamphlets called "Heart Talks," which have been incorporated as a company for which Anthony PATCH briefly tries to sell stock.

Carling Character in *TSOP*. A Princetonian whom Amory BLAINE encounters at the Knickerbocker Bar after his breakup with Rosalind CONNAGE.

Carlyle, Curtis Character in "The Offshore Pirate." Pseudonym of Toby Moreland, a young man who wins Ardita FARNAM by his imaginative stunt of posing as a robber fleeing his pursuers.

Carmatle, Governor Character in "The Room with the Green Blinds." Georgia governor who served in the cavalry under Nathan Bedford Forrest (1821–77) during the Civil War. He shoots John Wilkes BOOTH to avenge the death of his own son.

Carney, Doctor Howard Character in "Her Last Case." Bette WEAVER's fiancé, whom she leaves for Ben DRAGONET.

Caroline Character in "His Russet Witch." Girl whom Merlin GRAINGER watches through his apartment window and whom he calls Caroline. She comes to symbolize for him glamor and romance. Many years later he finds out that she was dancer Alicia Dare, now Mrs. Thomas Allerdyce.

Carraway, Nick Partially involved narrator of *GG*. Daisy BUCHANAN's cousin and Tom BUCHANAN's classmate at Yale; a bond salesman from an established Middle-Western family. Nick claims, "I am one of the few honest people that I have ever known" (p. 48). Although he begins by proclaiming his inclination to reserve judgments, he serves as the moral center of the novel and eventually passes judgment on all the major characters. Nick evaluates his role thus: "I was within and without, simultaneously enchanted and repelled by the inexhaustible variety of life" (p. 30).

Carroll, Peter Character in "Babes in the Woods." Hotchkiss student who is charmed by ISABELLE, unaware that she is really interested in Kenneth POWERS. This character is renamed Froggy PARKER in *TSOP*.

Carroll, Dr. Robert S. (1869–1949) Director of HIGHLAND HOSPITAL in ASHEVILLE, which Zelda FITZGERALD entered on April 8, 1936. Carroll's treatment for mental problems was based on his theory that they were caused by toxic substances, and Zelda responded to the treatment.

Carroll wrote *The Grille Gate* (1922), an autobiographical novel about hospital life, and several popular books on medical topics, including *The Mastery of Nervousness: Based Upon Self Reeducation* (1917), *Our Nervous Friends: Illustrating the Mastery of Nervousness* (1919), *The Soul in Suffering: A Practical Application of Spiritual Truths* (1919), *Old at Forty or Young at Sixty: Simplifying the Science of Growing Old* (1920), and *What Price Alcohol?* (1941).

Carson Character in "Basil and Cleopatra." Assistant coach of the Yale freshman football team. He gives Basil Duke LEE an opportunity to play during football practice.

Carstairs, Bill Character in *B&D*. A former beau of Gloria Gilbert [PATCH].

Carter, Eleanor Character in "Pat Hobby's Preview." Cute blonde tourist from Idaho whom Pat HOBBY takes to a movie preview.

Carton, James Character in "The Rough Crossing." Steward whom Eva SMITH finds sick in her cabin, who undergoes an appendectomy during the storm, and who dies and is buried at sea.

cartoonist (unnamed) Character in "An Alcoholic Case." Alcoholic who throws and breaks a bottle of gin when his NURSE tries to keep it from him.

Carver Character in "The Freshest Boy." Captain of the football team at ST. REGIS. He grabs Basil and rebukes him for shoving to get into the dining room, which everyone is doing.

Cary, Colonel Character in "On Your Own." Man who knew Evelyn LOVEJOY when she was a "party girl" and whose presence at dinner with George IVES and his mother makes Evelyn defensive.

Cary, Daisy Character in "The Bowl." A young movie actress in whom Dolly HARLAN becomes interested. Based on Lois MORAN, she is a preliminary sketch for Rosemary HOYT in *TITN*. Both Daisy and Rosemary are

required, in their acting jobs, to fall into a lagoon repeatedly despite having colds.

Cary, Edith Character in "The Passionate Eskimo." Beautiful, wealthy girl who invites Eskimo PAN-E-TROON to visit her home.

Cary, Esther Character in "A New Leaf." Julia ROSS's friend who becomes involved with Dick RAGLAND while Julia is out of town.

Cary, Jonquil Character in " 'The Sensible Thing.' " Southern girl who breaks her engagement to George O'KELLY because she fears a life of poverty and struggle; later, after he has become successful, she agrees to marry him.

Cary, Mr. and Mrs. Characters in " 'The Sensible Thing.' " Jonquil CARY's parents.

Cary, Mrs. Character in "That Kind of Party." The principal of Mrs. Cary's Academy. She rebukes Terrence R. TIPTON for correcting his teacher.

Casasus Character in *TITN*. Bank employee in PARIS who authorizes a check for Dick DIVER.

Case, Harold Character in "The Bowl." Vienna THORNE's date at the PRINCETON Senior Prom. She deserts him for Dolly HARLAN.

Cass, Mr. Character in "The Guest in Room Nineteen." Stroke victim and hotel guest who is suspicious of the mysterious GUEST in room nineteen.

Cassius Character in " 'Send Me In, Coach.' " Stout boy at Camp Rahewawa.

Castle, Mr. Character in "Magnetism." George HANNAFORD's lawyer, whom he consults about Margaret DONOVAN's blackmail attempt.

Castleton, Emily Character in "Majesty." Headstrong American heiress who leaves her socially acceptable fiancé, Brevoort BLAIR, at the altar and later marries Prince Gabriel PETROCOBESCO, the claimant to the throne of a tiny Middle-European kingdom.

Castleton, Harold, Jr. Character in "Majesty." Emily CASTLETON's brother, who shocks Olive MERCY by encouraging music, dancing, and drinking for his friends after Emily's canceled wedding.

Castleton, Harold, Sr. Character in "Majesty." Emily CASTLETON's father, who is distressed by her abandonment of Brevoort BLAIR at the altar.

Cathcart, Jim Character in "A Short Trip Home." Young man who tells Eddie STINSON that Joe VARLAND hit Joe JELKE with brass knuckles.

Catherine Character in *GG*. Myrtle WILSON's sister, who is at Myrtle's and Tom BUCHANAN's party. At the inquest following Jay GATSBY's death, she responds to MICHAELIS's testimony regarding George WILSON's suspicions of his wife by swearing that Myrtle was happy with her husband and had been into no mischief.

Catherine Character in "A Short Trip Home." Jim CATHCART's date at the Cotillion Club dance.

Caxter, Wessel Character in "Tarquin of Cheepside." An avid reader who offers SOFT SHOES refuge from his pursuers.

Cedric Character in "Rags Martin-Jones and the Pr-nce of W-les." Elevator-boy who poses as Baron MARCHBANKS, who is supposed to be the Prince of Wales in disguise.

"Cedric the Stoker (The True Story of the Battle of the Baltic)" Humor article by Fitzgerald and John BIGGS, Jr. *The PRINCETON TIGER,* 28 (November 10, 1917), 12; *In His Own Time.* Account of a stoker who throws himself into the furnace when the ship runs out of fuel during battle.

"Censorship or Not" *The Literary Digest,* 77 (June 23, 1923), 31, 61; *In His Own Time.* Includes Fitzgerald's statement that New York Supreme Court Justice Ford's campaign against "unclean books" will attack authors like Joseph HERGESHEIMER, Theodore DREISER, Sherwood ANDERSON, and James Branch Cabell (1879–1958), "whom they detest because they can't understand" and won't touch "really immoral books" such as *Simon Called Peter* (1921) by Robert Keable (1887–1927) (*In His Own Time,* p. 170).

Centennial The 1996 centennial of Fitzgerald's birth was celebrated around the world. ST. PAUL, Minnesota, hosted "F. Scott Fitzgerald's 100th Birthday: A Literature Festival" September 23–29. Events included tours of area sites identified with Fitzgerald; a marathon reading of *The Great Gatsby* and other Fitzgerald writings; a literature festival for students and adults featuring workshops with authors, including E. L. Doctorow (b. 1931) and Joseph Heller (b. 1923); the dedication of a bronze sculpture of Fitzgerald by Minnesotan Michael B. Price; a theater parade; "A Prairie Home Companion" radio show with Garrison Keillor (b. 1942), followed by The Great Gatsby Ball; and "Coming Apart at the Seams: Styles and Society in the 1920s," an

exhibition of 1920s fashions at the Goldstein Gallery, University of Minnesota. The United States Postal Service issued an F. Scott Fitzgerald Commemorative Stamp on September 27 in St. Paul. Two books were published in conjunction with the St. Paul festival: *F. Scott Fitzgerald and St. Paul: "Still Home to Me"* by Lloyd C. Hackl (Cambridge, Minn.: Adventure Publications, 1996) and *F. Scott Fitzgerald in Minnesota: Toward the Summit* by David Page and John Koblas (St. Cloud, Minn.: North Star Press, 1996).

PRINCETON UNIVERSITY and the F. SCOTT FITZGERALD SOCIETY sponsored an "F. Scott Fitzgerald Centennial Conference" at Princeton September 19–21. Events included lectures; panel discussions; reminiscences by people who knew Fitzgerald, including Honoria Murphy Donnelly, Frances KROLL Ring, and Budd SCHULBERG; a banquet with remarks by Senator Eugene J. McCarthy; and tours of Princeton. "A Centennial Exhibition in Celebration of F. Scott Fitzgerald (1896–1940), Class of 1917" at the Harvey S. Firestone Library was held May 5 to September 29.

The University of South Carolina in Columbia, South Carolina, hosted an "F. Scott Fitzgerald Centenary Celebration" September 24–26. Joseph Heller was the featured speaker at a banquet on Fitzgerald's birthday, September 24. Other events included a production of Fitzgerald's 1914 TRIANGLE CLUB musical, *Fie! Fie! Fi-Fi!*; a panel discussion on "The Influence and Example of Fitzgerald," moderated by novelist George Garrett (b. 1929), and featuring fiction writers Richard Bausch (b. 1945), Robert Bausch (b. 1945), and Sydney Blair (b. 1949); Vance Bourjaily (b. 1922) reading his story "Fitzgerald Attends My Fitzgerald Seminar"; Budd Schulberg speaking on "Working with Fitzgerald and Other Writers"; the opening of an exhibition, "F. Scott Fitzgerald and the Profession of Authorship," of materials from the BRUCCOLI COLLECTION at the Thomas Cooper Library, with Frederick Busch (b. 1941) as the featured speaker; the opening of an exhibition, "Double Vision: Fitzgerald's World of Realism and Imagination," at the McKissick Museum; an interactive teleconference for high-school students and teachers with Joseph Heller and James Dickey (1923–97); the premiere of a documentary, "Getting It Right," produced by Ed Breland; and readings from Fitzgerald's works and from an unproduced screenplay for *Tender Is the Night* by Malcolm Lowry (1909–57). On September 30 Columbia Postmaster Lawrence Jordan presented poster reproductions of the Fitzgerald stamp to university officials and distributed cancellations of the stamp during a reception at the university's Thomas Cooper Library. Several volumes were published in connection with the centennial celebration: an exhibition catalogue, *F. Scott Fitzgerald Centenary Exhibition* (University of South Carolina Press for the Thomas Cooper Library); *Tributes* (Thomas Cooper Library),

statements on Fitzgerald by contemporary writers; a facsimile of the acting script and musical score for *Fie! Fie! Fi-Fi!* (University of South Carolina Press for the Thomas Cooper Library); and *F. Scott Fitzgerald on Authorship*, ed. Matthew J. BRUCCOLI, with Judith S. Baughman (University of South Carolina Press). *A Young Reader's Guide to F. Scott Fitzgerald*, by Harriett S. Williams (Fitzgerald Centenary Committee of the University of South Carolina, in cooperation with the South Carolina Department of Education and South Carolina ETV), was distributed to South Carolina high schools.

ROCKVILLE, Maryland, where F. Scott and Zelda FITZGERALD are buried at St. Mary's Catholic Church, held community events with 1920s themes throughout 1996, including an original one-act play, *Great Scott*, by local author Nancy Nilsson on September 20; a "Flappers and Philosophers Ball" on September 27; an F. Scott Fitzgerald Literary Conference on September 28 at Montgomery College, Rockville campus, where William Styron (b. 1925) received the first F. Scott Fitzgerald Literary Award; a Second Day Issue of the F. Scott Fitzgerald Stamp on September 28; a staged reading of *Zelda, By Herself*, a one-act play by local playwright Patricia H. Lin, on October 19 and 20; and a December 18 ceremony at St. Mary's Church to commemorate Fitzgerald's death.

The Mercantile Library of New York and the F. Scott Fitzgerald Society sponsored "The Romantic American: F. Scott Fitzgerald and His World," a centennial lecture series, on April 10, 17, and 25 and May 1. Lectures included "A Crisis of Feeling: F. Scott Fitzgerald and The Jazz Age" by John Callahan, author of *The Illusions of a Nation: Myth and History in the Novels of F. Scott Fitzgerald*; "The Private and Public Lives of Scott and Zelda" by Ruth Prigozy, Executive Director of the F. Scott Fitzgerald Society; "F. Scott Fitzgerald and the Profession of Authorship" by Matthew J. Bruccoli; and "Fitzgerald in Hollywood" by Alan Margolies, editor of *F. Scott Fitzgerald's St. Paul Plays 1911–1914*. The Players sponsored an October 8 dinner and celebration of Fitzgerald's life and work in New York City; the program included talks, recitations, and reminiscences by Budd Schulberg, Ring Lardner, Jr., Keir Dullea, Sidney Zion, and Gwinn Owens. The Westhampton Beach Performing Arts Center and the Westhampton Cultural Consortium sponsored a December 6 staged reading from Budd Schulberg's revised theatrical adaptation of *The Disenchanted*.

"Fortunes and Misfortunes in the Life and Times of F. Scott Fitzgerald," an international conference held in ROME, Italy, on October 11 and 12, featured a keynote address by Matthew J. Bruccoli in addition to other lectures, music, an exhibit of Italian translations of Fitzgerald's work, and a roundtable discussion. Events were held at the University of Rome "La Sapienza," Villa Mirafiori, the National Library, the small

theater of the Palazzo delle Esposizioni, John Cabot University, and the American Studies Center. Bruccoli's appearance in Rome and his October 14 presentation at the University of Milan were sponsored by the United States Information Service.

See "F. Scott Fitzgerald Centenary Celebrations," *Dictionary of Literary Biography Yearbook: 1996* (Detroit: Bruccoli Clark Layman/Gale Research, 1997).

Chaffee, Book Character in "A Woman with a Past." Alabama boy with whom Josephine PERRY gets locked in a room at the Yale prom; they escape through a window.

Chambers, Miss Character in "A Woman with a Past." Teacher who chaperones Josephine PERRY, Lillian HAMMEL, and Adele CRAW on an errand to New Haven. She enlists Josephine to entertain Ernest WATERBURY.

Chambers, Mr. Character in " 'The Sensible Thing.' " Manager of the insurance company where George O'KELLY works. He fires George when the latter asks for vacation a second time in two weeks.

Chamson, André (1900–1983) French novelist, civil servant, and later a member of the French Academy to whom Sylvia BEACH introduced Fitzgerald in June 1928, beginning his only literary friendship with a Frenchman. Fitzgerald recommended Chamson's *Les Hommes de la Route* (1927) to editor Maxwell PERKINS, and SCRIBNERS published the novel as *The Road* in 1929. Fitzgerald introduced Chamson to American movie director King VIDOR, and the three planned a movie collaboration that was abandoned when Chamson declined an invitation to HOLLYWOOD.

See Chamson, *A Time to Keep* (London: Faber & Faber, 1957); trans. Erik de Mauny.

Chandelle, Jaques Character in "Shadow Laurels." Wealthy man who returns to PARIS after a 28-year absence to seek information about his dead father, Jean CHANDELLE.

Chandelle, Jean Character in "Shadow Laurels." Jaques CHANDELLE's father, who died five years after Jaques left France for America. A drunkard who was greatly loved by his friends for giving expression to their lives.

Chandler, Cora Character in "Presumption." San Juan CHANDLER's wealthy, snobbish cousin, who tries to discourage his interest in Noel GARNEAU.

Chandler, San Juan Character in "Presumption." Poor young man who aspires to marry wealthy Noel GARNEAU.

"A Change of Class" Fiction. Written July 1931. *The SATURDAY EVENING POST,* 204 (September 26, 1931), 6–7, 37–38, 41; *The Price Was High.* Barber Earl JOHNSON makes money on an investment based on a tip given him by his customer Philip JADWIN, but he loses his money in the stock market crash and returns to his work as a barber. He plans to use his remaining $2,000 in savings to buy his own shop in Jadwin's office building; but his wife, Violet JOHNSON, withdraws the money to run away with bootlegger Howard SHALDER. When Jadwin checks with the bank to verify Earl's account for the shop purchase, he is informed that Shalder is there to cash Violet's check, which will make Earl's check bounce. Jadwin tells the bank to go ahead and cash Violet's check, because he knows that Shalder's departure will free his wife, Irene SHALDER, with whom Jadwin was in love before she married. He accepts Earl's check, then destroys it so that Earl is able to purchase the barber shop anyway.

"The Changing Beauty of Park Avenue" Article by Zelda FITZGERALD. *Harper's Bazaar,* 62 (January 1928), 61–63; *Zelda Fitzgerald: The Collected Writings.* By-lined "Zelda and F. Scott Fitzgerald" but credited to Zelda in *Ledger.* Description of Park Avenue, which has "the essence of a pen-and-ink drawing of Paris" (*Collected Writings,* p. 403).

Chanler, Margaret (Mrs. Winthrop Chanler) (1862–1952) Mother of Theodore CHANLER. Monsignor FAY introduced Fitzgerald to the wealthy Mrs. Chanler, a close friend who had built a private chapel on her Hudson River estate for Fay's use. She may have been the model for Mrs. LAWRENCE in *TSOP.* Her memoirs include a description of Fay; see *Autumn in the Valley* (Boston: Little, Brown, 1936).

Chanler, Theodore (1902–1961) Son of Margaret CHANLER; young American composer who accompanied Fitzgerald to tea at Edith WHARTON's home outside PARIS in July 1925. Chanler, a friend of Gerald and Sara MURPHY and Archibald MACLEISH, became dissatisfied with his life in France—especially his drinking—and broke with his friends, saying he was tired of them. When he told Fitzgerald about the incident, Fitzgerald discussed it as the basis of a novel about a talented young American who experiences a breakdown after he is taken up by a group of charming EXPATRIATES. Chanler was a partial model for Francis Melarky, the protagonist of an early version of *TITN.*

Chapman, William Character in *Assorted Spirits.* Railroad contractor dressed as a devil who mistakenly enters Peter WETHERBY's home on his way home from a masquerade ball. He later offers to purchase Wether-

by's house for the railroad and proposes marriage to Cecile WETHERBY.

Charles Scribner's Sons *See* SCRIBNERS.

Chase, Walter Character in *GG*. Tom BUCHANAN'S friend who was involved in GATSBY and WOLFSHIEM'S illegal business.

chauffeur (unnamed) Character in "His Russet Witch." Man who is unable to identify correctly the first edition for which CAROLINE has sent him into the Moonlight Quill Bookshop.

"A Cheer for Princeton" Lyrics. Included in a newsstory not written by Fitzgerald, "Mass Meeting To-Night To Practice New Song," *The Daily Princetonian*, October 28, 1915, p. 1; *In His Own Time*. "A Cheer for Princeton," with lyrics by Fitzgerald and music by Paul B. DICKEY, won the fall 1915 competition for a new football song and was probably sung at the 1915 Yale-PRINCETON game, but it never caught on, perhaps because of its anticipation of defeat: "Ever ready/For defeat or victory." *Fitzgerald Newsletter* prints a reconstruction of the melody (pp. 221–22).

Cheever, Bessie Belle Character in "Basil and Cleopatra." Girl whom Minnie BIBBLE is visiting in Mobile, Alabama.

Chestnut, John M. Character in "Rags Martin-Jones and the Pr-nce of W-les." Young man who has been in love with Rags MARTIN-JONES for many years. He stages an elaborate spectacle in order to win her love.

Chevril, Mr. Character in "Diagnosis." Confederate veteran who offends Charlie CLAYHORNE by telling him that things were worse after the Civil War than they are now in the Depression.

Chillicheff, Prince Character in *TITN*. Aristocrat whom Tommy BARBAN has helped escape from Russia and to whom he introduces Dick DIVER in a Munich café.

Choynski, Mrs. Character in "Jacob's Ladder." Woman convicted of murder. Jenny DELEHANTY didn't know she was her sister until the trial.

Christopher Character in "The Passionate Eskimo." Edith CARY's butler, whom PAN-E-TROON prevents from stealing a tiara.

"City Dusk" Verse. *The* NASSAU LITERARY MAGAZINE, 73 (April 1918), 315; *In His Own Time, Poems*.

Civet, Doctor Webster Character in *GG*. Guest at GATSBY's party.

Clancy, Miss Character in "Hot & Cold Blood." Jim MATHER's secretary.

Clark, Amanda Rawlins Character in "No Flowers." Marjorie CLARK's mother, who grows wistful over her own memories of proms and her loss of Carter MCLANE.

Clark, Llewellyn Character in "The Adolescent Marriage." Young architect who temporarily separates from his wife, Lucy Wharton CLARK.

Clark, Lucy Wharton Character in "The Adolescent Marriage." Sixteen-year-old girl who elopes with twenty-year-old Llewellyn CLARK. She leaves him because she considers him selfish, but they are reunited.

Clark, Marjorie Character in "No Flowers." Girl who attends the prom with Billy JOHNS.

Clark, Robert D. (Bob) and Caroline Brother and sister who were childhood friends of Fitzgerald in ST. PAUL. Bob was a member of the ELIZABETHAN DRAMATIC CLUB. In November 1910 Fitzgerald noted in his *Thoughtbook* that Bob "is interesting to talk to because he lets me do a lot of talking (which I like)" (p. XX). Fitzgerald frequently visited the Clarks' summer home at White Bear Lake in DELLWOOD. When Bob wrote a letter urging him to write about "real people," Fitzgerald responded on February 9, 1920: "The Rosseaus, Marxes, Tolstois—men of thought, mind you, 'impractical' men, 'idealist' have done more to decide the food you eat and the things you think + do than all the millions of Roosevelts and Rockerfellars . . ." (*Life in Letters*, p. 45).

Clarkson, Elizabeth Childhood friend of Fitzgerald in ST. PAUL. On September 12, 1913, before the ELIZABETHAN DRAMATIC CLUB's performance of Fitzgerald's play *Coward*, her family gave a dinner in honor of the cast. Fitzgerald and Elizabeth corresponded while he was at PRINCETON.

Clay, Collis Character in *TITN*. Yale student from Georgia with whom Rosemary HOYT attended the prom the preceding fall and whom she sees in PARIS. He and Dick go out drinking in ROME; and when Dick is jailed, Baby WARREN summons Collis to stay with him while she arranges his release.

Clayhorne, Ben Character in "Diagnosis." Charlie CLAYHORNE's half-brother, whom he is bringing up and who attends PRINCETON.

Clayhorne, Charlie Character in "Diagnosis." Man whose personality is temporarily changed by the stress of the Depression but who returns to his old self after clearing up a family matter regarding his father's will.

Clayhorne, Dicky Character in "Diagnosis." Charlie CLAYHORNE's half-brother, whom he is bringing up and to whom Charlie's fiancée, Sara ETHERINGTON, brings expensive toy soldiers.

Clayhorne, Pete Character in "Diagnosis." Charlie CLAYHORNE's older half-brother. After his release from prison he bought a farm with the money that their father had hidden.

Clemens, Samuel Langhorne *See* Mark TWAIN.

Clothilde Character in "New Types." Emily HOLLIDAY's maid.

Codman, Russel Character in "Your Way and Mine." Henry MCCOMAS's right-hand man, whose proposal McComas urges his daughter, Honoria MCCOMAS, to reject because he is not his own man.

Cody, Dan Character in *GG*. Millionaire miner who employed young Jay GATSBY on his yacht for five years.

Cohalan, Miss Character in "Two Wrongs." Bill MCCHESNEY's secretary.

Cola, Mr. ("Capone") Character in "Indecision." Guest at the same hotel as Tommy MCLANE. He travels with a "harem" of his wife, daughters, and four other women, all of whom he has psychoanalyzed for constantly complaining.

Cole, Miss Character in "That Kind of Party." Terrence R. TIPTON's teacher, who says Mexico City is the capital of Central America. Terrence corrects her and is rebuked by the school principal. A similar incident is recorded in Fitzgerald's *Ledger* for September 1906 (p. 161).

Coles, Joel Character in "Crazy Sunday." Screenwriter who disgraces himself at director Miles CALMAN's party and who later becomes involved with Stella CALMAN. Based on Fitzgerald and screenwriter Dwight Taylor (1902–86).

College Humor This magazine published an essay—"Princeton" (December 1927)—and a parody—"My Old New England Homestead on the Erie" (August 1925)—by Fitzgerald, but none of his stories appeared in the magazine. However, five stories about various types of girls, written by Zelda FITZGERALD and revised

by Fitzgerald, appeared under their joint byline from July 1929 to January 1931 (*see* FITZGERALD, ZELDA—WRITINGS OF). In January 1925 Fitzgerald rejected a $10,000 offer from the magazine to serialize *GG* because he didn't want to delay book publication and also feared that "most people who saw it advertised in *College Humor* would be sure that Gatsby was a great halfback and that would kill it in book form" (to Harold OBER, rec. January 26, 1925; *As Ever*, p. 74). *College Humor* editor H. N. SWANSON later became Fitzgerald's first HOLLYWOOD agent.

Collier's Fitzgerald's story "The Curious Case of Benjamin Button" appeared in *Collier's* in May 1922. However, the magazine was a rival of *The SATURDAY EVENING POST*, Fitzgerald's best market; and in 1932 agent Harold OBER advised Fitzgerald against offending the *Post* by appearing in *Collier's* (January 6 and February 25, 1932; *As Ever*, pp. 184–185 and 188–190). In 1937, however, just before Fitzgerald went to HOLLYWOOD, *Collier's* editor Kenneth LITTAUER paid $1,500 down against a rewrite of "Thumbs Up," a Civil War story that had been declined by 13 magazines; Littauer rejected at least two revisions before accepting the version titled "The End of Hate" in June 1939, paying $1,000 more; and the story appeared in the June 1940 issue. In return for the advance against a temporarily unusable story, Ober promised *Collier's* an equal opportunity with the *Post* for Fitzgerald's stories for a time. In summer 1939 Fitzgerald informed Littauer that he would probably not write many more stories about young love, but was attempting to "open up a new well, a new vein" of fiction: "You see, I not only announced the birth of my young illusions in 'This Side of Paradise' but pretty much the death of them in some of my last Post stories like 'Babylon Revisited.' . . . Nevertheless, an overwhelming number of editors continue to associate me with an absorbing interest in young girls—an interest that at my age would probably land me behind the bars" (c. late July 1939; *Life in Letters*, p. 402).

Littauer declined the stories Fitzgerald offered, including "Design in Plaster," "Mike Van Dyke's Christmas Wish" (later titled "Pat Hobby's Christmas Wish"), "Three Hours Between Planes," "Last Kiss," and "Director's Special." Fitzgerald hoped that *Collier's* would serialize his Hollywood novel, financing his work with installment payments. On September 29, 1929 he sent a synopsis to Littauer and SCRIBNERS editor Maxwell PERKINS, but Littauer refused to advance any money without a substantial sample. On the basis of a 6,000-word sample consisting of the first chapter of *LT/LOLT* which Fitzgerald submitted in November, Littauer refused to commit *Collier's* to the serial, although he remained interested; and Fitzgerald went on a bender. (For more details and references about the *Collier's* negotiations, *see* LOLT entry.) *Collier's* published "Last

Kiss" in April 1949, awarding it a $1,000 bonus as the best story in that issue.

Collins, Captain Character in *B&D*. Army officer whom Gloria PATCH meets at Rachael BARNES's apartment and with whom she is surprised to find she is expected to spend the night; she leaves in disgust.

Collins, Marjorie Character in "The Bridal Party." Girl who tries to blackmail Hamilton RUTHERFORD before his wedding.

Collins, Miss Character in "In the Holidays." Nurse at whom patient Mr. MCKENNA makes a pass.

Colman, Ronald (1891–1958) Historical figure and character in "The Homes of the Stars." Famous actor who greets Pat HOBBY by his first name, impressing the tourists Pat is guiding.

Column, Phoebe Character in *TSOP*. One of two NEW YORK showgirls in whose apartment Amory BLAINE sees a devil figure.

Combrinck, Lady Sybil Character in "Two Wrongs." Woman who was involved with Bill MCCHESNEY but is no longer interested in him. When he crashes her party, her husband has him thrown out.

Combrinck, Lord Character in "Two Wrongs." Lady Sybil COMBRINCK's husband, who orders Bill MCCHESNEY to be thrown out of his party.

Commodore Hotel Apartment hotel in the SUMMIT AVENUE area of ST. PAUL, Minnesota. The Fitzgeralds lived here for several weeks after being evicted from their cottage in DELLWOOD in October 1921, and Scottie FITZGERALD was born at a nearby hospital during their stay here. The Fitzgeralds moved to the Commodore again in August 1922 after being asked to leave the WHITE BEAR YACHT CLUB; they stayed at the hotel until they moved to GREAT NECK in October.

Compson, Doctor Character in " 'Trouble.' " Doctor who fires TROUBLE at the request of Mrs. JOHNSTON.

"Confessions" Public letter to Fanny Butcher. *Chicago Daily Tribune*, May 19, 1923, p. 9; *In His Own Time*. In response to Fanny Butcher's inquiry, Fitzgerald noted that he would "rather have written" Joseph CONRAD's *Nostromo* (1904) "than any other novel" (*In His Own Time*, p. 168).

Connage, Alec Character in *TSOP*. A PRINCETON friend of Amory BLAINE and the brother of Rosalind and Cecelia CONNAGE. He shares a NEW YORK apartment with Amory and Tom D'INVILLIERS after the war.

When an Atlantic City hotel detective catches him in a room with Jill WAYNE, Amory claims the girl was with him to protect Alec's reputation.

Connage, Mr. and Mrs. Beverly Characters in *The Captured Shadow*. Parents of Hubert CONNAGE and owners of the house which "The SHADOW" is attempting to rob.

Connage, Cecelia Character in *TSOP*. Alec and Rosalind CONNAGE's 16-year-old sister, who smokes Rosalind's cigarettes.

Connage, Dorothy Character in *The Captured Shadow*. Hubert CONNAGE's sister, who finds the story of "The SHADOW" romantic.

Connage, Hubert Character in *The Captured Shadow*. Young man who comes home drunk with two crooks whom he promises to make aldermen. He is engaged to Helen MAYBURN.

Connage, Leland R. Character in *TSOP*. Father of Alec, Cecelia, and Rosalind CONNAGE.

Connage, Mrs. Leland R. Character in *TSOP*. Alec, Cecelia, and Rosalind CONNAGE's mother, who instructs Rosalind how to behave at her debut. She discourages Rosalind's relationship with Amory BLAINE and encourages her to marry wealthy Dawson RYDER.

Connage, Rosalind Character in *TSOP*. Alec CONNAGE's sister, a NEW YORK debutante with whom Amory BLAINE falls in love. They talk of marriage, but she eventually breaks up with him to marry wealthy Dawson RYDER because she fears a life of boredom and responsibility while Amory struggles to make his way. Based on a combination of Zelda FITZGERALD and Beatrice Normandy from H. G. WELLS's *Tono-Bungay* (1909). In a 1923 interview Zelda commented: "I love Scott's books and heroines. I like the ones that are like me! That's why I love Rosalind in *This Side of Paradise*. . . . I like girls like that. . . . I like their courage, their recklessness and spend-thriftness. Rosalind was the original American flapper" (*In His Own Time*, p. 259).

Conrad, Joseph (1857–1924) Polish-born English novelist who influenced Fitzgerald. As a gesture of homage, Fitzgerald and Ring LARDNER danced on the lawn of the Doubleday estate at Oyster Bay, Long Island, where Conrad was visiting in May 1923; but they were thrown off the property for trespassing before they could meet him. Fitzgerald included *Nostromo* (1904) in his 1923 list of "10 Best Books I Have Read," calling it "the great novel of the past fifty years" (*FSF on Authorship*, p. 86); he also identified it as the novel he would rather have written than any other (*see* "Confessions"). Fitzgerald's

use of Nick CARRAWAY as the partially involved narrator who judges Jay GATSBY derives from Conrad's Marlow in *Lord Jim* (1900) and "Heart of Darkness" (1902). In a letter to H. L. MENCKEN defending *TITN*, Fitzgerald acknowledged Conrad's influence: "The motif of the 'dying fall' was absolutely deliberate and did not come from any diminuition of vitality, but from a definite plan. That particular trick is one that Ernest Hemmingway and I worked out—probably from Conrad's preface to 'The Nigger'—and it has been the greatest 'credo' in my life, ever since I decided that I would rather be an artist than a careerist" (April 23, 1934; *Life in Letters,* p. 256). In response to HEMINGWAY's critique of *TITN*, Fitzgerald cited Conrad's theory "that the purpose of a work of fiction is to appeal to the lingering after-effects in the reader's mind" (June 1, 1934; *Life in Letters*, pp. 263–264). Fitzgerald explained his use of Cecelia BRADY as narrator of *LT/LOLT* to Kenneth LITTAUER: "I shall grant myself the privilege, as Conrad did, of letting her imagine the actions of the characters" (September 29, 1939; *Life in Letters,* p. 410).

See Frederick R. Karl, *Joseph Conrad: The Three Lives* (New York: Farrar, Straus & Giroux, 1979) and Jeffrey Meyers, *Joseph Conrad: A Biography* (New York: Scribners, 1991).

"The Continental Angle" Fiction by Zelda FITZGERALD. *The* NEW YORKER, 8 (June 4, 1932), 25; *Bits of Paradise*; *Zelda Fitzgerald: The Collected Writings*. A couple dining in France recalls the food and restaurants in America.

Cooley, Jim Character in "Not in the Guidebook." False war hero who received a medal for obtaining the German orders which in actuality he had stolen from Bill DRISCOLL. He justifies his mistreatment of his wife, Milly COOLEY, by claiming "shell shock."

Cooley, Milly Character in "Not in the Guidebook." Eighteen-year-old girl who is deserted by her husband, Jim COOLEY, and who later marries Bill DRISCOLL.

Coots, Mrs. Character in "Not in the Guidebook." Woman who wants to hire Milly COOLEY as a companion.

Copyright The term of American copyright for Fitzgerald's published writings is now 75 years from the year of publication. (*TSOP* went out of copyright in 1995, and *GG* will go out of copyright in 2000.) The term of British copyright is 50 years from Fitzgerald's death; thus all of his published work went out of copyright in the United Kingdom at the end of 1990.

Corcoran Character in "A Penny Spent." An "incurable spendthrift" whom Julius BUSHMILL hires to guide

his wife and daughter through EUROPE. Corcoran tells Hallie BUSHMILL: "When you were still playing who's got the button back in Ohio I entertained on a cruising trip that was so much fun that I had to sink my yacht to make the guests go home" (*Bits of Paradise*, p. 122).

Corcoran, Caroline Martin Character in "Flight and Pursuit." Virginia belle who is unhappily married to George CORCORAN but is reunited with her real love, Sidney LAHAYE, years later after leaving Corcoran.

Corcoran, Dexter Character in "Flight and Pursuit." Son of Caroline and George CORCORAN.

Corcoran, George Character in "Flight and Pursuit." Lieutenant from Ohio who marries Caroline Martin [CORCORAN].

Corcoran, Mrs. Character in "Flight and Pursuit." George CORCORAN's domineering mother, who dislikes his wife, Caroline CORCORAN.

Corker, Bill Character in "Two Old-Timers." Movie director who shoved Phil MACEDON into a shell hole and filmed him.

Correspondence *See* LETTERS.

Cortelyou, Henry Character in "Diagnosis." Charlie CLAYHORNE's employer and Sara ETHERINGTON's uncle.

"Cosmopolitan" In March 1940 Lester COWAN, an independent producer, paid $1,000 for the movie rights to "Babylon Revisited" (February 1931), one of Fitzgerald's best stories. Planning to produce the movie with the Columbia studio, Cowan hired Fitzgerald to write the screenplay for $500 a week with a bonus if the movie was made. The salary was low compared to what Fitzgerald had received from the studios; but he enjoyed working on the project, and "Cosmopolitan"—as he retitled it—is considered his best screenplay. His August 1940 second draft includes an "Author's Note" which explains: "This is an attempt to tell a story from a child's point of view without sentimentality. . . . Remember that it is a dramatic piece—not a homey family story. Above all things, Victoria is a child—not Daddy's little helper who knows all the answers" (PRINCETON UNIVERSITY LIBRARY). Fitzgerald's screenplay is not a close adaptation of his story, for he invented a new plot to provide action for the camera and expanded the role of Honoria WALES, renamed Victoria in honor of Budd SCHULBERG's baby daughter. Shirley Temple (b. 1928) was considered for the role of Victoria, and Fitzgerald discussed the screenplay with Temple and her mother in July; however, Cowan and Mrs. Temple failed to agree on terms. Fitzgerald's

screenplay was never produced, and Cowan later sold the rights to "Babylon Revisited," reportedly for $40,000, to MGM, which produced it in 1954 as *The Last Time I Saw Paris* from a new screenplay by Philip G. Epstein (1909–52), Julius J. Epstein (b. 1909), and Richard Brooks (1912–92).

In "Cosmopolitan" Charles Wales gets out of the stock market in October 1929 because his wife has suffered nervous strain from the demands of his work. While they are sailing to EUROPE with their daughter, Victoria, the market crashes. Wales tries to save a friend's investments by cable; and his wife, who sees this as evidence that their lives will always be dominated by the ticker tape, jumps overboard. In PARIS Wales has a nervous breakdown and turns Victoria over to his sister-in-law. Victoria later follows her father to SWITZERLAND, where his crooked partner has hired someone to murder Wales for his million-dollar insurance policy. A phone call from Victoria distracts the would-be murderer so that Wales can knock him out.

Fitzgerald's screenplay was published as *Babylon Revisited: The Screenplay*, with an introduction by Budd Schulberg and an afterword by Matthew J. BRUCCOLI (New York: Carroll & Graf, 1993).

Cosmopolitan On December 26, 1922 Fitzgerald signed a contract with *Cosmopolitan*, a Hearst magazine, for an option on all stories he wrote in 1923, with the magazine to accept at least six; he received $1,500 for the option and was to receive $1,875 for each story. However, the arrangement proved unsatisfactory, and the magazine rejected stories; all the stories accepted under this agreement were published in HEARST'S INTERNATIONAL. The contract gave *Cosmopolitan* first refusal on serial rights to *GG*, but on December 4, 1924 editor Ray Long declined the novel. In 1932 Harry Burton, the new editor of *Cosmopolitan*, asked Harold OBER for Fitzgerald's stories; but he declined "Crazy Sunday" because the Hearst organization feared it would offend their associates in the movie industry. In 1933 *Cosmopolitan* expressed interest in serializing *TITN*, but Fitzgerald chose to serialize the novel in SCRIBNER'S MAGAZINE. Fitzgerald's work never appeared in *Cosmopolitan*.

Costain, Thomas B. (1885–1965) An associate editor at *The SATURDAY EVENING POST* who was agent Harold OBER's primary contact at the magazine (*As Ever*, p. 195). The Canadian-born Costain later became a popular historical novelist with such works as *The Black Rose* (1945) and *The Silver Chalice* (1952).

Costello, Bill Character in "A Man in the Way." Pat HOBBY's old friend who is in Jack BERNERS' office when Hobby enters.

Cottage Club PRINCETON UNIVERSITY eating club to which Fitzgerald was elected in March 1915. Princeton had no fraternities, and the 18 eating clubs identified the social standing of their members. During spring elections each club admitted about 25 sophomores—a total of about 75 percent of the sophomore class. Cottage was one of the top clubs.

While on leave from the ARMY at the end of February 1918, Fitzgerald went to the Cottage Club to finish writing "The Romantic Egotist," an early version of *TSOP*. At the end of February 1920 he moved to the Cottage Club so he would be at Princeton when *TSOP* was published. On May 1, 1920, while Fitzgerald was visiting Princeton with Edmund WILSON and John Peale BISHOP, he was told that his Cottage Club membership had been suspended because he and Zelda FITZGERALD had disgraced the club during a recent campus visit as chaperones for a house party weekend; and club members shoved him out of the building. Nevertheless, Fitzgerald always considered himself a member of Cottage Club, and the suspension was later lifted. In late January 1928 he was invited to speak at a club dinner, but he was nervous and probably intoxicated, and he ended his speech after only a few sentences.

Count Charles (*See* also Bertram de VILLEFRANCHE.) Character in "In the Darkest Hour." PHILIPPE's deceased father, who was killed by a Spanish VIZIER.

"The Count of Darkness" Fiction—second PHILIPPE story. Written October 1934. REDBOOK, 65 (June 1935), 20–23, 68, 70, 72. Philippe organizes his supporters and makes plans for a camp. He requires a band of Syrian merchants to hand over a tenth of their goods in order to ford the River Loire, and he allows the local peasants a portion of the loot. He takes LETGARDE, the consort of the slain Norman chieftain, as his own consort; but when he mistreats her, she runs away and drowns trying to cross the river.

"A Couple of Nuts" Fiction by Zelda FITZGERALD. SCRIBNER'S MAGAZINE, 92 (August 1932), 80–84; *Bits of Paradise*; *Zelda Fitzgerald: The Collected Writings*. The marriage of musicians Larry and Lola deteriorates while they are in EUROPE. Lola becomes involved with their patron, Jeff Daugherty; and Larry later becomes involved with Jeff's ex-wife, Mabel. Larry and Mabel drown when her yacht sinks in a hurricane, but Lola survives.

Cousin Jo Character in "The Rich Boy." Paula LEGENDRE's cousin, who reports to Mrs. LEGENDRE that Anson HUNTER was drunk at a dinner party.

Cowan, Lester (1905–1990) Independent movie producer whose films include *My Little Chickadee* (Universal

Pictures, 1940), *Story of G. I. Joe* (United Artists, 1945), and *Main Street to Broadway* (MGM, 1953). He bought film rights to "Babylon Revisited" for $1,000 in March 1940 and paid Fitzgerald $500 a week to write the screenplay, called "Cosmopolitan." Cowan and Fitzgerald developed a good working relationship, but Fitzgerald's screenplay was never produced. Cowan later sold the rights to "Babylon Revisited" to MGM.

Coward Play. In *F. Scott Fitzgerald's St. Paul Plays, 1911–1914.* Performed by the ELIZABETHAN DRAMATIC CLUB on August 29, 1913 at the ST. PAUL Y.W.C.A. Auditorium, raising $150 for the Baby Welfare Association; and repeated "upon urgent request" at the WHITE BEAR YACHT CLUB in DELLWOOD on September 2, 1913. Fitzgerald played the roles of Lt. Charles DOUGLAS and Private WILLINGS, and was also listed in the program as Stage Manager. The play received favorable reviews from the local press, and Fitzgerald captioned the review clippings in his scrapbook "The GREAT EVENT" and "ENTER SUCCESS!" (*The Romantic Egoists,* pp. 18 & 19).

Act I (1861)
Judge DOUGLAS objects to Jim HOLWORTHY's attentions to his daughter Lindy DOUGLAS because Holworthy is not away fighting in the Civil War. Jim wants Lindy to marry him, but she explains that her father thinks he is a coward, so he resolves to enlist. Lindy's brother Charley DOUGLAS, a Confederate soldier, stops by the house while his regiment is retreating; he is carrying $12,000 which he stole from a Union commissary train that morning. Union soldiers search the house for him, and when they threaten Jim—who didn't enlist after all—he reveals Charley's hiding place in a chest, and Charley is taken prisoner of war. Jim realizes his cowardice and heads South to join the army.

Act II (1865)
Judge Douglas has died, and Lindy is teaching school to support the impoverished family. Charley returns home after the surrender of General Robert E. LEE at Appomattox, and Jim Holworthy—who saved Charley's life in the war—returns as an army captain. He proposes to Lindy again, but she refuses him when he confesses that he still retains a streak of cowardice. When two Union soldiers try to pillage the house, Jim confronts Private WILLINGS, who is trying to steal Lindy's necklace, and bluffs him by offering to let him choose between two pistols, only one of which is loaded. Lindy agrees he has had another chance to conquer his "yellow streak" and embraces him.

Cowley, Malcolm (1898–1989) American author, editor, and critic whose works include *Blue Juniata: Poems* (1929, revised and expanded as *Blue Juniata: Collected Poems,* 1968); *Exile's Return* (1934; revised edition, 1951); *The Literary Situation* (1954); and *A Second Flowering: Works and Days of the Lost Generation* (1973). He succeeded Edmund WILSON as literary editor of *The New Republic* in 1929, holding that post until 1944. He was active in left-wing politics in the 1930s, helping to found the League of American Writers in 1935; but he discontinued his political activity after World War II. In 1948 he became a literary adviser to Viking Press, and in 1950 he began a series of visiting professorships at various universities. Cowley promoted the work of William Faulkner (1897–1962), John Cheever (1912–82), Jack Kerouac (1922–69), and Ken Kesey (b. 1935).

In his review of *TITN,* Cowley noted Fitzgerald's "double personality" as both observer and participant: "Part of him is a guest at the ball given by the people in the big house; part of him has been a little boy peeping in through the window and being thrilled by the music and the beautifully dressed women—a romantic but hard-headed little boy who stops every once in a while to wonder how much it all cost and where the money came from" ("Breakdown," *The New Republic,* 79 [6 June 1934], 105–106; *FSF: The Critical Reception,* p. 324). He also suggested that the "technical faults" of *TITN* were due to Fitzgerald's working on it at intervals over nine years, during which his attitude changed so that he could not make the early and late parts agree.

In 1951 Cowley edited two volumes which contributed to the Fitzgerald REVIVAL: *The Stories of F. Scott Fitzgerald* and *Tender Is the Night* "With the Author's Final Revisions." The *TITN* edition was based on a copy of the novel which Fitzgerald had disbound, reassembling the pages in chronological order and noting on the front endpaper: "This is the <u>final version</u> of the book as I would like it." Fitzgerald had made some 40 corrections or revisions but had stopped annotating about halfway through the book. Cowley claimed that the chronological rearrangement improved the novel, but reviews of the revised edition were unenthusiastic, and it went out of print after 1959.

See Hans Bak, *Malcolm Cowley: The Formative Years* (Athens: University of Georgia Press, 1993).

"The Crack-Up" Autobiographical essay. ESQUIRE, 5 (February 1936), 41, 164; *CU.* Account of Fitzgerald's "crack-up," of his shift from believing that "life was something you dominated if you were any good" to the realization of his own emotional bankruptcy: "I had been mortgaging myself physically and spiritually up to the hilt" (*CU,* pp. 69 & 72).

This was the first of three confessional articles, including "Pasting It Together" and "Handle with Care," which Fitzgerald wrote for *Esquire* after the publication of *TITN* when he was having trouble writing stories for *The SATURDAY EVENING POST.* Reaction to the "Crack-

THE CRACK-UP

F. SCOTT FITZGERALD

With other Uncollected Pieces, Note-Books and Unpublished Letters

Together with Letters to Fitzgerald from Gertrude Stein, Edith Wharton, T. S. Eliot, Thomas Wolfe and John Dos Passos

And Essays and Poems by Paul Rosenfeld, Glenway Wescott, John Dos Passos, John Peale Bishop and Edmund Wilson

Edited by **EDMUND WILSON**

A New Directions Book

Title page for the 1945 collection that stimulated the reassessment of Fitzgerald's work (Bruccoli Collection, University of South Carolina)

Up" series was largely negative: magazine editors and movie people distrusted Fitzgerald's ability to deliver good work, and his friends found the articles embarrassing.

The Crack-Up: With Other Uncollected Pieces, Note-Books and Unpublished Letters Edited with poem of dedication by Edmund WILSON. New York: New Directions, 1945; Harmondsworth, U.K.: Penguin, 1965. Contents: "Echoes of the Jazz Age," "My Lost City," "Ring," " 'Show Mr. and Mrs. F. to Number ——,' " "Auction—Model 1934," "Sleeping and Waking," "The Crack-Up," "Handle With Care," "Pasting It Together," "Early Success," "The Note-books" [21 sections], "Letters to Friends," "Letters to Frances Scott Fitzgerald," "Three

Letters about 'The Great Gatsby,' " "A Letter from John Dos Passos," "A Letter from Thomas Wolfe," "F. Scott Fitzgerald" by Paul Rosenfeld, "The Moral of Scott Fitzgerald" by Glenway WESCOTT, "A Note on Fitzgerald" by John DOS PASSOS, "The Hours" by John Peale BISHOP. In an influential review of the volume, Lionel Trilling noted: "The root of Fitzgerald's heroism is to be found, as it sometimes is in tragic heroes, in his power of love" (*The Liberal Imagination* [New York: Viking, 1950], p. 244). Maxwell PERKINS had vetoed Wilson's earlier proposal to include the "Crack-Up" essays with *The Last Tycoon* because he felt they had damaged Fitzgerald's reputation, and he declined to publish *CU*. However, the publication of *CU* was a key event in triggering the Fitzgerald REVIVAL.

Craddock, Mr. Character in " 'The Sensible Thing.' " Young man who is waiting at the station with Jonquil CARY when George O'KELLY comes to visit her.

Craig, Charlie Character in "Strange Sanctuary." Dolly HAINES's uncle, whose home she visits. During his absence his house is occupied by thieves who call themselves Major REDFERN and Miss Willie SHUGRUE.

Craig House Sanitarium in BEACON, New York, with a resort-like atmosphere. The director, Dr. Clarence SLOCUM, was a friend of Dr. Oscar FOREL, who recommended Craig House to Fitzgerald. Zelda FITZGERALD was transferred there from PHIPPS CLINIC on March 8, 1934 but failed to improve. On May 19, 1934 she was transferred to SHEPPARD-PRATT HOSPITAL outside BALTIMORE in a catatonic state.

Craker, Captain Character in "The Last of the Belles." Soldier who has a date with Nancy LAMAR before his scheduled embarkation for France.

Craw, Adele Character in "A Woman with a Past." President of the senior class and the "ideal girl" at Miss BRERETON's School. She dates Dudley KNOWLETON, but they don't believe in getting engaged so young. Josephine PERRY is puzzled by this girl who is so different from herself.

Crawford, Jason Character in "Inside the House." Boy with whom Gwen BOWERS sneaks out to a movie.

Crawford, Mr. Character in *B&D*. Man whose phone call for Gloria PATCH is answered by Anthony PATCH, who has just returned from the army.

"Crazy Sunday" Fiction. Written January 1932. *The AMERICAN MERCURY*, 27 (October 1932), 209–220; *TAR*. Screenwriter Joel COLES attends an exclusive Sunday tea at the home of director Miles CALMAN, where he is

flattered by the attention of Calman's wife, Stella CAL-MAN. After drinking a couple of cocktails Joel makes a fool of himself by performing a humorous skit, for which he is booed by a famous actor. At a party the following Sunday, Stella tells Joel about Miles's affair with Eva GOEBEL, her best friend. Joel goes home with the Calmans, who discuss their marital troubles with him; and he realizes he is in love with Stella. She invites him to escort her to a dinner and theater party while Miles is out of town at a football game. After the party Stella invites Joel to her house and shares her doubt that Miles has really gone to the game; she thinks he may have faked several telegrams and really be in town spying on her. Just as Stella kisses Joel, the telephone rings with the news that Miles's plane has crashed and his body has been identified. Stella refuses to believe the news and begs Joel to stay with her. He phones for a doctor and leaves, but knows he will be back.

The incident at the Calmans' tea was based on Fitzgerald's alcohol-inspired exhibition at a party hosted by Irving THALBERG and Norma SHEARER. (See Dwight Taylor, "Scott Fitzgerald in Hollywood," *Harper's*, 218 [March 1959], 67–71.) "Crazy Sunday" was rejected by the mass-circulation magazines out of fear that well-known HOLLYWOOD figures might be recognized.

"The Credo of F. Scott Fitzgerald" *See* "Public letter to Thomas Boyd."

Cresswell, Clarke Character in "Strange Sanctuary." Fifteen-year-old boy who meets Dolly HAINES at the APPLETONS' house and who helps her break into her Uncle Charlie CRAIG's house when she suspects that his guests are lying to her about his illness.

Critical Reputation and Reception of Novels While Fitzgerald's early novels *This Side of Paradise* (1920) and *The Beautiful and Damned* (1922) have received critical attention chiefly for the insight they give into his development, the author has attained his reputation as a major American novelist on the basis of his achievement in *The Great Gatsby* (1925) and *Tender Is the Night* (1934). An evocative exploration of an era and of the "American dream," *GG* is widely recognized as Fitzgerald's masterpiece and as a classic American novel. However, the reputation of *TITN*, a novel with steadfast detractors as well as fierce partisans, is more problematic. For some, *TITN* is seriously flawed, "a brilliant failure," but others regard it as a great novel. "While *The Great Gatsby* represents Fitzgerald's most perfectly expressed insight into the fraud of his own dream of success," writes Otto Friedrich, "*Tender Is the Night* combines that new insight with a new understanding of how and why the dream disintegrates" ("F. Scott Fitzgerald: Money, Money, Money," *American Scholar*, 29 [Summer 1960], 401).

Even though Fitzgerald had written only drafts of 17 of its projected 30 episodes, his fifth novel, which Edmund WILSON edited and entitled *The Last Tycoon* (1941), has been hailed as an "unfinished masterpiece" and the best novel written about HOLLYWOOD, but it has also been seen as merely a promising start. Tracing the contemporary reception of Fitzgerald's novels, from *TSOP* through *LT*, provides necessary background for understanding the subsequent critical debate over his standing as a novelist and the nature of the "Fitzgerald REVIVAL": it is the story of how an author who once wanted "to write for the youth of his own generation" largely lost the audience of his own era but after his death began to win the appreciation of the critics and "the schoolmasters of ever afterward."

TSOP launched Fitzgerald not only as a novelist but also as a celebrated spokesman for his generation. The overwhelmingly positive reviews largely praised the book as a realistic portrayal of American youth, especially the collegiate set. "Beside it," wrote Burton Rascoe in the *Chicago Daily Tribune*, "Tarkington's 'Seventeen,' Johnson's 'Stover at Yale,' and Samuel Merwin's yarns are amusing and superficial sketches" ("A Youth in the Saddle," April 3, 1920, p. 11; *FSF: The Critical Reception*, p. 3). For the reviewer of *The Dartmouth*, Fitzgerald's novel fulfilled "the demands of readers who know undergraduate life at first-hand" (R.F.M., "Princeton Scene of Novel—'This Side of Paradise' Is True-to-Life Novel," April 24, 1920, p. 2; *FSF: The Critical Reception*, p. 16). While some critics professed shock—"If the parties to Amory's various love-affairs are faithful portraits of the modern American girl," warned the reviewer for *America*, "the country is going to the dogs rapidly" (23 [May 29, 1920], 139; *FSF: The Critical Reception*, p. 25)—most reviewers appreciated the ebullient individuality of Fitzgerald's approach and style. In *The SMART SET*, H. L. MENCKEN proclaimed *TSOP* "a truly amazing first novel—original in structure, extremely sophisticated in manner, and adorned with a brilliancy that is as rare in American writing as honesty is in American statecraft" (62 [August 1920], 140; *FSF: The Critical Reception*, p. 28). Most reviewers, even many with reservations, were aware of Fitzgerald's possible significance. The "biggest thing," concluded Maud Davis Walker in the *New York Call*, "is the promise of what the author will do in the future" (September 19, 1920, Section 2, p. 10; *FSF: The Critical Reception*, p. 31).

The most widely reviewed of Fitzgerald's works, *B&D* was regarded as a disappointment by most reviewers, who, like Edwin Francis Edgett of the *Boston Evening Transcript*, "reasonably" asked for "something better" in his second novel (March 11, 1922, Part 3, p. 10; *FSF: The Critical Reception*, p. 82). Some critics did credit Fitzgerald with improvement. In the *New York Herald*, John Peale BISHOP argued that "the book represents

both in plan and execution an advance" ("Mr. Fitzgerald Sees the Flapper Through," March 5, 1922, Section 8, p. 1; *FSF: The Critical Reception,* p. 74). And while Mencken believed that Fitzgerald's naturalistic novel lacked the "vast plausibility" of Theodore DREISER'S *Sister Carrie* (1900), he praised the young author for trying "something much more difficult" than he had previously done, noting that "even in its defects there is proof of hard striving" ("Fitzgerald and Others," *The Smart Set,* 67 [April 1922], 140–141; *FSF: The Critical Reception,* p. 107). But though many praised the novel's realism, more found the story and the characters tedious and depressing. "The author has filled a 400–page book with the affairs of an utterly selfish girl, married to an equally selfish but far weaker man," asserted the *Cleveland Plain Dealer* critic (P. B., "Young Married Crowd Is Trivial as the Flappers," March 11, 1922, p. 15; *FSF: The Critical Reception,* p. 81). "What earthly care," asked the reviewer for the *Yale Literary Magazine,* "has anyone of their progress from drunk to drunk toward the damnation of a flat on Claremont Avenue?" (T.C.C., 87 [March 1922], 204–205; *FSF: The Critical Reception,* p. 62).

The majority of reviewers recognized *GG* as a step toward artistic maturity for Fitzgerald, but few would have predicted that it would become a classic. For Isabel Paterson of *New York Herald Tribune Books,* the novel provided a "nice problem"—"to say plainly that it is neither profound nor durable, without producing the impression that it is insignificant (which it is not)" ("Up to the Minute," April 19, 1925, p. 6; *FSF: The Critical Reception,* p. 200). Fitzgerald's work, wrote Laurence Stallings in the *New York World,* "evidences an interest in the color and sweep of prose, in the design and integrity of the novel, in development of character, like nothing else he has attempted," but he did "not think for one moment in reading this book that 'here is a great novel' or even, that 'here is a fine book' " ("The First Reader—Great Scott," April 22, 1925, p. 13; *FSF: The Critical Reception,* pp. 203 & 204). Mencken in the *Baltimore Evening Sun,* while praising "the charm and beauty of the writing," nevertheless found the novel "in form no more than a glorified anecdote" ("As H.L.M. Sees It," May 2, 1925, p. 9; *FSF: The Critical Reception,* pp. 212 & 211). William Rose Benét's review in the *Saturday Review of Literature* was among the most perceptive because he recognized the sureness of the novelist's mature moral vision: "For the first time Fitzgerald surveys the Babylonian captivity of this era unblinded by the bright lights. He gives you the bright lights in full measure, the affluence, the waste, but also the nakedness of the scaffolding" ("An Admirable Novel," 1 [May 9, 1925], 739–740; *FSF: The Critical Reception,* p. 220). Most reviewers, however, believed that Fitzgerald had yet to prove himself a major artist. "If only he can refrain altogether in future from the sham romanticism and sham sophistication which the

magazines demand of him," opined Conrad Aiken in the *New Criterion,* "he may well become a first-rate novelist" (4 [October 1926], 775–776; *FSF: The Critical Reception,* p. 244).

TITN was published to mixed reviews nine years after *GG,* an interval Fitzgerald believed hurt his reputation "almost beyond repair" (to Zelda FITZGERALD, October 11, 1940; *Life in Letters,* p. 466). While a few reviewers such as Gilbert SELDES in the *New York Evening Journal* proclaimed *TITN* a "great novel" ("True to Type—Scott Fitzgerald Writes Superb Tragic Novel," April 12, 1934, p. 23; *FSF: The Critical Reception,* p. 292) and Fitzgerald's best, others faulted its structure, particularly the shift in focus from Rosemary HOYT to Dick DIVER, and the credibility of Dick's decline. John Chamberlain in the *New York Times* asserted that "the novel does not really begin until Rosemary is more or less out of the way" ("Books of the Times," April 13, 1934, p. 17; *FSF: The Critical Reception,* p. 295), while Fanny Butcher in the *Chicago Tribune* found the novel worth reading chiefly for its "first third" ("New Fitzgerald Book Brilliant; Fails as Novel," April 14, 1934, p. 10; *FSF: The Critical Reception,* p. 299). Clifton Fadiman in *The New Yorker* viewed Dick's "rapid acceptance of his failure" as unconvincing and argued that "the events of the narrative, tragic as they are, are insufficient to motivate his downfall. It is the failure to reach far, far back into his characters' lives that helps to prevent this novel from being the first-rate work of fiction we have been expecting" ("F. Scott Fitzgerald," 10 [April 14, 1934], 112–115; *FSF: The Critical Reception,* p. 302). Chamberlain interrupted his review of *Dr. Martino and Other Stories* (1934) by William Faulkner (1897–1962) to defend Fitzgerald's treatment of Dick Diver's collapse—"Compared to the motivation in Faulkner, it is logic personified"—and to register his consternation over the conflicting reviews the novel had received: "The critical reception . . . might serve as the basis for one of those cartoons on 'Why Men Go Mad.' No two reviews were alike; no two had the same tone" ("Books of the Times," *New York Times,* April 16, 1934, p. 15; *FSF: The Critical Reception,* pp. 312 & 311). The publication of Malcolm COWLEY's reordered edition of *TITN* in 1951 renewed the debate that the novel's first appearance had sparked.

Appearing posthumously in a volume that also included *GG* and five stories, *LT* offered reviewers the opportunity to reassess Fitzgerald's career—the very beginning, perhaps, of the popular and critical revival of his reputation. Save for a few, most reviewers were respectful, if not enthusiastic, echoing Edmund Wilson's judgment that the novel was Fitzgerald's "most mature" and praising the characterization of Monroe STAHR. Even James Gray of the *St. Paul Dispatch*—who predicted that a finished *LT* would "have been a failure measured by the standard that Fitzgerald had set for himself"—recognized its significance: "It is good that

some one at last has written seriously about Hollywood, some one who believed in its function, its technique, its poetry" ("Epitaph for Fitzgerald: Fascination and Faulty," October 27, 1941, p. 8; *FSF: The Critical Reception,* pp. 358 & 359). Of all the contemporary criticism Fitzgerald's work received throughout his career, however, none was more prescient than Stephen Vincent Benét's review in the *Saturday Review of Literature:* "You can take off your hats now, gentlemen, and I think perhaps you had better. This is not a legend, this is a reputation—and, seen in perspective, it may well be one of the most secure reputations of our time" ("Fitzgerald's Unfinished Symphony," 24 [December 6, 1941], 10; *FSF: The Critical Reception,* pp. 375–376).

by George P. Anderson

Critical Studies When Fitzgerald died in 1940, nine of his works were still in the SCRIBNERS warehouse. But the "Fitzgerald REVIVAL" commencing between 1945 and 1951 awakened appreciation of Fitzgerald as a substantial contributor to American literature. Since then, several aspects of his work have attracted critical and scholarly attention.

The annotated secondary checklists of Fitzgerald criticism provided in Jackson R. Bryer's *The Critical Reputation of F. Scott Fitzgerald* (Hamden, CT: Archon, 1967) and *Supplement One Through 1981* (Hamden, CT: Archon, 1984) document the shifting perceptions of Fitzgerald's achievement. Several significant contemporary reviews, essays, and editorials, as well as interviews, have been collected in the second half of *F. Scott Fitzgerald in His Own Time: A Miscellany,* edited by Matthew J. BRUCCOLI and Bryer (Kent, Ohio: Kent State University Press, 1971). Bryer also collected contemporary reviews of Fitzgerald's books in *F. Scott Fitzgerald: The Critical Reception* (New York: Burt Franklin, 1978).

The first book-length critical study of Fitzgerald was James E. Miller, Jr.'s *The Fictional Technique of F. Scott Fitzgerald* (The Hague: Nijhoff, 1957), later expanded as *F. Scott Fitzgerald: His Art and His Technique* (New York: New York University Press, 1964). Miller traces Fitzgerald's development from a novelist of saturation to one of selection, focusing especially on "development of theme, point of view, and the manner of representing events." Richard D. Lehan also discusses Fitzgerald's increasing control as a writer in *F. Scott Fitzgerald and the Craft of Fiction* (Carbondale: Southern Illinois University Press, 1966), illustrating "the Romantic quality of his imagination" and his transformation of personal experiences into art.

Kenneth Eble's *F. Scott Fitzgerald* (Boston: Twayne, 1963; revised edition, 1977) is an introductory survey of the life and work, part of Twayne's United States Authors Series. In *F. Scott Fitzgerald: A Critical Portrait* (New York: Holt, Rinehart & Winston, 1965), a biographical as well as critical study, Henry Dan Piper distinguishes between the "real" Fitzgerald and the

popular myth, and focuses on Fitzgerald's development as a writer. He also includes a chapter on Zelda FITZGERALD'S *Save Me the Waltz* (1932); he was one of the first to give scholarly attention to that work. Another critical study which incorporates biography is Joan M. Allen's *Candles and Carnival Lights: The Catholic Sensibility of F. Scott Fitzgerald* (New York: New York University Press, 1978), in which she analyzes the influence of his Catholic experience on his work. Sergio Perosa, in *The Art of F. Scott Fitzgerald* (Ann Arbor: University of Michigan Press, 1965; first published in Rome: Edizioni di Storia e Letterature, 1961), downplays biographical connections and examines the achievement of Fitzgerald's work independent of its relationship to his life.

Robert Sklar's *F. Scott Fitzgerald: The Last Laocoön* (New York: Oxford University Press, 1968) is an examination of Fitzgerald's re-creation of "the genteel romantic hero" throughout the body of his work. John B. Chambers, in *The Novels of F. Scott Fitzgerald* (New York: St. Martin's Press, 1989), argues against a prevalent notion that Fitzgerald "was an emotional rather than a conceptual thinker," suggesting instead that Fitzgerald sustained a consistent ironic philosophy, which he described in a letter to his daughter as "the wise and tragic sense of life" (October 5, 1940; *Life in Letters,* p. 465).

Fitzgerald's creative process and the evolution of his texts are examined in Bruccoli's *Apparatus for a Definitive Edition of Under the Red, White and Blue. [The Great Gatsby]* (Columbia, S.C.: University of South Carolina Press, 1974); introduction to *The Great Gatsby: A Facsimile of the Manuscript* (Washington: Bruccoli Clark/NCR Microcard Books, 1973); *The Composition of Tender Is the Night* (Pittsburgh: University of Pittsburgh Press, 1963); and *"The Last of the Novelists": F. Scott Fitzgerald and The Last Tycoon* (Carbondale: Southern Illinois University Press, 1977). These works illustrate Fitzgerald's craftsmanship, dispelling the notion that he was frivolous with his talent. Bruccoli's *Reader's Companion to F. Scott Fitzgerald's Tender Is the Night* (with Judith S. Baughman; Columbia, S.C.: University of South Carolina Press, 1996), details the novel's creation, clarifies its chronology, and identifies references to places, terms, and other details with which today's readers may be unfamiliar.

Fitzgerald, and some subsequent critics, tended to regard his short stories as inferior to his novels; but the stories are receiving some of the attention they merit. In *A Fortune Yet: Money in the Art of F. Scott Fitzgerald's Short Stories* (New York: Garland, 1991), Bryant Mangum examines the importance of the stories to Fitzgerald's career, both as an artistic workshop and as a vital source of income—Fitzgerald was both a literary artist and a professional writer. Bruccoli analyzes Fitzgerald as a professional/commercial short story writer in "The Man of Letters as Professional," *F. Scott Fitzgerald on Authorship,* ed. Bruccoli with Judith S.

Baughman (Columbia: S.C. University of South Carolina Press, 1996, pp. 11–22). Other sources are two collections of essays, *The Short Stories of F. Scott Fitzgerald: New Approaches in Criticism* (ed. Bryer; Madison: University of Wisconsin Press, 1982) and *New Essays on F. Scott Fitzgerald's Neglected Stories* (ed. Bryer; Columbia: University of Missouri Press, 1996); and Alice Hall Petry's *Fitzgerald's Craft of Short Fiction* (Ann Arbor: UMI Research Press, 1989).

Some attention has also been given to Fitzgerald's HOLLYWOOD work. *The Cinematic Vision of F. Scott Fitzgerald,* by Wheeler Winston Dixon (Ann Arbor: UMI Research Press, 1986), is a study of the screenwriting techniques that Fitzgerald developed, most significantly in the screenplay for "Infidelity," and how this writing style affected the style and structure of his fiction. Gene D. Phillips's *Fiction, Film, and F. Scott Fitzgerald* (Chicago: Loyola University Press, 1986) includes some assessment of Fitzgerald as a screenwriter, but is primarily an evaluation of the various film versions of Fitzgerald's works and life.

Fitzgerald was a writer particularly attuned to details of time and place. In *F. Scott Fitzgerald and the Art of Social Fiction* (London: Arnold, 1980), Brian Way calls Fitzgerald a social novelist in the tradition of Edith WHARTON and Henry James—observers of social relations and behaviors, manners and morals, and of the psychological effects these have on characters. Sarah Beebe Fryer's *Fitzgerald's New Women: Harbingers of Change* (Ann Arbor: UMI Research Press, 1988) is a study of the major female characters, who exist in a period of changing roles and expectations for women. This approach acknowledges Fitzgerald's reliability as a chronicler of his era.

There are several collections of essays on various aspects of Fitzgerald's work, including those edited by Bruccoli, *New Essays on the Great Gatsby* (Cambridge: Cambridge University Press, 1985) and *Profile of F. Scott Fitzgerald* (Columbus, Ohio: Merrill, 1971); Harold Bloom, *F. Scott Fitzgerald* (New York: Chelsea House, 1985), *F. Scott Fitzgerald's The Great Gatsby* (New York: Chelsea House, 1986), and *Gatsby,* analyses of the literary character (New York: Chelsea House, 1991); Marvin J. LaHood, *Tender Is the Night: Essays in Criticism* (Bloomington: Indiana University Press, 1969); Milton R. Stern, *Critical Essays on F. Scott Fitzgerald's Tender Is the Night* (Boston: Hall, 1986); and A. Robert Lee, *Scott Fitzgerald: The Promises of Life* (New York: St. Martin's Press, 1989). Another resource is the *Fitzgerald Newsletter,* which appeared from 1958 to 1968 and was published in one volume by NCR Microcard Books in 1969. It was followed by the *Fitzgerald/Hemingway Annual,* which appeared from 1969 to 1979.

by Tracy Simmons Bitonti

Critical Writings of Fitzgerald F. Scott Fitzgerald had a clear understanding of the craft of fiction and its application to his own work and the work of others. His ability to see the value in works from various periods and genres is evident in comments he made throughout his career in letters, notebooks, reviews, articles, reading lists, and passages in his fiction. (See *F. Scott Fitzgerald on Authorship.*)

Fitzgerald came to literature with a sense of wonder and a sense of what was of value. As Lionel Trilling observes in *The Liberal Imagination:* "It is hard to overestimate the benefit which came to Fitzgerald from his having consciously placed himself in the line of the great. . . . To read Fitzgerald's letters to his daughter . . . and to catch the tone in which he speaks about the literature of the past, or to read the notebooks he faithfully kept . . . and to perceive how continuously he thought about literature, is to have some clue to the secret of the continuing power of Fitzgerald's work" (New York: Viking, 1950, p. 243). Without that critical sense, Fitzgerald could not have become the great writer that he was.

On March 5, 1922, Fitzgerald wrote to Maxwell PERKINS about *The Mind in the Making* (1921) by James Harvey Robinson (1863–1936): "I think its a thoroughly excellent book. It states the entire case for modernity's lingering hope of progress. It is a depressing book, I think, as are Well's + Shaw's late things and all those of that brave company who started out in the nineties so full of hope and joy in life and faith in science and reason" (*Scott/Max,* p. 57). This seems a remarkable passage by the young writer of whom Malcolm COWLEY said in 1951, "He was not a student for all the books he read; not a theoretician and perhaps one should flatly say, not a thinker" (*Stories,* p. xvi). It is this kind of misunderstanding of Fitzgerald's critical ability that has endured from the publication of his first novel right up to the present.

Fitzgerald was indeed a thinker, sometimes rational and sometimes intuitive, whose lifelong concern with the craft of fiction helped to make him a critic of both his own work and the work of others. Aware of the accusations that he had a "fatal facility" in his early work, he said that he then "labored like a slave over every sentence so as not to be like that" ("Afternoon of an Author," August 1936; *AOAA,* p. 181).

Fitzgerald agreed with Joseph CONRAD's definition in his preface to *The Nigger of the "Narcissus"* (1897) of the writer's responsibility: "My task is by the power of the written word to make you hear, to make you feel—it is, before all, to make you see." He quotes it in his article "One Hundred False Starts" (March 1933), where he also observes: "Mostly we authors repeat ourselves—that's the truth. We have two or three great and moving experiences in our lives—experiences so great and moving that it doesn't seem at the time that anyone else has been so caught up and pounded and dazzled and astonished and beaten and broken and rescued and illuminated and rewarded and humbled

in just that way ever before" (*AOAA*, p. 132). Fitzgerald clearly believed that an author can only make a reader hear, feel, and see what the author has profoundly experienced himself. "I must start out with an emotion—one that's close to me and that I can understand" (*AOAA*, p. 132).

In *F. Scott Fitzgerald: His Art and His Technique,* James E. Miller, Jr. sees the change from *TSOP* to *GG* as a very conscious change in Fitzgerald's movement away from H. G. WELLS's technique of "saturation" toward Henry James's technique of "selection" (p. 2). Fitzgerald renounced Wells's influence in his review of John DOS PASSOS's *Three Soldiers* (1921), and his thinking through to "selection" as an essential aspect of the writer's craft accounts for his strong criticism of Thomas WOLFE's work (see Fitzgerald to Wolfe, mid–July 1937; *Life in Letters*, p. 332).

In his review of *Three Soldiers* Fitzgerald states: "This is all very careful work. There is none of that uncorrelated detail, that clumsy juggling with huge masses of material which shows in all but one or two pieces of American realism. The author is not oppressed by the panic-stricken necessity of using all his data at once lest some other prophet of the new revelation uses it before him" (*In His Own Time*, p. 123).

Fitzgerald was also concerned that some American writers had a tendency to emphasize material to the neglect of technique. In "How to Waste Material" (May 1926) he wrote:

Ever since Irving's preoccupation with the necessity for an American background, for some square miles of cleared territory on which colorful variants might presently arise, the question of material has hampered the American writer. For one Dreiser who made a single minded and irreproachable choice there have been a dozen like Henry James who have stupid-got with worry over the matter, and yet another dozen who, blinded by the fading tail of Walt Whitman's comet, have botched their books by the insincere compulsion to write "significantly" about America. (*AOAA*, p. 117)

Two striking examples of Fitzgerald's critical ability were his critiques of Ernest HEMINGWAY's *The Sun Also Rises* (1926) and *A Farewell to Arms* (1929). Even though *The Sun Also Rises* was already in proof, Fitzgerald made such a strong case against the opening that Hemingway eventually deleted the opening pages: "Why not cut the inessentials in Cohens biography? His first marriage is of no importance. When so many people can write well + the competition is so heavy I can't imagine how you could have done these first 20 pps. so casually" (June 1926; *Life in Letters*, p. 144).

Fitzgerald read *A Farewell to Arms* in typescript. He made a couple of dozen observations in the form of notes. One of the best:

Catherine is too glib, talks too much physically. In cutting their conversations cut some of her speeches rather than his.

I mean—you're still seeing her as you did in 1917 thru nineteen yr. old eyes. In consequence unless you make her a bit fatuous occasionally the contrast jars—either the writer is a simple fellow or she's Eleanora Duse disguised as a Red Cross nurse. (June 1929; *Life in Letters*, p. 166)

Fitzgerald became something of a professor of literature in the late 1930s as he tried to help educate his daughter, Scottie FITZGERALD, and Sheilah GRAHAM. He wrote to Scottie: "<u>Strange Interlude</u> is good. It was good the first time, when Shaw wrote it and called it <u>Candida.</u> On the other hand you don't pass an hour of your present life that isn't directly influenced by the devastating blast of light and air that came with Ibsen's <u>Doll's House</u>" (29 July 1940; *Life in Letters*, p. 457).

In an undated fragment from a letter evaluating something Scottie had written, he wrote: "There is as yet no honesty—the reader will say 'so what?' But when in a freak moment you will want to give the low-down, not the scandal, not the merely *reported* but the *profound* essence of what happened at a prom or after it, perhaps that honesty will come to you—and then you will understand how it is possible to make even a forlorn Laplander *feel* the importance of a trip to Cartier's!" (*Letters*, p. 101).

Sheilah Graham details Fitzgerald's tutelage in *College of One* (1967), which includes lists of all of the things Fitzgerald wanted her to read and a narrative laced with many comments he made about works and authors. He greatly admired Conrad's work. He commented on "Shaw's aloof clarity and brilliant consistency" (p. 83). He considered Theodore DREISER's *Sister Carrie* (1900) "almost the first piece of American realism" (p. 83). At another time he observed, "Tolstoy became too mystical, James too complex and intricate" (p. 86).

Fitzgerald was interested in the craft of fiction from an early age. He applied well-thought-out standards to both his own work and the work of others. He read widely, had a solid grasp of the history of ideas, and wrote sound criticism.

See John Kuehl, "Scott Fitzgerald's Critical Opinions," *Modern Fiction Studies,* 7 (Spring 1961), 3–18.

by Marvin J. LaHood

Cromwell, George Character in "The Lees of Happiness." Harry and Kitty CROMWELL's little boy.

Cromwell, Harry Character in "The Lees of Happiness." Jeffrey CURTAIN's closest friend, an unhappily married man. A frequent visitor during Jeffrey's illness, he is devoted to Roxanne CURTAIN.

Cromwell, Kitty Carr Character in "The Lees of Happiness." Harry CROMWELL's unattractive wife, who leaves him and marries another man after their divorce.

Crosby, Esther Character in "Six of One—". Gordon VANDERVERE's fiancée.

Crosby, Waldron Character in "The Smilers." Sylvester STOCKTON's old friend who has just lost all his money, whose wife is expecting a baby, and who persuades his friend Donny to hire him as a clerk.

"The Cruise of the Rolling Junk" Article. *Motor,* 41 (February, March, April 1924), 24–25, 58, 62, 64, 66; 42–43, 58, 72, 74, 76; 40–41, 58, 66, 68, 70; *The Cruise of the Rolling Junk* (Bloomfield Hills, Mich. & Columbia, S.C.: Bruccoli Clark, 1976). Three-part humorous travel article dealing with the Fitzgeralds' July 1920 trip from WESTPORT, Connecticut, to MONTGOMERY, Alabama, in a secondhand Marmon touring car dubbed "the Rolling Junk."

Crum, Hector Character in "Forging Ahead." Lewis CRUM's cousin, who attends Rhoda SINCLAIR's dinner party. While Hector is dancing with Rhoda at the Lake Club, Basil Duke LEE has a brief opportunity to be alone with Minnie BIBBLE.

Crum, Lewis Character in the Basil Duke LEE stories. In "The Freshest Boy" he is on the train with Basil on the way to ST. REGIS, where he will be a second-year student. Lewis, who hates the school, attempts to dampen Basil's enthusiasm and reminds him of his reputation for freshness at his previous school. In "He Thinks He's Wonderful" he rides with Joe GORMAN to Connie DAVIES' dance. In "Forging Ahead" he is a guest at Rhoda SINCLAIR's dinner party.

Cuba In April 1939, after a quarrel with Sheilah GRAHAM in HOLLYWOOD, Fitzgerald took Zelda FITZGERALD to Cuba. He drank heavily and was beaten for trying to stop a cockfight. They went to NEW YORK, where Fitzgerald continued drinking and was hospitalized. Zelda returned alone to HIGHLAND HOSPITAL, telling her doctors that Fitzgerald's lungs had required attention (he had tuberculosis). This trip was the last time the Fitzgeralds were together.

Cugat, Francis (F. Coradal-Cugat) (1893–1981) Artist born in Spain and raised in CUBA; the brother of orchestra leader Xavier Cugat (1900–90). He worked as a designer for Douglas Fairbanks (1883–1939) and as a technicolor consultant in HOLLYWOOD, and he had a one-man show in NEW YORK in 1942. He illustrated the dust jacket for *The Great Gatsby,* featuring a woman's face over a night scene at an amusement park. There has been much speculation about Fitzgerald's comment to Maxwell PERKINS: "For Christs sake don't give anyone that jacket you're saving for me. I've written it into the book" (c. August 25, 1924; *Life in Letters,* p. 79; *Scott/Max,* p. 76). See Appendix 3, "Note on the Dust Jacket," in *GG,* ed. Matthew J. BRUCCOLI (Cambridge: Cambridge University Press, 1991), pp. 209–210; D. Mesher, "Covering a Debt: F. Scott Fitzgerald and Francis Cugat," *Modern Fiction Studies,* 37 (Summer 1991), 235–239; and Charles Scribner III, "Celestial Eyes: From Metamorphosis to Masterpiece," *The Princeton University Library Chronicle,* 53 (Winter 1992), 140–155, which discusses and reproduces Cugat's preliminary artwork for the jacket. The final painting is at the PRINCETON UNIVERSITY LIBRARY; the preliminary artwork is in the Arlyn Bruccoli Collection. See *Francis Coradal-Cugat,* catalogue of a February 1994 exhibit at the McKissick Museum, University of South Carolina, Columbia, South Carolina.

Cupp, Walter Character in "Family in the Wind." Man whose house was destroyed by the second tornado.

"The Curious Case of Benjamin Button" Fiction. Written February 1922. *COLLIER'S,* 69 (May 27, 1922), 5–6, 22–28; *TJA.* Benjamin BUTTON, the first child of Mr. and Mrs. Roger BUTTON, a socially prominent couple in antebellum BALTIMORE, is born as an old man, about age seventy. His parents try to ignore or disguise his age as much as possible—feeding him only milk at first, buying him toys, and sending him to kindergarten. At age 18 he passes the entrance examinations for Yale but is not allowed to matriculate because he looks as if he is 50. He joins his father's hardware business and marries young Hildegarde MONCRIEF. As he grows older, Benjamin appears younger and takes up activities—such as dancing—which are appropriate for his apparent age. He attends and graduates from Harvard, but later goes to kindergarten with his own grandson. He grows younger and younger until he finally fades out.

Fitzgerald explained in the annotated table of contents for *TJA* that "this story was inspired by a remark of Mark Twain's to the effect that it was a pity that the best part of life came at the beginning and the worst part at the end" (p. ix).

Curly, Michael Character in "The Bridal Party." American in Paris who attends the wedding of Caroline DANDY, whom he had loved and lost.

Curtain, Jeffrey Character in "The Lees of Happiness." Author who has been happily married to actress Roxanne Milbank [CURTAIN] for a year when he suffers a stroke; he is paralyzed for 11 years, then dies.

Curtain, Roxanne Milbank Character in "The Lees of Happiness." Chorus girl and actress who marries Jeffrey CURTAIN and devotes herself to taking care of him during his 11-year paralysis.

Cushmael, T. Character in "The Pusher-in-the-Face." Charles David STUART's employer, who plans to fire Stuart for missing work while in jail for pushing a woman in the face.

"The Cut-Glass Bowl" Fiction. Written October 1919. *SCRIBNER'S MAGAZINE*, 67 (May 1920), 582–592; *F&P.* Evylyn PIPER's life is haunted by an enormous cut-glass bowl, a gift from a rejected suitor who told her the bowl was as hard, beautiful, empty, and easy to see through as she was. When Freddy GEDNEY, with whom she has just ended an affair, accidentally hits the bowl while attempting to slip out of the house, he is discovered by her husband, Harold PIPER. Her daughter, Julie PIPER, cuts her finger on the bowl, and her hand is amputated after she contracts blood-poisoning. Harold Piper's proposed business merger falls through after his cousin's husband, Tom LOWRIE, who is drunk on punch served in the bowl, is rude to Piper's prospective partner, Clarence AHEARN. When the Pipers' son, Donald PIPER, is killed in the war, the letter notifying them of his death is temporarily misplaced in the bowl. Desperate to be rid of the bowl, Evylyn tries to fling it into the yard but slips and crashes down the steps with it.

D

Dada (Horatio Frost) Character in *The Vegetable*. Jerry FROST's father, a Civil War veteran whose mind is failing and who is nearly blind and deaf. Jerry's appointment of Dada as Secretary of the Treasury is responsible for Idaho's demand that Jerry resign as President of the United States.

Daddy Character in "Outside the Cabinet-Maker's." Man who tells his daughter a tale of a fairy princess held captive by an ogre.

Dale, Dick Character in "Mightier Than the Sword." Movie director who hires Pat HOBBY to work on a script about composer Reginald de Koven (1861–1920).

Daley, Irene Character in "Six of One—". Actress who files a lawsuit for injuries received in a car wreck with Howard KAVENAUGH, Beau LEBAUME, Wister SCHOFIELD, and George WINFIELD.

Dalyrimple, Bryan Character in "Dalyrimple Goes Wrong." Young military hero who is dissatisfied with his job in the stockroom of a wholesale grocery and begins a secret life of burglary until offered a seat in the State Senate.

"Dalyrimple Goes Wrong" Fiction. Written September 1919. *The SMART SET*, 61 (February 1920), 107–116; *F&P*. Bryan DALYRIMPLE returns to his hometown as a military hero and seeks his first civilian job. Theron G. MACY employs him to work in the stockroom of his wholesale grocery, where Dalyrimple grows bored and discontented with his lack of progress. When Dalyrimple discovers that Macy's nephew, Tom EVERETT, has been given preferential treatment, he resolves to "get on"—no matter what it takes—so that he can buy happiness. He moonlights as a burglar until he is offered a seat in the State Senate by Alfred J. FRASER, who has watched and admired the steadiness with which he has persisted at his grocery work.

"Dalyrimple Goes Wrong" is Fitzgerald's first ironic examination of the Horatio Alger (1832–99) success story.

Damianakes, Cleon (Cleonikes) (1895–1979) Illustrator of the dust jackets for *All the Sad Young Men* and Zelda FITZGERALD's novel, *Save Me the Waltz* (1932). She also illustrated the dust jackets for Ernest HEMINGWAY's *The Sun Also Rises* (1926) and *A Farewell to Arms* (1929).

D'Amido, Elizabeth (Betsy) Character in "The Rough Crossing." Pretty girl to whom Adrian SMITH is attracted while sailing to France.

"The Dance" Fiction. Written June 1926. *REDBOOK*, 47 (June 1926), 39–43, 134, 136, 138; *Bits of Paradise*. Fitzgerald's first commercial mystery story; he considered changing the title to "In a Little Town." The NARRATOR, a girl from NEW YORK, relates how the dark underside of a small Southern town, which she calls Davis, had been revealed during her visit five years before. She had become interested in Charley KINCAID until she learned of his engagement to Marie BANNERMAN; then she had decided to leave town to avoid causing trouble. At a country club dance two nights before she was to leave, she and Charley had discovered Marie kissing Joe CABLE; shortly afterward Marie had been discovered murdered in a dressing-room. Charley had been arrested and believed guilty until the narrator solved the crime: Catherine JONES had killed Marie after she saw her kissing Joe Cable, with whom Catherine was in love. The narrator married Charley, and they live in New York.

Dance, Beatrice Stribling Married woman with whom Fitzgerald had an affair while living at the GROVE PARK INN in ASHEVILLE, North Carolina, in the summer of 1935. Dance, a wealthy Texan, was staying at the hotel with her sister, Eleanor; she fell in love with Fitzgerald, pushing their affair further than he wanted, according to his reports to his typist and confidante, Laura GUTHRIE. (Guthrie chronicled the Fitzgerald-Dance relationship in her diary; Dance was disguised as "Gloria Dart" in the diary excerpts published in the December 1964 *ESQUIRE* as "A Summer with F. Scott Fitzgerald.") When Dance's husband, Du Pre Rainey "Hop" Dance, came to Asheville there was a confrontation. Fitzgerald, who had always made it clear that he would never leave Zelda, ended the affair with a firm letter when Dance left Asheville in August. Dance and Fitzgerald contin-

ued to correspond, and she sent him gifts. PRINCETON UNIVERSITY LIBRARY acquired her correspondence with Fitzgerald in 1963.

Dandy, Caroline Character in "The Bridal Party." Young woman whom Michael CURLY loves but who marries Hamilton RUTHERFORD.

Dandy, Mrs. Character in "The Bridal Party." Caroline DANDY's mother, who had always liked Michael CURLY.

Dane, Oscar Character in "One Trip Abroad." Man who is interested in Nicole KELLY in Monte Carlo.

Dangeu, Doctor Character in *TITN*. Devereux WARREN's physician in LAUSANNE.

Danski, Mrs. Character in "The Adjuster." Charles and Luella HEMPLE's cook, who quits her job because it is too difficult. Luella refuses to pay her.

Danzer, Abe Character in " 'I Didn't Get Over.' " Officer who turned to drink after he was wrongly blamed for an accident in Georgia in which some men under his command drowned.

Darcy, Jack Character in *The Girl from Lazy J*. George KENDALL's nephew from San Francisco. He is concerned that his mother may not approve of his engagement to Leticia LARNED.

Darcy, Monsignor Thayer Character in *TSOP*. Catholic priest with whom Beatrice O'Hara [BLAINE] had a romance when he was a "pagan, Swinburnian young man" (p. 7) before entering the priesthood. "He was intensely ritualistic, startlingly dramatic, loved the idea of God enough to be a celibate, and rather liked his neighbor" (p. 24). He becomes Amory BLAINE's mentor and encourages his ambitions and introspection. Darcy's death and funeral near the end of the novel cause Amory to realize that he wants not to be loved and admired but to be indispensable and to give people a sense of security. Based on Monsignor Cyril Sigourney Webster FAY.

Dare, Alicia *See* CAROLINE.

Darrow, Clark Character in "The Ice Palace" and "The Jelly-Bean." A Georgia Tech graduate from TARLETON, Georgia, who drives an ancient Ford and spends his time loafing and discussing how to invest his small capital. In "The Ice Palace," he takes Sally Carrol HAPPER swimming. In "The Jelly-Bean," he invites Jim POWELL to a dance at the country club.

Dartmouth College College in Hanover, New Hampshire, where Fitzgerald and Budd SCHULBERG, his collaborator on *Winter Carnival,* traveled February 10–12, 1939 with producer Walter WANGER to get fresh ideas for their screenplay. Fitzgerald and Schulberg got drunk during the trip; Wanger fired both writers, but rehired Schulberg in California. The trip provided the basis for Schulberg's 1950 novel, *The Disenchanted.*

Dashiell, Alfred (1901–1970) Managing editor of *SCRIBNER'S MAGAZINE,* which serialized *TITN* January–April 1934.

Davey, George Character in "A Woman with a Past." Lillian HAMMEL's date for the Yale prom.

Davies, Connie Character in the Basil Duke LEE stories. In "The Scandal Detectives" she is one of the young people who gather in the Whartons' yard. In "He Thinks He's Wonderful" she hosts a dance at her family's lake house. In "The Captured Shadow" she plays Miss Saunders in Basil's play.

Davies, Gwendolyn (Mrs. Cornelius B. Hasbrouk; the Comptesse de Frejus) Character in "A Full Life." Woman whose adventures are followed by Dr. Harvey WILKINSON, who once treated her in the emergency room.

Davis, Annie Lee Character in "Lo, the Poor Peacock!" Jason DAVIS's invalid wife.

Davis, Jason Character in "Lo, the Poor Peacock!" Man who nearly commits suicide when his finances plummet, but whose fortunes improve.

Davis, Jo Character in "Lo, the Poor Peacock!" Jason and Annie Lee DAVIS's daughter, who is unjustly expelled from school.

Davis, Katherine Character in "Magnetism." Hostess of the party at which Kay HANNAFORD drinks too much and expresses interest in Arthur BUSCH in order to make her husband, George HANNAFORD, jealous.

Davis, Minna Character in *LT/LOLT*. Monroe STAHR's dead wife, an actress.

Day, Helen Character in "One Interne." Doctor Howard DURFEE's debutante fiancée, for whom he abandons Thea SINGLETON.

Dean, Elisabeth Childhood friend and confidante of Fitzgerald in ST. PAUL.

Dean, Philip Character in "May Day." Gordon STER-RETT's Yale classmate who refuses to lend him $300 but gives him $80. After the Gamma Psi dance he gets drunk and goes around with Peter HIMMEL as "Mr. In" and "Mr. Out."

"Dearly Beloved" Fiction. *Fitzgerald/Hemingway Annual* (1969), pp. 1–3; *Bits of Paradise; Dearly Beloved* (Iowa City: Windhover Press of the University of Iowa, 1969). Black golf champion and Pullman steward BEAUTY BOY marries LILYMARY, and they have a son after many years. When Beauty Boy's leg is amputated after an injury on the job, Lilymary works as a cook, and he becomes a night watchman. They both die of influenza and go to heaven, where his leg is restored and he becomes golf champion again.

"The Death of My Father" Unfinished essay. *The Princeton University Library Chronicle,* 12 (Summer 1951), 187–189; manuscript facsimiled in *Apprentice Fiction*. Fitzgerald adapted material from this essay about Edward FITZGERALD for use in *TITN* to describe the relationship between Dick DIVER and The Rev. DIVER.

DeBec, Mayall Character in "The Captured Shadow." He takes the role of leading man in Basil Duke LEE's play after Hubert BLAIR drops out.

Debris, Percy B. Character in *B&D*. Movie director who gives Gloria PATCH a screen test at the request of Joseph Black [BLOECKMAN] but who decides the role in question calls for a younger actress.

"A Debt of Honor" Fiction. *The ST. PAUL ACADEMY NOW AND THEN,* 2 (March 1910), 9–11; *Apprentice Fiction*. Confederate private Jack SANDERSON volunteers for sentry duty and falls asleep at his post. General Robert E. LEE condemns him to be shot, but then lets him off with a reprimand. Six weeks later Sanderson is killed by the enemy while heroically charging a house held by federal troops; before he dies he sets the house on fire, putting the enemy to flight.

Fitzgerald's interest in the Civil War was influenced by the reminiscences of his father, Edward FITZGERALD, who guided Confederate spies during his boyhood.

"The Debutante" Play. *The NASSAU LITERARY MAGAZINE,* 72 (January 1917), 241–252; revised for *The SMART SET,* 60 (November 1919), 85–96; incorporated into *TSOP; Apprentice Fiction*. A one-act play about self-absorbed belle Helen HALCYON on the evening of her debut. Helen's admission to her forlorn suitor, John CANNEL, that she enjoys the thrill of "going after" young men is the earliest example of an attitude char-acteristic of many Fitzgerald heroines. Fitzgerald included a revised and expanded version of the play in *TSOP* as the first meeting of Amory BLAINE and Rosa-lind CONNAGE.

de Caros Moros, Count Character in "Indecision." Young Greek whose attentions to Rosemary MERRI-WEATHER make Tommy MCLANE jealous.

Decker, Mary Character in "Family in the Wind." Girl whom Forrest JANNEY secretly loved, but who ran away with Pinky JANNEY, who later abandoned her.

de Coppet, Travis Character in the Josephine PERRY stories. In "First Blood" he and Josephine go for a car ride, but Josephine no longer wants to kiss him because she is now interested in Anthony HARKER. The previous summer Josephine and Travis had tried to elope but couldn't find a minister. In "Emotional Bankruptcy" Travis arrives at Josephine's house at the same time as Edward DICER.

Deems, Mr. Character in "Two for a Cent." Bank vice-president who is suspicious of all bank employees after a cashier disappears with $30,000 and whom Henry W. HEMMICK encounters while trying to replace a penny he has lost from a sum he is transporting for the bank.

Deering, Humphrey Character in "The Passionate Es-kimo." A World's Fair executive who spends the night at Edith CARY's house to protect the tiara which her father had lent to the fair.

Deering, Jeff Narrator of "The Bowl." Dolly HARLAN's roommate at PRINCETON.

"The Defeat of Art" Review of *The Boy Grew Older* by Heywood Broun (1888–1939). *St. Paul Daily News,* January 21 1923, section 2, p. 6; *FSF on Authorship*. Fitzgerald describes Broun's novel about a newspaper man as "a competently written, highly interesting and somewhat sketchy story" (*FSF on Authorship,* p. 79).

Deglen, Joris Character in "Design in Plaster." French-man with whom Mary HARRIS has an affair.

de la Guillet de la Guimpé, Marquis Eduard Charac-ter in "The Intimate Strangers." SARA's husband, whom she leaves briefly for KILLIAN.

de la Guillet de la Guimpé, Henri Character in "The Intimate Strangers." Son of Eduard and SARA DE LA GUILLET DE LA GUIMPÉ.

de la Guillet de la Guimpé, Marquise *See* SARA.

de la Guillet de la Guimpé, Miette Character in "The Intimate Strangers." Daughter of Eduard and SARA DE LA GUILLET DE LA GUIMPÉ.

de la Guillet de la Guimpé, Noel Character in "The Intimate Strangers." SARA'S sister-in-law, who tries to dissuade her from reuniting with KILLIAN after the death of Sara's husband, Eduard DE LA GUILLET DE LA GUIMPÉ.

de la Guillet de la Guimpé, Comte Paul Character in "The Intimate Strangers." Eduard DE LA GUILLET DE LA GUIMPÉ'S brother, who resents SARA'S reunion with KILLIAN because of the disgrace her actions bring on his brother's name.

de Lanclerc, Count Hennen Character in "Discard." Dolly BORDON'S husband, who leaves her for Phyllis BURNS.

de Lanclerc, Countess *See* Dolly BORDON.

Delauney, Madame Noel Character in "One Trip Abroad." Woman whom Nicole KELLY catches her husband, Nelson KELLY, kissing, and whom she accidentally strikes with a vase.

Delehanty, Jenny Character in "Jacob's Ladder." Shopgirl who becomes an actress with the help of Jacob BOOTH. She takes the name of Jenny Prince when she begins her acting career. Based on actress Lois MORAN.

Delihant, Cecilia *See* Cecilia Delihant TAYLOR.

Delihant, Eliza Edward FITZGERALD'S sister; mother of Cecilia Delihant TAYLOR and Thomas DELIHANT. Young Scott Fitzgerald visited her home, "Randolph," in Montgomery County, Maryland, in May 1902 and again in April 1903, the second time to be a ribbon holder at "Cousin Ceci's" wedding.

Delihant, Thomas Fitzgerald's cousin, the son of Eliza DELIHANT and brother of Cecilia Delihant TAYLOR; he was one of Fitzgerald's heroes for a time. Fitzgerald visited him at the Jesuit seminary in Woodstock, Maryland, at Easter in 1912, an experience which provided the basis for Fitzgerald's 1915 story "The Ordeal."

Dell, Henry Haven Character in "News of Paris—Fifteen Years Ago." Man who has a one-afternoon fling with Bessie WING, whom he meets when they share a taxi while he is waiting for a ship.

Dellwood, Minnesota Community on White Bear Lake outside ST. PAUL where young Fitzgerald frequently visited his friends' lake houses. Two of Fitzgerald's plays for the ELIZABETHAN DRAMATIC CLUB—*Coward* (1913) and *Assorted Spirits* (1914)—were performed at the WHITE BEAR YACHT CLUB in Dellwood. Scott and Zelda Fitzgerald rented a cottage in Dellwood August–October 1921, and they lived at the Yacht Club June–August 1922.

Demorest, Ethel Character in "Bernice Bobs Her Hair." Jim STRAIN'S fiancée, who won't marry him until he can hold down a job.

Dempster, Paul Character in "Emotional Bankruptcy." Josephine PERRY'S date for the PRINCETON prom. He is eventually offended by her excessive attention to Louie RANDALL.

Denzer, Catherine Character in "On an Ocean Wave." Gaston T. SCHEER'S mistress.

Derocco, Doctor Character in "The Swimmers." French physician who attends Henry Clay MARSTON after Marston's collapse.

de Sano, Marcel Screenwriter who collaborated with Fitzgerald at Metro-Goldwyn-Mayer studio in 1931 revising a script based on the novel *Red-Headed Woman* (1931) by Katharine Brush (1902–52). Fitzgerald described de Sano as a studio hack and claimed he was sabotaging his work; Fitzgerald wanted to appeal to Irving THALBERG for permission to work alone but was advised against it. The Fitzgerald/de Sano script was unsatisfactory, and the film was released in 1932 with the screenplay credited to Anita LOOS.

Deshhacker, Mrs. Character in "Lo, the Poor Peacock!" Grocer's wife who closes Jason DAVIS'S account at the store.

"Design in Plaster" Fiction. *ESQUIRE,* 12 (November 1939), 51, 169; *AOAA.* Martin and Mary HARRIS, separated for four months, are briefly drawn back together when he is in a body cast after his arm is dislocated in an accident. When he learns that she will be seeing Joris DEGLEN that night, he goes to her apartment, where he falls down the stairs and suffers new injuries. Mary's bitterness at Martin's jealousy leads her to invite Deglen into her bedroom.

This story was partly based on Fitzgerald's experience in a body cast after tearing his shoulder in a diving accident in 1936.

Destage Character in "Shadow Laurels." One of Jean CHANDELLE'S three closest friends, who tell Jaques CHANDELLE what Jean had meant to them.

detective Character in *The Vegetable*. Detective hired by Charlotte FROST to find her missing husband, Jerry FROST. He locates the wrong man.

DeTinc, Mr. Character in "Fun in an Artist's Studio." Powerful studio executive who lends Pat HOBBY to Princess DIGNANNI for an afternoon so she can paint his portrait.

De Vinci, Leonard Edward Davies ("Skiddy") Character in "The Perfect Life." Hard-drinking young man with whom Jobena DORSEY plans to elope; Basil Duke LEE foils their plan by getting Skiddy drunk.

Devlin Character in "Winter Dreams." Man who tells Dexter GREEN that Judy JONES is unhappily married and that her beauty has faded.

Devlin, Estelle (Mrs. John Devlin) Character in "No Harm Trying." Pat HOBBY's ex-wife, to whom he was married only three weeks. Once the best script girl at the studio, she has tried to cut her wrists and is in the hospital.

DeWitt, Marylyn Character in *TSOP*. Minneapolis girl who writes to Amory BLAINE at PRINCETON.

Deyo, Draycott Character in "Bernice Bobs Her Hair." Ministerial student whom BERNICE shocks with a bathtub story.

Deyo, Mrs. Character in "Bernice Bobs Her Hair." Draycott DEYO's mother, who regards bobbed hair as an abomination and who is hosting a dance the day after BERNICE has her hair bobbed.

"Diagnosis" Fiction. Written October 1931. *The SATURDAY EVENING POST,* 204 (February 20, 1932), 18–19, 90, 92; *The Price Was High.* Sara ETHERINGTON returns from a trip to EUROPE to find her fiancé, Charlie CLAYHORNE, changed by his worries about the Depression. At her request he goes to see Marston RAINES, a wise and perceptive man, then returns to his hometown of MONTGOMERY, Alabama, to settle what is bothering him. At the old family home he retrieves an unopened envelope which he had hidden after his father's death ten years before and which he believes contains his father's revised will, cutting him out and giving his imprisoned half-brother, Pete CLAYHORNE, control of the younger children, Dicky and Ben CLAYHORNE. Before he can open it, however, Pete appears and confesses that he had found and used $10,000 cash not mentioned in their father's will and offers to share the money with his three brothers. Charlie confesses about the hidden envelope, which they open to discover a note that says there is hidden money

which will go to whoever finds it. When Charlie returns to Sara he is his old self again.

"The Diamond as Big as the Ritz" Fiction. Written October 1921. *The SMART SET,* 68 (June 1922), 5–29; *TJA.* John T. UNGER spends the summer with his ST. MIDAS' classmate Percy WASHINGTON, who boasts that his father is the richest man in the world. The Washingtons' estate is hidden in the Montana Rockies, and their house rests on a diamond mountain. Though their lifestyle and surroundings are lavish, the Washingtons are hampered by the necessity of preserving the secret of their wealth. Percy's father, Braddock WASHINGTON, has imprisoned two dozen aviators who have discovered their estate; and he routinely arranges the deaths of his children's summer visitors. John and Percy's sister Kismine WASHINGTON fall in love; the night that Mr. Washington sees them together he arranges for John's death, but John escapes. That night the Washington estate falls under attack by a dozen airplanes, for an Italian teacher who escaped Washington's prison has revealed Washington's secret. John, Kismine, and her sister, Jasmine WASHINGTON, escape the family property; and John sees Braddock Washington attempting to bribe God to restore the secrecy of his wealth. Mr. and Mrs. Washington and Percy enter the mountain through a trapdoor; and the mountain, which is wired, explodes.

Fitzgerald's 1915 visit to his friend Sap DONAHOE's Montana ranch provided the setting for "Diamond." Fitzgerald noted in the annotated table of contents for *TJA* that this story "was designed utterly for my own amusement. I was in that familiar mood characterized by a perfect craving for luxury, and the story began as an attempt to feed that craving on imaginary foods" (p. viii).

Fitzgerald had difficulty selling "Diamond," which was rejected by the slick magazines, and he cut it from 20,000 words to 15,000. *The Smart Set* paid $300 for the story, and Fitzgerald wrote to Harold OBER: "I am rather discouraged that a cheap story like The Popular Girl written in one week while the baby was being born brings $1500.00 + a genuinely imaginative thing into which I put three weeks real entheusiasm like The Diamond in the Sky [the story's original title] brings not a thing" (February 5, 1922; *Life in Letters,* p. 54; *As Ever,* p. 36).

See David J. F. Kelley, "The Polishing of 'Diamond,' " *Fitzgerald Newsletter,* no. 40 (Winter 1968).

Diamond Dick See Diana DICKEY.

"Diamond Dick and the First Law of Woman" Fiction. Written December 1923. HEARST'S INTERNATIONAL, 45 (April 1924), 58–63, 134, 136; *The Price Was High.* At age 10 Diana DICKEY selected the name of "Diamond

Dick" as symbol of her "childish revolt against the softness of life" (*The Price Was High,* p. 80). (Diamond Dick was a character in the dime novels of George Charles Jenks [1850–1929], who wrote as W. B. Lawson.) At age 19 when she returns from a year in the Red Cross in France in 1919, she denies the rumor that she is engaged to Charley ABBOT; and she makes her debut and is a social success. Five years later Charley returns from PARIS, and Diana sees him with actress Elaine RUSSEL. Diana demands that he join her family for dinner the next evening; he comes and they discuss their old love, but he leaves to return to Elaine. Diana takes her father's pistol and, resuming her childhood persona of "Diamond Dick," goes to Elaine's apartment to find Charley, threatening to shoot Elaine and Charley if they don't cooperate with her. Diana reviews her relationship with Charley, whose memory of the events just before his plane crash in the war is unclear, and she begs him to remember. She reveals that they were married five years ago, and they soon have another wedding.

Diamond, Margaret Character in *TSOP.* Drunken woman who clings to Amory BLAINE at a restaurant.

"The Diary of a Sophomore" Humor article. *The PRINCETON TIGER,* 27 (March 17, 1917), 11; *In His Own Time.* Account of a college student waiting to receive bids from clubs.

"Dice, Brass Knuckles & Guitar" Fiction. Written January 1923. HEARST'S INTERNATIONAL, 43 (May 1923), 8–13, 145–149; *Bits of Paradise* (second edition—New York: Pocket Books, 1976); *The Price Was High.* Fitzgerald described this story to Maxwell PERKINS as "Exuberant Jazz in my early manner" (June 1, 1925; *Life in Letters,* p. 121; *Scott/Max,* p. 112). Jim POWELL, a native of TARLETON, Georgia, goes North for the summer and opens an academy offering lessons in crap-shooting, self-defense, and guitar-playing to the wealthy young people of Southampton, Long Island. Once his school is established, he sends for Amanthis POWELL, whom he had met on his way North, and offers to introduce her into society. While she becomes a social success, Jim is still an outsider, regarded as a servant. When he throws Martin VAN VLECK out of his school for drinking, two society women accuse him of running an immoral establishment and take all the girls home. Jim closes his academy. On his last night in town he has a date with Amanthis, who reveals that the dance from which he thinks they have both been excluded is being given for her and that she has been visiting her cousins there and had arranged for everyone to pretend not to know her. She urges him to come again next year; but he is eager to return to the South, where he feels at home. Amanthis's comment to Jim, "You're better than all of

them put together" (*The Price Was High,* p. 63), anticipates Nick CARRAWAY's assessment of Jay GATSBY in *GG.*

Dicer, Christine Character in "Emotional Bankruptcy." Josephine PERRY and Lillian HAMMEL meet Christine's cousin, Edward DICER, while waiting for dinner at her house.

Dicer, Captain Edward Character in "Emotional Bankruptcy." Christine DICER's cousin, an officer in the French aviation during World War I. He falls in love with Josephine PERRY, who believes she has finally found the right man. However, when he declares his love, she feels nothing and has nothing left to give him, for she has used up her emotional capacity in previous trivial relationships.

Dick Character in "A Nice Quiet Place." Josephine PERRY's boring cousin at Island Farms. He blackmails Josephine to kiss him by threatening to tell her mother about her conversation with Sonny DORRANCE.

Dickey, Breck Character in "Diamond Dick and the First Law of Woman." Diana DICKEY's younger brother, who wants to get his pilot's license.

Dickey, Diana Character in "Diamond Dick and the First Law of Woman." Girl who takes the name of "Diamond Dick" at the age of 10 and later resumes that persona to reclaim her husband, Charley ABBOT.

Dickey, Harry Character in "Fate in Her Hands." Man in whom Carol KASTLER was interested before the appearance of Billy RIGGS.

Dickey, Mr. and Mrs. Characters in "Diamond Dick and the First Law of Woman." Diana DICKEY's parents. Mr. Dickey offers Charley ABBOT a job.

Dickey, Paul (1893–1963) Fitzgerald's PRINCETON roommate during 1916–17, when Fitzgerald repeated his junior year. Dickey, a member of the Class of 1917, wrote the music for Fitzgerald's songs for three TRIANGLE CLUB shows.

Dignanni, Princess Character in "Fun in an Artist's Studio." Portrait painter who asks Pat HOBBY to pose for her.

Dillon, Jackson Character in "First Blood." Josephine PERRY, Constance PERRY, and their mother attend this young man's wedding to Mary JACKSON.

Dillon, Mr. and Mrs. Warren Characters in "Emotional Bankruptcy." Old friends who arrive at the PER-

RYS' house to meet Constance PERRY just before Edward DICER arrives to see Josephine PERRY.

D'Invilliers, Thomas Parke Character in *TSOP*. Poet and intellectual who becomes more conventional during his years at PRINCETON. He rooms with Amory BLAINE during their last two years of college and shares a NEW YORK apartment with Amory and Alec CONNAGE after the war, when he writes for *The New Democracy*. Fitzgerald attributes the epigraph poem in *GG* to this character. Based on John Peale BISHOP.

"Director's Special" *See* "Discard."

"A Dirge (Apologies to Wordsworth)" Humorous verse. *Judge*, 77 (December 20, 1919), 30; *In His Own Time; Poems*. Poem to a bar, now closed, that served liquor before Prohibition. Parody of "She dwelt among th' untrodden ways . . ." by William Wordsworth (1770–1850).

"Discard" Fiction. Written July 1939. *Harper's Bazaar*, 82 (January 1948), 103, 143–144, 146, 148–149; *The Price Was High*. George BAKER, who wants to be in the movies, admires his aunt, actress Dolly BORDON, who moves from HOLLYWOOD to NEW YORK to act on the stage. A couple of years later Dolly's husband, Count Hennen DE LANCLERC, leaves her for actress Phyllis BURNS, whom he meets while sailing to EUROPE. Dolly moves back to Hollywood and puts her mortgaged house up for sale; Phyllis, who holds the mortgage, wants to buy it. Dolly rejects a marriage proposal from director James JEROME because she doesn't want to give up her acting career, and she wins a major role in a movie.

Fitzgerald's title for this story was "Director's Special"; the title "Discard" was supplied by *Harper's Bazaar*. This story led to Fitzgerald's break with his agent, Harold OBER, over Ober's refusal to resume his practice of advancing Fitzgerald money against unsold stories.

Diver, Dick (Doctor Richard Diver) Character in *TITN*. Fitzgerald's 1932 sketch for *TITN* indicates his plan to "show a man who is a natural idealist, a spoiled priest, giving in for various causes to the ideas of the haute Burgeoise, and in his rise to the top of the social world losing his idealism, his talent and turning to drink and dissipation" (*F. Scott Fitzgerald Manuscripts IVb*, Part 1, p. 5). Dick Diver is educated at Yale, Johns Hopkins School of Medicine, Oxford University, in Vienna, and at the University of Zürich, after which he is commissioned in the United States Army. After his discharge from the army in spring 1919, he returns to Zürich, where he tells his friend Franz GREGOROVIOUS that he plans "to be a good psychologist—maybe to be

the greatest one that ever lived" (p. 138). He revises some pamphlets he had written earlier into a book and plans another ambitious volume. As he considers his future he reflects that "he wanted to be good, he wanted to be kind, he wanted to be brave and wise, but it was all pretty difficult. He wanted to be loved, too, if he could fit it in" (p. 140). His overwhelming desire to be loved leads him to marry Nicole Warren [DIVER], a wealthy mental patient who has fallen in love with him. They have two children and travel a great deal before settling at the VILLA DIANA on the RIVIERA. Dick's attractiveness is emphasized through the idealized view of young actress Rosemary HOYT, to whom "he seemed kind and charming—his voice promised that he would take care of her, and that a little later he would open up whole new worlds for her, unroll an endless succession of magnificent possibilities" (p. 20). He falls in love with Rosemary even though he protests that his complicated relationship with Nicole prevents their having an affair. He begins drinking too much, and he grows more and more dependent on Nicole's money, which he uses to finance his partnership with Franz Gregorovious in a psychiatric clinic. Dick's relationship with Nicole deteriorates, and when she suffers a relapse, he takes a leave of absence "for his soul's sake." "He had lost himself—he could not tell the hour when, or the day or the week, the month or the year. Once he had cut through things, solving the most complicated equations as the simplest problems of his simplest patients. Between the time he found Nicole flowering under a stone on the Zürichsee and the moment of his meeting with Rosemary the spear had been blunted" (p. 209). His father's death reinforces his growing awareness of his dissipation, yet he consummates his affair with Rosemary when he sees her in ROME after his return from his father's funeral in America. After a drunken altercation with a taxi driver he is beaten by the Rome police and jailed. When he returns to the clinic he and Franz dissolve their partnership after a patient is removed by his parents, who claim their son has twice smelled liquor on Doctor Diver's breath. The Divers return to the Riviera, where Nicole has an affair with Tommy BARBAN. Dick and Nicole quarrel, and he tells her, "I can't do anything for you any more. I'm trying to save myself" (p. 306). She calls him a coward and a failure and completes her psychological break from him: "The case was finished. Doctor Diver was at liberty" (p. 307). After their divorce Dick moves to America, where he moves from one small town to another practicing general medicine and claiming that he is working on his book.

Fitzgerald's notes show that Dick Diver's external qualities were based on Gerald MURPHY, Ernest HEMINGWAY, Ben FINNEY, Archibald MACLEISH, Charles MACARTHUR, and himself. Fitzgerald's depiction of the

decline of Dick Diver illuminates his own sense of a loss of purpose after the success of *GG*, as later chronicled in his 1936 "Crack-Up" essay. The two men share an emotional bankruptcy marked by drinking, a dislike of people, an increasing bigotry, and difficulty in completing the books they are writing.

Some critics charged that Diver's fall was unconvincing; *see* the portion of the entry for *TITN* dealing with the novel's reception.

Diver, Lanier Character in *TITN*. Son of Dick and Nicole DIVER.

Diver, Nicole Warren Character in *TITN*. Wealthy mental patient who marries Dick DIVER. After an incestuous episode with her father, Devereux WARREN, Nicole begins showing signs of mental illness at age 16; and her father takes her to DOHMLER's clinic in SWITZERLAND for psychiatric treatment. She meets Dick when he comes to the clinic to visit his friend, Franz GREGOROVIOUS, just before leaving for France with the army; she writes him many letters, and their correspondence contributes to her gradual recovery. When Dick returns to the clinic after his discharge from the army, Franz tells him that Nicole is apparently in love with him; and they agree that Dick should go away. However, Dick, who admits to being "half in love with her" (p. 148), is dissatisfied with this solution; when he encounters Nicole again, he realizes "her problem was one they had together for good now" (p. 165). They are married and have two children; Nicole suffers a relapse after the birth of each child. After several happy years together, their relationship begins to deteriorate as Dick grows more and more dependent on the Warren money, begins to drink more, and is attracted to other women. Reflecting on the decline of their relationship, Nicole thinks, "Why, I'm almost complete. . . . I'm practically standing alone, without him" (p. 294). She has an affair with Tommy BARBAN, divorces Dick, and marries Tommy.

Fitzgerald's notes indicate that Nicole is a "portrait of Zelda—that is, a part of Zelda"; however, there is no evidence that Zelda FITZGERALD was a victim of incest. His plan for the novel includes a chart comparing Nicole's and Zelda's case histories with the title "parallel between actual case and case in novel" (*F. Scott Fitzgerald Manuscripts IVb*, Part 1, p. 18).

Diver, The Reverend Character in *TITN*. Dick DIVER's father, who was Dick's "moral guide": "Dick loved his father—again and again he referred judgments to what his father would probably have thought or done" (p. 211). Dick learns of his father's death during his leave of absence from the clinic and travels to America for the funeral. His father's death reinforces Dick's grow-

ing awareness of his own dissipation; he wishes "he had always been as good as he had intended to be" (p. 212). Fitzgerald's description of the Rev. Diver and his relationship with his son is adapted from "The Death of My Father," an unfinished essay about Fitzgerald's father, Edward FITZGERALD.

Diver, Topsy Character in *TITN*. Daughter of Dick and Nicole DIVER.

Divine, Babe Character in "The Offshore Pirate." A mulatto who is Curtis CARLYLE's best friend.

Divine, Rodney Character in "Mister Icky." Wealthy young man who wants to marry Ulsa ICKY.

Dixon, Leslie Character in "New Types." Man who returns to America after spending several years in China and falls in love with Paula JORGENSEN.

doctor (unnamed) Character in "The Long Way Out." Man who tells the story of Mrs. George KING to the NARRATOR.

doctor (unnamed) Character in "Three Acts of Music." Man who is in love with a NURSE whom he never marries.

Dodd, Martha Character in *LT/LOLT*. Has-been actress whom Cecelia BRADY befriends in order to gain information about Kathleen MOORE, who sat at the same table as Martha at the screenwriters' ball.

"Does a Moment of Revolt Come Sometime to Every Married Man?" Article. MCCALL'S, 51 (March 1924), 21, 36; *In His Own Time*. Published with companion article with the same title by Zelda FITZGERALD. Fitzgerald suggests three reasons why husbands "revolt." First, as soon as they marry, they become "intensely self-conscious" about their wives and urge them to behave more conservatively. Second, they begin to realize that the welfare of the entire household depends on them. Third, they reach a stage of wanting to rest at home at night after working hard all day.

"Does a Moment of Revolt Come Sometime to Every Married Man?" Article by Zelda FITZGERALD. MCCALL'S, 51 (March 1924), 82; *Zelda Fitzgerald: The Collected Writings*. Published with companion article with the same title by F. Scott Fitzgerald. Asserts that "theoretically . . . every happy bridegroom revolts at the altar and from then on goes revolting through life with varying degrees of violence until his final revolt against life helps him briskly to extinguish himself" (*Collected Writings*, p. 395).

Dohmler, Doctor Character in *TITN*. Head of the Swiss psychiatric clinic where Dick DIVER meets Nicole Warren [DIVER].

Doldrum, Boscoe Character in "Jemina. . . ." Son of the family feuding with the Tantrums. He works a still on the opposite side of the stream from Jemina TANTRUM.

Dollard, Professor Character in "On an Ocean Wave." Man whom Gaston T. SCHEER sees embracing his wife, Minna SCHEER. Gaston Scheer arranges for Dollard to be thrown overboard.

Dolores Character in "Magnetism." George and Kay HANNAFORD's Mexican maid, who is attracted to George.

Donald Character in "A Snobbish Story." Mrs. MCRAE's nephew, whom she asks Josephine PERRY to introduce to the other young people at Lake Forest. He wins the tennis tournament.

Donilof Character in "Two Wrongs." Emmy PINKARD McChesney's ballet master, who urges her not to delay her debut by accompanying her husband West.

Donahoe, Charles W. (Sap) (1896–1973) Fitzgerald's classmate at the NEWMAN SCHOOL, where he played football and edited *The NEWMAN NEWS,* and at PRINCETON, where he was a member of the Class of 1917. In the summer of 1915, after his sophomore year at Princeton, Fitzgerald visited the Donahoe family's ranch in Montana, which provided the setting for "The Diamond as Big as the Ritz" (June 1922). In October 1918 Fitzgerald sent Donahoe five carbon-copy typescript chapters for "The Romantic Egotist"; these chapters are all that survive of this early version of *TSOP.* Donahoe was one of Fitzgerald's permanent heroes; Fitzgerald described him—without naming him—in "Pasting It Together" (March 1936): "another man represented my sense of the 'good life,' though I saw him once in a decade. . . . But in difficult situations I had tried to think what *he* would have thought, how *he* would have acted" (*CU,* p. 79).

Donnelly, Pop Character in *B&D.* Anthony PATCH's platoon sergeant.

Donohue, Elsie Character in "Last Kiss." Woman who sits with Jim LEONARD at the charity ball.

Donovan Character in "Magnetism." Margaret DONOVAN's brother, an ex-convict who helped her plan the blackmail scheme against George HANNAFORD.

Donovan, Margaret Character in "Magnetism." Script girl who has been in love with George HANNAFORD for years and who tries to kill herself after backing down from her attempt to blackmail him.

Doolan, Catherine Character in *LT/LOLT.* Monroe STAHR's secretary.

Doolan, Kit Character in "Pat Hobby's College Days." Athletic superintendent at U.W.C. (University of the Western Coast).

Doris Character in *The Vegetable.* Charlotte FROST's 19-year-old sister, who is newly engaged to Joseph FISH from Idaho, although she doesn't know much about him. In Act III Doris and Fish have been secretly married for three days.

Dorrance, Sonny Character in "A Nice Quiet Place." Handsome young man whom Josephine PERRY meets at Island Farms. He tells her his wife is black; she later learns that the story is an old line he always uses when he wants to avoid women while recovering from an affair.

Dorsey, George Character in the Basil Duke LEE stories; a student at ST. REGIS. In "The Perfect Life" he invites Basil to visit during Thanksgiving holidays but is offended by Basil's reforming efforts. In "Basil and Cleopatra" he rooms with Basil and Brick WALES at Yale.

Dorsey, Jobena Character in the Basil Duke LEE stories; George DORSEY's sister. In "The Perfect Life" she is so offended by Basil's priggish attempt to reform her that she agrees to elope with Skiddy DE VINCI; but Basil foils their plan by getting Skiddy drunk. In "Basil and Cleopatra" she urges Basil not to return to Minnie BIBBLE.

Dos Passos, John (1896–1970) Innovative American novelist; friend of Fitzgerald. His works include *Three Soldiers* (1921), an antiwar novel reviewed by Fitzgerald; *Manhattan Transfer* (1925), a stylistically experimental novel; and the *U.S.A.* trilogy (collected in 1938), consisting of *The 42nd Parallel* (1930), *1919* (1932), and *The Big Money* (1936). Dos Passos was inspired by left-wing politics; but the disillusionment of the Spanish Civil War of 1936–39 caused him to denounce the Communist party and become politically conservative, a move which led formerly favorable critics to condemn him and his work.

The Fitzgeralds met Dos Passos while house-hunting in New York in September 1922; and he accompanied them to GREAT NECK, Long Island, where they visited

Ring LARDNER. Dos Passos recalled his first impressions of Fitzgerald: "When he talked about writing his mind, which seemed to me full of preposterous notions, became clear and hard as a diamond" (*The Best Times* [New York: New American Library, 1966], p. 129). Dos Passos later rebuked Fitzgerald for his "Crack-Up" articles: "Christ, man, how do you find time in the middle of the general conflagration to worry about all that stuff? If you don't want to do stuff on your own, why not get a reporting job somewhere. After all not many people write as well as you do. . . . We're living in one of the damnedest tragic moments in history—if you want to go to pieces I think it's absolutely O.K. but I think you ought to write a first rate novel about it (and you probably will) instead of spilling it in little pieces for Arnold Gingrich" (October? 1936; *CU*, p. 311).

After Fitzgerald's death Dos Passos expressed admiration for *LT* in his 1945 *CU* essay, concluding, "Even in their unfinished state these fragments, I believe, are of sufficient dimensions to raise the level of American fiction to follow in some such way as Marlowe's blank verse line raised the whole level of Elizabethan verse" (p. 343).

See Townsend Ludington, *John Dos Passos: A Twentieth Century Odyssey* (New York: Dutton, 1980).

Dougall, Doctor Character in *TSOP.* ST. REGIS administrator who tells Amory BLAINE he could get the best marks in school if he wished.

Douglas, Lieutenant Charles, C.S.A. Character in *Coward.* Confederate soldier who steals $12,000 from a Union commissary train and who is taken prisoner of war while visiting his family during a retreat.

Douglas, Clara Character in *Coward.* Younger sister of Lindy and Charley DOUGLAS.

Douglas, Judge Character in *Coward.* Virginian who is unable to go to war because he is paralyzed from the waist down. He disapproves of Jim HOLWORTHY's attentions to his daughter Lindy DOUGLAS because Holworthy, though an able-bodied man, is not fighting in the war.

Douglas, Lindy Character in *Coward.* Judge DOUGLAS's daughter, who inspires Jim HOLWORTHY to enlist in the Confederate army when she rejects his marriage proposal because of his cowardice. After the war she changes her mind about him.

Douglas, Mrs. Character in *Coward.* Judge DOUGLAS's wife, who sees no harm in their daughter Lindy DOUG-LAS seeing Jim HOLWORTHY as long as they don't become intimate.

Douglas, Tommy Character in *Coward.* Younger brother of Lindy and Charley DOUGLAS.

Dragonet, Amalie Eustace Bedford Character in "Her Last Case." Ben DRAGONET's young daughter, who comes to live with him when her mother wants to get rid of her.

Dragonet, Ben Character in "Her Last Case." Bette WEAVER's last patient, a man who never got over World War I and who is harmed by the evil influence of his ex-wife.

Dragonet, Mrs. Ben Character in "Her Last Case." Ben DRAGONET's ex-wife and cousin, who has been a harmful influence on him since their childhood.

Drake, Fred Character in "Hot & Cold Blood." Businessman who refuses to lend Jim MATHER 50 dollars for a C.O.D. delivery. His policy of not lending money to friends makes Jim reconsider his own generosity.

Drake, Jane Character in "A Freeze-Out." Girl whom Forrest WINSLOW doesn't love but considers marrying before he falls in love with Alida RIKKER.

Dreiser, Theodore (1871–1945) Naturalistic American novelist, of whom Fitzgerald said, "Dreiser is rough, No Social grace at all, but my God, what a storyteller! He's the best of our generation!" (Sheilah GRAHAM, *College of One*, p. 84).

Dreiser's treatment of the deterioration of Hurstwood in *Sister Carrie* (1900)—which Fitzgerald described as "almost the first piece of American realism" (*College of One*, p. 83)—influenced Fitzgerald's depiction of Anthony PATCH in *B&D*; and *An American Tragedy* (1925) was a possible source for the murder plot of an early version of *TITN*. Fitzgerald and Dreiser met at a party which Dreiser gave in NEW YORK CITY in spring 1923.

See W. A. Swanberg, *Dreiser* (New York: Scribners, 1965).

Drinkwater, Theodore (Ted) Character in "Your Way and Mine." Henry MCCOMAS's business partner, who urges Henry to change his work habits.

Driscoll, William (Bill) Character in "Not in the Guidebook." Tour guide in PARIS who befriends and later marries Milly COOLEY. It was really Driscoll, rather than Milly's first husband, Jim COOLEY, who stole the German orders for which Jim received a medal.

du Cary, Edith Character in "On Schedule." René DU CARY's deceased wife, whose will specifies that he forfeits the income she bequeathed him if he remarries within seven years of her death.

du Cary, Noël Character in "On Schedule." René DU CARY's 12-year-old daughter, for whom he prepares an elaborate schedule.

du Cary, René Character in "On Schedule." Frenchman who is doing scientific research in an American university town and who plans to marry Becky SNYDER.

Duckney, Angela Character in "Strange Sanctuary." Debutante to whom Dolly HAINES introduces Major REDFERN.

Dudley, Thorton Hart Character in *The Captured Shadow*. Gentleman who bets $5,000 that he can prove the NEW YORK police incompetent by committing daring burglaries for two weeks and remaining uncaught. He disguises himself as "The SHADOW," and he always returns what he steals. While attempting to rob the Beverly CONNAGE home, he becomes attracted to Dorothy CONNAGE, who has read of him in the newspaper and finds his deeds romantic.

Duke of Guyenne Character in "The Kingdom in the Dark." Nobleman who is traveling with King LOUIS and who advises the king not to press PHILIPPE too hard in his search for GRISELDA, who has run away from the king.

Duke of Maine Character in "Gods of Darkness." Powerful man who owns property a hundred miles from PHILIPPE's land and whose attempt at invading Philippe's territory is foiled by the bond that his men share with Philippe's men as members of a witch cult.

Dulany, Tib Character in "The End of Hate." Confederate soldier who falls in love with Josie PILGRIM, an Ohio girl.

Dumphry, Royal Character in *TITN*. Homosexual whom Rosemary HOYT meets on the RIVIERA. Dumphry later encounters Dick DIVER in LAUSANNE and informs him that Nicole DIVER's father, Devereux WARREN, is dying.

Dunn, Sir Humphrey Character in "Two Wrongs." Bill MCCHESNEY's friend, who persuades Lady Sybil COMBRINCK's footman to admit Bill to the party.

Dunning, Captain Character in *B&D*. Army officer who promotes Anthony PATCH to corporal.

Dureal, Officer Leon Character in *The Captured Shadow*. Bumbling French detective whom "The SHADOW" locks into a closet in the Beverly CONNAGE home.

Durfee, Doctor Howard Character in "One Interne." Surgeon who abandons Thea SINGLETON to marry Helen DAY.

Dwan, Allan (1885–1981) Movie director who lived on Long Island; Fitzgerald listed him as a source for Chapter III of *GG*. Fitzgerald noted in his *Ledger* for July 1923: "Parties at Allen Dwans" (p. 177). In 1923 Fitzgerald wrote the titles for Dwan's silent film of Edith WHARTON's novel *Glimpses of the Moon* (1922). Dwan accompanied the Fitzgeralds and Ring and Ellis LARDNER to the opening of *The Vegetable*.

Earl Character in "The Passionate Eskimo." Bundle boy whom the department store SALESWOMAN instructs to take PAN-E-TROON to the five-and-ten store around the corner.

Earle, Helen Character in " 'Boil Some Water—Lots of It.' " Nurse whom Pat HOBBY takes to lunch at the studio commissary. She tends to Walter HERRICK after Hobby assaults him with a tray.

Early, General Jubal (1816–1894) Historical figure and character in "The End of Hate." Confederate general who instructs Doctor PILGRIM to pull Prince NAPOLEON's tooth.

"Early Success" Autobiographical essay. *American Cavalcade*, 1 (October 1937), 74–79; *CU*. Recollection of Fitzgerald's intertwined struggles to win Zelda Sayre [FITZGERALD] and to write his first novel. He recounts both the sense of "ineffable toploftiness and promise" (*CU*, p. 86) brought by the acceptance of *TSOP* for publication and how PRINCETON's negative reaction to the novel took the joy out of his success. He traces his evolution from amateur writer to professional who was conscious of all his experiences as material for fiction; and he shares the "conviction that life is a romantic matter" (p. 89), which resulted from his early success. Years later, however, he is a different person who has no more dreams of his own; and he looks back longingly to the time "when the fulfilled future and the wistful past were mingled in a single gorgeous moment—when life was literally a dream" (p. 90).

Earnings Fitzgerald's earnings have been much exaggerated, for it is generally believed that he made and squandered a fortune. He was unquestionably extravagant; but his income, though substantial by 1920s and 1930s standards, was not prodigious. The careful record he maintained in his *Ledger* reveals that his total income from 1919 to 1936, before he moved to HOLLYWOOD, was $374,922.58 (after deducting agent Harold OBER's 10 percent commission on magazine sales): This amounts to an annual average of $20,829 over 18 years of writing. It is impossible to convert the buying power of Fitzgerald's dollars into the value of 1990s dollars. Multiples of 8 or 10 are often used—in which case Fitzgerald's $20,000 would be worth $160–$200,000 today. Comparative figures: members of the House and Senate were paid $10,000 per year during the 1920s and the average salary for a public school teacher was $1,445 in 1929.

None of Fitzgerald's novels was a true best-seller. *TSOP* sold 47,075 copies in 1920–21 and made the *Publishers Weekly* best-seller list twice, reaching number four. Fitzgerald's royalty of 10 percent on the first 5,000 copies and 15 percent thereafter for the $1.75 book brought him about $12,445. *B&D* sold 50,000 copies in 1922 and made the *Publishers Weekly* list three times, reaching number six. The 15 percent royalty on this $2.00 book amounted to about $15,000. *GG* never made the list and did not break 24,000 copies in 1925. *TITN* was number 10 for April 1934 but sold 15,000 copies that Depression year. The total royalties on the four novels published during Fitzgerald's lifetime were about $41,000.

The subsidiary income from Fitzgerald's novels was meager by present standards. There were no mass-market paperbacks before 1939 and no book clubs before 1926. Movie rights brought comparatively little: $10,000 for *TSOP* (not produced—and it is uncertain whether all of the money was paid) and $2,500 for *B&D*. The most subsidiary income came from *GG*: about $6,900 from the play by Owen Davis and $16,200 for the movie rights—against $7,161 from the book sales.

Most of Fitzgerald's income came from his 160 stories—and most of that from his 65 SATURDAY EVENING POST stories. Before he went to work for the movies in 1937——the year after he sold his last *Post* story—magazine purchases of 116 stories brought Fitzgerald $241,453—of which $175,410 came from the *Post*. The royalties from his four collections added $12,400 to his short-story income. His first *Post* sale brought $400 for "Head and Shoulders" in 1919; the magazine paid $1,200 for "Gretchen's Forty Winks" in 1923; $2,500 for "Presumption" in 1925; $3,000 for "Jacob's Ladder" in 1927; and $4,000 for "At Your Age" in 1929. The peak *Post* payment of $4,000 worked out to about 80 cents per word. In 1932 the *Post* began cutting his fee, and his last appearance in the magazine brought $2,000 for " 'Trouble' " in 1937.

Fitzgerald's 18 months on the MGM payroll paid $91,000. After the MGM contract expired he freelanced as a screenwriter and sold short-shorts to ESQUIRE for $250 or $300. The greatest amount of earnings from Fitzgerald's writings came after his death.

M. J. B.

East Egg In *GG*, a fictional fashionable community on the North Shore of Long Island, New York, corresponding to Manhasset Neck, an old-money community. Tom and Daisy BUCHANAN live in East Egg, across the bay from WEST EGG.

"Echoes of the Jazz Age" Essay. SCRIBNER'S MAGAZINE, 90 (November 1931), 459–465; *CU*. Fitzgerald nostalgically recalls how the JAZZ AGE "bore him up, flattered him and gave him more money than he had dreamed of, simply for telling people that he felt as they did, that something had to be done with all the nervous energy stored up and unexpended in the War" (*CU*, p. 13). He then traces the development of the decade, which he characterizes thus: "It was an age of miracles, it was an age of art, it was an age of excess, and it was an age of satire" (p. 14). He explores the hedonism of an age marked by the loosening of sexual standards and an abundance of alcohol—despite Prohibition—and its decline into neurosis, violence, and wandering abroad. He concludes with a sense of loss "because we will never feel quite so intensely about our surroundings any more" (p. 22).

Eckleburg, Doctor T. J. Character in *GG*. This oculist's billboard overlooking the VALLEY OF ASHES is an important symbol in the novel; George WILSON regards the eyes on the billboard as the eyes of God. Fitzgerald's description of the eyes—"their retinas are one yard high"—is anatomically incorrect because the retina, which is at the back of the eye, cannot be seen. The correct reading is "irises" or "pupils."

Eddington, George Character in "Between Three and Four." Howard BUTLER's employer, who plans to fire him for firing Sarah SUMMER on his own whim.

Edgemoor, Delaware Community near WILMINGTON, Delaware, where the Fitzgeralds rented "ELLERSLIE" from March 1927 to March 1929.

Edison, Edgar Character in "Jemina. . . ." Stranger who wants to buy the TANTRUMS' land.

Editing Fitzgerald's Texts F. Scott Fitzgerald's published work is peppered with inconsistencies and factual errors. Apart from misspellings, there are arith-

metical errors, geographical errors, anatomical errors, and chronological errors. These blunders brought Fitzgerald a reputation for ignorance or irresponsibility that has interfered with the proper assessment of his genius. In his own time critics included lists of Fitzgerald's errors in their reviews of his books.

The blame must be divided between Fitzgerald and Charles SCRIBNER's Sons. Like other authors, Fitzgerald expected that his publishers would catch and correct errors of detail; but this expectation was blocked by the conditions of production and by the limitations of Scribners' editing. Since Fitzgerald rewrote *The Great Gatsby* and *Tender Is the Night* in proof, the production of the novels was necessarily rushed; moreover, editor Maxwell PERKINS was not much concerned with factual accuracy. Charles Scribner, Jr. has stated: "Perkins was totally useless when it came to copyediting or correcting a text. Such details meant very little to him. Consequently, the early editions of books such as Scott Fitzgerald's *The Great Gatsby* were textually corrupt to a nauseating degree" (*In the Company of Writers: A Life in Publishing* [New York: Scribners, 1990], p. 44). Fitzgerald's published work requires re-editing to provide emended texts that recover his intentions.

The idea of emending or correcting F. Scott Fitzgerald outrages Fitzgerald amateurs who assert that every printed word in a Fitzgerald text is sacrosanct—whether or not it is what he wrote or intended to have printed. But preserving incorrect readings, especially when the words are not what he wrote, is not an act of literary piety. Neither is it a service to Fitzgerald's readers to retain puzzling errors—such as the age of Pammy BUCHANAN in *GG*, which requires Daisy Fay BUCHANAN to have been at least nine months pregnant at the time of her marriage. Imputations of illegitimacy or a forced marriage are not what the author intended. The accumulation of simple errors and inconsistencies in a novel distracts good readers and undermines their confidence in the author. The description of one of the key symbols in *GG*, the billboard eyes of Dr. T. J. ECKLEBURG, is marred by the impossible statement that "their retinas are one yard high"; Fitzgerald wrote "retinas," but he meant "irises" or "pupils." *TITN* is seriously damaged by chronological inconsistencies that blur the structure of the novel. An emended edition of *TITN* requires 69 word corrections exclusive of spellings; 26 of these corrections are concerned with the time scheme. Editorial apparatus and a corrected time scheme are in Matthew J. BRUCCOLI's *Reader's Companion to F. Scott Fitzgerald's Tender Is the Night* (with Judith S. Baughman; Columbia: University of South Carolina Press, 1996); Bruccoli's emended edition of the novel was published by Everyman in England in 1996.

The substitution of the right word for the inadvertently wrong word—even when it is clear that Fitzgerald

wrote the incorrect word—is not rewriting. The Fitzgerald editor working now has the obligation to do what should have been done—what Fitzgerald expected would be done—by Scribners' editors when his books were first published.

Most readers do not notice the errors in books, but serious authors write for serious readers. The high incidence of errors in Fitzgerald's work does not indicate that he did not care about getting it right. One of the Fitzgerald paradoxes is that he was a social realist who understood the importance of accurate details yet had difficulty achieving them. It is therefore the editor's proper responsibility to impose accuracy on the flawed texts of Fitzgerald's writings when this can be achieved by simple correction or word substitution.

The preparation of what are loosely called "definitive editions"—"critical editions" is a better term—of Fitzgerald's writings is facilitated by the availability of much pre-book evidence. Because he saved manuscripts, typescripts, and revised proofs, it is possible to trace the transmission of his texts and recover words that Fitzgerald wrote—or was trying to write. Thus, in Episode 11 of *LT/LOLT*, Greek cameraman Pete ZAVRAS compares Monroe STAHR to several figures in Greek classical civilization, one of whom Fitzgerald wrote as "Diocenes" in manuscript. Editor Edmund WILSON emended "Diocenes" to "Euripides" for the first printing. The 1993 Cambridge edition recovers "Diogenes"—which was clearly Fitzgerald's intention.

The errors in a text may be functional or nonfunctional. A functional or meaningful error is intended by the author and serves a purpose in the work: GATSBY's claim that he grew up in a part of the Midwest called San Francisco signals the unreliability of his autobiography. But a nonfunctional error is unintentional and serves no purpose apart from puzzling the reader. Thus, the authorial statement in *TITN* that Dick DIVER sees the "Jugenhorn" from Montreux refers to a nonexistent mountain but is intended to be correct; it should read "Dent du Jaman."

Authorial errors in a work of fiction are internal or external. An internal error occurs within the invented world of fiction. EAST EGG and WEST EGG are invented places; therefore an editor should not attempt to emend the fictional geography. An external error occurs in the real world in which the fictional characters and events are embedded. Invented East Egg and West Egg are situated on actual Long Island. When Fitzgerald's characters leave their fictional venue, the details of the real world should be correct. Thus, Gatsby and Nick CARRAWAY cross the real Queensboro Bridge connecting the real Long Island City in Queens with 59th Street in Manhattan. Fitzgerald's incorrect placement of the Queens end of the bridge in ASTORIA must be emended. (The real Astoria is in another section of Queens.)

A concomitant of the reputation for authorial ignorance fostered by the bad texts of Fitzgerald's first editions is that later editors have been too quick to correct what does not require emendation. Edmund Wilson—who was Fitzgerald's friend for 25 years and regarded him as an ignoramus—altered "orgastic" to "orgiastic" in the coda of *GG*: "Gatsby believed in the green light, the orgastic future. . . ." But this is a case where Fitzgerald's intention can be verified. When Scribners queried "orgastic" in the 1925 proofs, Fitzgerald informed Perkins: " 'orgastic' is the adjective from 'orgasm' and it expresses exactly the intended ecstasy" (January 24, 1925; *Life in Letters*, p. 94; *Scott/Max*, p. 93). Wilson made necessary and unnecessary emendations in *The Last Tycoon* when he edited the work in progress in 1941.

In addition to emending or preserving the author's words, the Fitzgerald editor is required to set a policy for treating punctuation. Since Fitzgerald was an authentic case of a writer who composed by ear, an editor would be ill-advised to impose a conventionally correct system of punctuation on the writer's natural light pointing. Again, the manuscripts, revised typescripts, and proofs enable an editor to recover Fitzgerald's punctuation, which is crucial for a stylist whose rhythms affect the meanings of his prose.

THE CAMBRIDGE EDITION OF THE WORKS OF F. SCOTT FITZGERALD, edited by Bruccoli with the advice of Fredson Bowers, was planned as a critical edition. The editor of a critical edition establishes an emended text that recovers the author's intentions from the evidence and fulfills those intentions as affected by the several stages of transmission and production. A critical text also corrects nonfunctional authorial errors that confuse or distract readers. Editorial emendation should be conservative, but a critical edition provides necessary emendations in the endeavor to achieve the best text of the work. The concept of recovering authorial intention may seem mystical, but the editor's ambition to satisfy the author's expectations is realistic. Fitzgerald expected and required editorial help that he did not receive from Scribners. It is the responsibility of the scholar-editor to perform the services that were neglected when Fitzgerald's books were first published. After editing *The Great Gatsby* (1991) and *The Love of the Last Tycoon: A Western* (1993), Bruccoli withdrew from the Cambridge Edition because of interference with his editorial judgment.

See Bruccoli, "Getting It Right: The Publishing Process and the Correction of Factual Errors—with Reference to *The Great Gatsby*," *Essays in Honor of William B. Todd*, comp. Warner Barnes and Larry Carver (Austin: Harry Ransom Humanities Research Center, The University of Texas, 1991); revised edition separately published (Columbia, S.C.: privately printed, 1994).

M. J. B.

Egan, Mr. Narrator of "The Mystery of the Raymond Mortgage." Chief of police who is unable to solve the murder of Agnes RAYMOND.

Egorova, Lubov (1880–1972) Russian prima ballerina who married Prince Pavel Trubetskoy (1866–1938) and in 1923 began teaching ballet in PARIS, where she was head of the ballet school of the Ballet Russe of Serge Diaghilev (1872–1929). She was recommended to Zelda FITZGERALD by Gerald and Sara MURPHY, whose daughter, Honoria, studied ballet with Egorova. Zelda probably began taking lessons from Egorova while she and Fitzgerald were in Paris in the summer of 1928, and she resumed her studies when they returned to EUROPE the next spring. Zelda's 1929 series of "girl" stories for *COLLEGE HUMOR* was partly motivated by her desire to pay for her ballet lessons; she described the rigorous training in her novel, *Save Me the Waltz* (1932). Dr. Oscar FOREL, who treated Zelda at PRANGINS CLINIC in 1930–31, was convinced that Zelda's psychological recovery required that she abandon her hopes for a ballet career. On June 22, 1930 Fitzgerald wrote to Egorova for an assessment of Zelda's dancing (*Life in Letters,* pp. 185–186). Egorova responded that although Zelda had started training too late to become a first-class dancer, she was capable of becoming a good dancer in nonstarring roles. This report, although not as discouraging as Fitzgerald and Forel had expected, badly disappointed Zelda; and she did not resume her training.

See Gennady Smakov, "Lubov Egorova," *The Great Russian Dancers* (New York: Knopf, 1984), pp. 19–25.

Elgin, Paul Pseudonym under which Fitzgerald's story "On an Ocean Wave" was published. Fitzgerald had proposed the pseudonym "John Darcy" for "Between Planes" ("Three Hours Between Planes," July 1941) which *ESQUIRE* editor Arnold GINGRICH was holding for publication after the Pat HOBBY stories. Fitzgerald told Gingrich: "I'm awfully tired of being Scott Fitzgerald anyhow, as there doesn't seem to be so much money in it, and I'd like to find out if people read me just because I am Scott Fitzgerald or, what is more likely, don't read me for the same reason. In other words it would fascinate me to have one of my stories stand on its own merits completely and see if there is a response" (February 7, 1940; *Life in Letters,* p. 433). On June 25 Fitzgerald requested that Gingrich change the pseudonym to John Blue (*Correspondence,* p. 601). When Gingrich asked for a less obviously phony name, Fitzgerald suggested Paul Elgin on July 15 (*Life in Letters,* p. 454); and he submitted "On an Ocean Wave" under the name of Paul Elgin.

Elgin, Dr. William (b. 1905) Zelda FITZGERALD's doctor at SHEPPARD-PRATT HOSPITAL.

Eliot, T. S. (1888–1965) American-born poet and critic who became a British subject in 1927 and was awarded the Nobel Prize for literature in 1948. Fitzgerald greatly admired Eliot's *The Waste Land* (1922), a likely source for the VALLEY OF ASHES and Dr. T. J. ECKLEBURG in *GG.* In October 1925 Fitzgerald sent Eliot a copy of *GG* inscribed to the "Greatest of Living Poets from his enthusiastic worshipper" (*Life in Letters,* p. 128). In a letter of thanks and congratulations which was later included in *The Crack-Up,* Eliot said that *GG* "seems to me to be the first step that American fiction has taken since Henry James" (December 31, 1925; *CU,* p. 310). Eliot hoped that Faber & Faber, the British publishing house where he was an editor, could publish *GG* in England; but it was published by Chatto & Windus in 1926. Fitzgerald met him when Eliot lectured on the Metaphysical Poets at Johns Hopkins University in February 1933, and Fitzgerald read Eliot's poems aloud at a dinner which Bayard and Margaret TURNBULL gave for Eliot. On February 3 Eliot inscribed Fitzgerald's copy of *Ash-Wednesday* (1930) "with the author's homage" (*Correspondence,* p. 305). On May 21, 1934 Fitzgerald wrote to Eliot apologizing for SCRIBNERS' unauthorized use of a line from a personal letter on the *TITN* dust jacket, which read: "I have been waiting impatiently for another book by Mr. Scott Fitzgerald, with more eagerness and curiosity than I should feel towards the work of any of his contemporaries,

T. S. Eliot

except that of Mr. Ernest Hemingway" (*Correspondence*, pp. 362–363).

See Peter Ackroyd, *T. S. Eliot: A Life* (New York: Simon & Schuster, 1984).

Elizabethan Dramatic Club ST. PAUL theatrical group named for its founder, Elizabeth MAGOFFIN. Fitzgerald wrote four plays for the club: *The Girl from Lazy J* (1911), *The Captured Shadow* (1912), *Coward* (1913), and *Assorted Spirits* (1914).

Elkins, Mrs. Arthur (Lilah) Character in "Myra Meets His Family." Former school roommate with whom Myra HARPER discusses her desire to get married.

Elkins, Ed Character in *TITN*. Man with whom Dick DIVER shared an apartment in Vienna.

"Ellerslie" Nineteenth-century Greek Revival mansion at EDGEMOOR on the Delaware River near WILMINGTON, Delaware, which the Fitzgeralds rented for $150 a month from March 1927 to March 1929, spending summer 1928 in PARIS. Zelda FITZGERALD wrote in 1934: "The squareness of the rooms and the sweep of the columns were to bring us a judicious tranquility" ("Show Mr. and Mrs. F. to Number ——"; *CU*, p. 47). While at "Ellerslie," Zelda began ballet lessons and wrote a series of articles about various types of girls for *COLLEGE HUMOR* (*see* FITZGERALD, ZELDA—WRITINGS OF).

See Edmund Wilson, "A Weekend at Ellerslie," *The Shores of Light* (New York: Farrar, Straus and Young, 1952), pp. 373–383.

Ellinger, Mr. Character in *B&D*. First vice-president at Wilson, Hiemer and Hardy, where Anthony PATCH briefly works as a bond salesman.

Elliot, Emily Character in "Indecision." Twenty-five-year-old divorcée. One of two women in whom Tommy MCLANE is interested.

Ellis, Walker Mallum (1893–1948) A member of the PRINCETON Class of 1915 and president of the COTTAGE CLUB and TRIANGLE CLUB. He selected Fitzgerald's script *Fie! Fie! Fi-Fi!* for the Triangle Club's 1914–15 show and revised it with Fitzgerald, assigning himself sole credit for dialogue and characters, with Fitzgerald receiving credit for the plot and lyrics. Ellis took a law degree at Harvard and served as a pilot in World War I, but he abandoned the law for acting and moved to EUROPE in 1925, failing to fulfill the promise of his brilliant undergraduate career. Ellis was a model for Francis Melarky, the protagonist of an early version of *TITN*.

"Ellerslie," the Fitzgeralds' home near Wilmington, Delaware, 1927

Emile Character in *TITN*. Proprietor of an inn near where Nicole DIVER wrecks the car.

Emma Character in "Fate in Her Hands." Maid who informs Carol KASTLER of Jean KASTLER's narrow escape from a mad dog.

Emma Kate Character in *The Captured Shadow*. The Beverly CONNAGES' maid, whom housekeeper Miss SAUNDERS forces to reveal the conversation she overheard between Mr. and Mrs. Connage.

"Emotional Bankruptcy" Fiction—Josephine PERRY story. Written June 1931. *The SATURDAY EVENING POST*, 204 (August 15, 1931), 8–9, 60, 65; *B&J*. Josephine

Perry and Lillian HAMMEL attend the PRINCETON prom, where Josephine spends time with Louie RANDALL and Martin MUNN in addition to her date, Paul DEMPSTER. She tells Lillian how bored she has become with men because she realizes that she has been in control of all of her relationships: "It had been like that for almost a year—a game played with technical mastery, but with the fire and enthusiasm gone" (*B&J*, p. 276). Josephine falls in love with Captain Edward DICER and believes that she has finally found the right man. However, when he declares his love for her, Josephine feels nothing, for she has already had everything and has nothing left to give him.

The concept of emotional bankruptcy introduced in this story was a key idea for Fitzgerald, who believed that squandering one's emotional capital on trivial relationships leaves one unable to respond to the things that are worthy of deep emotion.

Encino, California Community in the San Fernando Valley, where Fitzgerald rented a cottage on "BELLY ACRES," the estate of actor Edward Everett Horton (1887–1970), from November 1938 to May 1940.

"The End of Hate" Fiction. *COLLIER'S*, 105 (June 22, 1940), 9–10, 63–64; *The Price Was High*. In summer 1936 Fitzgerald wrote a story titled "Thumbs Up" based on his father's memories of the Civil War. Thirteen magazines declined it before Kenneth LITTAUER of *Collier's* paid $1,500 in 1937 against an acceptable re-write. Littauer rejected at least two revisions before accepting the version called "The End of Hate" in June 1939, when he paid the remaining $1,000 due. Other titles Fitzgerald considered for the story include "When This Cruel War—," "Dentist Appointment," "No Time for That," "Two Minutes Alone," "Midst War's Alarms," "That Can Wait," and "Of All Times."

During the Civil War Captain Doctor PILGRIM and his sister, Josie PILGRIM, are traveling south from Ohio, unaware that the Confederates hold the territory they are entering. Confederate soldier Tib DULANY takes them to a house where Doctor Pilgrim is asked to pull Prince NAPOLEON's tooth, and Josie and Tib become interested in each other. When Union cavalry approach, Doctor Pilgrim alerts them to the presence of Rebel soldiers under the command of Colonel John Mosby (1833–1916), a Confederate leader particularly hated by Union troops. The Yankees string Tib up by his thumbs; later Josie cuts him down and drives away with him, and they plan to get married. When Tib discovers that Doctor Pilgrim has amputated his thumbs, he leaves Josie in anger, accusing her of trying to pay for what her brother did. Just after the war ends he seeks out Doctor Pilgrim, planning to shoot off his thumbs; but Josie intervenes, and she and Tib again plan to get married.

In February 1940 Fitzgerald unsuccessfully tried to interest Edwin KNOPF, a story editor at MGM, in an idea for a Civil War movie based on "The End of Hate" and "The Night before Chancellorsville" (*see Life in Letters*, pp. 430–431).

Engels, Crenshaw Character in "The Fiend." Man who seeks revenge on the FIEND who murdered his wife and son but grows dependent on his relationship with the killer.

Engels, Mrs. Crenshaw Character in "The Fiend." Crenshaw ENGELS's murdered wife.

Engels, Mark Character in "The Fiend." Mr. and Mrs. Crenshaw ENGELS's seven-year-old son, who was murdered with his mother.

Eric Character in "No Harm Trying." Callboy at the studio who sells a movie idea to Pat HOBBY and, when the idea is discovered to be his, is put on salary.

Esquire Men's magazine to which Fitzgerald began contributing in 1934, attracted by Ernest HEMINGWAY's role as its star contributor and the fact that it provided a ready source of income, although the top price Fitzgerald received was only $250 until he persuaded editor Arnold GINGRICH in 1940 to raise his price for the Pat HOBBY stories to $300—still much less than he received from *The SATURDAY EVENING POST*. Gingrich accepted nearly all of Fitzgerald's submissions; and Fitzgerald bypassed his agent Harold OBER to deal directly with Gingrich, frequently requesting advances. Fitzgerald shared a joint byline with Zelda FITZGERALD for his first two appearances in *Esquire*—" 'Show Mr. and Mrs. F. to Number——' " (May–June 1934) and "Auction—Model 1934" (July 1934)—autobiographical articles which she wrote and he polished. His *Esquire* essays include "Sleeping and Waking" (December 1934), "Author's House" (July 1936), and "Afternoon of an Author" (August 1936); best known are the confessional articles of spring 1936: "The Crack-Up," "Pasting It Together," and "Handle with Care." The "Crack-Up" series generated mostly negative reaction, embarrassing Fitzgerald's friends and making magazine editors and movie producers suspicious of his ability to produce good work. His *Esquire* fiction ranged from 1,100 to 2,250 words and was easier to turn out than his 5,000–6,000-word stories for the *Post*. *Esquire* published 28 Fitzgerald stories during his lifetime, including "The Fiend" (January 1935), "The Night Before Chancellorsville" (February 1935), "Financing Finnegan" (January 1938), "The Lost Decade" (December 1939), and 12 of the 17 Pat HOBBY stories, which helped finance Fitzgerald's work on *LT/LOLT*. The Hobby stories had become stockpiled, and five of them

were published in 1941. Other Fitzgerald pieces which *Esquire* published posthumously include "On an Ocean Wave" (as by Paul ELGIN, February 1941), "The Woman from Twenty-One" (June 1941), "Three Hours Between Planes" (July 1941), "Lo, the Poor Peacock!" (September 1971), and "On Your Own" (January 1979).

Este, Lord Charles Character in "Rags Martin-Jones and the Pr-nce of W-les." Official in Baron MARCHBANKS's entourage.

Estelle Character in "No Flowers." Girl whose date, STANLEY, discovers that his suit is missing.

Etherington, Sara Character in "Diagnosis." Charlie CLAYHORNE's fiancée, who is disturbed by the changes she sees in him when she returns from a trip to EUROPE.

"Eulogy on the Flapper" Article by Zelda FITZGERALD. *METROPOLITAN MAGAZINE*, 55 (June 1922), 38–39; *Zelda Fitzgerald: The Collected Writings*. Notes that the characteristics which originally set apart the flapper have now become commonplace: "Flapperdom has become a game; it is no longer a philosophy" (*Collected Writings*, p. 392). When the flapper first appeared, she was distinguished thus: "She flirted because it was fun to flirt and wore a one-piece bathing suit because she had a good figure; she covered her face with powder and paint because she didn't need it and she refused to be bored chiefly because she wasn't boring" (p. 391).

Europe The Fitzgeralds' first trip to Europe (May–July 1921) was "a bore and a disappointment" (to Shane LESLIE, May 24, 1921; *Letters*, p. 379) due to the couple's not having friends on the Continent. They returned to PARIS in the spring of 1924 for what would stretch into a two-and-a-half-year European stay (April 1924–December 1926) because Fitzgerald believed that time spent in Europe would be conducive to novel writing. The cost of living there was lower than in the United States, so he hoped he would not have to interrupt his work to turn out stories for ready income; and he expected few distractions while he wrote *GG*.

Although Fitzgerald did manage to write *GG* in the summer and fall of 1924, the couple's time in Europe was not the quiet sojourn the author had imagined. Instead, their second trip abroad and the two that followed (April–September 1928 and March 1929–September 1931) were filled with events and experiences that would profoundly influence the writing of some of his best stories, notably "One Trip Abroad" (October 1930) and "Babylon Revisited" (February 1931) as well as *TITN*. In the summer of 1924, Fitzgerald was rocked by his wife's romantic involvement with French aviator Edouard JOZAN. Also that summer, the Fitzgeralds began what became a close long-term friendship with

Gerald and Sara MURPHY, the attractive EXPATRIATE couple who served as partial models for Dick and Nicole DIVER in *TITN*. In April 1925 Fitzgerald met Ernest HEMINGWAY in the Dingo bar in Paris, thus initiating perhaps his most important, and certainly his most turbulent, literary friendship. During their years in Europe, the Fitzgeralds' marriage became increasingly strained: Zelda FITZGERALD complained about Fitzgerald's heavy drinking; and he resented his wife's dedication to her ballet practice, which proved to be the prelude to her mental breakdown in April 1930—the "crash" that changed their lives and deeply affected his career.

Despite the importance of his European experiences to his writing, Fitzgerald's involvement with expatriate writers other than Hemingway was limited. In Paris he attended Gertrude STEIN's receptions and dined on at least two occasions with James JOYCE. He became friends with Sylvia BEACH, the proprietress of Shakespeare and Co., the bookstore and gathering spot for the American expatriate writing community; but he remained largely aloof from the struggling writers of the Left Bank. He befriended one French writer, André CHAMSON, who with Fitzgerald's help became a SCRIBNERS author. On the RIVIERA he socialized with many writers, including Archibald MACLEISH, John DOS PASSOS, Charles MACARTHUR, Dorothy PARKER, and Robert BENCHLEY; but there is no evidence to suggest that these relationships influenced his literary development. Fitzgerald's friendship with Hemingway, then, was as singular as it was significant. "You were the first American I wanted to meet in Europe—" Fitzgerald wrote to his friend in the midst of his criticisms of *The Sun Also Rises* (1926), "and the last" (June 1926; *Life in Letters,* p. 143). In conversations in cafés and in their letters, the two men talked literature and craft.

Although upon his return to America in 1927 Fitzgerald professed a preference for life in France, his attitude toward Europe as reflected in his fiction became intertwined with his personal sense of dissipation and his wife's illness. When the Fitzgeralds arrived in HYÈRES in May 1924, he called the RIVIERA "the lovliest piece of earth I've ever seen without excepting Oxford or Venice or Princeton or anywhere" (to Thomas BOYD; *Life in Letters,* p. 68). In the first stories he wrote set in Europe—"Love in the Night" (March 1925), "A Penny Spent" (October 1925), and "Not in the Guidebook" (November 1925)—the Continent provides merely a backdrop for his commercial romances. However, five years later, at the beginning of his last period of living abroad, Europe as an idea had clearly become entwined with his fear of deterioration.

In a draft of the novel that would evolve into *TITN*, Lew Kelly, an accomplished motion picture director, sails with his wife to Europe in the typically American search for "culture"—"to learn something," Kelly tells

a fellow passenger on the transatlantic voyage. "I've been putting out for five years and I want to take in some cargo" (*F. Scott Fitzgerald Manuscripts IVa,* Part 2, p. 307):

> The idea of Europe seen from the sudden bareness he had discovered in their Hollywood house had seemed warm, unified and clear, a movement from the diverse and thin toward the definate and concrete. . . .
>
> He expected, in any case, a completed world, a world he would not have to make or mould. Europeans had drifted into Hollywood in the past few years and he felt that they had not to struggle as he had to see life or any segment of life as a progress from here to there. . . . And he knew that the Europeans were impressed with [Hollywood] as they were impressed with the sky scrapers, as something without human rythm or movement. They had left rythm behind them + it was there rythm he wanted. He was tired of his own rythm + the rythms of the people in Hollywood (pp. 329–330).

But the Europe Fitzgerald wrote of in his stories was not a place of culture or human rhythm. Instead Fitzgerald's Europe, as in "The Hotel Child" (January 1931), was populated by Europeanized Americans who "had reached a position where they could hardly be said to belong to any nation at all; certainly not to any great power, but perhaps to a sort of Balkanlike state composed of people like themselves" (*Bits of Paradise,* p. 249). As Fitzgerald had discovered and as Dick DIVER would find out, the life of the expatriate provided no answers to vexing personal questions or professional insecurities.

In Fitzgerald's stories Europe becomes a place where promising young Americans—Henry MARSTON in "The Swimmers" (October 1929), Bill MCCHESNEY in "Two Wrongs" (January 1930), Nicole and Nelson KELLY in "One Trip Abroad" (October 1930), Charlie WALES in "Babylon Revisited" (February 1931), and Dick RAGLAND in "A New Leaf" (July 1931)—lose their self-control and their dreams, a place "where very few things begin, but many things end" ("One Trip Abroad"; *AOAA,* p. 161). In "The Swimmers" Henry Marston's dislike for his own country has driven him to France. To an American friend who urged him to return to America to cash in on new opportunities, Marston "spoke vaguely about being able to live more comfortably in Paris and restrained himself from stating his frank opinion upon existence at home" (*Bits of Paradise,* p. 188). France, however, in the person of his promiscuous wife, Choupette MARSTON, offers only disillusionment. Marston eventually returns to America for a time to put his life right, reflecting that "the best of America was the best of the world" (p. 209). As the story concludes he is aboard a ship bound for Europe looking back on his native land:

He had come home as to a generous mother and had been profusely given more than he asked—money, release from an intolerable situation, and the fresh strength to fight for his own. Watching the fading city, the fading shore, from the deck of the Majestic, he had a sense of overwhelming gratitude and of gladness that America was there, that under the ugly debris of industry the rich land still pushed up, incorrigibly lavish and fertile, and that in the heart of the leaderless people the old generosities and devotions fought on, breaking out sometimes in fanaticism and excess, but indomitable and undefeated. . . . France was a land, England was a people, but America, having about it still that quality of the idea, was harder to utter—it was the graves at Shiloh and the tired, drawn, nervous faces of its great men, and the country boys dying in the Argonne for a phrase that was empty before their bodies withered. It was a willingness of the heart (pp. 209–210).

Like his character Marston, Fitzgerald's deepest feelings were for his own country. Even when his work was set in Europe, he wrote of the American character; life in Europe provided him with a new perspective on his country.

by George P. Anderson

Evelyn Character in "A Snobbish Story." John Boynton BAILEY's wife, who is angry that John isn't giving her a role in his play. Jealous of his attention to Josephine PERRY, she attempts suicide.

Everett, Tom Character in "Dalyrimple Goes Wrong." Theron MACY's nephew, who is given preferential treatment on the job.

The Evil Eye 17 song lyrics. Cincinnati, New York & London: The John Church Co., 1915. A two-act musical comedy presented by the PRINCETON TRIANGLE CLUB; opening performance December 18, 1915. Book by Edmund WILSON; music by Paul B. DICKEY and F. Warburton Guilbert; lyrics by Fitzgerald: Act I—"Opening," "I've Got My Eyes on You," "On Dreams Alone," "The Evil Eye," "What I'll Forget," "Over the Waves to Me," "On Her Eukalali," "Jump Off the Wall," "Finale"; Act II—"Opening," "Harris from Paris," "Twilight," "The Never, Never Land," "My Idea of Love," "Other Eyes," "The Girl of the Golden West," "With Me." Lyrics reprinted in *In His Own Time* and *Poems.* The show was set in a Normandy fishing village and concerned an amnesiac shipwreck survivor and her rescuer, reputed to have the evil eye. Fitzgerald's failure of a make-up exam in qualitative analysis made him ineligible to perform in the show, which opened on December 18, 1915; but he was involved with the production, writing new lyrics on demand during rehearsals; and there was a publicity photo of him in a showgirl costume.

Score for Fitzgerald's 1915 Triangle Club musical (Bruccoli Collection, University of South Carolina)

Ewing, Joe Character in "The Ice Palace" and "The Jelly-Bean." Young man from TARLETON, Georgia. In "The Ice Palace" he goes swimming with Clark DARROW, Sally Carrol HAPPER, and Marylyn WADE. In "The Jelly-Bean" he attends the country club dance with Marylyn.

Expatriates Although American artists, musicians, and writers have taken residence in EUROPE since the 18th century, the term *expatriate* is usually associated with the immigration of Americans to France—especially PARIS—during the 1920s. Among the reasons were the rejection of what was regarded as American "puritanism" (prohibition), the favorable rate of exchange, the desire to be with other creative people, and opportunities to have work published, performed, or exhibited. Among the American literary figures associated with the expatriate movement were Gertrude STEIN and Ezra Pound (1885–1972) (who went to Paris before the twenties), Sylvia BEACH, Harry and Caresse Crosby (1898–1929 and 1892–1970), Man Ray (1890–1976), Ernest HEMINGWAY, Robert MCALMON, T. S. ELIOT (in London), H.D. (1886–1961), and John DOS PASSOS.

Fitzgerald was classified as an expatriate on the basis of his extended residences in France between 1925 and 1931, but he took no part in expatriate literary schools and never wrote for the little magazines published in France.

F

F. Scott Fitzgerald Collection Notes Occasional publication of the Thomas Cooper Library, University of South Carolina, Columbia, S.C., 1995– . Describes acquisitions for the BRUCCOLI COLLECTION.

F. Scott Fitzgerald In His Own Time: A Miscellany Ed. Matthew J. BRUCCOLI and Jackson R. Bryer. Kent, Ohio: Kent State University Press, 1971. Contents: Part 1—Miscellany by Fitzgerald: " 'Football' "; *Fie! Fie! Fi-Fi!*—"Opening Chorus," "Gentlemen Bandits We," "A Slave to Modern Improvements," "In Her Eyes," "What the Manicure Lady Knows," "Good Night and Good Bye," " 'Round and 'Round," "Chatter Trio," "Finale Act I," "Rose of the Night," "Men," "In the Dark," "Love or Eugenics," "Reminiscence," "Fie! Fie! Fi-Fi!," "The Monte Carlo Moon," "Finale Act II"; "A Cheer for Princeton"; *The Evil Eye*—"Act I Opening Chorus," "I've Got My Eyes on You," "On Dreams Alone," "The Evil Eye," "What I'll Forget," "Over the Waves to Me," "On Her Eukalali," "Jump Off the Wall," "Finale Act I," "Act II Opening Chorus," "Harris from Paris," "Twilight," " 'The Never, Never Land,' " "My Idea of Love," "Other Eyes," "The Girl of the Golden West," "With Me"; *Safety First*—"(A) Prologue," "(B) Garden of Arden," "Act I Opening Chorus," "Send Him to Tom," "One-Lump Percy," "Where Did Bridget Kelly Get Her Persian Temperament?" "It Is Art," "Safety First," "Charlotte Corday," "Underneath the April Rain," "Dance, Lady, Dance," "(A) Safety First," "(B) Hello Temptation," "When That Beautiful Chord Came True," "Rag-Time Melodrama," "Scene II," "Take Those Hawaiian Songs Away," "The Vampires Won't Vampire for Me," "The Hummin' Blues," "Down in Front," "Finale"; "To My Unused Greek Book"; "Rain Before Dawn"; "Princeton—The Last Day"; "On a Play Twice Seen"; "The Cameo Frame"; "City Dusk"; "My First Love"; "Marching Streets"; "The Pope at Confession"; "A Dirge"; "Sleep of a University"; "To Anne"; untitled poem; "Lamp in a Window"; "Obit on Parnassus"; "There was once a second group student . . ."; "May Small Talk"; "How They Head the Chapters"; "The Conquest of America"; "Yais"; "Little Minnie McCloskey"; "One from Penn's Neck"; "A Litany of Slang"; " 'Triangle Scenery by Bakst' "; "Futuristic Impressions of the Editorial Boards"; " 'A glass of beer kills him' ";

"Oui, le backfield est from Paris"; " 'When you find a man doing a little more' "; "Things That Never Change. Number 3333"; "The Old Frontiersman"; "Boy Kills Self Rather Than Pet"; "Precaution Primarily"; "Things That Never Change No. 3982"; "McCaulay Mission—Water Street"; "Popular Parodies—No. 1"; "The Diary of a Sophomore"; "Undulations of an Undergraduate"; "Yale's swimming team will take its maiden plunge to-night"; "Kenilworth Socialism"; "True Democracy"; "A Few Well-Known Club Types And Their Futures"; "The Prince of Pests"; " 'These rifles*** will probably not be used . . .' "; " 'It is assumed that the absence of submarines . . .' "; "Ethel had her shot of brandy . . ."; "The Staying Up All Night"; "Intercollegiate Petting Cues"; "Our American Poets"; "Cedric the Stoker"; "Our Next Issue"; "The Usual Thing"; "Jemina"; review of *Penrod and Sam*; review of *David Blaize*; review of *The Celt and the World*; review of *Verses in Peace and War*; review of *God, the Invisible King*; review of *Prejudices. Second Series*; review of *Three Soldiers*; "Three Cities"; review of *Brass*; review of *Crome Yellow*; review of *Gentle Julia*; review of *Margey Wins the Game*; review of *The Oppidan*; review of *The Love Legend*; review of *Many Marriages*; review of *Being Respectable*; review of *Through the Wheat*; "How to Waste Material"; "F. Scott Fitzgerald Is Bored by Efforts at Realism in 'Lit' "; blurb for *Babel*; blurb for *Lily-Iron*; introduction to *GG*; blurb for *Cast Down the Laurel*; foreword to *Colonial and Historic Homes of Maryland*; blurb for *What Makes Sammy Run?*; blurb for *The Day of the Locust*; self-interview; "The Author's Apology"; "The Credo of F. Scott Fitzgerald"; "What I Was Advised To Do—And Didn't"; "How I Would Sell My Book If I Were a Bookseller"; "Confessions"; "In Literary New York"; "Censorship or Not"; "Fitzgerald Sets Things Right about His College"; "Unfortunate 'Tradition' "; "False and Extremely Unwise Tradition"; "Confused Romanticism"; "An Open Letter to Fritz Crisler"; comments on stories; statement on Huck Finn; "Anonymous '17"; letter to Harvey H. Smith; " 'Why Blame It on the Poor Kiss if the Girl Veteran of Many Petting Parties Is Prone to Affairs after Marriage?' "; "Does a Moment of Revolt Come Sometime to Every Married Man?"; "What Kind of Husbands Do 'Jimmies' Make?" " 'Wait Till You Have Children of Your Own!' "; "What Became of Our Flap-

pers and Sheiks?"; "Girls Believe in Girls"; "What I Think and Feel at 25"; "A Short Autobiography"; "This is a Magazine"; "Reminiscences of Donald Stewart"; *The St. Paul Daily Dirge*; "The Most Disgraceful Thing I Ever Did"; "Salesmanship in the Champs-Élysées"; *The True Story of Appomattox*; "A Book of One's Own"; testimonial for Constant Tras. Also material about Fitzgerald: interviews, reviews, essays, editorials, parodies, and obituaries.

F. Scott Fitzgerald: Inscriptions Edited with introduction by Matthew J. BRUCCOLI. Columbia, S.C.: 1988 (limited edition of 200 numbered copies). Facsimiles of inscriptions by Fitzgerald in his own books, as well as other authors' books which he gave to friends; also inscriptions to Fitzgerald from James Branch Cabell, John DOS PASSOS, T. S. ELIOT, James JOYCE, H. L. MENCKEN, Gertrude STEIN, and others. All but two of the items facsimiled in this volume are in the BRUCCOLI COLLECTION at the University of South Carolina.

"F. Scott Fitzgerald Is Bored by Efforts at Realism in 'Lit' " Review of March issue of *The NASSAU LITERARY MAGAZINE*. *The Daily Princetonian*, March 16, 1928, pp. 1, 3; *In His Own Time*. Fitzgerald notes that the stories in this issue of the *Lit* are "desperately similar to each other" because "they all take place on Nassau Street, no longer back than yesterday" (*In His Own Time*, p. 150). He finds the poetry better than the fiction, but concludes that "this is a dignified but on the whole unadventurous number of the oldest college magazine in America" (p. 151).

F. Scott Fitzgerald Manuscripts New York & London: Garland, 1990–91. Facsimiles of the novels, short stories, and essays in 18 volumes. All the volumes are edited with introductions by general editor Matthew J. BRUCCOLI, except for *B&D*, which is edited with an introduction by associate editor Alan Margolies.

Contents:

I. This Side of Paradise
Part 1: holograph draft of *TSOP*, Book One. Part 2: holograph draft of *TSOP*, Book Two; revised typescript and carbon copy of Chapters I, II, V, XII, XIV of "The Romantic Egotist"; carbon copy of Chapters I and II of *TSOP*.

II. The Beautiful and Damned
Part 1: holograph manuscript with revised typed inserts for Book One, Chapters I-III and Book Two, Chapter I. Part 2: holograph manuscript with revised typed inserts for Book Two, Chapters II–III and Book Three, Chapters I–III; carbon copies of galley inserts.

III. The Great Gatsby
Revised and rewritten galleys with revised typed inserts. [Note: *The Great Gatsby: A Facsimile of the Manuscript,*

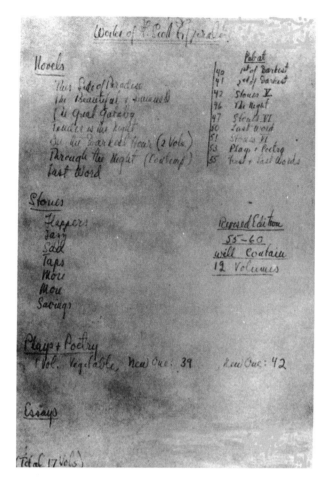

Fitzgerald's plan for a projected complete edition of his works, c. 1936 (Princeton University Library)

ed. Bruccoli, was previously published (Washington: Bruccoli Clark/NCR Microcard Books, 1973).]

IV. Tender Is the Night
a. The Melarky and Kelly Versions. Part 1: holograph for Francis Melarky version (first draft); revised typescript (second draft) for Melarky version. Part 2: holograph for Melarky narrator version (third draft); revised typescript for Melarky narrator version (fourth draft); holograph draft for two chapters of Lew Kelly version.

b. The Diver Version. Part 1: selected notes, holograph draft. Part 2: holograph draft (continued). Part 3: first revised typescript. Part 4: second revised typescript. Part 5: setting copy for the serial; revised serial galleys and revised typed inserts; revised book galleys.

V. The Last Tycoon
Part 1: holograph and revised typescript for Fitzgerald's preliminary and working notes; holograph draft for Episodes 1–17. Part 2: holograph draft for Episodes 1–

17 (continued); revised typescripts and revised carbon copies. Part 3: revised typescripts and revised carbon copies (continued); latest revised typescripts.

VI. The Vegetable, Stories, and Articles
Part 1: revised typescript for scenes deleted from *The Vegetable* before publication; holograph revisions for production of *The Vegetable;* incomplete holograph for "Babes in the Woods"; holograph for "Rags Martin-Jones and the Pr-nce of W-les"; revised typescript for "A Penny Spent" and "The Rich Boy"; holograph for "How To Waste Material: A Note on My Generation"; revised typescript for "The Love Boat," "A Night at the Fair," "He Thinks He's Wonderful," "The Captured Shadow," "The Perfect Life," and "The Last of the Belles." Part 2: revised typescript for "Forging Ahead"; holograph plan (previously unpublished) for Basil Duke LEE stories; revised typescript for "The Swimmers"; revised typescript (and possibly carbon copy) for "Two Wrongs"; revised typescript for "A Nice Quiet Place," "The Bridal Party," and "A Woman with a Past"; revised typescript (and possibly carbon copy) for "One Trip Abroad"; revised typescript for "The Hotel Child," "Babylon Revisited," and "Indecision." Part 3: revised typescript for "A New Leaf" and "Emotional Bankruptcy"; holograph notes (previously unpublished) for a projected volume of augmented Josephine PERRY stories; revised typescript for "Six of One—," "Diagnosis," and "Crazy Sunday"; holograph and revised typescript for "In the Darkest Hour"; holograph for "The Count of Darkness"; holograph and revised typed notes for PHILIPPE medieval stories; revised typescript for "The Crack-Up," "Early Success," and "The Woman from Twenty-One"; holograph for "Reunion at the Fair" (incomplete and previously unpublished Pat HOBBY story); holograph and revised typed notes (previously unpublished) on Pat Hobby stories.

Fitzgerald's manuscripts and revisions on typescripts and galleys demonstrate his painstaking process of rewriting and revising through multiple drafts and provide evidence of his careful craftsmanship (*See* EDITING FITZGERALD'S TEXTS). These facsimiles therefore provide an invaluable resource for the serious Fitzgerald scholar. Most of the material in this facsimile edition is in the F. Scott Fitzgerald Papers at PRINCETON UNIVERSITY LIBRARY.

F. Scott Fitzgerald on Authorship Edited with introduction by Matthew J. BRUCCOLI, with Judith S. Baughman. Columbia: University of South Carolina Press, 1996. One of the volumes published by USC Press to mark the CENTENNIAL of Fitzgerald's birth. Contents: Untitled review of *David Blaize* by E. F. Benson; untitled review of *The Celt and the World* by Shane LESLIE; untitled review of *Verses in Peace and War* by Shane Leslie; untitled review of *God, The Invisible King* by H. G. Wells;

"An Interview with F. Scott Fitzgerald"; "Contemporary Writers and Their Work, a Series of Autobiographical Letters—F. Scott Fitzgerald"; "Who's Who—and Why"; Public Letter to Thomas Boyd; "The Baltimore Anti-Christ," review of *Prejudices, Second Series* by H. L. MENCKEN; "*Three Soldiers*," review of the novel by John DOS PASSOS; "Three Cities"; "Poor Old Marriage," review of *Brass* by Charles G. Norris; "Reminiscences of Donald Stewart"; dust-jacket statement for John Cournos's *Babel;* "Aldous Huxley's *Crome Yellow*"; "Literary Libels—Francis Scott Key Fitzgerald" by Thomas A. BOYD; "What I Was Advised To Do—And Didn't"; "Tarkington's *Gentle Julia*"; "Homage to the Victorians," review of *The Oppidan* by Shane Leslie; "A Rugged Novel," review of *The Love Legend* by Woodward BOYD; "How I Would Sell My Book If I Were a Bookseller"; "The Defeat of Art," review of *The Boy Grew Older* by Heywood Broun; "Minnesota's Capital in the Role of Main Street," review of *Being Respectable* by Grace Flandrau; "Sherwood Anderson on the Marriage Question," review of *Many Marriages* by Anderson; "10 Best Books I Have Read"; "Confessions," public letter to Fannie Butcher; "Under Fire," review of *Through the Wheat* by Thomas Boyd; "Censorship or Not"; "Prediction Is Made about James Joyce Novel: F. S. Fitzgerald Believes *Ulysses* Is Great Book of Future"; "In Literary New York"; "How To Waste Material—A Note on My Generation," essay-review of *In Our Time* by Ernest HEMINGWAY; "Fitzgerald, Spenglerian" by Harry Salpeter; "F. Scott Fitzgerald Is Bored by Efforts at Realism in 'Lit,'" review of March 1928 issue of *The Nassau Literary Magazine;* "Fitzgerald Back from Riviera; Is Working on Novel"; Statement on *Huckleberry Finn;* "One Hundred False Starts"; "Ring"; Introduction to the Modern Library reprint of *The Great Gatsby;* "My Ten Favorite Plays"; "Fitzgerald's Letter of Recommendation for Nathanael West's Guggenheim Fellowship Application"; "Author's House"; "Afternoon of an Author"; "Early Success"; "Financing Finnegan"; dust-jacket statement for Budd SCHULBERG's *What Makes Sammy Run?;* excerpts from *Notebooks;* and excerpts from letters.

F. Scott Fitzgerald Society The first Fitzgerald Society was founded by Matthew J. BRUCCOLI in 1958 to sponsor the *Fitzgerald Newsletter;* it disbanded when the newsletter ceased publication in 1968. In 1990 a second F. Scott Fitzgerald Society was founded by Jackson R. Bryer (University of Maryland), Alan Margolies (John Jay College, CUNY), and Ruth Prigozy (Hofstra University) to assist and coordinate Fitzgerald studies through the Society's general meetings and other special conferences, the publication of a yearly newsletter—which includes a bibliography, and the support of similar activities approved by the Society. The Society sponsored a conference at Hofstra University in 1992, co-sponsored a conference in PARIS with the Ernest

HEMINGWAY Society in 1994, and commemorated Fitzgerald's 100th birthday with a conference at PRINCETON UNIVERSITY in 1996 (*see* CENTENNIAL). There were 325 members as of March 1996. Send all correspondence and requests for membership to Professor Ruth Prigozy, Executive Director, 107 Hofstra University, Hempstead, N.Y. 11550–1090.

F. Scott Fitzgerald's Ledger: A Facsimile Introduction by Matthew J. BRUCCOLI. Washington, D.C.: Bruccoli Clark/NCR Microcard Editions, 1973. A 9½″ x 14½″ business ledger in which Fitzgerald kept a record of his professional and personal activities in five categories: "Record of Published Fiction—Novels, Plays, Stories"; "Money Earned by Writing since Leaving Army"; "Published Miscelani (including movies) for which I was Paid"; "Zelda's Earnings"; "Outline Chart of my Life" (a monthly chronology beginning with his birth, with a yearly summary beginning with September 1910–August 1911). He probably began keeping the *Ledger* in late 1919 or early 1920, but he may have begun it in 1922 when he wrote to Harold OBER that he was "getting up a record of all my work" (*As Ever,* p. 46); he continued the record through 1936.

F. Scott Fitzgerald's Preface to This Side of Paradise Edited by John R. Hopkins. Iowa City, Iowa: Windhover Press/Bruccoli Clark, 1975 (limited edition of 150 copies); typescript previously facsimiled in *Fitzgerald/Hemingway Annual* (1971), pp. 1–2. Preface which Fitzgerald wrote in August 1919, before Maxwell PERKINS of SCRIBNERS accepted *TSOP* for publication. The preface, which was never published with the novel, describes the composition of the novel and Fitzgerald's unsuccessful early attempts at finding a publisher for it.

F. Scott Fitzgerald's St. Paul Plays, 1911–1914 Edited by Alan Margolies. Princeton, N.J.: Princeton University Library, 1978. Contents: *The Girl from Lazy J, The Captured Shadow, Coward,* and *Assorted Spirits.* Collection of four plays which Fitzgerald wrote for the ELIZABETHAN DRAMATIC CLUB in ST. PAUL.

Fairboalt, Mrs. Roger Character in "The Cut-Glass Bowl." Curious woman who visits Evylyn PIPER, who tells her the history of the bowl.

"The Family Bus" Fiction. Written September 1933. *The SATURDAY EVENING POST,* 206 (November 4, 1933), 8–9, 57, 61–62, 65–66; *The Price Was High.* Dick HENDERSON is great friends with his family's gardener's daughter, Jannekin MELON-LOPER, throughout their childhood. However, when Dick's older brother, Ralph HENDERSON, is killed in a car wreck while attempting to elope with Jannekin's sister, Kaethe MELON-LOPER,

the gardener's family moves away. Six years later Dick encounters Jannekin again in high school, where his fraternity brothers, who resent his superior social background and regard him as a snob, deface the old family car he drives. Jannekin's family becomes well-to-do and rises socially; Dick's family becomes poor, and he takes a job in an automobile plant in Detroit. He learns that the old family car was one of six with a special intake manifold that the manufacturer wishes to recover. Dick learns that Jannekin had bought the car but her chauffeur had resold it; Dick and Jannekin finally locate the stripped-down car and take it for a ride together.

"Family in the Wind" Fiction. Written April 1932. *The SATURDAY EVENING POST,* 204 (June 4, 1932), 3–5, 71–73; *TAR.* Gene JANNEY urges his brother, Forrest JANNEY, an alcoholic doctor who now runs a drugstore in his Alabama hometown, to operate on Gene's son Pinky JANNEY, who has been shot. Forrest agrees to look at Pinky but refuses to operate because of his resentment of Pinky's treatment of Mary DECKER, a girl whom Forrest had secretly loved but who had run away with Pinky. When Pinky had tired of her, he had turned her out; and she had died of starvation. After Forrest leaves his brother's house, a tornado devastates the town. When Pinky shows up at the hospital where Forrest is helping tornado victims, Forrest agrees to operate on him after all. A second tornado hits the town the same day, and Forrest decides to leave town and possibly resume his medical practice in the city. He plans to assume responsibility for Helen KILRAIN, a little girl who was orphaned by the storm.

"The Far-seeing Skeptics" *The SMART SET,* 67 (February 1922), 48. Excerpt from *B&D,* Book Two, Chapter II, "Symposium."

Farnam, Ardita Character in "The Offshore Pirate." Strong-minded girl who is won by the imaginative stunt of Toby Moreland, who poses as pirate Curtis CARLYLE.

Farnam, Mr. Character in "The Offshore Pirate." Ardita FARNAM's elderly uncle, whose yacht is taken by Curtis CARLYLE.

Farrelly, Billy Character in "Jacob's Ladder." Movie director who gives Jenny Prince [DELEHANTY] her first role.

fat man (unnamed) Character in "Head and Shoulders." Man who is impressed by Horace TARBOX's gymnastic performance and introduces him to agent Charlie PAULSON.

"Fate in Her Hands" Fiction. Written June–July 1935. *The American Magazine,* 121 (April 1936), 56–59, 168–

172; *The Price Was High.* When Carol [KASTLER] is 19, a FORTUNE-TELLER says that she will be married that month, that she will acquire great notoriety in about three years, and that something very bad will happen to her and her family in about six years in May. Wanting to disprove the predictions, Carol refuses to marry her fiancé, Billy RIGGS, until New Year's morning. On the way to the wedding, Billy's friend Ben KASTLER declares his love for Carol; and she marries him just before midnight on New Year's Eve. Three years later Carol is reminded of the second prediction, and when a photographer for a tabloid newspaper snaps her picture with a ragged woman outside a Junior League function she worries that her possible depiction as stingy and uncaring may harm Ben's chances of being selected as the new president of his university. She decides to leave town for a week and leaves a note of explanation for Ben. On her way home she learns that her maid has not delivered the note but rather asked for ransom for Carol's alleged kidnapping. Since Ben has just been named university president, the event makes newspaper headlines, fulfilling the second prophecy. Several years later Carol locates the original palmist, who reiterates her third prediction but tells her to forget it. When Ben escapes injury in his office building, which collapses shortly after he leaves it, Carol is relieved and allows her daughter, Jean KASTLER, to climb a tree, which protects Jean from being bitten by a rabid dog. At the end of the story there are six more hours until the first day of June, when the prophecy will have passed.

Fitzgerald's working title for this story was "What You Don't Know." The story was influenced by palmist Laura GUTHRIE, whom he met in ASHEVILLE, North Carolina, while he was writing it.

Fay, Daisy *See* Daisy Fay BUCHANAN.

Fay, Father Cyril Sigourney Webster (1875–1919) Intellectual Catholic priest, a former Episcopalian minister, and adviser to Cardinal Gibbons of BALTIMORE. Fitzgerald met Fay—who was later headmaster of the NEWMAN SCHOOL—in November 1912; the priest, who encouraged his ambitions, soon became his surrogate father. Fitzgerald wrote that Fay and author Shane LESLIE, to whom Fay introduced him, made the Catholic Church "a dazzling, golden thing, dispelling its oppressive mugginess and giving the succession of days upon gray days, passing under its plaintive ritual, the romantic glamour of an adolescent dream" ("Homage to the Victorians," May 1922; *In His Own Time,* p. 134). Fay was the model for Monsignor Thayer DARCY in *TSOP,* in which Fitzgerald described Amory BLAINE's first meeting with Darcy as "one of the memorable events in Amory's early life. . . . Monsignor called out the best that he had thought by question and suggestion, and Amory talked with an ingenious brilliance of

Father Cyril Sigourney Webster Fay, Fitzgerald's early mentor and model for Monsignor Darcy in This Side of Paradise
(Bruccoli Collection, University of South Carolina)

a thousand impulses and desires and repulsions and faiths and fears" (p. 28). Fitzgerald incorporated into the novel a Gaelic keen that Fay sent him on December 10, 1917 when Fitzgerald was in the ARMY, and the novel is dedicated to Fay.

In 1917 Fay, who was planning a secret mission to Russia designed to unify the Catholic Church, proposed to take Fitzgerald along as his aide. His August 22 letter to Fitzgerald details his scheme for traveling under cover of a Red Cross mission (*Correspondence,* pp. 19–21). Fitzgerald planned to accompany Fay and obtained a passport, but the mission was canceled. Pope Benedict XV made Fay a monsignor in 1918. Fay died of pneumonia on January 10, 1919; Fitzgerald, who was stationed at CAMP SHERIDAN, near MONTGOMERY, Alabama, was unable to attend the funeral.

Fay, Ted Character in "The Freshest Boy." Yale football captain, based on Yale star Ted Coy, whom Basil Duke LEE sees with an actress in NEW YORK.

Fay, Teeny Character in "I Got Shoes." Johanna BATTLES's friend whom she encounters on her way to interview Nell MARGERY; they discuss Miss Margery's shoe collection.

"The Feather Fan" Movie treatment. *Fitzgerald/Hemingway Annual* (1977), pp. 3–8. Probably in 1939, Fitzgerald wrote a treatment which he submitted to MGM for a movie set in 1919 about a Vassar student who finds a feather fan that will grant wishes. His proposal was declined.

Ferdie Character in *GG*. Daisy BUCHANAN's chauffeur, who drives her to Nick CARRAWAY's house for the surprise reunion with Jay GATSBY.

Ferrenby, Jesse Character in *TSOP*. PRINCETON student who becomes editor of the *Princetonian* newspaper when Amory BLAINE is disqualified because of failing a crucial exam. Ferrenby is later killed in the war.

Ferrenby, Mr. Character in *TSOP*. Jesse FERRENBY's father, the "big man" who gives Amory BLAINE a ride at the end of the novel and with whom Amory argues socialism.

Fiancé of Miss Hunter (unnamed) Character in "In the Holidays." Detective who poses as a resident doctor and who discovers Mr. MCKENNA's criminal identity by checking his fingerprints.

Fie! Fie! Fi-Fi! 17 song lyrics. Cincinnati, New York & London: The John Church Co., 1914; facsimile of acting script and song book (Columbia: University of South Carolina Press for the Thomas Cooper Library, 1996). A two-act musical comedy presented by the PRINCETON TRIANGLE CLUB; opening performance December 19, 1914. Music by D. D. Griffin, A. L. Booth, and Paul B. DICKEY; lyrics by Fitzgerald: Act I—"Opening Chorus," "Gentlemen Bandits We," "A Slave to Modern Improvements," "In Her Eyes," "What the Manicure Lady Knows," "Good-night and Good-bye," "Round and Round," "Chatter Trio," "Finale"; Act II—"Rose of the Night," "Men," "In the Dark," "Love or Eugenics," "Reminiscence," "Fie! Fie! Fi-Fi!," "The Monte Carlo Moon," "Finale." Lyrics reprinted in *In His Own Time* and *Poems*. Triangle Club president Walker ELLIS revised Fitzgerald's book with Fitzgerald and awarded himself sole credit for dialogue and characters. Fitzgerald corrected the credits in his own copy of the program to read: "Book and lyrics by F. Scott Fitzgerald, 1917. Revision by Walker Ellis, 1915." The plot involves an American con man, now prime minis-

Score for Fitzgerald's 1914 Triangle Club musical (Bruccoli Collection, University of South Carolina)

ter of Monaco, and his abandoned wife, a hotel manicurist in Monte Carlo, whose role was played by Ellis. Fitzgerald was cast as a dancer in a love subplot, but he failed a make-up exam in coordinate geometry and was excluded from extracurricular activities, including the Triangle Club's 3,500-mile Christmas tour after a premiere at Princeton on December 19, 1914. The *Baltimore Sun* noted, "The lyrics of the songs were written by F. S. Fitzgerald, who could take his place right now with the brightest writers of witty lyrics in America" (scrapbook, PRINCETON UNIVERSITY LIBRARY). The play was produced at the University of South Carolina in 1996 to celebrate the CENTENNIAL of Fitzgerald's birth; a video of the premiere performance is available from the University of South Carolina Press. The song book for *Fie! Fie! Fi-Fi!* has previously been procurable for about $2,000–3,000, but there were only two copies of the acting script, and only one copy with Fitzgerald's extra lyrics. The 1996 facsimile of the song book and acting script (Columbia: University of South Carolina Press for the Thomas Cooper Library) makes these items readily available to collectors and scholars.

Fielding, Cyrus Character in *B&D*. Young man with whom Dot RAYCROFT once had a brief affair.

"The Fiend" Fiction. Written September 1934. *ESQUIRE*, 3 (January 1935), 23, 173–174; *TAR*. Crenshaw ENGELS seeks revenge on the FIEND who murdered his wife and son. When his attempts to kill the murderer or have him sentenced to capital punishment fail, Engels resorts to psychological revenge. He begins by threatening the Fiend with the torments of hell and by bringing him horrifying and frustrating books to read. He then changes his tactics to raising false hopes of release or false fears of execution and threatening to kill the Fiend himself. After 30 years Engels, fearing that the Fiend may outlive him, determines to shoot him so that he will die slowly and painfully. When he arrives at the Fiend's cell with a smuggled pistol, he finds the man doubled over in pain. Engels calls for a doctor, but the Fiend dies of a ruptured appendix. Shocked and despairing, Engels speaks of the Fiend as "my only friend" and laments that he is alone.

the Fiend Character in "The Fiend." Murderer of Mrs. Crenshaw ENGELS and Mark ENGELS.

Filipino servant (unnamed) Character in *LT/LOLT*. Monroe STAHR's servant, who gives Stahr the letter which Kathleen MOORE had dropped in Stahr's car.

"Financing Finnegan" Fiction. Written June 1937. *ESQUIRE*, 9 (January 1938), 41, 180, 182, 184; *Stories*. Literary agent Mr. CANNON and editor George JAGGERS lend money to FINNEGAN, a brilliant author who has lately been unproductive. The NARRATOR overhears Cannon and Jaggers discussing Finnegan's prospects and realizes that "the two men had entered into a silent conspiracy to cheer each other up about Finnegan" (*Stories*, p. 464). Cannon and Jaggers finance Finnegan's trip to the North Pole, and he assigns his life insurance to them. Finnegan's party is reported lost in a blizzard; he is presumed dead. His son, who writes poetry, asks Jaggers for money. Finnegan turns up in Norway and cables Cannon to send him money for return passage.

Fitzgerald wrote this story partly as a joke about his financial dependence on editor Maxwell PERKINS and agent Harold OBER.

Fingarson Character in "The Honor of the Goon." Norwegian chauffeur whom Mister LEI CHAMORO instructs to beat up Bomar WINLOCK and Oates MULKLEY for insulting his relative, Ella LEI CHAMORO.

the Finn Character in *GG*. Nick CARRAWAY's servant.

Finnegan Character in "Financing Finnegan." Talented author who is no longer productive and who lives on loans from his agent, Mr. CANNON, and his editor, George JAGGERS.

Finney, Ben (b. 1900) Friend of Fitzgerald on the RIVIERA in summer 1926; Fitzgerald discussed his work-in-progress on *TITN* with him. Fitzgerald listed Finney as one of the models for Dick DIVER's external qualities. See Finney, *Feet First* (New York: Crown, 1971).

Finney, Eben (1897–1959) Friend of Fitzgerald at PRINCETON (Class of 1919) with whom he renewed his acquaintance while living at "LA PAIX" in 1932. Finney's daughter, Peaches FINNEY, became Scottie FITZGERALD's closest friend in BALTIMORE.

Finney, Margaret (Peaches) Daughter of Fitzgerald's PRINCETON friend Eben FINNEY; Scottie FITZGERALD's best friend and classmate at the Calvert School and the Bryn Mawr School in BALTIMORE. During some of her father's absences from Baltimore Scottie stayed with the Finneys. In August 1938 Scottie and Peaches traveled to California to visit Fitzgerald, who was living at MALIBU BEACH.

"First Blood" Fiction—Josephine PERRY story. Written January 1930. *The SATURDAY EVENING POST*, 202 (April 5, 1930), 8–9, 81, 84; *TAR*; *B&J*. Josephine Perry's sister, Constance PERRY, complains to their mother about Josephine's behavior with Travis DE COPPET. Josephine falls in love with Anthony HARKER, who is several years older than she is. Anthony, who is uneasy about being seen with Josephine, breaks off their relationship, but then sends her a passionate letter, which she destroys. Anthony frantically courts her until his family sends him West; and Josephine resolves to behave better.

Fischer, Anton Otto (1882–1962) Illustrator for "The Rough Crossing" (*The SATURDAY EVENING POST*, June 8, 1929). Celebrated for his maritime paintings, Fischer illustrated many sea-related stories for the *Post*, including the "Tugboat Annie" series by Norman Reilly Raine (1895–1971) and the "Glencannon" series by Guy Gilpatric (1896–1950).

Fish, Joseph Character in *The Vegetable*. DORIS's fiancé. In Act II he is a Senator from Idaho and delivers a telegram demanding Jerry FROST's resignation as President of the United States. In Act III he and Doris have been secretly married for three days.

Fisher, Harrison (1875–1934) Magazine illustrator who sketched life portraits of F. Scott and Zelda FITZGERALD (National Portrait Gallery). His popular drawings of beautiful women, known as "the Fisher Girl," rivaled "the Gibson Girl" created by Charles Dana Gibson (1867–1944). During the 1920s and 1930s

Fisher primarily painted magazine covers, most often for *The SATURDAY EVENING POST*. He never illustrated a Fitzgerald story, but in "The Freshest Boy" (*Post,* July 28, 1928), Basil Duke LEE decorates his room at prep school with "Harrison Fisher Girls."

by Park Bucker

fisherman (unnamed) Character in *LT/LOLT.* Black man whom Monroe STAHR and Kathleen MOORE encounter on the beach gathering grunion. His comment that he doesn't allow his children to go to the movies because "There's no profit" in them has a profound effect on Stahr, who changes his plans regarding several upcoming movies. This philosophical character, who reads Ralph Waldo Emerson (1803–82) and Rosicrucian literature, has links to BEAUTY BOY in Fitzgerald's story "Dearly Beloved" (1969).

Fitzgerald, Annabel (1901–1987) Fitzgerald's younger sister, born in SYRACUSE, New York, on July 21, 1901. Fitzgerald later recorded in his *Ledger* that his "first certain memory is the sight of her howling on a bed" (p. 155). Although Fitzgerald was never close to Annabel, who was at convent schools while he was at the NEWMAN SCHOOL and PRINCETON, during her teen years he attempted to refine her social skills, providing detailed instructions on popularity and improving her image. A 10-page letter, probably written in 1915, gives advice on conversation, poise, carriage, dancing, expression, dress, and personality (*Life in Letters,* pp. 7–10); Fitzgerald later noted that this letter was the basis of his 1919 story "Bernice Bobs Her Hair." Annabel married naval officer Clifton Sprague, who became an admiral and was a hero at the Battle of Leyte Gulf in World War II. See Patricia Sprague Reneau and Courtney Sprague Vaughan, *Remembered and Honored: Clifton A. F. "Ziggy" Sprague, U.S.N., 1896–1955* (Santa Cruz: privately printed, 1992) and John F. Wukovits, *Devotion to Duty* (Annapolis: Naval Institute Press, 1995).

Fitzgerald, Cecilia Ashton Scott (1832–1924) Fitzgerald's paternal grandmother, whose family could be traced back to the 17th century in Maryland to the first Scotts, Keys, Ridgelys, and Dorseys. Wife of Michael FITZGERALD.

Fitzgerald, Edward (1853–1931) Fitzgerald's father. He was born to Michael and Cecilia Ashton Scott FITZGERALD in 1853 at "Glenmary" Farm near ROCK-VILLE, Maryland. During the Civil War he guided Confederate spies; his son later became convinced that the disappointments of the war sapped his ambition. His stories of the war and the lost South sparked Scott's interest in history and made him a Confederate sympathizer. Edward Fitzgerald went West to seek his fortune after attending Georgetown College, and he married Mollie McQuillan [FITZGERALD] of ST. PAUL at her

F. Scott Fitzgerald and his father, Edward Fitzgerald

mother's house in Washington, D.C. on February 12, 1890. By 1893 he was president of the American Rattan and Willow Works, a St. Paul furniture manufacturing company, which failed in 1898; he then worked as a wholesale grocery salesman for Procter & Gamble in BUFFALO, New York. He was transferred to SYRACUSE in 1901 and back to Buffalo in 1903. Fitzgerald's *Ledger* for August 1906 notes "His father used to drink too much and then play baseball in the back yard" (p. 160). In March 1908, at age 55, Edward Fitzgerald lost his job with Procter & Gamble. His son commented in an interview 28 years later: "That morning he had gone out a comparatively young man, a man full of strength, full of confidence. He came home that evening, an old man, a completely broken man. He had lost his essential drive, his immaculateness of purpose. He was a failure the rest of his days" (Michel Mok, "The Other Side of Paradise"; *In His Own Time,* p. 296). The Fitzgerald family returned to St. Paul in the summer of 1908, and Edward Fitzgerald unprosperously sold wholesale

groceries from the real estate office of his McQuillan brother-in-law; the family's primary source of income after Procter & Gamble was Mollie's inheritance.

In the 1920s Edward, Mollie, and Annabel Fitzgerald moved to Washington, D.C., where Edward died on January 26, 1931; his son, who was living in SWITZERLAND, returned to America for the burial. Scott Fitzgerald expressed his feelings about his father in his 1931 story "On Your Own," from which he salvaged a passage to describe Dick DIVER's feelings about his father's death in *TITN*. Fitzgerald also described his father's influence in an unfinished essay, "The Death of My Father":

> I loved my father—always deep in my subconscious I have referred judgements back to him, what he would have thought or done. He loved me—and felt a deep responsibility for me—I was born several months after the sudden death of my two elder sisters + he felt what the effect of this would be on my mother, that he would be my only moral guide. He became that to the best of his ability. He came from tired old stock with very little left of vitality and mental energy but he managed to raise a little for me. (*Apprentice Fiction*, p. 178)

Fitzgerald, Frances Scott (Scottie) (1921–1986) When strangers commiserated with the Fitzgeralds' only child about what they regarded as her irregular childhood, Scottie—the form of her name that she always used—insisted that she had been insulated from her parents' problems by good nannies and governesses. She described herself as "a pampered darling" who was not exposed to her father's alcoholism until they were in BALTIMORE during 1934–35. Before Zelda FITZGERALD's ballet work absorbed her time and energy, she constructed dollhouses and painted a series of elaborate paper dolls for Scottie. After Scottie entered the Ethel Walker School in Connecticut in 1936, when her mother was hospitalized at HIGHLAND HOSPITAL in North Carolina and her father was living in the ASHEVILLE area and then in HOLLYWOOD, Harold and Anne OBER served as her foster parents. Their house in Scarsdale, New York, became her home when she was not at boarding school and college.

Determined to prevent Scottie from repeating his academic failures, Fitzgerald attempted to supervise her education by mail; while she was at prep school and at college, he wrote stern letters of advice to her, urging her to take difficult courses and reprimanding her for her lack of seriousness. Scottie later joked that if she had known that her father's letters would be regarded as models of paternal advice after they were published, she might have read them more obediently when she received them. Her ironic stance toward her role is expressed in her introduction to *Letters to His*

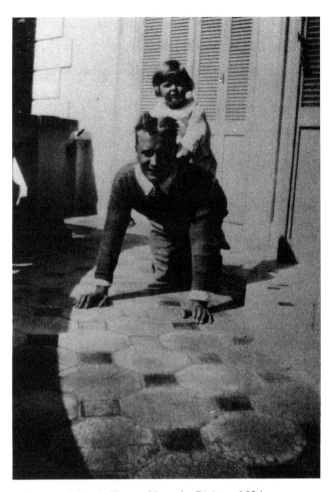

F. Scott and Scottie Fitzgerald on the Riviera, 1924

Daughter: "In my next incarnation, I may not choose again to be the daughter of a Famous Author. The pay is good, and there are fringe benefits, but the working conditions are too hazardous. People who live entirely by the fertility of their imaginations are fascinating, brilliant, and often charming, but they should be sat next to at dinner parties, not lived with" (p. ix). Despite his financial worries during the 1930s, Fitzgerald provided an expensive education with the intention of making Scottie an intellectual figure. Although she was highly intelligent, she was not a scholar: her interests and aptitudes were literary and social—like her father's. Her Vassar career resembled Fitzgerald's PRINCETON career, but she was not as irresponsible as he, and she did graduate in 1942. At college she organized the OMGIM Club (Oh, My God, It's Monday) to produce musical revues that she wrote and directed. Her song "The Right Person Won't Write" achieved Ivy League currency.

In 1943 Scottie married naval officer Samuel J. Lanahan (b. 1918), who became a lawyer. They had four

children: Timothy (1946–73), Eleanor (b. 1948), Samuel, Jr. (b. 1950), and Cecilia (b. 1951). The Lanahans moved from NEW YORK to the Washington, D.C., area in 1950. Scottie was an ardent Democrat, and politics became a consuming interest of her life. In 1952 she gave an anti-inauguration ball when Dwight D. Eisenhower defeated Adlai Stevenson.

Scottie inherited Fitzgerald's verbal fluency and wit. She worked on *The New Yorker,* the *Democratic Digest,* the *Northern Virginia Sun,* the *Washington Post,* and *The New York Times*—as well as writing and directing musical revues for Washington multiple sclerosis benefits. The demands of her family, political events, social activities, and journalism prevented Scottie from concentrating on literary work. Her novels remained unfinished, and the anticipated production of her musical about the Kennedy administration was cancelled by the assassination of the President. Her nonfiction book *Don't Quote Me: Washington Newswomen and the Power Society* (New York: Dutton, 1970) was written in collaboration with Winzola McLendon. Her play, *The Cat's Whiskers* (also titled *Love, Among Other Things*), was produced in 1988 at Auburn University in MONTGOMERY, Alabama, two years after her death.

Scottie's serious writing was impeded by a quality she shared with her father: a sense of responsibility for other people's enjoyment of life. She expended energy on her own entertainments and improved parties at which she was a guest. She cared about anyone who needed help, whether or not that person had any claim to her attention. When a wealthy friend's will failed to provide for an elderly chauffeur, Scottie put the man on retainer, although she was too afraid of his driving to ride with him.

Scottie was comfortable with a wide range of people and, like her father, had an authentic talent for being really interested in them. Among the notes for *LT/LOLT* Fitzgerald wrote a description of her style: "Scotty comes up to people when she meets them as if she were going to kiss them on the mouth, or walk right thru them, looking them straight in the eye—then stops a bare foot away and says her Hello, in a very disarming understatement of voice. This approach is her nearest to Zelda's personality. Zelda's was always a vast surprise" (*F. Scott Fitzgerald Manuscripts V,* Part 1, p. 60).

Scottie was and remains the principal patron and begetter of Fitzgerald scholarship. Following her father's death, while she was in college, Scottie resisted pressure to break up Fitzgerald's manuscripts and sell them for whatever they would fetch—not much at that time. She kept the great archive together and gave it to PRINCETON UNIVERSITY LIBRARY in 1950, thus facilitating Fitzgerald research.

Scottie became the sole heir to the Fitzgerald literary properties. She never attempted to cash in on her position as "daughter of," and she rejected all quick-money propositions for marketing her parents' names or cheapening their reputations. Scottie was secure and confident; she was able to joke about the responsibilities of "the best-paying job in the world." But she was patient, kind, and generous with literary enthusiasts as well as with scholars and students.

Scottie wrote about her parents reluctantly but well. Her introductions to *Six Tales of the Jazz Age* (1960) and *Letters to His Daughter* (1965) are admirable. In the 1970s she began working with Matthew J. BRUCCOLI on what she called "Daddy projects": *As Ever, Scott Fitz*— (1972), *Bits of Paradise* (1973), and *The Price Was High* (1979). She collaborated with Bruccoli and Joan P. Kerr on *The Romantic Egoists* (1974). She vetted Bruccoli's Fitzgerald biography, *Some Sort of Epic Grandeur* (1981), and provided the genealogical afterword.

The Lanahans' twenty-four-year marriage ended in divorce, as did Scottie's subsequent twelve-year marriage to C. Grove Smith. Scottie moved from Washington to Montgomery, Alabama, in 1973 to look after her mother's elderly sister Rosalind SAYRE Smith. In 1974 Scottie organized an exhibition of her mother's paintings at the Montgomery Museum of Art. She kept her battle against cancer from her friends' knowledge as long as possible, and she spent her final days arranging posthumous gifts. Her will created a TRUST to administer the F. Scott Fitzgerald literary properties.

Frances Scott Fitzgerald Smith was greatly loved and admired for reasons that had nothing to do with the literary fame or celebrity of her parentage.

See *In Memoriam: Frances Scott Fitzgerald Smith 1921–1986* (Privately printed, 1986) and Eleanor Lanahan, *Scottie, the Daughter of . . . : The Life of Frances Scott Fitzgerald Lanahan Smith* (New York: HarperCollins, 1995).

M. J. B.

Fitzgerald, Francis Scott Key (1896–1940) The dominant influences on F. Scott Fitzgerald were aspiration, literature, PRINCETON, Zelda Sayre FITZGERALD, and alcohol.

Francis Scott Key Fitzgerald was born in ST. PAUL, Minnesota, on September 24, 1896, the namesake and second cousin three times removed of the author of the National Anthem. His father, Edward FITZGERALD, was from Maryland, with an allegiance to the Old South and its values. Fitzgerald's mother, Mary (Mollie) McQuillan FITZGERALD, was the daughter of an Irish immigrant who became wealthy as a wholesale grocer in St. Paul. Both were Catholics.

Edward Fitzgerald failed as a manufacturer of wicker furniture in St. Paul, and he became a salesman for Procter & Gamble in upstate New York. After he was dismissed in 1908, when his son was 12, the family returned to St. Paul and lived comfortably on Mollie

Fitzgerald's inheritance. Fitzgerald attended the ST. PAUL ACADEMY; his first writing to appear in print was a detective story in the school newspaper when he was 13.

During 1911–13 he attended the NEWMAN SCHOOL, a Catholic prep school in New Jersey, where he met Father Sigourney FAY, who encouraged his ambitions for personal distinction and achievement. As a member of the PRINCETON Class of 1917, Fitzgerald neglected his studies for his literary apprenticeship. He wrote the scripts and lyrics for the TRIANGLE CLUB musicals and was a contributor to *The PRINCETON TIGER* humor magazine and *The NASSAU LITERARY MAGAZINE*. His college friends included Edmund WILSON and John Peale BISHOP. On academic probation and unlikely to graduate, Fitzgerald joined the ARMY in 1917 and was commissioned a second lieutenant in the infantry. Convinced that he would die in the war, he rapidly wrote a novel, "The Romantic Egotist"; the letter of rejection from Charles SCRIBNER's Sons praised the novel's originality and asked that it be resubmitted when revised.

In June 1918 Fitzgerald was assigned to CAMP SHERIDAN, near MONTGOMERY, Alabama. There he fell in love with a celebrated belle, 18-year-old Zelda Sayre [FITZGERALD], the youngest daughter of an Alabama Supreme Court judge. The romance intensified Fitzgerald's hopes for the success of his novel, but after revision it was rejected by Scribners a second time. The war ended just before he was to be sent overseas; after his discharge in 1919 he went to NEW YORK CITY to seek his fortune in order to marry. Unwilling to wait while Fitzgerald succeeded in the advertisement business and unwilling to live on his small salary, Zelda broke their engagement.

Fitzgerald quit his job in July 1919 and returned to St. Paul to rewrite his novel as *This Side of Paradise*; it was accepted by editor Maxwell PERKINS of Scribners in September. Set mainly at Princeton and described by its author as "a quest novel," *TSOP* traces the career aspirations and love disappointments of Amory BLAINE.

In the fall-winter of 1919 Fitzgerald commenced his career as a writer of stories for the mass-circulation magazines. Working through agent Harold OBER, Fitzgerald interrupted work on his novels to write money-making popular fiction for the rest of his life. *The SATURDAY EVENING POST* became Fitzgerald's best story market, and he was regarded as a "*Post* writer." His early commercial stories about young love introduced a fresh character: the independent, determined young

Gordon Bryant's portraits of Zelda and F. Scott Fitzgerald, c. 1921 (Arlyn Bruccoli Collection)

American woman who appeared in "The Offshore Pirate" and "Bernice Bobs Her Hair." Fitzgerald's more ambitious stories, such as "May Day" and "The Diamond as Big as the Ritz," were published in *The SMART SET*, which had a small circulation.

The publication of *This Side of Paradise* on March 26, 1920 made the 24-year-old Fitzgerald famous almost overnight, and a week later he married Zelda in New York. They embarked on an extravagant life as young celebrities. Fitzgerald endeavored to earn a solid literary reputation, but his playboy image impeded the proper assessment of his work.

After a riotous summer in WESTPORT, Connecticut, the Fitzgeralds took an apartment in New York City; there he wrote his second novel, *The Beautiful and Damned,* a naturalistic chronicle of the dissipation of Anthony and Gloria PATCH. When Zelda became pregnant, the Fitzgeralds took their first trip to EUROPE in 1921 and then settled in St. Paul for the birth of their only child: Frances Scott (Scottie) FITZGERALD was born in October 1921.

Fitzgerald expected to become affluent from his play, *The Vegetable,* in the fall of 1922 the Fitzgeralds moved to GREAT NECK, Long Island, in order to be near Broadway. The political satire—subtitled "From President to Postman"—failed at its tryout in November 1923, and Fitzgerald wrote his way out of debt with short stories. The distractions of Great Neck and New York prevented Fitzgerald from making progress on his third novel. During this time his drinking increased. Fitzgerald was an alcoholic, but he wrote sober. Zelda regularly got "tight," but she was not an alcoholic. There were frequent domestic rows, usually triggered by drinking bouts.

Literary opinion-makers were reluctant to accord Fitzgerald full marks as a serious craftsman. His reputation as a drinker fed the myth that he was an irresponsible writer, yet he was a painstaking reviser whose fiction went through layers of drafts. Fitzgerald's clear, lyrical, colorful, witty style evoked the emotions associated with time and place. His prose is recognizable by the warmth of the authorial voice. When critics objected to Fitzgerald's concern with love and success, his response was: "But, my God! it was my material, and it was all I had to deal with" (introduction to 1934 Modern Library edition of *GG; In His Own Time,* p. 156). The chief theme of Fitzgerald's work is aspiration—the idealism he regarded as defining American character. Another major theme was mutability or loss. As a social historian Fitzgerald became identified with "The Jazz Age": "It was an age of miracles, it was an age of art, it was an age of excess, and it was an age of satire."

The Fitzgeralds went to France in the spring of 1924 seeking tranquillity for his work. He wrote *The Great Gatsby* during the summer and fall in VALESCURE near ST. RAPHAËL, but the marriage was damaged by Zelda's involvement with a French naval aviator. The extent of the affair—if it was in fact consummated—is not known. On the RIVIERA the Fitzgeralds formed a close friendship with Gerald and Sara MURPHY.

The Fitzgeralds spent the winter of 1924–25 in ROME, where he revised *GG;* they were en route to PARIS from CAPRI when the novel was published in April. *GG* marked a striking advance in Fitzgerald's technique, utilizing a complex structure and a controlled narrative point of view. Fitzgerald's achievement received critical praise; however, sales of *GG* were disappointing, though the stage and movie rights brought additional income.

In Paris Fitzgerald met Ernest HEMINGWAY—then unknown outside the EXPATRIATE literary circle—with whom he formed a friendship based largely on his admiration for Hemingway's personality and genius. The Fitzgeralds remained in France until the end of 1926, alternating between Paris and the Riviera.

Fitzgerald made little progress on his fourth novel, a study of American expatriates in France, provisionally titled "The Boy Who Killed His Mother," "Our Type," and "The World's Fair." During these years Zelda's unconventional behavior became increasingly eccentric.

The Fitzgeralds returned to America to escape the distractions of France. After a short, unsuccessful stint of screenwriting in HOLLYWOOD, Fitzgerald rented "ELLERSLIE," a mansion near WILMINGTON, Delaware, in the spring of 1927. The family remained at "Ellerslie" for two years, interrupted by a visit to Paris in the summer of 1928; but Fitzgerald was still unable to make significant progress on his novel. At this time Zelda commenced ballet training, intending to become a professional dancer. In the spring of 1929 the Fitzgeralds returned to France, where Zelda's intense ballet work damaged her health and estranged them. In April 1930 she suffered her first breakdown. Zelda was treated at PRANGINS CLINIC in SWITZERLAND until September 1931, while Fitzgerald lived in Swiss hotels. Work on the novel was again suspended as he wrote short stories to pay for her psychiatric treatment.

Fitzgerald's peak story fee of $4,000 from *The SATURDAY EVENING POST* may have had in 1929 the purchasing power of $40,000 in 1994 dollars. Nonetheless, the general view of his affluence is distorted. Fitzgerald was not among the highest-paid writers of his time; his novels earned comparatively little, and most of his income before he went to Hollywood came from magazine stories. During the 1920s his income from all sources averaged under $25,000 a year—good money for that time, but not a fortune. Scott and Zelda Fitzgerald did spend money faster than he earned it; the author who wrote so eloquently about the effects of money on character was unable to manage his own finances.

The Fitzgeralds returned to America in the fall of 1931 and rented a house in Montgomery. Fitzgerald made a second unsuccessful trip to Hollywood in 1931. Zelda suffered a relapse in February 1931 and entered the PHIPPS CLINIC of JOHNS HOPKINS UNIVERSITY HOSPITAL in BALTIMORE. She spent the rest of her life as a resident or outpatient of sanitariums.

In 1932, while a patient at Phipps, Zelda rapidly wrote *Save Me the Waltz.* Her autobiographical novel generated considerable bitterness between the Fitzgeralds, for he regarded it as pre-empting the material that he was using in his novel-in-progress. Fitzgerald rented "LA PAIX," a house outside Baltimore, where he completed his fourth novel, *Tender Is the Night.* Published in 1934, his most ambitious novel was a commercial failure; and its merits were matters of critical dispute. Set in France during the 1920s, *TITN* examines the deterioration of Dick DIVER, a brilliant American psychiatrist, during the course of his marriage to a wealthy mental patient.

The 1935–37 period is known as "the crack-up" from the title of an essay Fitzgerald wrote in 1936. Ill, drunk, in debt, and unable to write commercial stories, he lived in hotels in the region near ASHEVILLE, North Carolina, where in 1936 Zelda entered HIGHLAND HOSPITAL. After Baltimore Fitzgerald did not maintain a home for Scottie. When she was 14 she went to boarding school, and the OBERS became her surrogate family. Nonetheless, Fitzgerald functioned as a concerned father by mail, attempting to supervise Scottie's education and to shape her social values.

Fitzgerald went to Hollywood alone in the summer of 1937 with a six-month Metro-Goldwyn-Mayer contract at $1,000 a week. He received his only screen credit for adapting *Three Comrades* (1938), and his contract was renewed for a year at $1,250 a week. This $91,000 from MGM was a great deal of money during the late Depression years, when a new Chevrolet coupe cost $619; nevertheless, although Fitzgerald paid off most of his debts, he was unable to save. His trips East to visit Zelda were disastrous. In California Fitzgerald fell in love with movie columnist Sheilah GRAHAM; their relationship endured despite his benders. After MGM dropped his option at the end of 1938, Fitzgerald worked as a freelance scriptwriter and wrote short-short stories for *ESQUIRE.* He began his Hollywood novel, *The Love of the Last Tycoon,* in 1939, and had written more than half of a working draft when he died of a heart attack in Graham's apartment on December 21, 1940. Zelda Fitzgerald perished in a fire in Highland Hospital in 1948.

F. Scott Fitzgerald died believing himself a failure. The obituaries were condescending, and he seemed destined for literary obscurity. The first phase of the Fitzgerald resurrection—"REVIVAL" does not properly describe the process—occurred between 1945 and 1950. By 1960 he had achieved a secure place among America's enduring writers: *The Great Gatsby,* a work that seriously examines the theme of aspiration in an American setting, defines the classic American novel.

<div align="right">M. J. B.</div>

(revised from *F. Scott Fitzgerald: A Life in Letters* [New York: Scribners, 1994] with permission of Scribner, an imprint of Simon & Schuster)

Fitzgerald/Hemingway Annual Edited by Matthew J. BRUCCOLI, 1969; Bruccoli and C. E. Frazer Clark, 1970–75; Bruccoli, 1976; Margaret M. Duggan and Richard Layman, 1977; Bruccoli and Layman, 1978–79. Washington: NCR Microcard Books, 1969–73; Englewood, Colo.: Information Handling Services, 1974–1976; Detroit: Gale Research, 1977–79. This bound volume published full-length articles, notes, and bibliographical information about Fitzgerald and Ernest HEMINGWAY.

Fitzgerald, Mary (Mollie) McQuillan (1860–1936)
Fitzgerald's mother. The eldest surviving child of Philip F. and Louisa Allen MCQUILLAN, Mollie was born in ST. PAUL, Minnesota in 1860. Her father's success as a

Fitzgerald's mother, Mollie McQuillan Fitzgerald

businessman enabled her to be educated at the Visitation Convent in St. Paul and Manhattanville in New York and to travel to EUROPE four times. On February 12, 1890 Mollie married Edward FITZGERALD at her mother's house in Washington, D.C. They had two daughters, Mary and Louise, who died in 1896 at the ages of one and three. Forty years later their son, Scott, assessed the impact of this event on his life: "Well, three months before I was born my mother lost her other two children and I think that came first of all though I don't know how it worked exactly. I think I started then to be a writer" ("Author's House," July 1936; *AOAA*, p. 184).

Scott was embarrassed by his mother, who was considered eccentric, dressed carelessly, and read sentimental and religious books, especially preferring poets Alice and Phoebe Cary (1820–71 and 1824–71). He described her as "a neurotic, half insane with pathological nervous worry" (to Maxwell PERKINS, February 20, 1926; *Life in Letters*, p. 138; *Scott/Max*, p. 135). Edward Fitzgerald's lack of success in business was one source of Mollie's anxiety; her money supplemented his income. She spoiled Scott, who later believed her indulgence had weakened his character. She discouraged his literary ambitions and destroyed most of his juvenilia: "My mother did me the disservice of throwing away all but two of my very young efforts—way back at twelve and thirteen, and later I found that the surviving fragments had more quality than some of the stuff written in the tightened-up days of seven or eight years later" (to Morton Kroll, August 9, 1939; *Letters*, p. 593).

Fitzgerald's second story collection, *Tales of the Jazz Age* (1922) was dedicated "QUITE INAPPROPRIATELY TO MY MOTHER." Mollie visited her son in PARIS in May 1931; the anxiety she expressed about him in her visits to "LA PAIX" irritated him. He began borrowing money from her in the summer of 1933.

Mollie, who had been living in Washington, suffered a stroke in June 1936. Fitzgerald moved her to a nursing home; after going through her possessions, he wrote to his sister, Annabel FITZGERALD: "Mother and I never had anything in common except a relentless stubborn quality, but when I saw all this it turned me inside out realizing how unhappy her temperament made her and how she clung, to the end, to all things that would remind her of moments of snatched happiness" (August 1936?; *Life in Letters*, p. 306). Mollie died in early September; Fitzgerald, who had a broken shoulder, was unable to attend her funeral. Before her death he had written an obituary story, "An Author's Mother," about an old woman who doesn't understand the modern world or her son's books; the story was published in ESQUIRE in September 1936. He later wrote about his mother: "She was a defiant old woman, defiant in her love for me in spite of my neglect of her, and it would have been quite within her character

to have died that I might live" (to Beatrice DANCE, September 15, 1936; *Letters*, p. 541).

Fitzgerald, Michael (d. 1855) Fitzgerald's paternal grandfather, husband of Cecilia Ashton Scott FITZGERALD. Almost nothing is known about him, but he may have kept a general store in Maryland. He died when his son, Edward FITZGERALD, was two years old.

Fitzgerald Newsletter Edited by Matthew J. BRUCCOLI and published quarterly (1958–68) to provide "a journal that would be open to both amateur and professional readers of Fitzgerald and that would attempt to record all references to Fitzgerald in the media of communication," with special attention to "Fitzgerald activity in the rare-book market." Superseded by the *Fitzgerald/Hemingway Annual*. The 40 issues of the *Fitzgerald Newsletter* were collected and revised in a 1969 volume (Washington: NCR Microcard Books).

Fitzgerald, Zelda Sayre (1900–1948) Zelda Sayre was born in MONTGOMERY, Alabama, on July 24, 1900. She was the youngest of five surviving children born to Minnie Machen SAYRE, the artistically inclined daughter of a Kentucky Senator, and Anthony Dickinson SAYRE, a judge who later served on the Alabama Supreme Court. She was named for a gypsy heroine in a novel, possibly *Zelda: A Tale of the Massachusetts Colony* (1866) by Jane Howard or *Zelda's Fortune* (1874) by Robert Edward Francillon (1841–1919). As a child, Zelda was free-spirited and undisciplined, enjoying the protection from censure that her socially privileged family afforded her. She was highly popular for her beauty and her fun-loving rebelliousness, and she graduated from Sidney Lanier High School in May 1918 having been voted "Prettiest" and "Most Attractive" in her class.

In July 1918 she met F. Scott Fitzgerald at the country club in Montgomery, and he noted in his *Ledger* that he fell in love with her on September 7 (p. 173). Their relationship became an informal engagement, which Zelda broke off in June 1919 because of her doubts about Fitzgerald's ability to provide for her. She was reassured by the acceptance for publication of *This Side of Paradise* and Fitzgerald's first magazine short stories. They were married in a small ceremony at St. Patrick's Cathedral in NEW YORK CITY on April 3, 1920, a week after the release of the novel.

The Fitzgeralds were almost immediately swept into a heady lifestyle of fame and success. Zelda inspired many of her husband's female characters. In his *Ledger* he recorded her words immediately after the birth of their daughter, Frances Scott (Scottie) FITZGERALD on October 26, 1921: "Oh God, goofo I'm drunk. Mark Twain. Isn't she smart—she has the hiccups. I hope its beautiful and a fool—a beautiful little fool" (p. 176);

Fitzgerald later ascribed the last part of this statement to Daisy BUCHANAN in *The Great Gatsby*. Zelda also occasionally offered advice on his work; for example, in December 1921 Fitzgerald wired his editor, Maxwell PERKINS, that she had suggested cutting the ending of *The Beautiful and Damned,* which in serial had concluded with a passage about Anthony and Gloria PATCH's idealism (*Correspondence,* p. 89). In her review of *B&D,* she asserted: "It seems to me that on one page I recognized a portion of an old diary of mine which mysteriously disappeared shortly after my marriage, and also scraps of letters which, though considerably edited, sound to me vaguely familiar. In fact, Mr. Fitzgerald—I believe that is how he spells his name—seems to believe that plagiarism begins at home" ("Friend Husband's Latest," *New York Tribune,* April 2, 1922, Section 5, p. 11; *FSF: The Critical Reception,* p. 111). Fitzgerald did use bits of her diary and letters for *B&D,* and later incorporated material from her letters in *TITN.* But she was not his collaborator. Fitzgerald contributed to some of her stories and essays, mainly in revision; but his work was his own.

In the summer of 1924, while the Fitzgeralds were living on the RIVIERA in France, their marriage suffered a serious crisis when Zelda became romantically inter-

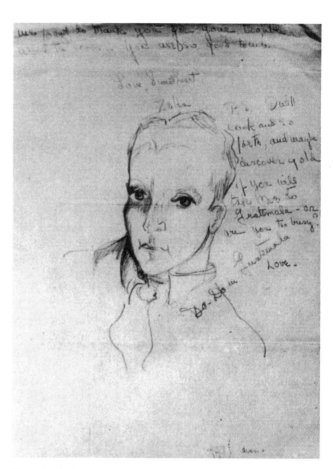

Portrait of Fitzgerald by his wife, 1934 (Princeton University Library)

ested in Edouard JOZAN, a French naval aviator. It is impossible to determine whether the affair was consummated, but it was nevertheless a damaging breach of trust. Zelda was similarly wounded in 1927 when Fitzgerald carried on a flirtation with Lois MORAN, a young actress. Fitzgerald admitted that part of his attraction to Moran was that she used her artistic talents constructively; this implied criticism made Zelda determined to accomplish something for herself.

In the summer of 1927, while the Fitzgeralds were living at "ELLERSLIE" near WILMINGTON, Delaware, Zelda began commuting to Philadelphia for dancing lessons with Catherine Littlefield (1904–51), director of the Philadelphia Opera Ballet. She had taken lessons as a child and had appeared in several local performances, but now she returned to ballet in earnest. In 1928 the Fitzgeralds spent the summer in PARIS, where Zelda studied with celebrated ballerina Lubov EGOROVA. But she was too old at 28 to become a first-rate dancer, though she punished her body in strenuous efforts to improve. She also turned to writing stories for *COLLEGE HUMOR,* hoping to earn the money for her lessons (*See* FITZGERALD, ZELDA—WRITINGS OF).

Self-portrait by Zelda Fitzgerald, c. 1932 (Princeton University Library)

Zelda Fitzgerald's gouache illustration of "The Lobster Quadrille" from Alice in Wonderland (Arlyn Bruccoli Collection)

She was a competent enough dancer to receive an offer in September 1929 from the San Carlo Opera Ballet Company in Naples, including a solo role in *Aïda*; but for unknown reasons, she declined. In April 1930 she broke down from the strain of her ballet work.

Friends had previously noticed some nervous habits and the erratic turns her conversations would take, but by 1930 her behavior was obsessive and out of control. She was hospitalized first at MALMAISON CLINIC near Paris, and then in VAL-MONT and PRANGINS in SWITZER-LAND. She suffered hallucinations and became suicidal; she also suffered physically from bouts of severe eczema and asthma. Dr. Oscar FOREL, an expert in mental illness, diagnosed her as schizophrenic. From this time forward, her medical expenses were a spur for Fitzgerald to maintain his short-story income, as he was determined that she should have the best care available. She was discharged from Prangins in September 1931, but in February 1932 she experienced a relapse and entered the PHIPPS CLINIC at the JOHNS HOPKINS UNIVERSITY HOSPITAL in BALTIMORE for a four-month stay. During her first six weeks there she wrote her novel, *Save Me the Waltz*, which was published on October 7, 1932. She also wrote a play, *Scandalabra,* that fall. She was hospitalized periodically for the rest of her life, in clinics in Baltimore and New York, and finally in HIGHLAND HOSPITAL in ASHEVILLE, North Carolina.

Several of the Fitzgeralds' long letters in the early 1930s to one another and to Zelda's psychiatrists show the couple trying to analyze what had happened to their marriage and their lives. The letters are sometimes recriminatory, but many emphasize the depth of the love that remained. In 1932, Fitzgerald wrote to Dr. Mildred SQUIRES, who was treating Zelda at Phipps Clinic: "Perhaps fifty percent of our friends and relatives would tell you in all honest conviction that my drinking drove Zelda insane—the other half would assure you that her insanity drove me to drink. Niether judgement would mean anything" (c. March 20, 1932; *Life in Letters,* p. 211). Two years earlier he had written to Zelda in a letter that may not have been sent: "We ruined ourselves—I have never honestly thought that we ruined each other" (Summer? 1930; *Life in Letters,* p. 189).

Besides writing and dancing, Zelda sought to express herself artistically through painting. When her hopes of becoming a dancer subsided, she returned to paint-

ing in earnest. She worked in watercolors, gouache, and oils; flowers were a favorite subject, as were religious themes. Fitzgerald helped to arrange for a showing of her work from March 29 to April 30, 1934: 13 paintings and 15 drawings were exhibited jointly with photographs by Dr. Marion Hines (1889–1982) of the Johns Hopkins Medical School in the New York gallery of Cary ROSS; there was also a smaller exhibit at the Hotel Algonquin. Among the paintings were two portraits of Fitzgerald, now lost. Many of Zelda's artworks have been destroyed. In 1942 she donated paintings to servicemen at CAMP SHERIDAN who could not afford materials; she intended for them to reuse the canvases. After her death, others were lost when a fire consumed the shed where they were stored. Some 100 works have survived, several of which are reproduced in *The Romantic Egoists* and in *Zelda, An Illustrated Life: The Private World of Zelda Fitzgerald.*

In 1940, Zelda moved to Montgomery to live quietly with her mother, returning to Highland Hospital as needed. She was at Highland on March 10, 1948 when a fire broke out, trapping and killing her and eight other women. She was buried with Fitzgerald in Rockville Union Cemetery in Maryland. In 1975 Scottie Fitzgerald Smith obtained permission for her parents to be reinterred in the Fitzgerald family plot at St. Mary's Church in ROCKVILLE.

by Tracy Simmons Bitonti

Fitzgerald, Zelda—Writings of Zelda FITZGERALD's desire for a creative identity of her own led her in three directions: she danced; she painted; and she wrote—stories, articles, a play, and a novel. She did not receive serious critical consideration as a writer during her lifetime, and only began to attract some scholarly notice when her novel, *Save Me the Waltz,* was republished in 1967 and 10 of her stories were collected in *Bits of Paradise* in 1974. The 1991 Scribners volume of her *Collected Writings* made all of her surviving completed work readily available for reassessment.

Zelda's writing career began with light articles commissioned as "celebrity pieces." The first of these was a 1922 "review" of *The Beautiful and Damned* for the *New York Tribune.* Her nonfiction was mostly witty commentaries on topics of the times, such as marriage and flappers: "Flapper wasn't a particularly fortunate cognomen. It is far too reminiscent of open galoshes and covered-up ears and all other proverbial flapper paraphernalia, which might have passed unnoticed save for the name" ("What Became of the Flappers?", *MCCALL'S,* 1925; *Collected Writings,* p. 397). Some of her work appeared under a joint byline with her husband because magazines insisted, although he recorded in his *Ledger* (p. 143) which pieces were hers. He analyzed

the "joint" pieces in a June 13, 1934 letter to Zelda in which he proposed a collection of her work, noting that one of her stories ("A Millionaire's Girl") "appeared under my name but actually I had nothing to do with it except for suggesting a theme and working on the proof of the completed manuscript. This same cooperation extends to other material gathered herein under our joint names, though often when published in that fashion I had nothing to do with the thing from start to finish except supplying my name" (*Correspondence,* p. 368). Two 1934 autobiographical essays for *ESQUIRE,* "Show Mr. and Mrs. F. to Number ——" and "Auction—Model 1934," were collaborations that present catalogues of their shared experiences.

Zelda also began writing short stories, studying her husband's work for technique and seeking his advice.

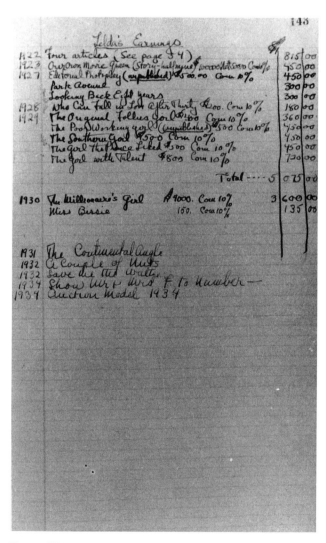

Fitzgerald's record in his Ledger *of his wife's literary sales* (Washington, D.C.: NCR Microcard Books/Bruccoli Clark, 1973)

Her first story, "Our Own Movie Queen," was revised by Fitzgerald and published under his name in 1925 (*Chicago Sunday Tribune*). In 1929 COLLEGE HUMOR commissioned a series of six stories about different types of girls, to be published under a joint byline, although they were not collaborations. This series included "The Original Follies Girl," "Southern Girl," "The Girl the Prince Liked," "The Girl with Talent," "A Millionaire's Girl," and "Poor Working Girl." "A Millionaire's Girl" was published as an F. Scott Fitzgerald story in *The SATURDAY EVENING POST*, where it brought $4,000, as opposed to the $400–800 the "joint" stories earned. There are records in the files of the Fitzgeralds' literary agent, Harold OBER, of eight additional Zelda Fitzgerald stories that were rejected by magazines such as *Delineator, Harper's Bazaar,* the *Post,* and SCRIBNER'S MAGAZINE (see Bruccoli, "Zelda Fitzgerald's Lost Stories," *Fitzgerald/Hemingway Annual* (1979), pp. 123–126).

In "Rivalry and Partnership: The Short Fiction of Zelda Sayre Fitzgerald" (*Fitzgerald/Hemingway Annual* (1977), pp. 19–42), W. R. Anderson traces the development of Zelda's literary technique in her stories, suggesting that she was gaining increasing control of aspects such as narrative perspective, description, and irony. "Miss Ella," published in *Scribner's* in 1931 and admired by editor Maxwell PERKINS, is the highly descriptive story of the tragedy behind a Southern woman's spinsterhood. The story is full of sensory details: "Upstairs, Miss Ella was deep in the cedar and lavender of a new trunk; fine linen nightgowns and drawnwork chemises were lifted preciously into the corners and little silk puffs of sachet perched tentatively over the newness" (*Collected Writings,* p. 348). "A Couple of Nuts" was her last published story, appearing in *Scribner's* in 1932 and depicting the dissipation of a married pair of entertainers in EUROPE. Thematically, this story is similar to some of F. Scott Fitzgerald's concerns—a marriage that self-destructs, and corruption under the glamor of "high society."

Zelda's continuing need to be a writer in her own right also produced her novel, *Save Me the Waltz,* written mainly in PHIPPS CLINIC in 1932. The book was not well received by readers or critics, who had difficulty with her unusual style. Maxwell Perkins had warned her (in an unpublished letter now in the Scribners Archives, PRINCETON UNIVERSITY LIBRARY) about her tendency to use too many metaphors that call attention to themselves rather than make an effective comparison. She also used words because she liked their sound. Many sentences require close attention; for example, her depiction of dancing at a party: "Spare, immaculate legs and a consciousness of rib, the vibrant suspension of lean bodies precipitated on the jolt of reiterant rhythmic shock, the violins' hysteria, evolved them-

selves to a tortured abstraction of sex" (*Collected Writings,* p. 106). But there are also some surprising gems embedded in her prose. For example, one characteristic of her description is synesthesia, a blending of the senses, as in her recital of flowers which heroine Alabama Beggs buys, including "cold blue hydrangeas clean as a newly calcimined wall, the crystalline drops of lily of the valley, a bowl of nasturtiums like beaten brass . . . lemon-yellow carnations perfumed with the taste of hard candy . . . the soft, even purr of black tulips" (*Collected Writings,* p. 130).

Fitzgerald had been furious about the first draft of *Save Me the Waltz,* which he felt was too openly autobiographical and too close to the material he wanted to use in *Tender Is the Night.* He was satisfied with Zelda's subsequent revisions, but he put limitations on what she could write next. The result was a play, *Scandalabra,* written in 1932 and performed for six nights by the VAGABOND JUNIOR PLAYERS in BALTIMORE in 1933. Billed as "A Farce Fantasy in a Prologue and Three Acts," it is uneven.

Zelda eventually began a second novel, "Caesar's Things," which occupied the last few years of her life. Nancy Milford describes this unfinished, fragmentary work in her biography, *Zelda,* adding that it can be read as "a fantasized memoir, a sort of parable about madness itself" (p. 409). The work also reflects Zelda's religiosity—she wrote to a friend about her "thematic intent of inducting the Biblical pattern of life into its everyday manifestations" (Milford, p. 354). The existing 135 pages of chapters and fragments depict the childhood and marriage of the heroine, Janno, including her strange visions, which make the novel "wildly incoherent" (Milford, p. 355).

by Tracy Simmons Bitonti

Fitzpatrick, Al Character in "The Love Boat." Mae PURLEY's date to the high school dance on the boat and later her husband.

Flagg, James Montgomery (1877–1960) One of the most famous American illustrators, Flagg painted the popular World War I recruiting poster depicting Uncle Sam pointing a finger with the caption "Uncle Sam Wants You!" He illustrated two Fitzgerald stories: "The Curious Case of Benjamin Button" (COLLIER'S, May 27, 1922) and "Diamond Dick and the First Law of Woman" (HEARST'S INTERNATIONAL, April 1924). An accomplished portrait painter, Flagg provided drawings of F. Scott and Zelda FITZGERALD for her article "Looking Back Eight Years" (COLLEGE HUMOR, June 1928).

See Susan E. Meyer, *James Montgomery Flagg* (New York: Watson-Guptill Publications, 1974).

by Park Bucker

Flappers and Philosophers Story collection. New York: Charles SCRIBNER'S Sons, 1920; London: Collins, 1922. Dedication: "TO ZELDA." Contents: "The Offshore Pirate," "The Ice Palace," "Head and Shoulders," "The Cut-Glass Bowl," "Bernice Bobs Her Hair," "Benediction," "Dalyrimple Goes Wrong," "The Four Fists." Published on September 10, 1920 in a first printing of 5,000 copies at $1.75, with a dust jacket illustrated by W. E. HILL (*see* p. 18). Fitzgerald's first story collection sold well—by November 1922 there were six printings totalling 15,325 copies—but received mixed reviews. H. L. MENCKEN called Fitzgerald "curiously ambidextrous" and was one of the earliest critics to note the split between his roles as entertainer and serious novelist (*The* SMART SET, 63 [December 1920], 140; *F. Scott Fitzgerald: The Critical Reception*, p. 48). Fitzgerald sent Mencken an inscribed copy of *Flappers and Philosophers* with his own ranking of the stories: "Worth reading: 'The Ice Palace,' 'The Cut Glass Bowl,' 'Benediction,' 'Dalyrimple Goes Wrong'; Amusing: 'The Offshore Pirate'; Trash: 'Head + Shoulders,' 'The Four Fists,' 'Bernice Bobs her Hair' (*Life in Letters*, p. 42). Other titles which Fitzgerald considered for *Flappers and Philosophers* were "We are Seven," "Table D'hote," "A La Carte," "Journeys and Journey's End," "Bittersweet," and "Short Cake."

Flieshacker, Mort Character in *LT/LOLT*. Company lawyer for the studio. Fitzgerald's notes for the unwritten episodes indicate that Cecelia BRADY was to have an affair with Flieshacker after Monroe STAHR broke off his relationship with her.

"Flight and Pursuit" Fiction. Written April 1931. *The* SATURDAY EVENING POST, 204 (May 14, 1932), 16–17, 53, 57; *The Price Was High*. Virginia belle Caroline Martin [CORCORAN] elopes with George CORCORAN after she is jilted by Sidney LAHAYE. George and Caroline move to Ohio to live with his mother, Mrs. CORCORAN, who dislikes Caroline. After three years of unhappiness Caroline receives a telephone call from Lahaye, whom she tells to leave her alone. When the phone rings again the next day she takes her young son, Dexter CORCORAN, and runs away. Two years later Caroline, who is working in NEW YORK as a stenographer, encounters Lahaye while visiting her friend Evelyn MURDOCK and rebukes him for his treatment of her. A few months later she takes a job as private secretary and traveling companion to Helen O'CONNOR. During her three years' employment with Mrs. O'Connor, Caroline begins to drink and stay out late; and she contracts tuberculosis. Lahaye, who had employed Mrs. O'Connor to hire Caroline, shows up and takes Caroline to a sanitorium, where she begins to recuperate. Several months later, when Caroline reads

in the newspaper that Lahaye may be lost at sea, she realizes that she loves him. She then receives a telegram that he is alive; and she summons him to her, declaring her love.

Flint, Bill Character in "The Family Bus." Man who tells Dick HENDERSON that the Henderson family car is one of six with a special intake manifold that the manufacturer's engineers are eager to see.

Flowing Boots Characters in "Tarquin of Cheepside." Two men who are pursuing SOFT SHOES.

Flynn, Maurice ("Lefty") and Nora (1893–1959 and 1890?–1955) Friends of Fitzgerald in TRYON, North Carolina, where he lived in February 1935; Scottie FITZGERALD stayed with the Flynns while her father lived at the OAK HALL HOTEL. Nora Flynn, a sister of Lady Astor (1879–1964), unsuccessfully urged Fitzgerald to try Christian Science treatment for his alcoholism. Lefty, a former Yale football hero, movie actor, and naval aviator, had trouble with alcohol and was on the wagon. The musically talented Flynns performed for their friends, and Fitzgerald's 1935 story "The Intimate Strangers" is based on the Flynns (see *Notebooks* #928). On October 28, 1936 Fitzgerald wrote to his childhood friend, Marie HERSEY Hamm, about Nora: "During the mood of depression that I seem to have fallen into about a year ago she was a saint to me; took care of Scottie for a month one time under the most peculiar circumstances, and is altogether, in my opinion, one of the world's most delightful women" (*Letters*, p. 546).

" 'Football' " Verse. *The* NEWMAN NEWS, 9 (Christmas 1911?), 19; *In His Own Time*; *Poems*. Fitzgerald wrote this 36-line poem, his first known contribution to *The Newman News*, after disgracing himself on the football field. Years later he explained the circumstances:

> I remember the desolate ride in the bus back to the train and the desolate ride back to school with everybody thinking I had been yellow on the occasion, when actually I was just distracted and sorry for the opposing end. That's the truth. I've been afraid plenty of times but that wasn't one of the times. The point is it inspired me to write a poem for the school paper which made me as big a hit with my father as if I had become a football hero. So when I went home that Christmas vacation it was in my mind that if you weren't able to function in action you might at least be able to tell about it, because you felt the same intensity—it was a back door way out of facing reality. ("Author's House," July 1936; *AOAA*, pp. 185–186)

"For Sheilah, a Beloved Infidel" *See* "To a Beloved Infidel."

Forel, Dr. Oscar (b. 1891) Psychiatrist who came to VAL-MONT CLINIC in GLION, SWITZERLAND for a consultation about Zelda FITZGERALD on June 3, 1930. He diagnosed her as a schizophrenic and agreed to treat her at his clinic, Les Rives de PRANGINS at NYON, Switzerland, on the condition that she agree to the transfer and to a temporary separation from her husband. She entered the clinic on June 5 and remained there for 15 months. Dr. Forel was convinced that Zelda's recovery required that she abandon her hopes for a ballet career; he asked Fitzgerald to ask her teacher, Lubov EGOROVA, for an assessment of her talent, hoping that the reply would be discouraging. Egorova's response, though not as negative as expected, was disappointing to Zelda. Dr. Forel recommended that Fitzgerald stop drinking, but Fitzgerald denied Zelda's claim that his drinking was responsible for her collapse. The correspondence between Fitzgerald and Forel on this and other matters indicates that Fitzgerald considered himself a consultant on his wife's case.

Forel, the son of noted psychiatrist August Forel (1848–1931), was on the faculty at the University of Geneva from 1925 to 1953. His books include *La Psychologie des neuroses* (1925) and *Manuel de Psychiatrie* (1940). Later in his life he became a naturalist and professional photographer; in 1945 Charles de Gaulle awarded him the Legion of Honor. Forel's autobiography, *La Mémoire du chêne,* was published in 1980.

"Forging Ahead" Fiction—Basil Duke LEE story. Written January 1929. *The SATURDAY EVENING POST,* 201 (March 30, 1929), 12–13, 101, 105; *AOAA; B&J.* Basil Duke Lee, age 16, decides to work his way through Yale after his mother tells him she can't afford to send him there. After a two-day stint at a railroad job, Basil takes a summer job at his uncle Benjamin REILLY's wholesale drug company. Escorting Reilly's unattractive step-daughter, Rhoda SINCLAIR, turns out to be part of the job. Minnie BIBBLE, who is visiting in town, doesn't understand why Basil pays so little attention to her; but when Basil's family's improved finances free him from the necessity of pleasing his uncle, he and Minnie are reunited.

Forney, Edward Character in "The Honor of the Goon." College dean whom Mister LEI CHAMORO confronts with the insults his relative, Ella LEI CHAMORO, has suffered from fellow students.

Forrest, Mrs. Hugh Character in "A Freeze-Out." Forrest WINSLOW's great-grandmother, a sensible and "entirely solid" woman who does her duty.

Forrester, Frank Character in "Indecision." Emily ELLIOT's cousin, who tells Tommy MCLANE that Emily thinks her ex-husband is spying on her.

Fort Leavenworth, Kansas Second Lieutenant F. Scott Fitzgerald reported for training at Fort Leavenworth on November 20, 1917; Dwight D. Eisenhower (1890–1969) was the captain in charge of his training platoon, but there is no record of how they responded to one another. Fitzgerald began writing "The Romantic Egotist," an early version of *TSOP,* while stationed there, writing during study period until he was caught, then writing in the officers' club from 1:00 p.m. to midnight on Saturdays and 6:00 a.m. to 6:00 p.m. on Sundays. He completed his novel at the COTTAGE CLUB at PRINCETON while on leave at the end of February 1918 and reported to CAMP ZACHARY TAYLOR on March 15.

fortune-teller (unnamed) Character in "Fate in Her Hands." Based on Laura GUTHRIE. Palmist who makes three predictions about Carol [KASTLER] which influence Carol's decisions and actions over the next several years.

Fossile, Chief Justice Character in *The Vegetable.* Supreme Court justice who pronounces the sentence of impeachment on President Jerry FROST.

"The Four Fists" Fiction. Written May 1919. *SCRIBNER'S MAGAZINE,* 67 (June 1920), 669–680; *F&P.* Samuel MEREDITH's character is progressively improved when he is punched four times over the course of two decades. His prep-school roommate, Gilly HOOD, hits him for being spoiled and generally unpleasant. While in college, he is punched by a WORKMAN at whom he snobbishly sneers for refusing to give up his horse-car seat to a woman. Several years after college, Meredith becomes involved with MARJORIE, a married woman whose husband hits him when he finds Meredith with Marjorie. While in his early thirties, Meredith is sent to the Southwest by his employer, Peter CARHART, to handle the forcible purchase of 17 adjoining ranches from their reluctant owners. After MCINTYRE, the leader of the ranchers, hits him, Meredith refuses to conclude the underhanded business and is promoted to be Carhart's partner.

Fitzgerald told one admirer that this story was written in financial desperation in order to give the magazine what it wanted. He told another correspondent that he disliked "The Four Fists" more than all but one of his stories because it was "so preachy + righteous" (Fall 1920; *Correspondence* p. 71).

Fowler, John Jackson Character in "John Jackson's Arcady." Mr. FOWLER's son, whom he named for his boss, John JACKSON.

Fowler, Ludlow (1897?–1961) Wealthy PRINCETON student, Townsend MARTIN's roommate, whom Fitzgerald met through his work with the TRIANGLE CLUB. Fowler served as best man at Fitzgerald's wedding and was part of the group of friends the newlywed Fitzgeralds partied with in NEW YORK. Fowler was the model for Anson HUNTER in "The Rich Boy" (January & February 1926). Fitzgerald wrote to him: "I have written a fifteen thousand word story about you called *The Rich Boy*—it is so disguised that no one except you and me and maybe two of the girls concerned would recognize, unless you give it away, but it is in large measure the story of your life, toned down here and there and symplified. Also many gaps had to come out of my imagination. It is frank, unsparing but sympathetic and I think you will like it—it is one of the best things I have ever one" (March 1925; *Correspondence*, p. 152). Fitzgerald sent a copy of the story to Fowler before its publication in REDBOOK, but he was unable to make the cuts Fowler requested until its appearance in *All the Sad Young Men*.

Fowler, Mr. Character in "John Jackson's Arcady." John JACKSON's chief clerk, who named his son for Jackson and who offers tribute to him at the Civic Welfare League meeting.

Fragelle, Gen. Sir Evelyne Character in "One Trip Abroad." Englishman who is outraged when Nelson KELLY turns on the hotel's electric piano again after Lady FRAGELLE turns it off.

Fragelle, Lady Character in "One Trip Abroad." Englishwoman who turns off the hotel's electric piano, which Nelson KELLY is playing.

France, Anatole (1844–1922) Nobel Prize–winning French novelist whom Fitzgerald admired; author of *Penguin Island* (1908) and *The Revolt of the Angels* (1914). On May 17, 1921 the Fitzgeralds unsuccessfully waited outside his house in PARIS for a glimpse of him. Fitzgerald invoked France in a December 10, 1921 letter to Maxwell PERKINS defending his inclusion of Maury NOBLE's skeptical account of the Bible in B&D. Fitzgerald included *Thaïs* (1890) in his April 1923 list of "10 Best Books I Have Read." In the opening of "The Offshore Pirate" (May 1920), Ardita FARNAM is reading *The Revolt of the Angels*.

Franklin, Sidney (1893–1972) MGM producer and director with whom Fitzgerald briefly worked on *Marie Antoinette* in 1938 and on *Madame Curie* in 1938–39. Fitzgerald used conversations between Franklin and novelist Aldous Huxley (1894–1963) as the basis for

Monroe STAHR's advice to George BOXLEY about screenwriting in *LT/LOLT*. See Kevin Brownlow, "The Modest Pioneer: Sidney A. Franklin," *Focus on Film*, no. 10 (Summer 1972), pp. 30–41.

Fraser, Alfred J. Character in "Dalyrimple Goes Wrong." Influential man who offers to put Bryan DALYRIMPLE in the State Senate.

Freeman Character in *TITN*. Black restaurateur in PARIS who is arrested when he is mistakenly identified as the man who stole some money from Abe NORTH. Morley CALLAGHAN notes in *That Summer in Paris* (New York: Coward-McCann, 1963) that Fitzgerald was involved in a similar experience, accusing the wrong man of stealing his wallet in a nightclub (p. 191).

"A Freeze-Out" Fiction. Written September 1931. *The SATURDAY EVENING POST*, 204 (December 19, 1931), 6–7, 84–85, 88–89; *The Price Was High*. Pierce and Charlotte WINSLOW discuss Chauncey RIKKER, who had gone bankrupt and left town and was later involved in various scandals and imprisoned for contempt of court, but who is rich again and has returned to town. Pierce Winslow and his son, Forrest WINSLOW, both decide to blackball Rikker from the Kennemore Club. Forrest changes his mind because he doesn't want to punish Rikker's beautiful daughter, Alida RIKKER; and his father backs down because he owes a favor to Walter HANNAN, the Rikkers' social sponsor. Despite his family's prejudice against the Rikkers, Forrest falls in love with Alida and wants to marry her. He knows his parents will disapprove; but his great-grandmother, Mrs. Hugh FORREST, tells him to marry her if she has a good character. Chauncey moves out of his parents' house and plans a small private wedding. His mother and sister plan to attend, but only at the last minute does his father decide to go so he won't be laughed at. Old Mrs. Forrest calls Alida after the wedding to wish her happiness and is satisfied that she has fulfilled her duty.

"The Freshest Boy" Fiction—Basil Duke LEE story. Written April 1928. *The SATURDAY EVENING POST*, 201 (July 28, 1928), 6–7, 68, 70, 73; *TAR*; *B&J*. Basil Duke Lee, age 15, is called "Bossy" and is extremely unpopular during his first year at ST. REGIS. After attending a play in NEW YORK he overhears an unhappy conversation between football star Ted FAY and an actress named JERRY, and he realizes that life is difficult even for apparently successful people. He thus forgoes a trip to EUROPE, which would have removed him from his painful school experience, because he is unwilling to give up his dream of "the conquest of the successive worlds of school, college and New York" (*TAR*, p. 50).

Back at school, some of his fellow students are a bit friendlier to him; and he gains the nickname "Lee-y."

Friar Brian *See* BROTHER BRIAN.

"Friend Husband's Latest" Review of *B&D* by Zelda FITZGERALD. *New York Tribune,* April 2, 1922, magazine section, p. 11; *Zelda Fitzgerald: The Collected Writings.* Zelda Fitzgerald's first professional publication. Although the review was partly a joke, she criticized the intellectual pretentiousness of her husband's second novel.

Frost, Charlotte Character in *The Vegetable.* Jerry FROST's nagging wife, age 30, who rebukes him for his lack of ambition. *"She talks in a pessimistic whine and, with a sort of dowdy egotism, considers herself generally in the right"* (p. 11).

Frost, Horatio *See* DADA.

Frost, Jerry (Jeremiah) Character in *The Vegetable.* Thirty-five-year-old railroad clerk whose childhood ambition was to be a postman but who has no ambition left. In an alcoholic fantasy he becomes President of the United States until he is impeached for appointing his father, DADA, Secretary of the Treasury. He briefly leaves his nagging wife, Charlotte FROST, to become a postman, which completely changes him and makes him confident. He brags, "I'm new but I'm good. . . . I'm the best one they ever had" (p. 133).

Frothington, Bill Character in "The Love Boat." One of three young Harvard graduates who board a boat where a high school dance is being held. He falls in love with Mae PURLEY but marries Stella [FROTHINGTON], a girl of his own social class.

Frothington, Mrs. Character in "The Love Boat." Bill FROTHINGTON's mother, who urges him not to disgrace the family name by marrying Mae PURLEY.

Frothington, Stella Character in "The Love Boat." Girl whom Bill FROTHINGTON marries despite his earlier attraction to Mae PURLEY.

Fulham, Mrs. Myra Character in "The Pierian Springs and the Last Straw." Woman who rejected George ROMBERT 15 years before and who despises him for letting her treat him like a dog. She later elopes with George the night before she is to marry another man.

"A Full Life" Fiction. Written c. 1936–37. *The Princeton University Library Chronicle,* 49 (Winter 1988), 158–172. Gwendolyn DAVIES is treated in the emergency room by Dr. Harvey WILKINSON when she jumps from a 53rd-story window in an inflatable rubber suit and is injured; she leaves the hospital abruptly and denies her name. Dr. Wilkinson recognizes her as the girl he had read about who had vanished from her hometown of Delphis, New York. Five years later he reads a newspaper report of a Comptesse de Frejus, the former Mrs. Cornelius B. Hasbrouk, jumping from an ocean liner, and recognizes her as the same woman. Nine years later he attends her performance as "the human shell" when she is shot out of a cannon. While he is questioning her about her past, she explodes and he is killed. Fitzgerald's working title for this story was "The Vanished Girl."

"Fun in an Artist's Studio" Fiction—Pat HOBBY story. Submitted June 25, 1940. *ESQUIRE,* 15 (February 1941), 64, 112; *PH.* Studio executive Mr. DE TINC persuades Pat Hobby to pose for Princess DIGNANNI, a painter. Pat keeps asking her whether she wants him to pose naked and whether she has ever painted a naked man. When he continues to make sexual suggestions, she calls in a police officer and says Pat had agreed to pose nude and is now refusing. When Pat has undressed and has only a turkish towel, his face again wears the expression that had originally intrigued her and made her want to paint him.

G

Gallup, Doctor Roswell Character in "The Unspeakable Egg." Psychiatrist who is hired to treat Fifi MARSDEN.

Galt, Mr. Character in "The Third Casket." Cyrus GIRARD's general manager, who sends Rip JONES to Chicago to handle some silver shipments.

Garden of Allah Hotel at 8152 Sunset Boulevard in HOLLYWOOD on property originally belonging to silent movie star Alla Nazimova (1879–1945). Fitzgerald rented half a bungalow for $400 a month from July 1937 to April 1938; screenwriter Edwin Justus MAYER lived in the other half. Fitzgerald met Sheilah GRAHAM on July 14, 1937 at a party which Robert BENCHLEY gave at the Garden of Allah to celebrate her engagement to the Marquess of Donegal.

Gardener, Nancy Childhood sweetheart whom Fitzgerald met in dancing school in BUFFALO. He mentioned Nancy in his *Ledger* for November and December 1905 (p. 160), and recalled their relationship in a *Thoughtbook* entry on "My girls" dated August 1910 (p. VIII).

Garland, Dodson Character in "The Trail of the Duke." Indolent young man whose fiancée, Mirabel WALMSLEY, sends him in search of "the Duke."

The Garden of Allah apartment hotel, where Fitzgerald lived at the start of his Hollywood residence in 1937

Garneau, Mrs. Clifton Character in "Dice, Brass-knuckles & Guitar." Fashionable Southampton woman who takes her daughter and other girls out of Jim POWELL's jazz school.

Garneau, Harold Character in "Presumption." Noel GARNEAU's father, who advises San Juan CHANDLER to get to work so he can support the wealthy girl he loves, but later calls him presumptuous when he discovers that the girl is his own daughter.

Garneau, Noel Character in "Presumption." Wealthy girl with whom San Juan CHANDLER is in love and who breaks her engagement to Brooks Fish TEMPLETON when Chandler, who has made money, declares his love for her.

Garnett, Chauncey Character in "The Adolescent Marriage." Elderly architect who intervenes to save the marriage of Lucy and Llewellyn CLARK.

Garovochi, Signor Character in "Gods of Darkness." Leader of a group of Italian merchants whom PHILIPPE charges 10 percent of their wares to ford the River Loire.

Garrod, H. G. Character in "Gretchen's Forty Winks." Important client whose business Roger HALSEY is trying to win.

Garvin Character in *TSOP*. The "little man" riding with Mr. FERRENBY.

Gaspar, Sergeant Character in "Two Old-Timers." Police sergeant who detains Phil MACEDON and Pat HOBBY after their automobile collision.

Gaspar, William ("Fat") Character in the Basil Duke LEE stories; a student at ST. REGIS. In "The Freshest Boy" he rudely refuses to accompany Basil to NEW YORK but later is nice to him. In "Basil and Cleopatra" Basil visits him in Mobile, Alabama, while Minnie BIBBLE is in town.

Gatsby, Jay Character in *GG*. Nick CARRAWAY'S wealthy neighbor, a mysterious man who inspires a great deal of speculation regarding his origins and the source of his wealth. As Nick becomes acquainted with him, Gatsby gradually reveals bits (sometimes false) of his background. He was born James Gatz but changed his name to Jay Gatsby at age 17 when he encountered wealthy miner Dan CODY, on whose yacht he worked for five years. He fell in love with Daisy Fay [BUCHANAN] while he was a poor army officer stationed in LOUIS-VILLE, Kentucky; but his love for her distracted him from his ambitions. While Gatsby was in Oxford, England, after World War I, Daisy married wealthy Tom BUCHANAN. Gatsby, soon wealthy himself, bought his mansion on Long Island to be near Daisy, who remains the object of his romantic quest. His goal is for Daisy to renounce her love for Tom and marry Gatsby just as if it were five years before. When Nick warns him that he can't repeat the past, Gatsby cries incredulously, "Can't repeat the past? . . . Why of course you can!" (p. 86). Gatsby and Daisy are reunited; but when Tom reveals the illegal nature of Gatsby's business (which includes selling alcohol and handling stolen securities), her resolve to leave Tom is shaken. Gatsby takes the blame for Myrtle WILSON'S death, although Daisy was the driver of the car that killed her; and George WILSON murders him.

Gatsby may have been based on Max GERLACH, Fitzgerald's Long Island acquaintance who was an alleged bootlegger. Gatsby's meeting with Dan Cody was based on the boyhood experience of Robert KERR, another Great Neck friend of Fitzgerald. Fitzgerald wrote to his friend, John Peale BISHOP: "You are right about Gatsby being blurred and patchy. I never at any one time saw him clear myself—for he started as one man I knew and then changed into myself—the amalgam was never complete in my mind" (c. August 9, 1925; *Life in Letters*, p. 126).

Jay Gatsby, who possessed "an extraordinary gift for hope, a romantic readiness" (p. 6), is one of the most recognizable characters in all of American literature.

See Harold Bloom, ed., *Gatsby* (New York: Chelsea House, 1991).

Gatz, Henry C. Character in *GG*. Jay GATSBY'S father, who arrives for his son's funeral and is awed by the splendor of his mansion. He eagerly shows Nick CARRA-WAY a schedule and list of resolves that Gatsby had written as a boy on a flyleaf of *Hopalong Cassidy* (1910).

Gatz, James (Jimmy) *See* Jay GATSBY.

Gauss, Christian (1878–1951) PRINCETON professor of Romance languages and later Dean of the College. He taught Fitzgerald's junior-year courses in French literature and was the only professor with whom Fitzgerald maintained a friendship after college. Gauss recalled that Fitzgerald showed him a novel in manuscript before leaving Princeton to report at FORT LEAV-ENWORTH, Kansas, and that he persuaded Fitzgerald not to publish it (Arthur MIZENER, *The Far Side of Paradise*, p. 70); but there is no evidence that Fitzgerald had completed a substantial portion of "The Romantic Egotist" (an early version of *TSOP*) at this time. More likely Fitzgerald showed him the manuscript in March 1918 when he was working on it at the COTTAGE CLUB. Years later Fitzgerald thanked Gauss for putting in "a good word for my first book, then bound for Scribners" and told him "you are one of the people for whom I, subconsciously, write" (April 23, 1934; *Letters*, p. 385). On May 1, 1920 Fitzgerald, Edmund WILSON, and John Peale BISHOP visited Princeton to attend a *NASSAU LITERARY MAGAZINE* banquet; and they called on Professor Gauss, bearing lyres and wreaths. Fitzgerald saw Gauss in PARIS and tried to arrange regular luncheon discussions with him and Ernest HEMINGWAY. In September 1934 Fitzgerald consulted with Gauss about presenting a lecture series "on the actual business of creating fiction" for the English department, but Gauss suggested that Fitzgerald speak to an undergraduate club because the university was unable to sponsor the lectures; Fitzgerald declined (September 7, 1934; *Life in Letters*, p. 269; see also September 26, 1934, *Life in Letters*, p. 270).

See Edmund Wilson, "Christian Gauss as a Teacher of Literature," *The Shores of Light* (New York: Farrar, Straus and Young, 1952), pp. 3–26, and *The Papers of Christian Gauss*, ed. Katherine Gauss Jackson and Hiram Haydn (New York: Random House, 1957).

Gausse Character in *TITN*. Proprietor of Gausse's Hôtel des Etrangers, based on the Grand-Hôtel du Cap on CAP D'ANTIBES. Gausse helps Dick DIVER get Mary [NORTH] Minghetti and Lady Caroline SIBLY-BIERS out of jail.

Gedney, Freddy Character in "The Cut-Glass Bowl." Young man with whom Evylyn PIPER has an affair.

George Character in "Fate in Her Hands." Child who is bitten by the mad dog from which Jean KASTLER narrowly escapes.

George Character in "The Passionate Eskimo." Salesman from whom PAN-E-TROON attempts to purchase some tobacco.

Gerlach (von Gerlach), Max Alleged bootlegger and acquaintance of Fitzgerald in Long Island; he may have been the source for Jay GATSBY'S lifestyle. Gatsby's characteristic expression, "old sport," appears in an

Newspaper clipping annotated by Max Gerlach, a source for Jay Gatsby (Princeton University Library)

autograph note from Gerlach to Fitzgerald on a newspaper clipping about the Fitzgeralds: "Enroute from the coast—Here for a few days on business—How are you and the family old Sport? Gerlach." The note, dated "7/20/23," preceded the final draft of *GG;* Fitzgerald kept the clipping in his scrapbook. (See Matthew J. BRUCCOLI, " 'How Are You and the Family Old Sport?'—Gerlach and Gatsby," *Fitzgerald/Hemingway Annual* [1975], pp. 33–36.) Gerlach was in the used car business in Flushing, New York, when he attempted suicide by shooting himself in 1939; he indicated in his suicide note that he had been an officer in World War I.

Gifford, Nancy Holmes (Mrs. Walter Gifford) Character in "Three Hours Between Planes." Woman whom Donald PLANT had loved when he was 12 and she was 10 and whom he visits during a wait between planes.

Gilbert, Catherine Character in *B&D.* Gloria Gilbert PATCH's mother, an adherent of a religion called BILPH-ISM. She dies in December after Gloria's marriage in June.

Gilbert, Gloria *See* Gloria Gilbert PATCH.

Gilbert, Russel Character in *B&D.* Gloria Gilbert PATCH's father and supervising manager of the Associ-

ated Mid-Western Film Materials Company. He dies in 1917.

Gillespie, Howard Character in *TSOP.* One of Rosalind CONNAGE's rejected suitors.

Gingrich, Arnold (1903–1976) *ESQUIRE* founding editor who accepted nearly everything Fitzgerald submitted to the magazine. He praised Fitzgerald's writing in a 1934 letter: "Regarding the written word like a musical instrument, you are the supreme virtuoso—nobody can draw a purer finer tone from the string of an English sentence" (*Correspondence,* p. 397). When Fitzgerald asked for advances in 1935, Gingrich responded that he could not forward money without something to show the accountants and "suggested that he put down anything that came into his head, as automatic writing in the Gertrude Stein manner, or that, if even that were beyond his powers of concentration, he simply copy out the same couple of sentences over and over, often enough to fill eight or ten pages, if only to say I can't write stories about young love for *The Saturday Evening Post*" (*The Armchair Esquire* [New York: Putnam, 1958], p. 93). Fitzgerald responded with a series of confessional articles including "The Crack-Up" (February 1936), "Pasting It Together" (March 1936), and "Handle with Care" (April 1936). Despite his admiration for Fitzgerald, Gingrich published Ernest HEMING-WAY's story "The Snows of Kilimanjaro" (*Esquire,*

August 1936), which included a contemptuous reference to Fitzgerald.

Fitzgerald provided a dust jacket blurb for Gingrich's 1935 novel *Cast Down the Laurel:* "Beautifully written, startling in form, and promising other equally good things to come. It pleases me beyond measure that Arnold Gingrich has brought off this book, which has the same scope and appeal of his editorial ventures" (*In His Own Time,* p. 158). Gingrich edited *The Pat Hobby Stories* (1962), which had appeared in *Esquire.*

See Gingrich, *Nothing But People: The Early Days at Esquire, A Personal History, 1928–1958* (New York: Crown, 1971).

Girard, Cyrus Character in "The Third Casket." Businessman who is seeking someone to succeed him when he retires. He sends for the sons of his three best friends to compete for the opportunity.

Girard, Lola Character in "The Third Casket." Cyrus GIRARD's daughter, who marries Rip JONES.

girl (unnamed) (*See* also LETGARDE.) Character in "In the Darkest Hour." ROBERT THE FROG's consort, who comes to PHILIPPE after Robert's death.

girl (unnamed) Character in "Love in the Night." Young woman whom Prince Val ROSTOFF meets on a yacht and marries several years later.

girl (unnamed) Character in "The Swimmers." American whom Henry Clay MARSTON tries to rescue from drowning in France, although he doesn't know how to swim, and who later teaches him to swim. He encounters her again in Virginia four years later and on the ship as he returns to EUROPE.

The Girl from Lazy J Play. In *F. Scott Fitzgerald's St. Paul Plays, 1911–1914.* Performed in August 1911 at the home of Elizabeth MAGOFFIN during the organizational meeting of the ELIZABETHAN DRAMATIC CLUB in ST. PAUL. Fitzgerald played the leading role of Jack DARCY, who is visiting his uncle, George KENDALL, at "Diamond O" Ranch in Texas. Kendall has inexplicably received a note from a prospective thief warning him that on the night of August 12 his $5,000 from a recent sale of steers will be stolen; and he asks Jack to wait up that night for a while and be on the lookout. When Jack falls asleep in his chair, Tony GONZOLES, a Mexican cowpuncher whom Kendall plans to fire, enters and ties Jack up. Leticia LARNED, Jack's fiancée from the neighboring "Lazy J" Ranch, enters masked and aims a gun at Tony, demanding that he hand over the letters he stole from her mother five years ago which he has been using to blackmail her. She burns the letters and ties up Tony. The Kendalls enter and untie Tony and

Jack. Jack prevents Tony from escaping and is amazed to find that the masked girl is Leticia.

"The Girl the Prince Liked" Fiction by Zelda FITZGERALD. COLLEGE HUMOR, no. 74 (February 1930), 46–48); *Bits of Paradise; Zelda Fitzgerald: The Collected Writings.* Bylined "F. Scott and Zelda Fitzgerald" but credited to Zelda in *Ledger.* Wealthy, ambitious Helena, whose husband doesn't complain about her flirtations with other men, grows bored with her life in the Middle West and travels with her family to Florida and then Chicago, where she attracts the Prince of Wales. They meet again in PARIS; and she later visits him at his palace, where he gives her a jeweled bracelet.

"The Girl With Talent" Fiction by Zelda FITZGERALD. COLLEGE HUMOR, no. 76 (April 1930), 50–52, 125–127; *Bits of Paradise; Zelda Fitzgerald: The Collected Writings.* Bylined "F. Scott and Zelda Fitzgerald" but credited to Zelda in *Ledger.* After her show closes in NEW YORK, Lou, a dancer, leaves her husband and child behind to perform at a PARIS nightclub with enormous success. She disappears with a man for five days, then reappears and gets a divorce; she later runs off to China with an Englishman.

"Girls Believe in Girls" Essay. LIBERTY, 7 (February 8, 1930), 22–24; *In His Own Time.* Fitzgerald analyzes the "modern and somewhat disturbing cult of the heroine" which has developed as "women have come to believe that they have nothing of value to learn from men" (*In His Own Time,* pp. 207 & 208). He adds that virtue is no longer identified with chastity and classifies Americans according to "two frames of mind: the first engaged in doing what it would like to do; the second pretending that such things do not exist" (p. 210).

Glion, Switzerland Zelda FITZGERALD was a patient at VAL-MONT CLINIC in Glion from May 22 to June 5, 1930. In *TITN* Dick DIVER encounters Nicole Warren [DIVER] and Baby WARREN on the Glion funicular.

"Gods of Darkness" Fiction—fourth PHILIPPE story. REDBOOK, 78 (November 1941), 30–33, 88–91. Published posthumously. The ABBOT warns Philippe that his followers are involved in a pagan cult and asks for Philippe's help in stamping it out. When the DUKE OF MAINE approaches Philippe's property with a large troop of horsemen, GRISELDA, whom Philippe plans to marry, urges him to let JACQUES handle the situation. By following Jacques' instructions, Philippe captures the Duke and his entourage. Griselda and Jacques take Philippe to a meeting of the Witch Cult, attended by followers of both Philippe and the Duke of Maine. When the chief witch, Becquette LE POIRE, denounces Philippe, Griselda reveals that she is really the chief priestess of the Witches of Touraine. Philippe resolves to use the cult to help his own cause.

Goebel, Eva　Character in "Crazy Sunday." Stella CAL-MAN's best friend, with whom Miles CALMAN has an affair.

Golden, Mr.　Character in "Gretchen's Forty Winks." Superintendent of Roger HALSEY's office building; he comes to Roger's office to collect the overdue rent.

Goldgreaves　Character in "In the Darkest Hour." ROBERT THE FROG's son, whose execution PHILIPPE orders to avoid any threat to his own leadership.

Golding, T. F.　Character in *TITN* and "One Trip Abroad." In *TITN* he is the owner of the *Margin*, a yacht on which Dick and Nicole DIVER crash a party and where they re-encounter Tommy BARBAN and meet Lady Caroline SIBLY-BIERS. In "One Trip Abroad" he hosts a party on his yacht in Monte Carlo.

Goldstein, Bertha Weinberg　*See* Bert BARR.

Golstein, Katie　Character in "The Dance." Catherine JONES's former nurse, now a maid at the country club, who provides an alibi for Catherine after Marie BAN-NERMAN's murder.

Golstein, Thomas　Character in "The Dance." Katie GOLSTEIN's brother, who reveals to the NARRATOR that Katie had been Catherine JONES's nurse.

Gone With the Wind　(Selznick International, with MGM, 1939) During the last three weeks of his MGM contract, which expired on January 27, 1939, Fitzgerald was loaned to David O. SELZNICK to polish Oliver H. P. Garrett's (1897–1952) revision of Sidney Howard's (1891–1939) screenplay for *Gone With the Wind,* using only dialogue from the 1936 novel by Margaret Mitchell (1900–49). He worked on the scenes from the bazaar through the burning of Atlanta, but was dismissed because Selznick was bringing in relays of writers, totaling 16; Sheilah GRAHAM noted in a lecture which Fitzgerald helped her write that he was dismissed because he couldn't find a way to make Aunt Pitty quaint enough for the cameras. Pages 50–111 of Fitzgerald's copy of the screenplay, with typed marginal annotations justifying his cuts and dialogue changes, are at PRINCETON UNIVERSITY LIBRARY. (See also his January 10, 1939 memos to David O. Selznick and January 24 memo to Barbara Keon, *Life in Letters*, pp. 377–382.)

Fitzgerald evaluated Mitchell's novel for his daughter, Scottie FITZGERALD: "It is a good novel—not very original, in fact leaning heavily on The Old Wives' Tale, Vanity Fair, and all that has been written on the Civil War. There are no new characters, new technique, new observations—none of the elements that make literature—especially no new examination into human emotions. But on the other hand it is interesting, surprisingly honest, consistent and workman like throughout, and I felt no contempt for it but only a certain pity for those who considered it the supreme achievement of the human mind" (January 1939; *Life in Letters,* p. 383).

Gonzoles, Tony　Character in *The Girl from Lazy J.* A "Mexican cowpuncher" whom George KENDALL plans to discharge. Under the alias of "D.S.H." (Dead Shot Hoskins), he attempts to rob Kendall, but is apprehended by neighboring cowgirl Leticia LARNED, whose mother he has been blackmailing.

Gooddorf, Harry　Character in "Pat Hobby's Christmas Wish." Studio executive whom Pat HOBBY tries to blackmail.

Goodrich, Frances　*See* Frances Goodrich HACKETT.

the Goon　*See* Ella LEI CHAMORO.

Gorman, Joe　Character in "He Thinks He's Wonderful." Basil Duke LEE admires Joe's singing, and Joe is impressed by Basil's popularity with the girls. While spending the night with Joe, Basil offends him by offering advice on how to be more popular; in retaliation Joe tells their friends that Basil thinks he's wonderful.

"Gracie at Sea"　Fitzgerald met George Burns (1896–1996) and Gracie Allen (1902–64) while they were on tour in BALTIMORE in 1934. He wrote a movie treatment, "Gracie at Sea," for them on speculation, collaborating with Robert Spafford; but they did not buy the treatment.

Grady, Henry　Character in " 'Send Me In, Coach.' " Boy at Camp Rahewawa.

Graham, Sheilah (1904–1988)　Fitzgerald's companion in HOLLYWOOD. Born Lily Sheil in an East End London slum and raised in an orphanage from age 6 to 14, she married John Graham Gillam, a 42-year-old unsuccessful businessman, when she was 18. He endeavored to improve her speech and manners and encouraged her to go on the stage. They selected the name Sheilah Graham for her stage name; and she became one of Cochran's Young Ladies, the English equivalent of a Ziegfeld Girl. They kept their marriage a secret to advance her career, and Gillam even encouraged her to date other men. As their marriage deteriorated, she went to America as a journalist, obtaining a divorce in 1937. She wrote a syndicated column, "Hollywood Today," for the North American Newspaper Alliance. Fitzgerald first saw her at a July 14, 1937 party hosted by Robert BENCHLEY to celebrate her

Sheilah Graham and Fitzgerald in Tijuana, Mexico

engagement to the Marquess of Donegal. Fitzgerald noticed her resemblance to Zelda FITZGERALD and, after leaving the party, mistakenly recalled that she had been wearing a silver belt—details he later used in *LT/ LOLT* for Monroe STAHR's first impression of Kathleen MOORE, a character based on Graham. Fitzgerald next saw Graham on July 22 at the Screen Writers Guild dinner dance at the Ambassador Hotel, where they spoke but didn't dance with one another. They met again on July 24 when screenwriter Edwin Justus MAYER invited Graham to have dinner with him and Fitzgerald at the Clover Club, where Fitzgerald and Graham danced together most of the evening. Fitzgerald called to cancel their upcoming dinner date because Scottie FITZGERALD was coming to visit, but Graham said she would like to meet his daughter. They took Scottie and some other young people to the Trocadero nightclub, where Fitzgerald corrected Scottie all evening. Graham initially concealed her past from Fitzgerald, telling him that she came from an upper-class English family; but when she revealed the truth he was fascinated rather

than appalled—although he was shocked by her admission that she had slept with eight men; and he offered to educate her.

Graham was initially unaware of Fitzgerald's alcoholism, but in October—by which time she had already committed herself to him by breaking her engagement—he fell off the wagon, a situation which distressed her because of her memories of drunken men from her childhood. In 1937 Sheilah agreed to do a weekly radio talk about the movies, and Fitzgerald accompanied her to Chicago for a trial broadcast. He caused trouble by directing her in the radio studio and hitting the sponsor, and he was ejected from the studio. When she returned to their hotel she found him drunk, and the airline refused to board him until he sobered up. In April 1938 Graham, who wanted him to get away from his apartment at the noisy GARDEN OF ALLAH, found him a house at 114 Malibu Beach, and she spent weekends with him there.

Fitzgerald was ambivalent about their relationship. He did not try to keep it secret: although he warned Scottie not to mention Graham to Zelda or the Sayres, he introduced Graham to Gerald and Sara MURPHY, Harold OBER, Maxwell PERKINS, and Edmund WILSON when they went East. However, he apologized to Helen HAYES for introducing Graham to her; and after his death Graham found that he had written "Portrait of a Prostitute" on the back of her photograph—almost certainly after one of his drunken quarrels with her. In "To a Beloved Infidel," a poem he wrote for her, he betrayed his uneasiness about her former lovers, although he thanked them for making her more desirable.

Fitzgerald devised a plan for educating Graham called "College of One," a two-year curriculum in the arts and humanities built around H. G. WELLS's *Outline of History* (1920) with readings in Wells and supplemental works of literature, all discussed in tutorial sessions. He planned for Graham to read Oswald SPENGLER's *Decline of the West* (Germany, 1918–22; first English translation, London, 1926–28) at the end of the two-year program. (Kathleen Moore's lover ["the MAN"] in *LT/LOLT* educated her with a view toward reading Spengler.) Fitzgerald encouraged Graham to write fiction; and they collaborated on "Dame Rumor," a play about a Hollywood gossip columnist, but it did not progress beyond the first act.

Fitzgerald and Graham led a quiet life in Hollywood, avoiding large cocktail parties but attending dinners, teas, and small parties with friends. When they studied music and art in the "College of One" they attended Hollywood Bowl concerts and visited museums. Graham did not try to make Fitzgerald divorce Zelda, although she believed he would marry her if she pushed the matter; and she shocked him by suggesting they have a child. Zelda was presumably unaware of

their relationship, although she probably suspected that Fitzgerald was involved with someone in California. Fitzgerald and Graham maintained separate residences for most of their relationship, but he moved to her apartment at 1443 North Hayworth Avenue after he suffered a heart attack about six weeks before his death, and it was there that he died on December 21, 1940.

Graham married Trevor Westbrook in 1941; they divorced in 1946. Her daughter, Wendy W. Fairey, reveals in *One of the Family* (New York: Norton, 1992) that British philosopher A. J. Ayer (1910–89), rather than Westbrook, was her father. Graham's son, Robert Westbrook, says in *Intimate Lies: F. Scott Fitzgerald and Sheilah Graham* (New York: HarperCollins, 1995) that Westbrook divorced Graham because he suspected that actor Robert Taylor (1911–69) was Robert Westbrook's father. Graham was married to W. S. Wojkiewicz in the 1950s. She eventually had a radio program and television show.

Graham chronicled her relationship with Fitzgerald in three memoirs: *Beloved Infidel* (with Gerold Frank; New York: Holt, Rinehart & Winston, 1958); *College of One* (New York: Viking, 1967); and *The Real F. Scott Fitzgerald Thirty-five Years Later* (New York: Grosset & Dunlap, 1976; London: W. H. Allen, 1976), a revision and expansion of portions of the two earlier volumes. Her other books include *The Rest of the Story* (New York: Coward-McCann, 1964), *The Garden of Allah* (New York: Crown, 1970), and *Hollywood Revisited* (New York: St. Martin's Press, 1984).

Grainger, Arthur Character in "His Russet Witch." Son of Merlin and Olive GRAINGER.

Grainger, Merlin Character in "His Russet Witch." Employee of the Moonlight Quill Bookshop who watches CAROLINE through his apartment window and encounters her at various times throughout his life.

Grainger, Olive Masters *See* Olive MASTERS.

Granby, Mr. and Mrs. Alec Characters in *B&D*. A couple who stop phoning Anthony and Gloria PATCH after Alec is too attentive to Gloria at a party.

Granby, John Character in "The Perfect Life." ST. REGIS alumnus and PRINCETON student who urges Basil Duke LEE to try to lead a perfect life and to exert a positive influence on his schoolmates.

grandson (unnamed) Character in "His Russet Witch." Young man whose grandmother, Caroline, has promised him $5,000 if he doesn't smoke before his majority; she catches him smoking when she enters the Moonlight Quill Bookshop to purchase a first edition.

Grange, "Red" Character in "No Flowers." Wealthy student whose suit Billy JOHNS borrows to attend the prom. Named after college and professional football star Harold "Red" Grange (1903–91).

Granny Character in "The Count of Darkness." Spokesman for the peasants who demand that PHILIPPE give them their tools so they can farm. Philippe later appoints her to divide among the peasants a share of the loot taken from the Syrian merchants who ford the river.

Granville, Bonita (1923–1988) Historical figure and character in "Pat Hobby, Putative Father." Actress whom John INDORE wishes to see. When Pat HOBBY sneaks John and his uncle into the set where she is acting, they are inadvertently filmed along with her.

The Great Gatsby Novel. New York: Charles SCRIBNER'S Sons, 1925; London: Chatto & Windus, 1926. Dedication: "ONCE AGAIN TO ZELDA." Fitzgerald began planning his third novel in June 1922 in DELLWOOD, Minnesota, reporting to Maxwell PERKINS: "Its locale will be the middle west and New York of 1885 I think. It will concern less superlative beauties than I run to usually + will be centered on a smaller period of time. It will have a catholic element" (*Life in Letters*, p. 60; *Scott/Max*, p. 61). No manuscript for the material he described survives. In July 1922 he informed Perkins: "I want to write something *new*—something extraordinary and beautiful and simple + intricately patterned" (*Correspondence*, p. 112).

Fitzgerald began writing an early version of the novel in GREAT NECK, Long Island, in June 1923. All that survives of this version are two pages which Fitzgerald sent to Willa Cather (1873–1947) in 1925, explaining that he had written a description of Daisy BUCHANAN before reading Cather's similar description of Marian Forrester in *A Lost Lady* (1923). The time and setting of Fitzgerald's novel is not specified in the pages; the characters are Jordan Vance (who anticipates Jordan BAKER), Ada (who anticipates Daisy), and Caraway, who is not the narrator. (See Matthew J. BRUCCOLI, " 'An Instance of Apparent Plagiarism': F. Scott Fitzgerald, Willa Cather, and the First *Gatsby* Manuscript," *The Princeton University Library Chronicle*, 39 [Spring 1978], 171–178.) Fitzgerald's work on the novel was interrupted by the September production of *The Vegetable* and the financial necessity of writing short stories after the play's failure. Several stories written during 1922–24 are closely related to the developing novel: "The Diamond as Big as the Ritz" (June 1922), "Winter Dreams" (December 1922), "Dice, Brass Knuckles & Guitar" (May 1923), "Absolution" (June 1924), and " 'The Sensible Thing' " (July 1924).

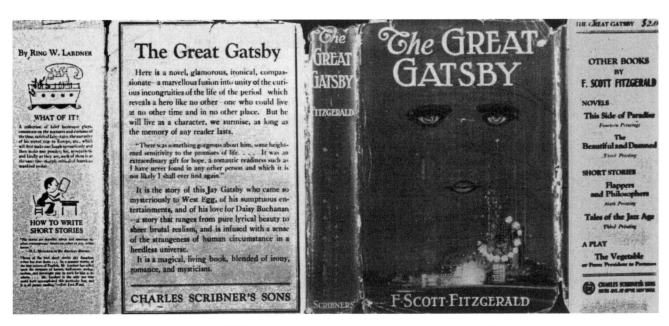

Francis Cugat's dust jacket for Fitzgerald's 1925 novel (Bruccoli Collection, University of South Carolina)

Around April 10, 1924 Fitzgerald notified Perkins that he was approaching his material from a "new angle"—by which he probably meant a new plot—and repeated his emphasis on technique: "This book will be a consciously artistic achievment + must depend on that as the 1st books did not" (*Life in Letters*, p. 67; *Scott/Max*, p. 70). He completed the first draft of the novel and revised the typescript while in France in the summer and fall of 1924, and in January–February 1925 he heavily revised and rewrote the galleys in ROME. Chapters VI, VII, and VIII were the most heavily rewritten: Fitzgerald moved portions of Jay GATSBY's biography to Chapter VI from Chapters VII and VIII, and he rewrote the PLAZA HOTEL confrontation between Gatsby and Tom BUCHANAN in Chapter VII. In December 1924 both Ray Long of COSMOPOLITAN and John Wheeler of LIBERTY declined serial rights to the novel (*As Ever*, p. 70). In January 1925 H. N. SWANSON of *COLLEGE HUMOR* offered $10,000 for the serial; but Fitzgerald declined to delay book publication for less than $20,000, and he was concerned that appearance in *College Humor* "would kill it in book form" (received January 26, 1925; *As Ever*, p. 74). *GG* was not serialized before publication.

At least 14 years after the composition of *GG*, Fitzgerald made notes on its sources on the endpaper of *Man's Hope* (1938) by André Malraux (1901–76). They include his acquaintances and experiences in NEW YORK CITY and Great Neck and his memory of Ginevra KING's wedding; only three chapters are described as "an invention" or "inv." Another source was his relationship with Zelda FITZGERALD—their

courtship and his loss of certainty in her fidelity caused by her interest in Edouard JOZAN. (Specific sources for characters are discussed in the entries for Jay Gatsby, Jordan Baker, and Meyer WOLFSHIEM. See also Joseph Corso, "One Not-Forgotten Summer Night: Sources for Fictional Symbols of American Character in *The Great Gatsby*," *Fitzgerald/Hemingway Annual* [1976], pp. 8–33.)

Fitzgerald considered several titles for his third novel, including "Among the Ash Heaps and Millionaires," "Gold-hatted Gatsby," "On the Road to West Egg," "The High-bouncing Lover," "Gatsby," "Trimalchio," and "Trimalchio in West Egg." Trimalchio was an ostentatious party-giver in *The Satyricon* (first century A.D.), a Latin work by Petronius Arbiter (d. 65 A.D.) which Fitzgerald may have read in 1922 when a translation published by his friend T. R. Smith of Boni & Liveright was charged with obscenity. As late as the first galleys, the novel's title was "Trimalchio," but Fitzgerald was dissuaded by objections that book-buyers would not understand the title or be able to pronounce it. He settled on *The Great Gatsby* in December 1924; but in January and March 1925 he continued to express his concern to Perkins about the title, cabling from CAPRI on March 19: "CRAZY ABOUT TITLE UNDER THE RED WHITE AND BLUE STOP WHART WOULD DELAY BE" (*Correspondence*, p. 153). Perkins replied that changing the title would delay publication by several weeks and urged that the title remain *The Great Gatsby*. Fitzgerald conceded in a 22 March cable.

The Great Gatsby was published on April 10, 1925 at $2.00, with a dust jacket by Francis CUGAT; and it

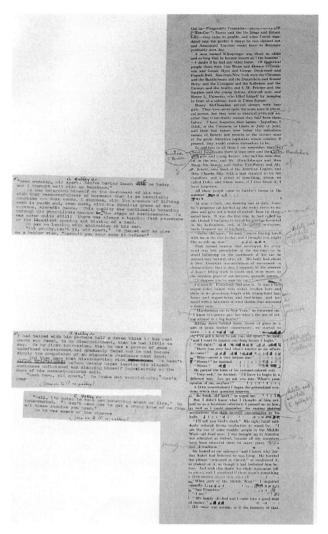

Corrected galley proof for The Great Gatsby (Princeton University Library)

received excellent reviews. Gilbert SELDES announced: "Fitzgerald has more than matured; he has mastered his talents and gone soaring in a beautiful flight, leaving behind him everything dubious and tricky in his earlier work, and leaving even farther behind all the men of his own generation and most of his elders" ("Spring Flight," *The Dial*, 79 [August 1925], 162–164; *FSF: The Critical Reception*, p. 239). (*See* also CRITICAL REPUTATION AND RECEPTION OF NOVELS.) However, sales were disappointing. After a first printing of 20,870 copies, there was a second printing of 3,000 copies in August. Some copies from the second printing were still in the Scribners warehouse when Fitzgerald died. In an April 24, 1925 letter to Perkins, Fitzgerald offered two explanations for the novel's poor sales: "1st The title is only fair, rather bad than good. 2nd And most important—the book contains no important woman character and women controll the fiction market at present. I don't think the unhappy end matters particularly" (*Life in Letters*, p. 107; *Scott/Max*, p. 101).

Owen Davis (1874–1956) dramatized *GG*. The play opened on February 2, 1926 at the Ambassador Theatre in New York, starring James Rennie (1890–1965) as Gatsby, Florence Eldridge (1901–88) as Daisy Buchanan, and Edward H. Wever (1899–1984) as Nick CARRAWAY. The play, which ran for 112 performances, was a success and received good reviews; Fitzgerald received $7,630, as well as $16,666 for rights to a 1926 movie adapted from the play.

When the Modern Library reissued *GG* in 1934, Fitzgerald wrote an introduction, in which he asserted:

> Now that this book is being reissued, the author would like to say that never before did one try to keep his artistic conscience as pure as during the ten months put into doing it. Reading it over one can see how it could have been improved—yet without feeling guilty of any discrepancy from the truth, as far as I saw it; truth or rather the *equivalent* of the truth, the attempt at honesty of imagination. I had just reread Conrad's preface to *The Nigger*, and I had recently been kidded half haywire by critics who felt that my material was such as to preclude all dealing with mature persons in a mature world. But, my God! it was my material, and it was all I had to deal with. (*In His Own Time*, p. 156)

Fifteen years after the original publication of *GG*, Fitzgerald tried to give his masterpiece another opportunity, writing to Perkins: "Would the 25 cent press keep Gatsby in the public eye—or is the book unpopular" (May 20, 1940; *Life in Letters*, p. 445; *Scott/Max*, p. 261). After Fitzgerald's death, the inclusion of *GG* with the first publication of *The Last Tycoon* and other editions in 1945 sparked a renewal of reader interest in *GG*.

Chapter I
In June 1922 Nick Carraway visits Tom and Daisy Buchanan and meets Jordan Baker, who mentions Jay Gatsby. When Nick returns home he catches a glimpse of Gatsby, who lives next door.

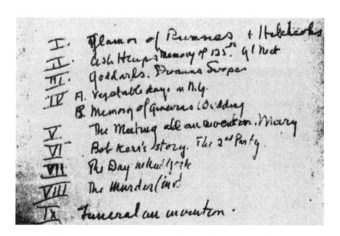

Fitzgerald's notes on the sources for the chapters in The Great Gatsby (Princeton University Library)

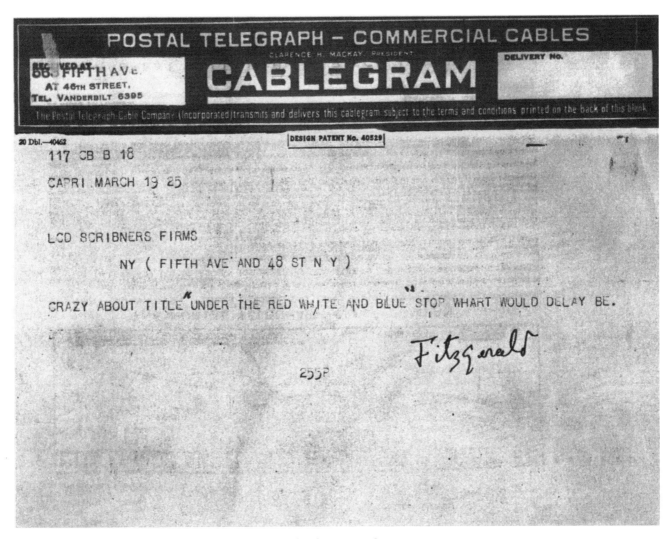

POSTAL TELEGRAPH – COMMERCIAL CABLES

CLARENCE H. MACKAY, PRESIDENT

CABLEGRAM

DELIVERY No.

RECEIVED AT
555 FIFTH AVE.
AT 46TH STREET,
TEL. VANDERBILT 6395

The Postal Telegraph Cable Company (Incorporated) transmits and delivers this cablegram subject to the terms and conditions printed on the back of this blank.

20 Dbl.—4462

DESIGN PATENT No. 40529

117 CB B 18

CAPRI MARCH 19 25

LCO SCRIBNERS FIRMS

NY (FIFTH AVE AND 48 ST N Y)

CRAZY ABOUT TITLE UNDER THE RED WHITE AND BLUE STOP WHART WOULD DELAY BE.

255P

Fitzgerald

Fitzgerald's wire asking to change the title of The Great Gatsby *was too late.* (Princeton University Library)

Chapter II

Nick and Tom stop in the VALLEY OF ASHES at George WILSON's garage, where Nick meets Myrtle WILSON, Tom's mistress. She accompanies them to New York, where she and Tom host an alcoholic party in an apartment he has rented. At the party Myrtle's sister CATHERINE mentions a rumor about Gatsby to Nick.

Chapter III

Nick attends a party at Gatsby's mansion, where he hears more speculation about his mysterious host and finally meets him. At the party Nick renews his acquaintance with Jordan, who is summoned by Gatsby for a private conversation. Later Nick reflects on "the racy, adventurous feel" (p. 46) of New York at night and on his relationship with Jordan.

Chapter IV

Nick enumerates the guests who attend Gatsby's parties. He rides to New York with Gatsby, who relates a bit of his personal history; they have lunch with Meyer Wolfshiem, who fixed the 1919 World's Series, and briefly encounter Tom Buchanan. Gatsby has asked Jordan to tell Nick the history of his relationship with Daisy Fay Buchanan. She explains how Gatsby and Daisy fell in love in 1917 when he was a young army officer stationed in LOUISVILLE, Kentucky. Gatsby was ordered abroad, and almost two years later Daisy married Tom Buchanan. Gatsby bought his mansion in WEST EGG to be near Daisy, and he throws his lavish parties in hopes that Daisy will attend one of them. Since she has not shown up, he wants Nick to invite her to his house and let Gatsby come over while she is there.

Chapter V

Nick invites Daisy to tea, where she is reunited with Gatsby. They all go to Gatsby's mansion, where he displays his wealth for Daisy and tosses his shirts into a heap for her and Nick to admire.

Chapter VI

Nick recounts Gatsby's early history as James Gatz (his real name), who was drifting along Lake Superior when he met Dan CODY, a wealthy miner who employed Gatsby on his yacht. Mr. SLOANE brings Tom Buchanan to Gatsby's house for a drink, and Gatsby mentions that he knows Tom's wife. Tom and Daisy attend Gatsby's next party, and Tom speculates that Gatsby is a bootlegger. After the party Gatsby shares with Nick his determination to repeat the past by Daisy's telling Tom she never loved him and marrying Gatsby at her home in Louisville as if it were five years before.

Chapter VII

Gatsby, Nick, and Jordan have lunch at the Buchanans' house; Daisy's indiscreet voice alerts Tom to her relationship with Gatsby. They all go to New York—Gatsby and Daisy in Tom's car, and the others in Gatsby's car. Tom stops at Wilson's garage for gas and discovers Wilson's suspicions of Myrtle and his plans to leave town with her. At the Plaza Hotel Tom confronts Gatsby, who tells him that Daisy has never loved him, but loves Gatsby. Daisy, who had hoped to avoid a confrontation, admits that she loved Tom once, but loved Gatsby too—a declaration that falls short of Gatsby's expectations. Tom undermines Daisy's resolve to leave him by revealing what he has discovered about Gatsby's illegal sale of alcohol. On the way home Daisy, driving Gatsby's car, kills Myrtle Wilson in a hit-and-run accident. Tom assumes that Gatsby was driving, but Nick guesses the truth. Gatsby keeps a vigil outside the Buchanan house in case Tom bothers Daisy about the afternoon's confrontation; but Nick, who looks through the window, sees Daisy and Tom conversing in an intimate, conspiratorial way.

Chapter VIII

Nick goes over to Gatsby's house at dawn. Gatsby tells him about his courtship of Daisy; how after the war he was mistakenly sent to Oxford, where he received word of Daisy's engagement to Tom; and his return visit to Louisville, now haunted by his memories of Daisy. Nick goes to work, where he quarrels on the phone with Jordan. Nick recounts what had happened at Wilson's garage the previous night after the accident—that Wilson had told his neighbor MICHAELIS that he had a way of finding out who had killed Myrtle. The afternoon after the accident Wilson murders Gatsby in his swimming pool, and then shoots himself.

Chapter IX

After Gatsby's murder, Nick discovers that the Buchanans have left town. Gatsby's father, who arrives for the funeral (September 1922), shares Gatsby's boyhood resolves with Nick. Wolfshiem recounts the beginning of his relationship with Gatsby, but Nick is unable to persuade him—or any of Gatsby's former guests—to attend the funeral. Nick plans to leave the East, which seems haunted to him after Gatsby's death, but he first makes a final break with Jordan. He encounters Tom and correctly guesses that Tom had told Wilson that Gatsby owned the car that killed Myrtle. In the novel's coda, Nick reflects on the American Dream and Gatsby's relation to it.

The narrative control that Fitzgerald exhibited through the use of Nick Carraway as the partially involved narrator—a technique he learned from English novelist Joseph CONRAD—marks his greatest technical advance over his previous novels. Nick relates bits and pieces of Gatsby's history as he learns them—out of chronological order—requiring the reader to reconstruct this essentially incredible character.

Much of the novel's significance is rooted in its exploration of the American Dream. Gatsby—a self-made man—achieves financial success, but he fails to understand how wealth works in society; he doesn't realize that his newly acquired money isn't as good as the Buchanans' family money. He believes in the promises of America—in "the orgastic future"—but his ambitions are undermined by and confused with his illusions about Daisy. In August 1924 Fitzgerald wrote to Ludlow FOWLER: "Thats the whole burden of this novel—the loss of those illusions that give such color to the world so that you don't care whether things are true or false as long as they partake of the magical glory" (*Life in Letters*, p. 78).

The Great Gatsby is widely regarded as one of the prime contenders for the title "the great American novel." Fitzgerald himself made a similar claim in a letter to Perkins: "I think my novel is about the best American novel ever written" (c. August 25, 1924; *Scott/Max*, p. 76).

See *The Great Gatsby*, ed. Matthew J. Bruccoli (Cambridge: Cambridge University Press, 1991); *The Great Gatsby: A Facsimile of the Manuscript; F. Scott Fitzgerald Manuscripts III:* "GG: The Revised and Rewritten Galleys"; Andrew T. Crosland, *A Concordance to F. Scott Fitzgerald's The Great Gatsby;* Frederick J. Hoffman, ed., *The Great Gatsby: A Study;* Ernest Lockridge, ed., *Twentieth Century Interpretations of The Great Gatsby;* Henry Dan Piper, ed., *Fitzgerald's The Great Gatsby: The Novel, the Critics, the Background;* Scott Donaldson, ed., *Critical Essays on F. Scott Fitzgerald's The Great Gatsby;* Bruccoli, ed., *New Essays on The Great Gatsby;* Harold Bloom, ed., *F. Scott Fitzgerald's The Great Gatsby;* Richard Lehan, *The Great Gatsby: The Limits of Wonder;* and Thomas A. Pendleton, *"I'm Sorry about the Clock": Chronology, Composition, and Narrative Technique in The Great Gatsby.*

Great Neck Town on the North Shore of Long Island, New York, where the Fitzgeralds rented a house at 6 Gateway Drive for $300 a month from mid-October 1922 to April 1924. Great Neck was the home of many show-business and journalism figures, including Her-

Zelda and Scottie Fitzgerald, probably at Great Neck, Long Island, 1923

bert Bayard SWOPE, executive editor of the *New York World* and a noted host. While living in Great Neck, Fitzgerald developed a close friendship with Ring LARDNER. Fitzgerald found Great Neck, 15 miles from NEW YORK CITY night life, expensive. In the summer of 1923 Fitzgerald began a draft of what became *The Great Gatsby,* and the Great Neck environment provided material for the novel. He revised *The Vegetable,* which was published in April 1923, but interrupted the start of his third novel while he waited for his play to be accepted by a producer; *The Vegetable* had a one-week run in November, leaving him in debt. Fitzgerald's 1924 essay "How to Live on $36,000 a Year" provides a humorous account of the Fitzgeralds' life-style in Great Neck.

Green, Dexter Character in "Winter Dreams." Ambitious young man whose dreams of success are intertwined with his love for wealthy, selfish Judy JONES. Green is a preliminary treatment of Jay GATSBY, with whom he shares a love for a beautiful but inconstant rich girl and the loss of his illusions.

Gregorovious, Franz Character in *TITN*. Swiss psychopathologist at DOHMLER's clinic. He and Dick DIVER

open a clinic together on the Zürichsee; Gregorovius later takes over the clinic when they dissolve their partnership.

Gregorovious, Kaethe Character in *TITN*. Dr. Franz GREGOROVIOUS's wife, who dislikes Nicole DIVER and tells Franz that Dick DIVER "is no longer a serious man" (p. 249).

Gregory, Doctor Character in "Gretchen's Forty Winks." Doctor who comes to see Gretchen HALSEY after she wakes from her drugged sleep. He informs the Halseys about George TOMPKINS's nervous breakdown.

Gregory, Walter Character in "Myra Meets His Family." Myra HARPER's cousin, who poses as a minister to perform a sham marriage ceremony for her and Knowleton WHITNEY.

Gregson Character in "The Mystery of the Raymond Mortgage." He is "supposed to be the ablest detective in the force" (*Apprentice Fiction,* p. 21). While staying in the Raymond house, he is knocked unconscious by a YOUNG MAN whom he finds kneeling by Agnes RAYMOND's body.

Gresham, John Character in "One Interne." Thea SINGLETON's fiancé, who had died of radium poisoning contracted during his own medical experiments.

"Gretchen's Forty Winks" Fiction. Written January 1924. *The SATURDAY EVENING POST,* 196 (March 15, 1924), 14–15, 128, 130, 132; *ASYM*. Roger HALSEY tells his wife, Gretchen HALSEY, that the next six weeks are the most important in his life because he has the opportunity to get some big accounts for his advertising business; she complains that he already works too much. They go to dinner with George TOMPKINS, an interior decorator who holds up his own "balanced life" as a model for Roger. During the next few weeks while Roger works overtime, Gretchen frequently goes out with George, until Roger confronts him and forbids him to return to their house. Desperate to complete one final day of work uninterrupted, Roger drugs Gretchen; and she sleeps through a whole day. He completes his work and wins one of the big accounts he has been seeking. Gretchen awakes confused and scared when she realizes she has lost a whole day. Roger sends for Doctor GREGORY, who informs Roger that he has never looked better in his life, but that George Tompkins has had a nervous breakdown.

Griebel, Louie Character in "A Man in the Way," "Teamed with Genius," "Pat Hobby and Orson Welles," "Pat Hobby's Secret," "Pat Hobby Does His Bit," "No Harm Trying," "On the Trail of Pat Hobby," "Pat Hobby's Preview," and "Pat Hobby's College Days." The studio bookie.

Griffin, Bob Character in "Last Kiss." Director with whom Pamela KNIGHTON refuses to cooperate.

Griffin, Mr. Character in "In the Holidays." Man whose murder is arranged by Mr. MCKENNA.

Griggs, Benjamin Childhood friend of Fitzgerald in ST. PAUL, a fellow student at ST. PAUL ACADEMY, and a member of William BAKER's dancing class.

Griselda Character in "The Kingdom in the Dark" and "Gods of Darkness." In "The Kingdom in the Dark" PHILIPPE protects her from discovery by LOUIS, King of the West Franks, from whom she has run away. In "Gods of Darkness" Philippe agrees to marry her. She persuades him to let JACQUES handle the approaching DUKE OF MAINE and reveals that she is the chief priestess of the Witches of Touraine.

Grit (Film Guild, 1924) Fitzgerald was paid $2,000 for his original story for this movie and received credit for providing the "source"; his story does not survive. The scenario was written by James Ashmore Creelman; the movie was directed by Frank Tuttle (1892–1963) and starred Glenn Hunter (1893–1945) and Clara Bow (1905–65). In this crook melodrama a young man who is afraid of guns exposes a gang of criminals and wins Orchid McGonigle, an underworld girl. Fitzgerald's friend Townsend MARTIN was a partner in the Film Guild.

Grove Park Inn Hotel in ASHEVILLE, North Carolina, where Fitzgerald lived in the summer of 1935 and July–December 1936. In summer 1935 he met Laura GUTHRIE, who became his typist and friend, and had an affair with Beatrice DANCE, whom he met at the inn. In July 1936 he broke his right shoulder in a diving accident and later developed arthritis in the shoulder after falling in the bathroom and lying on the tile floor. He drank a good deal and was regarded as a troublesome guest at the inn. After he fired a revolver in a suicide threat, the inn refused to let him stay without a nurse. He hired nurse Dorothy RICHARDSON and business manager Martha Marie SHANK while at the Grove Park Inn in 1936.

Gruger, F. R. (Frederic Rodrigo) (1871–1953) Prolific, versatile, and popular American illustrator. More

The Grove Park Inn, Asheville, N.C. (Bruccoli Collection, University of South Carolina)

than half of his output appeared in *The SATURDAY EVENING POST,* for which he provided both cover paintings and story illustrations. He illustrated two Fitzgerald stories: "One of My Oldest Friends" (*WOMAN'S HOME COMPANION,* September 1925) and "The Rich Boy" (*REDBOOK,* January & February 1926). He provided illustrations for more than four hundred authors, including Theodore DREISER, William Faulkner (1897–1962), O. Henry (1862–1910), Ben Hecht (1894–1964), Ring LARDNER, Edith WHARTON, and P. G. Wodehouse (1881–1975).

See Bernard Perlman, *The Golden Age of Illustration: F. R. Gruger and His Circle* (Westport, CT: North Light Publishers, 1978).

by Park Bucker

Gstaad, Switzerland Fitzgerald took his daughter, Scottie FITZGERALD, skiing at Gstaad during her 1930 Christmas vacation after an unhappy visit to Zelda FITZGERALD at PRANGINS CLINIC. The Gstaad trip provided the setting for Fitzgerald's 1931 story "Indecision" and for Book II, Chapter 13 in *TITN.*

Guesculin Character in "The Kingdom in the Dark." Squire who finds GRISELDA's gray horse and whom PHILIPPE and JACQUES kill to keep him from revealing her presence to King LOUIS.

"The Guest in Room Nineteen" Fiction. Written March 1937. *ESQUIRE,* 8 (October 1937), 56, 209; *The Price Was High.* Stroke victim Mr. CASS wonders about the mysterious hotel GUEST in room nineteen, whom the night WATCHMAN tells him comes in late every night and whose description matches that of Cass's partner, John CANISIUS. When the watchman collapses while lifting a heavy log, Cass suspects the guest of being involved. When Cass later meets the guest, he asks the man to help him lift a log; but Cass dies from the effort. The guest turns out to be the HOTEL MANAGER's brother.

guest in room nineteen (unnamed) Character in "The Guest in Room Nineteen." Mysterious hotel guest who comes in late each night and turns out to be the HOTEL MANAGER's brother.

Gunther, Amanda Character in "More Than Just a House." Girl whom Lew LOWRIE saves from being run over by a train and with whom he falls in love. She

marries George HORTON and four years later dies in childbirth.

Gunther, Bess Character in "More Than Just a House." The youngest of the Gunther girls. Lew LOWRIE proposes to her when he finds her alone and penniless eight years after he first meets the family.

Gunther, Jean Character in "More Than Just a House." The Gunther girl whom Lew LOWRIE encounters at a NEW YORK party and who calls herself "the child of the century" (*The Price Was High,* p. 463). She later marries and moves to China. In a letter of praise for the story, John O'HARA described her to Fitzgerald as "one of those girls for the writing about of whom you hold the exclusive franchise" (*Selected Letters of John O'Hara,* ed. Matthew J. BRUCCOLI [New York: Random House, 1978], pp. 75–76).

Gunther, Mr. Character in "More Than Just a House." Amanda, Jean, and Bess GUNTHER's father, who suffers from senile dementia and worries about twenty dollars he borrowed in 1892. He dies a year before Lew LOWRIE's third visit to the Gunther home.

Gunther, Mrs. Character in "More Than Just a House." Amanda, Jean, and Bess GUNTHER's mother, who insists that Amanda invite Lew LOWRIE to her dance after he saves her life. She dies between Lew's first and second visits to the Gunther home.

Guthrie, Laura Palmist whom Fitzgerald met at the GROVE PARK INN in ASHEVILLE, North Carolina, in the summer of 1935, an encounter which intrigued him because he was writing a story about a fortune-teller at the time ("Fate in Her Hands"; April 1936). Mrs. Guthrie, who was separated from her husband and had literary ambitions, became Fitzgerald's typist, companion, and confidante, although they were not romantically involved. She kept a journal about their meetings, which was later partly published (Laura Guthrie Hearne, "A Summer with F. Scott Fitzgerald," *ESQUIRE,* 62 [December 1964], 160–165, 232, 236, 237, 240, 242, 246, 250, 252, 254–258, 260). Her journal and correspondence with Fitzgerald were acquired by PRINCETON UNIVERSITY LIBRARY.

Gygsum Character in "The Diamond as Big as the Ritz." Slave who waits on John UNGER during his visit to Percy WASHINGTON's home.

H

Haedge, Mr. Character in "The Popular Girl." Man who informs Yanci BOWMAN of the dismal state of her deceased father's financial affairs.

Hackett, Albert and Frances Goodrich (b. 1900; 1891–1984) Screenwriters and playwrights who wrote the *Thin Man* movies and adapted *Anne Frank: The Diary of a Young Girl* (1952) for the stage as *The Diary of Anne Frank* (1955; Pulitzer Prize). Fitzgerald became friendly with the Hacketts while working at MGM in the summer of 1937, and he and Sheilah GRAHAM later attended dinners at their house. Frances Hackett had studied at Vassar, and Fitzgerald sought her advice on his letters to his daughter, Scottie FITZGERALD, who was a student there.

Hagerty, Peter Character in "The Rich Boy." Paula LEGENDRE'S second husband, with whom she is very happy.

Haggin, Mr. and Mrs. Characters in "New Types." Couple whom Emily HOLLIDAY asked to stand in the receiving line at the dance.

Haight, Marjorie Character in "The Jelly-Bean." Girl who, at a children's party, tactlessly mentions that Jim POWELL sometimes delivers groceries.

Haight, Mr. Character in *B&D*. Lawyer whom Anthony PATCH hires to break his grandfather Adam PATCH'S will.

Haines, Dolly Character in "Strange Sanctuary." Thirteen-year-old girl who is visiting various friends while her father is sick. She becomes friends with Clarke CRESSWELL, who helps her break into her Uncle Charlie CRAIG'S house when she suspects that his guests are lying to her about his illness.

Haines, Morton Character in "Strange Sanctuary." Dolly HAINES'S father, who is in New Mexico because of his arthritis.

Halbird, June Character in "The Rubber Check." Girl to whose house party Ellen MORTMAIN invites Val SCHUYLER.

Halbird, Mrs. Character in "The Rubber Check." Woman who tells Val SCHUYLER that he is too old to be socializing with the young people at her party and that most of the girls' mothers feel the same way.

Halcyon, Cecilia Character in "The Debutante." Helen HALCYON'S "socially precocious" younger sister, who smokes Helen's hidden cigarettes and drinks from Helen's hidden flask. This character is renamed Cecelia CONNAGE in *TSOP*.

Halcyon, Helen Character in "The Debutante." Self-absorbed young woman based on Ginevra KING. On the evening of her debut she rejects suitor John CANNEL because the novelty has gone out of their relationship. This character is renamed Rosalind CONNAGE in *TSOP*.

Halcyon, Mr. Character in "The Debutante." Helen HALCYON'S father. This character is renamed Leland R. CONNAGE in *TSOP*.

Halcyon, Mrs. Character in "The Debutante." Helen HALCYON'S mother, who instructs her bored daughter on how to behave at her debut. This character is renamed Mrs. CONNAGE in *TSOP*.

Hale, Musidora Character in "The Dance." Aunt whom the NARRATOR is visiting in a small Southern town.

Halklite, Mr. Character in "Lo, the Poor Peacock!" Vice-president of a large textile company who gives a big account to Jason DAVIS even though Davis is too ill to meet him.

Hallam Character in "Majesty." Harold CASTLETON, Sr.'s agent in EUROPE, who reveals Emily CASTLETON'S attachment to Prince PETROCOBESCO.

Halliburton, Miss Character in "The Captured Shadow." Teacher who coaches Basil Duke LEE'S play. Based on ST. PAUL drama buff Elizabeth MAGOFFIN.

Halloran Character in *B&D*. Bank manager who informs Anthony PATCH that the bank will have to close

his account because he has failed to maintain the required $500 balance.

Halsey, Gretchen Character in "Gretchen's Forty Winks." Selfish wife whose eagerness for social excitement hinders the business of her husband, Roger HAL-SEY, until he drugs her while he completes an important project.

Halsey, Maxy Character in "Gretchen's Forty Winks." Roger and Gretchen HALSEY's baby.

Halsey, Roger Character in "Gretchen's Forty Winks." Young man who is struggling to make his advertising business successful. He drugs his selfish wife, Gretchen HALSEY, so that he can complete a crucial project.

Hamil Character in "The Four Fists." Peter CARHART's employee in the Southwest who is in charge of a scheme to buy up ranches in New Mexico.

Hamilton, John Character in "Strange Sanctuary." Boy at the Halloween party which Dolly HAINES attends.

Hammel, Lillian Character in the Josephine PERRY stories. In "First Blood" she and Josephine, against the orders of their parents, go for a car ride with Howard PAGE and Travis DE COPPET. In "A Nice Quiet Place" she writes to Josephine that Ridgeway SAUNDERS has fallen in love with Evangeline TICKNOR while Josephine is at Island Farms. In "A Woman with a Past" Lillian goes to the Yale prom with George DAVEY. She is one of the girls who is leaning out the window at school talking to some boys, an incident in which Josephine is not involved but for which she unjustly gets put on probation. In "A Snobbish Story" Lillian is at the dance at Lake Forest. In "Emotional Bankruptcy" she and Josephine attend the PRINCETON prom, where Josephine steals away with Lillian's date, Martin MUNN. She is with Josephine when they meet Edward DICER.

Hammerton, Elsie Character in "A Snobbish Story." Woman whose play is rejected in favor of John Boynton BAILEY's "Race Riot."

Hancock, Thornton Character in *TSOP.* An agnostic, influential friend of Monsignor DARCY. Based on historian Henry Adams (1838–1918), a friend of Sigourney FAY.

"Handle with Care" Autobiographical essay. *ESQUIRE*, 5 (April 1936), 39, 202; *CU.* Sequel to "The Crack-Up" and "Pasting It Together." Fitzgerald describes with contempt his resolution to survive his crack-up by becoming a writer only, by ceasing "any attempts to be a person—to be kind, just or generous" (*CU*,

p. 82), by giving up "the old dream of being an entire man in the Goethe-Byron-Shaw tradition, with an opulent American touch, a sort of combination of J. P. Morgan, Topham Beauclerk and St. Francis of Assisi" (p. 84).

The titles of "Pasting It Together" and "Handle with Care" were transposed in the early printings of *CU.*

Hannaford, George Character in "Magnetism." Actor whose wife, Kay HANNAFORD, is jealous of his interest in actress Helen AVERY and who is blackmailed by script girl Margaret DONOVAN.

Hannaford, Kay Tompkins Character in "Magnetism." George HANNAFORD's wife, an actress. She expresses interest in Arthur BUSCH in retaliation for George's interest in Helen AVERY.

Hannaman, Clara Character in "Too Cute for Words." Helen HANNAMAN's niece and Gwen BOWERS's friend, with whom Gwen travels to PRINCETON.

Hannaman, Helen Character in "Too Cute for Words." Friend of Bryan BOWERS.

Hannan, Carly Character in *TITN.* Man whom Dick DIVER meets with Tommy BARBAN at a café in Munich.

Hannan, Helen Character in "A Freeze-Out." Girl with whom Alida RIKKER plays golf.

Hannan, Walter Character in "A Freeze-Out." Man who sponsors Chauncey RIKKER for membership in the Kennemore Club.

Hanson, Claud Character in "On an Ocean Wave." Gaston T. SCHEER's secretary, who cables that he would gladly die for Scheer.

Hanson, Mr. Character in "Dalyrimple Goes Wrong." Man to whom Bryan DALYRIMPLE reports on his first day at the wholesale grocery stockroom.

Happer, Sally Carrol Character in "The Ice Palace," "The Jelly-Bean," and "The Last of the Belles." Girl from TARLETON, Georgia. In "The Ice Palace" she travels North to visit her fiancé, Harry BELLAMY, but returns to the South after being trapped in an ice palace. In "The Jelly-Bean," where her last name is spelled "Hopper," she is Nancy LAMAR's inseparable friend. In "The Last of the Belles" she has a date with ANDY.

Harker, Anthony Character in "First Blood." A 22-year-old man with whom 16-year-old Josephine PERRY falls in love. At first he is uneasy about being seen with Josephine and breaks off their relationship, but then

he courts her frantically until his family sends him West.

Harlan, Dolly Character in "The Bowl." PRINCETON football player who hates the game and temporarily gives it up at the insistence of his fiancée, Vienna THORNE, but feels a sense of responsibility to return to the game and help his team.

Harlan, Genevieve Character in "Dice, Brassknuckles & Guitar." Young woman who attends Jim POWELL's jazz school.

Harlan, Madison Character in "Dice, Brassknuckles & Guitar." Ronald and Genevieve HARLAN's father, who invites Jim POWELL to lead the band for one number at his party for Amanthis POWELL.

Harlan, Ronald Character in "Dice, Brassknuckles & Guitar." Young man who attends Jim POWELL's jazz school and who is given a drink by Martin VAN VLECK.

Harland, Alice Character in "John Jackson's Arcady." John JACKSON's childhood sweetheart, now married, who refuses to leave her children to run away with him.

Harland, George Character in "John Jackson's Arcady." Alice HARLAND's husband, who owns a garage.

Harley, Ellen Character in "The Popular Girl." Old friend whom Yanci BOWMAN encounters on the train to PRINCETON.

Harman, Ned Character in " 'Boil Some Water—Lots of It.' " Production manager who tells Walter HERRICK, dressed as a Cossack, that the Big Table in the studio commissary is reserved.

Harmon, Dorothy Character in "A Luckless Santa Claus." Young woman who, on a whim, challenges her fiancé, Harry TALBOT, to give away twenty-five dollars to strangers on Christmas Eve.

Harper, Billy Character in "Presumption." Young man who accompanies Holly MORGAN to dinner at Noel GARNEAU's house.

Harper, Myra Character in "Myra Meets His Family." Popular girl who wishes to get married now that she is 21 and is tiring of her social life.

Harris, Ellen Character in "New Types." Leslie DIXON's cousin, with whom he discusses Paula JORGENSEN while they are at the beach.

Harris, Martin Character in "Design in Plaster." Studio electrical engineer who is briefly reunited with his estranged wife, Mary HARRIS, after his arm is dislocated in an accident.

Harris, Mary Character in "Design in Plaster." Martin HARRIS's estranged wife, who is briefly drawn back to him after his arm is dislocated in an accident.

Harris, Mike Character in "Last Kiss." Studio head who reports to Jim LEONARD that Pamela KNIGHTON is causing trouble.

Harrison, Doctor Character in "Her Last Case." Doctor who assigns Bette WEAVER to Ben DRAGONET's case.

Harrison, Edward Character in "Inside the House." Lawyer who falls ill while visiting Bryan BOWERS and who brings actress Peppy VELANCE to meet Gwen BOWERS.

Harry Character in "Too Cute for Words." Young man who sneaks Gwen BOWERS, Dizzy CAMPBELL, and Clara HANNAMAN into the PRINCETON prom in return for secrecy about his engagement to Marion LAMB.

Hart, Charley Character in "One of My Oldest Friends." Old friend of MICHAEL and MARION who was in love with Marion.

Hart, Mr. Character in "The Curious Case of Benjamin Button." Yale registrar who refuses to believe that Benjamin BUTTON is 18 years old and orders him out of town.

Hart, Mr. Character in "Winter Dreams." Man who gives 23-year-old Dexter GREEN a guest card to a private golf club and plays in a foursome with him. Dexter had once caddied for him.

Harvey, Josephine Character in "Bernice Bobs Her Hair." Marjorie HARVEY's mother and BERNICE's aunt.

Harvey, Marjorie Character in "Bernice Bobs Her Hair." BERNICE's cousin, who gives her lessons in popularity until she becomes jealous of Warren MCINTYRE's interest in Bernice. Marjorie, who is determined to succeed socially and is unwilling to be upstaged by her cousin, then spitefully reveals that Bernice's line about bobbing her hair is a bluff, causing Bernice to go through with the haircut.

Hatman, Mable Character in "Mightier Than the Sword." Dick DALE's script girl, who finds E. Brunswick HUDSON's script. When Hudson refuses to have his

name used, Dale decides to put Mable's name on it since he has been promising her a screen credit.

Hawkins, Mr. and Mrs. Characters in "Dalyrimple Goes Wrong." The mayor and his wife, with whom Bryan DALYRIMPLE stays when he first returns from the war.

Hayes, Helen (1900–1993) Broadway star and movie actress married to Fitzgerald's friend Charles MACARTHUR. In August 1937, while Fitzgerald was working in HOLLYWOOD, Hayes brought Scottie FITZGERALD to California for a visit, during which Scottie stayed with Hayes and MacArthur.

Hayward, Leland (1902–1971) Fitzgerald's HOLLYWOOD agent from December 1939 to February 1940. He was later a successful Broadway and Hollywood producer.

Hazeldawn Character in "Strange Sanctuary." Woman who escorts Dolly HAINES to Mrs. APPLETON's house.

"He Thinks He's Wonderful" Fiction—Basil Duke LEE story. Written July 1928. *The SATURDAY EVENING POST*, 201 (September 29, 1928), 6–7, 117–118, 121; *TAR*; *B&J*. Basil Duke Lee, age 15, returns home for the summer after an unhappy year at school. When Margaret TORRENCE tells everyone that Basil is wonderful, he suddenly becomes popular; and, in a game of Truth, all the girls name him as their favorite boy. Basil's popularity goes to his head; and when word spreads that he thinks he's wonderful, people begin snubbing him. While visiting Bill KAMPF, Basil meets Minnie BIBBLE; they kiss and make plans to see each other in the future. Basil loses an opportunity to go on a trip with Minnie's family when he talks too much about himself to Minnie's father. Basil borrows his grandfather's electric car and offers a ride to Imogene BISSEL, with whom he had earlier imagined himself in love.

"Head and Shoulders" Fiction. Written November 1919. *The SATURDAY EVENING POST*, 192 (February 21, 1920), 16–17, 81–82, 85–86; *F&P*. Horace TARBOX enters PRINCETON at age 13 and begins work on his Master of Arts at Yale at age 17. His chief interest is modern philosophy until he meets and falls in love with actress Marcia MEADOW, whom he soon marries. He finds a job as a clerk and Marcia continues her dancing act until she is five months pregnant. Then Horace, who had taken up gymnastics for his health at her suggestion, takes on additional work as a gymnastic performer. After the birth of their daughter, the book which Marcia wrote during her pregnancy is published;

she receives praise for her style and use of vernacular. When Marcia's publisher brings philosopher Anton LAURIER, Horace's idol, to meet Marcia, whose book he admires, Horace is shaken by the reversal in their roles as Head (now Marcia) and Shoulders (now Horace).

"Head and Shoulders" was Fitzgerald's first story in *The SATURDAY EVENING POST*. It was made into a lost movie (retitled *The Chorus Girl's Romance*) in 1920.

Hearne, Laura Guthrie *See* Laura GUTHRIE.

Hearst Character in "Reade, Substitute Right Half." Right tackle who is injured; READE substitutes for the halfback who takes Hearst's place.

Hearst's International On December 26, 1922 Fitzgerald signed a contract with Hearst's *COSMOPOLITAN* for an option on all stories he wrote in 1923, with the magazine to accept at least six; he received $1,500 for the option and was to receive $1,875 for each story. Although the contract was with *Cosmopolitan*, all the stories were published in *Hearst's International*: "Dice, Brass Knuckles & Guitar" (May 1923), "Hot & Cold Blood" (August 1923), "Diamond Dick and the First Law of Woman" (April 1924), and "The Baby Party" (February 1925). *Hearst's International* rejected stories and was slow in making payments, and Fitzgerald returned to writing for *The SATURDAY EVENING POST*.

Hedrick, T. A. Character in "Winter Dreams." Golfer whom young Dexter GREEN dreams of defeating. When he and Dexter play in a foursome together years later, Dexter feels superior to him. Hedrick is hit in the stomach by Judy JONES's golf ball.

Held, John Jr. (1889–1958) Cartoonist, illustrator, writer, and artist, best known for his figures of flappers and college boys; author of *Grim Youth* (1930), *The Flesh Is Weak* (1931), *Women Are Necessary* (1931), and *The Works of John Held, Jr.* (1932). Held provided the dust jacket illustrations for *Tales of the Jazz Age* and *The Vegetable*. Fitzgerald suggested the idea for the *Vegetable* jacket in a January 1923 letter to Maxwell PERKINS: "Cover something like the Jazz Age, with a different color background and little figures—Dada, Jerry, Doris, Charlotte, Fish, Snooks and Gen Pershing scattered over it" (*Scott/Max*, p. 65)

John O'HARA commented in his 1961 story "Mrs. Stratton of Oak Knoll":

> For years I've been hearing and reading people talking about John Held's girls and Fitzgerald's, as though they were one and the same thing. They just simply weren't. From the literary point of view, one of the worst things that ever happened to Fitzgerald was the simultaneous

Charles D. Mitchell's illustrations for Fitzgerald's February 21, 1920 Saturday Evening Post *story* (Bruccoli Collection, University of South Carolina)

popularity of John Held's drawings. Those damn editorial writers were largely to blame. Who would ever want to take Fitzgerald seriously if all they ever knew about him was that he wrote about those John Held girls? Held was a very good satirist, and he didn't *want* his girls to be taken seriously. Of course Fitzgerald was partly to blame. He called one book *Flappers and Philosophers,* and in the public mind the flapper was the John Held girl. Actually, of course, Fitzgerald and Held and the editorial writers were all misusing the word flapper. A flapper was English slang, and it meant a society girl who had made her debut and hadn't found a husband. On the shelf, they used to say. It wasn't an eighteen-year-old girl with flapping galoshes. (*Assembly* [New York: Random House, 1961], p. 19)

See Shelley Armitage, *John Held Jr., Illustrator of the Jazz Age* (Syracuse, NY: Syracuse University Press, 1987).

Hélène Character in "News of Paris—Fifteen Years Ago." Orphan whose convent education Henry Haven DELL is supporting.

Hemingway, Ernest (1899–1961) EXPATRIATE American sportsman, war correspondent, and author of novels, short stories, and nonfiction. Hemingway won the Pulitzer Prize in 1952 and the Nobel Prize in 1954 and is noted for his innovative, understated style and the code by which his characters live. Fitzgerald had not yet met Hemingway, who was just beginning his literary career, when he wrote about him to Maxwell PERKINS in October 1924: "This is to tell you about a young man named Ernest Hemmingway, who lives in Paris, (an American) writes for the transatlantic Review + has a brilliant future. Ezra Pount published a collection of his short pieces in Paris, at some place like the Egotist Press, I havn't it hear now but its remarkable + I'd look him up right away. He's the real thing" (c. October 10, 1924; *Life in Letters,* p. 82; *Scott/Max,* p. 78). The work Fitzgerald mentioned was *in our time* (Paris: Three Mountains Press, 1924), a collection of 18 vignettes published in an edition of 170 copies. Fitzgerald continued to mention Hemingway to Perkins, but the editor was unable to locate a copy of *in*

Ernest Hemingway, Charles Scribner III, and Maxwell Perkins, 1935

our time until he wrote to Hemingway at an old Paris address in February 1925.

Fitzgerald met Hemingway sometime before May 1, 1925 at the Dingo bar in PARIS. Hemingway's record of their meeting in *A Moveable Feast* (1964) depicts Fitzgerald as a drunk, a fool, and a nuisance; and his account of their subsequent excursion to Lyons is equally unflattering. However, Hemingway was impressed by *GG,* a copy of which Fitzgerald gave him a few days later: "When I had finished the book I knew that no matter what Scott did, nor how he behaved, I must know it was like a sickness and be of any help I could to him and try to be a good friend" (*A Moveable Feast,* p. 176). Nevertheless, Hemingway continued to condescend to Fitzgerald, who was both impressed by Hemingway's talent and intimidated by his reputation as an athlete and war hero. Zelda FITZGERALD and Hemingway disliked each other: he thought she was crazy, and she regarded him as bogus. In 1929 she charged that Fitzgerald and Hemingway were involved in a homosexual relationship; but there is no evidence to support this claim, which was made at a time when her sanity was deteriorating.

In the fall and winter of 1925 Fitzgerald and Hemingway spent time together arguing about writing, and Fitzgerald tried to advance Hemingway's career. Fitzgerald wrote an essay-review of *In Our Time* (1925) entitled "How to Waste Material: A Note on My Generation," concluding, "And many of us who have grown weary of admonitions to 'watch this man or that' have felt a sort of renewal of excitement at these stories

wherein Ernest Hemingway turns a corner into the street" (*AOAA,* p. 122). Hemingway had signed a three-book option with Boni & Liveright for *In Our Time,* which seemed to preclude bringing him to SCRIBNERS. However, Fitzgerald persuaded him to send stories to Perkins for SCRIBNER'S MAGAZINE and may have encouraged him to use *The Torrents of Spring*—a parody of Sherwood ANDERSON, a star Boni & Liveright author—as a contract breaker, although Hemingway denied that was his intent in writing the book. When Boni & Liveright declined the parody Hemingway was freed from his contract; and Fitzgerald persuaded Perkins to make an offer for *The Torrents of Spring* (1926) and *The Sun Also Rises* (1926), sight unseen, a deal that was concluded when Hemingway traveled to NEW YORK to meet Perkins in February 1926.

Sometime in 1925 or 1926 Fitzgerald urged novelist Glenway WESCOTT to "help launch Hemingway"; Wescott later remarked in his essay on Fitzgerald that Fitzgerald's enthusiastic admiration for Hemingway damaged him by causing him to cease writing seriously because "Hemingway could be entrusted with the graver responsibilities and higher rewards such as glory, immortality" ("The Moral of Scott Fitzgerald"; *CU,* pp. 324, 325). Wescott's conclusion exaggerates Hemingway's influence on Fitzgerald; their styles and material were too different for Fitzgerald to feel that Hemingway had made his own work unnecessary. Fitzgerald later designated Hemingway his artistic conscience, but stipulated that he was not directly influenced by his techniques: "a third contemporary had been an artistic conscience to me—I had not imitated his infectious style, because my own style, such as it is, was formed before he published anything, but there was an awful pull toward him when I was on a spot" ("Pasting It Together," March 1936; *CU,* p. 79). He also wrote to Perkins about Hemingway: "as an artist he is as near as I know for a final reference" (March 11, 1935; *Life in Letters,* p. 278; *Scott/Max,* p. 219).

In June 1926 the Hemingways joined the Fitzgeralds and Gerald and Sara MURPHY at JUAN-LES-PINS, where the Fitzgeralds turned over the VILLA PAQUITA to the Hemingways. Fitzgerald read *The Sun Also Rises,* which had already been sent to Scribners. In *A Moveable Feast* Hemingway denies that Fitzgerald's advice about the novel was helpful; but Fitzgerald's 10-page letter demonstrates that Hemingway did act on some of Fitzgerald's editorial suggestions in revising the proof, including cutting the initial expository material (see *Life in Letters,* pp. 142–145; and Charles Mann and Philip Young, "Fitzgerald's *Sun Also Rises:* Notes and Comment," *Fitzgerald/Hemingway Annual* [1970], pp. 1–9).

Hemingway and his second wife, Pauline (1895–1951), attended the PRINCETON-Yale football game at

Princeton with the Fitzgeralds on November 19, 1928 and spent the night at "ELLERSLIE"—their first meeting in two years. Hemingway described the occasion, including Fitzgerald's drunken behavior after the game and an altercation with the police at the WILMINGTON, Delaware, train station the next day, in an incomplete chapter intended for *A Moveable Feast*. On December 6, when Hemingway learned of his father's death, he wired Maxwell Perkins, Mike STRATER, and Fitzgerald from a train to send money so he could travel to the funeral; Fitzgerald delivered the money in person to the North Philadelphia train station.

When Hemingway was in Paris in 1929 he hurt Fitzgerald by concealing his address, as he and Pauline did not want to deal with Fitzgerald's drunken visits. Although Hemingway believed Fitzgerald's editorial advice would be worthless, he let him read a typescript of *A Farewell to Arms* (1929), probably in June after *SCRIBNER'S MAGAZINE* began the serial in May. Hemingway wrote "Kiss my ass" on Fitzgerald's nine-page holograph memo about the novel, but he acted on some of his suggestions while revising the novel in proof (see *Life in Letters*, pp. 164–167; and Charles Mann, "F. Scott Fitzgerald's Critique of *A Farewell to Arms*," *Fitzgerald/Hemingway Annual* [1976], pp. 141–152).

In June 1929 Fitzgerald served as timekeeper for a private boxing bout between Hemingway and Canadian novelist Morley CALLAGHAN and inadvertently let the second three-minute round go a minute overtime, during which Callaghan knocked down Hemingway. Hemingway reacted angrily, blaming Fitzgerald, who was troubled by the accusation. Callaghan provides a detailed account of the incident in *That Summer in Paris*. Hemingway altered his versions of the incident over the years; his August 28 report to Perkins (*Ernest Hemingway: Selected Letters*, pp. 302–303) differs from Callaghan's account, and he absurdly claimed in 1951 that Fitzgerald had let the round go 13 minutes (to Arthur MIZENER, January 4, 1951; *Ernest Hemingway: Selected Letters*, pp. 716–718). However, the Fitzgerald-Hemingway correspondence that summer is friendly, with no mention of the incident; Hemingway attempted to boost Fitzgerald's confidence at a time when Fitzgerald was concerned because his own novel (*TITN*) was unfinished after four years. Hemingway praised the parts of the novel he had read and explained his theory that Gilbert SELDES's favorable review of *GG* had blocked Fitzgerald's work on the novel by compelling him to attempt a masterpiece (September 4, 1929; *Ernest Hemingway: Selected Letters*, pp. 304–306).

In the fall of 1929 Gertrude STEIN strained Fitzgerald and Hemingway's friendship by telling them that Scott was the most talented writer of his generation and that his "flame" was stronger than Ernest's. Fitzgerald believed the comment was insincere as well as a slight to both him and Hemingway. Hemingway wrote to reassure Fitzgerald that Stein had been sincere and had never said anything unfavorable about Fitzgerald to him, adding that he did not resent her remark or feel competitive because "There can be no such thing" as comparing flames or feelings of superiority or inferiority "between serious writers—They are all in the same boat. Competition within that boat—which is headed toward death—is as silly as deck sports are—The only competition is the original one of making the boat and that all takes place inside yourself—You're on the boat but you're getting touchy because you haven't finished your novel—that's all—I understand it and you could be a hell of a lot more touchy and I wouldn't mind" (October 1929; *Ernest Hemingway: Selected Letters*, p. 310).

A delayed reaction to the Hemingway-Callaghan bout occurred when a November 24, 1929 *New York Herald Tribune* article alleged that Callaghan had knocked out Hemingway for disparaging his boxing stories. Callaghan's correction appeared in the *Tribune* on December 8, but meanwhile Fitzgerald—at Hemingway's insistence—had cabled Callaghan for a correction. Callaghan was angry; and although Maxwell Perkins tried to make peace among his three authors, Callaghan's friendship with Fitzgerald and Hemingway ended. The situation was complicated by Hemingway's suspicion that Callaghan had repeated Robert MCALMON's allegation that he and Fitzgerald were homosexuals; Fitzgerald believed that the gossip helped spoil his friendship with Hemingway. He wrote in his *Notebooks*, without naming Hemingway: "I really loved him, but of course it wore out like a love affair. The fairies have spoiled all that" (#62). On December 12, before the December 8 *Tribune* with Callaghan's correction reached France, Hemingway tried to mend his friendship with Fitzgerald by writing that he did not think Fitzgerald had deliberately let the round run overtime: "I know you are the soul of honor" (*Ernest Hemingway: Selected Letters*, p. 312).

Fitzgerald and Hemingway met again in October 1931, and it was around this time that they began relaying messages to one another through Perkins. They next met in New York in January 1933 for lunch with Edmund WILSON; a drunken Fitzgerald quarreled with both Hemingway and Wilson. This occasion may have prompted Fitzgerald's observation in his *Notebooks*: "I talk with the authority of failure—Ernest with the authority of success. We could never sit across the table again" (#1915). On March 4, 1934 Fitzgerald wrote to Perkins in a letter about *TITN*: "One time I had a talk with Ernest Hemingway, and I told him, against all the logic that was then current, that I was the tortoise and he was the hare, and that's the truth of the matter, that everything I have ever attained has been through long and persistent struggle while it is Ernest who has

a touch of genius which enables him to bring off extraordinary things with facility" (*Life in Letters,* pp. 248–249; *Scott/Max,* p. 194).

A month after the publication of *TITN* (April 12, 1934), Fitzgerald wrote to Hemingway: "Did you like the book? For God's sake drop me a line and tell me one way or another" (May 10, 1934; *Life in Letters,* p. 259). Hemingway responded on May 28 with a three-page typed assessment developing criticisms he had already shared with Perkins: the writing was wonderful, but *TITN* was fake because it distorted Gerald and Sara MURPHY, partial models for Dick and Nicole DIVER (*Ernest Hemingway: Selected Letters,* pp. 407–409). Fitzgerald replied on June 1, defending his method of composite characterization and acknowledging Hemingway's contribution to the novel's understated ending (*Life in Letters,* pp. 262–264). Fitzgerald had previously written to H. L. MENCKEN about his deliberate use of the "dying fall" motif, noting that he and Hemingway had worked out "that particular trick" with the influence of Joseph CONRAD's preface to *The Nigger of the "Narcissus"* (1897) (April 23, 1934; *Life in Letters,* 256).

In 1935 Hemingway wrote to Perkins: "How is Scott? I wish I could see him. A strange thing is that in retrospect his Tender is the Night gets better and better." Perkins relayed the message to Fitzgerald on April 8 (*Scott/Max,* p. 219), and Fitzgerald replied about Hemingway on April 15: "I'd like to see him too and I always think of my friendship with him as being one of the high spots of life. But I still believe that such things have a mortality, perhaps in reaction to their very excessive life, and that we will never again see very much of each other" (*Life in Letters,* p. 279; *Scott/Max,* pp. 219–220). On March 25, 1939 Hemingway wrote to Perkins about *TITN:* "It's amazing how excellent much of it is. If he had integrated it better it would have been a fine novel (as it is) much of it is better than anything else he ever wrote. How I wish he would have kept on writing. Is it really all over or will he write again? If you write him give him my great affection. (I always had a very stupid little boy feeling of superiority about Scott—like a tough little boy sneering at a delicate but talented little boy.) But reading that novel much of it was so good it was frightening" (*Ernest Hemingway: Selected Letters,* p. 483). Fitzgerald preserved Hemingway's comments in his scrapbook for *TITN.*

TITN character Tommy BARBAN probably has connections with Hemingway, although Fitzgerald did not list him as one of the models. Fitzgerald did stipulate Hemingway as the model for his medieval hero, PHILIPPE, writing in his *Notebooks:* "Just as Stendahl's portrait of a Byronic man made *Le Rouge et Noir* so couldn't *my* portrait of Ernest as Phillipe make the real modern man" (#1034).

Hemingway's story "The Snows of Kilimanjaro" mentioned Fitzgerald contemptuously: "The rich were dull and they drank too much or they played too much backgammon. They were dull and they were repetitious. He remembered poor Scott Fitzgerald and his romantic awe of them and how he had started a story once that began, 'The very rich are different from you and me.' And how someone had said to Scott, Yes they have more money. But that was not humorous to Scott. He thought they were a special glamorous race and when he found they weren't it wrecked him just as much as any other thing that wrecked him" (*Esquire,* 6 [August 1936], p. 200). Fitzgerald responded to Hemingway on July 16:

Dear Ernest:
 Please lay off me in print. If I choose to write de profundis sometimes it doesn't mean I want friends praying aloud over my corpse. No doubt you meant it kindly but it cost me a night's sleep. And when you incorporate it (the story) in a book would you mind cutting my name?
 It's a fine story—one of your best—even though the "Poor Scott Fitzgerald ect" rather spoiled it for me

Ever Your Friend
Scott
Riches have never facinated me, unless combined with the greatest charm or distinction. (*Life in Letters,* p. 302).

Arnold GINGRICH has described Hemingway's lost reply to Fitzgerald as "brutal" ("Scott, Ernest and Whoever," *Esquire,* 66 [December 1966], p. 187), and Fitzgerald told his friend Beatrice DANCE that Hemingway's response indicated "that he felt that since I had chosen to expose my private life so 'shamelessly' in *Esquire,* he felt that it was sort of an open season for me" (September 15, 1936; *Letters,* p. 542). Perkins wrote to his cousin Elizabeth LEMMON on August 16 calling Hemingway's reference to Fitzgerald "contemptible" and explaining the true circumstances of the incident described in "Snows." During lunch with Perkins and critic Mary Colum (1884–1957), Hemingway had said, "I am getting to know the rich"; Mrs. Colum had responded, "The only difference between the rich and other people is that the rich have more money" (A. Scott Berg, *Max Perkins: Editor of Genius,* p. 305). When Hemingway collected "The Snows of Kilimanjaro" in *The Fifth Column and the First Forty-Nine Stories* (1938), he wanted to drop "Fitzgerald" but retain "Scott"; Perkins intervened to have the name changed to "Julian." Despite Fitzgerald's hurt over the "Snows" reference, he asked Hemingway to help him when Michel MOK published a humiliating interview ("The Other Side of Paradise") in the *New York Post* on September 25, 1936 depicting Fitzgerald as a broken drunk. Hemingway, who was in Montana and had not seen the interview, offered his

help; but Fitzgerald replied that nothing could be done at long range.

On June 4, 1937 Fitzgerald traveled to New York from North Carolina to see Hemingway, who denounced fascism at a meeting of the American Writers' Congress at Carnegie Hall. In a note which he mailed from the train the next day, Fitzgerald urged Hemingway to include short stories in his forthcoming book, *To Have and Have Not* (1937), a plan which Hemingway was considering but finally rejected. Fitzgerald and Hemingway met for the last time on July 12, 1937, when Fitzgerald was present at Hemingway's showing of the propaganda movie *The Spanish Earth* at the home of actor Fredric March (1897–1975) in HOLLYWOOD. A later Fitzgerald-Hemingway reunion has been described, but it did not occur. Charles Marquis WARREN, who lived at Fitzgerald's MALIBU BEACH house for a short time in 1938, has stated that Hemingway was also boarding there that summer and that Fitzgerald was giving him an allowance while he worked on *For Whom the Bell Tolls*. Warren's account, which is included in Aaron Latham's *Crazy Sundays* (1971) is entirely untrue; Hemingway was in Key West and Wyoming in summer 1938 and did not begin writing *For Whom the Bell Tolls* until 1939 in CUBA.

When *For Whom the Bell Tolls* was published in October 1940, Hemingway sent Fitzgerald a copy inscribed "To Scott with affection and esteem Ernest" (BRUCCOLI COLLECTION). Fitzgerald sent a warm letter of thanks: "It's a fine novel, better than anybody else writing could do. . . . Congratulations too on your new book's great success. I envy you like hell and there is no irony in this . . . and I envy you the time it will give you to do what you want" (November 8, 1940; *Life in Letters*, pp. 469–470). Despite his comments to Hemingway, Fitzgerald considered *For Whom the Bell Tolls* "a thoroughly superficial book which has all the profundity of Rebecca" (*Notebooks* #2066). While working on *LT/LOLT* (1941), Fitzgerald noted: "I want to write scenes that are frightening and inimitable. I don't want to be as intelligible to my contemporaries as Ernest who as Gertrude Stein said, is bound for the Museums. I am sure that I am far enough ahead to have some small immortality if I can keep well" (*Notebooks*, #2068).

Although Fitzgerald's last novel, published in its unfinished form as *The Last Tycoon* in 1941, generally met with a favorable critical reception, Hemingway dissented in a November 15, 1941 letter to Perkins, complaining about the "impossible dramatic tricks" Fitzgerald planned for the novel, saying the writing was like moldy bacon, and comparing Fitzgerald to a pitcher with a dead arm, because he never understood life well enough to write a novel that didn't depend on magic (*Ernest Hemingway: Selected Letters*, pp. 527–529). After the publication of *CU* (1945), Hemingway wrote to Perkins asking for a copy, explaining that he was

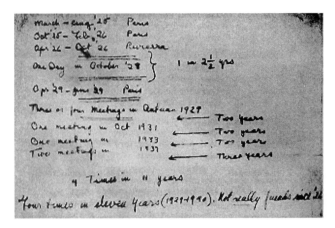

Fitzgerald's record of his friendship with Ernest Hemingway (Princeton University Library)

sorry he hadn't written about Scott because he knew him better than the people who were writing about him, but he couldn't write truly about him while Zelda was living (July 23, 1945; *Ernest Hemingway: Selected Letters*, pp. 593–595).

Fitzgerald had kept a chronology of his meetings with Hemingway from 1925 to 1937, noting at the end: "Four times in eleven years (1929–1940). Not <u>really</u> friends since '26" (PRINCETON UNIVERSITY LIBRARY).

Hemingway's comments about Fitzgerald are not always reliable. For example, in his account of his first 1925 meeting with Fitzgerald in *A Moveable Feast* he cites Fitzgerald's Princeton friend, Duncan Chaplin, as a witness; but Chaplin was not in EUROPE in 1925. Matthew J. BRUCCOLI provides corrections to the inaccurate legends about this famous literary relationship in *Fitzgerald and Hemingway: A Dangerous Friendship* (New York: Carroll & Graf, 1994; London: André Deutsch, 1995).

See Hemingway, "Scott Fitzgerald," "Hawks Do Not Share," and "A Matter of Measurements," *A Moveable Feast* (New York: Scribners, 1964), 147–193; Susanna Egan, "Lies, Damned Lies, and Autobiography: Hemingway's Treatment of Fitzgerald in *A Moveable Feast*," *A/B Auto/Biography Studies*, 9 (Spring 1994), 64–82; Carlos Baker, *Ernest Hemingway: A Life Story* (New York: Scribners, 1969); *Ernest Hemingway: Selected Letters, 1917–1961*, ed. Baker (New York: Scribners, 1981); and *The Only Thing That Counts: The Ernest Hemingway/Maxwell Perkins Correspondence*, ed. Bruccoli with Robert W. Trogdon (New York: Scribners, 1996).

Hemmick, Henry W. Character in "Two for a Cent." Southern man who was unable to go North because he had to stay in his hometown to clear his unjustly scarred reputation after losing a penny from a sum he was transporting for the bank where he was employed.

Hemple, Charles Character in "The Adjuster." Luella HEMPLE's husband, who suffers a nervous collapse.

Hemple, Chuck Character in "The Adjuster." Charles and Luella HEMPLE's young son, who dies some time after his father's nervous collapse.

Hemple, Luella Character in "The Adjuster." Bored and selfish young wife who learns responsibility after her husband, Charles HEMPLE, suffers a nervous collapse.

Henderson, Dick Character in "The Family Bus." Boy who has a long and friendly relationship with Jannekin MELON-LOPER over the years and throughout the changes in their families' fortunes.

Henderson, Ralph Character in "The Family Bus." Dick HENDERSON's older brother, who is killed in a car wreck while attempting to elope with Kaethe MELON-LOPER.

Henderson, Mrs. T. R. Character in "The Family Bus." Dick and Ralph HENDERSON's mother, who is displeased to see Ralph riding away with Kaethe MELON-LOPER.

Henderson, T. R. Character in "The Family Bus." Dick and Ralph HENDERSON's father, who tries to catch up with Kaethe MELON-LOPER and Ralph but encounters a policeman who informs him that Ralph has been killed in a car wreck.

Hendersonville, North Carolina Fitzgerald lived at the SKYLAND HOTEL in Hendersonville November–December 1935; he wrote "The Crack-Up" (February 1936) during his stay there.

Hendrix, Amelia Wetherby *See* Madame ZADA.

Hendrix, Josephus Character in *Assorted Spirits*. Peter WETHERBY's second cousin, who dresses as a devil to prove Wetherby's house is haunted so that he may buy it at a low price and resell it to the railroad.

"Her Last Case" Fiction. Written August 1934. *The SATURDAY EVENING POST*, 207 (November 3, 1934), 10–11, 59, 61–62, 64; *The Price Was High*. Bette WEAVER, a nurse who is engaged to marry Doctor Howard CARNEY in a month, takes Ben DRAGONET as her last case. Dragonet, who had been wounded in World War I, has trouble sleeping and wanders through the house at night. Dragonet and Bette get to know each other well; and when he tells her he is in love with her, she wonders whether she is falling in love with him, too.

Just then his ex-wife and daughter arrive; and his housekeeper, Jean KEITH, tells Bette that Dragonet's wife has always been evil and harmful to him. Mrs. DRAGONET leaves their daughter, Amalie Eustace Bedford DRAGONET, with her father, who is reluctant to keep her. Bette decides to leave; but her fiancé, after a brief visit, urges her to stay and finish the case. When he leaves she realizes that she is going to stay with Dragonet forever rather than marry Carney.

Dragonet's home in Warrenburg, Virginia, was inspired by Fitzgerald's visit to "Welbourne," a mansion in Middleburg, Virginia, where Maxwell PERKINS took Fitzgerald to visit his cousin, Elizabeth LEMMON, in July 1934. On September 6, 1934 Fitzgerald wrote to Lemmon: "This is the story that I got out of 'Welbourne,' with my novelist instinct to make copy out of social experience. I don't think for a moment that this does any justice to 'Welbourne' but it might amuse you as conveying the sharp impression that the place made on me during a few week-ends" (*Correspondence*, p. 383).

Hergesheimer, Joseph (1880–1954) American novelist whose works include *The Three Black Pennys* (1917), *Java Head* (1919), and *Linda Condon* (1919). Fitzgerald met Hergesheimer in Thomas BOYD's bookstore in ST. PAUL in the early 1920s, and Hergesheimer visited the Fitzgeralds at "ELLERSLIE."

Herrick, Walter Character in " 'Boil Some Water—Lots of It.' " Writer who dresses as a Russian Cossack and sits down at the Big Table in the studio commissary as a joke on Max LEAM. Pat HOBBY hits Herrick over the head with a tray.

Hersey, Marie (Mrs. William Hamm) A childhood friend and sweetheart of Fitzgerald in ST. PAUL; a member of William BAKER's dancing class. She was the model for Margaret TORRENCE in the Basil Duke LEE stories. Fitzgerald noted in his *Thoughtbook* for February 1911 that of his "two new crushes"—Margaret ARMSTRONG and Marie—Marie was the prettier (p. 35). Fitzgerald met Ginevra KING when she was visiting Marie, her classmate at Westover girls' school, during the Christmas holidays of 1914–15. Fitzgerald and Marie corresponded when they went away to school; and in December 1916 she visited him at PRINCETON to see the TRIANGLE CLUB musical *Safety First*, for which he had written the lyrics. When Zelda Sayre [FITZGERALD] arrived in NEW YORK CITY for her wedding to Fitzgerald, he enlisted Marie to guide her shopping expedition. When Marie wrote to Fitzgerald after *Time* reprinted Michel MOK's humiliating interview from the *New York Post* ("The Other Side of Paradise," September 25, 1936), he responded on October 28, 1936, "I think of you as about my oldest real friend, certainly my first

love" (*Letters*, p. 545). At the end of *The Great Gatsby*, Nick CARRAWAY recalls Christmas vacations and "the matching of invitations: 'Are you going to the Ordways'? the Herseys'? the Schultzes'?' " (p. 136).

Hesse, Mr. Character in "Dalyrimple Goes Wrong." Bookkeeper on whose desk Bryan DALYRIMPLE sees a list of salaries.

Hibben, John Grier (1861–1933) Fourteenth president of PRINCETON UNIVERSITY (1912–32), an ordained Presbyterian minister and author of *The Philosophy of the Enlightenment* (1910) and *A Defense of Prejudice* (1911)—essays on education. Hibben wrote to Fitzgerald on May 27, 1920 praising "The Four Fists" (1920), a didactic story which Fitzgerald disliked, and expressing his hope that Fitzgerald would further develop in his writings the "philosophy of the instinctive nobility of man" represented by that story. He then expressed how Fitzgerald's characterization of Princeton in *TSOP* had grieved him: "I cannot bear to think that our young men are merely living for four years in a country club and spending their lives wholly in a spirit of calculation and snobbishness. . . . From my undergraduate days I have always had a belief in Princeton and in what the place could do in the making of a strong vigorous manhood. It would be an overwhelming grief to me, in the midst of my work here and my love for Princeton's young men, should I feel that we have nothing to offer but the outgrown symbols and shells of a past whose reality has long since disappeared" (*Correspondence*, p. 58). Fitzgerald replied on June 3 (*Life in Letters*, pp. 37 & 40; *see* Princeton entry).

Hibbing Character in " 'I Didn't Get Over.' " Former officer who is self-conscious about not having gotten to EUROPE during World War I. He tells his classmates at a college reunion about the sinking of a ferry and its effect on Abe DANZER and later reveals to the NARRATOR that he was the "Captain Brown" who was responsible for the incident.

Higgins, Sybil *See* Pamela KNIGHTON.

"The High Cost of Macaroni" Article. *Interim*, 4, nos. 1–2 (1954), 6–15. This unfavorable account of the Fitzgeralds' 1924–25 visit to ITALY was intended as a companion piece to "How to Live on $36,000 a Year" (April 1924) and "How to Live on Practically Nothing a Year" (September 1924); but Harold OBER was unable to sell it to a magazine during Fitzgerald's lifetime. Fitzgerald incorporated two incidents from the article into *TITN*: a dispute over a table allegedly reserved for a princess, and a fight with taxi drivers and a policeman—which he treated seriously in *TITN*.

Highland Hospital Sanitarium in ASHEVILLE, North Carolina, which Zelda FITZGERALD entered on April 8, 1936. Director Dr. Robert S. CARROLL believed that mental problems were caused by toxic substances, and Zelda responded to the Highland regimen of controlled diet and exercise. She was discharged in mid-April 1940 and went to live with her mother, Minnie Machen SAYRE, in MONTGOMERY, Alabama. During periods of depression Zelda voluntarily returned to Highland, re-entering the hospital in November 1947. She died there in a fire on the night of March 10, 1948.

Hilda Character in "Winter Dreams." Eleven-year-old Judy JONES's nurse, who accompanies her to the golf course.

Hill, W. E. (William Ely) (1886–1962) Illustrator of the dust jackets for *This Side of Paradise, Flappers and Philosophers,* and *The Beautiful and Damned.* Fitzgerald told Maxwell PERKINS that he was glad Hill had done the cover for *TSOP*, noting, "I admire him more than any artist in the country" (c. January 10, 1920; *Scott/Max*, p. 24). However, Fitzgerald complained about the depiction of Anthony PATCH on the dust jacket of *B&D*, noting that Hill had gone "quite contrary to a detailed description of the hero in the book" (c. January 31, 1922; *Scott/Max*, p. 52). In 1916 Hill created a series of full-page cartoons for *The New York Tribune* titled *Among Us Mortals*. It was eventually syndicated to newspapers throughout the country until Hill's retirement in 1960.

by Park Bucker

Hilliard, George Character in "Pat Hobby Does His Bit." Director of the movie in which Pat HOBBY is required to act.

Hillis, Bill Character in *TITN*. Young man with whom Rosemary HOYT got into trouble on a train. Collis CLAY's report of this episode to Dick DIVER intensifies Dick's desire for Rosemary.

Himmel, Peter Character in "May Day." Yale undergraduate who escorts Edith BRADIN to the Gamma Psi dance, gets drunk, and goes around with Philip DEAN as "Mr. In" and "Mr. Out."

"His Russet Witch" Fiction. Written November 1920. *METROPOLITAN MAGAZINE*, 53 (February 1921), 11–13, 46–51; in *TJA* as " 'O Russet Witch!' " NEW YORK bookstore employee Merlin GRAINGER enjoys looking through his apartment window at CAROLINE, a young woman whose apartment building faces his. One day she comes to the Moonlight Quill Bookshop to see him, and she throws books around and wrecks the

store. A year and a half later, he proposes to fellow employee Olive MASTERS during dinner. Caroline, who has been drinking, comes to the restaurant with three men and dances on the table; Olive regards her as wicked. Merlin and Olive marry and have a baby, and Merlin is promoted to manager of the bookshop. As he reaches age 35 and becomes aware of the slowing down of his life, he sees Caroline causing a traffic jam outside a church as men swarm her car; again Olive disapproves. When he is 65 and sole owner of the bookshop, Caroline comes to the shop to buy a first edition; she and Merlin discuss what she has meant to him through the years. After she leaves, Merlin is startled when bookstore employee Miss MCCRACKEN identifies her as dancer Alicia Dare. He suddenly realizes that he has always been a fool and has wasted his opportunities for excitement and glamour.

Hitchcock, Tommy (1900–1944) Celebrated polo player and heroic military aviator whom Fitzgerald admired. Fitzgerald listed the "glamor" of the Hitchcocks as one of the sources for Chapter I of *GG*, and Hitchcock was one of several models for Tommy BARBAN in *TITN*. Fitzgerald noted in his *Ledger* for May 1923: "Met Mrs Rumsey + Tommy Hitchcock + went to parties there" (p. 177).

See Nelson Aldrich, Jr., *Tommy Hitchcock: An American Hero* (privately printed, 1984).

Hixson, Mrs. Character in "An Alcoholic Case." Agent who unsuccessfully tries to find a replacement for the NURSE who wishes to give up the case of the alcoholic CARTOONIST.

Hobby, Pat Character in a series of 17 stories which Fitzgerald wrote in HOLLYWOOD during 1939 and 1940. (*See The Pat Hobby Stories* and "Reunion at the Fair.") A 49-nine-year-old dishonest and illiterate writer who has been in the business of publicity and scriptwriting for 20 years. During the days of silent movies Pat achieved some financial success, but for the past 10 years (roughly 1929–39) he has had trouble finding work. He hangs around the studio in hopes of getting a job and because it seems like home to him.

Fitzgerald described Pat as "a complete rat" (to Arnold GINGRICH, December 19, 1939; *Life in Letters*, p. 426). When Fitzgerald's secretary Frances KROLL's brother Nathan was working on dramatizing the Hobby stories, Fitzgerald wrote to him that "the series is characterized by a really bitter humor and only the explosive situations and the fact that Pat is a figure almost incapable of real tragedy or damage saves it from downright unpleasantness. The play should attempt to preserve some of this flavor. It is the only thing actually new about the original conception" (May 6, 1940; *Correspondence*, p. 595).

The Pat Hobby stories should not be regarded as autobiographical; Pat Hobby is not Scott Fitzgerald. The stories did, however, provide an outlet for some of the bitterness which Fitzgerald felt about his experiences in Hollywood; and his income from the Hobby stories supported the writing of *LT/LOLT*.

Hodge, Katherine Character in "Teamed with Genius." Pat HOBBY's former secretary, who is now assigned to René WILCOX.

Hoffman, Phil Character in "A New Leaf." Young man who loves Julia ROSS and marries her a year after her fiancé Dick RAGLAND disappears at sea.

Holcome, Stuart Character in *B&D*. Former beau of Gloria Gilbert [PATCH] who had run away with her in his car and tried to make her marry him.

Holiday, Burne Character in *TSOP*. Kerry HOLIDAY's brother and a friend of Amory BLAINE at PRINCETON, where he leads the movement to abolish clubs. Based on Fitzgerald's Princeton classmate Henry (Mike) STRATER.

Holiday, Kerry Character in *TSOP*. Burne HOLIDAY's brother and a friend of Amory BLAINE at PRINCETON. He drops out of college to join the Lafayette Esquadrille in France and is killed in the war.

Holliday, Mrs. Emily Character in "New Types." Paula JORGENSEN's rich aunt, who hosts a dance for Paula but sleeps through it, causing Paula to think she is dead.

Hollister, Dean Character in *TSOP*. PRINCETON administrator in whose office a group of students assembles a taxicab as a prank.

Hollywood, California At one time Fitzgerald regarded Hollywood as "certainly one of the most romantic cities in the world" (to Harold OBER, February 8, 1936; *Life in Letters*, p. 297; *As Ever*, p. 250). Just months before his death, however, he wrote to Alice Wooton, "Isn't Hollywood a dump—in the human sense of the word. A hideous town, pointed up by the insulting gardens of its rich, full of the human spirit at a new low of debasement" (July 29, 1940; *F. Scott Fitzgerald Centenary Exhibition*, p. 82).

Fitzgerald was not a movie buff, although he attended movies, met movie people socially, and encountered even more in the studios. His correspondence suggests no extraordinary interest. If anything, he was critical of the movies in interviews, in essays such as " 'Wait Till You Have Children of Your Own!' " (July 1924) and "Echoes of the Jazz Age" (November 1931),

in situations in *The Beautiful and Damned* (1922) and *Tender Is the Night* (1934), and in short stories such as "Gretchen's Forty Winks" (March 1924) and "On Schedule" (March 1933). In "Pasting It Together" (March 1936) he noted:

> I saw that the novel, which at my maturity was the strongest and supplest medium for conveying thought and emotion from one human being to another, was becoming subordinated to a mechanical and communal art that . . . was capable of reflecting only the tritest thought, the most obvious emotion. It was an art in which words were subordinate to images, where personality was worn down to the inevitable low gear of collaboration. . . . There was a rankling indignity, that to me had become almost an obsession, in seeing the power of the written word subordinated to another power, a more glittering, a grosser power. (*CU,* p. 78)

Yet throughout his professional life Fitzgerald was associated with and influenced by the movies. During the 1920s, for example, two of his novels and five of his short stories were made into movies: *B&D* (1922; movie 1922), *GG* (1925; movie 1926), "Head and Shoulders" (1920; released that year as *The Chorus Girl's Romance*), "Myra Meets His Family" (1920; released that year as *The Husband Hunter*), "The Offshore Pirate" (1920; movie 1921), "The Camel's Back" (1920; released as *Conductor 1492* in 1924), and "The Pusher-in-the-Face" (1925; released as a two-reel sound movie in 1929).

Fitzgerald's earliest movie work included a scenario in 1920 for actress Dorothy Gish (1898–1968) that apparently was never made, a rejected synopsis for "Trans-Continental Kitty" for David O. SELZNICK in 1922, the titles for director Allan DWAN's 1923 Paramount silent movie *The Glimpses of the Moon* (based on a 1922 novel by Edith WHARTON), and a scenario for the Film Guild production *Grit* (1924). He was paid $10,000 in 1923 to write a treatment for a silent version of *TSOP,* but the movie was never made.

In April 1925, when editor Maxwell PERKINS cabled Fitzgerald that the sales situation for *GG* was "doubtful" (*Scott/Max,* p. 101), Fitzgerald responded with a depressed letter mentioning Hollywood as a potential source of financial stability: "In all events I have a book of good stories for the fall. Now I shall write some cheap ones until I've accumulated enough for my my next novel. When that is finished and published I'll wait and see. If it will support me with no more intervals of trash I'll go on as a novelist. If not I'm going to quit, come home, go to Hollywood and learn the movie business. I can't reduce our scale of living and I can't stand this financial insecurity" (c. April 24, 1925; *Life in Letters,* p. 107; *Scott/Max,* p. 102).

In 1927 Fitzgerald made his first trip to Hollywood, accompanied by his wife; they lived in a bungalow at the AMBASSADOR HOTEL. It was during this two-month Hollywood stay that Fitzgerald met actress Lois MORAN, to whom he became attracted. Producer John W. Considine (b. 1898) of United Artists had hired Fitzgerald to write a movie comedy titled "Lipstick" for actress Constance Talmadge (1900–73). The combination of a college campus, an innocent heroine who has just completed two years in jail to protect her guilty uncle, and a magic lipstick did not save an unsatisfactory script; this movie too was never made.

During the 1930s Fitzgerald devoted even more time to movies. He returned to Hollywood in November–December 1931 to work at Metro-Goldwyn-Mayer studios, revising a script based on the novel *Red-Headed Woman* (1931) by Katharine Brush (1902–52). This time he had a collaborator, Marcel DE SANO, who he claimed was sabotaging his work. The result was not satisfactory. The movie was released in 1932 with script written by Anita LOOS.

During the middle 1930s, Fitzgerald worked without success on several ideas for movies. In 1934, for example, he collaborated with the young Charles Marquis WARREN on a movie treatment for *TITN* (published in Matthew J. BRUCCOLI, *Some Sort of Epic Grandeur,* Appendix 1). That same year he collaborated with BALTIMORE writer Robert Spafford on "Gracie at Sea" intended for comedians George Burns (1896–1996) and Gracie Allen (1902–1964). Neither treatment was sold.

In 1937, when Fitzgerald once again journeyed to Hollywood, his life had changed. Scriptwriting was now his major source of income. He was no longer commanding high SATURDAY EVENING POST fees. He had experienced an emotional breakdown at least partly due to alcoholism. He had outstanding debts totaling at least $22,000 and was paying for his wife's hospital bills and his daughter's education. This time he was far more serious about movie work and spent time reading about filmmaking and viewing important movies. He was ambitious, too. He wrote to his daughter, Scottie FITZGERALD, assessing his previous work in Hollywood and planning his strategy for the third venture: "I must be very tactful but keep my hand on the wheel from the start—find out the key man among the bosses + the most malleable among the collaborators—then fight the rest tooth + nail until, in fact or in effect, I'm alone on the picture. That's the only way I can do my best work" (July 1937; *Life in Letters,* p. 331). A year later, however, he described his Hollywood work to Scottie as "the last tired effort of a man who once did something finer and better" (July 7, 1938; *Life in Letters,* p. 363). A year before his death he wrote to Scottie: "I expect to dip in and out of the pictures for the rest of my natural life, but it is not very soul-satisfying because it is a business of telling stories fit for children and this is only interesting up to a point.

Fitzgerald, 1937; photo by Carl Van Vechten (Yale University Library)

It is the greatest of all human mediums of communication and it is a pity that the censorship had to come along + do this, but there we are" (Winter 1939; *Life in Letters,* p. 384).

Shortly after arriving in Hollywood in July 1937, Fitzgerald met movie columnist Sheilah GRAHAM, who became his companion in his final years. His MGM stint began with work on another college movie, *A Yank at Oxford,* made in England but written in the United States. Fitzgerald's three weeks of script revisions resulted in at least two of his scenes appearing when the movie was released in 1938. Later in 1937 he was assigned to adapt *Three Comrades* (1937), a novel by Erich Maria Remarque (1898–1970), resulting in his only screen credit. Producer Joseph MANKIEWICZ designated writer E. E. PARAMORE, Jr. to work with Fitzgerald on the revisions, with Mankiewicz also contributing. Paramore eventually received joint script credit with Fitzgerald, who indicated his dissatisfaction with the result when he wrote Mankiewicz that the movie was "a flop." (*See* entries on Mankiewicz and *Three Comrades* for Fitzgerald's reaction and Mankiewicz's response.) The reviews, however, were mainly favorable; and *Three Comrades* was voted one of the 10 best movies of 1938.

In 1938, Fitzgerald spent much time working for producer Hunt STROMBERG on an adaptation of "Infidelity," a short story by Ursula Parrott (b. 1902). Fitzgerald and Stromberg never resolved possible censorship problems resulting from a plot that dealt with adultery; after many attempts at producing a satisfactory script, Stromberg gave up. That same year Fitzgerald worked for a short time revising *Marie Antoinette* (released 1938), a longer period partly with writer Donald Ogden STEWART on *The Women* (1939), and another short period on *Madame Curie* (1943). In January 1939 he was lent to Selznick International Productions and worked for David O. Selznick for two weeks revising the script for *Gone With the Wind* (1939). His MGM contract, which expired on January 27, was not renewed. He had worked for 18 months and had been paid a large sum: $1,000 a week for six months, then $1,250 a week. After his contract expired, Fitzgerald continued to submit original screenplay ideas to MGM producers but was not hired to develop any of them. His proposals included a musical based on the Basil Duke LEE stories to star Mickey Rooney (b. 1920), Judy Garland (1922–69), and Freddie Bartholomew (b. 1924); "Babes in Wonderland," about a group of aspiring actors and actresses hiding out in a studio; and "The Feather Fan," about a Vassar student who finds a feather fan that will grant wishes.

During the last two years of his life, Fitzgerald freelanced infrequently for the studios. In 1939, he worked with writer Budd SCHULBERG on Walter WANGER's production of *Winter Carnival* (1939). However, after a short period during which he was drinking as well as ill on location at DARTMOUTH, he was fired. Other brief stints included working again with Donald Ogden Stewart, this time at Paramount Pictures for a month on the script for "Air Raid," another movie which was never made; for Universal Pictures for a week writing "Open That Door," a treatment for a never-to-be-made movie based on *Bull by the Horns* (1937), a novel by Charles Bonner (1896–1965); for a week on the Samuel Goldwyn (1884–1974) movie *Raffles* (1940); and one day for Twentieth Century-Fox on *Everything Happens at Night* (1939). In 1940, he again worked for Twentieth Century-Fox studios, first commenting on the script for "Brooklyn Bridge," also not made, and then revising an adaptation of Emlyn Williams's (1905–87) play *The Light of Heart* (1940), released in 1942 as *Life Begins at Eight-Thirty* with script by Nunnally JOHNSON.

Meanwhile, in March 1940 Fitzgerald sold the movie rights to "Babylon Revisited" (February 1931) to producer Lester COWAN, who hired Fitzgerald to write the script, first called "Honoria," then "Babylon Revisited," and then "Cosmopolitan." Fitzgerald's final script differed greatly from its source, with Helen WALES committing suicide on board ship and Charles WALES becoming depressed and alcoholic, followed by Wales's

confinement, embezzlement by a partner, and an attempted murder. The movie was never made. (*See* "Cosmopolitan.")

Fitzgerald learned his craft—how to use movie devices such as montages, flashbacks, and close-ups, for example—and eventually learned how to write acceptable movie dialogue—despite director Mankiewicz's later statement that it was far too "literary." Critics differ about the merits of Fitzgerald's scripts, but there is general agreement that he never achieved the level of the best of the Hollywood screenwriters.

On the other hand, Fitzgerald profited greatly throughout his life from these movie experiences, using them as subject material for his fiction. Soon after Fitzgerald's 1927 stint in Hollywood, he wrote "Jacob's Ladder" (August 1927), in which wealthy Jacob BOOTH helps NEW YORK shopgirl Jenny PRINCE, modeled partly on Lois Moran, become a Hollywood star. The following year, Fitzgerald again used Hollywood as the background for a story, this time in "Magnetism" (March 1928), in which he wrote about blackmailed actor George HANNAFORD. In 1932, while working at MGM, Fitzgerald attended a party given by producer Irving THALBERG and his wife, actress Norma SHEARER; he later used parts of their personalities as well as an incident at the party in "Crazy Sunday" (October 1932), a story about scriptwriter Joel COLES, who has an affair with director Miles CALMAN's wife, Stella CALMAN. In *TITN*, Fitzgerald used aspects of Lois Moran's character for 18-year-old movie star Rosemary HOYT.

Fitzgerald's final stay in Hollywood offered even more material and gave new life to the author who had felt written out. The Pat HOBBY stories, brief vignettes of a broken-down scriptwriter—not an autobiographical character—came from Hollywood incidents that Fitzgerald had experienced or been told about, as did "Discard" (January 1948), "Last Kiss" (April 1949), and *The Last Tycoon* (1941). Union unrest at MGM, an earthquake that caused flooding in the studios, conversations between director Sidney FRANKLIN and novelist Aldous Huxley (1894–1963)—who was the model for screenwriter George BOXLEY—were only some of the events used by Fitzgerald in his last novel. The hero, Monroe STAHR, was based on Irving Thalberg. Narrator Cecelia BRADY, in addition to having some of Scottie FITZGERALD's characteristics, was also based partly on Budd Schulberg; and Kathleen MOORE resembled Sheilah Graham.

During his final stay in Hollywood, Fitzgerald lived at the GARDEN OF ALLAH until April 1938, when he rented a bungalow at MALIBU BEACH. In November 1938 he moved to "BELLY ACRES" in ENCINO, where he stayed until May 1940, when he moved to 1403 North Laurel Avenue in Hollywood. In November he moved into Sheilah Graham's first-floor apartment at 1443 North Hayworth after suffering a heart attack, and he died there of another heart attack on December 21, 1940.

The Hollywood years played an important role in the Fitzgerald REVIVAL. The posthumous publication of *The Last Tycoon* began a groundswell of praise.

Fitzgerald's secretary, Frances KROLL, gives an account of his life in Hollywood from April 1939 to his death in *Against the Current*. See also Aaron Latham, *Crazy Sundays;* Wheeler Winston Dixon, *The Cinematic Vision of F. Scott Fitzgerald;* and Gene D. Phillips, *Fiction, Film, and F. Scott Fitzgerald.*

by Alan Margolies

Holmes Character in *TITN*. Dick DIVER's father's curate, who cables the message that the Rev. DIVER has died.

Holt, Jerry Character in " 'The Sensible Thing.' " Young man who is waiting at the station with Jonquil CARY when George O'KELLY comes to visit her. Jerry takes them for a drive in his new car.

Holworthy, Jim Character in *Coward*. Able-bodied young man whom Judge DOUGLAS considers a coward for not going to war. When Lindy DOUGLAS rejects Holworthy's proposal, he considers enlisting, but fails to do so until he realizes his own cowardice in revealing the hiding place of her brother Charley DOUGLAS to the Yankees. Holworthy joins the army and is awarded a medal at the Battle of Petersburg. He returns from the war a captain and persuades Lindy to marry him when he scares away a Union soldier who is trying to steal her necklace.

"Homage to the Victorians" Review of *The Oppidan* by Shane LESLIE. *New York Tribune,* May 14, 1922, section 4, p. 6; *In His Own Time.* Fitzgerald comments that this novel about Eton in the late 1890s "interested me enormously" (*In His Own Time,* p. 135).

Home Page To commemorate the CENTENNIAL of Fitzgerald's birth, the University of South Carolina maintains an Internet web site. The site's address is: HTTP://WWW.SC.EDU/FITZGERALD/INDEX. HTML. It offers extensive information on Fitzgerald's writing and career, including primary and secondary bibliographies, detailed biographical material, and a history of the House of Scribner. The site also features quotations by and about the author, accompanied by photographs. It presents the complete texts of early short stories and features facsimiles of their original appearances in *The SATURDAY EVENING POST.* The site includes material on the career of Zelda FITZGERALD and provides Internet links to other author web sites.

by Park Bucker

"The Homes of the Stars" Fiction—Pat HOBBY story. Submitted March 28, 1940. *ESQUIRE,* 14 (August 1940), 28, 120–121; *PH.* Tourists Mr. and Mrs. Deering R. ROBINSON mistake Pat Hobby for a man who gives tours of the homes of HOLLYWOOD stars; and, since he needs money, he agrees to guide them. They are impressed when actor Ronald COLMAN greets him by name. When they ask to see the home of Shirley Temple (b. 1928), he takes them to the house next to hers, which he doesn't know belongs to producer Harold MARCUS. When Marcus arrives unexpectedly, Pat sneaks out and abandons the Robinsons.

"The Honor of the Goon" Fiction. Written April 1937. *ESQUIRE,* 7 (June 1937), 53, 216. Bomar WIN-LOCK, who is noted for his trick of falling down stairs, dislikes fellow college student, Ella LEI CHAMORO, a Malay, because she thought he was really hurt and tried to help; he was embarrassed and walked away rather than completing his trick. In consequence, he dubs her "the Goon," and she is ostracized. During her junior year, her relative, Mister LEI CHAMORO, comes to campus to avenge her. He goes to the dormitory room of Winlock and Oates MULKLEY, who also called Ella a "goon," and has his Norwegian chauffeur, FINGARSON, beat them up. Then he and Fingarson disfigure all the photographs of girls in the room, as well as photos of Winlock's father and dead mother.

Hood, Gilly Character in "The Four Fists." Samuel MEREDITH'S roommate at prep school and the first person to hit him. They eventually become good friends.

Hopkins, Lieutenant Character in *B&D.* A pompous officer in Anthony PATCH's army company.

Hopkins, Mr. *See* George VAN TYNE.

Hopper, Joe Character in "Pat Hobby's Christmas Wish." Man from the scenario department with whom Pat HOBBY chats briefly on Christmas Eve.

Hopper, Sally Carrol *See* Sally Carrol HAPPER.

Horton, George Character in "More Than Just a House." Man whom Amanda GUNTHER marries.

Horton, Mrs. Character in "Not in the Guidebook." Bill DRISCOLL's landlady, who takes in Milly COOLEY.

Hosain *See* Conte di MINGHETTI.

"Hot & Cold Blood" Fiction. Written April 1923. *HEARST'S INTERNATIONAL,* 64 (August 1923), 80–84, 150–151; *ASYM.* When Jaqueline MATHER discovers that her husband, Jim MATHER, has lent money to Ed BRON-SON, she rebukes him for being "an easy mark." On the streetcar on their way home, she is enraged when he gives his seat to a fat woman, who crowds her; and she calls him "a professional nice fellow." Their argument is forgotten until Jaqueline discovers that Ed Bronson has bought an expensive sportscar, although he hasn't repaid Jim's loan. Jaqueline, who is now pregnant, persuades Jim that she needs him more than the other people he helps do. When Fred DRAKE refuses to lend Jim $50, Jim decides Jaqueline has been right about his own excessive generosity and determines to change his ways. He refuses to lend much-needed money to his father's old friend, Edward LACY, and decides not to give up his seat on the streetcar to a woman swaying in the aisle. The woman, who faints, turns out to be Jaqueline; after taking her home to rest, Jim telephones Mr. Lacy to say he can lend him the money.

"The Hotel Child" Fiction. Written November 1930. *The SATURDAY EVENING POST,* 203 (January 31, 1931), 8–9, 69, 72, 75; *Bits of Paradise.* Fifi SCHWARTZ, an 18-year-old American girl, has been traveling in EUROPE with her mother and brother for three years. The other guests at the Hotel des Trois Mondes in SWITZERLAND criticize her behavior and elaborate clothes. When her mother suddenly plans for the family to return to America, Fifi decides to marry Count BOROWKI, but changes her mind when she discovers that he has robbed her mother.

Fitzgerald recycled material from this story for *TITN,* which shares its concern with the influence of corrupt European society on Americans. In "The Hotel Child" the corruption is personified as the Furies, who "were after Fifi now—after her childish complacency and her innocence, even after her beauty—out to break it all down and drag it in any convenient mud" (*Bits of Paradise,* p. 284). However, Fitzgerald offers hope for Fifi, concluding, "There was a certain doubt among the eldest and most experienced of the Furies if they would get her, after all" (p. 297).

In January 1931 Fitzgerald wrote to Harold OBER about this story: "Practically the whole damn thing is true, bizarre as it seems. Lord Allington + the famous Bijou O'Connor were furious at me putting them in + as for the lovely Jewess (real name Mimi Cohn) I don't dare tell her" (*As Ever,* pp. 174–175).

Hotel de la Paix Hotel in LAUSANNE, SWITZERLAND, where Fitzgerald lived in fall 1930.

Hotel des Princes Hotel at the Piazza di Spagna in ROME, ITALY, where the Fitzgeralds lived for $525 a month from October 1924 to February 1925.

hotel manager (unnamed) Character in "The Guest in Room Nineteen." Man who regrets the death of his guest, Mr. CASS.

Hotel Rennert BALTIMORE hotel where Fitzgerald lived from March 30 to May 20, 1932 at the beginning of Zelda FITZGERALD's hospitalization at PHIPPS CLINIC; he moved from the hotel to "LA PAIX."

Hotel Tiberio Hotel in CAPRI, ITALY, where the Fitzgeralds lived February–April 1925.

"How I Would Sell My Book If I Were a Bookseller" Article. *Bookseller and Stationer,* 18 (January 15, 1923), 8; *In His Own Time.* Fitzgerald notes that "the vogue of books like mine depends almost entirely on the stupendous critical power" of H. L. MENCKEN and his secondhand influence on other reviewers who "show the liberal tendencies which Mencken has popularized" (*In His Own Time,* p. 167). He suggests that a bookseller "with a real interest in better books" announce good books as he learns about them from the publisher and take advance orders from customers (p. 168).

"How to Live on Practically Nothing a Year" Essay. *The SATURDAY EVENING POST,* 197 (September 20, 1924), 17, 165–166, 169–170; *AOAA.* Sequel to "How to Live on $36,000 a Year." Humorous description of the Fitzgeralds' attempt to economize by living on the RIVIERA in the summer of 1924.

"How to Live on $36,000 a Year" Essay. *The SATURDAY EVENING POST,* 196 (April 5, 1924), 22, 94, 97; *AOAA.* Humorous description of the Fitzgeralds' financial irresponsibility while living in GREAT NECK, Long Island, New York in 1923. Fitzgerald makes their personal experience representative of the newly rich who populated that area. This essay depicts the Fitzgeralds' perpetual sense of never knowing where their money went.

"How to Waste Material: A Note on My Generation" Essay-review of *In Our Time* (1925) by Ernest HEMINGWAY. *The Bookman,* 63 (May 1926), 262–265; *AOAA.* Fitzgerald criticizes current trends in American writing, expressing his concern that material is being run through too quickly and is being published "raw and undigested." He sees hope for the future with the publication of Hemingway's *In Our Time,* which he praises for its objectivity and economy.

Howard Character in "Benediction." LOIS's lover, whom she is traveling to meet when she stops to visit her brother, KIETH.

Howard Character in "The Family Bus." The T. R. HENDERSONS' chauffeur, who teaches Dick HENDERSON about cars.

Howard Character in "No Flowers." Carter MCLANE's roommate, whose corsage Amanda Rawlins [CLARK] accepted in place of Carter's.

Howard, Miss Character in "The Hotel Child." Girl whom the TAYLORS are planning to present at court until she is caught running away with Count BOROWKI.

Howard, Mrs. Sigourney Character in *GG.* Jordan BAKER's aunt.

Howland, Mr. Character in *B&D.* Anthony PATCH's broker.

Hoyt, Rosemary Character in *TITN.* Eighteen-year-old actress from whose point of view most of Book I is presented, depicting an idealized version of Dick and Nicole DIVER. She is heavily influenced by her mother, Mrs. Elsie SPEERS, who handles the business matters of Rosemary's career. Rosemary falls in love with Dick and eventually has an affair with him. The character of Rosemary evolved from a combination of actress Lois MORAN and Francis Melarky, the protagonist of an early version of the novel. Although Melarky was a violent young man who was to murder his mother, none of his experiences which were transferred to Rosemary is inappropriate to her character.

Hubbard, Spud Character in "The Ice Palace." An athletic young man at the dinner party which Sally Carrol HAPPER attends on the first night of her visit to the North.

Hubbel, Mr. Character in "Two Wrongs." Mr. BRANCUSI's friend, to whom he introduces Bill MCCHESNEY.

Hubbel, Willard Character in "Zone of Accident." Local drama critic who gets AMY into the film contest in place of a girl who won the preliminary competition in Washington.

Hudson, E. Brunswick Character in "Mightier Than the Sword." Writer from the East who has difficulty adapting to screenwriting in HOLLYWOOD.

Hudson, Jewel Character in "May Day." Lower-class girl who is blackmailing Gordon STERRETT and who marries him while he is drunk.

Hughes, Easton Character in "Two Wrongs." Emmy PINKARD's friend, a dental student.

Hugo Character in "Dice, Brass Knuckles & Guitar." Jim POWELL's black bodyservant.

Hulda Character in *Assorted Spirits.* Peter WETHERBY's Swedish maid, who lets in burglar SECOND STORY SALLE

to steal the $10,000 which his guest, Josephus HENDRIX, has brought to purchase his house.

Hull, Joe Character in *B&D*. A man whom Richard CARAMEL and Maury NOBLE bring to Anthony and Gloria PATCH's house and who comes to Gloria's bedroom door drunk, causing her to run outside in the night.

Humbird, Dick Character in *TSOP*. A friend of Amory BLAINE at PRINCETON who was killed in a car wreck and whom Amory later sees as a devil figure in a hallucination at the apartment of showgirls Phoebe COLUMN and Axia MARLOWE.

Hume, Charles Character in "On Schedule." René DU CARY's chief assistant in his scientific research.

Hume, Dolores Character in "On Schedule." Charles HUME's wife, who is shocked to find Becky SNYDER in René DU CARY's bathtub.

Hunter, Anson Character in "The Rich Boy." Based on Ludlow FOWLER. Young man from a wealthy and socially prominent family. Anson's sense of personal superiority isolates him from love. His friend, the NARRATOR, evaluates him thus: "I don't think he was ever happy unless some one was in love with him, responding to him like filings to a magnet, helping him to explain himself, promising him something. What it

was I do not know. Perhaps they promised that there would always be women in the world who would spend their brightest, freshest, rarest hours to nurse and protect that superiority he cherished in his heart" (*ASYM*, p. 56).

Hunter, Edna Character in "The Rich Boy." Robert HUNTER's wife, who is having an affair with Cary SLOANE. When Anson HUNTER discovers the affair, he confronts his Aunt Edna and her lover and threatens to tell Uncle Robert and Sloane's father unless Sloane leaves town for six months.

Hunter, Miss Character in "In the Holidays." Nurse who asks Mr. MCKENNA to mail a letter for her; his fingerprints on the envelope are used to prove his criminal identity.

Hunter, Robert Character in "The Rich Boy." Anson HUNTER's uncle and the administrator of Anson's father's estate. He had been Anson's great friend during Anson's youth, but he gradually slips out of Anson's life as he is disappointed with the choices Anson makes after college and the war. He is unaware of his wife Edna HUNTER's affair, and Anson confronts Edna and her lover to prevent Uncle Robert from being hurt.

Hyères, France RIVIERA town where the Fitzgeralds stayed at the Grimm's Park Hotel in May 1924 before settling at the VILLA MARIE in VALESCURE in June.

I

" 'I Didn't Get Over' " Fiction. Written August 1936. *ESQUIRE,* 6 (October 1936), 45, 194–195; *AOAA.* At their 20th college reunion, several members of the Class of 1916 are discussing World War I when they are joined by HIBBING, who "didn't get over." He tells them about Abe DANZER, who had been a class hero but who had become a drunkard and ended up in Leavenworth, where he was shot trying to escape. Danzer had turned to drink after the sinking of a ferry and drowning of some men under his command in Georgia. Hibbing, who identifies himself as "Captain Brown" during the initial telling of the story, had been responsible for the incident but had blamed Danzer.

The ferry incident was based on the sinking of a ferry in the Talapoosa River near CAMP SHERIDAN in Alabama; Fitzgerald saved several lives during the accident.

"I Got Shoes" Fiction. Written July 1933. *The SATURDAY EVENING POST,* 206 (September 23, 1933), 14–15, 56, 58; *The Price Was High.* Johanna BATTLES, a former debutante who works for a newspaper, interviews actress Nell MARGERY, whom she asks about the rumor that she collects shoes. The actress tells how at age 10 she had worn the soles out of her shoes and injured her feet while accompanying her mother on a job interview. When the child outgrew her next pair of new shoes she had refused to discard them, and ever since then she had kept all of her old shoes. After discussing discipline and duty as part of professionalism, Miss Margery dismisses Johanna and talks with Warren LIVINGSTONE, who wants to marry her but with whom she is dissatisfied because he plays rather than working and earning money. Livingstone leaves in disgust, but telephones from the hotel lobby to say he can never love another woman. Miss Margery tells him to come back up; and she informs her maid, JACCY, that she can have her old shoes because she is not saving them anymore.

"The Ice Palace" Fiction. Written December 1919. *The SATURDAY EVENING POST,* 192 (May 22, 1920), 18–19, 163, 167, 170; *F&P.* Southern belle Sally Carrol HAPPER wants to leave the sleepy Southern town of

James H. Crank's illustration for "The Ice Palace" in The Saturday Evening Post *(Bruccoli Collection, University of South Carolina)*

TARLETON, Georgia, to "live where things happen on a big scale" (*F&P,* p. 54), where she won't feel she is wasting herself. On a January trip to visit her Yankee fiancé, Harry BELLAMY, she dislikes the cold and feels out of place. After she nearly freezes to death in an ice palace at the winter carnival, she returns to the familiar, warm, and lazy South.

"The Ice Palace," written after a visit to Zelda Sayre [FITZGERALD] in MONTGOMERY, Alabama, was the first of several stories in which Fitzgerald explored the differences between the North and South. Fitzgerald provides an account of writing "The Ice Palace" in "Contemporary Writers and Their Work, A Series of Autobiographical Letters—F. Scott Fitzgerald," *The Editor,* 53 (Second July Number, 1920), 121–122.

"ickle durls" (unnamed) Characters in "Indecision." Two California girls on vacation from their school in Montreux, SWITZERLAND, who convey messages about Rosemary MERRIWEATHER to Tommy MCLANE. In *TITN* Nicole DIVER contemptuously refers to the American schoolgirls in GSTAAD as "ickle durls."

Icky, Charles Character in "Mister Icky." Mr. ICKY's son who is going to sea.

Icky, Mr. Character in "Mister Icky." Old man and reformed arsonist who was given the glands of a young prisoner who was executed. His many children leave him.

Icky, Ulsa Character in "Mister Icky." Mr. ICKY's daughter who went to LONDON to be a typist.

Illustrations for Fitzgerald's Magazine Stories In the 1920s and 1930s mass-circulation magazines provided illustrations to accompany short stories and nonfiction articles. Illustrations both attracted readers to a story and established its tone. SATURDAY EVENING POST editor Wesley Stout described the artist's process: "He studies [the story] sometimes until he actually materializes a psychic portrait of the author, who subconsciously, had made himself the hero" ("Yes, We Read the Story," *Post*, 204 [June 25, 1932], p. 8). Because Fitzgerald was a top magazine writer, editors assigned top illustrators to his work, including Arthur William BROWN, James Montgomery FLAGG, and F. R. GRUGER.

The illustrations for Fitzgerald's stories often reflected the author's handsome and glamorous image through their depiction of idealized youth. The scenes that artists chose to illustrate also provide evidence about how he crafted serious or "adult" themes for a commercial audience that desired escapist and romantic literature. The drawings frequently depict glamorous young women and handsome tuxedoed youths in high society. In order to attract the reader's eye, the illustrations often portrayed a romantic aspect of the story, such as a flapper's dramatic entrance to a ball, or a lovers' quarrel set in a fashionable drawing room. The drawings usually carried a melodramatic caption or "legend" gleaned from the story.

The tragic aspects of "Babylon Revisited" may superficially appear too mature for most readers of *The Saturday Evening Post*, but the magazine placed it first in its February 21, 1932 issue. The illustrations highlight the elements that would appeal to the *Post*'s mainstream audience. Henrietta McCaig STARRETT's drawings for "Babylon Revisited" emphasize the hero's adorable young daughter rather than his debilitating alcoholism. The captions similarly reflect the story's sentimentality. Charlie WALES tells his daughter, Honoria WALES: "But you won't always like me best, Honey. You'll grow up and meet somebody your own age and go marry him, and forget you ever had a daddy" (p. 3). By stressing the daughter's role in the story, the *Post* focuses on Honoria's chance for a positive future rather than the final isolation of Wales.

For most authors the artists worked from a completed story or first installment of a series. In his unpublished memoirs illustrator Arthur William Brown recorded that Fitzgerald "was always late on deadlines and often I would have to make drawings from his vague descriptions" (*Correspondence*, p. 115). At the request of METROPOLITAN MAGAZINE editor Carl Hovey, Fitzgerald wrote a letter to Brown describing illustration ideas for his unfinished story "Winter Dreams" (December 1922). He also provided a rough sketch of Dexter GREEN and Judy JONES's first meeting on the golf course. The length and detail of his letter reveal Fitzgerald's attention to the illustrative aspects of his magazine fiction. Fitzgerald concluded, "It has been a most peculiar story—not nearly so obvious as it sounds here. I like all your work very much and was tremendously pleased at your illustrations for 'The Camel's Back' and for 'The Jellybean' " (Fall 1922; *Correspondence*, p. 114).

The heroes of Fitzgerald's magazine fiction conform to the idealized figures of the period's popular illustration. Fitzgerald referred to J. C. Leyendecker's famous portraits of exemplary male figures to describe the heroine's dead brother in "The Last of the Belles": "She showed me his picture—it was a handsome, earnest face with a Leyendecker forelock—and told me that when she met someone who measured up to him she'd marry" (*TAR*, p. 257). Leyendecker (1874–1951) painted many popular covers for the *Post* as well as successful Arrow Collar advertisements, but he did not illustrate individual stories, either for Fitzgerald or for other magazine writers of the period.

See Walt Reed and Roger Reed, *The Illustrator in America, 1880–1980: A Century of Illustration* (New York: Madison Square Press, 1993), and Wesley Stout, "Yes, We Read the Story," *The Saturday Evening Post*, 204 (June 25, 1932), 8–9, 34, 36, 38, 40.

by Park Bucker

"Image on the Heart" Fiction. Written September 1935. MCCALL'S, 63 (April 1936), 7–9, 52, 54, 57–58, 62; *The Price Was High*. When TUDY's husband drowns a week after their wedding, TOM, an old family friend, lends her the money to study in France for a year. As they grow closer through their correspondence, she accepts his proposal of marriage; and he travels to Provence for their wedding. When he arrives, however, he discovers that she has become interested in naval aviator Lieutenant de Marine RICCARD, who is almost Tom's double. While waiting for his mother to arrive for the wedding, Tom sends Tudy to PARIS to shop to get her away from Riccard. When she returns for their wedding, he finds out that Riccard flew to Paris to meet her at the station and ride back with her. Tudy protests her innocence; and Tom decides to go ahead and marry her, even though he can never be sure what really happened.

Fitzgerald's working titles for this story were "Finishing School" and "A Course in Languages." The story was based on the crisis in the Fitzgeralds' marriage brought on by Zelda FITZGERALD's involvement with French naval aviator Edouard JOZAN.

"Imagination—and a Few Mothers" Essay. *The Ladies' Home Journal*, 40 (June 1923), 21, 80–81. Fitzgerald describes the "average home" as "a horribly dull place" (*Ladies' Home Journal Treasury* [New York: Simon & Schuster, 1956], p. 121). He contrasts a nervous, depressing mother who imagines worrisome things about her children and husband with a charming woman who makes her home happy by enjoying life herself and treating her children as people.

"In the Darkest Hour" Fiction—first PHILIPPE story. Written April 1934. *REDBOOK*, 63 (October 1934), 15–19, 94–98; *The Price Was High*. Twenty-year-old Philippe, Count of Villefranche, who had been carried to Spain as an infant with his mother by the VIZIER who had killed his father, returns to his native France in 872 A.D. to find the country ravaged by invading Vikings. He gathers several villagers at the home of LE POIRE, the leader of the community, and reveals his claim to the land in that area, pledging to protect the people from foreign invaders in return for their service. When he discovers a Viking encampment, he enlists the aid of some monks and workmen and sends JACQUES, who had warned him of a plot against his life, to persuade Le Poire to gather other fighters; and the two groups successfully attack the Vikings. The Viking leader, ROBERT THE FROG, is killed in battle; and Philippe orders the execution of Robert's son, GOLDGREAVES, so that there will be no opposition to his leadership.

"In the Holidays" Fiction. Written February 1937. *ESQUIRE*, 8 (December 1937), 82, 184, 186; *The Price Was High*. On New Year's Eve hospital patient Mr. MCKENNA, a murderer, briefly leaves the hospital to get a drink; he tears up the letter which nurse Miss HUNTER has asked him to mail to her FIANCÉ. Around midnight Mr. GRIFFIN, a fellow patient in the hospital and a witness against McKenna, is murdered by McKenna's accomplices. The next day Miss Hunter's fiancé, a detective posing as a resident doctor, has McKenna's fingerprints, taken from the scraps of the envelope, checked; this confirms that he is criminal Joe Kinney.

"In Literary New York" Letter to Bernard Vaughan. *St. Paul Daily News*, December 23, 1923, section 2, p. 5; *In His Own Time*. Fitzgerald notes that "the real event of the year will, of course, be the appearance in January of the *American Mercury*," edited by H. L. MENCKEN and George Jean NATHAN (*In His Own Time*, pp. 169–170).

"Indecision" Fiction. Written January–February 1931. *The SATURDAY EVENING POST*, 203 (May 16, 1931), 12–13, 56, 59, 62; *The Price Was High*. Twenty-seven-year-old banker Tommy MCLANE visits SWITZERLAND in hopes of falling in love. He is attracted to both Emily ELLIOT, a 25-year-old divorcée, and Rosemary MERRIWEATHER, an 18-year-old Southerner; when he is with one of them, he thinks about the other. He is unable to choose between them until his jealousy of Rosemary's attention to Count DE CAROS MOROS swings the balance in her favor. He is suddenly called back to his job and is unable to locate Rosemary before he leaves the hotel; but he finds her on the same train he is taking and asks her to marry him, despite his final thoughts of Emily.

Fitzgerald borrowed material from this story for Dick and Nicole DIVER's Christmas trip to GSTAAD in *TITN*.

Indore, John Brown Hobby Character in "Pat Hobby, Putative Father." Pat HOBBY's putative son by his ex-wife Delia BROWN, to whom he had been married at the time of John's birth.

"Infidelity" Screenplay. *ESQUIRE*, 80 (December 1973), 193–200, 290–304. In early 1938 Metro-Goldwyn-Mayer assigned Fitzgerald to Hunt STROMBERG's production unit to work alone on a movie for Joan Crawford (1904–77), whose movies he studied in order to tailor the role to her acting abilities (see Fitzgerald to Gerald MURPHY, March 1938; *Letters*, pp. 427–428). MGM had acquired rights to "Infidelity," a short story by Ursula Parrott (b. 1902); but Fitzgerald was to write virtually an original story. He worked from February to May on a 104–page screenplay about wealthy Nicolas and Althea Gilbert. Althea discovers that Nicolas has had a one-night affair with a former sweetheart, and she develops a platonic relationship with a former suitor. The project was abandoned because the subject of marital infidelity was taboo in HOLLYWOOD in 1938. (See Fitzgerald to Stromberg, February 22, 1938; *Life in Letters*, pp. 348–349).

"Inside the House" Fiction—Gwen BOWERS story. Written April 1936. *The SATURDAY EVENING POST*, 208 (June 13, 1936), 18–19, 32, 34, 36; *The Price Was High*. Fourteen-year-old Gwen begs her father, Bryan BOWERS, to let her go to a movie with Jason CRAWFORD; but he refuses to let her date. When lawyer Edward HARRISON comes to dinner, he reveals that Gwen's idol, actress Peppy VELANCE, is a client of his. Harrison falls ill and is forced to stay with the Bowerses for several days; he tells Gwen that she looks like her mother, with whom he apparently was in love. Gwen sneaks away to a Peppy Velance movie with Jason. Just before the feature begins the theater roof caves in from the weight of snow, but everyone escapes unharmed. When Gwen

returns home, her father informs her that the visitor whom she had encountered on her way out and whom she had thought was a nurse for Mr. Harrison was really Peppy Velance, who had come to see her. After Gwen goes to bed disappointed, her father leaves her a note saying that Harrison and Velance will be there for dinner the next night.

"Institutional Humanitarianism" Unfinished play. Fitzgerald's August 21, 1937 MGM contract allowed him to "complete the writing of that certain play tentatively entitled 'Institutional Humanitarianism,' heretofore commenced" (PRINCETON UNIVERSITY LIBRARY). On December 7 Fitzgerald told Edwin KNOPF that he would have to rewrite the play, which had a prison background, because of its similarity to recent gangster films (*Correspondence*, p. 485). However, the only surviving material for the play is a notebook at Princeton University Library which contains a table of contents, a few notes, and a brief outline. See Alan Margolies, "F. Scott Fitzgerald's Prison Play," *Papers of the Bibliographical Society of America*, 66 (First Quarter 1972), 61–64.

"An Interview with F. Scott Fitzgerald" *Saturday Review*, 43 (November 5, 1960), 26, 56; in *In His Own Time* as "Self-Interview." Self-interview which Fitzgerald wrote in 1920 to publicize *TSOP*. Although the *Saturday Review* stated that the piece had not been used in 1920, it had partly appeared in Heywood Broun's "Books" (*New York Tribune*, May 7, 1920, p. 14) as quotes from an interview with Fitzgerald by Carleton R. Davis. The first two paragraphs of Fitzgerald's 1920 "Author's Apology" appeared in the self-interview in a slightly different form; and in *B&D* Anthony PATCH attributes the pronouncement about "the wise writer writing for the youth of his own generation, the critic of the next, and the schoolmaster of ever afterward" to an interview given by Dick CARAMEL after his early success as a novelist (*B&D*, p. 189).

"The Intimate Strangers" Fiction. Written February–March 1935. MCCALL'S, 62 (June 1935), 12–14, 36, 38, 40, 42, 44; *The Price Was High*. Twenty-one-year-old SARA runs away to North Carolina for a week with Cedric KILLIAN, who shares her love of music, before returning to France with her children and husband, Eduard DE LA GUILLET DE LA GUIMPÉ. During World War I, while Eduard is paralyzed from a wound, she encounters Killian again and sees him off to war. Eight years after the war, and a year after Eduard's death, Killian calls her while drunk in the middle of the night; and she

goes to his hotel suite. Her sister-in-law and brother-in-law, Comte Paul and Noel DE LA GUILLET DE LA GUIMPÉ, try to persuade her to give up Killian, but she runs away to marry him. She worries about his two unexplained absences, but when she finds him at the grave of his first wife, DOROTHY, and learns that he had been in love with Dorothy when they had met briefly during the war, she begins to understand their differences and loves him more.

"The Intimate Strangers" is loosely based on the relationship of Nora and Lefty FLYNN, friends of Fitzgerald in TRYON, North Carolina.

Ireland, Louis Character in "Six of One—". Brilliant scholar who is insubordinate and eccentric but whom Ed BARNES helps through college and who becomes a sculptor in EUROPE.

Irene Character in "The Cut-Glass Bowl." Evylyn PIPER'S sister, a guest at the Pipers' dinner party.

Irving, Gladys Character in "Six of One—". Young married woman with whom Charley SCHOFIELD has been flirting.

Isabelle Character in "Babes in the Woods." Sophisticated 16-year-old girl who is an experienced flirt; based on Ginevra KING. This character is renamed Isabelle BORGÉ in *TSOP*.

Italy The Fitzgeralds first visited Italy during their 1921 trip to EUROPE. They lived in ROME from October 1924 to February 1925 and in CAPRI February–April 1925. Fitzgerald disliked Italy and wrote to Harold OBER in response to a suggestion that he write about Rome: "I hate Italy and the Italiens so violently that I can't bring myself to write about them for the Post— unless they'd like an article called 'Pope Siphilis the Sixth and his Morons' or something like that" (received January 23, 1925; *Life in Letters*, p. 94; *As Ever*, p. 73). Ober was unable to place the article Fitzgerald eventually wrote; "The High Cost of Macaroni" was published posthumously.

Ives, George Character in "On Your Own." Wealthy lawyer who falls in love with Evelyn LOVEJOY, whom he meets on a ship from England to America.

Ives, Mrs. Character in "On Your Own." George IVES'S mother, who is offended by Evelyn LOVEJOY'S comments at dinner.

J

Jaccy Character in "I Got Shoes." Nell MARGERY's maid, to whom she gives her old shoes when she decides to relinquish them.

Jackson, Ellery Hamil Character in "John Jackson's Arcady." John JACKSON's son, who is unwelcome at many houses in town and who has been expelled from Yale.

Jackson, John Character in "John Jackson's Arcady." Discouraged man who feels he has gotten nothing out of life and who returns to his hometown to seek happiness. When he returns to the city after being rejected by his now-married childhood sweetheart, Alice HARLAND, he is cheered by the tribute paid to him at a meeting of the Civic Welfare League.

Jackson, Mary Character in "First Blood." Josephine PERRY, Constance PERRY, and their mother attend Mary's wedding to Jackson DILLON. Josephine, impressed by the purity of the bride, resolves to behave better.

Jackson, Norris (1895–1990) Childhood friend of Fitzgerald in ST. PAUL, a member of William BAKER's dancing class, and Fitzgerald's classmate at ST. PAUL ACADEMY and PRINCETON. He married another of Fitzgerald's childhood friends, Betty AMES.

Jackson, General Thomas Jonathan ("Stonewall") (1824–1863) Historical figure and character in "A Debt of Honor." Confederate general. In "A Debt of Honor" he grants Colonel BARROWS permission to assault a house held by federal troops.

"Jacob's Ladder" Fiction. Written June 1927. *The SATURDAY EVENING POST,* 200 (August 20, 1927), 3–5, 57–58, 63–64; *Bits of Paradise.* Thirty-three-year-old Jacob BOOTH meets 16-year-old shopgirl Jenny DELEHANTY after the trial of her sister, Mrs. CHOYNSKI, for murder. He suggests that she change her name to Jenny Prince and introduces her to director Billy FARRELLY, who hires her for one of three leading roles in his movie. She is then offered a two-year contract that requires her to leave NEW YORK for HOLLYWOOD. She weeps at parting with Jacob, who is in love with her; but she is excited about her prospects. Six months later Jacob visits her in California and perceives that she is no longer a child. He resents the attention which RAFFINO, a Latin actor, pays to Jenny. Jacob declares his love for her, but she says she doesn't love him the same way; and he dreams of the image he has created of her. Before he returns to New York he thwarts Choynski's attempt to blackmail Jenny. When Jenny comes to see him several months later he urges her to marry him, but she tells him she is in love and plans to marry the director of her most recent picture. When she leaves he goes to the theater to watch her latest movie, where he can recapture his image of her.

"Jacob's Ladder" has connections with *TITN,* into which Fitzgerald incorporated passages from the story. In early drafts of the novel Rosemary HOYT was named Jenny Prince.

Jacques (Jaques) Character in the PHILIPPE stories. In "In the Darkest Hour" this peasant warns Philippe of a plot against his life; and Philippe commissions him to enlist LE POIRE, a leader of the community, against the Vikings. In "The Count of Darkness" Jacques is a leader of Philippe's supporters. In "The Kingdom in the Dark" he and Philippe kill squire GUESCULIN to keep him from revealing to King LOUIS that GRISELDA, who has run away from the king, is nearby. In "Gods of Darkness" Jaques appeals to the common bond he shares with the followers of the DUKE OF MAINE who belong to the same witch cult to keep them from helping the Duke attack Philippe.

Jadwin, Philip Character in "A Change of Class." Wealthy and prominent businessman who reluctantly gives Earl JOHNSON a tip on the stock market.

Jaggers, George Character in "Financing Finnegan." Editor who lends money to author FINNEGAN. Based on Maxwell PERKINS.

Janney, Butch Character in "Family in the Wind." Gene and Rose JANNEY's son, who rebukes Forrest JANNEY for the way he had spoken to Rose.

Janney, Forrest Character in "Family in the Wind." Alcoholic doctor who gives up his medical practice and returns to his small Alabama hometown to run a drugstore.

Janney, Gene Character in "Family in the Wind." Forrest JANNEY's brother.

Janney, Pinky Character in "Family in the Wind." Gene and Rose JANNEY's worthless son, who has been shot in the head.

Janney, Rose Character in "Family in the Wind." Gene JANNEY's wife, who resents Forrest JANNEY's attitude toward her son, Pinky JANNEY.

Jaques *See* JACQUES.

Jaques, Leland Character in "At Your Age." Young man whom Tom SQUIRES asks about Annie LORRY.

Jarvis Character in "Benediction." One of KIETH's friends at the seminary.

Jazz Age The Jazz Age is impossible to discuss apart from Fitzgerald and his writings. He has come to be its eponymous figure and *The Great Gatsby* (1925) the representative Jazz Age novel. That Fitzgerald was made famous by the period has to a certain extent obscured his ambivalence about it, for he was one of its chief critics as well as chief celebrators. More than half a dozen biographies have raised what was once simple celebrity status to that of an American myth. His striving for material and literary success remains an American dream, even though he presented the drive for riches as morally bankrupt.

The Jazz Age lasted, according to Fitzgerald, from May 1919 to October 1929. He saw himself as its principal chronicler, writing to Maxwell PERKINS: "I claim credit for naming it + . . . it extended from the suppression of the riots on May Day 1919 to the crash of the Stock Market in 1929—almost exactly one decade" (c. May 15, 1931; *Scott/Max*, p. 171). His essay "Echoes of the Jazz Age" (November 1931) recapitulates the ambience: "It was an age of miracles, it was an age of art, it was an age of excess, and it was an age of satire" (*CU*, p. 14). Notwithstanding the ecstasy of this characterization, the moral side of Fitzgerald from the beginning rejected the time's lack of ethical fiber. In *TSOP* (1920), Amory BLAINE sees the devil himself in the company of a bibulous flapper; Anthony and Gloria PATCH in *B&D* (1922) deteriorate as a result of the dissipation characteristic of the period.

Underpinning the giddiness and glitter ("even when you were broke you didn't worry about money, because it was in such profusion around you" [*CU*, p. 21]) lay the profound optimism of the period. The "American dream" could be achieved; personal and material fulfillment was possible even in the edgy gaiety of a society disillusioned by the war. Fitzgerald's fiction idealizes and satirizes—sometimes at the same time—this optimism, the belief that "Life was something you dominated if you were any good" ("The Crack-Up," February 1936; *CU*, p. 69). The most perfect embodiment of this ambivalence comes in *GG*. Most characters in that novel aspire to a better life, a "piece" of the dream. *GG's* is a society on the make: from lower-class Myrtle WILSON to Jordan BAKER—who moves in the semi-elite milieu of successful sports figures—almost all aspire to riches and acclaim, moving in a fluid environment. Jay GATSBY himself is central, for he aspires more wildly than the others and comes closest to succeeding. As these characters, to varying degrees, achieve nobility through their struggles, Fitzgerald satirizes their credulousness by showing an almost pandemic dishonesty and by revealing that those at the top of the socioeconomic ladder, Tom and Daisy BUCHANAN, drift unhappily in moneyed purposelessness. Most notably, the dominating consciousness of the book, narrator Nick CARRAWAY, does not share those aspirations but maintains a critical, ironic stance toward them.

Fitzgerald's short fiction in the 1920s offers a similar although usually simpler view. In line with the commercial demands of *The* SATURDAY EVENING POST and the other magazines for which his short work was composed, the stories emphasize the successful aspirant. Constantly underpinning the upwardly mobile struggles of caddies, barbers, and businessmen in their quests, however, is the Jazz Age belief that wealth is attainable.

The term "Jazz Age" suggests that music was the force that lives revolved around. However, jazz *qua* jazz is only a small part of Fitzgerald's fictional world. Although he was a highly conscious manipulator of the rhythms of his own prose, jazz did not play the controlling role for him that it did for Vachel Lindsay (1879–1931), Langston Hughes (1902–67), or Kenneth Rexroth (1905–82). Rather, Fitzgerald used jazz in a general sense, as a metaphor for the spirit of the twenties. It is for this reason that he is sometimes called "the poet of the Jazz Age." Of course, with his consciousness of his times, Fitzgerald did weave popular songs into his narratives: *GG* includes lyrics from "Ain't We Got Fun" and "The Sheik of Araby" and mentions "The Beale Street Blues" (only the last of these is jazz). When the orchestra at Gatsby's party plays "Vladimir Tostoff's Jazz History of the World," there is no sense of what this composition is like as music, for Fitzgerald had no technical knowledge about jazz and didn't write about it. Fitzgerald is more concerned to satirize the self-importance of jazz as a

genre: in 1922, when *GG* takes place, people thought that jazz could in some way recapitulate the history of the world.

However, while not imitating its rhythms, Fitzgerald did identify some of his fiction with jazz, especially fiction less deeply ironical than his now better-known work. Writing to Perkins about the proposed contents of his third story collection, *All the Sad Young Men* (1926), he described "Dice, Brass Knuckles & Guitar" (considered but not finally included) as "Exuberant Jazz" and "Rags Martin-Jones and the Pr-nce of W-les" as "fantastic Jazz, so good that [*Saturday Evening Post* editor George Horace] Lorimer + [*Hearst's* editor Ray] Long refused it" (June 1, 1925; *Life in Letters,* p. 121; *Scott/Max,* p. 112).

Two years after the Depression began in October 1929 and put an end to the Jazz Age with its hedonism, "precocious intimacies," and "nervous stimulation," Fitzgerald began to see it in the nostalgic glow that was one of his deepest and steadiest emotions. "It all seems rosy and romantic to us who were young then, because we will never feel quite so intensely about our surroundings any more" ("Echoes of the Jazz Age," *CU,* p. 22) and "Come back, come back, O glittering and white!" ("My Lost City," *CU,* p. 33). He wrote in his *Notebooks:*

> It is the custom now to look back ourselves of the boom days with a disapproval that approaches horror. But it had its virtues, that old boom: Life was a great deal larger and gayer for most people, and the stampede to the spartan virtues in times of war and famine shouldn't make us too dizzy to remember its hilarious glory. There were so many good things. These eyes have been hallowed by watching a man order champagne for his two thousand guests, by listening while a woman ordered a whole staircase from the greatest sculptor in the world, by seeing a man tear up a good check for eight hundred thousand dollars. (#1769)

Fitzgerald's role as spokesman for and embodiment of the Jazz Age haunted him throughout his life. Many contemporary writers couldn't dissociate Fitzgerald from that era. As late as 1967, Paul Gallico (1897–1976) wrote, "Fitzgerald . . . had one fatal flaw as a novelist. The unquestioned poet of the Twenties, he could strike the bell of his generation but of no other" (*The Revealing Eye,* photographs by Nickolas Muray, text by Paul Gallico [New York: Atheneum, 1967], p. 106). Yet with the passage of time the twenties have reacquired their lost patina; they have become, largely because of Fitzgerald's writing, the lush romantic past he saw them as and are central to the American sense of self. Because of his art—his talent for language and metaphor, his ability to create a generation from its gestures and to place those gestures in a pattern more significant than any one of them—he transcends the era he portrayed and criticized, while retaining his identity with it. Like Nick Carraway in *GG,* he is "within

and without, simultaneously enchanted and repelled by the inexhaustible variety of life" (p. 30). Consequently, because of his life but even more because of his fiction, Fitzgerald encompasses the Jazz Age that was once thought to have encompassed him.

by Roger Lathbury

Jefferson (Jeff) Character in *Coward.* Black servant to Judge DOUGLAS's family. When he discovers the money which Charley DOUGLAS hid during the war, he thinks Charley will send it to General Robert E. LEE despite his own family's poverty; so he gives the money to Mrs. DOUGLAS and tells her that her now-deceased husband had entrusted it to him to give her after the war.

Jelke, Joe Character in "A Short Trip Home." Yale senior and one of the most eligible young men in ST. PAUL.

"The Jelly-Bean" Fiction. Written May 1920. METRO-POLITAN MAGAZINE, 52 (October 1920), 15–16, 63–67; *TJA.* Idler Jim POWELL, whose family's financial and social status has deteriorated through the generations, reluctantly accompanies Clark DARROW to a country club dance in TARLETON, Georgia. He is enchanted by Nancy LAMAR, who kisses him after he helps her win back the money she has lost shooting craps. His new love for Nancy inspires him to make something of himself, and he plans to go to work on his UNCLE DUN's farm. However, the day after the dance he hears that Nancy got drunk and married Ogden MERRITT, her date from Savannah; and he returns to loafing at the pool-hall. Fitzgerald described this as "the first story to really recreate the modern southern belle" (to Harold OBER, received February 2, 1928; *As Ever,* p. 109).

"Jemina A Story of the Blue Ridge Mountains By John Phlox, Jr." Prose parody. *The* NASSAU LITERARY MAGA-ZINE, 72 (December 1916), 210–215 (unsigned). Reprinted as "Jemina, the Mountain Girl (One of Those Family Feud Stories of the Blue Ridge Mountains with Apologies to Stephen Leacock)," *Vanity Fair,* 15 (January 1921), 44; in *TJA* as "Jemina the Mountain Girl." The Tantrums and the Doldrums are involved in a feud that started fifty years ago over a card game. When gold is discovered on the Tantrums' land, a stranger named Edgar EDISON tries to buy it. While he is in the Tantrum cabin, the Doldrums attack and set the cabin on fire. Jemina TANTRUM and Edison die in one another's arms.

John Fox, Jr. (1862–1919) of Kentucky wrote highly popular sentimental novels about Southern mountaineers. Stephen Leacock (1869–1944), an English-born Canadian author, was a political economist and humorist.

Jerome, James Character in "Discard." Movie director who is in love with actress Dolly BORDON.

Jerry Character in "The Freshest Boy." Actress who tells Ted FAY she has promised to marry BELTZMAN, the man who gave her the part in the play.

Jerry Character in "The Smilers." Hotel waiter whose former girlfriend is now a dancer at a cheap restaurant.

Jerryl, Rachael *See* Rachael Jerryl BARNES.

Jesuit novice (unnamed) Character in "The Ordeal." Young man who encounters an evil presence in the chapel as he prepares to enter the priesthood.

Jewett, Doctor Character in "The Lees of Happiness." Physician who comes in for a consultation on Jeffrey CURTAIN's condition.

Jimmy Character in "Benediction." One of KIETH's friends at the seminary. He wants LOIS to demonstrate the shimmy.

Joe Character in "Pat Hobby and Orson Welles." Barber who tells Pat HOBBY he looks like Orson Welles (1915–85).

"John Jackson's Arcady" Fiction. Written April 1924. *The SATURDAY EVENING POST,* 197 (July 26, 1924), 8–9, 100, 102, 105; *The Price Was High. See* also *John Jackson's Arcady.* John JACKSON, who has agreed to speak to the Civic Welfare League on "What Have I Got Out of Life," concludes privately that he has gotten nothing from life. His unhappiness is intensified by the dismissal of his son, Ellery Hamil JACKSON, from Yale. He wires his son not to come home, closes up his house, and travels to the small town of Florence, where he had been born. He finds Alice HARLAND, his now-married childhood sweetheart, and asks her to run away with him. She initially agrees; but when he arrives to take her away she says she could never leave her children. Despairing, he returns to the city and resolves to make his speech and to tell the audience that life has beaten him. Arriving late, he is seated half-hidden in the back. Since word has spread that he has gone away suddenly, several people come forward and pay tribute to him. Touched by the good will of people whom he has disliked, when he is discovered and called forward he tells the crowd that life has given him everything, then goes home and welcomes his son.

John Jackson's Arcady by F. Scott Fitzgerald: A Contest Selection arranged by Lilian Holmes Strack Boston: Walter H. Baker, 1928. Strack cut and revised Fitzgerald's story as a play for public reading. *See* "John Jackson's Arcady."

Johns Hopkins University Hospital Zelda FITZGERALD was a patient at the PHIPPS CLINIC of Johns Hopkins University Hospital in BALTIMORE, Maryland, from February 12 to June 26, 1932 and again in February 1934. Fitzgerald was admitted to Johns Hopkins Hospital in August 1932 with a tentative diagnosis of typhoid fever and was hospitalized there eight more times between 1933 and 1937 for alcoholism and chronic inactive fibroid tuberculosis: September 1–5, 1933, October 29–November 1, 1933; April 30–May 7, 1934; July 21–27, 1934; January 14–17, 1936; February 13–15, 1936; December 26, 1936–January 3, 1937; and January 11–14, 1937. Fitzgerald's time at Hopkins, as well as his conversations with Dr. Benjamin BAKER, yielded material for half a dozen stories, including "One Interne" (November 1932), "Zone of Accident" (July 1935), " 'Trouble' " (March 1937), and "In the Holidays" (December 1937); some of the stories were unsalable.

Johns, William Delaney (Billy) Character in "No Flowers." Marjorie CLARK's date to the prom, who has trouble finding a dinner jacket or suit to wear to the dance.

Johnson Character in "The Bridal Party." Friend who plans a practical joke on Hamilton RUTHERFORD at his bachelor party.

Johnson, Earl Character in "A Change of Class." Barber who makes money on a stock market tip but loses it in the crash.

Johnson, Nunnally (1897–1977) Former writer for *The SATURDAY EVENING POST* whom Fitzgerald, while drunk at a 1938 party after the cancellation of "Infidelity," attempted to persuade to leave HOLLYWOOD before it ruined him. Johnson replaced Fitzgerald on the screenplay for *The Light of Heart* in 1940 and later became a very successful writer, producer, and director; he wrote and produced *The Grapes of Wrath* (1940) and wrote, produced, and directed *The Three Faces of Eve* (1957). Johnson labeled Fitzgerald "next to useless" as a screenwriter (April 21, 1952; *The Letters of Nunnally Johnson,* ed. Doris Johnson and Ellen Leventhal [New York: Knopf, 1981], p. 80; see also November 8, 1974, pp. 249–250).

Johnson, Violet Character in "A Change of Class." Earl JOHNSON's wife, who runs away with bootlegger Howard SHALDER.

Johnston, Hamilton T. Character in "An Author's Mother." Author whose mother doesn't understand his writing.

Johnston, Mrs. Character in "An Author's Mother." Woman who doesn't understand the writing of her son,

Hamilton T. JOHNSTON. Based on Mollie McQuillan FITZGERALD.

Johnston, Mrs. Character in " 'Trouble.' " New superintendent of nurses who becomes angry when she finds TROUBLE and Doctor WHEELOCK in an operating room and who gets Trouble fired.

Jones, Catherine Character in "The Dance." Aspiring dancer who shoots Marie BANNERMAN.

Jones, Judy Character in "Winter Dreams." Selfish, wealthy girl who is "destined" to "bring no end of misery to a great number of men" (*ASYM*, p. 59) and with whom Dexter GREEN falls in love.

Jones, Mr. Character in *The Vegetable*. A "well-known politician" who informs Jerry FROST that he has received the Republican Party's unanimous nomination for President of the United States. He later serves as secretary to President Frost.

Jones, Mortimer Character in "Winter Dreams." Judy JONES's father, who tries to persuade Dexter GREEN not to quit his caddy job.

Jones, Rip (Oswald) Character in "The Third Casket." Industrious young man who becomes Cyrus GIRARD's partner and marries Lola GIRARD.

Jordan, Mr. Character in "Head and Shoulders." Magazine publisher who brings Anton LAURIER to meet Marcia MEADOW Tarbox.

Jorgensen, Paula (Lady Paula Tressiger) Character in "New Types." Young woman who desperately needs money for an operation for her husband, Eric TRESSIGER. She has made arrangements to receive payment for being photographed at a party at the home of her aunt, Emily HOLLIDAY. Just before the party Paula finds her aunt motionless in a chair and thinks she is dead, but she proceeds with the party.

Joyce, James (1882–1941) Irish novelist whom Fitzgerald admired. Joyce's technically and stylistically innovative *Ulysses* (Paris: 1922; London: 1922; New York: 1934) revolutionized the novel and influenced the development of the stream-of-consciousness technique. In 1922 Edmund WILSON wrote to Fitzgerald about *The Vegetable*: "By the way, the great question is, have you read James Joyce's *Ulysses*? Because if you haven't, the resemblance between the drunken-visions scene in it and your scene in the White House must take its place as one of the great coincidences in literature" (May 26, 1922; *Letters on Literature and Politics 1912–1972* [New York: Farrar, Straus & Giroux, 1977], p. 84). Fitzgerald

replied that he had not read *Ulysses*—which was banned in America at that time—and asked how he could obtain a copy (May 30, 1922; *Life in Letters*, pp. 58–59). Fitzgerald later included *Ulysses*, which he described as "the great novel of the future," and *A Portrait of the Artist as a Young Man* (New York: 1916; London: 1917) in his 1923 list of "10 Best Books I Have Read," in which he said Joyce "is to be the most profound literary influence in the next fifty years" (*FSF on Authorship*, p. 86). Fitzgerald met Joyce at a June 27, 1928 dinner hosted by Sylvia BEACH; he commemorated the occasion by drawing in Beach's copy of *GG* a picture of himself kneeling before Joyce, who wears a halo, with the caption "Festival of St. James" (*Life in Letters*, p. 156). The Joyces later dined at the Fitzgeralds' apartment, where Fitzgerald was annoyed by Zelda FITZGERALD's indifference to Joyce. On one occasion Fitzgerald offered to express his admiration for Joyce by jumping out the window—a gesture which distressed Joyce and to which he was probably referring in the November 7, 1928 note he enclosed with Fitzgerald's copy of *Ulysses:* "Here with is the book you gave me signed and

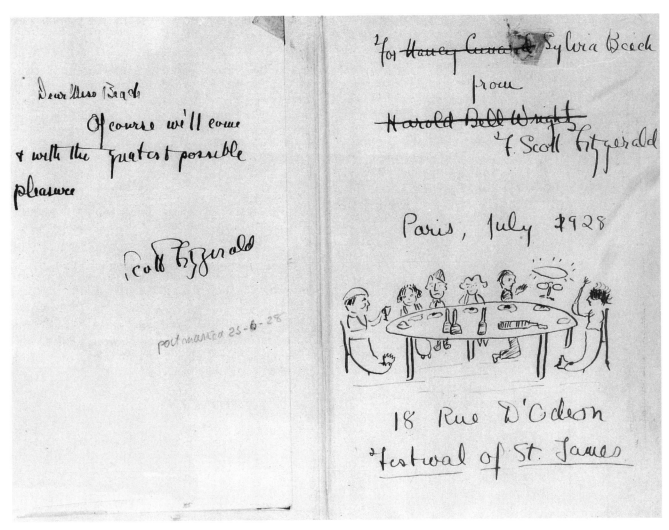

Fitzgerald's drawing in Sylvia Beach's copy of The Great Gatsby, *commemorating her dinner party for James Joyce. The figures at the table are Adrienne Monnier, the Chamsons, the Fitzgeralds, Joyce, and Beach.* (Beach Papers, Princeton University Library)

I am adding a portrait of the artist as a once young man with the thanks of your much obliged but most pusillanimous guest" (*Correspondence,* p. 219). Fitzgerald's annotated copy of *Ulysses* and a copy of *A Portrait of the Artist as a Young Man* which Joyce gave him are in the BRUCCOLI COLLECTION.

See Richard Ellmann, *James Joyce* (New York: Oxford University Press, 1959; revised edition, 1982).

Jozan, Edouard (b. 1899) French naval aviator with whom Zelda FITZGERALD became involved in July 1924 while the Fitzgeralds were living in VILLA MARIE in VALESCURE on the RIVIERA. The extent of their involvement is unknown. Jozan said it was merely a flirtation (Sara Mayfield, *Exiles from Paradise,* p. 97). In Zelda's fictionalized version in her novel, *Save Me the Waltz,* the affair is unconsummated; a French aviator wants

Alabama Beggs to be his mistress but does not urge her to leave her husband. Fitzgerald noted in his *Ledger,* "The Big crisis—13th of July" (p. 178). He later claimed that when Zelda asked for a divorce, Jozan avoided the confrontation which Fitzgerald demanded. Fitzgerald persuaded Zelda not to pursue a divorce; and in August he noted in his *Ledger,* "Zelda and I close together" (p. 178). However, Fitzgerald always felt she had destroyed the foundational trust of their marriage, later writing in his *Notebooks:* "That September 1924, I knew something had happened that could never be repaired" (#839).

Both Fitzgeralds elaborated and exaggerated the details of the crisis over Jozan. Zelda later said Fitzgerald had locked her in the villa for a month; near the end of his life Fitzgerald told Sheilah GRAHAM that he had dueled with Jozan and written it into *TITN.* Ernest

HEMINGWAY recalled: "This first version that he told me of Zelda and a French naval aviator falling in love was truly a sad story and I believe it was a true story. Later he told me other versions of it as though trying them for use in a novel, but none was as sad as this first one and I always believed the first one, although any of them might have been true. They were better told each time; but they never hurt you the same way the first one did" (*A Moveable Feast,* p. 172). Hemingway's first wife, Hadley (1891–1979), commented: "It was one of their acts together. I remember Zelda's beautiful face becoming very, very solemn, and she would say how he had loved her and how hopeless it had been and then how he had committed suicide. Scott would stand next to her looking very pale and distressed and sharing every minute of it" (Nancy Milford, *Zelda,* p. 114). In fact Jozan did not commit suicide; he was transferred to Indo-China in October and became vice-admiral of the French navy in 1952.

Fitzgerald's disillusionment with Zelda influenced *GG,* which he was working on during the time of the Jozan affair; and Jozan later served as one of the models for *TITN* character Tommy BARBAN, for whom Nicole DIVER leaves her husband, Dick DIVER. The Jozan crisis also served as the source for a minor 1935 story, "Image on the Heart."

Juan-les-Pins, France RIVIERA town where the Fitzgeralds rented VILLA PAQUITA from March to May or June 1926, when they turned it over to Ernest HEMINGWAY and moved to VILLA ST. LOUIS, where they stayed until their return to America at the end of the year. While in Juan-les-Pins Fitzgerald worked on an early version of *TITN.*

Jubal Character in "Basil and Cleopatra." Basil Duke LEE's Yale classmate whom Minnie BIBBLE dates after leaving Littleboy LE MOYNE.

Julia Character in "Diagnosis." Servant whom Charlie CLAYHORNE saw in his father's room signing a document which he believed to be a revised will.

Jumbo Character in "The Camel's Back." Black waiter who performs a mock wedding between Betty MEDILL and the camel, but whose status as a Baptist minister makes the ceremony legal.

Kagle, Miss Helen Character in "Pat Hobby's Christmas Wish." Pat HOBBY's new secretary, who formerly worked for Harry GOODDORF. She offers Pat information with which he attempts to blackmail Gooddorf.

Kahler Character in *B&D*. Self-important assistant secretary at Wilson, Heimer and Hardy, where Anthony PATCH briefly works as a bond salesman.

Kalman, Oscar and Xandra Wealthy ST. PAUL couple with homes on SUMMIT AVENUE and at DELLWOOD with whom the Fitzgeralds became friends when they lived at Dellwood outside St. Paul in the summer of 1921 while awaiting the birth of Scottie FITZGERALD. Xandra was Zelda's only close friend in St. Paul; she helped with preparations for Scottie's birth and was Scottie's godmother. The Kalmans visited the Fitzgeralds in GREAT NECK, New York, in 1923 and in PARIS in March 1930. Oscar Kalman lent Fitzgerald $7,500 in 1936 while Fitzgerald was awaiting his inheritance following his mother's death.

In April 1924 Zelda wrote to Oscar: "Scott's story 'Winter Dreams' written about you and Sandra has just been published in an anthology." Oscar Kalman replied: "I could not see how it in any way described Xandra or me but that may be because I was too close to the situation or perhaps don't know what goes on" (Minnesota Historical Society). No other evidence suggests a connection between the Kalmans and this story. "At Your Age" (August 1929) was probably based on the Kalmans; Oscar was considerably older than Xandra.

Kaluka Character in *TSOP*. Homely girl whom Kerry HOLIDAY picks up on a trip to the shore with PRINCETON friends.

Kamp, Doctor Character in "In the Holidays." Physician who inadvertently reveals to Mr. MCKENNA that Mr. GRIFFIN is in the same hospital.

Kampf, William S. (Bill) Character in the Basil Duke LEE stories. Based on Fitzgerald's ST. PAUL friend Paul BALLION. In "The Scandal Detectives," Basil Duke Lee

and Riply BUCKNER recruit him to help them in a plot to waylay Hubert BLAIR. In "He Thinks He's Wonderful" Bill invites Basil for a weekend visit while his cousin Minnie BIBBLE is staying at his house. In "The Captured Shadow" he plays a crook in Basil's play. In "Forging Ahead" Minnie Bibble is visiting his family.

Kane, Muriel Character in *B&D*. A vampish friend of Gloria PATCH who constantly sways to any music she hears and who is a bridesmaid at Gloria's wedding. She works for the Red Cross during the war.

Kapper, Lee Character in *LT/LOLT*. Art director who is present when Monroe STAHR views the rushes.

Karger, Dolly Character in "The Rich Boy." Wild young woman with whom Anson HUNTER becomes involved, though—as he frequently tells her—he is not in love with her. His memory of Paula LEGENDRE twice prevents them from consummating their relationship.

Karr, Ede (Mrs. Alphonse Karr) Character in "The Adjuster." Luella HEMPLE's friend, who listens to Luella's tale of boredom with her child and husband.

Kastler, Professor Benjamin (Ben) Character in "Fate in Her Hands." Billy RIGGS's friend, a college professor whom Carol [KASTLER] marries instead of Billy.

Kastler, Carol Character in "Fate in Her Hands." Woman whose decisions and actions for several years are influenced by three predictions of a FORTUNE-TELLER.

Kastler, Jean Character in "Fate in Her Hands." Ben and Carol KASTLER's daughter, who narrowly escapes being bitten by a mad dog.

Katie Character in *LT/LOLT*. Catherine DOOLAN's assistant. Rose MELONEY once refers to Doolan as "Katy," causing possible confusion.

Katzby, Martha Character in "Dice, Brass Knuckles & Guitar." Sixteen-year-old girl who attends Jim POWELL's jazz school.

Katzby, Mrs. Poindexter Character in "Dice, Brass Knuckles & Guitar." Southampton woman who takes her daughter and other girls out of Jim POWELL's jazz school.

Kavenaugh Character in "Six of One—". Howard KA-VENAUGH's younger brother, who can't get into college and who marries a manicurist.

Kavenaugh, Howard Character in "Six of One—". Wealthy young man who is expelled from Yale for his involvement in a drunk-driving accident. He elopes with a girl whom he later divorces.

Kaye, Ella Character in *GG*. Newspaperwoman who was involved with Dan CODY and who inherited his money. Based on journalist "Nellie Bly" (Elizabeth Cochrane Seaman, 1867–1922). See Brooke Kroeger, *Nellie Bly* (New York: Times Books, 1994).

Kearns, Doctor Character in "Two Wrongs." Bill MCCHESNEY's physician, who diagnoses his tuberculosis and orders him West to recuperate.

Keats, John (1795–1821) English Romantic poet whom Fitzgerald greatly admired and whose rhythms and imagery influenced Fitzgerald's writing. Fitzgerald explained to his daughter, Scottie FITZGERALD: "All fine prose is based on the verbs carrying the sentences. They make sentences move. Probably the finest technical poem in English is Keats' Eve of Saint Agnes. A line like: The Hare limped trembling through the frozen grass, is so alive that you race through it, scarcely noticing it, yet it has colored the whole poem with its movement—the limping, trembling, and freezing is going on before your own eyes" (Spring 1938; *Life in Letters,* p. 357). While Scottie was in college Fitzgerald wrote to her about Keats:

> Poetry is either something that lives like fire inside you—like music to the musician or Marxism to the Communist—or else it is nothing, an empty, formalized bore around which pedants can endlessly drone their notes and explanations. The Grecian Urn is unbearably beautiful with every syllable as inevitable as the notes in Beethoven's Ninth Symphony or it's just something you don't understand. It is what it is because an extraordinary genius paused at that point in history and touched it. I suppose I've read it a hundred times. About the tenth time I began to know what it was about, and caught the chime in it and the exquisite inner mechanics. Likewise with The Nightingale which I can never read through without tears in my eyes; likewise the Pot of Basil with its great stanzas about the two brothers, "Why they were proud, etc."; and The Eve of St. Agnes, which has the richest, most sensuous imagery in English, not excepting Shakespeare. And

finally his three or four great sonnets, Bright Star and the others.

> Knowing those things very young and granted an ear, one could scarcely ever afterwards be unable to distinguish between gold and dross in what one read. In themselves those eight poems are a scale of workmanship for anybody who wants to know truly about words, their most utter value for evocation, persuasion or charm. For awhile after you quit Keats all other poetry seems to be only whistling or humming (August 3, 1940; *Life in Letters,* pp. 460–461).

Fitzgerald considered the title "The Beautiful Lady Without Mercy" for *The Beautiful and Damned*; one preliminary title page for the novel's manuscript includes a canceled epigraph from Keats's "La Belle Dame Sans Merci." The title *Tender Is the Night* is taken from Keats's "Ode to a Nightingale," which also provided the epigraph for the novel: "Already with thee! tender is the night . . . / . . . But here there is no light, / Save what from heaven is with the breezes blown / Through verdurous glooms and winding mossy ways."

See Walter Jackson Bate, *John Keats* (Cambridge, Mass.: Harvard University Press, 1963).

Keatts, Lily Character in "Pat Hobby Does His Bit." English actress who leaves the country before it is discovered that Pat HOBBY was inadvertently filmed in a scene with her.

Keene, Doctor Character in "The Curious Case of Benjamin Button." Family physician who delivers Benjamin BUTTON, then refuses to have anything else to do with the Button family.

Keith, Jean Character in "Her Last Case." Ben DRAGONET's housekeeper.

Kelly Character in "Myra Meets His Family." Actor who poses as Knowleton WHITNEY's mother. He came up with the details of the plot to scare away Myra HARPER.

Kelly, Mr. Character in "A Snobbish Story." Constable who comes to the PERRYS' house to tell John Boynton BAILEY that his wife, EVELYN, has attempted suicide.

Kelly, Nelson Character in "One Trip Abroad." Young American who deteriorates as he travels abroad with his wife, Nicole KELLY.

Kelly, Nicole Character in "One Trip Abroad." Young American woman who deteriorates as she travels abroad with her husband, Nelson KELLY. In an early version of *TITN*, protagonist Lew Kelly's wife is also named Nicole.

Kendall, George Character in *The Girl from Lazy J.* Owner of the "Diamond O" Ranch and uncle of Jack

DARCY. Kendall has received a note warning him of an intended robbery at his ranch.

Kendall, Mrs. George Character in *The Girl from Lazy J.* Jack DARCY's aunt, who is surprised yet pleased to learn of Jack's engagement to Leticia LARNED.

Kenyon, Mary Character in "Fate in Her Hands." Friend with whom Carol KASTLER spends four days in an isolated cabin while trying to avoid publicity.

Keogh, Nat Character in "Crazy Sunday." Hard-drinking screenwriter who attends the CALMANS' party.

Kerr, Robert GREAT NECK friend of Fitzgerald who provided the basis for Jay GATSBY's meeting with Dan CODY in *GG*. At the age of 14, Kerr had warned Major Edwin R. Gilman that his yacht would be stuck in Brooklyn's Sheepshead Bay when the tide went out. Gilman hired Kerr, who lived on the yacht for three years. Fitzgerald wrote to Kerr: "The part of what you told me which I am including in my novel is the ship, yatch I mean, + the mysterious yatchsman whose mistress was Nellie Bly I have my hero occupy the same position you did + obtain it in the same way" (June 1924; *Life in Letters*, p. 75). See Joseph Corso, "One Not-Forgotten Summer Night: Sources for Fictional Symbols of American Character in *The Great Gatsby*," *Fitzgerald/Hemingway Annual* (1976), pp. 6–33.

Key, Carrol Character in "May Day." Gus ROSE's friend, a recently discharged soldier.

Key, George Character in "May Day." Carrol KEY's brother, a waiter at Delmonico's.

Keyster, Doctor Character in "Lo, the Poor Peacock!" Annie Lee DAVIS's physician, who thinks she will never get well.

Kieth Character in "Benediction." LOIS's older brother, who has been preparing for the priesthood for 17 years and who has idealized his sister.

Killian, Cedric Character in "The Intimate Strangers." Man with whom SARA falls in love and whom she marries after the death of her first husband, Eduard DE LA GUILLET DE LA GUIMPÉ.

Killian, Mrs. Cedric *See* SARA.

Killian, Dorothy Character in "The Intimate Strangers." Cedric KILLIAN's first wife, whom his second wife, SARA, never realizes he had really loved until she finds him at Dorothy's grave.

Kilrain, Helen Character in "Family in the Wind." Eight-year-old girl who is devoted to her cat and who is orphaned by the second tornado.

Kimberly, Scott Character in "The Popular Girl." Wealthy young man who falls in love with Yanci BOWMAN.

Kincaid, Charley Character in "The Dance." Marie BANNERMAN's fiancé, who marries the NARRATOR.

King, Clara Character in *Assorted Spirits*. Josephus HENDRIX's ward, who smokes cigarettes and has been engaged three times. She is unsuccessfully wooed by Dickie WETHERBY.

King, George Character in "The Long Way Out." Man who dies from injuries received in a car accident on his way to pick up his wife at the sanitarium.

King, Mrs. George Character in "The Long Way Out." Woman who suffers a coma and schizophrenia after the birth of her second child. While in the sanitarium she waits every day for her husband to meet her for a trip and refuses to believe the news of his death in a car accident.

King, Ginevra Fitzgerald's main romantic attachment while he was at PRINCETON. She was the inspiration for many of his fictional heroines, including Isabelle BORGÉ in *TSOP*, Judy JONES in "Winter Dreams" (December 1922), and Josephine PERRY. A 16-year-old debutante from Lake Forest, Illinois, Ginevra was wealthy, beautiful, and already popular at Ivy League colleges when she came to ST. PAUL to spend Christmas vacation with Marie HERSEY, a classmate at Westover, a girls' school in Connecticut. Fitzgerald met Ginevra on January 4, 1915 at the Town and Country Club at a party in her honor; he later based a short story, "Babes in the Woods" (May 1917), on this meeting, and incorporated the story material into *TSOP*. Fitzgerald and Ginevra went to the movies the next afternoon before he returned to Princeton, and he began writing to her almost daily. "Basil and Cleopatra" (April 1929) incorporates his memory of his first glimpse of Ginevra during his February 1915 visit to her at Westover. In June 1915 Ginevra went with Fitzgerald to the Princeton Prom and to NEW YORK, where they had dinner at the Ritz, saw *Nobody Home*, and went to the Midnight Frolic cabaret. He also visited her in Lake Forest on his way home to St. Paul. In his *Ledger* he summarized his sophomore year at Princeton as "Ginevra-Triangle year" (p. 169).

In October 1915 Ginevra and Fitzgerald attended the Yale-Princeton football game at New Haven. In

Ginevra King

In September Ginevra married Ensign William Hamilton Mitchell, a wealthy Chicagoan and instructor at a naval air station; Fitzgerald preserved in his scrapbook the wedding invitation and a piece of Ginevra's handkerchief with the comment "THE END OF A ONCE POIGNANT STORY" (*The Romantic Egoists*, p. 27). He later listed "Memory of Ginevra's Wedding" as a source for the fourth chapter of *GG*.

In October 1937, Ginevra, who had divorced Mitchell in 1936, contacted Fitzgerald during a visit to Santa Barbara, California. Fitzgerald wrote to Scottie: "She was the first girl I ever loved and I have faithfully avoided seeing her up to this moment to keep that illusion perfect, because she ended up by throwing me over with the most supreme boredom and indifference. I don't know whether I should go or not" (October 8, 1937; *Life in Letters*, p. 338). He did go to see Ginevra and drank too much during their meeting; he telephoned her for several days, but they did not meet again. Fitzgerald wrote to Scottie that Ginevra, "the love of my youth," was "still a charming woman" (November 4, 1937; *Life in Letters*, p. 340). Ginevra later married John Pirie of the Carson, Pirie, Scott department store in Chicago.

"The Kingdom in the Dark" Fiction—third PHILIPPE story. Written November 1934. REDBOOK, 65 (August 1935), 58–62, 64, 66–68. While surveying his land to determine its boundaries, Philippe meets GRISELDA, who has run away from LOUIS, King of the West Franks. The King arrives with his entourage, and Philippe shows him and the DUKE OF GUYENNE his fort. Philippe tries to hide Griselda's gray horse so the royal party will be unaware of her presence, but two of the King's men find the horse. Philippe denies any knowledge of the girl, and in retaliation the King orders his men to burn Philippe's fort.

Kingsley, Mr. Character in "Gretchen's Forty Winks." Druggist who supplies Roger HALSEY with the drugs to knock out his wife, Gretchen HALSEY.

Kinkallow, Marquis (Bopes) Character in "The Hotel Child." Man who, with Lady CAPPS-KARR, is thrown out of the hotel for inadvertently starting a fire. Based on Napier Alington (1896–1940), a friend of Bijou O'CONOR.

Kinney, Joe *See* Mr. MCKENNA.

Klipspringer, Ewing Character in *GG*. A frequent guest at Jay GATSBY's house, thus known as "the boarder"; he plays the piano when Daisy BUCHANAN first goes to Gatsby's house. Nick CARRAWAY is angered by his unwillingness to attend Gatsby's funeral.

March 1916 Ginevra was expelled from Westover, an event Fitzgerald recounted in "A Woman with a Past" (September 1930) and reflected on in a 1937 letter to his daughter, Scottie FITZGERALD: "It was in the cards that Ginevra King should get fired from Westover—also that your mother should wear out young" (c. July 5, 1937; *Letters*, p. 16). Fitzgerald visited Ginevra in Lake Forest in August 1916, but he was no longer her most favored suitor, and she was being courted by wealthy young men. Someone remarked in his hearing, "Poor boys shouldn't think of marrying rich girls," as he noted in his *Ledger* (p. 170). In November Ginevra went to the Yale game with Fitzgerald, and he noted in his *Ledger* for January 1917, "Final break with Ginevra" (p. 171). His play "The Debutante," which was inspired by Ginevra, was published in January 1917 and later incorporated into *TSOP*.

Fitzgerald learned of Ginevra's engagement in June 1918, shortly before he met Zelda Sayre [FITZGERALD].

knight (unnamed) Character in "The Kingdom in the Dark." Member of King LOUIS's entourage whom PHILIPPE warns that the Normans are nearby.

Knighton, Pamela Character in "Last Kiss." English actress whose real name is Sybil Higgins. She causes trouble on various pictures and is blacklisted in HOLLYWOOD. Partly based on Sheilah GRAHAM.

Knopf, Edwin (1899–1981) Half-brother of publisher Alfred A. Knopf (1892–1984); writer of *The Wedding Night,* a 1935 movie which presented a thinly disguised portrait of Fitzgerald. In June 1937 Knopf, then an MGM story editor, interviewed Fitzgerald; and the studio hired Fitzgerald in July for six months with an option for another year. In October 1938 Fitzgerald wrote to Knopf proposing a musical based on his Basil Duke LEE stories, but the project was not developed. In 1940 Fitzgerald unsuccessfully tried to interest Knopf in an idea for a Civil War movie based on his stories "The Night before Chancellorsville" (February 1935) and "The End of Hate" (June 1940) (February 1, 1940; *Life in Letters,* pp. 430–431).

Knowles, Bill Character in "The Last of the Belles." Yankee aviator whom Ailie CALHOUN considers marrying.

Knowleton, Dudley Character in "A Woman with a Past." Captain of the Yale baseball team and a member of Skull and Bones. Josephine PERRY falls in love with him, but he has always considered Adele CRAW his ideal girl. He is the first man whom Josephine has failed to win.

Kresge, Jim Character in "Pat Hobby's College Days." Man who introduces Pat HOBBY to Kit DOOLAN.

Kretching, Lieutenant Character in *B&D.* A popular officer who drills Anthony PATCH's army company.

Kroll (Ring), Frances (b. 1918) Secretary whom Fitzgerald hired in April 1939 while he was living at "BELLY ACRES" in ENCINO, California, and who worked for him until his death. Fitzgerald was writing *The Love of the Last Tycoon* during the time Kroll worked for him. Her memoir, *Against the Current: As I Remember Scott Fitzgerald,* corrects popular misconceptions about Fitzgerald's HOLLYWOOD life and is especially useful for her descriptions of his writing habits: "Now and again he would ask me to read a page he had written out loud so he could listen to it for cadence. How it sounded was as important as the sight of the words on paper, as if a blind person had to hear it and a deaf one to read it" (pp. 41–42).

Kurman Character in "No Flowers." Tailor who refuses to hand over Billy JOHNS' dinner jacket except for cash.

L

La Borwits, Jaques Character in *LT/LOLT*. An assistant producer. Based on MGM producer Joseph L. MANKIEWICZ, whom Fitzgerald blamed for ruining *Three Comrades*.

Lacy, Edward Character in "Hot & Cold Blood." Old man who had once lent money to Jim MATHER's father. Now a failure, he asks Jim for a loan to save his insurance policy, but Jim initially refuses.

Lacy, Mr. and Mrs. Character in *B&D*. A wild young couple at whose house drunken Anthony and Gloria PATCH stumble over empty milk bottles.

Ladislau, Doctor Character in *TITN*. Physician at Dick DIVER and Franz GREGOROVIOUS's clinic whom Dick dislikes. He is unable to pacify Mr. MORRIS, who comes to remove his son, Von Cohn MORRIS, from the clinic.

lady (unnamed) Character in "Outside the Cabinet-Maker's." Woman who delivers plans for her daughter's doll house to the cabinet-maker.

Lafarge, Miss Character in "Jemina. . . ." Schoolteacher who died of delirium tremens.

LaGatta, John (1894–1977) Popular illustrator of the 1930s known for his idealized pictures of the female form. He illustrated three Fitzgerald stories for *The SATURDAY EVENING POST*: "The Last of the Belles" (March 2, 1929), "Majesty" (July 13, 1929), and "The Bridal Party" (August 9, 1930).

Lahaye, Sidney Character in "Flight and Pursuit." Man who regrets jilting Caroline Martin [CORCORAN] and contacts her through the years until she discovers that she still loves him.

Lake Annecy, France The Fitzgeralds spent two weeks at Lake Annecy in July 1931 while Zelda FITZGERALD was on leave from PRANGINS CLINIC. She later described this vacation: "[We] said at the end that we'd never go there again because those weeks had been perfect and no other time could match them. . . . It was like the good gone times when we still believed in summer hotels and the philosophies of popular songs" (" 'Show Mr. and Mrs. F. to Number——' ", May & June 1934; *CU*, pp. 52–53).

Lamar, Doctor Character in "The Jelly-Bean." Nancy LAMAR's father, who is distressed by her sudden marriage.

Lamar, Nancy Character in "The Jelly-Bean" and "The Last of the Belles." A beautiful, popular girl who is proud of being wild and hard. Like many of Fitzgerald's female characters, she is daring and charming but harmful to the men who love her. In "The Jelly-Bean" she says that her model is Lady Diana Manners (1892–1986), a famous English beauty and eccentric who starred in a pageant entitled *The Miracle* and was married to politician Duff Cooper (1890–1954). Nancy shoots craps, flirts with Jim POWELL, and marries Ogden MERRITT while drunk. In "The Last of the Belles" she has a date with Captain CRAKER.

Lamarque Character in "Shadow Laurels." One of Jean CHANDELLE's three closest friends, who tell Jaques CHANDELLE what Jean had meant to them.

Lamb, Marion Character in "Too Cute for Words." Debutante whom Gwen BOWERS, Dizzy CAMPBELL, and Clara HANNAMAN see on the train to PRINCETON and whom they later overhear getting engaged to HARRY.

Lamb, Nancy Character in "The Rubber Check." Debutante at whose dance girls begin to decline to dance with Val SCHUYLER because of the rumors about his bounced check.

"Lamp in a Window" Verse. *The NEW YORKER*, 11 (March 23, 1935), 18; *CU*; *In His Own Time*; *Poems*. Nostalgic poem addressed to Zelda FITZGERALD recalling their life together before her breakdowns.

Langueduc, "Slim" Character in *TSOP*. A football player at PRINCETON who attends tutoring school with Amory BLAINE.

"La Paix" Fifteen-room Victorian frame house which the Fitzgeralds rented on the 28-acre estate of Bayard TURNBULL at RODGERS FORGE, TOWSON, Maryland, outside BALTIMORE, from May 1932 to November 1933. Until her June 26 discharge from PHIPPS CLINIC, Zelda FITZGERALD spent mornings at "La Paix" and returned to Phipps after lunch. She described the house in a letter to Maxwell PERKINS: "We have a soft shady place here that's like a paintless play-house abandoned when the family grew up. It's surrounded by apologetic trees and [morning] meadows and creaking insects and is gutted of its aura by many comfortable bed rooms which do not have to be floated up to on alcoholic inflation past the cupolas and cornices as did the ones at 'Ellerslie' " (PRINCETON UNIVERSITY LIBRARY). At "La Paix" Zelda resumed painting and practiced ballet. Her novel, *Save Me the Waltz*, written at Phipps Clinic, was published in October 1932; and her play, *Scandalabra*, was produced by the VAGABOND JUNIOR PLAYERS in Baltimore June 26–July 1, 1933. Fitzgerald hired a secretary, Isabel OWENS, and resumed work on *TITN*. Owens recalled Fitzgerald's working habits at "La Paix": "If he was sober, he worked well and very smoothly. He was disciplined and would write for two hours and then stop and go back to it later. If he was drinking, he had a hard time sitting still. He'd be in and out of his office" (John F. Kelly, "Memories of Scott and Zelda," *Pittsburgh Press Roto* [February 6, 1983], 16, 18). Fitzgerald devoted attention to his daughter, Scottie FITZGERALD, and spent time with the Turnbull children, Eleanor, Frances, and Andrew; Andrew TURNBULL wrote a biography, *Scott Fitzgerald,* in 1962. Fitzgerald resented Zelda's withdrawal from family life, and they quarreled frequently. In August 1933 there was an accidental fire at "La Paix" when Zelda burned some papers in a disused fireplace, and the second floor was damaged; the fire ruined many of Fitzgerald's

history books, but no important manuscripts were destroyed. After completing *TITN* Fitzgerald gave up "La Paix" and moved to a rented town house at 1307 Park Avenue in Baltimore.

Lardner, Ring (1885–1933) American sportswriter, humorist, and short story writer noted for his use of the American vernacular and best known for his story collection *You Know Me Al* (1916). He and Fitzgerald became close friends when they both lived in GREAT NECK, Long Island, New York in 1922; both alcoholics, they drank together. Fitzgerald admired Lardner's work and tried to promote his reputation, bringing together Lardner and editor Maxwell PERKINS and providing the title for Lardner's first SCRIBNERS volume, *How to Write Short Stories* (1924), a collection which sparked a reassessment of Lardner's fiction. He nominated Lardner "as America's most popular humorist" for the *Vanity Fair* Hall of Fame, writing to Edmund WILSON:

> Because he is really inimitable, as is shown by the lamentable failure of his many imitators,
> Because he does not subscribe to a press-clipping bureau and is quite unaware of the critical approval he is recieving in recondite circles,
> Because he is frequently covered with bruises from being the Yale football team against his four Harvard-bound boys,
> And finally because with a rare, true ear he has set down for the enlightenment of posterity the American language as it is talked today (*Life in Letters*, pp. 63–64; the published caption in *Vanity Fair,* 20 [March 1923], 71 was revised and condensed).

Lardner and his wife, Ellis, traveled to Atlantic City with the Fitzgeralds for the November 1923 tryout of Fitzgerald's play *The Vegetable;* and they visited the Fitzgeralds on the RIVIERA in September 1924. Lardner remarked in an article about his European trip: "Mr. Fitzgerald is a novelist and Mrs. Fitzgerald a novelty" (*What of It?* [New York & London: Scribners, 1925], p. 18). Fitzgerald dedicated his 1926 story collection, *All the Sad Young Men,* "TO RING AND ELLIS LARDNER." The character of Abe NORTH in *TITN* is based on Lardner.

When Lardner died in 1933, Fitzgerald wrote a tribute for *The New Republic,* in which he expressed his regret for Lardner's failure to live up to his potential (*see* "Ring"). Perkins asked Fitzgerald to select material and write the introduction for a collection of Lardner's work, but he declined because he was busy seeing *TITN* through the press. Fitzgerald was disappointed in *First and Last* (1934), edited by Gilbert SELDES, whom he had recommended; but the volume was well received. On May 31, 1934 Fitzgerald wrote to Seldes proposing a project in which two of Lardner's nonsense plays would be alternated with "something macabre" using

"La Paix," Towson, Maryland

Ring Lardner

the technique of the Grand Guignol, but nothing came of the plan (*Letters,* pp. 512–513).

See Donald Elder, *Ring Lardner* (Garden City, NY: Doubleday, 1956) and Jonathan Yardley, *Ring: A Biography of Ring Lardner* (New York: Random House, 1977).

Larned, Leticia　Character in *The Girl from Lazy J.* Cowgirl from the "Lazy J" ranch who is engaged to Jack DARCY and who apprehends Tony GONZOLES, who is trying to rob Jack's uncle, George KENDALL.

Larrabee, Ceci　Character in *B&D*. Philadelphia millionairess whom Maury NOBLE is going to marry.

Lascalles, Evylyn　Character in "Pat Hobby's College Days." Pat HOBBY's secretary, whom he has told to dispose of the empty liquor bottles in his office.

"Last Kiss"　Fiction. *COLLIER'S,* 123 (April 16, 1949), 16–17, 34, 38, 41, 43–44; *Bits of Paradise.* Agent Joe

BECKER introduces English actress Pamela KNIGHTON to Jim LEONARD, who has just been promoted to producer. She hopes that Jim will give her a part; although he avoids her at first, he finally offers her a part, which she accepts after being let go from another picture for causing trouble. When Pamela also causes trouble on Jim's picture, he visits her home and discovers that she is residing with an elderly Englishman, Chauncey WARD, who has been advising her to fight for her rights. She loses her part in Jim's movie and is blacklisted in HOLLYWOOD. After she dies of pneumonia her ghost visits Jim for a goodnight kiss.

COSMOPOLITAN declined "Last Kiss" in 1940; Fitzgerald changed the title to "Pink and Silver Frost" and later stripped the story for *LT/LOLT.* When *Collier's*—which had previously declined the story—published "Last Kiss" several years after Fitzgerald's death, the magazine awarded it a $1,000 bonus as the best story in that issue.

"The Last of the Belles"　Fiction. Written November 1928. *The SATURDAY EVENING POST,* 201 (March 2, 1929), 18–19, 75, 78; *TAR.* ANDY recounts his experiences in TARLETON, Georgia, when he was stationed at the army camp there 15 years before, during World War I. He became Southern belle Ailie CALHOUN's escort and confidant when her beau Bill KNOWLES left town. When Knowles returned to town while on leave, aviator Horace CANBY, who was in love with Ailie, crashed his plane. When Bill left town again, Ailie became attracted to Lieutenant Earl SCHOEN, despite his lower-class qualities. After the war Ailie broke up permanently with Bill and later broke up with Earl when, minus his uniform, his unattractive qualities stood out more than ever. Six years later Andy returned to Tarleton to see Ailie, who had changed her line to keep up with the new South. Andy realized he had always been in love with her, but she told him she was planning to marry a Savannah man the next month. Ailie rode with Andy to the former site of his army camp, where he "stumbled here and there in the knee-deep underbrush, looking for my youth in a clapboard or a strip of roofing or a rusty tomato can" (*TAR,* pp. 273–274). He realized that with Ailie's marriage the South would forever be empty for him.

"The Last of the Belles," Fitzgerald's final fictional study of the South and its women, is one of his most frequently anthologized stories. It was made into a movie for television in 1994: *The Last of the Belles,* a Herbert Brodkin production, written for television by James Costigan. North Hollywood: Hollywood Select Video, 1994. Distributed by Timeless Video.

The Last Tycoon　Novel. Edited by Edmund WILSON. New York: Charles SCRIBNER's Sons, 1941; London:

Grey Walls Press, 1949. *See The Love of the Last Tycoon: A Western.*

Laurier, Anton Character in "Head and Shoulders." French philosopher; Horace TARBOX's idol, who is charmed by Marcia MEADOW Tarbox's book.

Lausanne, Switzerland Fitzgerald lived in the HOTEL DE LA PAIX in Lausanne in fall 1930 in order to be near Zelda FITZGERALD, who was a patient at PRANGINS CLINIC at NYON. In *TITN* Dick DIVER travels to Lausanne to interview a prospective patient.

Lawrence, Mrs. Character in *TSOP*. Monsignor DARCY's friend whom Amory BLAINE visits at her home on Riverside Drive after his breakup with Rosalind CONNAGE. May be based on Margaret CHANLER.

Leam, Max Character in " 'Boil Some Water—Lots of It.' " Producer who hires Pat HOBBY for a three-week polish job. Writer Walter HERRICK, dressed as a Russian Cossack, plays a joke on Leam by attempting to join the powerful men seated at the Big Table in the studio commissary.

Leaming, Elwood Character in the Basil Duke LEE stories. In "The Scandal Detectives" Basil Duke Lee and Riply BUCKNER record that he has been to a burlesque show several times. In "A Night at the Fair" Basil and Riply join him in picking up two girls at the State Fair. In "He Thinks He's Wonderful" he takes Margaret TORRENCE to Connie DAVIES' dance.

Leanbaum Character in *LT/LOLT*. Studio executive.

Lebaume, Beau Character in "Six of One—". Young man whose life becomes a mess after he is suspended from Yale for his involvement in a drunk-driving accident.

Lee, Alice Riley Character in the Basil Duke LEE stories; Basil's mother. (His father is dead.) Her maiden name is spelled "Riley" in "A Night at the Fair," but in "Forging Ahead" her father and uncle spell it "Reilly." In "A Night at the Fair" she doesn't understand Basil's urgent need for long pants but agrees to let him buy them. In "The Freshest Boy" she is described as "an indulgent mother" who had given Basil "no habits of work" (p. 51). In "The Captured Shadow" she prays for God to help Basil because she can't help him anymore. In "Forging Ahead" she tells Basil she can't afford to send him to Yale.

Lee, Basil Duke Character in a series of eight stories written in 1928 and 1929: "The Scandal Detectives,"

"A Night at the Fair," "The Freshest Boy," "He Thinks He's Wonderful," "The Captured Shadow," "The Perfect Life," "Forging Ahead," and "Basil and Cleopatra." (*See* also "That Kind of Party" and *The Basil and Josephine Stories*.) His name is taken from Basil Wilson Duke (1838–1916), the brother-in-law and biographer of Confederate General John Hunt Morgan (1825–64), who was the first cousin of Zelda FITZGERALD's grandmother, Musidora Morgan SAYRE; Duke's biography of Morgan was in Zelda's parents' library. Basil Duke Lee is closely based on Fitzgerald, and many of the major events in the stories are drawn from autobiographical episodes recorded in Fitzgerald's *Ledger*. The series follows Basil from age 14 through prep school in the East to his first semester at Yale at age 17. He is imaginative, romantic, "fiercely competitive" ("A Night at the Fair," *AOAA*, p. 21), and ambitious; he dreams of being "a great athlete, popular, brilliant, and always happy" ("He Thinks He's Wonderful," *TAR*, p. 53). Throughout the series he struggles for popularity, success, recognition, and love, gradually maturing until in "Basil and Cleopatra" he is able to relinquish the beautiful and destructive Minnie BIBBLE so that he may pursue his own ambitions.

On October 26, 1938 Fitzgerald wrote to MGM editor Edwin KNOPF proposing a musical about young people who give an amateur play, using characters and situations similar to those in "He Thinks He's Wonderful," "The Captured Shadow," and "The Perfect Life," and starring Mickey Rooney (b. 1920), Judy Garland (1922–69), and Freddie Bartholomew (b. 1924). The Fitzgerald Papers at PRINCETON UNIVERSITY LIBRARY include two pages of plans for the movie, but the project was not developed.

Lee, Margery Character in "The Ice Palace." Young woman buried in the TARLETON, Georgia, graveyard whom Sally Carrol HAPPER imagines comes to comfort her while she is trapped in the ice palace.

Lee, Lieutenant General Robert E. (1807–1870) Historical figure and character in "A Debt of Honor." General-in-chief of the Confederate armies. In "A Debt of Honor" he sentences private Jack SANDERSON to death for falling asleep while on sentry duty, but then decides to let him off with a reprimand.

"The Lees of Happiness" Fiction. Written July 1920. *Chicago Sunday Tribune*, December 12, 1920, Blue Ribbon Fiction section, pp. 1, 3, 7; *TJA*. Author Jeffrey CURTAIN and former chorus girl Roxanne Milbank CURTAIN have been happily married for a little over a year when he suffers a stroke. He becomes a hopeless invalid, and she devotes herself to his care. Their friend Harry CROMWELL, who is unhappily married and later

divorced, is a frequent visitor. Jeffrey dies after eleven years, and Roxanne plans to run a boardinghouse.

Legendre, Mrs. Character in "The Rich Boy." Paula LEGENDRE's mother, who is distressed by COUSIN JO's report that Anson HUNTER was drunk.

Legendre, Paula Character in "The Rich Boy." Wealthy and beautiful girl to whom Anson HUNTER is engaged before he goes abroad to war. When he returns, they quarrel frequently and break their engagement. When Anson hears of Paula's interest in Lowell THAYER, he visits her and considers asking her again to marry him; but he delays since he feels he is in control of the relationship. Paula soon marries Thayer, whom she later divorces. She then quickly marries Peter HAGERTY, with whom she is very happy; but she dies in childbirth.

Lei Chamoro, Ella Character in "The Honor of the Goon." Malay college student whom Bomar WINLOCK dubs "the Goon" and whose relative, Mister LEI CHAMORO, avenges the insults she has suffered.

Lei Chamoro, Mister Character in "The Honor of the Goon." Relative of Ella LEI CHAMORO who avenges the insults she has suffered by having his Norwegian chauffeur, FINGARSON, beat up two of her fellow college students.

Lemmon, Elizabeth Maxwell PERKINS's cousin, whom he took Fitzgerald to meet in Middleburg, Virginia, in July 1934. After a visit to the Lemmon family home, "Welbourne," Fitzgerald wrote *The True Story of Appomattox* (July 1934); and the mansion served as the setting for "Her Last Case," written in August and published in November. Perkins's biographer, A. Scott Berg, has written that Perkins and Lemmon had a longstanding platonic love affair (*Max Perkins: Editor of Genius*).

Le Moyne, Littleboy Character in "Basil and Cleopatra." Boy with whom Minnie BIBBLE, who formerly liked Basil Duke LEE, falls in love. Fat GASPAR tells Basil about Minnie and Littleboy getting into trouble in a locked train compartment. Basil insults Littleboy while playing against him in the Yale-PRINCETON freshman football game.

Leonard, James (Jim) Character in "Last Kiss." Producer who befriends Pamela KNIGHTON.

Le Poire Character in "In the Darkest Hour." Villefranche community leader who resents the return of PHILIPPE and who is killed in battle with the Vikings.

Le Poire, Becquette Character in "Gods of Darkness." Chief witch who denounces PHILIPPE for killing her father, LE POIRE, although he was actually killed by the invading Northmen.

Leslie, Shane (1885–1971) Anglo-Irish writer and lecturer, a first cousin of Winston Churchill (1874–1965), and a Catholic convert whom Fitzgerald met at the home of Father Sigourney FAY in Washington in November 1912. Fitzgerald reviewed Leslie's *The Celt and the World* (New York: 1917) and *Verses in Peace and War* (London: 1916; New York: 1917) for *The NASSAU LITERARY MAGAZINE* in 1917. In his 1922 review of Leslie's *The Oppidan* (London & New York: 1922), Fitzgerald recalled his early impression of Leslie: "He first came into my life as the most romantic figure I had ever known. He had sat at the feet of Tolstoy, he had gone swimming with Rupert Brooke, he had been a young Englishman of the governing classes when the sense of being one must have been, as Compton McKenzie says, like the sense of being a Roman citizen" ("Homage to the Victorians"; *In His Own Time*, p. 134). Fay and Leslie attempted to influence Fitzgerald to enter the priesthood and become an American counterpart to English priest-novelist Robert Hugh BENSON, who had been a classmate of Leslie's at Cambridge.

Leslie offered to recommend Fitzgerald's first novel to his publisher, Charles SCRIBNER's Sons; he corrected grammar and spelling in the typescript which Fitzgerald sent him, then forwarded "The Romantic Egotist" (an early version of *TSOP*) to Charles SCRIBNER on May 6, 1918 with a letter that read, in part:

> I have read it through and in spite of its disguises it has given me a vivid picture of the American generation that is hastening to war. I marvel at it's crudity and its cleverness. It is naive in places, shocking in others, painful to the conventional and not without a touch of ironic sublimity especially toward the end. About a third of the book could be omitted without losing the impression that it is written by an American Rupert Brooke. I knew the poetic Rupert Brooke and this is a prose one, though some of the lyrics are good and aparently original. It interests me as a boy's book and I think gives expression to that real American youth that the sentimentalists and super patriots are so anxious to drape behind the canvas of the Y.M.C.A. tent. Though Scott Fitzgerald is still alive it has a literary value. Of course when he is killed it will also have a commercial value" (*Correspondence*, p. 29).

Fitzgerald later used Leslie's letter about Monsignor Fay's funeral (which Fitzgerald was unable to attend) as the basis for his description of Monsignor DARCY's funeral in *TSOP* (January 16, 1919; *Correspondence*, pp. 36–37). *B&D* is dedicated "TO SHANE LESLIE, GEORGE JEAN NATHAN AND MAXWELL PERKINS IN APPRECIATION OF MUCH LITERARY HELP AND ENCOURAGEMENT."

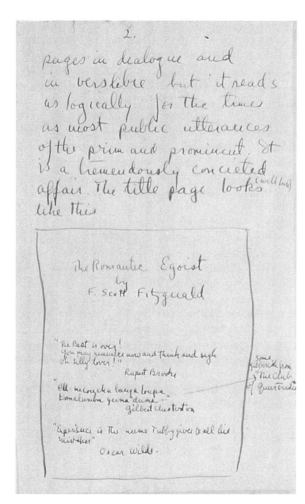

Fitzgerald's December 1917 letter to Shane Leslie illustrated the proposed title page of a novel that after extensive revision became This Side of Paradise. *(Bruccoli Collection, University of South Carolina)*

Letgarde (*See* also GIRL [unnamed] from "In the Darkest Hour.") Character in "The Count of Darkness." Consort of the slain Norman chieftain; PHILIPPE takes her as his own consort. When Philippe mistreats her, she runs away and drowns trying to cross the river.

"Let's Go Out and Play" Antiwar radio drama which Fitzgerald wrote for the Columbia Broadcasting Company for $700 in September 1935. It was broadcast on the Squibb "World Peaceways" program on WABC in New York on October 3, 1935 at 9:30 p.m. No copy of the script which was offered to listeners has been located, but there is a typescript of the play in PRINCETON UNIVERSITY LIBRARY.

Letters There are six collections of Fitzgerald's correspondence: *The Letters of F. Scott Fitzgerald,* ed. Andrew TURNBULL (New York: Charles SCRIBNER'S Sons, 1963; London: Bodley Head, 1964); *Dear Scott/Dear Max,* ed. John Kuehl and Jackson R. Bryer (New York: Charles

Scribner's Sons, 1971; London: Cassell, 1973)—correspondence between Fitzgerald and editor Maxwell PERKINS; *As Ever, Scott Fitz—,* ed. Matthew J. BRUCCOLI, with Jennifer McCabe Atkinson; foreword by Scottie FITZGERALD Smith (Philadelphia & New York: Lippincott, 1972; London: Woburn, 1973)—correspondence between Fitzgerald and agent Harold OBER; *Correspondence of F. Scott Fitzgerald,* ed. Matthew J. Bruccoli and Margaret M. Duggan, with Susan Walker (New York: Random House, 1980)—includes previously uncollected letters and letters Fitzgerald received; *F. Scott Fitzgerald: A Life in Letters,* ed. Matthew J. Bruccoli, with Judith S. Baughman (New York: Charles Scribner's Sons, 1994)—"the standard one-volume edition"—arranged chronologically, with an emphasis on autobiographical content; *Letters to His Daughter,* ed. Andrew Turnbull, with an introduction by Frances Fitzgerald Lanahan (New York: Charles Scribner's Sons, 1965)—reprints letters to Scottie Fitzgerald which had previously been published in *The Letters of F. Scott Fitzgerald.*

Le Vigne, Carl Character in "No Harm Trying." Studio executive who puts Pat HOBBY on the payroll to help Pat's ex-wife, Estelle DEVLIN.

Lewis, Sinclair (1885–1951) American novelist; the first American to win the Nobel Prize for literature (1930). Lewis's novels published in the same years as *TSOP, B&D, GG,* and *TITN—Main Street* (1920), *Babbitt* (1922), *Arrowsmith* (1925), and *Work of Art* (1934)—greatly outsold Fitzgerald's novels. Lewis visited the Fitzgeralds at the WHITE BEAR YACHT CLUB in DELLWOOD near ST. PAUL in summer 1922. Fitzgerald inscribed a copy of *GG* for Lewis: "I've just sent for Arrowsmith. My hope is that this The Great Gatsby will be the second best American book of the Spring" (April 1925; *Life in Letters,* p. 103).

See Mark Schorer, *Sinclair Lewis: An American Life* (New York: McGraw-Hill, 1961).

Libby, Malcolm Character in "A Nice Quiet Place." Constance PERRY's fiancé, who is found in a compromising situation with Josephine PERRY. He and Constance are reconciled, and the wedding goes on.

Liberty Weekly magazine that published three Fitzgerald stories and one article: " 'The Sensible Thing' " (July 1924), "The Passionate Eskimo" (June 1935), "Strange Sanctuary" (December 1939), and "Girls Believe in Girls" (February 1930). Fitzgerald suggested to Harold OBER that *Liberty* would be the best market for serializing *GG* because the novel "is a love story and it is sensational" (October 25, 1924; *As Ever,* p. 67); but editor John N. Wheeler (1886–1973) declined the offer on December 16, 1924, noting: "It is too ripe for us. Running only one serial as we do, we could not publish this story with as many mistresses and as much adultery as there is in it" (to Paul Revere REYNOLDS; *As Ever,* p. 70). In April 1926 Fitzgerald optimistically told Ober that *TITN* would be ready for serialization the following January, and Ober offered *Liberty* a first-refusal agreement. *Liberty* was prepared to offer $30–40,000, but the magazine changed ownership during the period before *TITN* was completed; Ober was able to obtain a release from the contract when Fitzgerald decided he preferred to have *TITN* appear in SCRIBNER'S MAGAZINE.

Life Begins at Eight-Thirty (Twentieth Century-Fox, 1940) Fitzgerald's last screenwriting assignment. He worked for Twentieth Century-Fox in 1940 on an adaptation of the 1940 play *The Light at Heart* by Emlyn Williams (1905–87); his screenplay was rejected. The movie, directed by Irving Pichel (1891–1954), was released with screenplay by Nunnally JOHNSON. Monty Woolley (1888–1963) starred as an alcoholic former actor who takes a job as a street-corner Santa Claus.

Lilymary Character in "Dearly Beloved." BEAUTY BOY's wife.

Lincoln, Sol Character in "Two Wrongs." Man who cancels lunch with Bill MCCHESNEY, leaving McChesney free to take Emmy PINKARD to lunch.

"Lipstick" Screenplay. *Fitzgerald/Hemingway Annual* (1978), pp. 3–35. In January 1927 United Artists producer John W. Considine (b. 1898) hired Fitzgerald to write an original flapper comedy for actress Constance Talmadge (1900–73), paying him a $3,500 advance with an additional $12,500 to be paid on acceptance of the script. Fitzgerald and Zelda moved to HOLLYWOOD, where they lived at the AMBASSADOR HOTEL for two months while he worked on the project; during this stay he met actress Lois MORAN. Fitzgerald's script is set in PRINCETON and stars an unjustly imprisoned girl who has a magic lipstick that makes men want to kiss her. It was rejected, and he was not paid the $12,500 balance.

Littauer, Kenneth (1894–1968) COLLIER'S fiction editor who in 1937 accepted Fitzgerald's story originally titled "Thumbs Up"—which had been declined by 13 other magazines—paying $1,500 against an acceptable rewrite; Littauer rejected at least two revisions before accepting the version titled "The End of Hate" in June 1939. Fitzgerald hoped to develop a connection with *Collier's* through Littauer, but the editor declined all the stories he submitted in the summer of 1939, when Fitzgerald tried to persuade him that he was opening a "new vein" of fiction and no longer writing stories about young love (c. late July 1939; *Life in Letters,* p. 402). Fitzgerald hoped that *Collier's* would serialize his HOLLYWOOD novel (*LT/LOLT*), and on September 29, 1939 he sent Littauer a synopsis (*Life in Letters,* pp. 408–412). After receiving a 6,000–word sample in November, Littauer declined to make an advance without seeing more of the novel.

little girl (unnamed) Character in "The Count of Darkness." Child who was orphaned by the Norman invaders and whom PHILIPPE adopts.

little girl (unnamed) Character in "Outside the Cabinet-Maker's." Six-year-old child whose DADDY tells her a story of a fairy princess held captive by an ogre.

"Lives of the Dancers" *Notebooks,* #1599. Ballet synopsis about the Russian ballet before the 1917 Revolution and some Russian dancers who move to PARIS and eventually America after the war. Fitzgerald referred to this synopsis in a 1936 letter to Harold OBER as "something that I wrote gratuitously for a Russian dancer some years ago" (February 8, 1936; *Life in Letters,* p. 296; *As Ever,* pp. 248–249).

Livingstone, Warren Character in "I Got Shoes." Society man who wants to marry Nell MARGERY.

Llewellen, Frank Character in "Two Wrongs." Actor who becomes involved with Irene RIKKER.

"Lo, the Poor Peacock!" Fiction. Written 1935. ES-QUIRE, 76 (September 1971), 154–158; *The Price Was High.* Jason DAVIS, who has lost a lot of money, is forced to give up his secretary, take his daughter, Jo DAVIS, out of private school, and move to a small apartment. When the grocer closes his account and the doctor tells him that his wife, Annie Lee DAVIS, who is hospitalized for heart trouble, will never get any better, Davis plans to kill himself; but when the phone interrupts him with notice that Jo has been expelled from her public high school, he changes his mind. Annie Lee's family farm, formerly noted for its sausage, becomes profitable again when the original recipe is used again; Jo's school discovers it erred in expelling her; Davis wins a big account in the textile industry; and Annie Lee comes home from the hospital.

The *Esquire* text was abridged and revised by an editor; Fitzgerald's text appears in *The Price Was High.*

Lockheart, Andy Character in "The Captured Shadow." Yale student and champion athlete who is at Evelyn BEEBE's house when Basil Duke LEE and Riply BUCKNER stop by to ask her to star in Basil's play. He is also mentioned in "Forging Ahead."

Lois Character in "Benediction." Girl who visits her older brother, KIETH, at a seminary and almost decides to give up her lover, HOWARD.

London, England The Fitzgeralds began their first trip to EUROPE in May 1921 with a visit to London, where they stayed at the Cecil Hotel. They dined with John Galsworthy (1867–1933), to whom Maxwell PERKINS had provided an introduction; but Fitzgerald found Galsworthy disappointing. SCRIBNERS' London representative Charles Kingsley arranged meetings with other literary people, and Shane LESLIE took the Fitzgeralds on a tour of the London docks at night. Lady Randolph Churchill (1854–1921) invited the Fitzgeralds to lunch, and Zelda had a long conversation with Winston Churchill (1874–1965). After visiting PARIS and ITALY, the Fitzgeralds returned to London on June 30, staying at Claridge's and the Cavendish. Collins had published *TSOP* on May 26, and Fitzgerald wanted to observe its English reception, which was disappointing. The Fitzgeralds returned to America in early July. They briefly visited London again in November 1925.

Long, Jimmy Character in "The Popular Girl." Old friend with whom Yanci BOWMAN goes out in order to make Scott KIMBERLY jealous; she is shocked by his gauche appearance.

"The Long Way Out" Fiction. Written May 1937. ES-QUIRE, 8 (September 1937), 45, 193; *Stories.* Mrs. KING goes into a coma at the birth of her second child, emerges with schizophrenia, and is sent to a sanitarium. As her condition improves she is given permission to take a trip with her husband, George KING, but he is injured in a car accident on his way to see her. The doctors decide simply to tell her that her husband has been delayed, and they continue this story for several days. When her husband dies the doctors finally tell her the truth, but she laughs it off as an attempt to see whether she is still sick. Over the years she dresses every day in the same suit and waits for her husband to arrive.

"Looking Back Eight Years" Article by Zelda FITZGER-ALD. COLLEGE HUMOR, 14 (June 1928), 36–37; *Zelda Fitzgerald: The Collected Writings.* Bylined "F. Scott and Zelda Fitzgerald" but credited to Zelda in *Ledger.* Analysis of the impact of World War I on the "Younger Generation," who are "haunted and harassed by a sense of unfulfilled destiny" and have "a baffled feeling of frustration" (*Collected Writings,* p. 409).

Loos, Anita (1893–1981) Screenwriter and author of *Gentlemen Prefer Blondes* (1925). Her screenplay for *Red-Headed Woman* (1931) was used instead of Fitzgerald's screenplay, which was considered too serious. Fitzgerald had known Loos in the 1920s, and he sometimes lunched with her and other writers at the MGM commissary. Loos and Jane Murfin (1893–1955) replaced Fitzgerald and Donald Ogden STEWART when it was decided that the screenplay for *The Women* (1938) required female screenwriters.

See Gary Carey, *Anita Loos: A Biography* (New York: Knopf, 1988).

Lorimer, George Horace (1867–1937) Editor of *The SATURDAY EVENING POST,* the primary market for Fitzgerald's short fiction. In 1938 Fitzgerald commented in an unsent letter to Eddie Mannix and Sam Katz at MGM, in which he complained about changes in his screenplay for *Three Comrades* (1938): "In writing over a hundred and fifty stories for George Lorimer, the great editor of *The Saturday Evening Post,* I found he made a sharp distinction between a sordid tragedy and a heroic tragedy—hating the former but accepting the latter as an essential and interesting part of life" (*Letters,* p. 565).

See John Tebbel, *George Horace Lorimer and The Saturday Evening Post* (Garden City, NY: Doubleday, 1948).

Lorry, Annie Character in "At Your Age." Debutante who is briefly engaged to 50-year-old Tom SQUIRES.

Lorry, Arthur Character in "At Your Age." Annie LORRY's father.

Lorry, Mabel Tollman Character in "At Your Age." Annie LORRY's mother, who objects to Annie's relationship with Tom SQUIRES.

"The Lost Decade" Fiction. Written 1939. ESQUIRE, 12 (December 1939), 113, 228; *Stories.* Orrison BROWN's boss asks him to take to lunch Louis TRIMBLE, a once-famous architect who has "been away" during the 1930s. Trimble, who spent the decade drunk, tries to recover a sense of reality: "I simply want to see how people walk and what their clothes and shoes and hats are made of. And their eyes and hands" (*Stories,* p. 485).

Louis II (Louis the Stammerer) (846–879) Historical figure and character in "The Kingdom in the Dark." King of the West Franks and grandson of Charlemagne (742–814). When PHILIPPE gives shelter to GRISELDA, who has run away from Louis, Louis orders his men to burn Philippe's fort.

Louisville, Kentucky Fitzgerald was stationed at CAMP ZACHARY TAYLOR near Louisville in March and April 1918. In *GG* Daisy Fay [BUCHANAN] and Jordan BAKER grew up in Louisville.

"The Love Boat" Fiction. Written August 1927. *The SATURDAY EVENING POST,* 200 (October 8, 1927), 8–9, 134, 139, 141; *The Price Was High.* Three young Harvard graduates—Bill FROTHINGTON, Ellsworth AMES, and Hamilton ABBOT—board a boat where a high-school dance is being held. Bill falls in love with high-school student Mae PURLEY, who abandons Al FITZPATRICK for Bill. Bill and Mae date for two months, and he wants to marry her but hesitates because of the wide difference in their social classes. They quarrel and part; after serving in the war, Bill marries a girl of his own set, Stella [FROTHINGTON]. After eight years of marriage Bill feels restless and recalls the moonlit night on the boat with Mae as the symbol of his youth. He goes to visit Mae, who is now married to Al Fitzpatrick, then gets drunk and boards a boat with another high-school dance, where he gets into a fight and is thrown overboard. When he returns home the next afternoon he discovers that Stella has left him.

"Love in the Night" Fiction. Written November 1924. *The SATURDAY EVENING POST,* 197 (March 14, 1925), 18–19, 68, 70; *Bits of Paradise.* Seventeen-year-old Val ROSTOFF, a Russian prince, experiences his first love when he meets a GIRL on the yacht *The Privateer* in the harbor at CANNES. They do not reveal their names; and after she kisses him, she tells him that she has recently married a 60-year-old man. After Val's parents' death in the Russian Revolution, he returns destitute to Cannes, working first as a taxi driver and then in a bank. He takes his vacation the last two weeks of every April in memory of his encounter with the girl; in 1922 he learns that the girl, now widowed, has also returned to the Cannes harbor in April for the past two years. He doesn't wish her to see him as a failure, but on his way out of town he stops at the American consulate to learn her name in case his fortunes ever improve. She has instructed the consulate to notify her if anyone inquires for her, and while he is there she arrives. They marry and settle in NEW YORK, where Val operates a thriving taxi business, and they return every April to the RIVIERA.

"Love in the Night" was Fitzgerald's first story set abroad, and it began a series of stories in which he contrasted America and EUROPE. Fitzgerald salvaged some material from the story for *TITN,* including the evocation of the pre-Revolution Russian colony on the Riviera.

The Love of the Last Tycoon: A Western (*See* also *The Last Tycoon.*) Novel. Edited by Matthew J. BRUCCOLI (Cambridge: Cambridge University Press, 1993). When Fitzgerald died with his fifth novel unfinished, he had not yet decided on a title. Edmund WILSON provided the title *The Last Tycoon* when he edited the work for its original publication (New York: Charles SCRIBNER's Sons, 1941), but there is no evidence that this title was the author's final choice. The only typed title page in Fitzgerald's draft material names the novel "STAHR/A Romance." When Sheilah GRAHAM, Fitzgerald's companion in HOLLYWOOD, sent his manuscripts to editor Maxwell PERKINS, she told him the working title was "Stahr." She further noted that a few weeks before his death Fitzgerald had asked what she thought of "The Love of the Last Tycoon." Frances KROLL, Fitzgerald's secretary, referred to the novel as "Stahr" three times and wrote to Edmund Wilson that "Scott satirically considered the alternative title for the book 'The Last of the Tycoons' " (June 11, 1941; *LOLT,* p. lv). A page of notes in Fitzgerald's handwriting headed <u>Title</u> includes "The Last Tycoon"; but it and all other notes are crossed out except for "The Love of the Last Tycoon/A Western," which is the only title on the list written in title-page format with subtitle and author's name. Fitzgerald wrote and deleted this note next to the title: "This is the familiar Fitzgerald formula but the boy grows tired" (*LOLT,* p. xvi). Bruccoli explains his choice of this title for his critical edition of the novel: It is "preferable because it is close to the title by

which the novel has been known and because it has the Fitzgerald bouquet. Fitzgerald was in fact writing a western—a novel about the last American frontier, where immigrants and sons of immigrants pursued and defined the American dream. It is appropriate that these tycoons made movie westerns: they too were pioneers" (*LOLT,* p. xvii).

Although the seed for *LOLT* was planted as early as his January 1927 meeting with producer Irving THAL-BERG, the model for protagonist Monroe STAHR, Fitzgerald did not begin writing the novel until the termination of his MGM contract in January 1939. On May 29, he reported to Harold OBER, "I have blocked out my novel completely with a rough sketch of every episode and event and character" (*Life in Letters,* p. 393; *As Ever,* p. 389); and on October 14 he wired Perkins: "I THINK I CAN WRITE THIS BOOK AS IF IT WAS A BIOGRAPHY BECAUSE I KNOW THE CHARACTER OF THIS MAN" (*Life in Letters,* p. 414). Fitzgerald hoped that *COLLIER'S* would serialize the novel; on September 29 he sent a synopsis to *Collier's* editor Kenneth LITTAUER, stating: "I hope it will be something new, arouse new emotions perhaps even a new way of looking at certain phenomena. I have set it safely in a period of five years ago to obtain detachment, but now that Europe is tumbling about our ears this also seems to be for the best. It is an escape into a lavish, romantic past that perhaps will not come again into our time" (*Life in Letters,* p. 412). Littauer was interested but declined to make an advance without a substantial sample, for which he offered $5,000 if *Collier's* accepted the novel after seeing the sample, with another $5,000 advance for the next 20,000 words (October 10, 1939; *Correspondence,* pp. 550–551). The terms Littauer proposed totaled at least $20,000 for serial rights to the novel, but the final price was to be negotiated later. Fitzgerald was dissatisfied with the offer and asked Maxwell Perkins to negotiate for a larger advance. In November Fitzgerald sent Littauer and Perkins a 6,000–word sample consisting of the first chapter of the novel. Littauer wired on November 28: "FIRST SIX THOUSAND PRETTY CRYPTIC THERE-FORE DISAPPOINTING. BUT YOU WARNED US THIS MIGHT BE SO. CAN WE DEFER VERDICT UNTIL FURTHER DEVELOPMENT OF STORY? IF IT HAS TO BE NOW IT HAS TO BE NOW. REGARDS" (*Correspondence,* p. 561). Fitzgerald replied an hour later: "NO HARD FEELINGS THERE HAS NEVER BEEN AN EDITOR WITH PANTS ON SINCE GEORGE LORIMER" (*Life in Letters,* p. 421). That day Fitzgerald wired Perkins to send the sample to *The SATURDAY EVENING POST,* which declined the serial rights. The next day he wired Perkins to show the synopsis to agent Leland HAYWARD, hoping for an advance from a studio for movie rights; but Hayward

Page of Fitzgerald's notes on possible titles for The Love of the Last Tycoon (Princeton University Library)

said he could do nothing until the novel was written.

On October 31, 1939 Fitzgerald wrote to his daughter, Scottie FITZGERALD: "Look! I have begun to write something that is maybe great. . . . It may not <u>make</u> us a cent but it will pay expenses and it is the first labor of love I've undertaken since the first part of 'Infidelity.' . . . And I think when you read this book, which will encompass the time when you knew me as an adult, you will understand how intensively I knew your world—not <u>ex</u>tensively, because I was so ill and unable to get about" (*Life in Letters,* p. 419).

Fitzgerald's work on the novel was interrupted by the financial necessity of writing the Pat HOBBY stories and other short pieces for *ESQUIRE,* as well as by his work on the unproduced screenplay for his story "Baby-lon Revisited" (*see* "Cosmopolitan"). Although he was careful not to use novel material in the Hobby stories, several of his other Hollywood stories have connections to *LOLT.* Miles CALMAN, the brilliant movie director in

"Crazy Sunday" (October 1932), is partly based on Irving Thalberg. Pamela KNIGHTON of "Last Kiss" (unpublished until 1949) is, like Kathleen MOORE in *LOLT*, based on Sheilah GRAHAM. BEAUTY BOY in "Dearly Beloved" (unpublished until 1969) has connections with the philosophical FISHERMAN in the novel.

On October 23, 1940 Fitzgerald wrote to Zelda FITZGERALD: "I am deep in the novel, living in it, and it makes me happy. It is a <u>constructed</u> novel like <u>Gatsby</u>, with passages of poetic prose when it fits the action, but no ruminations or side-shows like <u>Tender</u>. Everything must contribute to the dramatic movement" (*Life in Letters*, p. 467). When Fitzgerald died of a heart attack on December 21, 1940, he had written drafts of 17 of the projected 30 episodes for the novel.

Perkins, who wanted to publish the novel both as a memorial to Fitzgerald and to earn money for the author's estate, was unsure about the best way to present the work in progress. He considered having another writer complete the novel, but both John O'HARA and Budd SCHULBERG declined the task. It was arranged for Edmund Wilson to edit the work; extant documents show that he styled the punctuation, corrected spelling, altered names, replaced words, moved two scenes, and combined episodes into chapters, conveying the impression of a more finished work than Fitzgerald's working drafts represent. He also provided the title without specifying a source. (For a more complete discussion of Fitzgerald's work in progress, as well as the editing and publication process, see Matthew J. Bruccoli's introduction to *The Love of the Last Tycoon: A Western* and Bruccoli, *"The Last of the Novelists": F. Scott Fitzgerald and The Last Tycoon*.

*THE LAST TYCOON/*AN UNFINISHED NOVEL*/ BY/*F. SCOTT FITZGERALD*/*TOGETHER WITH*/ THE GREAT GATSBY/*AND SELECTED STORIES was published on October 27, 1941 at $2.75. The volume included "May Day," "The Diamond as Big as the Ritz," "The Rich Boy," "Absolution," and "Crazy Sunday," as well as Wilson's foreword, his synopsis of the unwritten episodes, and 30 pages of edited selections from Fitzgerald's notes for the novel. The first printing was less than 5,000 copies; the volume was reprinted in 1941, 1945, 1947, and 1948. Most of the reviews were favorable, and the positive responses of Stephen Vincent Benét and James THURBER may have contributed to the Fitzgerald REVIVAL. Benét wrote: "Had Fitzgerald been permitted to finish the book, I think there is no doubt that it would have added a major character and a major novel to American fiction. As it is, 'The Last Tycoon' is a great deal more than a fragment. It shows the full powers of its author, at their height and at their best. . . . You can take off your hats now, gentlemen, and I think perhaps you had better. This is not a legend, this is a reputation—and, seen in perspective, it may well be one of the most secure reputations of our time" ("Fitzgerald's Unfinished Symphony," *Saturday Review of Literature*, 24 [December 6, 1941], 10; *FSF: The Critical Reception*, pp. 375–376). John DOS PASSOS expressed admiration for the novel in his 1945 *Crack-Up* essay, concluding, "Even in their unfinished state these fragments, I believe, are of sufficient dimensions to raise the level of American fiction to follow in some such way as Marlowe's blank verse line raised the whole level of Elizabethan verse" (*CU*, p. 343). (*See* also CRITICAL REPUTATION AND RECEPTION OF NOVELS.)

Fitzgerald had not perfected his narrative plan for the novel when he died. Cecelia BRADY, daughter of producer Pat BRADY, serves as the narrator, as Fitzgerald explained to Littauer: "I shall grant myself the privilege, as Conrad did, of letting her imagine the actions of the characters. Thus, I hope to get the verisimilitude of a first person narrative, combined with a Godlike knowledge of all events that happen to my characters" (September 29, 1939; *Life in Letters*, p. 410). Cecelia relates much of the story, sometimes stipulating her sources; but she was to be allowed greater flexibility than *GG* narrator Nick CARRAWAY, who witnesses or cites a source for everything except Jay GATSBY's murder. In *LOLT* the point of view shifts, with some of the material being presented by the authorial voice. Twice Fitzgerald inserted awkward transitions—possibly reminders to himself—that at these points Cecelia was resuming the narrative. He also considered a narrative frame in which Cecelia, a patient in a tuberculosis sanitarium, tells the story to a fellow patient who retells it to the reader.

Note: The following synopsis is keyed to the episode and section designations in Fitzgerald's latest revised typescripts (these designations are utilized in the Cambridge critical edition of the novel); Wilson's chapter designations (which appear in all other editions) are provided in brackets.

Chapter I
Cecelia Brady tries to explain Hollywood by relating the events of five years ago (around 1935). While flying home to Hollywood for the summer vacation from Bennington College, Cecelia meets screenwriter Wylie WHITE and Mannie SCHWARTZE, the former head of a Hollywood combine. When the plane is grounded in Nashville, Wylie takes Cecelia and Schwartze to visit the Hermitage, home of President Andrew Jackson (1767–1845). Schwartze does not return to the plane with the others, and they later learn that he has shot himself. Back on the plane, Cecelia talks with her father's partner, Monroe STAHR, with whom she is secretly in love and to whom Schwartze had sent a note of warning against his enemies. Stahr, who has identified himself as "Mr. SMITH" on this plane ride, lectures the pilot on decision making (an episode based on Fitzgerald's first meeting with Irving Thalberg).

Fitzgerald's final outline-plan for The Love of the Last Tycoon (Princeton University Library)

Dust jacket for the volume posthumously published in 1941 (Bruccoli Collection, University of South Carolina)

Episodes 4 and 5 [Chapter 2]
On a July night a month later, Cecelia is in her father's office at the studio when an earthquake occurs. Stahr, who was asleep in his own office when the quake hit, calls in trouble-shooter "Robby" ROBINSON.

Episode 6 [Chapter 2]
Stahr and Robby arrive at the flooded back lot, where they see two women floating on the head of the god Siva, a movie prop. Stahr is struck by the resemblance of one of the women to his dead wife, Minna DAVIS.

Episode 7 [Chapter 3]
To give a glimpse of Stahr functioning, Cecelia begins to describe "a producer's day." In the morning Stahr is informed that cameraman Pete ZAVRAS jumped off the balcony of the Administration Building and broke his arm in a failed suicide attempt. Stahr asks his secretary, Catherine DOOLAN, to find out whether MALONE, the policeman who had put the two women off the back lot last night, knows their names; but Malone has no helpful information.

Episode 8 [Chapter 3]
Stahr meets with English novelist George BOXLEY, who is struggling to write for the movies. Gag man Mike

VAN DYKE demonstrates a slapstick routine. Mr. RODERI-GUEZ, an impotent actor, comes to Stahr for advice.

Episode 9 [Chapter 3]
Stahr holds a conference with writers Rose MELONEY and Wylie White, supervisor Joe RIENMUND, and director John BROACA. He explains his dissatisfaction with a script scheduled for production in two weeks and offers suggestions for its improvement. Robinson leaves a message that one of the women from the back lot said she had just moved to Los Angeles and that her name was Smith or Brown or Jones; Stahr recalls that the woman wore a silver belt. Stahr asks Miss Doolan about Pete Zavras, who is rumored to be going blind.

Episode 10 [Chapter 3]
Danish Prince AGGE, who is visiting the studio, has lunch at the commissary with 11 of the most powerful men of the studio, including Stahr, Pat Brady, studio executives MARCUS and LEANBAUM, company lawyer Mort FLIESHACKER, and theater owner Joe POPOLOUS. Stahr shocks the others by proposing a quality picture that will lose money. Robinson remembers that the woman's name was Smith, and Stahr assigns Miss Doolan to call all the Smiths who have taken new phones in the last month.

For Episode 11 [Chapter 4]
Stahr replaces director Red RIDINGWOOD because Ridingwood can't handle the star actress in his movie.

Episode 11 [Chapter 4]
Stahr and others watch the day's rushes and screen tests in his projection room. Stahr's oculist, to whom he had sent Pete Zavras, reports that Zavras has nearly perfect vision and gives him a letter to dispel the rumors. Stahr placates the MARQUANDS, writers who are upset that they are not working alone on the script, a situation that "shocks their sense of unity"; he tells Prince Agge, "I'm the unity" (p. 58). Stahr receives a phone call from Edna SMITH, the woman with the silver belt; she reluctantly agrees to meet him at a drugstore that night. Pete Zavras thanks Stahr for "saving" him and offers to help if he ever wants anybody's throat cut.

Episode 12 [Chapter 4]
Stahr meets Edna Smith and sees no resemblance to Minna. He offers to take her home; and she asks him to drop her off at the house of her friend, Kathleen MOORE. When Stahr sees Kathleen, he realizes that she is the one who looks like Minna and that he had been mistaken about the belt. Stahr lingers to talk with Kathleen and invites her to visit the studio.

Episode 13 [Chapter 5]
A week later Wylie White drives Cecelia to the studio, where she is disappointed by Stahr's rejection of her invitation to the screenwriters' ball.

13 (continued) [Chapter 5]
At the ball Cecelia sees Stahr dancing with Kathleen and tries to find out who she is. Stahr walks Kathleen to her car, and she agrees to meet him the next day.

Section 14 [Chapter 5]
Stahr and Kathleen meet the next afternoon; and they go for a drive, stopping for a Coke at a restaurant with a trained seal. He takes her to the house he is building on the beach, where he receives a phone call alleged to be from the President of the United States, but which turns out to be from an orangutan who resembles President William McKinley (1843–1901).

Section 14 (2nd part) [Chapter 5]
Stahr and Kathleen drive back to the city. After they kiss at her door they get back in the car to return to his house.

Section 14 (Part iii) [Chapter 5]
Back at Stahr's house, he and Kathleen make love. She tells him about "the MAN" she once lived with and how he educated her. Stahr and Kathleen walk along the beach, where they encounter a black fisherman who says he never goes to movies or lets his children go because "There's no profit" (p. 93). Stahr is profoundly affected by the man's comments and changes his plans about several forthcoming movies as a result. When Stahr takes Kathleen home she looks in his car for an envelope she thinks fell out of her purse, but she doesn't find it. Stahr returns home, where his FILIPINO servant brings him a letter that fell out of the car. After reading scripts for three hours, Stahr opens the letter, which Kathleen had written before their date and in which she reveals that she is to be married soon.

Section 15 (first part) [Chapter 5]
Cecelia visits Rose Meloney and tells her that she has a rival for Stahr's affections. Rose agrees to call Martha DODD, a faded star who had been at the same table with Kathleen at the ball.

15 (second part) [Chapter 5]
Cecelia and Rose meet Martha Dodd for lunch, and Cecelia takes Martha to meet her father in hopes of getting her work. Cecelia finds her father's secretary, Birdy PETERS, naked in a closet in his office. Martha takes Cecelia to Kathleen's house, but Kathleen is not at home.

Episode 16, First Part [Chapter 5]
Stahr lectures George Boxley on writing for the movies, then takes him to Jaques LA BORWITS' office, where Boxley's suggestion inspires the other writers to get back to work on a problematic script.

Episode 16 (Part 2) [Chapter 5]
Doctor BAER conducts Stahr's weekly examination and reflects that Stahr, who has heart trouble, will surely die soon. Kathleen calls Stahr; and though he expresses his outrage over her letter, he agrees to pick her up later that night. While they ride in his limousine she tells him that the man she had lived with was a king and discusses her upcoming marriage to an AMERICAN. He suggests that she go somewhere with him for the weekend, but she hesitates. Stahr resists his inclination to persuade her that their future lies together, resolving to wait until the next day to settle things. The next afternoon he receives a telegram from Kathleen announcing that she was married at noon.

Episode 17 [Chapter 6]
Stahr asks Cecelia to help him meet a Communist Party member; she arranges for BRIMMER to meet Stahr at her house, where Stahr complains about Communist interference with his writers. The three go to dinner, where Stahr, miserable over the loss of Kathleen, gets drunk. When they return to the Brady house Stahr announces that he is going to beat Brimmer up, but Brimmer knocks him down. After Brimmer leaves, Stahr invites Cecelia to visit Douglas Fairbanks' (1883–1939) ranch with him.

The Unwritten Episodes

When he died, Fitzgerald had written 17 of his projected 30 episodes for the novel, and much of the plot was undeveloped. His outline and working notes indicate that he planned for Pat Brady to blackmail Stahr, who resumes his affair with Kathleen after her marriage, and for Stahr to retaliate with information about Brady. When Stahr learns that Brady is planning to have him murdered, he arranges for Brady's murder during his own absence from Hollywood. On the plane Stahr rejects his plan but is unable to call off the murder because his plane crashes. Fitzgerald originally planned to end the novel by having children who plunder the plane wreckage be influenced by the possessions they take. This conclusion was apparently discarded or altered in favor of ending with Stahr's funeral, for which has-been actor Johnny SWANSON is mistakenly invited to be a pallbearer, with the result that his career is revived on the basis of his supposed closeness to Stahr.

Fitzgerald wrote in his notes for the novel, "I am the last of the novelists for a long time now" (*Notebooks,* #2001). This conception of himself may be illuminated by the character of Monroe Stahr, the last tycoon. Stahr, a self-made man who represents integrity, honor, courage, and responsibility, shares Fitzgerald's allegiance to traditional American ideals. Matthew J. Bruccoli writes, "Sensing that the politics of the Thirties and the impending world war would terminate the romantic reactions to life that had inspired his fiction, Fitzgerald saw himself as the last of a certain kind of novelist writing about the last of the old American heroes. Nurturing a heroic sense of American character, he found his essential American figure in his last novel" (*Some Sort of Epic Grandeur,* p. 554).

Fitzgerald's sense of America is revealed in the following comment: "I look out at it—and I think it is the most beautiful history in the world. It is the history of me and of my people. And if I came here yesterday like Sheilah I should still think so. It is the history of all aspiration—not just the American dream but the human dream and if I came at the end of it that too is a place in the line of the pioneers" (*Notebooks,* #2037).

See *F. Scott Fitzgerald Manuscripts V* (3 vols): "*LT:* Manuscript and Revised Typescript for the First 17 Episodes, with the Author's Plans and Notes," and Matthew J. Bruccoli, *"The Last of the Novelists": F. Scott Fitzgerald and The Last Tycoon.*

Lovejoy, Evelyn Character in "On Your Own." Actress who falls in love with George IVES while sailing to America for her father's funeral. Her behavior on shipboard is based on Bert BARR.

Lowrie, Jessie Piper Character in "The Cut-Glass Bowl." Harold PIPER'S cousin, who tells him about his wife's affair with Freddy GEDNEY.

Lowrie, Lewis (Lew) Character in "More Than Just a House." Young man on his way up socially when he meets the GUNTHER family.

Lowrie, Tom Character in "The Cut-Glass Bowl." Jessie Piper LOWRIE'S husband, who drunkenly speaks to Mr. and Mrs. Clarence AHEARN about their being kept out of the Country Club.

Lucienne Character in *TITN.* The DIVERS' maid, who has difficulty operating the heater for the bathwater during their visit to the MINGHETTIS' home.

Lucille Character in *GG.* Party guest to whom Jay GATSBY sent a new evening gown after she tore her gown on a chair at one of his parties.

"A Luckless Santa Claus" Fiction. *The NEWMAN NEWS,* 9 (Christmas 1912), 1–7; *Apprentice Fiction.* Dorothy HARMON challenges her fiancé, Harry TALBOT, to give away $25 to strangers on Christmas Eve. Harry encounters great difficulties in finding people to accept his money; finally two men beat him up. Dorothy is charmed by what Harry did for her; but he leaves with the two men who beat him up, whom he has invited home for Christmas. This story marks the first appearance of Fitzgerald's theme of a man's servitude to a woman.

Lucy Character in "No Flowers." Marjorie CLARK'S grandmother, who broke up with Phil SAVAGE when he was asked to leave college for cheating.

Luther Character in "No Flowers." Steward whom Carter MCLANE asks to search for a missing corsage.

Lytell, Pete Character in *B&D.* An acquaintance whom Anthony PATCH meets at "Sammy's."

M

MacArthur, Charles (1895–1956) Playwright and screenwriter; he collaborated with Ben Hecht (1894–1964) on *The Front Page* (1928). MacArthur and Fitzgerald played alcholic pranks on the RIVIERA in the summer of 1926. MacArthur was later a guest at the house party the Fitzgeralds gave for Lois MORAN and her mother at "ELLERSLIE" in May 1927. When Fitzgerald returned to America from EUROPE in early 1931 for his father's funeral, he visited MacArthur and his wife, actress Helen HAYES, in NEW YORK; Fitzgerald and MacArthur were ejected from the play *Grand Hotel* for being drunk. When Scottie FITZGERALD visited her father in HOLLYWOOD in August 1937, she stayed with Hayes and MacArthur. Fitzgerald listed MacArthur as one of six sources for the external qualities of Dick DIVER in *TITN,* and he also used some of MacArthur's characteristics for Abe NORTH.

See Ben Hecht, *Charlie: The Improbable Life and Times of Charles MacArthur* (New York: Harper, 1957).

MacDowell, Thomas J. Character in "John Jackson's Arcady." Man with whom John JACKSON has argued over municipal affairs for 20 years. Despite their quarrels, at the Civic Welfare League meeting MacDowell offers tribute to Jackson as an honorable man.

Macedon, Phil Character in "Two Old-Timers." Actor who had been a star in the silent movies.

Machen, Victoria Mims (1838–1895) Zelda Sayre FITZGERALD's maternal grandmother, the third wife of Senator Willis B. MACHEN.

Machen, Willis B. (1810–1893) Zelda Sayre FITZGERALD's maternal grandfather, a U. S. Senator from Kentucky. Husband of Victoria Mims MACHEN.

Mackenzie, Compton (1883–1972) English author of novels, poems, essays, biography, journalism, and travel books. When Edmund WILSON read the typescript of *TSOP* in November 1919, he described it as "an exquisite burlesque of Compton Mackenzie with a pastiche of Wells thrown in at the end" (*Letters on Literature and Politics 1912–1972* [New York: Farrar, Straus & Giroux,

1977], p. 45). Mackenzie's *Sinister Street* (1913–14) was one of the "quest novels" which influenced both Fitzgerald and Amory BLAINE of *TSOP.* When critic Frances Newman wrote in the *Atlanta Constitution* in February 1921 that *TSOP* was a "desecration" of *Sinister Street,* Fitzgerald responded by acknowledging the novel's influence but denying that the specific details she mentioned were borrowed from Mackenzie: "I was also hindered by a series of resemblances between my life and that of Michael Fane [the protagonist of *Sinister Street*] which, had I been a more conscientious man, might have precluded my ever attempting an autobiographical novel. . . . When I was twenty-one and began *This Side of Paradise* my literary taste was so unformed that *Youth's Encounter* [vol. 1 of the American edition of *Sinister Street*] was still my 'perfect book.' My book quite naturally shows the influence to a marked degree" (February 26, 1921; *Letters,* pp. 468–469). In 1922 Fitzgerald wrote to a fan that Mackenzie and Booth TARKINGTON "together taught me all I know about the English language" (to Hazel McCormack, n.d., postmarked June 26, 1922; PRINCETON UNIVERSITY LIBRARY).

Fitzgerald met Mackenzie on CAPRI in 1925 but was disappointed by the meeting and reproached his former idol for abandoning serious fiction. Fitzgerald wrote to John Peale BISHOP about the meeting: "I found him cordial, attractive and pleasantly mundane. You get no sense from him that feels his work has gone to pieces. He's not pompous about his present output. I think he's just tired. The war wrecked him as it did Wells and many of that generation" (April 1925; *Life in Letters,* p. 101).

See Kenneth Young, *Compton Mackenzie* (London: Longmans, Green, 1968).

MacLeish, Archibald (1892–1982) American poet and dramatist who won Pulitzer Prizes for *Conquistador* (1932), *Collected Poems, 1917–1952* (1952), and *J.B.* (1958). He was an EXPATRIATE during the 1920s and was a friend of Fitzgerald and Gerald and Sara MURPHY; he dedicated his poem "American Letter" to Gerald Murphy. MacLeish served as Librarian of Congress (1939–44), director of the U.S. Office of Facts

and Figures (1941–42), Assistant Director of the U.S. Office of War Information (1942–43), and Assistant Secretary of State (1944–45), participating in the founding of UNESCO, the United Nations Educational, Scientific and Cultural Organization; and he was Boylston Professor of Rhetoric and Poetry at Harvard (1949–62).

Fitzgerald listed MacLeish as one of the sources for the external qualities of Dick DIVER in TITN. MacLeish wrote to Fitzgerald about TITN: "Great God Scott you can write. You can write better than ever. You are a fine writer. Believe it. Believe It—not me" (The Romantic Egoists, p. 200).

See Scott Donaldson, Archibald MacLeish: An American Life (Boston: Houghton Mifflin, 1992).

Macy, Martin Character in "The Camel's Back." Man who drinks champagne in BAILY's room.

Macy, Theron G. Character in "Dalyrimple Goes Wrong." Owner of a wholesale grocery business who gives Bryan DALYRIMPLE a job in his stockroom.

Madame Curie (MGM, 1943) Fitzgerald's last MGM assignment, in November 1938, was writing *Madame Curie* for Greta Garbo (1905–90). Aldous Huxley (1894–1963) had prepared a treatment, but he and Fitzgerald did not work together. On January 3, 1939 Fitzgerald submitted a 74-page screenplay that went up to the Curies' decision to marry, but the project was shelved. (In 1943 Greer Garson [b. 1908] starred in MGM's *Madame Curie*, directed by Mervyn Le Roy [1900–87], with a screenplay by Paul Osborn [1901–88] and Paul H. Rameau). Fitzgerald later explained that he and producer Sidney FRANKLIN "were bucking [executive producer] Bernie Hyman's preconception of the thing as a love story" (to Phil BERG–Bert Allenberg Agency, February 23, 1940; *Life in Letters,* p. 435). During work on the project MGM declined to pick up the second option on Fitzgerald's contract, which expired on January 27, 1939.

Magoffin, Elizabeth Clay Rogers (Mrs. Peter Garnett) (1891–1951) ST. PAUL drama buff who organized a theatrical group which was soon named the ELIZABETHAN DRAMATIC CLUB in her honor. Fitzgerald's first play for the group, *The Girl from Lazy J* (1911), was performed in the Magoffin home at the organizational meeting of the club. Magoffin was probably the model for Miss HALLIBURTON in "The Captured Shadow." In 1911 Magoffin gave Fitzgerald a photograph inscribed "To Scott— 'He had that Spark— Magnetic Mark—' With the best love of the one who thinks so" (The Romantic Egoists, p. 18). Magoffin's transcriptions of the four plays Fitzgerald wrote for the club were ob-

tained by PRINCETON UNIVERSITY LIBRARY from her family after her death. (See Alan Margolies' introduction to *F. Scott Fitzgerald's St. Paul Plays 1911–1914,* pp. 3–10.)

"Magnetism" Fiction. Written December 1927. *The SATURDAY EVENING POST,* 200 (March 3, 1928), 5–7, 74, 76, 78; *Stories.* Actor George HANNAFORD's wife, Kay HANNAFORD, is jealous of his interest in actress Helen AVERY. At a party George sees Kay, who has drunk too much, holding hands with writer-director Arthur BUSCH, who has loved her for years. When the Hannafords arrive home after the party, the brother of Margaret DONOVAN, the script girl at the studio, tries to blackmail George for $50,000 on the basis of some documents George had signed that afternoon without reading; Margaret had told him they were script changes, but they were really love letters she had drafted from him to her. The next morning George refuses to talk with Kay and Busch about their situation and goes for a car ride just to get away. He happens to pass Margaret Donovan's apartment, where he stops to confront her about the letters. She tears up the letters and tells George she has loved him for years, and he leaves. When he returns home Kay expresses her indignation at the blackmail attempt and confesses that she is not really interested in Busch but had just been mad at George. They learn that Margaret Donovan has tried to kill herself, and George goes to the hospital to see her.

Fitzgerald recycled several passages from this story for use in TITN.

"Majesty" Fiction. Written May 1929. *The SATURDAY EVENING POST,* 202 (July 13, 1929), 6–7, 57–58, 61–62; *TAR.* At age 24, wealthy Emily CASTLETON, aware that most of her friends are married, consents to marry William Brevoort BLAIR. An elaborate society wedding is planned; but just before the ceremony Emily shares her sadness with her cousin, Olive MERCY, who is secretly in love with Brevoort. Emily leaves Brevoort at the altar, causing a scandal; and he asks Olive to marry him. Emily runs away to EUROPE, where she becomes involved with Prince Gabriel PETROCOBESCO, a man whom her father's agent describes as "a dissipated ne'er-do-well." Mr. CASTLETON sends Brevoort and Olive to Europe to bring Emily home. They find her with Petrocobesco in a dirty room in Czjeck-Hansa, a tiny Middle-European country with rich magnesium deposits. While the Blairs are there, Petrocobesco receives word that the national assembly has voted him king, as he is next in line for the crown; and Emily agrees to marry him. Two years later the Blairs watch Emily, now a queen, and her husband in a royal procession in LONDON; and Olive can't help but admire her cousin's achievement.

"Make Yourself at Home" *See* "Strange Sanctuary."

Makova, Paul Character in "Two Wrongs." Dancer who wants Emmy PINKARD McChesney to dance with him at the Metropolitan.

Malibu Beach, California In April 1938 Fitzgerald moved to a bungalow at 114 Malibu Beach, which he rented for $300 a month until November, when he moved to "BELLY ACRES" at ENCINO. Sheilah GRAHAM spent weekends with Fitzgerald at Malibu; and they gave a party there after "Infidelity," a screenplay on which he was working, was canceled.

Malmaison Clinic Psychiatric clinic outside PARIS which Zelda FITZGERALD entered on April 23, 1930. The clinic report reads:

> Mrs. FITZ-GERALD entered on 23 April 1930 in a state of acute anxiety, restlessness, continually repeating: "This is dreadful, this is horrible, what is going to become of me, I have to work, and I will no longer be able to, I must die, and yet I have to work. I will never be cured, let me leave. I have to go see 'Madame' (dance teacher), she has given me the greatest joy that can exist, it is comparable to the light of the sun that falls on a block of crystal, to a symphony of perfume, the most perfect chord from the greatest composer in music." . . .
>
> Finally, we are in the presence of a lady exhausted from work in an environment of professional dancers. Some obsessive ideas, the main one of which is her fear of becoming a homosexual. She thinks she is in love with her dance teacher (Madame X) as she had already thought in the past of being in love with another woman. [Translated from the French] (PRINCETON UNIVERSITY LIBRARY)

On May 11, Zelda discharged herself from Malmaison against her doctor's advice; and on May 22 she entered VAL-MONT CLINIC at GLION, SWITZERLAND.

Malone Character in *LT/LOLT.* Policeman who puts Edna SMITH and Kathleen MOORE off the studio lot after the earthquake.

man (unnamed) Character in "The Offshore Pirate." Man with a bad reputation whom Ardita FARNAM loves for his imagination.

the Man (unnamed) Character in *LT/LOLT.* Former king whose mistress had been Kathleen MOORE until she ran away from him. His passion for educating her reflects Fitzgerald's "College of One" plan for educating Sheilah GRAHAM.

"A Man in the Way" Fiction—Pat HOBBY story. Submitted September 16, 1939. *ESQUIRE,* 13 (February 1940), 40, 109; *PH.* Pat Hobby pitches Priscilla SMITH's idea about an old painter to producer Jack BERNERS as his own, and Berners puts him on the payroll. Later Smith reveals the idea to Berners as her own.

Manfred, Jeff Character in "No Harm Trying." Associate producer who got his job through family connections.

Mankiewicz, Joseph (1909–1993) MGM producer for whom Fitzgerald was assigned to write the screenplay for *Three Comrades* in 1937. In a 1969 interview Mankiewicz explained: "I hired Scott for *Three Comrades* because I admired his work. More than any other writer, I thought that he could capture the European flavor and the flavor of the twenties and early thirties that *Three Comrades* required. I also thought that he would know and understand the girl" (quoted in Aaron Latham, *Crazy Sundays,* p. 123). Fitzgerald asked Mankiewicz to allow him to work without a collaborator; although Mankiewicz agreed in a telegram to let Fitzgerald work alone, he assigned E. E. PARAMORE to work with him. Mankiewicz heavily revised their screenplay, and Fitzgerald resented his interference, as he indicated in an emotional letter that he may not have sent (January 20, 1938; *Life in Letters,* pp. 343–345). Mankiewicz defended himself in a 1967 interview: "I personally have been attacked as if I had spat on the flag because it happened once that I rewrote some dialogue by F. Scott Fitzgerald. But it needed it! The actors, among them Margaret Sullavan, absolutely could not read the lines. It was very literary dialogue, novelistic dialogue that lacked all the qualities required for screen dialogue. The latter must be 'spoken.' Scott Fitzgerald really wrote very bad spoken dialogue" (Jacques Bontemps and Richard Overstreet, "Measure for Measure: Interviews with Joseph Mankiewicz," *Cahiers du Cinema in English,* 18 [February 1967], 31).

See Kenneth L. Geist, *Pictures Will Talk: The Life and Films of Joseph Mankiewicz* (New York: Scribners, 1978) and Bernard F. Dick, *Joseph L. Mankiewicz* (Boston: Twayne, 1983).

Maplewood Character in "The Freshest Boy." A new student at ST. REGIS with whom Basil Duke LEE becomes friends after Christmas. They quarrel.

Maranda, Mr. Character in "A Patriotic Short." Pat HOBBY's next-door neighbor back in the days of Pat's success. He had invited Pat to a luncheon for the President of the United States.

Marbrooke, Eleanor Character in "Sentiment—and the Use of Rouge." The late Dick SYNEFORTH's fiancée, who explains to Clay SYNEFORTH the moral changes

the war has brought to England and who sleeps with him before he returns to the war.

Marchbanks, Baron Character in "Rags Martin-Jones and the Pr-nce of W-les." Pseudonym of the man who John M. CHESTNUT tells Rags MARTIN-JONES is the Prince of Wales but who is really an elevator-boy named CEDRIC.

"Marching Streets" Verse. *The NASSAU LITERARY MAGAZINE*, 74 (February 1919), 103–104; *In His Own Time; Poems*. Included in *A BOOK OF PRINCETON VERSE II*; Fitzgerald's revisions of this poem in his copy are facsimiled in *Fitzgerald/Hemingway Annual* (1979), pp. 28–29.

Marcus, Harold Character in "Pat Hobby and Orson Welles," "The Homes of the Stars," and "On the Trail of Pat Hobby." Powerful movie producer for whom Pat had been press agent two decades ago. In "Pat Hobby and Orson Welles" he gives a ride to Pat, who asks him for a studio pass. In "The Homes of the Stars" Pat takes a tourist couple into Marcus's house on the pretense that it is the home of Shirley Temple (b. 1928). In "On the Trail of Pat Hobby" Pat steals a hat which he doesn't realize belongs to Marcus.

Marcus, Mr. Character in *LT/LOLT*. Elderly studio executive.

Margery, Nell Character in "I Got Shoes." Actress who is unwilling to part with any of her old shoes.

" 'Margey Wins the Game' " Review of *Margey Wins the Game* by John V. A. Weaver (1893–1938). *New York Tribune*, May 7, 1922, section 4, p. 7; *In His Own Time*. After imitating Weaver's "semi-dialect prose" style, Fitzgerald describes this novel as "a highly amusing, swiftly moving tale of the jazz-nourished generation" (*In His Own Time*, p. 133).

Margot Character in "The Intimate Strangers." Nurse who cares for SARA's young son and who later marries Paul PECHARD.

Margotson, Findle Character in *TSOP*. Yale man whom Axia MARLOWE greets at Bistolary's café.

Margotson, Mr. Character in *TSOP*. Senior master at ST. REGIS. He tells Amory BLAINE that Amory is unpopular because he is too fresh.

Marie Antoinette (MGM, 1938) In May 1938 Fitzgerald worked briefly on *Marie Antoinette*, a former project of Irving THALBERG, for MGM producer Sidney FRANKLIN. The movie was released with screenplay by Claudine

West (1884?–1943), Donald Ogden STEWART, and Ernest Vajda (1887–1954); directed by W. S. Van Dyke (1889–1943) and produced by Hunt STROMBERG.

Marietta, New York In *B&D*, fictional town in the New York countryside where Anthony and Gloria PATCH rent a house in the summertime. Based on WESTPORT, Connecticut.

Marion Character in "One of My Oldest Friends." Woman with whom Charley HART—one of the oldest friends of her and her husband, MICHAEL—was in love.

Marjorie Character in "The Four Fists." A young wife with whom Samuel MEREDITH becomes involved and whose husband is the third person to hit Meredith.

Mark Twain *See* TWAIN, MARK.

Markey, Billy Character in "The Baby Party." Mr. and Mrs. Joe MARKEY's two-year-old son, whose birthday is the occasion of the baby party.

Markey, Joe Character in "The Baby Party." Billy MARKEY's father, who fights his neighbor John ANDROS after their children get into a tussle and their wives exchange insults.

Markey, Mrs. Joe Character in "The Baby Party." Billy MARKEY's mother, who is offended by Edith ANDROS's laughter and calls Ede ANDROS a brat.

Marlowe, Axia Character in *TSOP*. One of two NEW YORK showgirls in whose apartment Amory BLAINE sees a devil figure.

Marmora, Tino Character in *TITN*. Italian count whom Dick DIVER encounters with Nicole Warren [DIVER] on the GLION funicular.

Marquand, Mr. and Mrs. Characters in *LT/LOLT*. A husband-and-wife team of writers who are upset when they discover they are not the only writers working on a particular script. Possibly based on Albert and Frances Goodrich HACKETT. The Marquands' name was changed to "Tarleton" in the first edition of *LT* because Harold OBER was concerned that readers would think "Marquand" referred to writer John P. Marquand (1893–1960).

Marsden, Cal Character in "The Unspeakable Egg." Fifi MARSDEN's aunt, who is distressed by her interest in a tramp.

Marsden, Fifi Character in "The Unspeakable Egg." Young woman who breaks and renews her engagement to George VAN TYNE.

Marsden, Josephine Character in "The Unspeakable Egg." Fifi MARSDEN's aunt, who is distressed by her interest in a tramp.

Marston, Choupette Character in "The Swimmers." Henry Clay MARSTON's French wife, whom he divorces after her repeated infidelities.

Marston, Henry Clay Character in "The Swimmers." Virginian living in PARIS who suffers a nervous collapse when he discovers his French wife, Choupette MARSTON, in a compromising situation. When she is again unfaithful during their three-year stay in America, he divorces her and returns to EUROPE.

Martha Character in "Discard." Passenger on the ship on which George BAKER and Count Hennen DE LANCLERC travel to EUROPE.

Martin, Caroline *See* Caroline Martin CORCORAN.

Martin, Townsend (1895–1951) Wealthy PRINCETON student, a member of the Class of 1917, whom Fitzgerald met through his work with the TRIANGLE CLUB. Martin was Ludlow FOWLER's roommate and a member of the Quadrangle Club. He was part of the group the newlywed Fitzgeralds partied with in NEW YORK. He later wrote for the movies and wrote a successful Broadway play, *A Most Immoral Lady* (1928).

Martin-Jones, Rags Character in "Rags Martin-Jones and the Pr-nce of W-les." Wealthy, beautiful young woman who craves excitement and believes she will never find it with an American man. However, John M. CHESTNUT wins her love by staging an elaborate spectacle for her.

"Martin's Thoughts" Poem. *Fitzgerald Newsletter,* no. 13 (Spring 1961), 1; *Poems.* Thoughts of the girls liked by Martin Amorous, Fitzgerald's classmate at the NEWMAN SCHOOL.

Marvis, Julie Character in "Porcelain and Pink." Girl in a bathtub who is mistaken for her sister, Lois MARVIS, by Lois's date, Mr. CALKINS.

Marvis, Lois Character in "Porcelain and Pink," Julie MARVIS's conservative older sister, who has a date with Mr. CALKINS.

Masters, Olive Character in "His Russet Witch." Stenographer at the Moonlight Quill Bookshop who marries Merlin GRAINGER.

Mather, Jaqueline Character in "Hot & Cold Blood." Woman who rebukes her husband, Jim MATHER, for

letting people abuse his generosity, saying that she needs him to save himself for her.

Mather, Jim Character in "Hot & Cold Blood." Man who temporarily abandons his natural generosity when his wife, Jaqueline MATHER, rebukes him for letting people take advantage of him.

Matsko, James Character in "Six of One—". Industrious young man whom Ed BARNES persuades to study money and banking at Columbia and who becomes a partner in a Wall Street brokerage house.

Maude Character in *LT/LOLT.* One of three secretaries in Pat BRADY's outer office.

Mavromichaelis *See* MICHAELIS.

"May Day" Fiction. Written March 1920. *The SMART SET,* 62 (July 1920), 3–32; *TJA.* On May 1, 1919, Gordon STERRETT, a Yale graduate and failed artist, asks his wealthy classmate, Philip DEAN, for $300 because his lower-class girlfriend, Jewel HUDSON, is blackmailing him. Dean, repelled by his friend's deterioration, refuses the loan but gives him $80. Two recently discharged soldiers, Carrol KEY and Gus ROSE, briefly join an antisocialist demonstration but slip away to get liquor from Carrol's brother, George KEY, a waiter at Delmonico's, where the Yale fraternity Gamma Psi is hosting a dance. At the dance Gordon encounters his former girlfriend, Edith BRADIN, who has been falling in love with her memory of him until she sees him drunk and forlorn at the dance. Peter HIMMEL, Edith's date whom she has rebuffed for his attempt to kiss her, gets drunk with Key and Rose, who are hiding in a side room. Jewel tracks Gordon down at Delmonico's and makes him leave with her. Edith slips away from the dance to visit her brother, Henry BRADIN, at the office of the radical newspaper for which he writes. While she is there, a crowd of antisocialist soldiers—including Key and Rose—attacks the office. Key falls out of a window to his death, and Henry Bradin's leg is broken. Rose, Dean, Himmel, Sterrett, and Jewel all end up at the same café in the early morning hours of May 2. Dean shakes his finger condemningly at Sterrett and Jewel, who leave. Dean and Himmel, who are both drunk, leave together to retrieve Himmel's coat from Delmonico's, where they appropriate signs reading "In" and "Out" from the coatroom doors and place them in their vests, labeling themselves "Mister In" and "Mister Out." After being refused a second bottle of champagne for breakfast at Delmonico's, they proceed to the Biltmore Hotel, where they see Edith, who spots Gus Rose and identifies him as the man who broke her brother's leg. Gordon Sterrett wakes with a hangover in

a hotel room and realizes that he is married to Jewel. He purchases a revolver and kills himself.

Fitzgerald revised this story heavily between periodical and book publication, tightening his prose and improving his depiction of characters. The most significant change was in the ending: in the *Smart Set* version Sterrett's suicide is only implied, but in *Tales of the Jazz Age* it is depicted. See Colin Cass, "Fitzgerald's Second Thoughts about 'May Day,' " *Fitzgerald/Hemingway Annual* (1970), pp. 69–95.

"May Day" exhibits the influence of naturalism, a literary movement emphasizing that human behavior is determined by forces beyond the control of the characters. It shares this element with *B&D*, which, like "May Day," is concerned with character deterioration.

Mayburn, Helen Character in *The Captured Shadow*. Dorothy CONNAGE's friend and Hubert CONNAGE's fiancée.

Mayer, Edwin Justus (1896?–1960) Screenwriter with whom Fitzgerald shared an apartment unit at the GARDEN OF ALLAH in HOLLYWOOD from July 1937 to April 1938. His screenplays include *So Red the Rose* (1935) and *To Be or Not to Be* (1942).

Mayer, Lou (b. 1869) METROPOLITAN MAGAZINE cover artist whose painting of Gloria PATCH appeared on the magazine's cover for the first installment of *The Beautiful and Damned* (September 1921).

McAlmon, Robert (1896–1956) American EXPATRIATE novelist, poet, and publisher; as co-founder of Contact Editions in PARIS he published Ernest HEMINGWAY, William Carlos Williams (1883–1963), Ezra Pound (1885–1972), and Gertrude STEIN, among others. McAlmon spread the false rumor that Fitzgerald and Hemingway were homosexuals—gossip which Fitzgerald believed contributed to the decline of his friendship with Hemingway. Fitzgerald wrote to Maxwell PERKINS, who had reported that McAlmon said "mean things about Ernest" to him (October 30, 1929; *Scott/Max*, p. 158): "McAlmon is a bitter rat and I'm not surprised at anything he does or says. He's failed as a writer and tries to fortify himself by tieing up to the big boys like Joyce and Stien and despising everything else" (c. November 15, 1929; *Life in Letters*, p. 171; *Scott/Max*, pp. 158–159). It is possible that Albert MCKISCO in *TITN* was intended as a satirical reference to McAlmon.

See McAlmon, *Being Geniuses Together* (London: Secker & Warburg, 1938). Revised edition with chapters by Kay Boyle (Garden City, NY: Doubleday, 1968).

McBeth, Mr. Character in *TITN*. Manager-owner of the PARIS hotel where Jules PETERSON is murdered. Because Dick DIVER had previously made an effort to ingratiate himself with him, McBeth arranges for Dick's and Rosemary's names to be kept out of the situation.

McCaffray Character in "The Family Bus." Engineer who designed the intake manifold on the T. R. HENDERSONS' family car.

McCall's Magazine which published three Fitzgerald stories—"Rags Martin-Jones and the Pr-nce of W-les" (July 1924), "The Intimate Strangers" (June 1935), and "Image on the Heart" (April 1936)—as well as two articles—"Does a Moment of Revolt Come Sometime to Every Married Man?" (March 1924; with companion article by Zelda FITZGERALD) and "Our Young Rich Boys" (October 1925; with companion article by Zelda, "What Became of the Flappers?"). In 1925 *McCall's* expressed interest in serializing Fitzgerald's fourth novel, but *TITN* was ultimately serialized in *SCRIBNER'S MAGAZINE*. In 1929 editor Otis Wiese (1905–72) commissioned Fitzgerald to write an article about the "present day status of the Flapper"; but he rejected Fitzgerald's submission—"Girls Believe in Girls"—as too serious (see *As Ever*, p. 156). Fitzgerald and Ober were outraged by the magazine's failure to accept and pay for a commissioned article which had taken Fitzgerald's time away from his novel and stories, and Fitzgerald wanted to bring a lawsuit. However, Ober advised him that a suit would be difficult and that it would be better to sell the article elsewhere; *LIBERTY* published the piece in February 1930. Having given up the idea of a lawsuit, Fitzgerald considered publishing the correspondence about the issue in the Authors' League Bulletin, but Ober discouraged him because he felt it would be potentially embarrassing to *Liberty* (see *As Ever*, pp. 156–164).

McCarthy, Gyp Character in "Pat Hobby Does His Bit." Actor from whom Pat HOBBY tries to borrow money.

McChesney, Bill Character in "Two Wrongs." Broadway producer who forfeits his health and success by a dissipated lifestyle. He marries aspiring dancer Emmy PINKARD.

McChesney, Billy Character in "Two Wrongs." Son of Bill and Emmy [PINKARD] MCCHESNEY.

McChesney, Emmy Pinkard *See* Emmy PINKARD.

McClurg, Glenola *See* TROUBLE.

McComas, Henry Character in "Your Way and Mine." Businessman who suffers a collapse and paralysis when he is forced to change his idiosyncratic work habits.

McComas, Honoria Character in "Your Way and Mine." Daughter of Henry and Stella MCCOMAS. Her father urges her to marry Max VAN CAMP rather than Russel CODMAN.

McComas, Stella Character in "Your Way and Mine." Henry MCCOMAS's wife, who tries to get him to change his ways.

McCracken, Miss Character in "His Russet Witch." Clerk at the Moonlight Quill Bookshop.

McCrary, Miss Character in "Lo, the Poor Peacock!" Secretary whom Jason DAVIS lets go because of financial constraints.

McCutcheon, Mr. Character in "Lo, the Poor Peacock!" Principal who unjustly expels Jo DAVIS from high school.

McDavitt, Elizabeth Childhood friend of Fitzgerald; a member of the ELIZABETHAN DRAMATIC CLUB. She gave the January 4, 1915 party at the Town and Country Club, followed by supper at her home, at which Fitzgerald met Ginevra KING, who became his first serious love.

McDowell Character in *TSOP*. Arrogant sophomore in PRINCETON tutoring school with Amory BLAINE.

McGinness, Officer Character in *The Captured Shadow*. Bumbling detective who is unable to apprehend "The SHADOW."

McGovern, Miss Character in *B&D*. Gloria PATCH's trained nurse while she has flu and double pneumonia.

McIlvaine, Bee Character in "On the Trail of Pat Hobby." Writer whose picture needs a title.

McIntyre Character in "The Four Fists." Leader of the New Mexico ranchers; the fourth person to hit Samuel MEREDITH.

McIntyre, Warren Character in "Bernice Bobs Her Hair." Marjorie HARVEY's beau, who becomes interested in BERNICE.

McKaig, Alexander (b. 1895) Friend whom Fitzgerald met at PRINCETON (Class of 1917), where McKaig was active on *The Daily Princetonian* and *The NASSAU LITERARY MAGAZINE* and was a member of the Quadrangle Club. He was later part of the group the newlywed Fitzgeralds partied with in NEW YORK. His diary, which records many observations about the Fitzgeralds, is

quoted in Andrew TURNBULL's *Scott Fitzgerald*, pp. 112–115.

McKee, Chester Character in *GG*. Photographer and guest at Tom BUCHANAN and Myrtle WILSON's party.

McKee, Lucille Character in *GG*. Wife of Chester MCKEE; guest at Tom BUCHANAN and Myrtle WILSON's party.

McKenna, Mr. Character in "In the Holidays." Alias of murderer Joe KINNEY, who arranges the death of witness Mr. GRIFFIN while they are both in the hospital.

McKibben, Mr. Character in *TITN*. Man whom Dick DIVER meets with Tommy BARBAN at a café in Munich.

McKisco, Albert Character in *TITN*. American novelist whom Rosemary HOYT meets on the RIVIERA. His duel with Tommy BARBAN gives him the self-confidence that becomes the basis for his future success. It is possible that McKisco was intended as a satirical reference to Robert MCALMON.

McKisco, Violet Character in *TITN*. Albert MCKISCO's wife, who finds Nicole DIVER behaving hysterically in the bathroom at the VILLA DIANA and whose comments about the scene lead to the duel between Albert McKisco and Tommy BARBAN.

McLane, Carter Character in "No Flowers." Man with whom Amanda Rawlins [CLARK] was in love but who withdrew his proposal after he discovered she had accepted HOWARD's corsage in place of his.

McLane, Tommy Character in "Indecision." Twenty-seven-year-old banker who goes to SWITZERLAND to fall in love. He is unable to choose between Emily ELLIOT and Rosemary MERRIWEATHER until his jealousy of Rosemary's attention to another man leads him to propose to her.

McQuillan, Annabel (1866–1963) Sister of Fitzgerald's mother, Mollie McQuillan FITZGERALD. She may have paid Fitzgerald's tuition to the NEWMAN SCHOOL; but her offer to finance his education at Catholic Georgetown University failed to attract him, since his heart was set on PRINCETON. Fitzgerald called her "the real matriarch of my family, a dried up old maid, but with character and culture" (Andrew TURNBULL, *Scott Fitzgerald*, p. 37).

McQuillan, Clara (1868–1911) Sister of Fitzgerald's mother, Mollie McQuillan FITZGERALD. She paid young Scott Fitzgerald 25 cents a day for eating a raw egg daily while on vacation in the Catskill Mountains. He

used the money to buy books by G. A. Henty (1832–1902), the author of boys' stories largely based on military history.

McQuillan, Louisa Allen (1841–1913) Fitzgerald's maternal grandmother, an Irish immigrant carpenter's daughter who married Philip F. MCQUILLAN in 1860. After Fitzgerald's father, Edward FITZGERALD, lost his job with Procter & Gamble in March 1908, the family returned to ST. PAUL in the summer; Scott and his sister, Annabel FITZGERALD, lived with Grandmother McQuillan while their parents stayed with nearby friends. When Louisa McQuillan died in 1913, Mollie FITZGERALD's inheritance made it possible for the Fitzgerald family to live comfortably in the SUMMIT AVENUE area of St. Paul and provided tuition money for Fitzgerald to attend PRINCETON.

McQuillan, Philip Francis (1834?–1877) Fitzgerald's maternal grandfather. In 1843, when Philip was nine years old he and his parents emigrated from County Fermanagh, Ireland, and settled in Galena, Illinois. In 1857 he moved to ST. PAUL, where he worked as a bookkeeper for two years before opening his own general store. He married Louisa Allen [MCQUILLAN] in 1860 and by 1862 was a prosperous grocery wholesaler. As his business expanded he built a three-story house and a four-story warehouse that was one of the largest buildings in the city. He died at age 43, leaving a personal estate of $266,289.49 and a business with annual billings of two million dollars. When the Fitzgerald family returned to St. Paul in 1908 after Edward FITZGERALD lost his job at Procter & Gamble, Mollie FITZGERALD frequently commented to young Scott, "If it weren't for your Grandfather McQuillan, where would we be now?"

McRae, Mrs. Jenny Character in the Josephine PERRY stories. In "First Blood," she didn't want to invite Josephine to that year's dancing class because Josephine's reputation was so bad and invited her only because of her sister, Constance PERRY. In "A Snobbish Story" she wants to omit from the vaudeville Josephine's usual dance with Travis DE COPPET because of the circumstances surrounding Josephine's departure from school. Her husband persuades her to reconsider; and she asks Josephine to introduce her nephew, DONALD, to the other young people at Lake Forest.

McTeague Character in "Your Way and Mine." Henry MCCOMAS's business competitor, whom Max VAN CAMP tries to buy out.

McVitty, Mr. Character in "The Love Boat." High-school principal and dance chaperone.

Meadow, Marcia Character in "Head and Shoulders." An actress, famous for her shimmy, who marries Horace TARBOX. She achieves widespread recognition for her book, *Sandra Pepys, Syncopated,* which she writes during her pregnancy after giving up dancing.

Medill, Betty Character in "The Camel's Back." Perry PARKHURST's girlfriend, who marries him while he is in a camel costume.

Medill, Cyrus Character in "The Camel's Back." Betty MEDILL's father, known as "the Aluminum Man."

Melon-Loper, Jan Character in "The Family Bus." The T. R. HENDERSONS' gardener, who later prospers in industry.

Melon-Loper, Mrs. Jan Character in "The Family Bus." Jannekin and Kaethe MELON-LOPER's mother, who is displeased to see Kaethe ride away with Ralph HENDERSON.

Melon-Loper, Jannekin (Janny) Character in "The Family Bus." Gardener's daughter with whom Dick HENDERSON is good friends for many years.

Melon-Loper, Kaethe Character in "The Family Bus." Jannekin MELON-LOPER's older sister, who escapes uninjured from the car wreck that kills Ralph HENDERSON.

Meloney, Jane *See* Rose MELONEY.

Meloney, Rose Character in *LT/LOLT.* A writer who had been a friend of Minna DAVIS and who is a friend of Cecelia BRADY. She arranges for Cecelia to have lunch with Martha DODD, who has met Kathleen MOORE. Rose Meloney may have been based on a combination of screenwriter Bess Meredyth (1890?–1969) and writer Dorothy PARKER. Her first name was changed to "Jane" in the first edition of *LT* because Harold OBER said "Rose Meloney" was the name of a real person (who has not been identified).

Mencken, H. L. (1880–1956) Influential American literary critic who coedited *The SMART SET* with George Jean NATHAN from 1914 to 1923 and founded *The AMERICAN MERCURY* with Nathan in 1924. His books include *The American Language* (1919, revised 1921, 1923, 1936; supplementary volumes, 1945, 1948) and six series of *Prejudices* (1919–27). In his 1921 review of *Prejudices, Second Series,* Fitzgerald said Mencken "has done more for the national letters than any man alive" ("The Baltimore Anti-Christ"; *In His Own Time,* p. 121).

Fitzgerald sent Mencken a copy of *TSOP* in March 1920, explaining in the inscription: "As a matter of fact, Mr. Menken, I stuck your name in on Page 224 in

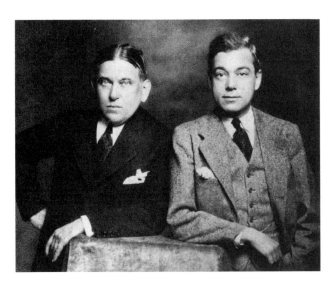

H. L. Mencken and George Jean Nathan

the last proof—partly, I suppose, as a vague bootlick and partly because I have since adopted a great many of your views. . . ." (*Life in Letters,* p. 39). Mencken's review called *TSOP* "the best American novel that I have seen of late" (*The Smart Set,* 62 [August 1920], p. 140; *FSF: The Critical Reception,* p. 28). In his review of *Flappers and Philosophers* Mencken was one of the earliest critics to note the split between Fitzgerald's roles as entertainer and serious novelist: "Fitzgerald is curiously ambidextrous. Will he proceed via the first part of 'This Side of Paradise' to the cold groves of beautiful letters, or will he proceed via 'Head and Shoulders' into the sunshine that warms Robert W. Chambers and Harold MacGrath?" (*The Smart Set,* 63 [December 1920], 140; *FSF: The Critical Reception,* p. 48). Mencken's enthusiasm for Theodore DREISER and Joseph CONRAD influenced Fitzgerald; and Mencken was partly responsible for Fitzgerald's foray into determinism with *B&D,* which Mencken reviewed for *The Smart Set:* "There are a hundred signs in it of serious purpose and unquestionable skill. Even in its defects there is proof of hard striving. Fitzgerald ceases to be a *Wunderkind,* and begins to come into his maturity" (67 [April 1922], pp. 140–141; *FSF: The Critical Reception,* p. 107). Mencken's review of *GG* says the "obviously unimportant" story is given distinction by "the charm and beauty of the writing" (*Baltimore Evening Sun,* May 2, 1925, p. 9; *FSF: The Critical Reception,* p. 212). Mencken had high hopes for Fitzgerald but feared he would not fulfill his promise unless he gave up Zelda FITZGERALD and alcohol.

Fitzgerald included Mencken's *The Philosophy of Friedrich Nietzsche* (1908) on his list of "10 Best Books I Have Read" in 1923. In his 1926 essay-review of Ernest HEMINGWAY's *In Our Time,* "How to Waste Material: A Note on My Generation," Fitzgerald wrote that

Mencken "has yet done more for American letters than any man alive" but blamed his forceful criticism for spawning a band of imitators who were "insensitive, suspicious of glamour, preoccupied exclusively with the external, the contemptible, the 'national' and the drab, whose style was a debasement of his least effective manner and who, like glib children, played continually with his themes in his maternal shadow" (*AOAA,* p. 119).

When Fitzgerald lived in the BALTIMORE area in the 1930s he visited Mencken and asked for his recommendations of a bootlegger and a doctor (Mencken recommended Dr. Benjamin BAKER). Mencken had married Sara Haardt (1898–1935), whom Zelda had known in MONTGOMERY; Mrs. Mencken was an invalid, and the Menckens' need for a quiet life limited their contact with Fitzgerald.

See William Manchester, *Disturber of the Peace: The Life of H. L. Mencken* (New York: Harper, 1950).

Mercy, Olive Character in "Majesty." Emily CASTLETON's poor cousin, who marries Brevoort BLAIR when Emily leaves him at the altar.

Meredith, Samuel Character in "The Four Fists." Man whose character is improved by being hit four times.

Meridien, Francois Character in "Shadow Laurels." One of Jean CHANDELLE's three closest friends, who tell Jaques CHANDELLE what Jean had meant to them.

Merriam, Constance Shaw and Eric Characters in *B&D.* Friends of Anthony and Gloria PATCH.

Merril, Mimi Character in "The Offshore Pirate." The woman to whom the MAN Ardita FARNAM loves had given a bracelet which he had promised to Ardita.

Merritt, Ogden Character in "The Jelly-Bean." Savannah man whom Nancy LAMAR marries while drunk.

Merriweather, Rosemary Character in "Indecision." Eighteen-year-old Southerner whom Tommy MCLANE asks to marry him.

Metropolitan **magazine** In May 1920 *Metropolitan,* hoping to increase its circulation, took an option on Fitzgerald's stories for $900 each in an attempt to lure him away from *The SATURDAY EVENING POST,* which was then paying him $500 per story. In 1920–21 Fitzgerald submitted five stories under this contract before the magazine went into receivership: "The Jelly-Bean" (October 1920), "His Russet Witch" (February 1921), "Two for a Cent" (April 1922), "The Curious Case of Benjamin Button" (declined), and "Winter Dreams" (December 1922). *Metropolitan* also bought the serial rights

to *B&D* for $7,000, publishing the novel in seven installments from September 1921 through March 1922. Editor Carl Hovey (1875–1956) cut the 130,000–word typescript by 40,000 words.

Meyer, Dr. Adolf (1866–1950) Director of the PHIPPS CLINIC at JOHNS HOPKINS UNIVERSITY HOSPITAL in BALTIMORE, which Zelda FITZGERALD entered in February 1932. Zelda did not respond well to Meyer; and Fitzgerald, who wanted to participate in his wife's treatment, was unable to establish a collaborative relationship with Meyer. Meyer insisted that it was crucial to Zelda's cure for Fitzgerald to give up drinking and referred to Fitzgerald as "a potential but unwilling patient" (April 18, 1933; PRINCETON UNIVERSITY LIBRARY). Fitzgerald refused psychiatric treatment and defended his drinking. (See Fitzgerald's April 10 and Spring 1933 letters to Meyer; *Life in Letters,* pp. 228–233.)

Michael Character in "One of My Oldest Friends." Man who is crushed by the revelation of his old friend Charley HART's interest in his wife, MARION.

Michaelis Character in *GG.* A young Greek who owns the restaurant near George WILSON's garage. He stays with Wilson for a while after Myrtle's death and tries to comfort him. At the inquest following Jay GATSBY's death he reveals Wilson's suspicions about his wife. He was named "Mavromichaelis" in the manuscript, but Fitzgerald changed the name in proof.

"Mightier than the Sword" Fiction—Pat HOBBY story. Submitted December 25, 1939. *ESQUIRE,* 15 (April 1941), 36, 183; *PH.* Director Dick DALE dismisses writer E. Brunswick HUDSON and hires Pat Hobby to work on a script about composer Reginald de Koven (1861–1920). When Dale and Pat's script is rejected, Dale again asks Hudson if he still has his own script about de Koven; but Hudson, who has already been given another job at the studio and is working in Pat's old office, refuses to help. Dale's script girl, Mable HATMAN, finds Hudson's script; and Dale plans to put her name on it. Pat, whom Dale has fired, sympathizes with Hudson and tells him HOLLYWOOD wants writers, not authors.

Milbank, Hat Character in "The Woman from Twenty-One." Friend of Raymond TORRENCE.

Milbank, Roxanne *See* Roxanne Milbank CURTAIN.

Miles, Liddell and Cardine Characters in "One Trip Abroad." Couple whom Nelson and Nicole KELLY meet in Algeria and with whom they go to see the Ouled Naïls dancing girls.

Military Service of F. Scott Fitzgerald *See* ARMY.

Miller, Carl Character in "Absolution." Rudolph MILLER's ineffectual father, a freight agent.

Miller, Mrs. Carl Character in "Absolution." Rudolph MILLER's mother.

Miller, Rudolph Character in "Absolution." Eleven-year-old boy who creates for himself an alternate persona named Blatchford Sarnemington and who is frightened over the implications of having told a lie in confession. His encounter with the deranged Father Adolphus SCHWARTZ confirms his sense of a glamour separate from God.

"A Millionaire's Girl" Fiction by Zelda FITZGERALD. *The* SATURDAY EVENING POST, 202 (May 31, 1930), 8–9, 118, 121; *Bits of Paradise; Zelda Fitzgerald: The Collected Writings.* Bylined "F. Scott Fitzgerald" but credited to Zelda in *Ledger.* The publication of this story under Fitzgerald's name was the responsibility of his agent, Harold OBER (see March 14, 1930; *As Ever,* p. 166). Caroline and wealthy Barry break their engagement after she accepts a check and a car from his father, presumably for giving up Barry. She goes to HOLLYWOOD to seek success so that she can win him back. On the night of her successful movie debut she attempts suicide when she learns of Barry's engagement to an heiress, and he leaves his fiancée to marry Caroline.

Minghetti, Conte di (Hosain) Character in *TITN.* Mary NORTH's second husband, a wealthy Eastern ruler with a papal title.

Minghetti, Mary *See* Mary NORTH.

Minghetti, Tony Character in *TITN.* The Conte di MINGHETTI's ill son. Lanier DIVER's assertion that he was bathed in Tony's dirty bathwater leads to a quarrel between the Divers and Mary [NORTH] Minghetti.

"Minnesota's Capital in the Role of Main Street" Review of *Being Respectable* by Grace Flandrau (d. 1971). *The Literary Digest International Book Review,* 1 (March 1923), 35–36; *In His Own Time.* Fitzgerald criticizes the novel for being "clumsy in its handling of an enormous quantity of material" (*In His Own Time,* p. 140) and for dealing with too many characters without one to draw the whole book together; but he praises it as "thoroughly interesting and capable" (p. 142).

"Miss Ella" Fiction by Zelda FITZGERALD. SCRIBNER'S MAGAZINE, 90 (December 1931), 661–665; *Bits of Paradise; Zelda Fitzgerald: The Collected Writings.* In her youth, Miss Ella, now an "essentially Victorian" spinster, had broken her engagement to Mr. Hendrix when she fell

in love with Andy Bronson. On the day she was to marry Bronson, Hendrix had shot himself in her garden.

"Mister Icky The Quintessence of Quaintness in One Act" Humorous play. Written November 1919. *The* SMART SET, 61 (March 1920), 93–98; *TJA*. Young PETER is talking with Mr. ICKY, a reformed arsonist. Rodney DIVINE appears in search of Ulsa ICKY, whom he wishes to marry. Ulsa returns from LONDON; she and Divine argue but are reconciled. Charles ICKY wants to go to sea, and the other Icky children—crying "Life" and "Jazz"—prepare to leave their father. Mr. Icky lies down on the steps of his cottage and dies.

Fitzgerald noted in his *Ledger* that his 1916 NASSAU LITERARY MAGAZINE parody "The Usual Thing" was a source for this play.

Mitchell, Charles D. (Davis) (1887–1940) Fitzgerald's first magazine illustrator, for "Head and Shoulders" (*The* SATURDAY EVENING POST, February 21, 1920). He illustrated three more Fitzgerald stories for the *Post:* "The Popular Girl" (February 11 & 18, 1922), "Gretchen's Forty Winks" (March 15, 1924), and "The Third Casket" (May 31, 1924).

Mizener, Arthur (1907–1988) Author of *The Far Side of Paradise* (Boston: Houghton Mifflin, 1951), the first biography of Fitzgerald. Mizener also edited *Afternoon of an Author* (Princeton, N.J.: Princeton University Library, 1957; New York: Scribners, 1958; London: Bodley Head, 1958) and *F. Scott Fitzgerald: A Collection of Critical Essays* (Englewood Cliffs, N.J.: Prentice-Hall, 1963).

Mok, Michel (1888–1961) Journalist who interviewed Fitzgerald on his 40th birthday at the GROVE PARK INN. Mok's humiliating article, which depicted Fitzgerald as a broken drunk, appeared on the front page of the *New York Post* on September 25, 1936 and was reprinted in *Time* ("The Other Side of Paradise/Scott Fitzgerald, 40/Engulfed in Despair/Broken in Health He Spends Birthday Re-/gretting That He Has Lost Faith in His Star"). After reading the interview Fitzgerald took an overdose of morphine, which he vomited up. Fitzgerald explained the circumstances of the interview in a letter to Harold OBER: "I was in bed with temp about 102 when the [obliterated] phone rang and a voice said that this party had come all the way from N. Y to interview me. I fell for this like a damn fool, got him up, gave him a drink + accepted his exterior good manners. He had some relative with mental trouble (wife or mother) so I talked freely about treatments symtoms ect, about being depressed at advancing age and a little desperate about the wasted summer with this shoulder and arm—perhaps more freely than if had been well" (received October 5, 1936; *Life in Letters*, p. 308; *As Ever*, p. 282). A shortened version of the interview is included in *In His Own Time* as "A Writer Like Me Must Have an Utter Confidence, an Utter Faith in His Star."

Moncrief, General Character in "The Curious Case of Benjamin Button." Hildegarde MONCRIEF's father, who is outraged by her engagement to Benjamin BUTTON.

Moncrief, Hildegarde Character in "The Curious Case of Benjamin Button." Young woman who marries Benjamin BUTTON. He becomes tired of her as she ages and he grows younger, and she leaves him to live in ITALY.

Monte Character in "Rags Martin-Jones and the Prnce of W-les." Man who warns John CHESTNUT that he is being sought for murder; this is part of the spectacle Chestnut is staging for Rags MARTIN-JONES.

Montgomery, Alabama Zelda Sayre [FITZGERALD] was born at South Street in Montgomery on July 24, 1900; in 1907 the Sayre family moved to 6 Pleasant Avenue,

Scottie Fitzgerald Smith in front of 6 Pleasant Avenue, Montgomery, Alabama, where her father courted her mother in 1918 (Bruccoli Collection, University of South Carolina)

Zelda's home until her marriage. She met F. Scott Fitzgerald at a country club dance in Montgomery in July 1918 while he was stationed at nearby CAMP SHERIDAN. The Fitzgeralds rented a house at 819 Felder Avenue (now the Fitzgerald Museum) in Montgomery from September 1931 through Spring 1932; Fitzgerald left Zelda and Scottie FITZGERALD there when he traveled to HOLLYWOOD in November for five weeks to work on the screenplay for *Red-Headed Woman* (MGM, 1932). Zelda was admitted to the PHIPPS CLINIC in BALTIMORE in February, and in March Fitzgerald moved to Baltimore to be near her. Zelda returned to Montgomery near the end of her life when she was discharged from HIGHLAND HOSPITAL in mid-April 1940; she lived with her mother, Minnie Machen SAYRE, at 322 Sayre Street, where she remained—with intermittent visits to Highland—until her return to Highland in November 1947.

Moon, Charlie Character in "Head and Shoulders." Horace TARBOX's cousin, who bribes actress Marcia MEADOW to visit Horace.

Moon, Doctor Character in "The Adjuster." Mysterious doctor whom Charles HEMPLE asks to speak to his wife, Luella HEMPLE. Moon urges a sense of responsibility upon Luella and, when he believes she has finally grown up, tells her she must be responsible for making her home happy.

Moore, Albert Character in "That Kind of Party." Terrence R. TIPTON accidentally bloodies the nose of this boy, the son of his mother's best friend.

Moore, Carpenter Character in "That Kind of Party." Albert MOORE's bad-tempered older brother, who is in a wheelchair and uses a cane. At Joe SHOONOVER's party he enlists the other children in a plot against Terrence R. TIPTON.

Moore, Charley Character in "Dalyrimple Goes Wrong." Lazy fellow-worker who is responsible for training Bryan DALYRIMPLE in the grocery stockroom.

Moore, Doctor Character in "Zone of Accident." Intern on duty when Loretta BROOKE is brought to the accident room at the hospital.

Moore, Kathleen Character in *LT/LOLT*. Irish girl who resembles Minna DAVIS and with whom Monroe STAHR falls in love. The former mistress of a king ("The MAN"), she marries an AMERICAN after her affair with Stahr. Based on Sheilah GRAHAM, Fitzgerald's companion in HOLLYWOOD. Fitzgerald was concerned about making Stahr's attraction to Kathleen convincing, as shown by his note: "Where will the warmth come from

in this. Why does he think she's warm. Warmer than the voice in Farewell. My girls were all so warm and full of promise. The sea at night. What can I do to make it honest and different?" (*F. Scott Fitzgerald Manuscripts V*, Part 1, p. 63).

Moran, Lois (1909–1990) Seventeen-year-old actress whom Fitzgerald met in HOLLYWOOD in early 1927 and to whom he was attracted. Fitzgerald was never alone with Moran, whose widowed mother was present at all their meetings; his interest in her sparked several quarrels between the Fitzgeralds. When Fitzgerald said he admired the actress because she used her talents in a way that required work and discipline, Zelda FITZGERALD burned her clothes in the bathtub. After another quarrel over Moran, Zelda threw her platinum wristwatch—her first expensive gift from Fitzgerald—out of a train window on their return to the East from Hollywood. The Fitzgeralds hosted a house party for Moran and her mother at "ELLERSLIE" on the weekend of May 21, 1927, and Zelda did not show her resentment. Moran was the model for Jenny Prince [DELE-

Lois Moran, the model for Rosemary Hoyt in Tender Is the Night *(Bruccoli Collection, University of South Carolina)*

HANTY] in "Jacob's Ladder" (August 1927) and Rosemary HOYT in *TITN*; and Rosemary's first movie, *Daddy's Girl,* is based on *Stella Dallas* (United Artists, 1925), in which Moran played her first significant role. Moran's other movies included *Reckless Lady* (1926), *Love Hungry* (1928), *Mammy* (1930), and *West of Broadway* (1931). She starred on Broadway in *Of Thee I Sing* (music and lyrics by George and Ira Gershwin), which opened on December 26, 1931 and had 441 performances. She married aviation executive Clarence M. Young (1889–1973) in 1935.

"More Than Just a House" Fiction. Written April 1933. *The SATURDAY EVENING POST,* 205 (June 24, 1933), 8–9, 27, 30, 34; *The Price Was High.* Lew LOWRIE becomes acquainted with the Gunther family in 1925 when he pulls Amanda GUNTHER out of the path of a train. When he later asks Amanda to marry him, she reveals that she has just become engaged to George HORTON. Four years later he encounters Jean GUNTHER at a party in NEW YORK. When he goes to her home to visit her, he learns that Mr. GUNTHER is suffering from senile dementia and that Bess GUNTHER is primarily responsible for his care. While he is there the family receives the news that Amanda has died in childbirth.

Poster for the June 24, 1933 issue of The Saturday Evening Post *(Bruccoli Collection, University of South Carolina)*

Four years later he returns to the house to find that Jean has married and lives in China, and Bess tells him she is getting married herself next week. However, he learns that she is not engaged and is in desperate financial straits, and he asks her to marry him. Throughout the story the girls' feelings about the house symbolize the gradual decline of their family.

Moreland, Colonel Character in "The Offshore Pirate." Toby Moreland's [Curtis CARLYLE'S] father.

Moreland, Toby *See* Curtis CARLYLE.

Morfit, Garrison (Garry Moore) (1915–1993) While living in BALTIMORE in 1934, Fitzgerald invited 18-year-old Morfit to work with him on a project combining Ring LARDNER's nonsense plays with horror plays. Morfit worked with Fitzgerald in the evenings for four months, writing down dialogue which Fitzgerald dictated; but he quit when Fitzgerald showed an amorous interest in Morfit's sister, who was helping him as a secretary one night. Morfit later became a prominent announcer and panelist on radio and television.

Morgan, Holly Character in "Presumption." Girl to whom San Juan CHANDLER pays attention, which makes Noel GARNEAU jealous.

Morris, Mr. Character in *TITN.* Australian who removes his son, Von Cohn MORRIS, from Dick DIVER and Franz GREGOROVIOUS's clinic after his son reports smelling alcohol on Dr. Diver's breath.

Morris, Von Cohn Character in *TITN.* Alcoholic and kleptomaniac patient whose parents remove him from Dick DIVER and Franz GREGOROVIOUS's clinic after he reports that he has smelled alcohol on Dr. Diver's breath. This event precipitates the dissolution of the partnership between Dick and Franz.

Morrison, Hep J. Character in "Strange Sanctuary." Major REDFERN's "business rival," whose presence in BALTIMORE persuades Redfern to try Atlanta instead.

Mortmain, Ellen Character in "The Rubber Check." Wealthy girl with whom Val SCHUYLER falls in love but who decides not to elope with him after a bounced check damages his reputation.

Mortmain, Mrs. Character in "The Rubber Check." Ellen MORTMAIN's mother, who initially accepts Val SCHUYLER because he knows his place.

Morton, Junie Character in "The Ice Palace." An athletic young man at the dinner party that Sally Carrol

HAPPER attends on the first night of her visit to the North.

"The Most Disgraceful Thing I Ever Did: 2. The Invasion of the Sanctuary"
Humor article. *Vanity Fair*, 21 (October 1923), 53; *In His Own Time*. One of 10 unsigned articles on the same topic by different authors; readers who identified the authors won prizes. Fitzgerald recalls that during his Christmas vacation in ST. PAUL in 1913, he went to a church on Christmas Eve after getting tight and walked up the aisle looking for a friend to sit with, telling the minister, "Don't mind me . . . go on with the sermon" (*In His Own Time*, p. 234).

Mother Character in "Image on the Heart." TOM's mother, who suggests that TUDY may need a little firmness after she marries Tom.

Mother Character in *LT/LOLT*. Cecelia BRADY's mother and Pat BRADY's wife. It is unclear whether she is still living.

Movies *See* HOLLYWOOD and Bibliography sections on "Movie Projects" and "Adaptations of Fitzgerald's Work."

Mowat, H. J. (Harold James) (1879–1949) Popular illustrator for *The SATURDAY EVENING POST* and *Ladies' Home Journal*. He illustrated "Love in the Night" (March 14, 1925) and "A New Leaf" (July 4, 1931) for the *Post*.

Mridle Character in "Reade, Substitute Right Half." Quarterback on READE's football team.

Muchhause Character in *TITN*. Bank employee in PARIS.

Mulkley, Oates Character in "The Honor of the Goon." Bomar WINLOCK's roommate, who is beaten up by FINGARSON for insulting fellow student Ella LEI CHAMORO.

Muller, Mr. Character in "Between Three and Four." Less competent employee whom Howard BUTLER had temporarily retained when he fired Sarah SUMMER.

Mulligan Character in *Assorted Spirits*. Policeman who enters Peter WETHERBY's house to apprehend burglar SECOND STORY SALLE.

Munn, Martin Character in "Emotional Bankruptcy." Lillian HAMMEL's date at the PRINCETON prom. He and Josephine PERRY steal away to a dark room, but she doesn't enjoy his kiss, and she realizes this is the first time that she has had no feeling at all about a man she is with.

Murdock, Evelyn Character in "Flight and Pursuit." Caroline CORCORAN's friend, at whose home she encounters Sidney LAHAYE several years after her marriage to George CORCORAN.

Murphy, Gerald and Sara (1888–1964 and 1883–1975) American EXPATRIATES whom the Fitzgeralds met in the summer of 1924 and who became their closest friends in France. The Murphys—whose motto was the Spanish saying "Living well is the best revenge"—lived in luxury on inherited money, were noted for their hospitality, and were seriously interested in the arts. They studied painting with Natalia Goncharova (1881–1962), and art historians credit Gerald Murphy with anticipating the Pop art school in his own work.

Fitzgerald came to regard Gerald Murphy as his social conscience, as he described in "Pasting It Together" (March 1936): "A fourth man had come to dictate my relations with other people when these relations were successful: how to do, what to say. How to make people at least momentarily happy (in opposition to Mrs. Post's theories of how to make everyone thoroughly uncomfortable with a sort of systematized vulgarity). This always confused me and made me want to go out and get drunk, but this man had seen the game, analyzed it and beaten it, and his word was good enough for me" (*CU*, p. 79).

Gerald Murphy's letter to the Fitzgeralds after their departure from the RIVIERA describes the close friendship between the two couples: "We four communicate by our presence rather than any means: so that where we meet and when will never count. Currents race between us regardless: Scott will uncover for me values in Sara, just as Sara has known them in Zelda through her affection for Scott" (September 19, 1925; *Correspondence*, p. 178). Fitzgerald named Honoria WALES in "Babylon Revisited" (1931) after the Murphys' daughter, Honoria (b. 1917).

As Fitzgerald began planning the novel that would become *Tender Is the Night*, he chose the Murphys as models for Seth and Dinah Roreback, characters who evolved into Dick and Nicole DIVER. Fitzgerald's questions and analysis irritated Sara Murphy, who complained in a June 1926 letter: "You can't expect anyone to like or stand a *Continual* feeling of analysis + subanalysis, + criticism—on the whole unfriendly—Such as we have felt for quite awhile. It is definitely in the air,— + quite unpleasant" (*Correspondence*, p. 196). Although the Murphys were models for the Rorebacks, Fitzgerald shifted away from them as he worked through three versions of the novel. The Divers share some of the Murphys' social characteristics, but their lives derive more from the Fitzgeralds. The Murphys'

Gerald and Sara Murphy with their children

VILLA AMERICA at CAP D'ANTIBES contributed to the description of the Divers' VILLA DIANA. *TITN* is dedicated: "GERALD AND SARA/MANY FÊTES."

Ernest HEMINGWAY wrote to Maxwell PERKINS on April 30, 1934 that *TITN* was unsound because of the way the Divers begin as the Murphys and then become the Fitzgeralds (Matthew J. BRUCCOLI, *Fitzgerald and Hemingway*, pp. 166–168). When Fitzgerald asked for his response to *TITN*, Hemingway replied on May 28 that, although the novel was wonderful in places, a writer can't start with real people and change them into other people: "You took liberties with peoples' pasts and futures that produced not people but damned marvellously faked case histories. You, who can write better than anybody can, who are so lousy with talent that you have to—the hell with it. Scott for gods sake write and write truly no matter who or what it hurts but do not make these silly compromises. You could write a fine book about Gerald and Sara for instance if you knew enough about them and they would not have any feeling, except passing, if it were true" (*Ernest Hemingway: Selected Letters 1917–1961*, p. 407).

Fitzgerald defended his use of Sara Murphy in an August 15, 1935 letter to her:

> In my theory, utterly opposite to Ernest's, about fiction i.e. that it takes half a dozen people to make a synthesis strong enough to create a fiction character—in that theory, or rather in despite of it, I used you again and again in <u>Tender</u>:
> "Her face was hard + lovely + pitiful"
> and again
> "He had been heavy, belly-frightened with love of her for years"
> —in those and in a hundred other places I tried to evoke not <u>you</u> but the effect that you produce on men—the echoes and reverberations—a poor return

for what you have given by your living presence, but nevertheless an artist's (what a word!) sincere attempt to preserve a true fragment rather than a "portrait" by Mr. Sargent. And someday in spite of all the affectionate skepticism you felt toward the brash young man you met on the Riviera eleven years ago, you'll let me have my little corner of you where I know you better than anybody—yes, even better than Gerald" (*Life in Letters*, p. 288).

The Murphys ended their residence on the Riviera in 1933 when they returned to the United States to seek treatment for their son, Patrick (1920–37), who had tuberculosis. After the deaths of Patrick and their other son, Baoth (1919–35), Gerald Murphy stopped painting. Although the Murphys visited France again, they gave up the expatriate life.

See Honoria Murphy Donnelly with Richard N. Billings, *Sara & Gerald: Villa America and After* (New York: Times Books, 1982); Calvin Tomkins, *Living Well Is the Best Revenge* (New York: Viking, 1971); and *Letters from the Lost Generation: Gerald and Sara Murphy and Friends*, ed. Linda Patterson Miller (New Brunswick, N.J.: Rutgers University Press, 1991).

"My First Love" Verse. *The NASSAU LITERARY MAGAZINE*, 74 (February 1919), 102; *In His Own Time*, Poems. Included in *A BOOK OF PRINCETON VERSE II*.

my friend Character in "Shaggy's Morning." SHAGGY's friend, a dog who is hit by a car.

"My Generation" Essay. *ESQUIRE*, 70 (October 1968), 119, 121, 123; *Profile of F. Scott Fitzgerald*. Fitzgerald notes that the America into which he was born "passed away somewhere between 1910 and 1920; and the fact gives my generation its uniqueness—we are at once prewar and postwar" (*Esquire*, p. 121). His generation "inherited two worlds—the one of hope to which we had been bred; the one of disillusion which we had discovered early for ourselves" (p. 121). He discusses the heroes, composers, writers, critics, and playwrights of his generation and notes the future writers and leaders whom he had known at the NEWMAN SCHOOL and at PRINCETON.

"My Lost City" Essay. Written in late 1935 or early January 1936. *CU*. Account of the changes in Fitzgerald's feelings for NEW YORK CITY, from his early symbols of triumph and romance to a profound sense of loss: "I can only cry out that I have lost my splendid mirage. Come back, come back, O glittering and white!" (*CU*, p. 33).

"My Old New England Homestead on the Erie" Parody. *COLLEGE HUMOR*, 6 (August 1925), 18–19. Humorous account of renovating "the house of our dreams"

by replacing all the modernized parts with antique structures and furnishings.

"My Ten Favorite Plays" Article. *New York Sun,* September 10, 1934, p. 19; *FSF on Authorship.* Fitzgerald's list includes Charles Chaplin (1889–1977) in *The Pilgrim* (1923) by Chaplin; an obscure actor (unnamed) in a c. 1906 performance of *Secret Service* (written 1895) by William Gillette (1855–1937); his own performance in a magic show at age nine; Greta Garbo (1905–90) "in her first big role" (possibly *The Temptress* [1926] or *Love* [1927]); E. H. Sothern (1859–1933) in a 1908 performance of *Our American Cousin* (written 1858) by Tom Taylor (1817–80); George M. Cohan (1878–1942) in *The Little Millionaire* (1911) by Cohan; Ina Claire (1892–1985) in *The Quaker Girl* (1911) by James T. Tanner (d. 1915), Lionel Monckton (1861–1924), Adrian Ross (1859–1933), and Percy Greenbank (1878–1968); Hortense Alden (1903–78) in the stage version of *Grand Hotel* (1930) by Vicki Baum (1896–1960); Ernest Truex (1890–1973) in Fitzgerald's *The Vegetable* (1923); and D. W. Griffith's (1875–1948) face as Fitzgerald imagines it during the filming of *The Birth of a Nation* (1915).

Myers, Carmel (1899–1980) The Fitzgeralds formed a friendship with this actress in ROME in 1924 while she was acting in *Ben-Hur* (1926). While in HOLLYWOOD in January and February 1927, the Fitzgeralds shared a four-apartment bungalow at the AMBASSADOR HOTEL with Myers, Carl VAN VECHTEN, and John Barrymore (1882–1942). See Myers, "Scott and Zelda," *Park East* (May 1951), pp. 18, 32–33.

Myers, Dick and Alice Lee Friends whom the Fitzgeralds met through Gerald and Sara MURPHY; they lived in France in the 1920s. Their daughter, Fannie, was a friend of Scottie FITZGERALD, whom Alice Lee Myers chaperoned on a trip to EUROPE in summer 1938.

Myers, Gus Character in "What a Handsome Pair!" Man who hires Stuart OLDHORNE to manage his racing stable.

"Myra Meets His Family" Fiction. Written December 1919. *The SATURDAY EVENING POST,* 192 (March 20, 1920), 40, 42, 44, 46, 49–50, 53; *The Price Was High.*

Rewritten from an abandoned story, "Lilah Meets His Family," which was written in April 1919. Myra HARPER, at age 21, has grown tired of prom-trotting and decides to find a husband. She becomes engaged to wealthy Knowleton WHITNEY but is shocked by his family's eccentricity during her visit to their home. She faints when Knowleton tells her that his great-grandmother is Chinese. When Myra awakens she overhears Knowleton talking with Warren APPLETON and KELLY, two actors who have been posing as his parents. She discovers that everything that has happened during her visit has been part of a plot to scare her away, since Knowleton thought she was just after his money. Later, feeling guilty, Knowleton confesses the plot but tells her he is now in love with her. She agrees to marry him that day and arranges for her cousin, Walter GREGORY, to perform the ceremony. On the way to their honeymoon, Myra leaves Knowleton on the train and rejoins her cousin, who is not really a minister, saying that she is letting Knowleton get off far too easily.

Fitzgerald told Harold OBER that he had never liked this story and did not intend to republish it in book form (November 29, 1921; *As Ever,* p. 30). It was made into a lost movie (retitled *The Husband Hunter*) in 1920.

"The Mystery of the Raymond Mortgage" Fiction. Written June 1909. *The ST. PAUL ACADEMY NOW AND THEN,* 2 (October 1909), 4–8; limited edition of 750 copies (New York: Random House, 1960) distributed on September 2, 1960 by Random House to promote *Ellery Queen's 15th Mystery Annual* (New York: Random House, 1960), in which the story appeared; *Apprentice Fiction.* Chief of police EGAN tells how reporter John SYREL solves the murder of Agnes RAYMOND, which baffled the police. Syrel discovers that Raymond family servant John STANDISH shot Agnes RAYMOND, who didn't return his love, and that Mrs. RAYMOND then shot Standish and fled town with the assistance of a YOUNG MAN whom Agnes Raymond had loved. When Syrel tracks down Mrs. Raymond, she takes poison and dies.

Fitzgerald recalled his excitement over the publication of this story, his first appearance in print: "I read my story through at least sic times, and all day I loitered in the corridors and counted the number of men who were reading it, and tried to ask people casually, 'If they had read it'?" ("The Romantic Egotist," Chapter I, p. 21; PRINCETON UNIVERSITY LIBRARY).

Nana Character in "The Curious Case of Benjamin Button." Benjamin BUTTON's nurse during his infancy.

Napoleon, Prince Character in "The End of Hate." Napoleon Bonaparte's cousin, who invites Doctor PILGRIM to practice in PARIS after Pilgrim pulls a tooth for him. Possibly based on Napoleon III (Louis Napoleon Bonaparte, 1808–73), the nephew of Napoleon Bonaparte (1769–1821).

narrator (unnamed) Character in "The Dance." Girl from NEW YORK who solves a murder while visiting a small Southern town.

narrator (unnamed) Narrator of "Financing Finnegan." Writer who has the same agent and editor as FINNEGAN.

narrator (unnamed) Character in " 'I Didn't Get Over.' " Classmate to whom HIBBING reveals that he was the "Captain Brown" who had been responsible for the sinking of the ferry in the story he had told earlier.

narrator (unnamed) Narrator of "The Long Way Out." Person to whom the DOCTOR tells the story of Mrs. George KING.

narrator (unnamed) Character in "The Rich Boy." Partially involved narrator, similar to Nick CARRAWAY in *GG*. A middle-class man who is an outsider in Anson HUNTER's world, he envies Anson and resents his wealth and power. He meets Anson when they are both officers in naval aviation in Pensacola, Florida in 1917. At various points in the narrative he explains that Anson has told him the events he is relating. At the end of the story he sails for EUROPE with Anson.

Narry Character in "The Debutante." Seamstress for the HALCYON family.

The Nassau Literary Magazine PRINCETON UNIVERSITY student publication, founded in 1842. The plays, stories, poems, and book reviews which Fitzgerald wrote for the *Lit* mark the commencement of his serious literary apprenticeship. He developed close friendships with editors Edmund WILSON and John Peale BISHOP. Fitzgerald's *Lit* contributions, which include "Shadow Laurels" (1915), "Sentiment—and the Use of Rouge" (1917), "The Pierian Springs and the Last Straw" (1917), "To My Unused Greek Book" (1916), "Rain before Dawn" (1917), "On a Play Twice Seen" (1917), "The Cameo Frame" (1917), "City Dusk" (1918), "My First Love" (1919), "Marching Streets" (1919), "The Pope at Confession" (1919), "Sleep of a University" (1920), "Our Next Issue" (1916), "The Usual Thing" (1916), and five book reviews, are reprinted in *The Apprentice Fiction of F. Scott Fitzgerald, F. Scott Fitzgerald In His Own Time,* and *Poems 1911–1940.* Fitzgerald recycled some of his *Lit* pieces for later publication in magazines and books: "The Ordeal" (1915) was revised as "Benediction" in *The SMART SET* (1920) and collected in *F&P;* "Jemina" (1916; *Vanity Fair,* 1921) and "Tarquin of Cheapside" (1917; *The Smart Set,* 1921) were revised and collected in *TJA;* "The Debutante" (1917; *The Smart Set,* 1919), "Babes in the Woods" (1917; *The Smart Set,* 1919), and "Princeton—The Last Day" (1917) were incorporated into *TSOP.*

See Christian GAUSS, "Edmund Wilson—The Campus and the Nassau 'Lit,' " *The Princeton University Library Chronicle,* 5 (February 1944), 41–50.

Nathan, George Jean (1882–1958) Influential American literary critic who coedited *The SMART SET* with H. L. MENCKEN from 1914 to 1923 and founded *The AMERICAN MERCURY* with Mencken in 1924. The Fitzgeralds became friends with Nathan while living in NEW YORK as newlyweds, and he visited them at their home in WESTPORT, Connecticut, in the summer of 1920; his flirtation with Zelda FITZGERALD annoyed Fitzgerald. Nathan was the model for Maury NOBLE in *B&D;* the novel is dedicated to "SHANE LESLIE, GEORGE JEAN NATHAN AND MAXWELL PERKINS IN APPRECIATION OF MUCH LITERARY HELP AND ENCOURAGEMENT."

Neall, Adelaide W. (1884–1957) Fiction editor at *The SATURDAY EVENING POST* who was one of Fitzgerald's and Harold OBER's contacts at the magazine.

Nell Character in "The Night before Chancellorsville." NORA's friend, a prostitute who takes a train to Virginia during the Civil War.

Nelson, Dr. Clarence H. One of Fitzgerald's doctors in HOLLYWOOD. He had been scheduled to examine Fitzgerald on December 21, 1940, the day of the author's death; and it was he who pronounced Fitzgerald dead at 5:15 p.m.

Nelson, Paul (1895–1979) Friend of Fitzgerald at the NEWMAN SCHOOL and PRINCETON UNIVERSITY (Class of 1917), where Fitzgerald and Nelson both roomed at 15 University Place their freshman year. Nelson became president of the TRIANGLE CLUB; Fitzgerald had expected to be president but was ineligible because he failed a makeup exam.

"A New Leaf" Fiction. Written April 1931. *The SATURDAY EVENING POST*, 204 (July 4, 1931), 12–13, 90–91; *Bits of Paradise.* Julia ROSS is attracted to Dick RAGLAND, a handsome alcoholic who promises to go on the wagon on his upcoming 28th birthday; but she refuses to see him after he shows up drunk for their first date. When they sail for America on the same ship, she realizes that she loves him regardless of his past. They begin to go out together, and she agrees to announce their engagement after he stays sober for six months and to marry him after another six months. Their mutual friend, Phil HOFFMAN, warns her not to marry Dick because people don't change; and Phil forces Dick to confess that he had become involved with Esther CARY during Julia's two-month absence. Dick plans a business trip to LONDON to give Julia time to consider whether she still wants to marry him, and he disappears at sea. Phil Hoffman, who informs Julia of Dick's disappearance, decides not to tell her that Dick had been drinking again in the past few months. Phil and Julia get married a year later with her illusions of Dick still intact.

Dick Ragland's analysis of his drinking reflects Fitzgerald's own growing dependence on alcohol: "I found that with a few drinks I got expansive and somehow had the ability to please people, and the idea turned my head. Then I began to take a whole lot of drinks to keep going and have everybody think I was wonderful" (*Bits of Paradise*, p. 302).

New Orleans, Louisiana In January 1920 Fitzgerald moved from ST. PAUL to a rooming house at 2900 Prytania Street in New Orleans to escape the Minnesota winter. During his brief stay he corrected proofs for *TSOP*, wrote "The Camel's Back" (April 1920) and "Bernice Bobs Her Hair" (May 1920), and began a seduction novel—now lost—called "Darling Heart."

During his visits to MONTGOMERY, Alabama, he and Zelda Sayre [FITZGERALD] resumed their engagement. In February 1920 he moved to NEW YORK CITY.

"New Types" Fiction. Written July 1934. *The SATURDAY EVENING POST*, 207 (September 22, 1934), 16–17, 74, 76, 78–79, 81; *The Price Was High.* Leslie DIXON returns to America after many years in China and meets Paula JORGENSEN, who invites him to a dance at the home of her aunt, Mrs. Emily HOLLIDAY. Leslie and his cousin, Ellen HARRIS, overhear Paula talking with a man about receiving payment for being photographed at the party. Just before the party is to begin, Paula discovers Aunt Emily motionless in a chair and thinks she is dead; however, she locks the room and proceeds with the party. At the dance Paula and Leslie kiss, and afterwards he comes upstairs to find her in her aunt's room. Just as Paula explains to Leslie that she knew her aunt was dead during the party, Aunt Emily wakes up from a deep sleep. Leslie persuades Paula to leave with him for NEW YORK. In the taxi she explains that she went ahead with the party to get money for an operation for her husband, Eric TRESSIGER, who has been an invalid for seven years, since a week after their secret wedding. Tressiger dies in the operating room, and Paula decides that her home is with Leslie now.

New York City, New York When Fitzgerald was discharged from the ARMY in February 1919, he moved to New York City, which he described to Zelda Sayre FITZGERALD as "THE LAND OF AMBITION AND SUCCESS" (after February 22, 1919; *Life in Letters*, p. 22). He lived in a room at 200 Claremont Avenue near Columbia University in Manhattan. He hoped to succeed in journalism so that he could marry Zelda as soon as possible, but after unsuccessfully seeking a newspaper job he went to work for the Barron Collier agency writing trolley-car advertising cards. In spring 1919 he wrote 19 stories and received 122 rejections; he was further discouraged by Zelda's hesitation to marry him. "May Day" (July 1920) reflects the despair of this stay in New York, which he recalled in 1936 as "the four most impressionable months of my life" ("My Lost City"; *CU*, p. 25). After Zelda broke their engagement in June, he quit his job in July and returned to ST. PAUL, where he rewrote *TSOP* while living with his parents. After a brief stay in NEW ORLEANS in January 1920 he returned to New York, living at the Murray Hill Hotel and later at the Allerton. He and Zelda resumed their engagement; and they were married on April 3, 1920 at the rectory of St. Patrick's Cathedral in New York, with a honeymoon at the Biltmore Hotel. When the Biltmore asked them to leave because they disturbed other guests, they moved to the Commodore Hotel two blocks away on 42nd Street. They moved to

WESTPORT, Connecticut, May–September 1920, then returned to New York in October to live in an apartment at 38 West 59th Street, ordering meals from the nearby PLAZA HOTEL. In May 1921 they left New York for their first trip to EUROPE. "My Lost City," an essay Fitzgerald wrote in late 1935 or early January 1936 (unpublished until 1945; *CU*), describes his changing feelings about the city over the years.

The New Yorker On October 21, 1929 Harold OBER suggested that, despite the low rate of pay, Fitzgerald write occasionally for *The New Yorker,* a magazine "which has a very different audience from the Saturday Evening Post and an audience that would be very keen to see something from you, and I think it would help you in the long run" (*As Ever,* p. 152). Fitzgerald rejected the magazine's suggestion that he write a profile of Ring LARDNER (see *As Ever,* pp. 157 & 163) and instead submitted "Salesmanship in the Champs-Élysées" (February 1930). *The New Yorker* also published "A Short Autobiography (With Acknowledgments to Nathan)" (May 1929); "A Book of One's Own" (August 1937); "Lamp in a Window" (March 1935); and "Obit on Parnassus" (June 1937). The magazine frequently asked Ober for prose or verse by Fitzgerald, but rejected "Thousand-and-First Ship" (1945) and "Thank You for the Light" (unpublished story) in 1936.

The Newman News NEWMAN SCHOOL magazine to which Fitzgerald contributed "Football" (1911), "A Luckless Santa Claus" (1912), "Pain and the Scientist" (1913), "The Trail of the Duke" (1913), and two untitled news features. He preserved clippings of these pieces in his scrapbooks, but there is no complete run of the magazine. The three stories are collected in *The Apprentice Fiction of F. Scott Fitzgerald,* and "Football" appears in *F. Scott Fitzgerald In His Own Time* and *Poems 1911–1940.*

See Henry Dan Piper, "Scott Fitzgerald's Prep-School Writings," *The Princeton University Library Chronicle,* 17 (Autumn 1955), 1–10.

Newman School Boarding school in Hackensack, New Jersey, which aimed to be the Catholic equivalent of prestigious Protestant prep schools in New England and which Fitzgerald entered in September 1911; yearly tuition was $850. Fitzgerald was bossy, unpopular, and unhappy during his first year at Newman—an experience reflected in his 1928 Basil Duke LEE story "The Freshest Boy"; but his behavior and popularity improved in his second year. He did poorly academically, failing four courses in two years; but he won medals for elocution and track. While at Newman Fitzgerald developed a close friendship with Charles W. ("Sap") DONAHOE, editor of the school magazine,

The NEWMAN NEWS, to which Fitzgerald contributed; and in November 1912 he met Father Cyril Sigourney Webster FAY, who became his mentor. Other Newman friends included Stephan PARROTT and Paul NELSON. Newman was the model for ST. REGIS, a prep school in several of Fitzgerald's stories.

"News of Paris—Fifteen Years Ago" Fiction. Written c. 1940. *Furioso,* 3 (Winter 1947), 5–10; *AOAA.* Henry Haven DELL, waiting for a ship, says goodbye to RUTH and has a one-afternoon fling with Bessie WING, who has just broken her engagement to another man. When he leaves Bessie and finds he still has to wait for the ship, he calls on HÉLÈNE, an orphan whose convent education he has supported for three years, and is jealous of her interest in an American reporter.

"A Nice Quiet Place" Fiction—Josepine PERRY story. Written March 1930. *The* SATURDAY EVENING POST, 202 (May 31, 1930), 8–9, 96, 101, 103; *TAR; B&J.* Josephine Perry's parents plan the family's summer vacation at Island Farms in Michigan instead of Lake Forest because they realize she knows her way around Lake Forest too well. Josephine is bored at Island Farms until she meets handsome Sonny DORRANCE; but then the Perrys return to Lake Forest for Constance PERRY's wedding to Malcolm LIBBY. Josephine resolves to do something awful so her family will send her away; she is found with Malcolm's arm around her, and after the wedding she returns to Island Farms.

Nick Character in "No Harm Trying." Pat HOBBY's landlord.

Nick Character in "The Rich Boy." Bartender with whom Anson HUNTER reminisces at the PLAZA HOTEL.

Nicotera Character in *TITN.* Actor who is appearing in *The Grandeur That Was Rome* with Rosemary HOYT in ROME. He wants to marry Rosemary, and his attention to her makes Dick DIVER jealous.

"A Night at the Fair" Fiction—Basil Duke LEE story. Written May 1928. *The* SATURDAY EVENING POST, 201 (July 21, 1928), 8–9, 129–130, 133; *AOAA; B&J.* Basil Duke Lee, age 15, and Riply BUCKNER are at the State Fair. Riply, who has been wearing long pants for a week, belittles Basil—still in short pants—who has previously dominated him. They join Elwood LEAMING in picking up two girls, and Basil is gradually eliminated from the group. The next evening Basil's new suit, with long pants, arrives just in time for him to go to the fireworks, where he sits with Gladys VAN SCHELLINGER and generously urges Riply's aunt not to tell Riply's mother about his unseemly behavior at the fair.

Fitzgerald noted in his *Ledger* for September 1911, when he was 15, "Attended state fair and took chicken on roller-coaster" (p. 166).

"The Night before Chancellorsville" Fiction. Written November 1934. *ESQUIRE*, 3 (February 1935), 24, 165; in *TAR* as "The Night of Chancellorsville." NORA, a prostitute, recounts her experience while traveling with a trainload of prostitutes to Virginia. The train arrives in Chancellorsville, Virginia, during the Union retreat but manages to return safely to Washington. Nora is outraged that the public is only interested in what happened to the army and that the "attack" on the train is never reported in the newspapers.

In February 1940 Fitzgerald unsuccessfully tried to interest Edwin KNOPF, an editor at MGM, in an idea for a Civil War movie based on "The Night before Chancellorsville" and "The End of Hate" (June 1940) (see *Life in Letters*, pp. 430–431).

"No Flowers" Fiction. Written May 1934. *The SATURDAY EVENING POST*, 207 (July 21, 1934), 10–11, 57–58, 60; *The Price Was High*. When Marjorie CLARK attends her first prom she resents that hard economic times demand that the prom not be as luxurious as the ones her mother, Amanda Rawlins CLARK, has told her of attending in her own youth. When Marjorie's date, Billy JOHNS, leaves her for a moment in the Engagement Room, she has a vision of her grandmother, LUCY, breaking up with Phil SAVAGE, who has been asked to leave college for cheating—a story she has heard from her grandmother. The next day in the same room, Amanda Clark recalls how she had accepted HOWARD's corsage in place of Carter MCLANE's, which she was unaware contained his mother's engagement ring which he planned to give her that night, and how Carter had left her when he discovered the switch. On the day of the prom, when Billy discovers that he can't get his dinner jacket from the tailor, he steals a suit from the student laundry; but when Marjorie overhears the owner's date's disappointment at not being able to go to the prom, she makes Billy return the suit. When Billy's friend "Red" GRANGE passes out, Billy takes his suit; and he and Marjorie attend the prom.

"No Harm Trying" Fiction—Pat HOBBY story. Submitted October 27, 1939. *ESQUIRE*, 14 (November 1940), 30, 151–153; *AOAA*; *PH*. Studio executive Carl LE VIGNE tells Pat Hobby that Pat's ex-wife Estelle DEVLIN is in the hospital after trying to cut her wrists and that he has put Pat on the studio payroll in order to help Estelle. Pat buys an idea from ERIC, the callboy, and assembles Jeff MANFRED, Dutch WAGGONER, and Harmon SHAVER to work on a script to star Lizzette STARHEIM. When Shaver and the others present the idea to Le Vigne, Le Vigne reveals that Miss Starheim, a for-

eigner, can speak only three English sentences; that Waggoner isn't reliable because of drug use; and that Manfred is at the studio only because of a family connection. Le Vigne reveals to Pat that he had walked in when Estelle was typing Eric's story idea and has put Eric on salary.

Noble, Maury Character in *B&D*. Anthony PATCH's Harvard classmate and one of his best friends. A cynic who believes there is "no ultimate goal for man" (p. 255). He snubs Anthony after Anthony becomes poor. Based on George Jean NATHAN.

Nolak, Mr. and Mrs. Characters in "The Camel's Back." Proprietors of the costume shop where Perry PARKHURST rents a camel costume; they both refuse to wear the back part of the costume.

Nora Narrator of "The Night before Chancellorsville." Prostitute who takes a train to Virginia during the Civil War.

Norris, Charles G. (1881–1945) Realistic American novelist and brother of Frank NORRIS. Fitzgerald described Charles Norris's 1917 novel *Salt* as "a most astounding piece of realism" (to Alida BIGELOW, September 23, 1919; *Life in Letters*, p. 33); it influenced his depiction of Anthony PATCH in *B&D*. However, Fitzgerald found *Brass* (1921) disappointing (*see* "Poor Old Marriage").

Norris, Frank (1870–1902) Naturalistic American novelist whose *Vandover and the Brute* (1914) influenced Fitzgerald's depiction of Anthony PATCH in *B&D*. In October 1920 Fitzgerald wrote to H. L. MENCKEN proposing a collected edition of Norris's work (*Correspondence*, pp. 69–70); Mencken offered to help, but Fitzgerald's plan never developed further. (He was not involved in the 10-volume Norris edition which Doubleday published in 1928.)

Fitzgerald had tried to interest Zelda Sayre [FITZGERALD] in Norris's *McTeague* (1899) during their courtship, but she found the novel distasteful (February 1920; *Correspondence*, p. 52). At the end of his life Fitzgerald sent Edmund WILSON a copy of *McTeague* marked to demonstrate how John Steinbeck (1902–68) had imitated it in *Of Mice and Men* (1937). *The Octopus* (1901) was one of the books Fitzgerald assigned Sheilah GRAHAM to read in the "College of One"; he wrote in her copy: "Frank Norris after writing three great books died in 1902 at the age of just thirty. He was our most promising man and might have gone further than Drieser or the others. He claimed to be a diciple of Zola the naturalist, but in many ways he was better than Zola" (*Life in Letters*, p. 423).

North, Abe Character in *TITN*. Friend of Dick and Nicole DIVER; an alcoholic composer whose career lags after a brilliant start. He is beaten to death in a NEW YORK speakeasy. Based on Ring LARDNER, whose death and unfulfilled genius Fitzgerald mourns through his depiction of Abe. Fitzgerald also used some of Charles MACARTHUR's characteristics for Abe.

North Africa The Fitzgeralds traveled to North Africa in February 1930, primarily to provide rest for Zelda FITZGERALD, who was approaching her first breakdown. They visited Algiers, Bou Saada, Biskra, and El Kantara. Zelda later wrote: "It was a trying winter and to forget bad times we went to Algiers. The Hôtel de l'Oasis was laced together by Moorish grills; and the bar was an outpost of civilization with people accentuating their eccentricities" (" 'Show Mr. and Mrs. F. to Number ——' ", May–June 1934; *CU*, p. 51). Fitzgerald utilized material from this trip in "One Trip Abroad" (October 1930).

North, Mary Character in *TITN*. Friend of Dick and Nicole DIVER. Wife of Abe NORTH and later of the Conte di MINGHETTI.

Norton, Doctor Character in "One Interne." Medical professor whom Bill TULLIVER idolizes.

Nosby, Claude Character in "A Penny Spent." Hallie BUSHMILL's fiancé.

"Not in the Guidebook" Fiction. Written December 1924; rewritten February 1925. *WOMAN'S HOME COMPANION*, 52 (November 1925), 9–11, 135–136; *The Price Was High*. Jim and Milly COOLEY, unhappily married for six months, sail to EUROPE, where Jim says he has found a job. Jim, a war hero who claims "shell shock" to justify his unpleasant behavior to Milly, deserts her on the train to PARIS. Tour guide Bill DRISCOLL rescues her from two disreputable-looking men on the street and finds her a place to stay with his own landlady. When Milly accompanies him on a tour of the Château-Thierry battlefield, she learns that it was

really Bill who had stolen the German orders for which Jim had taken credit. Milly gets a divorce from Jim and marries Bill.

The Notebooks of F. Scott Fitzgerald Edited by Matthew J. BRUCCOLI. New York & London: Harcourt Brace Jovanovich/Bruccoli Clark, 1978. Fitzgerald probably began assembling his *Notebooks* after moving to "LA PAIX" outside BALTIMORE, Maryland, in May 1932. His secretaries typed the pages from his manuscript notes and from marked tearsheets of his stories. When he decided not to reprint one of his stories, he salvaged passages for use in his novels, storing them in his *Notebooks,* which also include story ideas, miscellaneous observations, and autobiographical material. Edmund WILSON published 60 percent of the entries, with silent alterations, in *The Crack-Up* (1945). The 1978 volume includes the complete *Notebooks* in unemended texts, as well as a selection of the loose notes that are with *LT/ LOLT* manuscripts at PRINCETON UNIVERSITY LIBRARY. Fitzgerald's classification of notes includes: Anecdotes; Bright Clippings; Conversation and Things Overheard; Description of Things and Atmosphere; Epigrams, Wise Cracks and Jokes; Feelings & Emotions (without girls); Descriptions of Girls; Descriptions of Humanity (Physical); Ideas; Jingles and Songs; Karacters; Literary; Moments (What people do); Nonsense and Stray Phrases; Observations; Proper Names; Rough Stuff; Scenes and Situations; Titles; Unclassified; Vernacular; Work References; Youth and Army.

nurse (unnamed) Character in "An Alcoholic Case." Woman who considers giving up the case of the alcoholic CARTOONIST to whom she is assigned but who goes back to him when her agent is unable to find a replacement for her.

nurse (unnamed) Character in "Three Acts of Music." Woman who contemplates marrying a DOCTOR but rises in her profession instead.

Nyon, Switzerland Zelda FITZGERALD was a patient at PRANGINS CLINIC in Nyon, June 1930–September 1931.

O

" 'O Russet Witch!' " *See* "His Russet Witch."

Oak Hall Hotel Hotel in TRYON, North Carolina, a resort town where Fitzgerald stayed for a couple of weeks in February 1935; Scottie FITZGERALD stayed with her father's friends Lefty and Nora FLYNN in Tryon while he was at the hotel. Fitzgerald returned to Oak Hall in January 1937, and remained there until his departure for HOLLYWOOD in July.

Ober, Harold (1881–1959) Fitzgerald's literary agent. On October 28, 1919, at the suggestion of ST. PAUL writer Grace Flandrau (d. 1971), Fitzgerald sent a story typescript to the Paul Revere REYNOLDS literary agency in NEW YORK; and in November he became the client of Ober, a partner in the agency who was responsible for new or young clients. Fitzgerald had already contracted with SCRIBNERS for *TSOP*, and he continued to deal directly with Scribners about the publication of his books; Ober handled magazine and movie sales, receiving a 10 percent commission. In September 1929 Ober left the Reynolds agency to open his own literary agency, which became Harold Ober Associates in 1949; Fitzgerald wired: "FOLLOWING YOU NATURALLY" (September 24, 1929; *Life in Letters*, p. 170; *As Ever*, p. 147). Ober's clients eventually included William Faulkner (1897–1962), Catherine Drinker Bowen (1897–1973), and J. D. Salinger (b. 1919). Ober acted strictly as a middleman for the sale of Fitzgerald's stories until the mid-1930s, when Fitzgerald began to send him material that was unsalable and Ober began making editorial recommendations. For example, he sent Fitzgerald a list of 29 suggestions for revisions in "The Pearl and the Fur," an unpublished story about Gwen BOWERS (April 25, 1936; *As Ever*, pp. 265–267). When Scottie FITZGERALD began attending the Ethel Walker School in Simsbury, Connecticut, in 1936, Ober and his wife, Anne, became her foster parents, visiting her at school and welcoming her to their home in Scarsdale during holidays. On September 4, 1938, Anne Ober wrote to Fitzgerald about Scottie: "I know you think Harold and I spoil her, but so far Scottie trusts me and I think I have at least part of her confidence. It is an important relationship to me and while she may not realize it, I think it is to Scottie too"

(*As Ever*, pp. 368–369). (See Scottie's foreword to *As Ever, Scott Fitz—*.) *Taps at Reveille* (1935) is dedicated to Harold Ober.

In the early 1920s Fitzgerald began requesting payment when he delivered a story to Ober, before it was sold to a magazine; the arrangement evolved into a system whereby Ober advanced Fitzgerald money against unwritten stories. By the summer of 1936 Fitzgerald owed Ober $11,000. Ober, whose business was suffering from the Depression and who was concerned about educating his two sons, tried to convince Fitzgerald that he could not continue to advance money; but Fitzgerald still sent desperate requests for $50 or $100 when his bank account was overdrawn. Fitzgerald's financial dependence on Ober and editor Maxwell PERKINS is depicted in "Financing Finnegan" (January 1938). In June 1937 Ober arranged for Edwin KNOPF to interview Fitzgerald, resulting in a six-month contract with MGM. When Fitzgerald went to HOLLYWOOD, he owed Ober $12,511.69; but he paid off both Ober and Perkins by the end of 1938.

In June 1939 Ober sent Fitzgerald his requested $500 advance against his next story. Unwilling to resume the cycle of debt, Ober composed a firm letter explaining his inability to make further advances; but he never mailed the letter (June 21, 1939; *As Ever*, pp. 393–395). Around July 3 Ober refused another advance, and Fitzgerald turned to Perkins for funds, commenting: ". . . OBER HAS DECIDED NOT TO BACK ME THOUGH I PAID BACK EVERY PENNY AND EIGHT THOUSAND COMMISSION. . . . PLEASE DO NOT ASK OBERS COOPERATION" (*Life in Letters*, p. 395). On July 13 Fitzgerald tried Ober again: "STILL FLABBERGASTED AT YOUR ABRUPT CHANGE IN POLICY AFTER 20 YEARS ESPECIALLY WITH STORY IN YOUR HANDS STOP MY COMMERCIAL VALUE CANT HAVE SUNK FROM 60 THOUSAND TO NOTHING BECAUSE OF A SLOW HEALING LUNG CAVITY STOP AFTER 30 PICTURE OFFERS DURING THE MONTHS I WAS IN BED SWANSON NOW PROMISES NOTHING FOR ANOTHER WEEK STOP CAN'T YOU ARRANGE A FEW HUNDRED ADVANCE FROM A MAGAZINE SO I CAN EAT TODAY AND TOMORROW STOP WONT YOU WIRE SCOTT" (*Life in Letters*, pp. 395–396; *As Ever*, p. 400). Ober wired a

Harold Ober, Fitzgerald's agent (Bruccoli Collection, University of South Carolina)

refusal on July 14 and explained in a letter on July 18 that his expenses were increasing, he had two boys to send to college, and the profit margin of his agency was too small to accommodate loans. He suggested that Fitzgerald work more in Hollywood and save money to live on when he got ready to write later; and he assured him, "I haven't lost faith in your being able to write" (*As Ever,* p. 401).

Fitzgerald broke off their business relationship in a July 19 letter: "This is not a request for any more backing—there will be no more requests. I am quite sure that you would be as stubborn in any decision that I am through as you were up to 1934 about the value of my stories. Also I am writing this letter with, I hope, no touch of unpleasantness—simply from a feeling that perhaps you share, that I have depended too long on backing and had better find out at the source whether my products are considered deficient and why" (*Life in Letters,* p. 400; *As Ever,* p. 402).

When Perkins offered to lend Fitzgerald $1,000 later that year, Fitzgerald reflected: "Max, you are so kind.

When Harold withdrew from the questionable honor of being my banker I felt completely numb financially and I suddenly wondered what money was and where it came from. There had always seemed a little more somewhere and now there wasn't" (December 19, 1939; *Life in Letters,* p. 427; *Scott/Max,* p. 260).

Although he had asked Perkins to recommend other agents, Fitzgerald began acting as his own agent; Ober handled the business for Fitzgerald's already published work. When Fitzgerald died on December 21, 1940, Sheilah GRAHAM called Ober, whom Scottie was visiting in Scarsdale; Ober called Zelda FITZGERALD in MONT-GOMERY. Fitzgerald had appointed Ober and PRINCETON classmate John BIGGS as his executors in his 1937 will, but on November 10, 1940 he had substituted Perkins's name for Ober's. Ober and Perkins both withdrew as executors to avoid legal complications, but they helped Biggs administer Fitzgerald's literary affairs. The Obers continued to look after Scottie; and Ober, Maxwell PERKINS, and Gerald MURPHY lent her the money to finish her education at Vassar. Ober and later Harold Ober Associates handled Fitzgerald's literary affairs after Fitzgerald's death; Harold Ober Associates still handles them.

The Fitzgerald/Ober correspondence, which is at the Lilly Library of Indiana University, Bloomington, Indiana, is collected in *As Ever, Scott Fitz—,* ed. Matthew J. BRUCCOLI with Jennifer M. Atkinson.

"Obit on Parnassus" Verse. *The NEW YORKER,* 13 (June 5, 1937), 27; *In His Own Time, Poems.* A chronicle of authors who died in their thirties, forties, fifties, and so on.

O'Connor, Helen Character in "Flight and Pursuit." Woman who is employed by Sidney LAHAYE to hire Caroline CORCORAN as a private secretary and traveling companion.

O'Conor, Bijou (1896–1975) Englishwoman with whom Fitzgerald allegedly had an affair in SWITZER-LAND in fall 1930 while Zelda FITZGERALD was in PRAN-GINS CLINIC. In 1975 O'Conor gave a taped interview about her relationship with Fitzgerald (*Bijou O'Conor Remembers F. Scott Fitzgerald* [London: Audio Arts, 1975]). O'Conor was a partial model for Lady Caroline SIBLY-BIERS in *TITN* and was the model for Lady CAPPS-KARR in "The Hotel Child" (January 1931). See "The Quest for Bijou O'Conor," Appendix III in Jeffrey Meyers, *Scott Fitzgerald: A Biography.*

"The Offshore Pirate" Fiction. Written February 1920. *The SATURDAY EVENING POST,* 192 (May 29, 1920), 10–11, 99, 101–102, 106, 109; *F&P.* Ardita FARNAM rudely refuses her uncle's request to meet Toby Moreland, the son of his friend, because she is in love with

Leslie L. Benson's illustrations for Fitzgerald's May 29, 1920 Saturday Evening Post *story* (Bruccoli Collection, University of South Carolina)

another man whose imagination she admires. Her uncle leaves his yacht, which is soon commandeered by Curtis CARLYLE and his Six Black Buddies, all fugitives from justice. During the three days they are together, Carlyle tells Ardita his history and his ambitions of aristocracy. They fall in love, and Ardita asks Carlyle to take her with him as he flees to Peru and India. A revenue boat finds their hideout in a secluded bay, and Ardita's uncle and Colonel MORELAND come aboard. Carlyle reveals that he is really Toby Moreland and that his entire story was invented. Impressed by his imagination, Ardita asks him to lie to her sweetly for the rest of her life.

This is the first appearance of Fitzgerald's recurring plot of an unattainable woman who is won by a man's performance of a great or imaginative feat. The story originally ended with the explanation that it was all a dream; but when the *Post* complained, Fitzgerald provided a new conclusion which ends, "She kissed him softly in the illustration"—which he regarded as "one of the best *lines* I've ever written" (to Harold

OBER, February 21, 1920; *As Ever,* p. 12). "The Offshore Pirate" was made into a lost movie in 1921.

O'Flaherty, Sergeant Character in "Sentiment—and the Use of Rouge." Dying Irish soldier who discusses religion and the difference between the English and the Irish with Clay SYNEFORTH.

O'Flarity Character in *Assorted Spirits*. Policeman who enters Peter WETHERBY's house to apprehend burglar SECOND STORY SALLE.

O'Hara, John (1905–1970) American short-story writer and novelist; friend of Fitzgerald. His works include *Appointment in Samarra* (1934), *Butterfield 8* (1935), *Pal Joey* (stories, 1940; libretto, 1952), and *Ten North Frederick* (1955). O'Hara was 15 years old when he read *TSOP*; later he recalled the impression Fitzgerald's novel made on him in his introduction to *The Portable F. Scott Fitzgerald:* "A little matter of twenty-five years ago I, along with half a million other men and women

between fifteen and thirty, fell in love with a book" (p. vii). His earliest located letter to Fitzgerald was written June 25, 1933 to praise "More Than Just a House" (June 24, 1933): "Miss Jean Gunther, of the More Than Just a House Gunthers, was one of those girls for the writing about of whom you hold the exclusive franchise, if you can puzzle out that sentence. . . . And that easily we get to the second thing you've done so well: Lowrie, the climber; and I wonder why you do the climber so well. Is it the Irish in you? *Must* the Irish always have a lot of climber in them?" (*Selected Letters of John O'Hara*, ed. Matthew J. BRUCCOLI [New York: Random House, 1978], pp. 75–76). Fitzgerald's July 18 reply included an analysis of his own social insecurities, which he attributed to the clash between his "black Irish" and "old American" ancestors: "So if I were elected King of Scotland tomorrow after graduating from Eton, Magdalene to the Guards with an embryonic history which tied me to the Plantagonets, I would still be a parvenue" (*Life in Letters*, p. 233).

When Fitzgerald was in NEW YORK in January and February 1934 to work on proofs for *TITN*, he spent time with O'Hara, who was trying to complete *Appointment in Samarra*, his first novel. O'Hara declined a loan that Fitzgerald offered, but he appreciated Fitzgerald's encouragement, as he stated in an April 1934 letter: "You helped me finish my novel. I finished it yesterday. The little we talked when you were in New York did it. I reasoned that the best parts of my novel will be said to derive from Fitzgerald, and I think I have muffed my story, but I became reconciled to having done that after talking to you and reading Tender Is the Night in proof. No one else can write like that, and I haven't tried, but the best parts of my novel are facile pupils of The Beautiful and Damned and The Great Gatsby" (*Correspondence*, p. 348). Fitzgerald provided a blurb that was used in advertisements for *Appointment in Samarra*: "John O'Hara's novel indicates the tremendous strides that American writers have taken since the war" (*New York Herald-Tribune Books*, October 7, 1934, section 7, p. 17; Matthew J. Bruccoli, *The O'Hara Concern* [New York: Random House, 1975], p. 111).

O'Hara expressed his admiration for *TITN* after reading the novel in proof: "I will say now that Tender Is the Night is in the early stages of being my favorite book, even more than This Side of Paradise. As I told you once before, I don't read many books, but the same ones over again. Right now I can't think of any other book clearly enough to make a comparison between it and Tender Is the Night, and I guess in its way that is the most important thing I've ever said about any book" (April 1934; *Correspondence*, p. 348). Years later O'Hara offered this explanation for the disappointing reception of *TITN*: "The book came out at precisely the wrong time in the national history. No matter how good it was, it was about the Bad People,

the well fed, well housed, well educated, well born— the villains of the depression. It was a time for Odets and the imitators of Odets, and of Steinbeck and the imitators of Steinbeck. . . . I am proud to say I did not go along with the gutless thinking that all but destroyed TENDER IS THE NIGHT and without a doubt broke Fitzgerald's heart' " (August 12, 1957; *Selected Letters of John O'Hara*, p. 266).

When Fitzgerald invited O'Hara and his wife, Belle (1915?-1954), for lunch at "BELLY ACRES," probably in late 1939, O'Hara read Fitzgerald's work-in-progress on *LT/LOLT*. He recalled the occasion in his 1941 *New Republic* tribute to Fitzgerald:

He was terribly nervous, disappearing for five and ten minutes at a time, once to get a plaid tie to give my wife because she was wearing a Glen plaid suit. Once to get a volume of Thackeray because I'd never read Thackeray, another time to get some tome about Julius Caesar which he assured me was scholarly but readable—but which he knew I would never read. Then we went out and took some pictures, and when we finished

Fitzgerald and John O'Hara in Hollywood, 1939; photo by Belle O'Hara (Bruccoli Collection, University of South Carolina)

that he suddenly said, "Would you like to read what I've written, but first promise you won't tell anyone about it. Don't tell them anything. Don't tell them what it's about, or anything about the people. I'd like it better if you didn't even tell anyone I'm writing another novel." So we went back to the house and I read what he had written. He saw that I was comfortable, with pillows, cigarettes, ashtrays, a coke. And sat there tortured, trying to be casual, but unhappy because he did not know that my dead pan was partly due to my being an extremely slow reader of good writing, and partly because this *was* such good writing that I was reading. When I had read it I said, "Scott, don't take any more movie jobs until you've finished this. You work so slowly and this is so good, you've got to finish it. It's real Fitzgerald." Then, of course, he became blasphemous and abusive, and asked me if I wanted to fight. I saw him a few times after that day, and once when I asked him how the book was coming he only said, "You've kept your promise? You haven't spoken to anyone about it?" ("Certain Aspects," *The New Republic*, 104 [March 3, 1941], 311; *"An Artist Is His Own Fault,"* ed. Matthew J. Bruccoli [Carbondale & Edwardsville: Southern Illinois University Press, 1977], p. 137).

O'Hara later described his friend's final years in HOLLYWOOD: "Scott should have been killed in a Bugatti in the south of France, and not to have died of neglect in Hollywood, a prematurely old little man haunting bookstores unrecognized (as he was the last-but-one time I saw him.)" (October 23, 1958; *Selected Letters of John O'Hara*, p. 279). After Fitzgerald's death, editor Maxwell PERKINS approached O'Hara and Budd SCHULBERG about completing *LT/LOLT,* but they declined.

In his introduction to *The Portable F. Scott Fitzgerald* O'Hara summarized: "All he was was our best novelist, one of our best novella-ists, and one of our finest writers of short stories" (p. xiv). He later wrote to John Steinbeck (1902–68): "Fitzgerald was a better just plain writer than all of us put together. Just words writing" (June 2 or 3, 1949; *Selected Letters of John O'Hara*, p. 224).

See Matthew J. Bruccoli, *The O'Hara Concern* (New York: Random House, 1975; revised edition, Pittsburgh: University of Pittsburgh Press, 1995).

O'Kane Character in "On an Ocean Wave." Gaston T. SCHEER's confidential secretary.

O'Kelly, George Character in " 'The Sensible Thing.' " Young man whose fiancée, Jonquil CARY, breaks their engagement because he is a failure. After he becomes a successful engineer, their engagement is renewed. Although he realizes their love has lost its original freshness, he is willing to accept love's mutability.

the Old Man Character in " 'Send Me In, Coach.' " Man who runs Camp Rahewawa and who warns counselor RICKEY to stay away from his wife.

Old Wise One Character in "The Passionate Eskimo." PAN-E-TROON's father, who reluctantly lets his son explore Chicago and asks him to purchase some tobacco.

Oldhorne, Helen Van Beck *See* Helen VAN BECK.

Oldhorne, Stuart Character in "What a Handsome Pair!" Sportsman whose marriage to Helen VAN BECK dissolves into rivalry.

Olive Character in "A Night at the Fair." Girl whom Elwood LEAMING, Riply BUCKNER, and Basil Duke LEE pick up at the State Fair. On the following night she deserts Riply for a date with "Bill Jones" (Hubert BLAIR).

Olson Character in *TSOP.* Atlantic City hotel house detective who forces Amory BLAINE and Jill WAYNE to leave the hotel when Amory pretends Jill has been with him rather than with Alec CONNAGE.

"On a Play Twice Seen" Verse. *The NASSAU LITERARY MAGAZINE*, 73 (June 1917), 149; *In His Own Time*; *Poems*; incorporated in *TSOP.*

"On an Ocean Wave" Fiction. Written summer 1940. *ESQUIRE*, 15 (February 1941), 59, 141; *The Price Was High*. Published as by "Paul ELGIN"; the only Fitzgerald story published under a pseudonym. Gaston T. SCHEER is traveling from NEW YORK to France; both his wife, Minna SCHEER, and his mistress, Catherine DENZER, are on board the ship. When he finds Minna embracing Professor DOLLARD, he summons Dollard to his cabin and has him thrown overboard, while Minna eagerly awaits Dollard on deck.

"On Schedule" Fiction. Written December 1932. *The SATURDAY EVENING POST*, 205 (March 18, 1933), 16, 17, 71, 74, 77, 79; *The Price Was High*. René DU CARY prepares a schedule for his daughter, Noël DU CARY, so that he can be free to pursue his scientific research. He emphasizes the importance of the schedule to Noël and her companion, Becky SNYDER, a 19-year-old girl whom he plans to marry in seven months. The wait for their wedding is necessitated by a provision in his deceased wife's will that he forfeit the income she bequeathed him if he remarries within seven years after her death. One day his chief assistant's wife, Dolores HUME, is shocked to discover Becky in the bathtub in du Cary's house, where she is bathing because the water isn't running where she boards. On a

cold day the water in the jars for du Cary's experiments freezes, and he panics at the possible loss of his research until he discovers that Becky has been in his laboratory for nearly an hour trying to start the furnace to save the jars. At that time he tells Dolores Hume of his engagement to Becky.

"On the Trail of Pat Hobby" Fiction. Submitted February 14, 1940. ESQUIRE, 15 (January 1941), 36, 126; *PH*. Writer Bee MCILVAINE tells Pat HOBBY about a $50 reward for a title for the movie she is working on about what goes on in tourist cabins. Pat is startled, because he has secretly been employed as a night clerk for tourist cabins that had been raided that morning. When Bee calls producer Jack BERNERS to her office to discuss title ideas, Pat suggests *Grand Motel,* which Berners says wins the prize.

"On Your Own" Fiction. Written spring 1931. ES-QUIRE, 91 (January 30, 1979), 56–67; *The Price Was High*. Actress Evelyn LOVEJOY sails to America from EUROPE to attend the funeral of her father in Rocktown, Maryland. On the ship she becomes attracted to George IVES, who is also from Maryland; he returns her interest. After her father's funeral she asks him to take her to the Washington train station, where she will leave for NEW YORK; en route she is offended by his insistence that he kiss her. She doesn't find much success in New York and is considering an English offer when she hears from Ives, who she learns is wealthy and important. When he takes her to dinner with his mother, Evelyn is uncomfortable because of the presence of Colonel CARY, who had known her when she was a "party girl" whom businessmen hired to entertain clients; she becomes unnecessarily defensive about being an actress and is rude to Mrs. IVES. As a result George decides to end their relationship, but when he sees her crying he returns to her.

Fitzgerald wrote this story as "Home to Maryland" after he returned to Europe from his father's funeral in ROCKVILLE, Maryland. It was declined by seven magazines—which hadn't happened since his apprentice days. He recycled some of Evelyn's reaction to her father's funeral for Dick DIVER in *TITN*.

"One Hundred False Starts" Essay. *The SATURDAY EVENING POST*, 205 (March 4, 1933), 13, 65–66; *AOAA*. Discussion of discarded story ideas, with an analysis of Fitzgerald's necessity for emotional involvement with his material: "Mostly, we authors must repeat ourselves—that's the truth. We have two or three great and moving experiences in our lives—experiences so great and moving that it doesn't seem at the time that anyone else has been so caught up and pounded and dazzled and astonished and beaten and broken and rescued and illuminated and rewarded and humbled

in just that way ever before. Then we learn our trade, well or less well, and we tell our two or three stories—each time in a new disguise—maybe ten times, maybe a hundred, as long as people will listen" (*AOAA*, p. 132).

"One Interne" Fiction. Written August 1932. *The SAT-URDAY EVENING POST*, 205 (November 5, 1932), 6–7, 86, 88–90; *TAR*. Bill TULLIVER begins his medical internship and falls in love with Doctor Howard DUR-FEE's girlfriend, Thea SINGLETON. When Durfee announces his engagement to debutante Helen DAY, Thea explains to Bill that she had once been engaged to John GRESHAM, who had died from his own medical experiments, and that her continued love for him prevented her from loving Durfee. While examining a patient, Bill collapses with stomach pain; he protests violently when his former classmate George SCHOATZE examines him. Thea convinces Bill to submit to an operation, which heals him.

"One of My Oldest Friends" Fiction. Written March 1924. *WOMAN'S HOME COMPANION*, 52 (September 1925), 7–8, 120, 122; *The Price Was High*. MICHAEL and MARION plan a party for Charley HART, one of their oldest friends, who is planning to get married. When he tells them he is sick and can't come to the party, they drop in at his apartment and discover that he is throwing a large party himself. When they return home Marion reveals to Michael that Charley was in love with her and wished Michael out of the way. When, after some time, Charley asks Michael for $2,000 to help him out of a difficulty that could land him in jail, Michael refuses. After Charley leaves, threatening suicide, Michael regrets his own lack of mercy and follows Charley into the night, preventing him from throwing himself in front of a train.

"One Trip Abroad" Fiction. Written August 1930. *The SATURDAY EVENING POST*, 203 (October 11, 1930), 6–7, 48, 51, 53–54, 56; *AOAA*. When Nelson KELLY inherits half a million dollars, he and his wife of eight months, Nicole KELLY, travel abroad for him to paint and her to study singing. Over the next four years they gradually deteriorate as they travel through NORTH AFRICA, ITALY, Monte Carlo, and PARIS; and they occasionally notice a vaguely familiar young couple who are also growing more dissipated. The Kellys, who have lost "peace and love and health, one after the other," end up in SWIT-ZERLAND, "a country where very few things begin, but many things end" (*AOAA*, pp. 164 & 161). As they resolve to try to renew their lives together, they realize that the young couple are themselves.

"One Trip Abroad" has close ties to *TITN*, and Fitzgerald revised passages from the story for the novel.

O'Neill (Wilson), Rose Cecil (1875–1944) Celebrated primarily as the creator of the Kewpie doll, O'Neill illustrated "The Baby Party" (February 1925) for HEARST'S INTERNATIONAL. O'Neill's depiction of John ANDROS bears a strong resemblance to Fitzgerald.

"Open That Door" In July or August 1939 Fitzgerald worked for Universal for one week, preparing a treatment for the 1937 novel *Bull by the Horns* by Charles Bonner (1896–1965); but the movie was not made.

Oral, Mrs. Character in "The Popular Girl." Woman who handles arrangements for Tom BOWMAN's funeral.

"The Ordeal" Fiction. *The NASSAU LITERARY MAGAZINE*, 71 (June 1915), 153–159; *Apprentice Fiction*; incorporated into "Benediction." In the hour before taking his first vows, a JESUIT NOVICE contemplates his vocation and what he is giving up to enter the priesthood. Then, during the service in the chapel, he senses an overpowering presence of evil in a candle flame but stands firm against the spiritual attack until the candle goes out. This story, which grew out of Fitzgerald's 1912 visit to his cousin Thomas DELIHANT at the Jesuit seminary in Woodstock, Maryland, expresses Fitzgerald's awareness of evil as a supernatural force.

Ordway, Katherine One of Fitzgerald's childhood friends in ST. PAUL. At the end of *The Great Gatsby*, Nick CARRAWAY recalls Christmas vacations and "the matching of invitations: 'Are you going to the Ordways'? the Herseys'? the Schultzes'?'" (p. 136).

"The Original Follies Girl" Fiction by Zelda FITZGERALD. *COLLEGE HUMOR*, 17 (July 1929), 40–41, 110; *Bits of Paradise*; *Zelda Fitzgerald: The Collected Writings*. Bylined "Zelda and F. Scott Fitzgerald" but credited to Zelda in *Ledger*. Gay, an actress and "an adventuress of a quiet order" (*Collected Writings*, p. 294), wanders about from NEW YORK to LONDON, Biarritz, and PARIS, where she dies in childbirth.

Ormonde, Otis Character in "Bernice Bobs Her Hair." Boy who is stuck with BERNICE at a dance but is later smitten with her and who inadvertently precipitates the bobbing of her hair.

Ormsby, Captain, U.S.A. Character in *Coward*. Union officer who takes Charley DOUGLAS prisoner.

O'Rourke, Jerry Character in "The Popular Girl." Young man whose marriage proposal Yanci BOWMAN rejects.

O'Sullivan, Eddie Character in "On Your Own." Actor who is in the same show as Evelyn LOVEJOY.

"Other Names for Roses" Fiction by Zelda FITZGERALD. *Zelda Fitzgerald: The Collected Writings*. Jayce and Fedora Jones move to southern France when Jayce tires of living on his wife's family's money. Jayce becomes involved with ballerina Belanova, and Fedora becomes involved with poet Tillyium. When Jayce tires of Belanova and learns that she is married to Tillyium, he returns to Fedora.

Otis Character in *B&D*. An usher at Anthony and Gloria PATCH's wedding.

"Our American Poets" Verse parodies. *The PRINCETON TIGER*, 28 (November 10, 1917), 11; *In His Own Time*; *Poems*. Parodies of Robert W. Service (1874–1958) and Robert Frost (1874–1963).

"Our April Letter" Verse. *Notebooks* #885; *Poems*. Includes Fitzgerald's analysis of his short stories: "I have asked a lot of my emotions—one hundred and twenty stories. The price was high, right up with Kipling, because there was one little drop of something not blood, not a tear, not my seed, but me more intimately than these, in every story, it was the extra I had. Now it is gone and I am just like you now" (*Poems*, p. 114).

"Our Next Issue" Prose parody. *The NASSAU LITERARY MAGAZINE*, 72 (December 1916), unpaged; *In His Own Time*. Unsigned—attributed to Fitzgerald on the basis of a clipping in the Fitzgerald Papers at PRINCETON UNIVERSITY LIBRARY. Humorous list of forthcoming articles in "Chaopolitan," a burlesque of COSMOPOLITAN.

"Our Own Movie Queen" Fiction by Zelda FITZGERALD. Written November 1923. *Chicago Sunday Tribune*, June 7, 1925, magazine section, pp. 1–4; *Bits of Paradise*; *Zelda Fitzgerald: The Collected Writings*. Published as by F. Scott Fitzgerald, but he noted in his *Ledger*: "Two thirds written by Zelda. Only my climax and revision" and elsewhere "half mine" (pp. 7 & 143). Twenty-year-old Gracie Axelrod and her father sell fried chicken and beer in a shanty on the unfashionable side of the river until Gracie takes a job at the Blue Ribbon department store and is chosen Grand Popularity Queen. She is disappointed when her promised leading role in a movie about her hometown turns out to be insignificant. Assistant director Joe Murphy, who is in love with her, offers her a chance to get back at Mr. Blue Ribbon because the director, Decourcey O'Ney, is angry that he wasn't paid what he had been promised. They reshoot and re-edit the film between the preliminary showing and the first public performance; and the completed movie features Gracie prominently and attacks the Blue Ribbon store. O'Ney is temporarily

committed to an asylum; Gracie marries Murphy, and they operate a profitable restaurant.

"Our Young Rich Boys" Article. MCCALL'S, 53 (October 1925), 12, 42, 69; *In His Own Time*. Published with Zelda FITZGERALD's "What Became of the Flappers?" under the joint title "What Becomes of Our Flappers and Sheiks?" Copyrighted as "The Little Brother of the Flapper." Fitzgerald traces the circumstances that cause America's young rich boys to grow up "perfectly useless," assuming "all the privileges of aristocracy without any of its responsibilities" (*In His Own Time,* p. 205).

"Outside the Cabinet-Maker's" Fiction. Written c. December 1927. *The Century Magazine,* 117 (December 1928), 241–244; *AOAA.* While his wife is delivering doll-house plans to the cabinet-maker, DADDY tells his LITTLE GIRL a story of a fairy princess held captive by an ogre. Fitzgerald was undecided as to whether to classify this piece as nonfiction or a story.

Owens, Isabel Fitzgerald's first full-time secretary, whom he hired in 1932 while living at "LA PAIX" and working on *TITN.* She also looked after Scottie FITZGERALD while Zelda FITZGERALD was hospitalized and served as companion to Zelda after her release from PHIPPS CLINIC. See John F. Kelly, "Memories of Scott and Zelda," *Pittsburgh Press Roto* (February 6, 1983), 16, 18.

Owl Eyes Character in *GG.* Drunken, bespectacled, stout guest whom Nick CARRAWAY and Jordan BAKER encounter in the library at Jay GATSBY's party and who is later in a car accident. He is the only former party guest to attend Gatsby's funeral, and he delivers the eulogy "The poor son-of-a-bitch" (p. 136). A connection has been suggested between this character and Ring LARDNER, who was called "Owl Eyes" when he was a sportswriter; but Lardner did not wear glasses and was not stout.

Rose O'Neill's illustration for "The Baby Party"; the father resembles Fitzgerald.

P

Packman, George Character in "The Bridal Party." Friend who hosts a party for Hamilton RUTHERFORD and Caroline DANDY.

Page, Clara Character in *TSOP*. Amory BLAINE's widowed third cousin, the mother of two young children. Amory finds her delightful and admirable and briefly thinks of marrying her. Based on Fitzgerald's cousin Cecilia Delihant TAYLOR.

Page, Howard Character in the Josephine PERRY stories. In "First Blood" he goes for a car ride with Lillian HAMMEL, Travis DE COPPET, and Josephine Perry. In "A Snobbish Story" he is at the PERRYS' house when John Boynton BAILEY joins them for lunch.

"Pain and the Scientist" Fiction. *The NEWMAN NEWS* (1913), 5–10; *Apprentice Fiction*. Walter Hamilton BARTNEY injures his ankle on his way to meet his neighbor, Dr. Hepezia SKIGGS, a Christian Scientist, who refuses to help him but charges him $3.00 for "treating" him by telling him he feels no pain. Bartney later catches Skiggs picking flowers on his property; Bartney shakes him violently, forces him to say he feels no pain, and makes Skiggs pay him $2.00.

"Paint and Powder" Article by Zelda FITZGERALD. *The SMART SET*, 84 (May 1929), 68; *Zelda Fitzgerald: The Collected Writings*. Bylined "F. Scott Fitzgerald" only, but written by Zelda in 1927 as "Editorial on Youth" for *Photoplay*, which did not publish it; credited to Zelda in *Ledger*. Argument that paint and powder stand for the desire of women "to choose their destinies—to be successful competitors in the great game of life" (*Collected Writings*, p. 416).

Palmer, Clothilde Sayre *See* Clothilde SAYRE.

Palmer, Fats Character in "That Kind of Party." Messenger boy who provides a blank telegram for Terrence R. TIPTON and Joe SHOONOVER to use to lure Joe's mother out of town during their party. Fats refuses to deliver a forged telegram himself, but he gets his sister to do the job. She mistakenly delivers it to Terrence's mother rather than Joe's.

Pan-e-troon Character in "The Passionate Eskimo." Eskimo from Lapland who is in Chicago for the World's Fair and who prevents the theft of a valuable tiara from the home of Edith CARY.

Paramore, E. E. (Ted) (1895?–1956) Screenwriter, best known for "The Ballad of Yukon Jake," a parody of the poems of Robert W. Service (1874–1958). Fitzgerald knew Paramore, who was a friend of Edmund WILSON's, in 1920 and caricatured him as Frederick E. PARAMORE in *B&D*. In 1937 PARAMORE was assigned to collaborate with Fitzgerald on *Three Comrades*. Fitzgerald, who had asked to continue working on the project alone, resented Paramore's assumption of equal authority and argued with him over control of the screenplay. Fitzgerald and Paramore shared screen credit for the movie.

Paramore, Frederick E. Character in *B&D*. Anthony PATCH's Harvard classmate, a social worker who gets drunk at the party which Anthony's grandfather, Adam PATCH, interrupts. A caricature of E. E. PARAMORE.

Paris, France The Fitzgeralds visited Paris in May 1921 during their first trip to EUROPE. During their longer second European trip they visited Paris in May 1924 before settling on the RIVIERA. In late April 1925 they returned to Paris, living in an apartment at 14 rue de Tilsitt on the Right Bank near the Arc de Triomphe; and Fitzgerald met Ernest HEMINGWAY in the Dingo Bar in Montparnasse in May. The Fitzgeralds went out almost nightly to various Paris cafés and cabarets. Fitzgerald completed "The Rich Boy," which he had begun in CAPRI, and began planning *TITN*. In August they left Paris for a month at CAP D'ANTIBES with Gerald and Sara MURPHY, returning to Paris in September. They visited LONDON in November and left Paris in January 1926. They returned to Paris in April 1928, renting an apartment at 58 rue de Vaugirard on the Left Bank. Zelda began studying ballet with Lubov EGOROVA, and Fitzgerald wrote the Basil Duke LEE stories for *The SATURDAY EVENING POST*. They returned to America on October 7, 1928. They made their fourth trip to Europe in March 1929, settling in Paris in April

The Fitzgeralds in Paris, Christmas 1925

in an apartment on the rue Mézières near St. Sulpice until June, when they moved to the Riviera. In October they returned to Paris, renting an apartment at 10 rue Pergolèse near the Bois de Boulogne. Fitzgerald made no significant progress on *TITN*, and he resented Zelda's obsession with ballet. They visited NORTH AFRICA in February 1930. Back in Paris, Zelda suffered her first breakdown and entered MALMAISON CLINIC on April 23; she discharged herself from Malmaison on May 11 and entered VAL-MONT CLINIC in GLION, SWITZERLAND on May 22, and was transferred to PRANGINS CLINIC at NYON, Switzerland on June 5. Fitzgerald commuted between Paris and Switzerland that summer and settled in LAUSANNE in the fall. After traveling to America in January-February 1931 for his father's funeral, Fitzgerald returned to Europe, dividing his time between Paris and Switzerland until he and Zelda returned to America after her September 15 release from Prangins.

Parke Character in *GG*. Young man who was caught handling stolen securities. SLAGLE's report of this event reveals one aspect of Jay GATSBY's illegal activities.

Parker, Dorothy (1893–1967) American dramatic and literary critic and writer; friend of Fitzgerald. Fitzgerald saw Parker in 1926 in France, in January and February 1934 while in NEW YORK to work on the proofs for *TITN*, and in 1937 in HOLLYWOOD. In 1933 she praised his tribute to Ring LARDNER: "I think your piece about Ring is the finest + most moving thing I have ever read" (after October 11, 1933; *Correspondence*, p. 318); and she once noted that although he could write a bad story, Fitzgerald could not write badly. He was her guest at the July 22, 1937 Screen Writers Guild dinner dance where he saw Sheilah GRAHAM for the second time. In 1945 Parker edited *The Portable F. Scott Fitzgerald*, for which she asked John O'HARA to write the introduction.

See Marion Meade, *Dorothy Parker: What Fresh Hell Is This?* (New York: Villard, 1988).

Parker, Froggy Character in *TSOP*. A friend of young Amory BLAINE in Minneapolis who later attends Harvard. He is fascinated by Isabelle BORGÉ, but she is interested only in Amory.

Parkhurst, Perry Character in "The Camel's Back." Lawyer who unsuccessfully presses Betty MEDILL to marry him, then marries her while disguised as a camel at a costume party.

Parks, Allen Character in "More Than Just a House." Man with whom Lew LOWRIE overhears Jean GUNTHER talking about going to NEW YORK.

Parmelee, Eddie Character in "Forging Ahead." He helps Basil Duke LEE get a job at the railroad. Basil pays him $10 to go to Rhoda SINCLAIR's party in Basil's place, but Eddie sends Mr. UTSONOMIA instead.

Parrish, John Hardwick Character in "The Third Casket." One of three young men competing to take over Cyrus GIRARD's business when he retires.

Parrott, Stephan ("Peevie") NEWMAN SCHOOL student with whom Fitzgerald was close because of their mutual mentor, Father FAY. Parrott was a partial model for Stephen Palms, the first-person hero of "The Romantic Egotist," an early version of *TSOP*. Fitzgerald sent him a carbon copy of the novel, and Parrott responded in an April 1919 letter (*Correspondence*, pp. 41–42). Fitzgerald visited Parrott in Boston in June 1919 after Zelda Sayre [FITZGERALD] broke their engagement. A break occurred in Fitzgerald and Parrott's friendship while they were both in France in 1925; it was never mended, although Fitzgerald had inscribed a portrait of himself to Parrott "from his brother" some time after 1920 (*Correspondence*, p. 64). Parrott lived most of his mature years abroad.

Paskert Character in *TSOP*. ST. REGIS student with whom Amory BLAINE attends a play in NEW YORK.

"The Passionate Eskimo" Fiction. Written February 1935. *LIBERTY*, 12 (June 8, 1935), 10–14, 17–18. PAN-E-TROON, an Eskimo who is at the World's Fair, explores Chicago on his last day before returning to Lapland; he purchases tobacco for his father and a lock for himself. On a whim, beautiful Edith CARY invites him to her house. Another guest, World's Fair executive Humphrey DEERING, is concerned about the possible theft of a tiara, formerly the property of Elizabeth the Second, which Edith's father had lent to the fair. Pan-e-troon suspects both Deering and another guest, Edith's former suitor WESTGATE, of planning to steal the tiara, so he locks them in their rooms for the night. During the night Pan-e-troon catches the Carys' butler, CHRISTOPHER, attempting to steal the tiara, which Pan-e-troon retrieves and restores to Edith in the morning.

"Pasting It Together" Autobiographical essay. *ESQUIRE*, 5 (March 1936), 35, 182–183; *CU*. Sequel to "The Crack-Up." Exploration of the factors that contributed to Fitzgerald's crack-up, including his dropping out of PRINCETON due to illness and the difficulty which his lack of money imposed on his courtship of Zelda Sayre [FITZGERALD]—a situation that left him with "an abiding distrust" of the rich. He confesses that he had done "very little thinking, save within the problems of my craft" and attributes to five friends his intellectual, artistic, and political conscience; his sense of the good life; and his social relations. He concludes: "So there was not an 'I' any more—not a basis on which I could organize my self-respect—save my limitless capacity for toil that it seemed I possessed no more. It was strange to have no self . . ." (*CU*, p. 79).

The titles of "Pasting It Together" and "Handle with Care" were transposed in the early printings of *CU*.

"Pat Hobby and Orson Welles" Fiction. Submitted February 6, 1940. *ESQUIRE*, 13 (May 1940), 38, 198–199; *PH*. Pat HOBBY has trouble getting into the movie studio, and he begins to think of actor-director Orson Welles (1915–85) as being responsible for edging him out. People inexplicably begin to address him as "Orson," although the resemblance is faint. Jeff BOLDINI makes up Pat with a beard like Welles and drives him to the studio, placing a sign bearing Welles's name in the car window. Pat, who is unaware of the sign, doesn't understand the crowds staring at him. He flees to a bar where he buys a drink for every bearded man.

"Pat Hobby Does His Bit" Fiction. Submitted March 18, 1940. *ESQUIRE*, 14 (September 1940), 41, 104; *PH*. While in a studio, attempting to borrow money from Gyp MCCARTHY, Pat HOBBY is inadvertently filmed in a scene with Lily KEATTS, who leaves for England immediately after the shooting. Because Pat is in the scene with Keatts, producer Jack BERNERS requires him to play a bit part in some related shots, including one in which he is to be run over by a car. Pat wakes up alone on the ground and is unable to get up because of the protective metal doublet he is wearing. He is discovered by a POLICEMAN, who explains that Pat must have been forgotten in the excitement when the star broke his leg. Despite his rage, Pat feels pride in having once again saved a movie.

"Pat Hobby, Putative Father" Fiction. Submitted November 13, 1939. *ESQUIRE*, 14 (July 1940), 36, 172–174; *PH*. Producer Jack BERNERS asks Pat HOBBY to give a tour of the studio lot to Sir Singrim Dak RAJ and John Brown Hobby INDORE, Pat's putative son, who was born to Pat's ex-wife Delia BROWN when she was married to Pat. In an attempt to give John a chance to see actress Bonita GRANVILLE, Pat inadvertently interferes with the shooting of a movie. John later tells Pat that he and his uncle have decided to give him 50 sovereigns ($250) a month for the rest of his life, except in case of war. The next morning Pat reads that England has declared war (the beginning of World War II).

The Pat Hobby Stories Story collection. New York: Charles SCRIBNER's Sons, 1962; Harmondsworth, U.K.: Penguin, 1967. Contents: Introduction by Arnold GINGRICH; "Pat Hobby's Christmas Wish," "A Man in the Way," " 'Boil Some Water—Lots of It,' " "Teamed with Genius," "Pat Hobby and Orson Welles," "Pat Hobby's Secret," "Pat Hobby, Putative Father," "The Homes of the Stars," "Pat Hobby Does His Bit," "Pat Hobby's Preview," "No Harm Trying," "A Patriotic Short," "On the Trail of Pat Hobby," "Fun in an Artist's Studio," "Two Old-Timers," "Mightier than the Sword," "Pat Hobby's College Days"; Appendix: Fitzgerald's revision of "A Patriotic Short."

These stories were originally published in 17 consecutive issues of *ESQUIRE*, January 1940 through May 1941. Fitzgerald revised them and altered the order in which he wished them to be published.

"Pat Hobby's Christmas Wish" Fiction. Submitted October 14, 1939. *ESQUIRE*, 13 (January 1940), 45, 170–172; *PH*. Pat HOBBY's new secretary, Helen KAGLE, tells him of a letter which she believes indicates that studio executive Harry GOODDORF killed director William Desmond Taylor (1877–1922) 18 years before in a famous unsolved HOLLYWOOD crime. Hobby attempts to blackmail Gooddorf into making him a producer—his Christmas wish. Gooddorf explains that the letter was not a murder confession and agrees not to tell anyone about the blackmail attempt.

"Pat Hobby's College Days" Fiction. Submitted November 8, 1939. *ESQUIRE*, 15 (May 1941), 55, 168–169; *PH*. Studio bookie Louie GRIEBEL tells Pat HOBBY that Jack BERNERS wants to make a movie about U.W.C. (University of the Western Coast). Pat meets Athletic Superintendent Kit DOOLAN, who takes him to a Faculty Committee meeting to pitch his idea, based on the disciplinary case they are discussing. Dean Samuel K. WISKITH is appalled by the suggestion. A proctor brings in Evylyn LASCALLES, Pat's secretary, who has been caught with a pillowcase full of Pat's empty liquor bottles, which she has been trying to dispose of. Pat leaves with the bottles and tells the committee to think over his idea.

"Pat Hobby's Preview" Fiction. Submitted October 14, 1939. *ESQUIRE*, 14 (October 1940), 30, 118, 120; *PH*. Pat HOBBY asks producer Jack BERNERS for tickets to the preview of a movie for which he is sharing credit with Ward WAINWRIGHT. Berners tells Pat that he may have to take Pat's name off the picture when it is released because Wainwright is angry that Pat, who made only slight revisions, is sharing his screen credit. When Pat goes to Berners' office to pick up his tickets, the secretary tells Pat that the tickets she is giving him belonged to Wainwright, who was so angry that he wouldn't go to the preview. When Pat and his date, Eleanor CARTER, a cute blonde tourist, arrive at the preview, she is flattered by the attention of the crowd, who think she is a movie star. The doorman refuses to let Pat enter, telling him his tickets are for a burlesque show. Ward Wainwright storms out of the theater and gives Pat his ticket stubs, saying he doesn't want his name on the picture.

"Pat Hobby's Secret" Fiction. Submitted March 9, 1940. *ESQUIRE*, 13 (June 1940), 30, 107; *PH*. Producer BANIZON has forgotten the movie ending told to him by writer R. Parke WOLL, who now refuses to talk unless offered an eight-week contract. Banizon pays Pat HOBBY to find out the ending; Pat tracks down Woll in a bar, where Pat tricks him into revealing the idea. While trying to hit Pat, Woll inadvertently hits Mr. SMITH, the bouncer, who kills him. Pat hires an agent and asks Banizon for $3,000 to reveal the idea. When Banizon agrees to pay him $1,000 to see if he really knows, Pat has forgotten the idea.

Patch, Adam J. Character in *B&D*. Anthony PATCH's millionaire grandfather, a reformer known as "Cross Patch," from whom Anthony expects to inherit a fortune. He disinherits Anthony after unexpectedly interrupting a drunken party at Anthony's house. After Patch's death Anthony hires a lawyer to break the will; but by the time he wins the case on the second appeal, Anthony is a broken man.

Patch, Adam Ulysses Character in *B&D*. Anthony PATCH's father, who dies when Anthony is 11 years old.

Patch, Alicia Withers Character in *B&D*. Anthony PATCH's grandmother, who dies by the time he is 11.

Patch, Anthony Comstock Character in *B&D*. After the death of his mother, Henrietta Lebrune PATCH, when he is five, Anthony and his father, Adam Ulysses PATCH, live with his grandfather, Adam J. PATCH; his father dies when Anthony is 11. From ages 14 through 16 Anthony travels in EUROPE with a private tutor. He then enters Harvard, where he is something of a loner until his senior year, when he begins going out and drinking quietly. In 1912 he returns from a trip to ROME because of his grandfather's illness and settles in an apartment in NEW YORK. He marries beautiful Gloria Gilbert [PATCH], and they live a life of leisure and wild parties, expecting to become wealthy when his grandfather dies. As they gradually sell bonds to finance their lifestyle they become poorer and poorer, yet Anthony makes only brief efforts to earn a living. He is disinherited after his grandfather unexpectedly interrupts a drunken party at his house, and Anthony hires a lawyer to break the will. As he awaits the settlement of the case, he continues to spend money recklessly and drinks more and more. When America declares war on Germany, Anthony is drafted and sent to CAMP HOOKER in South Carolina, where he has an affair with Dot RAYCROFT, a lower-class girl. The war ends before he is sent overseas, and he and Gloria are reunited, but their relationship is empty. They become poorer and poorer, and Anthony, who has resigned from all his old clubs and now frequents a speakeasy called Sammy's, is drunk every day and hates to be sober. By the time the trial is settled in his favor on the second appeal, he is broken in body and mind. He and Gloria sail to Europe, and ironically he rejoices that he had refused to "submit to mediocrity" despite the urging of his friends that he go to work: "I showed them. . . . It was a hard fight, but I didn't give up and I came through!" (p. 449).

Patch, Gloria Gilbert Character in *B&D*. A beautiful Kansas City girl who marries Anthony PATCH and contributes to his decline by their extravagant lifestyle. "She had been, probably, the most celebrated and sought-after beauty in the country" (p. 81), but her beauty fades as she grows older: "She was being bent by her environment into a grotesque similitude of a housewife" (p. 424). Fitzgerald used bits of Zelda FITZGERALD's diary for Gloria's diary. Years after the publication of the novel Fitzgerald wrote to his daughter, Scottie FITZGERALD, about the relationship between Gloria and Zelda: "Gloria was a much more trivial and vulgar person than your mother. I can't really say there

was any resemblance except in the beauty and certain terms of expression she used, and also I naturally used many circumstantial events of our early married life. However the emphases were entirely different. We had a much better time than Anthony and Gloria had" (June 14, 1940; *Life in Letters,* p. 453).

Patch, Henrietta Lebrune Character in *B&D*. Anthony PATCH's mother, "the Boston Society Contralto," who dies when he is five years old.

Paterson, Director Character in " 'Boil Some Water—Lots of It.' " Walter HERRICK, dressed as a Cossack, sits down next to Paterson at the Big Table in the studio commissary.

"A Patriotic Short" Fiction—Pat HOBBY story. Submitted January 8, 1940. *ESQUIRE,* 14 (December 1940), 62, 269; *Stories; PH*. Producer Jack BERNERS hires Pat Hobby to work on a short picture called *True to Two Flags* about General Fitzhugh Lee (1835–1905), a Confederate officer who later fought for the United States against Spain. Pat's mind keeps drifting back to the time many years ago when the President of the United States had visited the studio. Pat had attended a luncheon for the President, who had later remarked on Pat's swimming pool, now a symbol to Pat of his lost success. Hurt by his present failure and lack of respect, Pat revises the movie script so that Lee rejects the United States commission offered to him by President William McKinley (1843–1901).

Patt, Larry Character in "Six of One—". Golfer who drops out of college and opens a chain of sporting-goods stores.

Patton, Roger Character in "The Ice Palace." University professor who befriends Sally Carrol HAPPER during her visit to the North.

Paul Character in "Babylon Revisited." Head barman at the RITZ in PARIS.

Paul Character in *TITN*. Concessionnaire at the RITZ BAR who talks with Abe NORTH.

Paulson, Charley Character in "Bernice Bobs Her Hair." Young man sitting next to BERNICE at the dinner party during which she first announces that she plans to bob her hair.

Paulson, Charlie Character in "Head and Shoulders." Horace TARBOX's agent for his gymnastic performances.

Paxton, Speed Character in "A Night at the Fair." Basil Duke LEE and Riply BUCKNER see this wild young man drive away with a blonde in a red sportscar. Their envy of him leads them to pursue the companionship of Elwood LEAMING.

Payson, Mr. Character in "No Flowers." Phil SAVAGE's friend, who asks him to leave college after he is caught cheating on an examination.

Pechard, Paul Character in "The Intimate Strangers." Man who marries MARGOT and whom SARA had nursed during the war.

"A Penny Spent" Fiction. Written July 1925. *The SATURDAY EVENING POST,* 198 (October 10, 1925), 8–9, 160, 164, 166; *Bits of Paradise*. Ohio manufacturer Julius BUSHMILL hires destitute "incurable spendthrift" CORCORAN, whom he meets in a PARIS bar, to guide his wife and daughter, Hallie BUSHMILL, on a month-long tour of Belgium and Holland on their way to meet Hallie's fiancé, Claude NOSBY. Julius Bushmill presents the job as an opportunity for Corcoran to learn to spend money responsibly and requires him to keep a record of all his expenditures. When Hallie expresses boredom with the inexpensive, historically informative excursions Corcoran plans, he resolves to show her that he knows how to entertain; and he spends money lavishly to provide her with a whirlwind of activities with socially prominent people. Mr. Bushmill rebukes Corcoran for his spending but, at Hallie's insistence, consents to allow him to guide them and Nosby through ITALY as well. In Italy Corcoran keeps Hallie, Mrs. Bushmill, and Nosby from being captured by bandits by throwing money in the air for the bandits to chase. He and Hallie are married, and he works in his father-in-law's purchasing department.

Pepin, Mrs. George Character in "The Rubber Check." Val SCHUYLER's mother, who has just married her fourth husband.

Percy Character in "The Unspeakable Egg." Josephine and Cal MARSDEN's yard man.

Perelman, S. J. (1904–1979) American humorist and screenwriter whose small parties Fitzgerald and Sheilah GRAHAM enjoyed in HOLLYWOOD and from whom Fitzgerald purchased a 1937 Ford convertible.
 See Dorothy Herrmann, *S. J. Perelman: A Life* (New York: Putnam, 1986).

"The Perfect Life" Fiction—Basil Duke LEE story. Written October 1928. *The SATURDAY EVENING POST,* 201 (January 5, 1929), 8–9, 113, 115, 118; *TAR; B&J*. After Basil Duke Lee, age 16, plays well in a ST. REGIS football game, alumnus John GRANBY urges him to try to lead a perfect life and to exert a positive influence on his schoolmates. While visiting George DORSEY, Basil

tries to reform George's sister, Jobena DORSEY; but she is so offended by Basil's priggishness that she agrees to elope with Skiddy DE VINCI, a hard-drinking young man to whom she had once been engaged. When Basil overhears Jobena describing him as "a nasty little prig," he abandons his attempt at perfection and stops her elopement by getting Skiddy drunk.

Perkins, Maxwell (**1884–1947**) Editor at Charles SCRIBNER'S Sons whose authors included Fitzgerald, Ernest HEMINGWAY, Ring LARDNER, and Thomas WOLFE. Scribners rejected Fitzgerald's novel, "The Romantic Egotist," on August 19, 1918 in a long letter signed "Charles Scribner's Sons" but probably written by Perkins, who wanted to publish the novel but was overruled by senior editors; the letter suggested changes and invited Fitzgerald to resubmit after revision (*The Romantic Egoists,* p. 34). Perkins rejected the revised novel in an October telegram which Fitzgerald captioned "The end of a dream" in his scrapbook (*The Romantic Egoists,* p. 35). On July 26, 1919 Fitzgerald wrote to Perkins that he had completed the first draft of a novel called "The Education of a Personage" (*Life in Letters,* p. 28; *Scott/Max,* p. 17); and on August 16 he informed Perkins of the new title, *This Side of Paradise* (*Life in Letters,* p. 30; *Scott/Max,* p. 18). On September 4 Fitzgerald sent the typescript to NEW YORK with a friend, Thomas Daniels. At the Scribners editorial meeting, only Perkins was in favor of publishing Fitzgerald's novel. Charles SCRIBNER initially refused to put his name on a book he felt lacked literary merit, and senior editor William C. Brownell (1851–1928) found the material frivolous. Perkins in effect threatened to resign: "My feeling is that a publisher's first allegiance is to talent. And if we aren't going to publish a talent like this, it is a very serious thing. . . . If we're going to turn down the likes of Fitzgerald, I will lose all interest in publishing books" (A. Scott Berg, *Max Perkins, Editor of Genius,* pp. 15–16). Scribner reconsidered, and Perkins accepted the novel on September 16:

> I am very glad, personally, to be able to write you that we are all for publishing your book, "This Side of Paradise". Viewing it as the same book that was here before, which in a sense it is, though translated into somewhat different terms and extended further, I think that you have improved it enormously. As the first manuscript did, it abounds in energy and life and it seems to me to be in much better proportion. I was afraid that, when we declined the first manuscript, you might be done with us conservatives. I am glad you are not. The book is so different that it is hard to prophesy how it will sell but we are all for taking a chance and supporting it with vigor (*Scott/Max,* p. 21).

Perkins's editorial method is indicated by his disagreement with Fitzgerald over Maury NOBLE's depiction of the Bible in *B&D* in a manner which Perkins thought would be unnecessarily offensive to readers (December 6, 1924; *Scott/Max,* p. 45). Fitzgerald was upset by his objection and responded with an emotional letter suggesting Perkins was intimidated by possible opposition and invoking George Bernard Shaw (1856–1950), Anatole FRANCE, and Mark TWAIN (c. December 10, 1921; *Scott/Max,* pp. 46–47). Perkins replied on December 12: "Don't ever *defer* to my judgment. You won't on any vital point, I know, and I should be ashamed, if it were possible to have made you; for a writer of any account must speak for himself." Yet he urged Fitzgerald to realize that he would "impair the effectiveness of the passage" by making it flippant and contemptuous (*Scott/Max,* pp. 47–48). Fitzgerald apologized, admitting to flippancy and noting several revisions which he had made (c. December 16, 1921; *Scott/Max,* p. 49); and the revised version was printed in the novel. *B&D* is dedicated "TO SHANE LESLIE, GEORGE JEAN NATHAN AND MAXWELL PERKINS IN APPRECIATION OF MUCH LITERARY HELP AND ENCOURAGEMENT."

On November 20, 1924 Perkins sent Fitzgerald a detailed response to the typescript of *GG*, suggesting that Jay GATSBY and the source of his wealth be made less vague and that some of his biography be presented bit by bit in the course of the narrative rather than in one long section. He also offered praise for Fitzgerald's achievement:

> The presentation of Tom, his place, Daisy and Jordan, and the unfolding of their characters is unequalled so far as I know. The description of the valley of ashes adjacent to the lovely country, the conversation and the action in Myrtle's apartment, the marvelous catalogue of those who came to Gatsby's house,-these are such things as make a man famous. And all these things, the whole pathetic episode, you have given a place in time and space, for with the help of T. J. Eckleberg and by an occasional glance at the sky, or the sea, or the city, you have imparted a sort of sense of eternity. You once told me you were not a *natural* writer—my God! You have plainly mastered the craft, of course; but you needed far more than craftsmanship for this" (*Scott/Max,* p. 84).

Perkins's advice was in accord with the existing narrative structure of the novel; but Fitzgerald, who followed his suggestions in revising and rewriting the novel in galley proofs, gave him generous credit after the publication of *GG:* "Max, it amuses me when praise comes in on the 'structure' of the book—because it was you who fixed up the structure, not me" (c. July 10, 1925; *Scott/Max,* pp. 117–118). Years later Perkins told Fitzgerald that *GG* "was as perfect a thing as I ever had any share in publishing.-One does not seem to get such satisfactions as that any more" (March 9, 1938; *Scott/Max,* p. 242).

Fitzgerald became discouraged over his lack of progress with the novel that would become *Tender Is the Night*. Around January 15, 1932 he wrote to Perkins that he was planning to spend five consecutive months on the novel: "Don't tell Ernest or anyone—let them think what they want—you're the only one whose ever consistently felt faith in me anyhow" (*Life in Letters*, p. 208; *Scott/Max*, p. 173). Perkins never lost confidence in Fitzgerald and sought to encourage him, writing in 1933: "Whenever any of these new writers come up who are brilliant, I always realize that you have more talent and more skill than any of them;- but circumstances have prevented you from realizing upon the fact for a long time" (August 4, 1933; *Scott/Max*, p. 180).

Fitzgerald's series of confessional "Crack-Up" articles in *ESQUIRE* attracted wide attention, and in March 1936 Simon & Schuster expressed interest in publishing a collection of Fitzgerald's autobiographical articles. Fitzgerald wrote to Perkins offering Scribners the first opportunity to publish such a volume (March 25, 1936; *Scott/Max*, pp. 227–228). Perkins, who found the "Crack-Up" articles embarrassing, suggested that Fitzgerald write "a reminiscent book" instead (March 26, 1936;*Scott/Max*, p. 228). Fitzgerald responded that he didn't have time to rewrite the material for a new book and proposed a collection of 15 articles plus the "Crack-Up" series (April 2, 1936; *Scott/Max*, pp. 228–230). Perkins believed such a collection would preempt a reminiscent book; and after Gilbert SELDES wrote to Fitzgerald in June opposing the plan—probably at Perkins's request—the project was dropped.

Although Perkins wrote Fitzgerald in October 1934 that Scribners would no longer be able to advance money against future books, he continued to make small personal loans to Fitzgerald. Fitzgerald's financial dependence on Perkins and agent Harold OBER is depicted in the 1937 story "Financing Finnegan." Fitzgerald owed Perkins $1,150 when he went to work for MGM in July 1937; he paid off the debt at the end of 1938, but he borrowed at least $1,500 more from Perkins before his death. When Ober refused to advance Fitzgerald any more money in July 1939, Fitzgerald turned to Perkins for loans. On November 10, 1940 Fitzgerald emended his will to substitute Perkins for Ober as coexecutor with John BIGGS. After Fitzgerald's death Ober and Perkins both withdrew as executors to avoid legal complications, but they helped Biggs administer Fitzgerald's literary affairs. Perkins, along with Ober and Gerald MURPHY, lent Scottie FITZGERALD the money to finish her education at Vassar.

In November 1939, when *COLLIER'S* editor Kenneth LITTAUER refused to make an advance for serial rights to Fitzgerald's HOLLYWOOD novel (*LT/LOLT*), Perkins sought to encourage Fitzgerald, wiring on November 29: "A BEAUTIFUL START. STIRRING AND NEW. CAN WIRE YOU TWO HUNDRED FIFTY AND A THOUSAND BY JANUARY" (Charles Scribner's Sons Archives, PRINCETON UNIVERSITY LIBRARY). He followed up with a letter the next day: "I thought the book had the magic that you can put into things. The whole transcontinental business, which is so strong and new to people like me, and to most people, was marvellously suggested, and interest and curiosity about Stahr was aroused, and sympathy with the narratress. It was all admirable, or else I am no judge any more" (*Scott/Max*, p. 259).

When Fitzgerald died of a heart attack on December 21, 1940, he had written drafts of 17 of the projected 30 episodes for *LT/LOLT*. Perkins wanted to publish the novel both as a memorial to Fitzgerald and to earn money for the author's estate, but he was unsure about the best way to present the work in progress. He considered having another writer complete the novel; but both John O'HARA and Budd SCHULBERG declined the task; and it was arranged for Edmund WILSON to edit the work, which was published in its unfinished form in 1941 as *The Last Tycoon*.

The Fitzgerald/Perkins correspondence, which is at the Princeton University Library, is collected in *Dear Scott/Dear Max*, ed. John Kuehl and Jackson R. Bryer. See also A. Scott Berg, *Max Perkins: Editor of Genius*; *Editor to Author: The Letters of Maxwell Perkins*, ed. John Hall WHEELOCK (New York: Scribners, 1979); and Malcolm COWLEY, *Unshaken Friend: A Profile of Maxwell Perkins* (Boulder, Colo.: Roberts Rinehart, 1985).

Perrin Character in *TITN*. Bank employee in PARIS.

Perry, Constance Character in the Josephine PERRY stories; Josephine's older sister. In "First Blood" she complains to her mother about Josephine's behavior and is offended by Josephine's interest in Anthony HARKER. In "A Nice Quiet Place" she marries Malcolm LIBBY. In "Emotional Bankruptcy" Mr. and Mrs. Warren DILLON arrive at the Perry home to visit Constance just before Edward DICER comes to see Josephine; Constance eventually leads her guests upstairs so that Edward and Josephine can be alone.

Perry, Mr. and Mrs. George (Herbert T.) Characters in the Josephine PERRY stories; Josephine's parents. In "First Blood" they decide to send Josephine east to school after the first of the year. In "A Nice Quiet Place" they plan the family's summer vacation at quiet Island Farms in Michigan instead of Lake Forest. In "A Woman with a Past" Mr. Perry removes Josephine from Miss BRERETON's School after she is twice unjustly accused of misbehavior. In "A Snobbish Story" Josephine is shocked when she sees her father at lunch with a peroxide blonde. It turns out that he was bribing the woman to leave Mrs. Perry's brother alone.

Perry, Josephine Character in a series of five stories written in 1930 and 1931: "First Blood," "A Nice Quiet Place," "A Woman with a Past," "A Snobbish Story," and "Emotional Bankruptcy." (*See also The Basil and Josephine Stories.*) Josephine, a young woman in Chicago at the time of World War I, is "an unconscious pioneer of the generation that was destined to 'get out of hand' " ("First Blood," *TAR*, p. 134) and has a scandalous reputation. She cares only about "being in love and being with the person she currently loved" ("A Nice Quiet Place," *TAR*, p. 156). The series follows her from age 16 to almost 18 through a string of love affairs in which, with the exception of Dudley KNOWLE-TON, she consistently has the upper hand. By the time she meets the right man in "Emotional Bankruptcy," she has used up her emotional capacity and has nothing left to give him. Josephine is based on Fitzgerald's first serious love, Ginevra KING, who commented: "I was too thoughtless in those days & too much in love with love to think of consequences. These things he has emphasized—and over-emphasized in the Josephine stories but it is only fair to say I asked for some of them" (Ginevra King Pirie to Arthur MIZENER, November 1947; *The Far Side of Paradise*, p. 327).

The Young and Beautiful (New York: Samuel French, 1956), a play by Sally Benson (1900–72) based on the Josephine stories, opened on October 1, 1955 at the Longacre Theatre in NEW YORK.

Peter Character in "Mister Icky." Little boy who places a mothball on Mr. ICKY's corpse.

Peters, Birdy Character in *LT/LOLT*. One of three secretaries in Pat BRADY's outer office. Cecelia BRADY finds her naked in Brady's office closet.

Peters, Elsie Character in "Babylon Revisited." Daughter of Lincoln and Marion PETERS.

Peters, Lincoln Character in "Babylon Revisited." Charlie WALES's brother-in-law, who wants Charlie to have custody of Honoria WALES. Husband of Marion PETERS.

Peters, Marion Character in "Babylon Revisited." Wife of Lincoln PETERS. Marion distrusts her brother-in-law Charlie WALES because of how he treated her sister, Helen WALES; and she resents his prosperity and free spending during a time when she and her husband were financially strapped. She refuses to relinquish guardianship of Charlie's daughter, Honoria WALES. Based on Zelda FITZGERALD's sister Rosalind SAYRE Smith, who thought Fitzgerald was unfit to raise Scottie FITZGERALD; Fitzgerald told Harold OBER that "Babylon Revisited" was "founded on a real quarrel with my sister-in-law" (received January 2, 1931; *As Ever,* p. 175).

Peters, Richard Character in "Babylon Revisited." Son of Lincoln and Marion PETERS.

Peterson, Jules Character in *TITN*. Black man who is variously identified as being from Stockholm and from Copenhagen; a failed manufacturer of shoe polish who is shot and found dead in Rosemary HOYT's hotel room after he helps Abe NORTH incorrectly identify the man who stole some money from Abe. Dick DIVER removes the body from Rosemary's room to protect her reputation and movie career; he gives the bloody bedclothes to Nicole DIVER to wash, a situation which triggers her second relapse in a fortnight.

Petrocobesco, Prince Gabriel (Tutu) Character in "Majesty." Disreputable claimant to the throne of a Middle European kingdom who marries Emily CASTLE-TON after he is given the title of king.

Philippe Character in "In the Darkest Hour," "The Count of Darkness," "The Kingdom in the Dark," and "Gods of Darkness." Based on Ernest HEMINGWAY, as Fitzgerald indicated in his *Notebooks:* "Just as Stendahl's portrait of a Byronic man made *Le Rouge et Noir* so couldn't *my* portrait of Ernest as Phillipe make the real modern man" (#1034). After the publication of *TITN* Fitzgerald planned a historical novel, to be called "The Castle," based on a series of connected stories about Philippe and covering the time from 880 to 950 A.D. Harold OBER had trouble selling the series to *REDBOOK* and expressed to Fitzgerald his reservations about the project since Fitzgerald was known for stories about contemporary society (December 5, 1934; *As Ever,* pp. 205–207). In 1938 Fitzgerald considered rewriting the Philippe stories as a novelette to lead a collection of stories, telling Maxwell PERKINS that Philippe "is one of the best characters I've ever 'drawn' (December 24, 1938; *Life in Letters,* p. 374; *Scott/Max,* p. 251). He discussed the plan in a January 4, 1939 letter to Perkins but indicated his preference for writing a modern novel (*Life in Letters,* pp. 375–376; *Scott/Max,* pp. 253–254).

In "In the Darkest Hour" Philippe, Count of Ville-franche, returns from Spain to his native France in 872 A.D. at the age of twenty to find it ravaged by Vikings. He stakes his claim to the land of Villefranche in the Loire valley fifty miles west of Tours and drives out a band of Viking invaders.

In "The Count of Darkness" Philippe organizes his supporters and makes plans for a camp. He requires a band of Syrian merchants to hand over a tenth of their goods in order to ford the Loire River, and he allows the local peasants a portion of the loot. He takes LETGARDE, the consort of the slain Norman chieftain, as his own consort; but she drowns when she runs away after he mistreats her.

In "The Kingdom in the Dark" he gives shelter to GRISELDA, who has run away from LOUIS, King of the West Franks; in retaliation, Louis instructs his men to burn Philippe's fort.

In "Gods of Darkness" Philippe agrees to marry Griselda and follows her advice to let JAQUES handle a possible attack by the DUKE OF MAINE. When Griselda reveals that she is the chief priestess of the witch cult of which Jaques is also a member, Philippe resolves to use the cult for his own purposes.

In 1935 Fitzgerald planned four more Philippe stories, as described in his notes:

> 5 Decision to build castle leads to raid to kidnap artisans + fight to death
> 6 Called to serve King. His Castle Stormed (Usurper has made surfs mutiny) The Fief absolute
> 7 Hard boiled Counts with Eclessiastics inventing Bogus rights to give chivalry a sacrosanct aspect
> 8 Love story
> (*F. Scott Fitzgerald Manuscripts VI,* Part 3, p. 406)

His notes also include a list of books he consulted for the medieval material, as well as notes he made from his reading; See *F. Scott Fitzgerald Manuscripts VI,* Part 3, pp. 400–407.

See Janet Lewis, "Fitzgerald's 'Philippe, Count of Darkness,'" *Fitzgerald/Hemingway Annual* (1975), pp. 7–32.

Phipps Clinic Zelda FITZGERALD entered the Henry Phipps Psychiatric Clinic of the JOHNS HOPKINS UNIVERSITY HOSPITAL in BALTIMORE, Maryland, on February 12, 1932, after her second breakdown. The Fitzgeralds did not have a good relationship with Dr. Adolf MEYER, director of the clinic; but Zelda was close to Dr. Mildred SQUIRES, to whom she dedicated her novel, *Save Me the Waltz* (1932), which she completed while at Phipps. Dr. Thomas RENNIE also treated Zelda at Phipps. She was discharged on June 26 but was not considered cured; she and Fitzgerald returned to Phipps for meetings with her doctors. After her third breakdown she reentered the clinic on February 12, 1934 but was transferred to CRAIG HOUSE on March 8 after she failed to improve.

Pickman, Josephine Character in "The Bowl." Vienna THORNE's friend and Jeff DEERING's date after the Yale game.

Pierce Character in *TITN.* Bank employee in PARIS.

"The Pierian Springs and the Last Straw" Fiction. *The NASSAU LITERARY MAGAZINE,* 73 (October 1917), 173–185; *Apprentice Fiction.* George ROMBERT is a successful novelist until he marries Myra FULHAM, who rejected him many years before; after their marriage he stops writing. This story is Fitzgerald's first analysis of the conflict between love and achievement; and it develops one of his major themes—the ruin of a gifted man by a selfish woman.

Pierre Character in "Gods of Darkness." Son of JAQUES, who sends him to tell the followers of the DUKE OF MAINE that the duke is PHILIPPE's prisoner.

Pilgrim, Captain Doctor Character in "The End of Hate." Ohio physician who amputates Confederate soldier Tib DULANY's thumbs.

Pilgrim, Josie Character in "The End of Hate." Ohio girl who falls in love with Confederate soldier Tib DULANY.

Pinkard, Emmy Character in "Two Wrongs." Aspiring dancer from South Carolina who marries Bill MCCHESNEY.

Piper, Donald Character in "The Cut-Glass Bowl." Harold and Evylyn PIPER's son, who is killed in the war.

Piper, Evylyn Character in "The Cut-Glass Bowl." Woman whose life is haunted by a cut-glass bowl that was a gift from a rejected suitor.

Piper, Harold Character in "The Cut-Glass Bowl." Evylyn PIPER's husband, a wholesale hardware dealer.

Piper, Julie Character in "The Cut-Glass Bowl." Harold and Evylyn PIPER's daughter, whose hand is amputated after contracting blood-poisoning from cutting her thumb on the bowl.

Piper, Milton Character in "The Cut-Glass Bowl." Harold PIPER's younger brother, who tries to keep Tom LOWRIE from telling Clarence AHEARN about the Country Club matter.

Pirie, Dr. Character in "The Long Way Out." Mrs. George KING's doctor, who allows her to keep waiting for her husband every day when she refuses to accept the news of his death.

Pitou Character in "Shadow Laurels." Wine dealer who tells Jaques CHANDELLE that his father, Jean CHANDELLE, was a drunkard and who introduces him to his father's friends.

Plage de la Garoupe Beach at CAP D'ANTIBES, France, which Gerald MURPHY had raked and where the Murphys and their friends, including the Fitzgeralds, swam.

Plant, Donald Character in "Three Hours Between Planes." Man who visits his childhood love, Nancy Holmes GIFFORD, during a wait between planes. He finds that she has confused him with Donald BOWERS.

Playwright, Fitzgerald as Much of Fitzgerald's early work was as a playwright. As a teenager he wrote four plays for the ELIZABETHAN DRAMATIC CLUB in ST. PAUL: *The Girl from Lazy J* (1911), *The Captured Shadow* (1912), *Coward* (1913), and *Assorted Spirits* (1914) (see *F. Scott Fitzgerald's St. Paul Plays*). While at PRINCETON he was active in the TRIANGLE CLUB, for which he wrote the book and lyrics for *Fie! Fie! Fi-Fi!* (1914–15), as well as lyrics for *The Evil Eye* (1915–16) and *Safety First* (1916–17). Some of his earliest professionally published pieces were short plays for *The SMART SET*: "The Debutante" (November 1919; revised from *The NASSAU LITERARY MAGAZINE*, January 1917), "Porcelain and Pink" (January 1920), and "Mister Icky" (March 1920). His first two novels, *This Side of Paradise* (1920) and *The Beautiful and Damned* (1922), included sections of dramatic dialogue with stage directions.

Fitzgerald hoped that his 1923 play, *The Vegetable*, would make his fortune; and he was disappointed when it failed. Matthew J. BRUCCOLI assesses Fitzgerald's writing in *The Vegetable*: "Despite Fitzgerald's apprenticeship as a playwright, his talent was novelistic—not dramatic. His stage dialogue does not stand up alone, and many of his jokes depend on the stage directions" (*Some Sort of Epic Grandeur*, p. 197).

Despite the failure of *The Vegetable*, Fitzgerald considered writing more plays. He informed Max PERKINS in February 1925 that he planned to "try another play" after writing three stories (*Life in Letters*, p. 96; *Scott/Max*, p. 94), but there is no evidence that he began a play at that time. In 1935 he wrote to Harold OBER: "If I ever get out of debt I want to try a second play. It's just possible I could knock them cold if I let go the vulgar side of my talent" (received July 2, 1935; *Life in Letters*, p. 284; *As Ever*, p. 221). In February 1937 he suggested to Perkins that a play might be his best option for getting out of debt: "I am thinking of putting aside certain hours and digging out a play, the ever-appealing mirage. At 40 one counts carefully one's remaining vitality and rescources and a play ought to be within both of them" (*Life in Letters*, p. 318; *Scott/Max*, p. 235). Later that year he planned a prison play (*see* "Institutional Humanitarianism"). He emphasized that "the playwriting venture is of great importance to me in keeping my name known during this time when I will be behind the comparative anonymity of the screen" (to Edwin KNOPF, December 7, 1937; *Correspondence*, p. 485), but he evidently did not proceed further than an outline and a few brief notes. In 1938 he and Sheilah GRAHAM collaborated on "Dame Rumor," an unfinished play. In 1940 Fitzgerald and Edward Everett

Horton (1886–1970) discussed a possible play based on the Pat HOBBY stories (to Arnold GINGRICH, February 23, 1940; *Life in Letters*, p. 434), but nothing came of the plan.

Plaza Hotel NEW YORK hotel where the Fitzgeralds stayed while house-hunting in September 1922 and during trips to New York while living at "ELLERSLIE" in 1927–28. In *GG* the confrontation between Tom BUCHANAN and Jay GATSBY takes place at the Plaza.

Poe, Edgar Allan, Jr. (1896–1983) A fellow student of Fitzgerald at PRINCETON (Class of 1918) and later his lawyer when Fitzgerald lived in Maryland. Poe helped Fitzgerald find "LA PAIX."

Poems 1911–1940 Edited by Matthew J. BRUCCOLI; foreword by James Dickey. Bloomfield Hills, Mich. & Columbia, S.C.: Bruccoli Clark, 1981. Includes poems from the publications of the NEWMAN SCHOOL and PRINCETON UNIVERSITY, 1911–19; poems published by Fitzgerald, 1919–37; poems from Fitzgerald's *Notebooks* which were not published in his lifetime; previously unpublished poems and posthumously published poems, 1913–40; and fragments and unfinished poems. Contents: "Football"; *Fie! Fie! Fi-Fi!* lyrics—"Act I Opening Chorus," "Gentlemen Bandits We," "A Slave to Modern Improvements," "In Her Eyes," "What the Manicure Lady Knows," "Good Night and Good Bye," " 'Round and 'Round," "Chatter Trio," "Finale Act I," "Rose of the Night," "Men," "In the Dark," "Love or Eugenics," "Reminiscence," "Fie! Fie! Fi-Fi!," "The Monte Carlo Moon," "Finale Act II"; "May Small Talk"; "A Cheer for Princeton"; *The Evil Eye* lyrics—"Act I Opening Chorus," "I've Got My Eyes on You," "On Dreams Alone," "The Evil Eye," "What I'll Forget," "Over the Waves to Me," "On Her Eukalali," "Jump Off the Wall," "Finale Act I," "Act II Opening Chorus," "Harris from Paris," "Twilight," "The Never, Never Land," "My Idea of Love," "Other Eyes," "The Girl of the Golden West," "With Me"; "To My Unused Greek Book"; "One from Penn's Neck"; Untitled—"Oui, le backfield . . ."; *Safety First* lyrics—"Prologue," "Garden of Arden," "Act I Opening Chorus," "Send Him to Tom," "One-Lump Percy," "Where Did Bridget Kelly Get Her Persian Temperament?" "It Is Art," "Safety First," "Charlotte Corday," "Underneath the April Rain," "Finale Act I Dance, Lady, Dance," "Act II Safety First," "Hello Temptation," "When That Beautiful Chord Came True," "Rag-Time Melodrama," "Scene II," "Take Those Hawaiian Songs Away," "The Vampires Won't Vampire for Me," "The Hummin' Blues," "Down in Front," "Finale"; "Rain Before Dawn"; From "Precaution Primarily"; "Popular Parodies—No. 1"; "Undulations of an Undergraduate"; Untitled—"Ethel had her shot of brandy . . ."; "Princeton—The Last Day"; "On

a Play Twice Seen"; "The Cameo Frame"; "Our American Poets"; "City Dusk"; "The Pope at Confession"; "My First Love"; "Marching Streets": First Printed Text, Revised *Notebooks* Text; "We keep you clean in Muscatine"; "A Dirge"; Verse included in *This Side of Paradise*—Untitled—"Marylyn and Sall*ee* . . . ," Untitled— "So the gray car crept . . . ," "In a Lecture-Room," Untitled—"Victorians, Victorians, who never learned to weep . . . ," Untitled—"Songs in the time of order . . . ," Untitled—"We leave to-night . . . ," "Boston Bards and Hearst Reviewers," Untitled—"The February streets . . . ," Untitled—"When Vanity kissed Vanity . . . ," "A Poem That Eleanor Sent Amory Several Years Later," "A Poem Amory Sent to Eleanor and Which He Called 'Summer Storm,'" Untitled—"A fathom deep in sleep I lie . . ."; Untitled—"Carrots and peas . . ."; Untitled—"Oh down— . . ."; "Sleep of a University"; "To Anne"; Untitled—"For the lads of the village triumph . . ."; Untitled—"Then wear the gold hat, if that will move her . . ."; Untitled—"We sing not soft, we sing not loud . . ."; Untitled—"Oh—oh—oh—oh . . ."; "Lamp in a Window"; "Obit on Parnassus"; "A Blues"; "Answer to a Poem"; "Apology to Ogden Nash"; Untitled—"The barber's too slick . . ."; "Beg You to Listen"; "Clay Feet"; Untitled— "Colors has she in her soul . . ."; Untitled—"Come in! Come in! . . ."; "Counter Song to the 'Undertaker'"; Untitled—"Don't you worry I surrender . . ."; "The Earth Calls"; Untitled—"Everytime I blow my nose I think of you . . ."; Untitled—"First a hug and tease and a something on my knees . . ."; "For a Long Illness"; Untitled—"For Song—Idea—"; Untitled—"For the time that our man spent in pressing your suit . . ."; Untitled—"A god intoxicated fly . . ."; "Half-and-Half Girl"; Untitled—"Hooray . . ."; "Hortense—To a Cast-Off Lover"; Untitled—"I don't need a bit assistance . . ."; Untitled—"If Hoover came out for the N. R. A. . . ."; Untitled—"If you have a little Jew . . ."; Untitled—"I hate their guts . . ."; Untitled— "In a dear little vine-covered cottage . . ."; Untitled— "Keep the Watch! . . ."; Untitled—"Life's too short to . . ."; Untitled—"Listen to the hoop la . . ."; Untitled—"Little by little . . ."; Untitled—"Mr. Berlin wrote a song about forgetting to remember . . ."; Untitled—"Mother taught me to—love things . . ."; Untitled—"Now is the time for all good men to come to the aid of the party . . ."; "Oh, Sister, Can You Spare Your Heart?"; Untitled—"Oh where are the boys of the boom-boom-boom . . ."; "One Southern Girl"; "Our April Letter"; "Pilgrimage"; Untitled—"Pretty Boy Floyd . . ."; "Prizefighter's Wife"; "Refrain for a Poem. How to Get to So and So"; "Sad Catastrophe"; Untitled—"Scott Fitzgerald so they say . . ."; Untitled— "She lay supine among her Pekinese . . ."; "Song"; "Song—"; "A Song Number Idea"; Untitled—"'Sticking along.' The voice so faint sometimes I could

scarcely hear it . . ."; "Thousand-and-First Ship"; "To Carter, a Friendly Finger"; Untitled—"Touchdown song based on . . ."; Untitled—"Truth and—consequences . . ."; Untitled—"You'll be reckless if you . . ."; Untitled—"You'll never know . . ."; Untitled—"You've driven me crazy . . ."; "Martin's Thoughts"; Untitled— "My mind is all a-tumble . . ."; "On My Ragtime Family Tree"; Untitled—"My Very Very Dear Marie . . ."; "For Dolly"; "A Letter to Helen"; Untitled—"Ruth . . ."; Untitled—"There was a young lady named Ruth . . ."; "When We Meet Again"; "Ellerslie"; Untitled—"Ah May, Shall I splatter my thoughts in the air . . ."; "1st Epistle of St. Scott to the Smithsonian"; "To the Ring Lardners"; "[Dog! Dog! Dog!]"; Untitled—"Of wonders is Silas M. Hanson the champ . . ."; Untitled—"There was a young man of Quebec . . ."; Untitled—"All the girls and mans . . ."; Untitled—"Orange pajamas and heaven's guitars . . ."; Untitled—"'Oh papa— . . .'"; Untitled—"DON'T EXPECT ME . . ."; "Momishness"; Untitled—"East of the sun, west of the moon . . ."; "For 2nd Stanza Baoth Poem"; "Because"; Untitled—"Oh Misseldine's, dear Misseldine's . . ."; "Spring Song"; "Lines on Reading Through an Autograph Album"; Untitled—"Valentine was a Saint . . ."; Untitled—"SING HOTCH-CHA SING HEY-HI NINNY . . ."; "Some Interrupted Lines to Sheilah"; Untitled— "This book tells that Anita Loos . . ."; "For Mary's Eighth Birthday"; "Les Absents Ont Toujours Tort"; "To a Beloved Infidel"; "The Big Academy Dinner"; "Lest We Forget"; Untitled—"From Scott Fitzgerald . . ."; Untitled—"Frances Kroll . . ."; "On Watching the Candidates in the Newsreels"; Untitled—"Now your heart is come so near . . ."; "[Vowels]"; "Tribute"; "Choke down another Hic and Hail the king"; "Colds in the Head"; "Dopey Sal + Penthouse Jerry"; "The girls I met at the Chicago Fire"; Untitled—"Mr. McDonald was keen to lay eyes on his daughter . . ."; Untitled— "Strombergs assorted pickels gather near . . ."; Untitled—"There was no firelight . . ."; "To My Grandfather."

Poetry Fitzgerald's PRINCETON classmate John Peale BISHOP tutored him in poetry, an influence which Fitzgerald later acknowledged to his daughter, Scottie FITZGERALD: "I had always dabbled in 'verse' but he made me see, in the course of a couple of months, the difference between poetry and non-poetry." In the same letter he noted, "Poetry is either something that lives like fire inside you—like music to the musician or Marxism to the Communist—or else it is nothing, an empty, formalized bore around which pedants can endlessly drone their notes and explanations," and listed eight poems by John KEATS as "a scale of workmanship for anybody who wants to know truly about words" (August 3, 1940; *Life in Letters,* pp. 460–461). Fitzgerald's own poetry was derivative, though he re-

garded his efforts as formative on his prose style: "I don't think anyone can write succinct prose unless they have at least tried and failed to write a good iambic pentameter sonnet, and read Browning's short dramatic poems, etc.—but that was my personal approach to prose" (to Scottie, undated; *Letters*, p. 101). He noted that his talent was in large part the poetic kind that matures early (to Scottie, July 18, 1940; *Life in Letters*, p. 455).

Fitzgerald wrote poems for the *The NEWMAN NEWS* and *The NASSAU LITERARY MAGAZINE*, lyrics for TRIANGLE CLUB musicals at Princeton, and humorous verse for *The PRINCETON TIGER*. In his 1920 essay "Who's Who—and Why" he recalled spring 1917 at Princeton: "I had decided that poetry was the only thing worth while, so with my head ringing with the meters of Swinburne and the matters of Rupert Brooke I spent the spring doing sonnets, ballads and rondels into the small hours. I had read somewhere that every great poet had written great poetry before he was twenty-one. I had only a year and, besides, war was impending. I must publish a book of startling verse before I was engulfed" (*AOAA*, p. 84). By fall 1917 he turned his attention to writing a novel which became *TSOP*, into which he incorporated several of his poems.

All of Fitzgerald's prep-school and college poems, plus other miscellaneous published poems, as well as unpublished and posthumously published poems, are collected in *Poems 1911–1940*.

Poindexter, Mrs. Morton (Aunt Jo) Character in "Presumption." Noel GARNEAU's aunt, who tries to send San Juan CHANDLER away until she realizes that he is the young man whom Noel really wishes to see.

policeman (unnamed) Character in "Pat Hobby Does His Bit." Officer who finds Pat HOBBY stranded after a movie stunt.

"Poor Old Marriage" Review of *Brass* by Charles NORRIS. *The Bookman*, 54 (November 1921), 253–254; *In His Own Time*. Fitzgerald found this novel disappointing: "It is a decent, competent, serious piece of work—but excite me it simply doesn't" (*In His Own Time*, p. 127).

"Poor Working Girl" Fiction by Zelda FITZGERALD. *COLLEGE HUMOR*, no. 85 (January 1931), 72–73, 122; *Bits of Paradise*; *Zelda Fitzgerald: The Collected Writings*. Bylined "F. Scott and Zelda Fitzgerald" but credited to Zelda in *Ledger*. Eloise Everette Elkins takes a job caring for the young daughter of Mr. and Mrs. Goatbeck; she plans to save money to study in NEW YORK but squanders it. Because she has been neglecting her duties, she is dismissed from her job four days before the Goatbecks go abroad. She returns home rather than going to New York and ultimately takes a job in the local power plant.

"The Pope at Confession" Verse. *The NASSAU LITERARY MAGAZINE*, 73 (February 1919), 105; *In His Own Time*; *Poems*. Included in *A BOOK OF PRINCETON VERSE II*.

Popolous, Joe Character in *LT/LOLT*. Greek-born theater owner. Probably based on Spyros Skouras (1893–1971), head of Twentieth Century-Fox.

"The Popular Girl" Fiction. Written November 1921. *The SATURDAY EVENING POST*, 194 (February 11 & 18, 1922), 3–5, 82, 84, 86, 89; 18–19, 105–106, 109–110; *Bits of Paradise*. When 21-year-old Yanci BOWMAN is left with only a thousand dollars after the sudden death of her father, she goes to NEW YORK to attempt to win Scott KIMBERLY—and the money and stability he represents—by conveying an illusion of prosperity and popularity. After turning down several dates with him to increase his desire for her, she agrees to have tea with him; since she has just spent her last dime, she knows this is her last chance to win him. He no longer seems interested in her, and she thinks she has lost him. As she rides away in a taxi she realizes she has no money with which to pay the fare. When she tells the driver she has no money, Scott appears to rescue her and reveals to Yanci that he has known of her predicament all along.

Fitzgerald regarded "The Popular Girl," his only two-part story for the *Post*, as "cheap." He told Harold OBER, "The Popular Girl hasn't the vitality of my earlier popular stories even tho I've learned my tricks better now and am technically proficient. . . . I was merely repeating the matter of an earlier period without being able to capture the exuberant manner" (January 24, 1921; *As Ever*, p. 34).

"Porcelain and Pink (A One-Act Play)" Written October 1919. *The SMART SET*, 61 (January 1920), 77–85; *TJA*. Julie MARVIS is in the bathtub when her sister's date, Mr. CALKINS, looks through the window. He can see only the wallpaper and doesn't realize the room is a bathroom; and he converses with Julie while thinking she is Lois MARVIS. Lois enters the room and, horrified to see him at the window, faints. The play ends just before Julie rises out of the tub.

The Portable F. Scott Fitzgerald Collection. Selected by Dorothy PARKER, with introduction by John O'HARA. New York: Viking, 1945. Also published as *The Indispensable F. Scott Fitzgerald*. New York: The Book Society, 1949. Contents: *The Great Gatsby*, *Tender Is the Night*, "Absolution," "The Baby Party," "The Rich Boy," "May Day," "The Cut-Glass Bowl," "The Offshore Pirate,"

"The Freshest Boy," "Crazy Sunday," "Babylon Revisited." This volume contributed to the Fitzgerald REVIVAL.

Porterfield, James One of Fitzgerald's closest childhood friends in ST. PAUL; a member of the ELIZABETHAN DRAMATIC CLUB.

Potter Character in "The Smilers." Stockbroker who informs Waldron CROSBY that he has lost all his money.

Powell, Amanthis Character in "Dice, Brass Knuckles & Guitar." New Jersey girl whom Jim POWELL invites to his jazz school in Southampton. She is the HARLANS' cousin.

Powell, Jim Character in "Dice, Brass Knuckles & Guitar." Southern young man who heads North for the summer and opens an academy offering lessons in dice, self-defense, jazz, and Southern accent. Apparently not the same character as Jim POWELL in "The Jelly-Bean"; they are both from TARLETON, Georgia, and have the same name but different personalities.

Powell, Jim Character in "The Jelly-Bean." An idler and accomplished crap-shooter who is briefly inspired to reform by his love for Nancy LAMAR. Apparently not the same character as Jim POWELL in "Dice, Brass Knuckles & Guitar"; they are both from TARLETON, Georgia, and have the same name but different personalities.

Powers, Kenneth Character in "Babes in the Woods." College freshman who is attracted to ISABELLE at a Christmas party. This character is replaced by Amory BLAINE in *TSOP*.

Prangins Clinic Les Rives de Prangins Clinic at NYON, SWITZERLAND, on Lake Geneva between Geneva and LAUSANNE. Zelda FITZGERALD was transferred from VALMONT CLINIC to Prangins, a resort-like facility run by Dr. Oscar FOREL, on June 5, 1930. Zelda wrote short stories while at Prangins; Harold OBER tried to sell them, but only "Miss Ella" was published (*SCRIBNER'S MAGAZINE*, December 1931). Fitzgerald suggested selling them under the blanket title "Stories from a Swiss Clinique." Zelda was discharged from Prangins on September 15, 1931.

"Precaution Primarily" Burlesque musical comedy. *The PRINCETON TIGER*, 27 (February 3, 1917), 13–14; *In His Own Time*. Burlesque of a TRIANGLE CLUB performance. Includes comments by actors behind the scenes and competition among the authors, composers, and lyricist watching from the back of the theater.

preceptor (unnamed) Character in "The Spire and the Gargoyle." Instructor whom a failing UNDERGRADUATE perceives as a gargoyle.

Preston, Kitty Character in "The Last of the Belles." Girl who dates Earl SCHOEN until he becomes interested in Ailie CALHOUN.

Preston, May Wilson (1873–1949) Magazine illustrator known for airy and witty drawings. She illustrated two early Fitzgerald stories for *The SATURDAY EVENING POST*: "Myra Meets His Family" (March 20, 1920) and "Bernice Bobs Her Hair" (May 1, 1920). She also illustrated stories by Mary Robert Rinehart (1876–1958) for the *Post*.

"Presumption" Fiction. Written November 1925. *The SATURDAY EVENING POST*, 198 (January 9, 1926), 3–5, 226, 228–229, 233–234; *The Price Was High*. San Juan CHANDLER is in love with wealthy Noel GARNEAU, whom he met at a dude ranch in Montana. He sees her again while visiting his snobbish cousin Cora CHANDLER, who warns him that he is too poor to get any ideas about Noel. While playing golf he is joined by Noel's father, Harold GARNEAU, who—unaware that San Juan is speaking of Noel—advises him to get to work so he can support the wealthy girl he loves. As a result San Juan drops out of college and moves to Boston, where he quickly becomes prosperous. When he reads a newspaper announcement of Noel's engagement to Brooks Fish TEMPLETON, San Juan urges her to marry him instead. Mr. Garneau calls him presumptuous and sends him away; Noel, distraught by the encounter, leaves town. San Juan manages to locate her at the home of her aunt, who tries to send him away until she realizes that he is not Templeton, whom Noel now despises, but San Juan, whom Noel wishes to see.

The Price Was High: The Last Uncollected Stories of F. Scott Fitzgerald Edited with introduction by Matthew J. BRUCCOLI. New York & London: Harcourt Brace Jovanovich/Bruccoli Clark, 1979; London: Quartet, 1979. Story collection. Contents: "The Smilers," "Myra Meets His Family," "Two for a Cent," "Dice, Brass Knuckles & Guitar," "Diamond Dick and the First Law of Woman," "The Third Casket," "The Pusher-in-the-Face," "One of My Oldest Friends," "The Unspeakable Egg," "John Jackson's Arcady," "Not in the Guidebook," "Presumption," "The Adolescent Marriage," "Your Way and Mine," "The Love Boat," "The Bowl," "At Your Age," "Indecision," "Flight and Pursuit," "On Your Own," "Between Three and Four," "A Change of Class," "Six of One—," "A Freeze-Out," "Diagnosis," "The Rubber Check," "On Schedule," "More than Just a House," "I Got Shoes," "The Family Bus," "In the Darkest Hour," "No Flowers," "New Types," "Her Last Case," "Lo, the

Poor Peacock!", "The Intimate Strangers," "Zone of Accident," "Fate in Her Hands," "Image on the Heart," "Too Cute for Words," "Inside the House," "Three Acts of Music," " 'Trouble,' " "An Author's Mother," "The End of Hate," "In the Holidays," "The Guest in Room Nineteen," "Discard" ["Director's Special"], "On an Ocean Wave," and "The Woman from Twenty-One."

The title for this volume is taken from Fitzgerald's comment in "Our April Letter": "I have asked a lot of my emotions—one hundred and twenty stories. The price was high, right up with Kipling, because there was one little drop of something not blood, not a tear, not my seed, but me more intimately than these, in every story, it was the extra I had" (*Notebooks* #885).

Prince, Jenny *See* Jenny DELEHANTY.

"The Prince of Pests A Story of the War" Humor article. *The PRINCETON TIGER*, 27 (April 28, 1917), 7; *In His Own Time*. Account of the German Kaiser and his "board of directors" planning World War I.

"Princeton" Essay. COLLEGE HUMOR, 13 (December 1927), 28–29, 130–131; *AOAA*. Part of a *College Humor* series on American colleges. Fitzgerald reflects on the "deep and imperishable love" which PRINCETON arouses in the hearts of its students. He explores various aspects of the school and its history, including the rise of football in America, the wealth of many of Princeton's students, changes in its admission standards, student publications and organizations (such as the *The NASSAU LITERARY MAGAZINE* and the TRIANGLE CLUB), the honor system, and the clubs. He then focuses on what Princeton was like when he was there in early 1917, just before World War I. Fitzgerald concludes that Princeton preserves "much of what is fair, gracious, charming and honorable in American life" (*AOAA*, p. 79).

"Princeton—The Last Day" Verse. *The NASSAU LITERARY MAGAZINE*, 73 (May 1917), 95; *In His Own Time*; *Poems*; incorporated in *TSOP* in prose format at the end of Book I. Edmund WILSON praised the poem, saying that it "possesses a depth and dignity of which I didn't suppose you capable" (October 7, 1917; *Letters on Literature and Politics 1912–1972* [New York: Farrar, Straus & Giroux, 1977], p. 30).

The Princeton Tiger PRINCETON UNIVERSITY humor magazine for which Fitzgerald wrote. He was elected to the editorial board in 1915; and his 1917 roommate, John BIGGS, edited the magazine. Fitzgerald's *Tiger* contributions, which include jokes, parodies, and verse, are collected in *F. Scott Fitzgerald In His Own Time* and *Poems 1911–1940*. Fitzgerald contributed an

The Princeton Tiger *editorial board. Fitzgerald stands at center behind John Biggs, Jr.*

unidentified piece to the first fall 1913 issue, and his work probably appeared in the magazine throughout his freshman year. However, due to the absence of bylines, none of his pre-1915 contributions is known; the clippings he preserved in his scrapbook are the primary source for identifying his *Tiger* material.

Princeton University While a student at the NEWMAN SCHOOL, Fitzgerald first noted his interest in Princeton in his scrapbook, captioning his ticket stub for the November 4, 1911 Harvard-Princeton game—the first since 1896—"Sam White decides me for Princeton" (*The Romantic Egoists*, p. 16). White starred in the 8–6 Princeton victory with a 95–yard touchdown run after a blocked kick. Another attraction was the TRIANGLE CLUB, which produced an original musical comedy each year. Fitzgerald was not interested in his aunt Annabel MCQUILLAN's offer to finance his education at Georgetown University, and he was discouraged by the possibility that he might be sent to the University of Minnesota to save money. However, Fitzgerald's grandmother, Louisa MCQUILLAN, died in summer 1913, and Mollie FITZGERALD's inheritance provided funds for college tuition. Fitzgerald was not interested in Harvard or Yale; he later distinguished the Big Three universities in *TSOP*: "I don't know why, but I think of all Harvard men as sissies, like I used to be, and all Yale men as wearing big blue sweaters and smoking pipes. . . . I think of Princeton as being lazy and good-looking and aristocratic—you know, like a spring day" (p. 27).

In May 1913 Fitzgerald took the Princeton entrance examinations in French, history, mathematics, science, three in Latin, two in English, and three in algebra and plane geometry. His scores were insufficient for admission; and he was required to travel to Princeton for make-up exams and a personal interview, in which he persuaded the admissions committee that it would be cruel to deny him entrance on his birthday. He was admitted with conditions in algebra, Latin, French, and physics, for which he had to take exams in December; 66 percent of the 430 freshmen were admitted with conditions. On September 24, 1913 he wired home: "ADMITTED SEND FOOTBALL PADS AND SHOES IMMEDIATELY PLEASE WAIT TRUNK" (*The Romantic Egoists*, p. 20). Fitzgerald's football career was short-lived: one account explains that he had to withdraw from the freshman squad after wrenching his knee during practice; another version is that he was cut from the team on the first day of practice. His athletic ambitions denied, he went out for the Triangle Club and *The PRINCETON TIGER*, a humor magazine.

During Fitzgerald's freshman year the university lacked sufficient dormitory space; he roomed alone off campus at 15 University Place, where Newman classmates Sap DONAHOE and Paul NELSON also lived. His first-term courses were Latin 103 (historical literature of Rome—Livy, Sallust, Cicero), Mathematics 101 (plane trigonometry), English 101 (readings in English literature—composition and rhetoric), Physics 101 (general physics), French 203 (survey of French literature), Hygiene 101 (personal hygiene), and physical education, as well as Mathematics 105 (algebra) to prepare for clearing his entrance condition. Instruction was by the preceptorial system—in addition to attending course lectures, students met in groups of three to six for weekly one-hour meetings with preceptors. Grading was by groups: 1, highest standing; 2, high standing; 3, satisfactory; 4, below average; 5, poor; 6, unsatisfactory; 7, very unsatisfactory. Fitzgerald's first-term average of 5.17 was barely passing: 5 in Latin; failed/failed/passed in trigonometry; 4 in English; 5 in physics; 5 in French; failed/passed in hygiene; failed/failed/passed in algebra. In addition to satisfying his entrance conditions, Fitzgerald had to make up failed courses—a pattern that grew worse every term. He passed all of his second-term exams except coordinate geometry (he was absent from the exam and his term grade was unsatisfactory); he made a 3 in English, 4 in French and hygiene, and 5 in Latin and physics.

Fitzgerald was critical of the English department, which he later characterized as "surprisingly pallid . . . top-heavy, undistinguished and with an uncanny knack of making literature distasteful to young men," noting: "Dr. Spaeth, one of several exceptions, . . . aroused interest and even enthusiasm for the romantic poets, an interest later killed in the preceptorial rooms where

mildly poetic gentlemen resented any warmth of discussion and called the prominent men of the class by their first names" ("Princeton," December 1927; *AOAA*, p. 75). Fitzgerald's contempt for his professors is exemplified by two poems he incorporated into *TSOP*: "In a Lecture-Room" (pp. 117–119) and "Songs in the time of order . . ." (pp. 165–166). In 1940 he wrote to his daughter, Scottie FITZGERALD, "Some of the professors who were teaching poetry really hated it and didn't know what it was about. I got in a series of endless scraps with them so that finally I dropped English altogether" (August 3, 1940; *Life in Letters*, p. 460).

Though his academic record was undistinguished, Fitzgerald was educating himself through wide reading—including the writings of Robert Hugh BENSON, H. G. WELLS, Compton MACKENZIE, and George Bernard Shaw (1856–1950)—as well as practicing his craft of writing, probably contributing to the *Tiger* throughout his freshman year and writing the book and lyrics for the 1914–15 Triangle Club show, *Fie! Fie! Fi-Fi!*. A strong influence on his education was classmate John Peale BISHOP, whom he met in April 1914 and who tutored him in poetry. Other Princeton friends included Townsend MARTIN, Ludlow FOWLER, Alexander MCKAIG, and Edmund WILSON. Fitzgerald summarized his freshman year as "A year of work and vivid experience" (*Ledger*, p. 168).

Fitzgerald began his sophomore year by failing the make-up exam in coordinate geometry; he was ruled ineligible for extracurricular activities and was not permitted to appear in *Fie! Fie! Fi-Fi!*, which premiered on December 19, 1914. He roomed alone at 71 Patton Hall; and his first-term courses were philosophy (logic), Latin (Roman comedy, Plautus and Terence), chemistry (inorganic), English (survey of English literature), French (17th-century literature), and another Latin course to meet his entrance condition. During his Christmas vacation in ST. PAUL, he met Ginevra KING, who became his primary love interest during his college years; he wrote her many lost letters instead of studying. Returning to Princeton in January, he passed five of his six courses, skipping the chemistry exam; his grades were 3 in English and logic and 5 in the other courses. His spring schedule included psychology, Latin (Horace and Catullus), chemistry (qualitative analysis), English (survey of English literature), French (17th-century literature), coordinate geometry (to make up his previous failure), and an unidentified history course as a penalty for exceeding the 50-cut limit in the fall. On February 26 he was elected secretary of the Triangle Club; and in March he was elected to the COTTAGE CLUB, also receiving bids from Cap and Gown, Quadrangle, and Cannon. He was elected to the editorial board of the *Tiger* and began contributing to *The NASSAU LITERARY MAGAZINE*. While working on the *Lit*, Fitzgerald's friendship with Edmund Wilson, who was

the 1915–16 chairman, deepened; they collaborated on *The Evil Eye* for the Triangle Club. In June Fitzgerald passed only four exams on the first try: psychology (4), English (3), French (4), and history (5). He passed the Latin exam on the third attempt, coordinate geometry on the second, and failed qualitative analysis three times. Ginevra King came to the Princeton prom in June, and Fitzgerald summarized the year as "A year of tremendous rewards that toward the end over-reached itself and ruined me. Ginevra-Triangle year" (*Ledger*, p. 169).

Fitzgerald's junior year began with his failure of the qualitative analysis make-up exam, which made him ineligible for campus offices, including the presidency of the Triangle Club. In 1936 he recalled his disappointment and its effects:

> To me college would never be the same. There were to be no badges of pride, no medals, after all. It seemed on one March afternoon that I had lost every single thing I wanted—and that night was the first time that I hunted down the spectre of womanhood that, for a little while, makes everything else seem unimportant.
>
> Years later I realized that my failure as a big shot in college was all right—instead of serving on committees, I took a beating on English poetry; when I got the idea of what it was all about, I set about learning how to write. On Shaw's principle that "If you don't get what you like, you better like what you get," it was a lucky break—at the moment it was a harsh and bitter business to know that my career as a leader of men was over. ("Pasting It Together"; *CU*, p. 76)

That fall Fitzgerald roomed alone at 32 Little Hall. His courses included English (the Renaissance—Spenser, Marlowe, Sidney), English (Chaucer), Italian (grammar, composition, and reading), French (the Romantic Movement from Rousseau to France), philosophy (history of philosophy), and ancient art (for exceeding the cut limit). After college Fitzgerald maintained a friendship with Christian GAUSS, who taught his French literature course. Although Fitzgerald was ineligible to perform in *The Evil Eye,* he was involved in the production of the show. He wrote for the *Tiger* and won the competition for a new football song with "A Cheer for Princeton." In November he was in the infirmary twice, diagnosed with malaria; it may actually have been a mild case of tuberculosis. He attended his last class on November 28 and went home early for Christmas; he dropped out for the rest of the year to recuperate. His transcript indicates: "Mr. Fitzgerald was required to withdraw from the University January 3, 1916 for scholastic deficiencies." However, in May he persuaded Dean Howard McClennan to write a general letter explaining that he had withdrawn voluntarily "because of ill health and that he was fully at liberty, at that time, to go on with his class, if his health had

permitted"; McClennan included a note to Fitzgerald: "This is for your sensitive feelings. I hope you will find it soothing" (*The Romantic Egoists*, p. 29). While in St. Paul in the spring Fitzgerald continued to send contributions to the *Tiger* and the *Lit,* but his book for a Triangle Club show was declined. He summarized 1915–16 as "A year of terrible disappointments + the end of all college dreams. Everything bad in it was my own fault" (*Ledger*, p. 170).

Fitzgerald returned to Princeton in September 1916 to repeat his junior year, rooming at 185 Little Hall with Paul B. DICKEY. Although Fitzgerald officially dropped back to the Class of 1918, he always considered himself part of the Class of 1917. He repeated four courses from the previous year—the English Renaissance, Chaucer, the French Romantic Movement, and history of philosophy—as well as European history and qualitative analysis (which he had failed his sophomore year). He wrote the lyrics for the Triangle Club show, *Safety First,* but was ineligible for the tour. Ginevra King came to the Yale game in November, but they broke up in January. He failed three of his six courses: history, philosophy, and chemistry; his other grades were English Renaissance (2), Chaucer (3), and French (2). Although his plans for the future were uncertain, he told Edmund Wilson, "I want to be one of the greatest writers who ever lived, don't you?" (Wilson, "Thoughts on Being Bibliographed," *The Princeton University Library Chronicle,* 5 [February 1944], p. 54). His spring 1917 courses included Shakespeare, history of the English language, French (the second term of the Romantic Movement), history of philosophy (Descartes to Kant), and qualitative analysis. His writing appeared in the *Nassau Lit* 13 times; and he explored his feelings about Princeton in a February short story, "The Spire and the Gargoyle." He was not involved in the anti-club movement of the spring—which led students to resign from the eating clubs because they were considered snobbish and contrary to Princetonian ideals; but he was friendly with two of the leaders, one of whom—Henry H. STRATER—became a model for Burne HOLIDAY in *TSOP.* America entered World War I on April 6, 1917; in May Fitzgerald signed up for a three-week program of intensive military training, receiving full credit (with third-group grades) for all his dropped courses. Although he was no longer officially part of the Class of 1917, he was included in the graduating class yearbook, *Nassau Herald Class of 1917.* His statement of future plans indicates: "He will pursue graduate work in English at Harvard, then he will engage in newspaper work" (p. 100). In the class poll he won two votes for Most Brilliant, two for Handsomest, five for Prettiest, two for Thinks He Is Best Dressed, eight for Thinks He Is Biggest Politician, and six as the class's Favorite Dramatist (*Nassau Herald Class of 1917,* pp. 343–345, 347–348). He summarized his second junior

year as "pregnant year of endeavor. Outwardly failure, with moments of anger but the foundation of my literary life" (*Ledger*, p. 171).

In September 1917 Fitzgerald returned to Princeton to await his ARMY commission, rooming in Campbell Hall with John BIGGS, Jr., who had coauthored the book for *Safety First*. Fitzgerald's transcript lists no courses for the fall 1917 term; he wrote for the *Tiger* and the *Nassau Lit*. His commission as a second lieutenant in the infantry is dated October 26, 1917, and he reported to FORT LEAVENWORTH in Kansas for training in November. In February 1918 he received leave and returned to Princeton, finishing his novel, "The Romantic Egotist" (an early version of *TSOP*), at the Cottage Club. He returned to the Cottage Club in February 1920 in order to be in Princeton when *TSOP* was published.

After the publication of *TSOP*, which describes Princeton as "the pleasantest country club in America" (p. 40), Princeton president John Grier HIBBEN wrote to Fitzgerald to express his distress (May 27, 1920; *Correspondence*, pp. 58–59). Fitzgerald replied on June 3:

> It was a book written with the bitterness of my discovery that I had spent several years trying to fit in with a curriculum that is after all made for the average student. . . .
>
> I don't mean at all that Princeton is not the happiest time in most boys lives. It is of course—I simply say it wasn't the happiest time in mine. I love it now better than any place on earth. . . . I have no fault to find with Princeton that I can't find with Oxford and Cambridge. I simply wrote out of my own impressions, wrote as honestly as I could a picture of its beauty. That the picture is cynical is the fault of my temperment. . . .
>
> I must admit however that This Side of Paradise does over accentuate the gayiety + country club atmosphere of Princeton. For the sake of the readers interest that part was much over stressed, and of course the hero not being average reacted rather unhealthily I suppose to many perfectly normal phenomena. To that extent the book is inaccurate. It is the Princeton of a Saturday night in May. Too many intelligent class mates of mine have failed to agree with it for me to consider it really photographic any more, as of course I did when I wrote it (*Life in Letters*, pp. 37 & 40).

On April 25, Fitzgerald and his bride, Zelda Sayre FITZGERALD, visited Princeton as chaperones for a weekend house party. Fitzgerald introduced her as his mistress to shock undergraduates, and he received a black eye during a scuffle in Harvey Firestone's car. When he returned to Princeton on May 1 with Wilson and Bishop to visit Professor Gauss, the Cottage Club informed him that he and his wife had disgraced the club and that his membership had been suspended,

and members shoved him out a window; the suspension was later lifted.

In 1927 Fitzgerald recalled the history of Princeton and his years there in an essay for *College Humor* (*see* "Princeton"). In late January 1928 he was invited to speak at a Cottage Club dinner, but he was nervous and probably intoxicated, and he ended his speech after only a few sentences. During this visit he learned that the honor system was being weakened, which troubled him; he arrived home drunk and crying about the speaking incident and the honor system.

In September 1934 he wrote to Professor Gauss offering to present eight lectures at Princeton on "the actual business of creating fiction" and promising to avoid drinking "to safeguard you from my elaborate reputation" (September 7, 1934; *Life in Letters*, p. 269). Gauss responded with a suggestion that Fitzgerald speak to an undergraduate club because the university was unable to sponsor the lectures; but Fitzgerald declined, indicating that the "authoritative aegis of the University" was more desirable for the formal lecture series he had planned (September 26, 1934; *Life in Letters*, p. 270).

After Fitzgerald's death, Princeton made an inadequate offer for the purchase of his papers; but his daughter, Scottie, refused to sell. She later donated the archive to Princeton (*see* PRINCETON UNIVERSITY LIBRARY).

Princeton University Library The most extensive archive of original research materials documenting the life and works of F. Scott Fitzgerald is the "F. Scott Fitzgerald Papers" in the Department of Rare Books and Special Collections, Princeton University Libraries. Of paramount importance are Fitzgerald's own papers (catalog #C0187), including 25.65 cubic feet (57 boxes and 8 flat cases) of holograph drafts, manuscripts, revised typescripts, correspondence, memorabilia, and other materials in his possession at the time of his death in 1940. Most of these papers were presented by Frances Scott (Scottie) FITZGERALD Lanahan in 1950 to the Princeton University Library. (See Matthew J. BRUCCOLI, "Where They Belong: The Acquisition of the F. Scott Fitzgerald Papers," *The Princeton University Library Chronicle*, 50 [Autumn 1988], 30–37.)

The Fitzgerald Papers include the manuscript and revised galleys of *GG*; 17 stages of manuscript and typescript drafts for *TITN*, as well as a partial galley proof; manuscripts and revised typescripts of *TSOP*, *B&D*, and *LT/LOLT*; manuscripts and revised typescripts of short stories, poems, and scripts for stage, screen, and radio; and juvenilia. Fitzgerald's extensive correspondence includes 16 boxes of letters received and carbons of typewritten letters sent. His correspondence is the best source for information about his relationships with Zelda FITZGERALD, Scottie Fitzger-

ald, John Peale BISHOP, Arnold GINGRICH, Ernest HEM-INGWAY, Ring LARDNER, Maxwell PERKINS, and Edmund WILSON. Hundreds of his letters to Zelda Fitzgerald are in her papers (C0183). Also included in the Fitzgerald Papers are drawings and photographs; family records; and topically organized scrapbooks, with many photographs later reproduced in *The Romantic Egoists: A Pictorial Autobiography from the Scrapbooks and Albums of Scott and Zelda Fitzgerald.*

Fitzgerald is extremely well documented in Princeton collections other than the Fitzgerald Papers. Foremost among ancillary materials in the Manuscripts Division is the extensive Fitzgerald correspondence in the author files of the Charles SCRIBNER's Sons Archives (C0101), principally with his editor Maxwell E. Perkins from 1919 to 1940, and also "third-party references" to Fitzgerald in Perkins's private correspondence with Elizabeth H. LEMMON (C0655). Publication, royalties, and other business aspects of Fitzgerald's creative work during his life and after his death may be traced in both the Scribners archives and those of his literary agent, Harold OBER (C0129). Selected correspondence and manuscripts of Fitzgerald from 1938 to 1940 acquired from *ESQUIRE* magazine and from Bert BARR are in the Fitzgerald Additional Papers (C0188).

Other collections offer information about Fitzgerald's literary estate, the acquisition and early use of the papers, new editions and posthumous publications, cinematic adaptations, and critical reception of his works. Also available are the Fitzgerald estate papers amassed by Judge John BIGGS (C0628), who was Fitzgerald's roommate at Princeton and the executor of his estate; and Arthur MIZENER's research files for *The Far Side of Paradise: A Biography of F. Scott Fitzgerald* (C0634). Additional Fitzgerald correspondence was acquired from his daughter, Scottie, as well as from Sheilah GRAHAM and Martha Marie SHANK (1959), Laura GUTHRIE Hearne (1967), Hazel McCormack (1986), and Frances KROLL Ring (1988). Letters written by Fitzgerald to Princeton-connected friends and others whose papers are now in the Department of Rare Books and Special Collections can be found by using indexing records in the department's MASC database. The University Archives includes information about Fitzgerald's life as a Princeton undergraduate (Class of 1917), such as his entrance examination and academic transcript, relevant records of the COTTAGE CLUB and the TRIANGLE CLUB, and scrapbooks of classmates.

Important new evidence about Zelda Fitzgerald has been provided in recently acquired medical files from CRAIG HOUSE for 1932–34 (C0745), including letters and notes from F. Scott Fitzgerald to Dr. Clarence V. SLOCUM and copies of medical files and psychiatric evaluations forwarded to Slocum by Dr. Oscar L. FOREL (PRANGINS CLINIC) and Dr. Thomas A. C. RENNIE

(PHIPPS CLINIC). Especially revealing about the Fitzgeralds' marital difficulties are a 10-page undated letter from Fitzgerald to Rennie and a 114-page "Stenographic Report of Conversation between Mr. and Mrs. F. Scott Fitzgerald and Dr. Thomas A. C. Rennie" dated May 28, 1933. All correspondence and files relating to Zelda Fitzgerald's illness and hospitalization are open, although these materials will not be photoduplicated for researchers.

In the area of printed materials are books from Fitzgerald's personal library, including those annotated by him, such as his own copies of *GG* and *TITN*. Of special interest are the 246 volumes (some inscribed or annotated by Fitzgerald) in the "College of One" Collection, which Fitzgerald used during the last years of his life to educate Sheilah Graham, who donated them in 1968.

A finding aid for the Fitzgerald Papers (C0187) is available through the Princeton University Libraries' World Wide Web Home Page. Collection-level bibliographic records are available in the RLIN/AMC national online database. For other information about Fitzgerald materials at Princeton, including the availability of photocopies and microfilm, contact the Reference Librarian, Department of Rare Books and Special Collections, Princeton University Libraries, Princeton, New Jersey 08544; (609) 258–3184.

by Don C. Skemer, Princeton University Libraries

Pruit, Miss Character in *Coward.* Tommy and Clara DOUGLAS's governess, who objects to her role in their war games.

Public letter to Thomas Boyd *St. Paul Daily News,* February 20, 1921, feature section, p. 8; reprinted as "The Credo of F. Scott Fitzgerald," *Chicago Daily News,* March 9, 1921, and as "How the Upper Class Is Being Saved by 'Men Like Mencken,' " *Baltimore Sun,* March 22, 1921, section C, p. 2; *In His Own Time.* Comment on the status of American literature, complaining that the "history of a young man" is "the overworked artform at present" and noting that the "so-called upper class" will read what H. L. MENCKEN recommends (*In His Own Time,* p. 165).

Purley, Mae Character in "The Love Boat." Lower-class high-school girl with whom Bill FROTHINGTON falls in love.

"The Pusher-in-the-Face" Fiction. Written March 1924. *WOMAN'S HOME COMPANION,* 52 (February 1925), 27–28, 143–144; *The Price Was High.* Charles David STUART is arrested for pushing Mrs. George D. ROBINSON in the face when she annoys him at the theater, but the judge decides that the assault was justified and dismisses the case. Stuart then pushes all the people who annoy him, such as a phony beggar. Stuart's em-

ployer, T. CUSHMAEL, plans to fire him in a few days; but after Stuart foils a burglary attempt by pushing an obnoxious customer in the face, Cushmael promotes him; and waitress Edna SCHAEFFER agrees to go to the theater with him.

"The Pusher-in-the-Face" was made into a lost movie in 1928.

Pushing, Mr.　Character in *The Vegetable*. Jerry FROST's employer, who fires him after a week's absence from his job as a railroad clerk. In Act II he is Major-General Pushing, who informs President Jerry FROST that he and two other generals have voted to have a war. He tells Jerry that the country needs a military man as a leader.

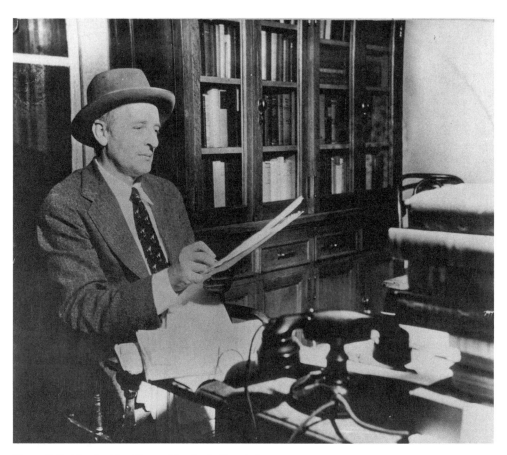

Maxwell Perkins in his office at Charles Scribner's Sons

Q

Quarrles, Lorraine Character in "Babylon Revisited." Friend from Charlie WALES's days of dissipation. Her drunken arrival at the home of Charlie's sister-in-law, Marion PETERS, causes Marion to change her mind about returning Honoria WALES to Charlie.

Quill, Mr. Moonlight Character in "His Russet Witch." Proprietor of the Moonlight Quill Bookshop, which he leaves to Merlin GRAINGER when he dies.

R

Raffino Character in "Jacob's Ladder." Latin actor whose attentions to Jenny Prince [DELEHANTY] are resented by Jacob BOOTH.

Raffles (Samuel Goldwyn, 1939) In September 1939 Fitzgerald worked for Samuel Goldwyn (1884–1974) on *Raffles* for a week; his assignment was cut short because of a disagreement between Goldwyn and director Sam Wood (1883–1949). The movie was released with screenplay by John Van Druten (1901–57) and Sidney Howard (1891–1939), based on stories about a gentleman thief by E. W. Hornung (1866–1921).

Ragland, Dick Character in "A New Leaf." Handsome alcoholic who is unable to keep his promise to stop drinking.

"Rags Martin-Jones and the Pr-nce of W-les" Fiction. Written December 1923. *MCCALL's*, 51 (July 1924), 6–7, 32, 48, 50; *ASYM*. A story reminiscent of "The Offshore Pirate"; Fitzgerald described it to Maxwell PERKINS as "Fantastic Jazz" (June 1, 1925; *Life in Letters*, p. 121; *Scott/Max*, p. 112). Wealthy and beautiful Rags MARTIN-JONES returns to America after five years in EUROPE. She tells John M. CHESTNUT, who is in love with her, that she wants "a man who's capable of a gallant gesture" (*ASYM*, p. 139) and that Americans lack imagination. He stages an elaborate spectacle for her, including an introduction to a man who she is led to believe is the Prince of Wales. When John is supposedly being sought for murder, Rags attempts to arrange for the Prince to transport John and herself to Canada in a "runaway marriage." John reveals that he is responsible for the entire performance, and Rags is charmed that he had orchestrated "a perfectly useless, gorgeous thing, just for me" (*ASYM*, p. 158).

Rahill Character in *TSOP*. Class president and friend and "co-philosopher" of Amory BLAINE at ST. REGIS.

"Rain Before Dawn" Verse. *The NASSAU LITERARY MAGAZINE*, 72 (February 1917), 321; *In His Own Time, Poems*. Fitzgerald included line 11 of this poem in *TSOP* in "A Poem Amory Sent to Eleanor and Which He Called 'Summer Storm.'"

Raines, Marston Character in "Diagnosis." Wise man whose counsel Sara ETHERINGTON asks Charlie CLAYHORNE to seek.

Raj, Sir Singrim Dak Character in "Pat Hobby, Putative Father." John Brown Hobby INDORE's uncle, the third-richest man in India.

Raleigh, Henry Patrick (1880–1944) Prolific illustrator of magazine stories, particularly Fitzgerald's. He illustrated 10 Fitzgerald stories for *The SATURDAY EVENING POST*, including "Jacob's Ladder" (August 20, 1927), "A Snobbish Story" (November 29, 1930), "The Hotel Child" (January 31, 1931), "Indecision" (May 16, 1931), "A Freeze-Out" (December 19, 1931), "Diagnosis" (February 20, 1932), "What a Handsome Pair!" (August 27, 1932), "I Got Shoes" (September 23, 1933), "No Flowers" (July 21, 1934), and "Her Last Case" (November 3, 1934). He also illustrated "His Russet Witch" for *METROPOLITAN MAGAZINE* (February 1921).

by Park Bucker

Ralston, Mrs. Character in "John Jackson's Arcady." Woman who has solicited charitable contributions from John JACKSON and who offers tribute to him at the Civic Welfare League meeting.

Randall, Louie Character in "Emotional Bankruptcy." Boy whom Josephine PERRY asks to show up at the PRINCETON prom even though she has a date with Paul DEMPSTER. She pretends that she didn't know that Louie would follow her there, but she spends time with him all weekend.

Raudenbush, Miss Character in "Pat Hobby, Putative Father." Pat HOBBY's secretary.

Rawlings, Marjorie Kinnan (1896–1953) American novelist best known for her Pulitzer Prize–winning novel *The Yearling* (1938). SCRIBNERS editor Maxwell PERKINS relayed to Fitzgerald Rawlings' response to *TITN*: "I am totally unable to analyze the almost overpowering effect that some of his passages create—some of them about quite trivial people and dealing with

trivial situations. There is something terrifying about it when it happens, and the closest I can come to understanding it is to think that he does, successfully at such times, what I want to do—that is, visualizes people not in their immediate setting, from the human point of view—but in time and space—almost, you might say, with the divine detachment" (February 14, 1934; *Scott/Max*, p. 193).

In 1936 Perkins asked Rawlings—who he hoped could encourage Fitzgerald since she had fought depression herself—to look up Fitzgerald; the two authors met in ASHEVILLE, North Carolina, that fall. After their meeting Rawlings wrote to Fitzgerald that she had reread *GG:* "The book resolves itself into the strangest feeling of a crystal globe, or one of the immense soap bubbles we achieved as children, if it could hold its shape and color without breaking—It is so beautiful, it is so clairvoyant, it is so heart-breaking—" (*Correspondence*, p. 459). Fitzgerald later wrote to Perkins about *The Yearling:* "The Marjorie Rawlings' book fascinated me. I thought it was even better than "South Moon Under" and I envy her the ease with which she does action scenes, such as the tremendously complicated hunt sequence, which I would have to stake off in advance and which would probably turn out to be a stilted business in the end. Hers just simply flows; the characters keep thinking, talking, feeling and don't stop, and you think and talk and feel with them" (April 23, 1938; *Life in Letters*, pp. 358–359; *Scott/Max*, p. 244).

Rawlings described her meeting with Fitzgerald in an October 26, 1936 letter to Perkins and a March 18, 1948 letter to Arthur MIZENER (*Selected Letters of Marjorie Kinnan Rawlings*, ed. Gordon E. Bigelow and Laura V. Monti [Gainesville: University Presses of Florida, 1983], pp. 125–127 & 308–311).

See Rawlings, *Cross Creek* (New York: Scribners, 1942).

Ray, Mrs. Charles Wrotten Character in "Too Cute for Words." Dizzy CAMPBELL's aunt, who calls off the dance she has planned.

Ray, Esther Character in "Too Cute for Words." Dizzy CAMPBELL's cousin, who takes Dizzy, Gwen BOWERS, and Clara HANNAMAN to the Harvard-PRINCETON concert since their dance has been called off.

Ray, Tommy (Shorty) Character in "Too Cute for Words." Dizzy CAMPBELL's cousin, with whom Gwen BOWERS dances at the PRINCETON prom and who gets her into the football game although she doesn't have her ticket.

Raycroft, Dorothy (Dot) Character in *B&D*. A lower-class Southern girl with whom Anthony PATCH has an affair while he is in the army. Her reappearance on the day the trial concerning Adam PATCH's will is to be settled precipitates Anthony's collapse.

Raymond, Agnes Character in "The Mystery of the Raymond Mortgage." Young woman who was murdered by John STANDISH.

Raymond, Mr. Character in "The Mystery of the Raymond Mortgage." Agnes RAYMOND's father, who found his murdered daughter's body. The mortgage which he had placed in a drawer disappeared around the time of the murder.

Raymond, Mrs. Character in "The Mystery of the Raymond Mortgage." Agnes RAYMOND's mother, who shoots John STANDISH for killing her daughter.

Raymond, Robert Calvin Narrator of "The Room with the Green Blinds." Young man who inherits his grandfather's house, where he discovers John Wilkes BOOTH hiding.

Read, Cecil (1896–1959) One of Fitzgerald's closest childhood friends in ST. PAUL; a member of William BAKER's dancing class. He was later Fitzgerald's fellow student at PRINCETON (Class of 1919) and a member of the COTTAGE CLUB. He was the model for Riply BUCKNER in the Basil Duke LEE stories. Fitzgerald staged some of his youthful plays in the attic of the Read home and began two of the clubs he started—the Gooserah (May 1910) and the Scandal Detectives (March 1911)—there. Fitzgerald frequently visited the Reads' summer cottage at White Bear Lake in DELLWOOD.

Reade Character in "Reade, Substitute Right Half." A small football player who is called off the bench and leads his team to victory.

"Reade, Substitute Right Half" Fiction. *The ST. PAUL ACADEMY NOW AND THEN*, 2 (February 1910), 10–11; *Apprentice Fiction*. Fitzgerald's second publication. READE, a small boy who is called into the football game when another player is injured, leads his team to victory. Football was a symbol of unattainable glory for Fitzgerald, who was learning to substitute writing for action, as he acknowledged in "Author's House" (July 1936). (*See* also " 'Football.' ")

Real, Francisco Character in *TITN*. Alcoholic homosexual from Chile whose father asks Dick DIVER to cure him; Dick refuses the case.

Real, Pardo Ciudad Character in *TITN*. Francisco REAL's father, who appeals to Dick DIVER for help.

Reardon, Mr. Character in *TSOP*. French teacher in Minneapolis in whose class Amory BLAINE shows off.

Red-Headed Woman (MGM, 1932) In November 1931 Metro-Goldwyn-Mayer offered Fitzgerald $750 a week for six weeks to rewrite a screenplay for Jean Harlow (1911–37) by Bess Meredyth (1890?–1969) and C. Gardner Sullivan (1879–1965), based on the 1931 novel *Red-Headed Woman* by Katharine Brush (1902–52). Fitzgerald was reluctant to delay work on his novel (*TITN*) and to leave Zelda FITZGERALD, who had been released from PRANGINS CLINIC in September; but he accepted the offer when it was raised to $1,200 a week because Irving THALBERG wanted him for the job. Fitzgerald argued with his collaborator, Marcel DE SANO, but finished the screenplay in five weeks, returning to MONTGOMERY for Christmas although MGM asked him to stay on for rewrites. His screenplay was considered too serious a treatment of a woman who advances by sex; and the movie, directed by Jack Conway (1887–1952), was made from a new screenplay by Anita LOOS. Fitzgerald's experiences during this HOLLYWOOD stay provided the material for his 1932 story "Crazy Sunday," which he wrote instead of an article on "Hollywood Revisited" he had planned for *SCRIBNER'S MAGAZINE*.

Redbook Magazine that Fitzgerald characterized as most hospitable to his "more serious work" (to Harold OBER, rec. November 30, 1925; *As Ever*, p. 82). *Redbook* published "The Adjuster" (September 1925), "The Rich Boy" (January & February 1926), "The Dance" (June 1926), and "Six of One—" (February 1932), as well as four PHILIPPE stories: "In the Darkest Hour" (October 1934), "The Count of Darkness" (June 1935), "The Kingdom in the Dark" (August 1935), and "Gods of Darkness" (November 1941). Fitzgerald's delays in meeting deadlines for the Philippe stories caused difficulties for editor Edwin Balmer (1883–1959).

Redfern, Major Character in "Strange Sanctuary." Thief who poses as Charlie CRAIG's houseguest and tells Craig's niece, Dolly HAINES, that her uncle (who is not really at home) is too ill to see her.

Regan Character in "Benediction." KIETH's best friend at the seminary.

Reilly, Benjamin Character in "Forging Ahead." Basil Duke LEE's great-uncle, who gives Basil a summer job at the Reilly Wholesale Drug Company and expects Basil to escort his step-daughter Rhoda SINCLAIR.

Reilly, Everett Character in "A Night at the Fair" and "Forging Ahead." Basil Duke LEE's uncle; brother of Basil's mother, Alice Riley LEE. In "A Night at the Fair" he meets Basil at the clothing store to help him select some suits with long pants. In "Forging Ahead" he tells Basil's mother that he, she, and their father have lost a lot of money, which means that she can't afford to send Basil to Yale.

Reilly, Grandfather Character in the Basil Duke LEE stories. In "The Freshest Boy" he wants to take Basil and Basil's mother to Europe with him for the rest of the year, but Basil decides not to go. In "He Thinks He's Wonderful," he lets Basil drive his electric car. In "Forging Ahead" he thinks Basil should attend the state university rather than Yale.

Reilly, Mrs. Character in "Forging Ahead." She persuades her husband, Benjamin REILLY, to give Basil Duke LEE a summer job so that Basil will be obligated to escort her unattractive daughter, Rhoda SINCLAIR.

"Reminiscences of Donald Stewart" Parody. *St. Paul Daily News*, December 11, 1921, City Life Section, p. 6; *In His Own Time*. Humorous account of Fitzgerald's friendship with Donald Ogden STEWART when they were both living in ST. PAUL, Minnesota, in 1919.

Renaud Character in "The Count of Darkness." Man whom PHILIPPE appoints to go to the settlement and bring back girls to cook and clean and be wives to his men.

Rennard, Jules Character in "Magnetism." George HANNAFORD's best friend, with whom he plans a fishing trip.

Rennie, Dr. Thomas (1904–1956) Psychiatrist at PHIPPS CLINIC to whom Fitzgerald sent analyses of Zelda FITZGERALD's behavior while she was at "LA PAIX" in the summer of 1932. On May 28, 1933 the Fitzgeralds and Dr. Rennie met at "La Paix" for an angry discussion of the problems in their marriage, particularly regarding Fitzgerald's insistence that he be allowed to control Zelda's writing. Dr. Rennie reminded Zelda that he had warned her all along not to write about psychiatric material. A stenographer prepared a 114–page typescript of the session (PRINCETON UNIVERSITY LIBRARY; extracts printed in Matthew J. BRUCCOLI, *Some Sort of Epic Grandeur*, pp. 409–415).

"Reunion at the Fair" Fiction—unfinished Pat HOBBY story. Holograph notes and incomplete draft facsimiled in *F. Scott Fitzgerald Manuscripts VI*, Part 3, pp. 438–450. Pat Hobby and producer George Poupolous visit the Golden Gate World's Fair, where Pat meets a swimmer with the Aquacade. Pat and Poupolous encounter director Ligorna on their way to an art gallery.

Review of *The Celt and the World* by Shane LESLIE *The NASSAU LITERARY MAGAZINE*, 73 (May 1917), 104–105; *In His Own Time*. Fitzgerald calls Leslie's book "a sort of bible of Irish patriotism" (*In His Own Time*, p. 115) and notes its emphasis on mysticism.

Review of *David Blaize* by E. F. Benson *The NASSAU LITERARY MAGAZINE*, 72 (February 1917), 343–344; *In His Own Time*. Fitzgerald suggests that this novel about an English schoolboy by E. F. Benson (1867–1940) "perhaps" belongs to the class of "really good boys' stories" (*In His Own Time*, p. 114). He points out the influence of Compton MACKENZIE and Rudyard Kipling (1865–1936) and concludes that "the first two-thirds of the book is immensely entertaining, the last third disappointing" (p. 115).

Review of *God, The Invisible King* by H. G. WELLS *The NASSAU LITERARY MAGAZINE*, 73 (June 1917), 153; *In His Own Time*. Fitzgerald states that Wells "has added very little" to the "fad of rediscovering God"; he suggests that the book should be welcomed "as an entertaining addition to our supply of fiction for light summer reading" (*In His Own Time*, p. 118).

Review of *Penrod and Sam* by Booth TARKINGTON *The NASSAU LITERARY MAGAZINE*, 72 (January 1917), 291–292; *In His Own Time*. Fitzgerald notes: "Mr. Tarkington has done what so many authors of juvenile books fail to do: he has admitted the unequalled snobbishness of boyhood and has traced the neighborhood social system which, with Penrod and Sam at the top, makes possible more than half the stories" (*In His Own Time*, p. 113).

Review of *Verses in Peace and War* by Shane LESLIE *The NASSAU LITERARY MAGAZINE*, 73 (June 1917), 152–153; *In His Own Time*. Fitzgerald suggests that the "same undercurrent of sadness" found in Leslie's prose gives his poetry "a most rare and haunting depth" (*In His Own Time*, p. 117).

Revival of Fitzgerald's Literary Reputation Before Fitzgerald died on December 21, 1940, he was aware that his salability and reputation had diminished even though nine of his titles were available from SCRIBNERS. In a May 20, 1940 letter to editor Maxwell PERKINS, he lamented his market decline: "I wish I was in print. It will be odd a year or so from now when Scottie assures her friends I was an author and finds that no book is procurable. . . . Would the 25 cent press keep Gatsby in the public eye—or is the book unpopular. Has it had its chance? Would a popular reissue in that series with a preface not by me but by one of its admirers— I can maybe pick one—make it a favorite with class rooms, profs, lovers of English prose—anybody. But to

die, so completely and unjustly after having given so much. Even now there is little published in American fiction that doesn't slightly bare my stamp—in a small way I was an original" (*Life in Letters*, p. 445; *Scott/Max*, p. 261). His last royalty check from Scribners was for $13.13. In *Dukedom Large Enough* (New York: Random House, 1969), David A. Randall, the head of the Scribners Rare Book Department, recounts the settling of Fitzgerald's estate. He notes that PRINCETON UNIVERSITY LIBRARY had offered only $750 for the entire collection of manuscripts and Fitzgerald's personal library, which included a copy of *Ulysses* that James JOYCE had inscribed to Fitzgerald. Randall voiced his objection to the offer and recalls that Julian Bond, then librarian at Princeton, responded that it was not the library's obligation to purchase the collections of " 'second-rate, Midwest hacks' just because they happened to have been lucky enough to have attended Princeton" (p. 254).

From 1945 through the next 20 years Fitzgerald's popularity and place in the literary market far exceeded what even he had dreamed of. Interest in him during that time swelled in two divergent but influential paths, for he underwent both popular and, later, academic resurrections. Part of what sparked the interest was that the man who had known newspaper celebrity in his youth had virtually disappeared from the newsstands; so the sensational appeal of his early death, in reduced circumstances, along with postwar nostalgia, have been credited for the resurgence of interest in him. But far more influential than such intangibles as these were the specific publishing events that were the impetus for what would soon be called the "Fitzgerald Revival."

After Fitzgerald's death Perkins decided to publish the novel-in-progress (*The Love of the Last Tycoon: A Western*) in its incomplete state, but he realized that the buying public would be more likely to buy a collection of Fitzgerald's work than a single unfinished novel. He decided to include *The Great Gatsby* and a selection of Fitzgerald's stories along with the HOLLYWOOD novel in an omnibus collection edited by Fitzgerald's college friend and influential literary critic Edmund WILSON, who provided the title *The Last Tycoon*. Furthermore, Wilson orchestrated a series of obituary-tributes in the February and March 1941 issues of *The New Republic* by authors who had known Fitzgerald and respected his work: John DOS PASSOS, John Peale BISHOP, John O'HARA, Glenway WESCOTT, and Budd SCHULBERG.

The early Fitzgerald Revival occurred in two phases, marked by the years 1945 and 1951. Evidence that Fitzgerald's posthumous career was strengthening began when Wilson further stimulated interest in Fitzgerald with the publication of *The Crack-Up* in 1945. This collection of Fitzgerald's autobiographical essays and selections from his *Notebooks*, as well as letters and

tributes to him from other authors, provides insight into Fitzgerald as a writer and as a man of literary intelligence, dignity, and humor. *The Crack-Up* has not gone out of print since its initial publication, despite Perkins's belief that it would receive no more than temporary interest. The next significant event was the publication of *The Portable F. Scott Fitzgerald* by Viking Press (1945). Again, Fitzgerald's literary friends were essential in promoting him, for the volume's contents were selected by Dorothy PARKER and introduced by John O'Hara. This collection included *GG* and *TITN* and nine stories. O'Hara's praise for Fitzgerald is exuberant: "All he was was our best novelist, one of our best novella-ists, and one of our finest writers of short stories" (xiv). Furthermore, the 1945–46 publication of *GG* and *"The Diamond as Big as the Ritz" and Other Stories* in the Armed Services Editions, which provided for more than 150,000 copies of each volume to be distributed free to troops during wartime, gave Fitzgerald a much larger and more diverse audience than ever before.

The popular market was also actively involved with the publication of Fitzgerald's works in the 1940s. The most significant event was the decision by Bantam in 1945 to print *GG* as number eight of its first 10 paperback titles. The other means by which Fitzgerald was marketed to a mass audience were radio, the motion picture industry, and television. In 1949 *GG* was adapted for a film starring Alan Ladd (1913–64). When the film was released, the publishing and film worlds intersected, for Grosset and Dunlap added a band to its *GG* to announce the film, and Bantam added a dust jacket featuring Ladd to the cover of its paperback *GG*.

The next period of the Fitzgerald Revival was the early 1950s; again, the events that attested to the growth of serious evaluations of Fitzgerald's work were identifiable occurrences in the publishing industry. Scottie FITZGERALD Lanahan donated her father's papers to the Princeton University Library in 1950, and the gift stimulated scholarly interest in Fitzgerald. Arthur MIZENER published the first book-length Fitzgerald biography, *The Far Side of Paradise*, in January 1951. Additionally, Scribners published a new collection of Fitzgerald's short stories edited by critic Malcolm COWLEY. Later that year Cowley published the so-called "author's final version" of *TITN* with chapters reordered in straight chronology.

Not only did Fitzgerald receive attention from serious critics such as Wilson and Cowley, but Budd Schulberg fed the popular interest with a novel based on Fitzgerald in Hollywood, *The Disenchanted* (1950). Also, Bantam added *TITN* to its list of titles, and Penguin in England added *GG* to its paperback line. Television, too, gave attention to Fitzgerald, for adaptations of his novels and short stories were produced and broadcast throughout the 1950s.

Once the revival of the 1940s and 1950s solidified into a canonized reputation, scholarship on the work and life of F. Scott Fitzgerald flourished. In the five and one-half decades since Fitzgerald's death, his stories have been reprinted in many collections and anthologies, while thousands of articles and more than 60 book-length studies, as well as unpublished theses and dissertations, have focused on his life and writings. Much of the academic attention has been biographical, from studies of his entire life to more narrowly focused examinations, such as his years in Hollywood. Other studies have been textual analyses of the novels and short stories; examination of Fitzgerald in relation to other writers; or explorations of specific topics, such as studies of his female characters, his use of religion, myth, and setting, or his narrative technique. (*See* BIOGRAPHICAL STUDIES and CRITICAL STUDIES.)

Although Fitzgerald remains visible in popular media, with frequent references to him on television and in magazines, his reputation stands firm in the classrooms and academic journals.

See Scottie Fitzgerald Smith, "Notes About My Now-Famous Father," *Family Circle,* 84 (May 1974), 118–120.

<div align="right">by Catherine E. Lewis</div>

Reynolds, Paul Revere On October 28, 1919, at the recommendation of ST. PAUL writer Grace Flandrau (d. 1971), Fitzgerald sent a story to Paul Revere Reynolds in NEW YORK CITY. The Reynolds agency specialized in placing fiction with popular magazines—a circumstance which strongly influenced Fitzgerald's career. Reynolds sold "Head and Shoulders" to *The SATURDAY EVENING POST* for $400, resulting in Fitzgerald's first publication in a high-circulation magazine on February 21, 1920. In mid-November Fitzgerald became the client of Harold OBER, a partner at the Reynolds agency who handled new or young clients; when Ober left the firm in September 1929 to start his own agency, Fitzgerald followed him.

Riccard, Lieutenant de Marine Character in "Image on the Heart." Based on Edouard JOZAN. Naval aviator in whom TUDY becomes interested a week before her fiancé, TOM, is to arrive for their wedding.

"The Rich Boy" Fiction. Written April–August 1925. *REDBOOK,* 46 (January & February 1926), 27–32, 144, 146; 75–79, 122, 124–126; *ASYM.* Novelette which, like *GG,* explores how wealth affects character, as well as how wealth operates in America. A partially involved unnamed NARRATOR begins the story of his friend, Anson HUNTER, a young man of wealth and privilege with a strong sense of personal superiority, by analyzing the "very rich": "They are different from you and me. They possess and enjoy early, and it does something to them, makes them soft where we are hard, and cynical where we are trustful, in a way that, unless you were

born rich, it is very difficult to understand. They think, deep in their hearts, that they are better than we are because we had to discover the compensations and refuges of life for ourselves" (*ASYM,* pp. 1–2).

After graduating from Yale, Anson serves a brief wartime stint as an officer in the naval aviation, then joins a NEW YORK brokerage firm, where he eventually becomes a partner. He falls in love with Paula LEGENDRE; and the day after they agree to marry she reveals that she, too, is rich. However, Anson's drinking troubles her, and they eventually break their engagement. When Anson hears of Paula's interest in Lowell THAYER, he visits her and considers asking her again to marry him, but he delays since he feels he is in control of the relationship. Anson cries when Paula later writes to him of her engagement to Thayer. Anson has an affair with Dolly KARGER, but the memory of Paula is still too strong for him to be happy with Dolly; they break up, and Dolly marries another man. Anson offers advice to his young married friends and intervenes to end his aunt Edna HUNTER's affair with Cary SLOANE. As he becomes older and his friends no longer need him, Anson becomes lonely and dissatisfied. In the PLAZA HOTEL he encounters Paula, who has divorced Thayer and married Peter HAGERTY and is expecting her fourth child; the Hagertys invite Anson to visit them in their summer house at Rye, where he sees how happy they are together. Anson's business partners insist that he vacation abroad that summer; just before he sails he learns of Paula's death in childbirth.

Fitzgerald wrote "The Rich Boy" on CAPRI while awaiting publication of *GG* and revised it in PARIS. Before its publication in *Redbook* he sent a copy to Ludlow FOWLER, the model for Anson Hunter; but he was unable to make the cuts Fowler requested until its appearance in *ASYM.* Fitzgerald revised the story heavily between periodical and book publication, increasing Anson's self-centeredness and Paula's appeal. Ring LARDNER told Fitzgerald that he should have made it into a novel, but Fitzgerald insisted that would have been impossible. Fitzgerald considered "The Rich Boy" "one of the best things" he had ever done (to Fowler, March 1925; *Correspondence,* p. 152).

Fitzgerald's pronouncement about how the very rich are different is often misquoted. Ernest HEMINGWAY contemptuously misquoted it in his 1936 story "The Snows of Kilimanjaro": "He remembered poor Scott Fitzgerald and his romantic awe of [the rich] and how he had started a story once that began, 'The very rich are different from you and me.' And how someone had said to Scott, Yes they have more money" (*ESQUIRE,* 6 [August 1936], p. 200). This anecdote has been widely reported, with Hemingway identified as having delivered the rejoinder; but Maxwell PERKINS explained that when he, Hemingway, and critic Mary Colum (1884–1957) were having lunch, Hemingway remarked, "I am getting to know the rich," and Mrs. Colum responded, "The only difference between the rich and other people is that the rich have more money" (A. Scott Berg, *Max Perkins: Editor of Genius,* p. 305).

Richard Character in *TSOP.* Myra ST. CLAIRE's chauffeur, who drives her and Amory BLAINE to the Minnehaha Club.

Richardson, Dorothy Nurse whom Fitzgerald hired while living at the GROVE PARK INN in ASHEVILLE, North Carolina, in 1936. Fitzgerald was not confined to bed, and Miss Richardson's responsibilities were to attempt to limit his drinking and to provide company. He prepared reading lists for her. (See "The Education of Dorothy Richardson," *Fitzgerald/Hemingway Annual* [1979], pp. 227–228.)

Rickey Character in " 'Send Me In, Coach.' " Handsome, athletic counselor at Camp Rahewawa whom the OLD MAN warns to stay away from his wife and who has an agreement with the Old Man to play football at the state college the coming fall.

Ridingwood, Red Character in *LT/LOLT.* Director whom Monroe STAHR replaces because he can't handle the star actress in his movie.

Rienmund, Joe Character in *LT/LOLT.* A supervisor. May be based on MGM producer Hunt STROMBERG, for whom Fitzgerald worked.

Riggs, Billy Character in "Fate in Her Hands." Fiancé of Carol [KASTLER], who abandons him for Ben KASTLER.

Rikker, Alida Character in "A Freeze-Out." Beautiful girl with whom Forrest WINSLOW falls in love and whom he marries despite his parents' prejudice against her family.

Rikker, Cathy Chase Character in "A Freeze-Out." Chauncey RIKKER's wife and Alida and Teddy RIKKER's mother.

Rikker, Chauncey Character in "A Freeze-Out." Man who returns to his Minnesota hometown after business scandals that prejudice the townspeople against him. Husband of Cathy Chase RIKKER and father of Alida and Teddy RIKKER.

Rikker, Irene Character in "Two Wrongs." Actress who is engaged to Bill MCCHESNEY until she becomes involved with Frank LLEWELLEN.

Rikker, Teddy Character in "A Freeze-Out." Alida RIKKER's brother, who invites Forrest WINSLOW to their dance.

"Ring" Essay. *The New Republic,* 76 (October 11, 1933), 254–255; *CU.* Tribute to Ring LARDNER in which Fitzgerald expresses his personal sense of loss as well as regret for Lardner's failure to live up to his potential, which Fitzgerald attributed to Lardner's cynical attitude and to his early work as a baseball reporter: "Ring got less percentage of himself on paper than any other American of the first flight" (*CU,* p. 38). He also recalled his friend's personality: "Proud, shy, solemn, shrewd, polite, brave, kind, merciful, honorable—with the affection these qualities aroused he created in addition a certain awe in people. His intentions, his will, once in motion, were formidable factors in dealing with him—he always did every single thing he said he would do. Frequently he was the melancholy Jaques, and sad company indeed, but under any conditions a noble dignity flowed from him, so that time in his presence always seemed well spent" (*CU,* p. 38).

Ring, Frances Kroll *See* Frances KROLL.

Riply Buckner's aunt (unnamed) Character in "A Night at the Fair." She witnesses Riply BUCKNER cavorting at the State Fair and plans to tell his mother; Basil Duke LEE tries to dissuade her.

Ritz Bar Bar in the PARIS Ritz Hotel favored by wealthy Americans. In a draft of a 1930 letter to Zelda FITZGERALD that may not have been sent, Fitzgerald described the Ritz as a place "where I got back my self esteem for half an hour, often with someone I had hardly ever seen before" during their 1928 stay in Paris (*Life in Letters,* p. 188). In "Babylon Revisited" (February 1931) Charlie WALES patronizes the Ritz Bar, and in *TITN* Abe NORTH spends a day there (Book I, Chapter 23).

Riviera Mediterranean resort area of southeastern France. On their second trip to EUROPE in 1924, the Fitzgeralds stopped briefly in PARIS in May before traveling to HYÈRES on the Riviera, where they stayed at

The Riviera

the Grimm's Park Hotel. In June they settled at VILLA MARIE in VALESCURE, where Fitzgerald worked on *GG* and Zelda FITZGERALD became involved with French naval aviator Edouard JOZAN. That summer the Fitzgeralds met Gerald and Sara MURPHY at CAP D'ANTIBES; in October they moved to ROME. Fitzgerald's 1924 essay "How to Live on Practically Nothing a Year" humorously describes their attempts at economizing on the Riviera that summer. In April 1925 they moved to Paris, where they stayed most of the rest of the year; in August they spent a month with the Murphys at Cap d'Antibes, probably staying at the Grand-Hôtel du Cap. After a two-month stay at SALIES DE BÉARN in January–February 1926, the Fitzgeralds returned to the Riviera in March, renting VILLA PAQUITA at JUAN-LES-PINS; they stayed there until May 1926, when they moved to VILLA ST. LOUIS, where they remained until their return to America in December. While at Juan-les-Pins Fitzgerald worked on the matricide version of *TITN,* which he had begun in Paris. In March 1929 they made their fourth trip to Europe, spending a month at the Beau Rivage hotel in Nice before settling in Paris in April. In June they returned to the Riviera, renting VILLA FLEUR DES BOIS in CANNES through September and returning to Paris in October. The Riviera provided the setting and some of the material for *TITN.*

Robbie, Martha Character in "That Kind of Party." A tomboy who breaks up Joe SHOONOVER's party by telling the mothers that the boys are trying to embrace the girls by force.

Robbins Character in "Head and Shoulders." Cabaret singer who did a song and dance routine with Marcia MEADOW.

Robbins, Stella *See* Jill WAYNE.

Robby *See* ROBINSON.

The Fitzgeralds and Scottie's nanny on the Riviera, c. 1924

Robert the Frog Character in "In the Darkest Hour." Viking leader who is slain in battle with PHILIPPE.

Robinson (Robby) Character in *LT/LOLT.* Troubleshooter whom Monroe STAHR calls in after the earthquake. Budd SCHULBERG has identified the source for this character as Otto Lovering, the second-unit head who went to DARTMOUTH for the location filming of *Winter Carnival* (1939). Fitzgerald's early notes for the novel indicate that he considered having Robinson have an affair with Kathleen MOORE and having him be Pat BRADY's agent to murder Stahr.

Robinson, Mr. and Mrs. Deering R. Characters in "The Homes of the Stars." Tourists who ask Pat HOBBY to take them on a tour of the homes of HOLLYWOOD stars.

Robinson, Mrs. George D. Character in "The Pusher-in-the-Face." Woman who annoys Charles David STUART at the theater by talking loudly and jostling his seat. He is arrested for pushing her in the face.

Rockville, Maryland Fitzgerald's father, Edward FITZGERALD, was born at "Glenmary Farm" near Rockville in 1853 and was buried at St. Mary's Church in Rockville in 1931. Because F. Scott Fitzgerald was not a practicing Catholic when he died in 1940, an official of the Baltimore Diocese refused to grant permission to bury him in the family plot at St. Mary's Church; and he was buried at Rockville Union Cemetery, as was Zelda FITZGERALD in 1948. In 1975 Scottie FITZGERALD Smith obtained permission for her parents to be reinterred in the Fitzgerald family plot at St. Mary's Church. In 1996, Rockville celebrated the CENTENNIAL of Fitzgerald's birth with a variety of commemorative events.

Roderiguez, Mr. Character in *LT/LOLT.* Impotent actor who comes to Monroe STAHR for advice. Fitzgerald did not name this character; the name Roderiguez was supplied in the first printing of *LT,* presumably by editor Edmund WILSON.

Rodgers Forge, Maryland Community in TOWSON, outside BALTIMORE, where Fitzgerald rented "LA PAIX" in 1932 and 1933.

Rogers, Alan Character in "Two Wrongs." Playwright who gives Emmy PINKARD a letter of introduction to Bill MCCHESNEY.

Rogers, Mrs. Orrin Character in "The Popular Girl." Woman who introduces Yanci BOWMAN to Scott KIMBERLY, her husband's cousin.

The Romantic Egoists: A Pictorial Autobiography from the Scrapbooks and Albums of Scott and Zelda Fitzgerald Edited by Scottie FITZGERALD Smith, Matthew J. BRUCCOLI, and Joan P. Kerr; introduction by Smith. New York: Charles SCRIBNER's Sons, 1974. Includes material from Fitzgerald family photo albums, Zelda FITZGERALD's scrapbook from birth through the first years of her marriage, and F. Scott Fitzgerald's five scrapbooks, which include reviews, interviews, letters, pictures, and memorabilia: for the years before his marriage ("A Scrap book record compiled from many sources of interest to and concerning one F. Scott Fitzgerald"); for *This Side of Paradise* and *Flappers and Philosophers*; for *The Beautiful and Damned, The Vegetable,* and *Tales of the Jazz Age*; for *The Great Gatsby* and *All the Sad Young Men*; and for *Tender Is the Night* and *Taps at Reveille*. The scrapbooks and albums are in the PRINCETON UNIVERSITY LIBRARY. A chronology and excerpts from Fitzgerald's *Ledger* provide a framework for the scrapbook material.

Rombert Narrator of "The Pierian Springs and the Last Straw." Young man who finally meets his legendary Uncle George ROMBERT.

Rombert, George Character in "The Pierian Springs and the Last Straw." Hard-drinking, philandering author of scandalous novels who stops writing when he marries Myra FULHAM, who had rejected him many years before.

Rombert, Mr. and Mrs. Thomas Characters in "The Pierian Springs and the Last Straw." ROMBERT's parents, whom he overhears discussing his Uncle George ROMBERT.

Rome, Italy After reading *Roderick Hudson* (1876) by Henry James (1843–1916), Zelda FITZGERALD wanted to spend winter 1924–25 in Rome. The Fitzgeralds lived at the HOTEL DES PRINCES from October 1924 to February 1925, when they moved to CAPRI to escape the damp winter in Rome. While in Rome Fitzgerald wrote stories and revised and rewrote *GG*. He was beaten by the police, an experience which he later transferred to Dick DIVER in *TITN*.

"The Room with the Green Blinds" Fiction. *The* ST. PAUL ACADEMY NOW AND THEN, 3 (June 1911), 6–9; *Apprentice Fiction*. An alternate version of the fate of John Wilkes BOOTH. Robert Calvin RAYMOND inherits his grandfather's house, with the puzzling provision that he not open a particular room "until Carmatle falls." Raymond discovers the initials "J.W.B." on the door of that room and asks Governor CARMATLE of Georgia if he knows anything about them. Carmatle accompanies Raymond to his house, where he shoots John Wilkes Booth, who had been hiding in the locked room. Carmatle explains that Booth had stolen his son's horse and uniform and that it was his son, in Booth's clothes, who had been shot in a barn and identified as Booth. Raymond agrees to keep silent about Carmatle's killing Booth.

Rooney, Mr. Character in "The Freshest Boy." Football coach and history teacher at ST. REGIS who gets drunk when he accompanies Basil Duke LEE to NEW YORK.

Rooney, Mr. Character in *TSOP*. PRINCETON tutor whose class in conic sections Amory BLAINE fails.

Rose, Gus Character in "May Day." Carrol KEY's friend, a recently discharged soldier.

Rosenthal, Rosy Character mentioned in *GG*. Meyer WOLFSHIEM's friend who was murdered in front of the Metropole hotel, an event based on the 1912 murder of Herman Rosenthal in Times Square.

Ross, Cary Friend of Fitzgerald in PARIS. On January 21, 1930 Fitzgerald recommended Ross's poems to SCRIBNERS editor Maxwell PERKINS (*Life in Letters*, p. 175; *Scott/Max*, p. 163). In 1934 Fitzgerald arranged an exhibit of Zelda FITZGERALD's paintings at Ross's art gallery in NEW YORK CITY; the show ran from March 29 to April 30 and also included photographs by Dr. Marion Hines (1889–1982) of the Johns Hopkins Medical School.

Ross, Julia Character in "A New Leaf." Young woman who wants to marry Dick RAGLAND if he can stay sober.

Rostoff, Prince Paul Serge Boris Character in "Love in the Night." Prince Val ROSTOFF's Russian father, a distant relative of Peter the Great (1672–1725).

Rostoff, Princess Character in "Love in the Night." Prince Val ROSTOFF's wealthy American mother, who looks down on her native country.

Rostoff, Prince Val Character in "Love in the Night." Russian prince who falls in love with a GIRL whom he meets on a yacht. Based partly on Fitzgerald's friend Prince Val Engalitcheff, who committed suicide in 1923.

Rothstein, Arnold (1882–1928) Gambler and racketeer, known as "The Brain" and "The Bankroll," who was the source for Meyer WOLFSHIEM in *GG*. Although many criminal activities, including fixing sporting events and dealing in stolen bonds, were attributed to Rothstein, he was never convicted of any crime.

Rothstein was murdered in 1928, and the case was never solved. In July 1937 Fitzgerald wrote: "In *Gatsby* I selected the stuff to fit a given mood or 'hauntedness' or whatever you might call it, rejecting in advance in *Gatsby,* for instance, all of the ordinary material for Long Island, big crooks, adultery theme and always starting from the *small* focal point that impressed me— my own meeting with Arnold Rothstein for instance" (to Corey Ford; *Letters,* p. 551); nothing is known about the meeting.

See Leo Katcher, *The Big Bankroll: The Life and Times of Arnold Rothstein* (New York: Harper, 1959) and Eliot Asinof, *Eight Men Out: The Black Sox and the 1919 World Series* (New York: Holt, Rinehart & Winston, 1977).

"The Rough Crossing" Fiction. Written March 1929. *The* SATURDAY EVENING POST, 201 (June 8, 1929), 12–13, 66, 70, 75; *Stories.* Americans Adrian and Eva SMITH and their children are sailing to France. During the stormy passage they quarrel because of Adrian's interest in fellow passenger Betsy D'AMIDO; and Eva tosses her pearls, a gift from Adrian, into the sea. Adrian and Eva are reconciled after they are both knocked unconscious when a wave washes over the boat, and they resolve to believe that the whole trip was a nightmare.

The stormy voyage is based on the Fitzgeralds' 1928 return from EUROPE.

Rousseau, Miss Character in "Between Three and Four." Substitute secretary at Howard BUTLER's office during Miss WIESS's vacation.

"The Rubber Check" Fiction. Written May 1932. *The* SATURDAY EVENING POST, 205 (August 6, 1932), 6–7, 41–42, 44–45; *The Price Was High.* Val SCHUYLER, who is unable to succeed in business, falls in love with wealthy, prominent Ellen MORTMAIN. When she tells him she is leaving for LONDON in a month, they decide to elope instead. However, when a check that he writes on his mother's account and that is accepted on the recommendation of Ellen's relatives, the Charles M. TEMPLETONS, bounces because his mother temporarily refuses to honor it, he is unable to face Ellen, and she leaves town. Mrs. TEMPLETON spreads word of the bounced check, and the story grows out of proportion so that Val seems like a major swindler; girls begin to decline to dance with him because of his bad reputation. Just after he loses his job, his mother dies; and he inherits a little money. When he travels to London to propose to Ellen, he discovers that her family's fortune has disappeared; she rejects his proposal because she is engaged to another man. When he leaves her he discovers that he, too, has lost his money in the Depression; he appeals to Charles Templeton for a job, since Mrs. Templeton's rumors had hurt his reputation.

Templeton gives him a job on a farm; and his daughter, Mercia TEMPLETON, becomes interested in Val.

Rudd, Chinyman Character in *The Captured Shadow.* Crook who works as a spy for "The SHADOW." Hubert CONNAGE, while drunk, brings Rudd home with him and promises to make him an alderman.

"A Rugged Novel" Review of *The Love Legend* by Woodward BOYD. *The Literary Review of the New York Evening Post,* October 28, 1922, pp. 143–144; *In His Own Time.* An excerpt from this review was used as an advertisement in the *Chicago Daily News,* November 22, 1922, p. 13. Fitzgerald, who had recommended the novel to Scribners, generously called it "easily the best picture of Chicago since 'Sister Carrie' " (*In His Own Time,* p. 136). He excused the book's formlessness as permissible in first novels, and noted that although it was not perfect, it was "honest, well written, if raggedy, and thoroughly alive" (p. 137).

Rumsey, Charles Cary (1879–1922) Rumsey, a sculptor and polo player, and his wife, heiress Mary Harriman (1881–1934), had an estate at Westbury, Long Island, New York. Fitzgerald listed the "glamor" of the Rumseys as a source for Chapter I of *GG.* He noted in his *Ledger* for May 1923 "Met Mrs Rumsey + Tommy Hitchcock + went to parties there" (p. 177) and for November 1923 "More Rumsey parties" (p. 178).

Russel, Elaine Character in "Diamond Dick and the First Law of Woman." Actress who dates Charley ABBOT while he doesn't remember that he is married to Diana DICKEY.

Ruth Character in "News of Paris—Fifteen Years Ago." Woman whom Henry Haven DELL has been seeing in PARIS.

Rutherford, Hamilton Character in "The Bridal Party." Caroline DANDY's fiancé, who loses his money but proceeds with an elaborate wedding reception.

Rutherford, Mr. Character in "The Bridal Party." Hamilton RUTHERFORD's father, whom Michael CURLY meets at a wedding party.

Ruthven, Mrs. Cassius Character in "What a Handsome Pair!" Woman who is critical of Helen VAN BECK.

Ryan, Brigadier General J. A. (James Augustine) (1867–1956) General to whom Fitzgerald served as aide at CAMP SHERIDAN in MONTGOMERY.

Ryder, Dawson Character in *TSOP.* Wealthy young man whom Rosalind CONNAGE marries instead of Amory BLAINE.

S

Safety First Cincinnati, New York & London: The John Church Co., 1916. 21 song lyrics. A two-act musical comedy presented by the PRINCETON TRIANGLE CLUB; opening performance December 15, 1916. Book by John BIGGS, Jr., and J. F. Bohmfalk; music by Paul B. DICKEY, F. Warburton Guilbert, and E. Harris; lyrics by Fitzgerald: "Prologue," "Garden of Arden"; Act I—"Opening Chorus," "Send Him to Tom," "One-Lump Percy," "Where Did Bridget Kelly Get Her Persian Temperament?," "It Is Art," "Safety First," "Charlotte

Score for Fitzgerald's 1916 Triangle Club musical (Bruccoli Collection, University of South Carolina)

Corday," "Underneath the April Rain," "Finale—Dance, Lady, Dance"; Act II, Scene 1—"Safety First," "Hello, Temptation," "When That Beautiful Chord Came True," "Rag-Time Melodrama"; Scene 2—"Opening," "Take Those Hawaiian Songs Away," "The Vampires Won't Vampire for Me," "The Hummin' Blues," "Down in Front," "Finale." Lyrics reprinted in *In His Own Time* and *Poems*. For academic reasons Fitzgerald was ineligible to participate in the tour of *Safety First*, a satire set in "a Futurist art community."

St. Claire, Mrs. Character in *TSOP*. Myra ST. CLAIRE's mother.

St. Claire, Myra Character in *TSOP*. Minneapolis girl who invites young Amory BLAINE to a bobbing party and whom he kisses. She later writes to him at PRINCETON.

St. Midas' School near Boston which John UNGER and Percy WASHINGTON attend in "The Diamond as Big as the Ritz." St. Midas' is "the most expensive and the most exclusive boys' preparatory school in the world" (*TJA*, p. 142).

St. Paul, Minnesota Birthplace of F. Scott Fitzgerald, who was born at 3:30 p.m. on September 24, 1896 at 481 Laurel Avenue in a building called the San Mateo Flats in the SUMMIT AVENUE neighborhood. The Fitzgerald family left St. Paul for BUFFALO, New York, in April 1898 after Edward FITZGERALD's wicker furniture factory failed, and returned to St. Paul in July 1908 after Edward Fitzgerald lost his job with Procter & Gamble in March. Fitzgerald and his sister, Annabel FITZGERALD, lived with their grandmother, Louisa Allen MCQUILLAN, at 294 Laurel Avenue, while their parents lived nearby with a friend until April 1909, when Grandmother McQuillan went abroad and the family was reunited at her apartment. In September they rented a house at 514 Holly Avenue and moved almost yearly in the Summit Avenue area, living in rental houses or apartments, including 509 Holly Avenue, 499 Holly Avenue, and 593 Summit Avenue. Fitzgerald entered ST. PAUL ACADEMY in September 1908 and was

active in the ELIZABETHAN DRAMATIC CLUB, for which he wrote four plays. His boyhood experiences in St. Paul provided material for the Basil Duke LEE stories (1928–29).

After Zelda Sayre [FITZGERALD] broke their engagement in June 1919, Fitzgerald quit his advertising job in NEW YORK CITY and returned to St. Paul in July to live with his parents at 599 Summit Avenue, where he rewrote "The Romantic Egotist" as *This Side of Paradise*. He left St. Paul for NEW ORLEANS, Louisiana, in January 1920. In August 1921 Scott and Zelda Fitzgerald moved to a cottage in DELLWOOD on White Bear Lake outside St. Paul to await the birth of their daughter; they were evicted from the lake house in October because of damage from a burst water pipe, and they moved to the COMMODORE, an apartment hotel in the Summit Avenue neighborhood. Scottie FITZGERALD was born on October 26, 1921 at the Miller Hospital in St. Paul. In November 1921 the Fitzgeralds rented a Victorian frame house at 626 Goodrich Avenue in the Summit Avenue area, where they lived until they moved to the WHITE BEAR YACHT CLUB in June 1922. When they were asked to leave the club in August, they returned to the Commodore, remaining there until October, when they moved to GREAT NECK, Long Island, New York. While in St. Paul in 1921–22 Fitzgerald revised *The Beautiful and Damned* for book publication.

On October 4, 1934 Fitzgerald wrote to his childhood friend Marie HERSEY Hamm: "I no longer regard St. Paul as my home any more than the Eastern seaboard or the Riviera. This is said with no disloyalty but simply because after all my father was an Easterner and I went East to college and I never did quite adjust myself to those damn Minnesota winters. It was always freezing my cheeks, being a rotten skater etc.—though many events there will always fill me with a tremendous nostalgia" (*Life in Letters*, pp. 270–271).

See David Page and John Koblas, *F. Scott Fitzgerald in Minnesota: Toward the Summit* (St. Cloud: North Star Press, 1996) and Lloyd C. Hackl, *F. Scott Fitzgerald and St. Paul: "Still Home to Me"* (Cambridge, Minn.: Adventure Publications, 1996).

St. Paul Academy Private boys' school at 25 North Dale Street in ST. PAUL, Minnesota, which Fitzgerald entered in September 1908, attending the school for three years before transferring to the NEWMAN SCHOOL in 1911. In 1909 the school newspaper, *The ST. PAUL ACADEMY NOW AND THEN*, printed this note: "If anybody can poison Scotty or stop his mouth in some way, the school at large and myself will be obliged" (I, 4 [Easter 1909]; signed by Sam Kennedy). Fitzgerald played football and baseball and became a debater but was a poor student. However, he achieved his first appearance in print in the October 1909 issue of the *Now and Then*, which included his story, "The Mystery

of the Raymond Mortgage." Headmaster C.N.B. WHEELER recalled Fitzgerald as "a sunny light-haired boy full of enthusiasm who fully foresaw his course in life even in his schoolboy days. . . . I helped him by encouraging his urge to write adventures. It was also his best work, he did not shine in other subjects. He was inventive in all playlets we had and marked his course by his pieces for delivery before the school. He wasn't too popular with his schoolmates. He saw through them too much and wrote about it. . . . I imagined he would become an actor of the variety type, but he didn't. . . . It was his pride in his literary work that put him in his real bent" (in Andrew TURNBULL, *Scott Fitzgerald*, p. 20).

The St. Paul Academy Now and Then ST. PAUL ACADEMY newspaper, which featured Fitzgerald's first appearance in print—"The Mystery of the Raymond Mortgage" (October 1909). His other contributions were a news article, "S.P.A. Men in College Athletics" (1910), and three more stories: "Reade, Substitute Right Half" (1910), "A Debt of Honor" (1910), and "The Room with the Green Blinds" (1911). The four stories are collected in *The Apprentice Fiction of F. Scott Fitzgerald*. In addition, five unsigned limericks may be by Fitzgerald: "There was a young fellow named Ware" (February 1910); "Craw Bryant's a studious boy" (February 1910); "There is an old Lady next door" (June 1910); "There is a young man who's not sour" (June 1910); "Paul Briggs is a cute little (?) lad" (June 1910). See Matthew J. BRUCCOLI, "Fitzgerald's St. Paul Academy Publications: Possible Addenda," *Fitzgerald/Hemingway Annual* (1975), pp. 147–148.

The St. Paul Daily Dirge Facsimiled in *In His Own Time*; 200 copies facsimiled by the *Fitzgerald Newsletter* (Columbus, Ohio, 1968). Parody newspaper written and privately printed by Fitzgerald as a joke; distributed on Friday, January 13, 1922, at the Bad Luck Ball at the University Club in ST. PAUL, Minnesota. The paper reported the dance with the headline "COTILLION IS SAD FAILURE" and included gag stories about local people.

St. Petersburg, Florida In January 1932 the Fitzgeralds vacationed at the Don Ce-Sar Hotel in St. Petersburg, seeking relief for Zelda FITZGERALD's asthma. While in Florida she suffered her second breakdown, resulting in her entering the PHIPPS CLINIC in BALTIMORE in February.

St. Raphaël, France The Fitzgeralds rented VILLA MARIE in VALESCURE, near St. Raphaël on the RIVIERA, June–October 1924.

St. Regis Fictional prep school in *TSOP*, "The Family Bus," "Inside the House," "The Freshest Boy" and "The

Perfect Life"; based on the NEWMAN SCHOOL. In "The Family Bus" St. Regis is described as "America's most expensive school" (*The Price Was High*, p. 497).

"Salesmanship in the Champs-Élysées" Humor article. *The NEW YORKER*, 5 (February 15, 1930), 20; *In His Own Time*. A French car salesman describes his profession. Written as if translated literally from the French.

saleswoman Character in "The Passionate Eskimo." Woman who sends PAN-E-TROON to the five-and-ten store when he is unable to afford a toy airplane in the department store.

Salies de Béarn Spa in the French Pyrenees where Zelda FITZGERALD, who had been having abdominal pains, took a cure in January–February 1926. Fitzgerald described it as "a lost little village" which had "the strongest salt springs in the world—and out of season nothing much else" (to Harold OBER, received February 4, 1926; *Life in Letters*, p. 135; *As Ever*, p. 84).

Sam Character in "Diagnosis." Servant whom Charlie CLAYHORNE saw in his father's room signing a document that Charlie believed to be a revised will.

Scott and Scottie at Salies de Béarn, Pyrenees, 1926

Sammy (Samuele Bendiri) Character in *B&D*. Proprietor of a speakeasy which Anthony PATCH frequents after resigning from his prestigious clubs.

Sanderson, Carl Character in "The Bowl." Suitor whom Vienna THORNE rejects because of his drinking and who shoots himself in the shoulder when she dismisses him.

Sanderson, John (Jack) Character in "A Debt of Honor." Confederate private who falls asleep on sentry duty but later redeems himself by heroically leading a charge.

Sandwood, Mr. Character in "Winter Dreams." One of the foursome with whom Dexter GREEN plays golf.

Sara (Marquise de la Guillet de la Guimpé; Mrs. Cedric Killian) Character in "The Intimate Strangers." Woman who has an affair with Cedric KILLIAN, whom she marries after the death of her first husband, the Marquis DE LA GUILLET DE LA GUIMPÉ.

Sarnemington, Blatchford *See* Rudolph MILLER.

Sarolai, Count Chiki Character in "One Trip Abroad." Austrian who lives with Nelson and Nicole KELLY in PARIS for a while until he hosts a large party at their expense.

The Saturday Evening Post High-paying magazine edited by George Horace LORIMER, with a circulation of 2,750,000 in the 1920s. Contributors in the 1920s and 1930s included William Faulkner (1897–1962), Thomas WOLFE, Ring LARDNER, Joseph HERGESHEIMER, and John P. Marquand (1893–1960). The *Post* was Fitzgerald's primary short story market from 1920 to 1937, printing 65 of the 113 Fitzgerald stories published during that period (in addition to four articles); and he became known as a *Post* author (see *As Ever*, pp. 191–193). After 1924 his agent, Harold OBER, offered the *Post* first refusal on Fitzgerald's stories. The *Post* published some of Fitzgerald's best stories, including "The Last of the Belles" (March 2, 1929), "The Swimmers" (October 19, 1929), "One Trip Abroad" (October 11, 1930), and "Babylon Revisited" (February 21, 1931); but it declined three of his masterpieces: "May Day" (*The SMART SET*, 1920), "The Diamond as Big as the Ritz" (*The Smart Set*, 1922), and "The Rich Boy" (*REDBOOK*, 1926). In May 1926, when Fitzgerald was considering possible serialization of the early matricide version of the novel that became *TITN*, he wrote to Harold Ober: "It is highly sensational. Not only would this bar it from the Post but also they are hostile, as you know, to the general cast of thought that permeates my serious work" (*As Ever*, p. 90).

Fitzgerald was paid $400 for his first *Post* appearance—"Head and Shoulders" in the February 21, 1920 issue; his price steadily increased until it peaked at $4,000 for "At Your Age" (August 17, 1929). He regarded stories as a way to finance work on his novels and grew to resent and denigrate his magazine work. (*See* SHORT STORY WRITER, FITZGERALD AS.) Ernest HEMINGWAY reports in *A Moveable Feast* (1964) that Fitzgerald claimed he wrote real stories then cheapened them for the *Post*, but there is no evidence of this procedure in extant manuscripts of Fitzgerald's stories. In the early 1930s the *Post* began to complain to Ober that the stories he was submitting were not up to Fitzgerald's usual standard, and in 1932 his price fell to $2,500, his 1925 rate. Fitzgerald's final *Post* appearance came on March 6, 1937 with " 'Trouble.' " His later story submissions were rejected, as was an offer of serial rights to *LT/LOLT*. In 1940 when Zelda FITZGERALD suggested that he begin writing *Post* stories again, Fitzgerald replied "I lost the knack of writing the particular kind of stories they wanted" (May 18, 1940; *Life in Letters,* p. 444). He later observed to Zelda: "I think the nine years that intervened between <u>The Great Gatsby</u> and <u>Tender</u> hurt my reputation almost beyond repair because a whole generation grew up in the meanwhile to whom I was only a writer of Post stories" (October 11, 1940; *Life in Letters,* p. 466).

See Jan Cohn, *Creating America: George Horace Lorimer and The Saturday Evening Post* (Pittsburgh: Pittsburgh University Press, 1989) and Otto Friedrich, *Decline and Fall* (New York: Harper & Row, 1970).

Saunders, Miss Character in *The Captured Shadow.* Housekeeper whom Mr. CONNAGE dismisses after he discovers that she has been obtaining private information from the other servants and that she threw his cigars out the window.

Saunders, Ridgeway Character in the Josephine PERRY stories. In "A Nice Quiet Place," while Josephine is away at Island Farms, he falls in love with Evangeline TICKNOR. At Ed BEMENT's house party, Josephine wins him back. In "A Woman with a Past" Josephine goes to the Yale prom with Saunders but becomes interested in Dudley KNOWLETON instead.

Savage, Eleanor Character in *TSOP.* A reckless, romantic atheist whom Amory BLAINE meets in Maryland. She was "the last time that evil crept close to Amory under the mask of beauty" (p. 222). His interest in her fades when, on their last night together before his return to NEW YORK, she nearly rides off a cliff to prove she won't call for God's help on her deathbed. See Elizabeth Beckwith MacKie, "My Friend Scott Fitzgerald," *Fitzgerald/Hemingway Annual* (1970), pp. 16–27.

Savage, Phil Character in "No Flowers." Young man who was expelled from college and with whom Marjorie CLARK's grandmother LUCY broke up as a result.

Savage, Ramilly Character in *TSOP.* Eleanor SAVAGE's grandfather.

Save Me the Waltz Novel. New York: Charles SCRIBNER'S Sons, 1932. Zelda FITZGERALD's only completed novel, written mainly in a six-week period in February and March 1932 in the PHIPPS CLINIC. Like F. Scott Fitzgerald's fiction, this book is autobiographical; Fitzgerald was initially angry about what he perceived as his wife's encroachment on material that was his. Alabama Beggs, a coddled Southern belle, marries David Knight, a handsome Yankee artist whom she meets during World War I; and they have a daughter, Bonnie. David's work is successful, and they live a hectic, glamorous, but ultimately unfulfilling "high life" in NEW YORK and EUROPE: "Nobody knew whose party it was. It had been going on for weeks. When you

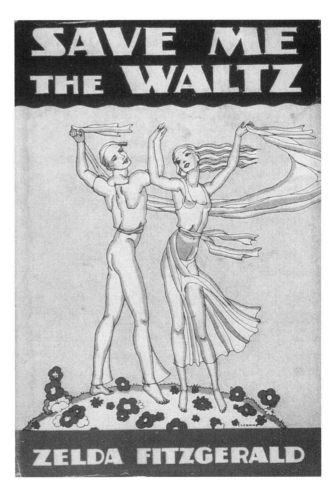

Cleon's dust jacket for Zelda Fitzgerald's only novel, Save Me the Waltz *1932* (Bruccoli Collection, University of South Carolina)

Dust-jacket photo for Zelda Fitzgerald's Save Me the Waltz, *1932* (Bruccoli Collection, University of South Carolina)

felt you couldn't survive another night, you went home and slept and when you got back, a new set of people had consecrated themselves to keeping it alive" (*Collected Writings*, p. 95). Alabama has a brief, unconsummated affair with a French aviator; and David is also unfaithful. Restless and dissatisfied, Alabama decides to embark on a career in ballet, enduring the physical pain of rigorous training and the emotional pain of separation from David and Bonnie. She accepts an offer from the San Carlo Opera Ballet Company in Naples, but blood poisoning from an infected blister in her foot ends her dancing career. She, David, and Bonnie return home to the South, where her father is dying. His loss forces them to begin asking themselves, " 'Why have we practically wasted the best years of our lives?' " (*Collected Writings*, p. 191). At the end of the novel, David and Alabama are sitting together in the twilight and the debris of yet another party, feeling older and, perhaps, even a little wiser.

Save Me the Waltz, published on October 7, 1932 at $2.00, was a commercial failure, selling only about 1,400 copies of its initial printing of 3,010. After the cost of proof revisions was subtracted, the book earned

$120.73. The novel was badly copyedited and riddled with errors; readers also reacted against the sometimes difficult, lushly metaphorical style of Zelda Fitzgerald's prose. Interest in this novel was reawakened with its republication in 1967 by the Southern Illinois University Press. Zelda Fitzgerald's novel stands as a companion volume to Fitzgerald's work, an examination of their life from a different perspective, and an expression of her own voice.

See Henry Dan Piper, *F. Scott Fitzgerald: A Critical Portrait* (New York: Holt, Rinehart and Winston, 1965), pp. 193–204, and Meredith Cary, "*Save Me the Waltz* as a Novel," *Fitzgerald/Hemingway Annual* (1976), pp. 65–78.

by Tracy Simmons Bitonti

Sayre, Anthony D., Jr. (1894–1933) Zelda Sayre FITZGERALD's brother, who was six when she was born. He became an engineer and committed suicide in 1933.

Sayre, Anthony Dickinson (1858–1931) Zelda Sayre FITZGERALD's father, whom she described as a "living fortress" (*Save Me the Waltz*, p. 3). He was born in Tuskegee, Alabama, in 1858; his father was editor of the *Montgomery Post*. Sayre graduated from Roanoke College, was admitted to the bar in 1881, and married Minnie Machen [SAYRE] in 1884. He served in the Alabama legislature, where he was president of the State Senate for a term, and was a City Court judge in MONTGOMERY. In 1909 he was appointed to the Alabama Supreme Court; he was elected to the court the following year and was reelected for the rest of his life. Anxious about providing for his large family, he had a nervous breakdown that was seldom mentioned. He was disturbed by Zelda's unconventional behavior, but she ignored his prohibitions. Judge and Mrs. Sayre discouraged Zelda's interest in F. Scott Fitzgerald, whom they believed lacked the stability to take care of her properly. Fitzgerald later worried that the Sayres believed he was responsible for Zelda's nervous collapse; on December 1, 1930 he reported to them the results of a consultation with Dr. Paul Eugen BLEULER, including, "because I know you despise certain weaknesses in my character," Dr. Bleuler's assurance to him: "This is something that began about five years ago. Let us hope it is only a process of re-adjustment. Stop blaming yourself. You might have retarded it but you couldn't have prevented it" (*Life in Letters*, pp. 203 & 204). Judge Sayre's death on November 17, 1931 probably triggered Zelda's relapse in early 1932.

Sayre, Clothilde (Tilde) (Mrs. John Palmer) (b. 1891) One of Zelda Sayre FITZGERALD's older sisters; she was nine when Zelda was born.

Sayre, Daniel (1808–1888) Zelda Sayre FITZGERALD's paternal grandfather, the husband of Musidora Morgan SAYRE. He edited the *Montgomery Post* and was influential in Masonic politics.

Sayre, Marjorie (Mrs. Minor Williamson Brinson) (b. 1882) One of Zelda Sayre FITZGERALD's older sisters; she was 18 when Zelda was born. Marjorie was a delicate child and suffered from nervous illness much of her life. She accompanied Zelda to NEW YORK for Zelda's wedding.

Sayre, Minnie Buckner Machen (1860–1958) Zelda Sayre FITZGERALD's indulgent mother. Born in Eddyville, Kentucky, in 1860 to Kentucky Senator Willis B. MACHEN and Victoria Mims MACHEN, she was musical and literary in her youth and was once offered a stage role, which her father refused to allow. She married Anthony D. SAYRE at "Mineral Mount" near Eddyville in June 1884. In a July 7, 1938 letter to his daughter, Scottie FITZGERALD, Fitzgerald said that he had made a mistake in marrying Zelda and that "for a long time I hated <u>her</u> mother for giving her nothing in the line of good habit—nothing but 'getting by' and conceit. I never wanted to see again in this world women who were brought up as idlers" (*Life in Letters*, p. 363). In 1939 and 1940 Mrs. Sayre and her other daughters wanted Zelda to be released from HIGHLAND HOSPITAL and to live in MONTGOMERY, an idea which Fitzgerald opposed in a bitter correspondence with them. In an angry letter to Zelda which was not mailed, he criticized her mother: "I loved you—romantically—like your mother, for your beauty + defiant intelligence; but unlike her I wanted to make it useful. I failed, as she did, but my intentions were a hell of a lot purer and since you could have left me at any time I'd like to discover the faintest basis for your family's accusation that I drove you crazy. In so far as it was the conscious work of man, that old witch drove you crazy" (Fall 1939; *Correspondence*, p. 559). When Zelda was discharged from Highland in April 1940 she went to live with her mother in Montgomery, where she remained—with periodic voluntary returns to Highland during times of depression—until her final return to Highland in November 1947.

Sayre, Musidora Morgan (1817–1907) Zelda Sayre FITZGERALD's paternal grandmother, the wife of Daniel SAYRE and the sister of Alabama Senator John Tyler Morgan (1824–1907).

Sayre, Rosalind ("Tootsie") (Mrs. Newman Smith) (b. 1889) One of Zelda Sayre FITZGERALD's older sisters; she was 11 years old when Zelda was born. She later worked at the First National Bank, becoming the first MONTGOMERY girl of a "good family" to hold a job other than teaching. Rosalind served as matron of honor at the Fitzgeralds' wedding. She and her husband were living in Brussels and represented the Sayre family during Zelda's psychiatric treatment in SWITZERLAND. Newman Smith accompanied the Fitzgeralds when Zelda entered PRANGINS CLINIC on June 5, 1930. On June 8 Rosalind, who blamed Fitzgerald's drinking for Zelda's breakdown, wrote to him, "I would almost rather she die now than escape only to go back to the mad world you and she have created for yourselves" (PRINCETON UNIVERSITY LIBRARY; Fitzgerald's draft of a response is printed in *Correspondence*, p. 236). Marion PETERS in "Babylon Revisited" (1931) is based on Rosalind, who regarded Fitzgerald as unfit to raise his daughter, Scottie FITZGERALD.

Sayre, Zelda *See* Zelda Sayre FITZGERALD.

"The Scandal Detectives" Fiction—Basil Duke LEE story. Written March 1928. *The SATURDAY EVENING POST*, 200 (April 28, 1928), 3–4, 178, 181–182, 185; *TAR; B&J*. Basil Duke Lee, age 14, and Riply BUCKNER keep a "Book of Scandal" in which they record the wrongdoings of their fellow townspeople. Basil falls in love with Imogene BISSEL and offers her his school ring; but when she sees him with Margaret TORRENCE she leaves with Hubert BLAIR. Consequently Basil, Riply, and Bill KAMPF disguise themselves and plot to tie up Hubert and put him in his own garbage can; but Basil backs down from the plan when he discovers he likes Hubert after all. The experience makes Basil feel "morally alone" and causes him to reconsider his ambition of being a gentleman burglar.

Sources for this story are noted in Fitzgerald's *Ledger* for March 1911—"The founding of The Scandal Detectives"—and April—"The Scandal detectives go after Reuben" (p. 165).

Scandalabra Play. Bloomfield Hills, Mich. & Columbia, S.C.: Bruccoli Clark, 1980. Written by Zelda FITZGERALD in 1932 after her novel, *Save Me the Waltz*, had been accepted for publication by SCRIBNERS. She had wanted to begin another novel, but Fitzgerald adamantly opposed her use of subject material he felt was his, so she turned to light drama. The result was this "Farce Fantasy in a Prologue and Three Acts." Andrew Messogony and his wife, Flower, stand to inherit $40 million from his uncle. The catch is that they must live an irresponsible life of drinking and misbehaving, which is the opposite of their inclinations. To make herself appear disreputable, Flower telephones the tabloids with a scandalous story about herself and a man whose name she picks from the telephone directory—Peter Consequential. When Andrew says he has had enough of the dissipated charade, the butler reveals that Andrew's resistance was the result his uncle really

wanted, so the fortune is won. The play's dialogue is self-consciously clever, with epigrams such as, "Life without pretensions leaves us facing the basic principles, which are usually a good deal worse and harder to unravel" (*Collected Writings*, p. 222). Zelda's love of language and wit is evident even in the stage directions. For example, at the beginning of Act Two, Scene 2, the stage description includes: "*A promontory juts out like a theory of nebular physics trimming the blue stage with a bias fold such as blue sailor collars chew and left the rest an azure wash*" (*Collected Writings*, p. 241).

Scandalabra was performed by the VAGABOND JUNIOR PLAYERS in BALTIMORE June 26–July 1, 1933. Fitzgerald did what he could to encourage the production, including trimming the over-long script. But the play was still rather confusing, and the reviews were not favorable. *Scandalabra* was first published in a limited edition by Bruccoli Clark in 1980. It includes Meredith Walker's discussion of the differences in the two surviving texts of the play. The play was republished in the 1991 Scribners volume of Zelda Fitzgerald's *Collected Writings*.

by Tracy Simmons Bitonti

Schaeffer, Duncan Character in "Babylon Revisited." Friend from Charlie WALES's days of dissipation. His drunken arrival at the home of Charlie's sister-in-law, Marion PETERS, causes her to change her mind about returning Honoria WALES to Charlie.

Schaeffer, Edna Character in "The Pusher-in-the-Face." Waitress at T. CUSHMAEL's restaurant whom Charles David STUART likes.

Schaffer, May Character in "The Love Boat." Popular high-school girl with whom Bill FROTHINGTON dances at the second high-school dance on a boat.

Scharnhorst Character in "Jacob's Ladder." Mrs. CHOYNSKI's lawyer, whose attempt to blackmail her sister Jenny DELEHANTY after Jenny has become a successful actress is thwarted by Jacob BOOTH.

Scheer, Gaston T. Character in "On an Ocean Wave." Man who has his wife's lover, Professor DOLLARD, thrown overboard.

Scheer, Minna Character in "On an Ocean Wave." Gaston T. SCHEER's wife, who becomes involved with Professor DOLLARD on a transatlantic voyage.

Scheerer, Irene Character in "Winter Dreams." Dexter GREEN's fiancée, whom he abandons when Judy JONES again shows interest in him.

Scheerer, Mrs. Character in "Winter Dreams." Irene SCHEERER's mother.

Schlach, Otto Character in "Six of One—". A farmer's son whom Ed BARNES helps through the Massachusetts Institute of Technology and who becomes a prominent consulting engineer.

Schmiel, Rosemary Character in *LT/LOLT*. One of three secretaries in Pat BRADY's outer office.

Schoatze, George Character in "One Interne" and "Zone of Accident." In "One Interne" he is Bill TULLIVER's medical school classmate who correctly diagnoses Bill's illness. In "Zone of Accident" he is a fellow doctor to whom Bill TULLIVER announces his engagement to AMY.

Schoen, Lieutenant Earl Character in "The Last of the Belles." Lower-class Yankee soldier who pursues Ailie CALHOUN.

Schofield, Charley Character in "Six of One—". Jack SCHOFIELD's younger son, who was expelled from Hotchkiss for smoking. He enters Yale with the encouragement of Gladys IRVING, a young married woman with whom he has been flirting. After graduation he runs his father's business.

Schofield, Jack Character in "Six of One—". Man whose boasting about his sons and their friends leads Ed BARNES to help six boys from his hometown through college to see if they turn out as well.

Schofield, Wister Character in "Six of One—". Jack SCHOFIELD's older son, who is expelled from Yale after having a wreck while driving drunk, and who lacks ambition.

Schroeder, Pete Character in "Magnetism." Studio executive who, as a joke, has Gwen BECKER call George HANNAFORD and claim he spent the night with her.

Schulberg, Budd (b. 1914) Dartmouth graduate and screenwriter who was Fitzgerald's collaborator on *Winter Carnival*. Producer Walter WANGER went with the writers to DARTMOUTH in February 1939 to get fresh ideas; Fitzgerald was drunk during the entire trip. Wanger fired them both, but rehired Schulberg in California. The trip provided the basis for Schulberg's 1950 novel, *The Disenchanted*. He has insisted that his character Manley Halliday is a combination of several HOLLYWOOD writers, including Fitzgerald, but the novel has been regarded as a biographical treatment of Fitzgerald. Fitzgerald's letter about Schulberg's Hollywood novel, *What Makes Sammy Run?* (1941), was used on the dust jacket: "It is a grand book, utterly fearless and with a great deal of beauty side by side with the most bitter satire. Such things *are* in Hollywood—and Budd

Budd Schulberg and Ann Sheridan on the set of Winter Carnival

reports them with fine detachment. . . . Especially toward the end it gets the feeling of Hollywood with extraordinary vividness" (to Bennett Cerf, December 13, 1940; *Letters,* p. 605; *In His Own Time,* p. 159).

Schulberg, the son of B. P. Schulberg (1892–1957), former production head at Paramount, provided inside information about Hollywood for Fitzgerald's work-in-progress on *LT/LOLT*; and narrator Cecelia BRADY was intended as a combination of Schulberg and Scottie FITZGERALD. After Fitzgerald's death editor Maxwell PERKINS approached Schulberg and John O'HARA about finishing *LT/LOLT,* but they declined.

See Schulberg, *Moving Pictures: Memories of a Hollywood Prince* (New York: Stein & Day, 1981).

Schulze, Katherine Childhood friend of Fitzgerald in ST. PAUL; a member of the ELIZABETHAN DRAMATIC CLUB. At the end of *The Great Gatsby,* Nick CARRAWAY recalls Christmas vacations and "the matching of invitations: 'Are you going to the Ordways'? the Herseys'? the Schultzes'?' " (p. 136).

Schurmeier, Gustave (Bobby) One of Fitzgerald's closest childhood friends in ST. PAUL; a member of the ELIZABETHAN DRAMATIC CLUB and William BAKER'S dancing class.

Schuyler, Val Character in "The Rubber Check." Young man whose social reputation is ruined by a bounced check, the story of which is blown out of proportion as it is spread.

Schwartz, Father Adolphus Character in "Absolution." Deranged priest whose ravings confirm Rudolph MILLER'S sense of the existence of a glamour separate from God.

Schwartz, Fifi Character in "The Hotel Child." American girl who doesn't want to leave Europe. Her behavior is criticized by the other hotel guests, and Mr. WEICKER wrongly suspects her of starting a fire in the hotel.

Schwartz, John Character in "The Hotel Child." Fifi SCHWARTZ'S 19-year-old brother, whom she frequently has to retrieve from a café where he drinks with a Russian woman who claims to be a countess.

Schwartz, Mrs. Character in "The Hotel Child." Mother of Fifi and John SCHWARTZ.

Schwartze, Mannie Character in *LT/LOLT.* Former head of a HOLLYWOOD combine who warns Monroe STAHR on the plane about his enemies and who shoots himself.

Screenwriter, Fitzgerald as *See* HOLLYWOOD.

Scribner II, Charles (1854–1930) President of Charles SCRIBNER'S Sons, Fitzgerald's publisher. When Fitzgerald submitted *TSOP* to Scribners in September 1919, Scribner initially declined to put his name on a book which he thought lacked literary merit; editor Maxwell PERKINS'S implied threat of resignation caused Scribner to reconsider, and Perkins accepted the novel on September 16. Fitzgerald expressed his gratitude for financial assistance in a June 1926 letter to Scribner: "For the first time in over four years I am no longer in financial debt to you—or rather I won't be when the money from my short story book becomes due me. But in another sense I shall always be in your debt—for

your unfailing kindness and confidence and obligingness to me in all my exigencies during that time" (*Letters,* p. 205). When Scribner died, Fitzgerald wrote to Perkins that he would miss "his fairness toward things that were of another generation, his general tolerance and simply his being there as titular head of a great business" (May 1930; *Life in Letters,* p. 181).

Scribners Charles Scribner's Sons, Fitzgerald's publisher. When Fitzgerald finished writing "The Romantic Egotist," an early version of *TSOP,* he sent the typescript to Shane LESLIE, who recommended it to Charles SCRIBNER on May 6, 1918. All of the Scribners were PRINCETON alumni, and Fitzgerald hoped the connection would work in his favor. Charles Scribner's Sons rejected the novel and a subsequent revised version. In July 1919 Fitzgerald wrote to Maxwell PERKINS about "The Education of a Personage" (later retitled *This Side of Paradise*), and he sent the typescript to Scribners in September. Only Perkins supported the novel at the Scribners editorial meeting; but at his insistence Scribners accepted the novel, which was published on March 26, 1920.

Fitzgerald maintained a close working relationship with Perkins and the Scribners firm, recommending promising young writers to his publisher. He was instrumental in Ernest HEMINGWAY's shift from Boni & Liveright to Scribners; and he also recommended John BIGGS, Peggy BOYD, Thomas BOYD, Erskine Caldwell (1903–87), André CHAMSON, and Ring LARDNER. In April 1922 he sent Charles Scribner a plan for a cheap reprint series, similar to the Modern Library and Lambskin Library, restricted to Scribners titles (April 19, 1922; *Life in Letters,* pp. 56–58); but the firm was not interested in competing with the established series.

Fitzgerald dealt directly with Scribners regarding the publication of his books; his agent, Harold OBER, specialized in placing his short stories and articles with magazines. Fitzgerald regularly borrowed from Scribners against anticipated royalties—a customary Scribners substitute for large advances (see Perkins to Fitzgerald, May 2, 1921; *Scott/Max,* p. 37). Royalties on the first printing of *GG* canceled Fitzgerald's $6,000 debt to the publisher at that time. However, he accumulated more debt to Scribners through advances and loans. In July 1936 he assigned $1,500 of his life insurance to Scribners in return for payment of two premiums; and while waiting for the settlement of his mother's estate after her death in 1936 he borrowed $2,000 from the publisher. By the time he went to HOLLYWOOD in summer 1937 he owed Scribners at least $9,000; and he arranged for $50 of his weekly MGM paycheck to be paid against the debt. At his death a list of his debts showed that he still owed the firm $5,456.92.

Fitzgerald expressed his loyalty to his publisher when he wrote to Perkins on June 1, 1925 regarding a rumor that he was switching to Boni & Liveright:

> Yesterday arrived a letter from T. R. Smith [an editor at Boni & Liveright] asking for my next book—saying nothing against the Scribners but just asking for it: 'if I happened to be dissatisfied they would be delighted' ect. ect. I answered at once saying that you were one of my closest friends and that my relations with Scribners had always been so cordial and pleasant that I wouldn't think of changeing publishers.
>
> * * *
>
> Now, Max, I have told you many times that you are my publisher, and permanently, as far as one can fling about the word in this too mutable world. If you like I will sign a contract with you immediately for my next three books. The idea of leaving you has never for <u>one single moment</u> entered my head.
>
> <u>First</u>. Tho, as a younger man, I have not always been in sympathy with some of your publishing ideas (which were evolved under the pre-movie, pre-high-literacy-rate conditions of twenty to forty years ago), the personality of you and of Mr. Scribner, the tremendous squareness, courtesy, generosity and open-mindedness I have always met there and, if I may say it, the special consideration you have all had for me and my work, much more than make up the difference.
>
> <u>Second</u> You know my own idea on the advantages of one publisher who backs you and not your work. And my feeling about uniform books in the matter of house and binding.
>
> <u>Third</u> The curious advantage to a rather radical writer in being published by what is now an ultra-conservative house.
>
> <u>Fourth</u> (and least need of saying) Do you think I could treat with another publisher while I have a debt, which is both actual and a matter of honor, of over $3000.00? (*Life in Letters,* pp. 115–116; *Scott/Max,* pp. 107–108).

Scribners published all of Fitzgerald's books during his lifetime, as well as posthumous volumes; Scribners also published Zelda FITZGERALD's novel, *Save Me the Waltz* (1932).

See *Dear Scott/Dear Max* and Roger Burlingame's history of Scribners, *Of Making Many Books* (New York: Scribners, 1946).

Scribner's Magazine Magazine that published two of Fitzgerald's early, didactic stories: "The Cut-Glass Bowl" (May 1920) and "The Four Fists" (June 1920). However, the monthly magazine could not accept much fiction, and editor Robert Bridges (1858–1941) declined most of Fitzgerald's submissions; furthermore, it paid only $150 per story, and Fitzgerald began to seek more lucrative markets with the help of agent Harold OBER. In October 1919 Fitzgerald inquired whether *Scribner's* would be interested in serializing "a literary forgery purporting to be selections from the

note-books of a man who is a complete literary radical. . . . It will be in turns cynical, ingenious, life saturated, critical, and bitter. It will be racy and startling with opinions and personalities" (October 25, 1919; *Life in Letters,* p. 35). "The Diary of a Literary Failure" was not published, and none of it survives. In August 1922 Fitzgerald asked SCRIBNERS editor Maxwell PERKINS about serializing his play *Gabriel's Trombone* (later retitled *The Vegetable*) in *Scribner's Magazine;* Perkins responded that it would be unusual for the magazine to publish a play but that he would like to consider the possibility and would discuss it with Bridges (*Life in Letters,* p. 62; *Scott/Max,* pp. 62–63). Nothing came of the proposal, and the play was not serialized. *Scribner's Magazine* published Fitzgerald's article "Echoes of the Jazz Age" in November 1931 and serialized *TITN* January–April 1934 for $10,000. *LIBERTY* and *COSMOPOLITAN* had both expressed interest in serializing the novel, but Fitzgerald regarded *Scribner's Magazine* as a quality publication that would be a better venue for his most ambitious novel. Managing editor Alfred DASHIELL dealt with the serial.

Second Story Salle Character in *Assorted Spirits.* Burglar whom Peter WETHERBY's maid, HULDA, lets into his house to steal the $10,000 that his guest, Josephus HENDRIX, has brought to purchase the house.

Sedgewick, Earl Character in "The Family Bus." Boy at whose house Dick HENDERSON's high-school classmates assemble for the Harvest Picnic. While Dick is there, his fraternity brothers paint insulting slogans on his car.

Seldes, Gilbert Vivian (1893–1970) American literary critic to whom Fitzgerald read part of *GG* in the summer of 1924. Ernest HEMINGWAY believed that Seldes's glowing review of the novel (*see GG* entry) made Fitzgerald so self-conscious that he felt compelled to make his next novel a masterpiece, causing his delay in completing *TITN* (September 4, 1929; *Ernest Hemingway: Selected Letters,* p. 305). In his review of *TITN* Seldes concluded: "He has gone behind generations, old or new, and created his own image of human beings. And in doing so has stepped again to his natural place at the head of the American writers of our time" (*New York Evening Journal,* April 12, 1934, p. 23; *FSF: The Critical Reception,* p. 293).

In 1936 Seldes wrote to Fitzgerald to discourage him from publishing a collection of his autobiographical articles, such as the "Crack-Up" essays: "You seem more and more to me an essential figure in America and sooner or later you will have to say your complete say, not only in fiction, but in the facts about yourself and the part you played at the beginning and what you think of it now. And that sort of book, of supreme importance, will have all the edge taken off it, if you now publish the raw material, the mere fact without the thought" (June 26, 1936; *Correspondence,* p. 436). Fitzgerald, who had been discussing such a collection with editor Maxwell PERKINS—who had mentioned it to Seldes—dropped the project. After Fitzgerald's death, when Perkins considered enlisting Hemingway's help to finish Fitzgerald's work-in-progress on *LT/LOLT,* Zelda FITZGERALD suggested Seldes instead; after conferring with Seldes, Perkins decided to publish the novel as Fitzgerald left it.

Seldes was managing editor of *The Dial* (1919–23) and later a regular drama critic for the magazine (1923–29). His books include *The Seven Lively Arts* (1924) and *The Movies and the Talkies* (1929); he edited *First and Last* (1934), a collection of Ring LARDNER's writings.

"Self-Interview" *See* "An Interview with F. Scott Fitzgerald."

Selznick, David O. (1902–1965) Producer who in March 1922 asked Fitzgerald to write a movie synopsis for actress Elaine Hammerstein (1897–1948); he rejected the 1,500–word synopsis for "Trans-Continental Kitty" which Fitzgerald submitted in April. In January 1939, during the last weeks of his MGM contract, Fitzgerald was loaned to Selznick to revise the screenplay for *Gone With the Wind.* Although he was dismissed after a short time, Fitzgerald regarded Selznick International as "the pleasantest studio that I have worked in" (to Leland HAYWARD, December 6, 1939; *Life in Letters,* p. 425).

See David Thomson, *Showman: The Life of David O. Selznick* (New York: Knopf, 1992).

" 'Send Me In, Coach' " Fiction. Written October 1936. *ESQUIRE,* 6 (November 1936), 55, 218–221. At Camp Rahewawa, CASSIUS, BUGS, Bill WATCHMAN, and Henry GRADY are rehearsing a play about a baseball team whose star player, Playfair, is disqualified because he played professional ball in the summer. Bill Watchman learns that his father has committed suicide after being acquitted at a trial. The OLD MAN who runs the camp warns counselor RICKEY to stay away from his wife; he has arranged for Rickey's board and tuition at the state college in the coming fall so that Rickey can play football there.

" 'The Sensible Thing' " Fiction. Written November 1923. *LIBERTY,* 1 (July 5, 1924), 10–14; *ASYM.* George O'KELLY, who has always wanted to be an engineer, has left an engineering job to work as an insurance clerk so he can earn enough money to marry Jonquil CARY, the Southern girl he loves. When he receives a letter that indicates she is having doubts about marrying him,

he asks for vacation time to go visit her, and he loses his job. During his visit she breaks their engagement because "it doesn't seem to be the sensible thing" (*ASYM*, p. 226). More than a year later he returns to her, having risen rapidly in an engineering job in Peru and also being on his way to a great opportunity for success in NEW YORK. She agrees to marry him; and although he realizes that he can never recapture the freshness of their early love, he is content—unlike Jay GATSBY—to accept that there is "never the same love twice)" (p. 238).

Fitzgerald told Maxwell PERKINS that this was a "Story about Zelda + me. All true" (June 1, 1925; *Life in Letters*, p. 121; *Scott/Max*, p. 113).

"Sentiment—And the Use of Rouge" Fiction. *The NASSAU LITERARY MAGAZINE*, 73 (June 1917), 107–123; *Apprentice Fiction*. Clay SYNEFORTH briefly returns to England after two years of military service in World War I and is disturbed by the changes he encounters in moral values. After sleeping with his dead brother's fiancée, Eleanor MARBROOKE, he returns to the war and is fatally wounded. As he is dying he reflects on the "muddle" the world is in—thoughts that were transferred to Amory BLAINE in the final chapter of *TSOP*.

Seymour, McNeil V. (Mac) Childhood friend of Fitzgerald in ST. PAUL; a member of the ELIZABETHAN DRAMATIC CLUB and William BAKER's dancing class.

"The Shadow" Character in *The Captured Shadow*. Alias of Thorton Hart DUDLEY who, on a bet, acts as a burglar for two weeks and baffles the NEW YORK police.

"Shadow Laurels" Play. *The NASSAU LITERARY MAGAZINE*, 71 (April 1915), 1–10; *Apprentice Fiction*. Jaques CHANDELLE, who left France for America 28 years before, returns to PARIS to seek information about his dead father. In PITOU's wine shop he learns that his father was a drunkard and meets his father's three closest friends, who loved him for giving expression to their lives.

"Shadow Laurels" was Fitzgerald's first literary exploration of his feelings about his father, Edward FITZGERALD.

Shaggy Character in "Shaggy's Morning." Dog who seeks amusement while his owners, the BRAIN and the BEARD, are away for the day.

"Shaggy's Morning" Fiction. Written March 1935. *ESQUIRE*, 3 (May 1935), 26, 160. A dog named SHAGGY looks for amusement while his owners, the BRAIN and the BEARD, are away for the day. He socializes with two dogs referred to as the SQUIRT and MY FRIEND, the

latter of which is hit by a car. Possibly intended as a parody of Ernest HEMINGWAY's work.

Shalder, Howard Character in "A Change of Class." Bootlegger who runs away with Violet JOHNSON.

Shalder, Irene Character in "A Change of Class." Woman with whom Philip JADWIN had been in love when she was a typist in his office but to whom he had failed to propose because of the difference in their social classes.

Shank, Martha Marie Owner of a secretarial service in ASHEVILLE, North Carolina, whom Fitzgerald hired as his business manager in 1936. She saved his working drafts and donated them to PRINCETON UNIVERSITY LIBRARY in 1959.

Shaver, Harmon Character in "No Harm Trying." Would-be producer who joins Pat HOBBY in assembling a production unit for a movie based on ERIC's idea.

Shearer, Norma **(1900–1983)** Academy Award–winning movie star and wife of producer Irving THALBERG. Fitzgerald's drunken behavior at a party hosted by the Thalbergs was the basis for his 1932 story "Crazy Sunday." The day after the party Shearer sent him a telegram: "I THOUGHT YOU WERE ONE OF THE MOST AGREEABLE PERSONS AT OUR TEA" (c. December 1931; *Correspondence*, p. 282). A draft of the inscription he planned for a copy of *LT/LOLT* to give to Shearer explains his use of Thalberg as a model for Monroe STAHR (*Life in Letters*, p. 468).

Shenton, Edward (1895–1977) Popular and prolific artist who specialized in black-and-white illustrations. His style perfectly suited book illustration. Shenton's portrait of Fitzgerald appeared on the cover of *SCRIBNER'S MAGAZINE* for the first *TITN* installment (January 1934). Fitzgerald liked his woodcut illustrations for the serial so much that he requested they be used in the book; he wrote to Maxwell PERKINS on January 13, 1934: "What do you think of the idea of using twenty-four of those wood-cuts, which illustrate the serial, as head and tail pieces for chapters in the book or, alternatively, interspersing them though the novel? I think it is comparatively an innovation in recent fiction and might give the book a certain distinction. I've gotten very fond of the illustrations" (*Life in Letters*, p. 244; *Scott/Max*, pp. 188–189). Fitzgerald also wired to Perkins his dissatisfaction with the dust jacket illustration and expressed his preference for a Shenton woodcut (January 28, 1934; *Correspondence*, p. 325); the jacket on the published book is by an unidentified artist. Shenton praised the novel in a letter to Fitzger-

ald: "The pattern of disintegration you've created, is so subtle, adroit, so technically proficient—and so completely moving—that the book seems to have a new form; something entirely it's own. . . . I am delighted to have my drawings a permanent part of the book" (Fall 1933; *Correspondence,* p. 319).

Shenton also provided illustrations for other novels, including *Green Hills of Africa* (1935) by Ernest HEMINGWAY, *The Unvanquished* (1938) and *Big Woods* (1955) by William Faulkner (1897–1962), and *The Yearling* (1938) and *Cross Creek* (1942) by Marjorie Kinnan RAWLINGS.

by Park Bucker

Sheppard-Pratt Hospital On May 19, 1934 Zelda FITZGERALD was transferred in a catatonic state from CRAIG HOUSE to Sheppard and Enoch Pratt Hospital in TOWSON, Maryland, outside BALTIMORE; her physician was Dr. William ELGIN. Zelda attempted suicide during her stay; and on April 8, 1936 she was transferred to HIGHLAND HOSPITAL in ASHEVILLE, North Carolina.

"Sherwood Anderson on the Marriage Question" Review of *Many Marriages* by Sherwood ANDERSON. *New York Herald,* March 4, 1923, section 9, p. 5; *In His Own Time.* Fitzgerald describes the method as "Anderson's accustomed transcendental naturalism" (*In His Own Time,* p. 139) and notes that the novel "casts a curious and startling light on the entire relation between man and woman" (p. 140).

the Shevlins Characters in "The Curious Case of Benjamin Button." Hosts of the dance where Benjamin BUTTON meets Hildegarde MONCRIEF.

Shinn, Everett (1876–1953) Respected and popular painter who began his career as a magazine and newspaper illustrator. A member of the "Ash-Can School," he is best known for his depiction of lower-class subjects. He illustrated "Hot & Cold Blood" (August 1923) for *HEARST'S INTERNATIONAL.*

Shoonover, Joe Character in "That Kind of Party." Boy whom Terrence R. TIPTON persuades to host a party for the purpose of kissing games.

Shoonover, Mrs. Character in "That Kind of Party." Joe SHOONOVER's mother, who offers to play the piano for "Clap-in-and-clap-out."

"A Short Autobiography (With Acknowledgments to Nathan)" Prose sketch. *The NEW YORKER,* 5 (May 25, 1929), 22–23. Yearly inventory of Fitzgerald's drinks from 1913 to 1929.

Short Story Writer, Fitzgerald as "The problem was a magazine story," explains the author of "Afternoon of

an Author" (*ESQUIRE,* August 1936), an autobiographical essay Fitzgerald sold for $250, "that had become so thin in the middle that it was about to blow away" (*AOAA,* p. 178). Over the course of his 20-year career, Fitzgerald doubtless faced such a problem many times, for he wrote some 160 stories, selling more than 90 to the high-paying or "slick" magazines (65 of these to *The SATURDAY EVENING POST*). Even as the money his short stories commanded rose through the 1920s, Fitzgerald with increasing bitterness complained of the "trash" he felt compelled to write, once even comparing himself to "an old whore" turning $4,000 tricks (to Ernest HEMINGWAY, September 9, 1929; *Life in Letters,* p. 169). Taking their cue from Fitzgerald's own remarks, many critics have ignored or dismissed the bulk of his stories as hack work. But as "Afternoon of an Author" suggests, for Fitzgerald writing short stories was neither easy work nor easy money. His stories, even those most blatantly "made for the trade" (to Maxwell PERKINS, March 26, 1935; *Correspondence,* p. 406), contained something of their author: "there was one little drop of something not blood, not a tear, not my seed, but me more intimately than these, in every story, it was the extra I had" (*Notebooks,* #885).

In the beginning of his career, Fitzgerald evidently enjoyed the challenge of cracking *The Saturday Evening Post,* then the country's most competitive and remunerative market for magazine fiction. More than just entertainment, Fitzgerald's best slick fiction was a vehicle for sharp social observation. In such early *Post* stories as "Bernice Bobs Her Hair" (May 1, 1920), "The Ice Palace" (May 22, 1920), and "The Offshore Pirate" (May 29, 1920), all appearing later in the first of Fitzgerald's four story collections, *Flappers and Philosophers* (1920), the young author charmed his audience and began to fill his destined role as spokesman for his generation. Moreover, through the creation of his female characters—conventional BERNICE, restless Sally Carrol HAPPER, and courageous Ardita FARNAM—he treated with seriousness the conflicts and desires of young American women struggling toward a new identity in the still traditional society of the 1920s.

Complaining to his literary agent Harold OBER "that the magazines want only flapper stories from me" (received September 11, 1922; *As Ever,* p. 48), Fitzgerald lost the exuberance with which he wrote his first stories for the *Post* as he learned that the slicks would not accept too dark a view of society or too unconventional an approach. His naturalistic "May Day" (July 1920) was evidently too strong for the slicks and had to be sold to H. L. MENCKEN's low-paying magazine *The SMART SET.* Fitzgerald was particularly discouraged when "The Popular Girl" (February 11 & 18, 1922), a story he considered "cheap," brought $1,500 from the *Post* while "The Diamond as Big as the Ritz" (*The Smart Set,* June 1922), a sharp satire on American materialism

that he considered "genuinely imaginative" (February 5, 1922; *Life in Letters,* p. 54; *As Ever,* p. 36), was rejected by the slicks and brought only $300 from Mencken's magazine. These two disturbing stories were the strongest of those he chose for his second collection, *Tales of the Jazz Age* (1922).

Fitzgerald wanted to be both a popular success and a serious artist, and though he sometimes thought of his stories solely as a means of making money, he was often able to write his popular stories with artistic purpose. Clearly at times he catered to the conventions of magazine fiction. Written to finance a trip to EUROPE and a summer of work on *GG* (1925), such stories as "The Third Casket" (*The Saturday Evening Post,* May 31, 1924), "The Unspeakable Egg" (*The Saturday Evening Post,* July 12, 1924), and "One of My Oldest Friends" (*WOMAN'S HOME COMPANION,* September 1925) use surprise endings, are marred by contrivance or coincidence, and fall into sentimentality. Yet in other stories—"Winter Dreams" (*METROPOLITAN MAGAZINE,* December 1922), "Absolution" (*The AMERICAN MERCURY,* June 1924), and " 'The Sensible Thing' " (*LIBERTY,* July 1924)—Fitzgerald was able to explore themes and ideas that were related to his novel. Although in his correspondence Fitzgerald had settled into the pose of the split man—half serious novelist, half slave to the commercial short story—the chasm between even his most acclaimed novel and his most contrived stories was not absolute: he lifted a striking description of the moonlight on Long Island Sound out of the otherwise weak story "Diamond Dick and the First Law of Woman" (*HEARST'S INTERNATIONAL,* April 1924) and placed it directly into *GG.* The stories Fitzgerald selected for his third story collection, *All the Sad Young Men* (1926), including the powerful study "The Rich Boy" (*REDBOOK,* June 1926), reveal an author who regularly achieves the often uneasy balance between financial necessity and artistic integrity.

In the nine years that passed between the publication of *GG* and *TITN* (1934), Fitzgerald wrote 55 stories, all but a handful of which appeared in the *Post,* reaching his peak story price of $4,000 with "At Your Age" (*The Saturday Evening Post,* August 17, 1929). Although he later came to believe that this interval permanently damaged his reputation "because a whole generation grew up in the meanwhile to whom [he] was only a writer of Post stories" (to Zelda FITZGERALD, October 11, 1940; *Life in Letters,* p. 466), many of the stories he wrote for the magazine were splendid. His last and richest story collection, *Taps at Reveille* (1935), includes such acclaimed stories as "The Last of the Belles" (*The Saturday Evening Post,* March 2, 1929), "Babylon Revisited" (*The Saturday Evening Post,* February 21, 1931), and "Crazy Sunday" (*The American Mercury,* October 1932).

In the final five years of his career, Fitzgerald, as he explained to Zelda, "lost the knack" (May 18, 1940; *Life*

in Letters, p. 444) of writing stories for the *Post* and began submitting his work to *Esquire,* a magazine that paid little but preferred shorter stories and permitted Fitzgerald greater flexibility in subject and approach. Although some of Fitzgerald's efforts of this period are the weakest of his career, he was able at times to produce memorable works such as "Afternoon of an Author" (*Esquire,* August 1936) and the haunting story "The Lost Decade" (*Esquire,* December 1939).

Readers of Fitzgerald's stories will find wit, a warm and graceful style, and keen observation. In addition, the stories provide insight into the man and his career. Weak and strong, the stories chronicle not only the times in which Fitzgerald lived but also his struggle as an artist in the literary marketplace.

See Jackson R. Bryer, ed., *The Short Stories of F. Scott Fitzgerald: New Approaches in Criticism,* and Bryant Mangum, *A Fortune Yet: Money in the Art of F. Scott Fitzgerald's Short Stories.*

by George P. Anderson

"A Short Trip Home" Fiction. Written October 1927. *The SATURDAY EVENING POST,* 200 (December 17, 1927), 6–7, 55, 57–58; *TAR.* Set in ST. PAUL, Minnesota. Ellen BAKER breaks a date with Joe JELKE for the Cotillion Club dance to meet a mysterious, sinister man (Joe VARLAND), who hits Joe with brass knuckles when he interferes. Eddie STINSON asks where she met the man; she says she met him on the train and warns Eddie to mind his own business. The next day Eddie sees the man outside a pool hall; but the man disappears and no one else has seen him. Eddie is relieved when Ellen's mother tells him that Ellen is leaving that night to visit friends in Chicago on her way back to school, until he remembers that those friends are in Florida for Christmas. He follows Ellen to Chicago and tries to keep her from meeting the man. He notes a change in her behavior and expression whenever they discuss the man, and he senses an evil presence. When he leaves Ellen's train compartment, he encounters the man, who warns him to get off the train. Eddie realizes that the man, who seems to be fading except when he draws strength from preying on people, is a ghost. The man collapses, and Eddie sees that the sleeping Ellen is herself again. Three months later Eddie returns to the pool hall, in search of information about the man. He discovers that the man, named Joe Varland, had died last winter and that he had made money by preying on girls traveling alone on trains.

Fitzgerald described "A Short Trip Home" as "the first real ghost story I ever wrote" (late October 1927; *As Ever,* p. 102). He borrowed the first description of Joe Varland for the newsvendor in *TITN* (Book I, Chapter 21) and included a footnote with the story in *TAR* apologizing for seeming to serve "warmed-over fare." In his review of *The Last Tycoon,* which included five of Fitzgerald's stories, James THURBER noted, "I

mourn the absence of 'A Short Trip Home' whether you do or not" ("Taps at Assembly," *The New Republic*, 106 [February 9, 1942], 211–212; *FSF: The Critical Reception*, p. 382).

Shorty Character in "A Short Trip Home." Man at a pool hall who informs Eddie STINSON that Joe VARLAND is dead and tells him about Varland's racket.

" 'Show Mr. and Mrs. F. to Number——' " Autobiographical article. *ESQUIRE*, 1 & 2 (May & June 1934), 19, 154B; 23, 120; *CU*. Bylined "F. Scott and Zelda Fitzgerald," but credited to Zelda FITZGERALD in *Ledger*; written by Zelda and revised by Fitzgerald. Description of the hotels which the Fitzgeralds visited during their travels over the years.

Shugrue, Miss Willie Character in "Strange Sanctuary." Thief who poses as Charlie CRAIG's trained nurse and tells Craig's niece, Dolly HAINES, that her uncle (who is not really at home) is too ill to see her.

Shuttleworth, Edward Character in *B&D*. Adam PATCH's secretary, the executor of his estate, and recipient of his largest bequest. He shoots himself when Anthony PATCH successfully contests his grandfather's will after two appeals.

Sibly-Biers, Lady Caroline Character in *TITN*. Corrupt Englishwoman whom Dick and Nicole DIVER meet on T. F. GOLDING's yacht. Dick offends her, and she observes that he was seen in questionable company in LAUSANNE, where he was interviewing a homosexual prospective patient. She is later arrested with Mary [NORTH] Minghetti for picking up two girls while dressed as sailors, and Dick arranges for their release from jail. Partially based on Bijou O'CONOR.

Simmons, Rabbit Character in *The Captured Shadow*. Crook who works as a spy for "The SHADOW." Hubert CONNAGE, while drunk, brings Simmons home with him and promises to make him an alderman.

Simms, Lud Character in "Winter Dreams." Judy JONES's husband, who drinks and runs around.

Sinclair, Rhoda Character in "Forging Ahead." Mrs. REILLY's unattractive daughter, whom Basil Duke LEE is required to escort because his great-uncle Benjamin REILLY, Rhoda's step-father, gives him a summer job.

Singleton, Thea Character in "One Interne." Anaesthetist who is Doctor Howard DURFEE's girlfriend until he announces his engagement to Helen DAY.

"Six of One—" Fiction. Written July 1931. *REDBOOK*, 58 (February 1932), 22–25, 84, 86, 88; *The Price Was*

High. Jack SCHOFIELD brags to his friend Ed BARNES about his sons and their friends—Wister SCHOFIELD, Charley SCHOFIELD, Howard KAVENAUGH, another KAVENAUGH, Larry PATT, and Beau LEBAUME—who he says remind him of "young knights." Barnes doesn't share Schofield's optimism about their future; he says he could pick six boys from the high school in his little Ohio hometown who could match them. Barnes chooses Otto SCHLACH, James MATSKO, Jack STUBBS, George WINFIELD, Louis IRELAND, and Gordon VANDERVERE and helps them through college. All six of them achieve a measure of success; but of Schofield's six, only his son Charley and Larry Patt turn out well. Barnes reflects on the fates of the six boys who were "brought up as princes with none of the responsibilities of princes" and regrets "all that waste at the top" (*The Price Was High*, p. 381).

"Six of One—", written as "Half a Dozen of the Other," is one of the strongest expressions of Fitzgerald's regret that wealth and privilege are seldom combined with seriousness and responsibility.

Skiggs, Dr. Hepezia Character in "Pain and the Scientist." Walter Hamilton BARTNEY's neighbor, a Christian Scientist.

Skyland Hotel Hotel in HENDERSONVILLE, North Carolina where Fitzgerald rented a cheap room November–December 1935 and wrote "The Crack-Up" (February 1936).

Slagle Character in *GG*. Man whose telephone call after Jay GATSBY's death reveals that Gatsby had been involved in handling stolen securities.

"Sleep of a University" Verse. *The NASSAU LITERARY MAGAZINE*, 76 (November 1920), 161; *In His Own Time*, *Poems*. This was Fitzgerald's "paraphrase" of "Princeton Asleep" by Aiken Reichner, published in the same issue of the *Nassau Lit* (p. 158).

"Sleeping and Waking" Autobiographical essay. *ESQUIRE*, 2 (December 1934), 34, 159–160; *CU*. An account of Fitzgerald's insomnia. Though he attempts to induce sleep through dreams of glory on the football field or in war, he is haunted instead by a sense of "Waste and horror—what I might have been and done that is lost, spent, gone, dissipated, unrecapturable" (*CU*, p. 67). The happy dream that finally comes with sleep includes a six-line poem that has become Fitzgerald's best-known verse and which he incorporated into "Thousand-and-First-Ship."

Sloane, Cary Character in "The Rich Boy." Dissolute young man with whom Edna HUNTER is having an affair. When Edna's nephew Anson HUNTER confronts them and threatens to tell Edna's husband and

Sloane's father, Sloane kills himself by jumping off a bridge.

Sloane, Fred Character in *TSOP*. Amory BLAINE'S PRINCETON friend with whom he visits the apartment of two NEW YORK showgirls, Phoebe COLUMN and Axia MARLOWE, an occasion on which Amory has a hallucination of a devil figure.

Sloane, Mr. Character in *GG*. Man who brings Tom BUCHANAN to Jay GATSBY'S house for a drink.

Slocum, Dr. Clarence (**1873–1950**) Director of CRAIG HOUSE sanitarium in BEACON, New York, where Zelda FITZGERALD was a patient March–May 1934.

Slocum, Mr. and Mrs. Characters in "On Schedule." René DU CARY'S next-door neighbors, with whom he arranges for Becky SNYDER to board until he can marry her.

The Smart Set: A Magazine of Cleverness Magazine, edited by H. L. MENCKEN and George Jean NATHAN from 1914 to 1923, which had a significant influence on the literary and critical community despite its comparatively small circulation (about 20,000). *The Smart Set* printed Fitzgerald's first professional publication: "Babes in the Woods" (September 1919), a story revised from *The NASSAU LITERARY MAGAZINE* (May 1917), and his only sale in spring 1919. After completing *TSOP* that fall, Fitzgerald submitted more stories and plays— some revised from the *Nassau Lit*—to *The Smart Set*, including "The Debutante" (November 1919), "Porcelain and Pink" (January 1920), "Benediction" (February 1920), and "Dalyrimple Goes Wrong" (February 1920), but because *The Smart Set* paid only $35–40 per story, he began to seek more lucrative markets. In an undated letter to Harold OBER, he inquired: "Is there any market at all for the cynical or pessimistic story except <u>Smart Set</u> or does realism bar a story from any well-paying magazine no matter how cleverly its done?" (*As Ever*, p. 7). He returned to *The Smart Set* with two masterpieces which were declined by the high-paying slicks: "May Day" (July 1920) and "The Diamond as Big as the Ritz" (June 1922).

Smidy Character in "The Mystery of the Raymond Mortgage." Boy whom John SYREL employs to locate Mrs. RAYMOND.

"The Smilers" Fiction. Written September 1919. *The SMART SET*, 62 (June 1920), 107–111; *The Price Was High*. Sylvester STOCKTON is continually annoyed by the smiles of friends and strangers. He assumes people are smiling because they are unacquainted with misery and think they'll always be happy; he doesn't realize that the people he encounters, such as Betty TEARLE, Waldron

CROSBY, and a waiter named JERRY, have their own problems.

Smith, Adrian Character in "The Rough Crossing." Man who quarrels with his wife, Eva SMITH, over his interest in Betsy D'AMIDO during their voyage to France.

Smith, Edna Character in *LT/LOLT*. Kathleen MOORE'S friend whom Monroe STAHR initially mistakes for Kathleen because he is confused about which woman was wearing a silver belt with stars cut out of it.

Smith, Eva Character in "The Rough Crossing." Woman who quarrels with her husband, Adrian SMITH, over his interest in Betsy D'AMIDO during their voyage to France.

Smith, Mr. Character in *LT/LOLT*. Name by which Monroe STAHR identifies himself on the airplane in the first chapter.

Smith, Mr. Character in "Pat Hobby's Secret." Doorman/bouncer who kills R. Parke WOLL.

Smith, Mrs. Character in "Pat Hobby's Secret." Mr. SMITH'S wife, who warns Pat HOBBY against serving as a witness against her husband, who is on trial for killing R. Parke WOLL.

Smith, Priscilla Character in "A Man in the Way." HOLLYWOOD writer whose idea is stolen by Pat HOBBY.

Smith, Rosalind Sayre See Rosalind SAYRE.

"A Snobbish Story" Fiction—Josephine PERRY story. Written September 1930. *The SATURDAY EVENING POST*, 203 (November 29, 1930), 6–7, 36, 38, 40, 42; *B&J*. While at Lake Forest, Josephine Perry meets reporter John Boynton BAILEY, who asks her to be in his play, "Race Riot," which she asks her father to back financially. Bailey's wife, EVELYN, jealous of his attention to Josephine, attempts suicide; and Mr. and Mrs. PERRY worry about how close Josephine came to scandal. Josephine decides that her value lies "in the immediate, shimmering present" and throws in her lot with "the rich and powerful of this world forever" (*B&J*, p. 269).

Snooks (Snukes) Character in *The Vegetable*. Bootlegger who sells gin to Jerry FROST. In Act II he is Ambassador to the United States from Irish Poland and strikes up a deal to trade the Buzzard Islands for Idaho.

Snyder, Becky Character in "On Schedule." Nineteen-year-old girl whom René DU CARY plans to marry and who is serving as a companion to his daughter, Noël DU CARY.

Soft Shoes Character in "Tarquin of Cheepside." Man who writes the story of his evening's escapade; its identification as "The Rape of Lucrece" indicates that he is William Shakespeare (1564–1616).

"Some Interrupted Lines to Sheilah" Poem. Fair-copy manuscript facsimiled on the rear endpaper of *Beloved Infidel* by Sheilah GRAHAM and Gerold Frank (New York: Holt, 1958); *Poems 1911–1940*. Poem for Graham, Fitzgerald's companion in HOLLYWOOD.

"Southern Girl" Fiction by Zelda FITZGERALD. *COLLEGE HUMOR*, 18 (October 1929), 27–28, 94, 96; *Bits of Paradise*; *Zelda Fitzgerald: The Collected Writings*. Bylined "F. Scott and Zelda Fitzgerald" but credited to Zelda in *Ledger*. Harriet runs her family's boarding house in the Southern town of Jeffersonville. Dan Stone, a soldier from Ohio, breaks his engagement to Louise when he falls in love with Harriet. When Harriet later visits Dan in Ohio, she seems out of place in his wealthy, quiet family home; and he breaks his engagement to Harriet to marry Louise. Harriet returns to the South and later elopes with Charles, who is from Ohio; she names their baby Dan.

Speers, Mrs. Elsie Character in *TITN*. Based on Lois MORAN's mother, Gladys Dowling Moran. Rosemary HOYT's mother, twice widowed. She has a great influence on Rosemary and decides business matters for her, but she is ready for Rosemary to be "spiritually weaned" (p. 16). She encourages Rosemary to pursue her interest in Dick DIVER.

Spengler, Oswald (1880–1936) German author of *Decline of the West* (1918–22), a book about the philosophy of history which Fitzgerald admired. Fitzgerald wrote to Maxwell PERKINS about Spengler in 1940: "I read him the same summer I was writing 'The Great Gatsby' and I don't think I ever quite recovered from him" (June 6, 1940; *Scott/Max*, p. 263). (Since *Decline of the West* was not translated into English until 1926, and Fitzgerald did not read German, he must have read about Spengler's work.) Fitzgerald planned for Sheilah GRAHAM to read *Decline of the West* at the end of the two-year "College of One" educational program he designed for her; and Kathleen MOORE's lover ("the MAN") in *LT/LOLT* educated her with a view toward reading Spengler.

Spiegel, Doris (b. 1907) Illustrator of the dust jacket for *Taps at Reveille* (1935). She also provided illustrations for *The NEW YORKER* magazine.

Spigot, Miss Character in *Assorted Spirits*. Will CHAPMAN's doting aunt, who calls on the Peter WETHERBYS and thinks they were all drunk when HULDA, their maid, tells her about all the "spirits" the previous night.

Spillman, Mr. Character in "Fate in Her Hands." Ben KASTLER's secretary, who telephones to say that Ben's office building collapsed shortly after he left.

"The Spire and the Gargoyle" Fiction. *The NASSAU LITERARY MAGAZINE*, 72 (February 1917), 297–307; *Apprentice Fiction*. Some material from this story was incorporated into *TSOP* in the segment titled "A Damp Symbolic Interlude." An UNDERGRADUATE who flunks out of the university has three encounters with the PRECEPTOR who grades his final exam: immediately after the exam, five years later in a NEW YORK museum, and on a train returning to the university campus. The preceptor, who left for a higher-paying job teaching high school, regrets his departure from the university; but the undergraduate senses a greater loss because the campus symbolizes aspirations left unfulfilled. Although PRINCETON is not named in the story, it clearly expresses Fitzgerald's love for Princeton and his regret at wasted opportunities there.

Spirelli, Lieutenant Character in "A Change of Class." Italian-American officer whose presence at the SHALDERS' party makes Earl JOHNSON wonder whether he has really risen socially.

Squires, Dr. Mildred Taylor Psychiatrist who treated Zelda FITZGERALD at PHIPPS CLINIC in 1932. When Zelda sent the typescript of her novel, *Save Me the Waltz* (1932), to editor Maxwell PERKINS without consulting her husband, Fitzgerald wrote to Dr. Squires expressing his anger over Zelda's use of material he was also using in his work-in-progress on *TITN* (March 14, 1932; *Life in Letters*, pp. 208–210). *Save Me the Waltz* is dedicated to Dr. Squires.

Squires, Tom Character in "At Your Age." Fifty-year-old man who seeks to restore some youth to his life by dating young Annie LORRY.

the squirt Character in "Shaggy's Morning." Little dog who lives next door to SHAGGY.

Stacomb, Mr. Character in "The Rough Crossing." Fellow passenger who invites Adrian SMITH to play in the deck-tennis tournament.

Stahr, Monroe Character in *LT/LOLT*. Based on MGM producer Irving THALBERG. Pat BRADY's business partner, a HOLLYWOOD movie producer and self-made man, the "boy wonder" of the industry. He suffers from heart trouble and is working himself to death. As a paternalistic employer who represents personal responsibility, Stahr is under attack by communists; and as a creative artist who cares more about the quality of pictures than their profit-making potential, he is under attack by the money men of his studio. A lonely man since the death of his wife, actress Minna DAVIS, Stahr

falls in love with Kathleen MOORE, who resembles Minna and whom he first sees after an earthquake hits the movie studio. However, he hesitates to commit himself to Kathleen, and she marries the AMERICAN to whom she is engaged.

Fitzgerald portrays Stahr as a heroic figure, comparing him to an emperor, prince, and king, and associating him with great American leaders by references to presidents throughout the novel. Stahr "was a marker in industry like Edison and Lumière and Griffith and Chaplin. He led pictures way up past the range and power of the theatre, reaching a sort of golden age before the censorship in 1933" (p. 28). Stahr sees himself as "the unity" which holds the whole process together.

After Fitzgerald's death, Zelda FITZGERALD wrote to Maxwell PERKINS an explanation of Fitzgerald's conception of Stahr: "The book was a story of Irving Thalberg, as Scott may have told you. Those minds which so nearly control the direction of public sentiment engaged Scott deeply. He wanted to render tangible the indominatable constancy of purpose and the driving necessity to achievement and the capacity for judicious and dextrous juggling of majesterous forces that distinguished such men from others" (January 27, 1941; Charles SCRIBNER's Sons Archives, PRINCETON UNIVERSITY LIBRARY).

Standish, John Character in "The Mystery of the Raymond Mortgage." Servant who shoots Agnes RAYMOND, apparently because she loved someone else. He is later shot by Mrs. RAYMOND.

Stanley Character in "No Flowers." Student whose suit is temporarily appropriated by Billy JOHNS.

Starheim, Lizzette Character in "No Harm Trying." Foreign actress who can speak only three English sentences.

Starrett, Henrietta McCaig (b. 1893) Fitzgerald's most frequent illustrator, Starrett provided drawings for 13 of his stories in *The SATURDAY EVENING POST*, including the entire Basil Duke LEE series (1928–29), "Babylon Revisited" (February 21, 1931), "Flight and Pursuit" (May 14, 1932), "Too Cute for Words" (April 18, 1936), "Inside the House" (June 13, 1936), and " 'Trouble' " (March 1937), Fitzgerald's final *Post* appearance. Starrett began her career as a fashion illustrator. Her illustrations appeared regularly in the *Post* throughout the 1930s, accompanying both fiction and nonfiction articles. As with May Wilson PRESTON, her casual style suited the sentimental aspects of Fitzgerald's magazine fiction. See "Who's Who and Why," *The Saturday Evening Post*, 201 (August 4, 1928), 36, 40.

by Park Bucker

"The Staying Up All Night" Humor article. *The PRINCETON TIGER*, 28 (November 10, 1917), 6; *In His Own Time*. List of what takes place when someone stays up all night.

Steele, Frederic Dorr (1873–1944) Prolific illustrator best known for his portrayal of Arthur Conan Doyle's (1859–1930) Sherlock Holmes in *COLLIER'S* magazine. He illustrated "Dice, Brass Knuckles & Guitar" (May 1923) for *HEARST'S INTERNATIONAL*. He also illustrated stories by Mark TWAIN, Rudyard Kipling (1865–1936), O. Henry (1862–1910), and Joseph CONRAD.

Stein, Gertrude (1874–1946) Influential and innovative EXPATRIATE American author whose works include *Three Lives* (1909), *Tender Buttons* (1914), and *The Making of Americans* (Paris, 1925; New York: 1926). Ernest HEMINGWAY introduced Fitzgerald to Stein in 1925, and her May 22, 1925 letter about *GG* was included in *CU:*

Gertrude Stein and Alice B. Toklas

Here we are and have read your book and it is a good book. I like the melody of your dedication and it shows that you have a background of beauty and tenderness and that is a comfort. The next good thing is that you write naturally in sentences and one can read all of them and that among other things is a comfort. You are creating the contemporary world much as Thackeray did his in *Pendennis* and *Vanity Fair* and this isn't a bad compliment. You make a modern world and a modern orgy strangely enough it was never done until you did it in *This Side of Paradise*. My belief in *This Side of Paradise* was alright. This is as good a book and different and older and that is what one does, one does not get better but different and older and that is always a pleasure" (*CU*, p. 308).

Stein and her companion, Alice B. Toklas (1877–1967), visited the Fitzgeralds in BALTIMORE in December 1934.

See James R. Mellow, *Charmed Circle: Gertrude Stein and Company* (New York: Praeger, 1974).

Stella Character in *GG*. Meyer WOLFSHIEM's receptionist, who tries to send Nick CARRAWAY away.

Sterrett, Gordon Character in "May Day." Failed artist who asks his friend Philip DEAN for money to pay off his blackmailing girlfriend, Jewel HUDSON. He gets drunk, wakes up married to Jewel, and shoots himself.

Stewart, Donald Ogden (1894–1980) American humorist, playwright, and screenwriter; author of *Perfect Behavior: A Parody Outline of Etiquette* (1922) and *Mr. and Mrs. Haddock Abroad* (1924). Bill Gorton in Ernest HEMINGWAY's *The Sun Also Rises* (1926) is based on Stewart.

Stewart and Fitzgerald became friends when they were both living in ST. PAUL in summer 1919, while Fitzgerald was working on *TSOP* and before Stewart began his own writing career, which Fitzgerald helped to launch. Stewart included a parody of Fitzgerald in his 1921 book, *A Parody Outline of History* ("The Courtship of Miles Standish—In the Manner of F. Scott Fitzgerald," reprinted in *In His Own Time*, pp. 449–454); and Fitzgerald wrote a parody, "Reminiscences of Donald Stewart."

In 1938 Fitzgerald and Stewart worked together on the screenplay for *The Women* (1939) but were replaced by Jane Murfin (1893–1955) and Anita LOOS; and in March 1939 they worked together for a month on "Air Raid," a Paramount movie for Madeleine Carroll (1906–87) which was not made. Stewart won an Academy Award for *The Philadelphia Story* (1940). His involvement in left-wing politics jeopardized his career during the investigation of Communists in HOLLYWOOD begun by the House Committee on Un-American Activities in 1947; he was blacklisted by 1950 and moved permanently to London in 1951.

See Stewart, *By a Stroke of Luck: An Autobiography* (New York: Paddington Press/Two Continents, 1975).

Stinson, Eddie Narrator of "A Short Trip Home." Yale sophomore from ST. PAUL who rescues Ellen BAKER from the spectre of Joe VARLAND.

Stirling, George Character in "John Jackson's Arcady." Taxi driver and childhood playmate of John JACKSON, whom he drives to a hotel during Jackson's visit to his hometown.

Stivers, Harley Ennis Illustrator of five Fitzgerald stories for *The SATURDAY EVENING POST*, including "The Adolescent Marriage" (March 6, 1926), "One Trip Abroad" (October 11, 1930), and three Josephine PERRY stories: "A Nice Quiet Place" (May 31, 1930), "A Woman with a Past" (September 6, 1930), and "Emotional Bankruptcy" (August 15, 1931). He also illustrated "Lions Are Lower Today" (*Post*, February 15, 1930) by James Gould Cozzens (1903–78).

by Park Bucker

Stockton, Sylvester Character in "The Smilers." Man who is irritated by the smiles of other people.

Stockton, Violet Southern girl with whom Fitzgerald had a youthful romance while she was visiting her aunt in ST. PAUL. Fitzgerald noted "affair with Violet" in his *Ledger* for July 1908, and in September 1910 he wrote a seven-page "story of Violet Stockton" in his *Thoughtbook* (pp. XI–XVII).

Stoddard, G. Reese Character in "Bernice Bobs Her Hair." Lawyer and eligible bachelor.

The Stories of F. Scott Fitzgerald Story collection. Selected with an introduction by Malcolm COWLEY. New York: Charles SCRIBNER's Sons, 1951. Contents: "The Diamond as Big as the Ritz," "Bernice Bobs Her Hair," "The Ice Palace," "May Day," "Winter Dreams," " 'The Sensible Thing,' " "Absolution," "The Rich Boy," "The Baby Party," "Magnetism," "The Last of the Belles," "The Rough Crossing," "The Bridal Party," "Two Wrongs," "The Scandal Detectives," "The Freshest Boy," "The Captured Shadow," "A Woman with a Past," "Babylon Revisited," "Crazy Sunday," "Family in the Wind," "An Alcoholic Case," "The Long Way Out," "Financing Finnegan," "A Patriotic Short," "Two Old-Timers," "Three Hours Between Planes," "The Lost Decade." This collection contributed to the Fitzgerald REVIVAL.

Strain, Jim Character in "Bernice Bobs Her Hair." Ethel DEMOREST's fiancé, who can't keep a job.

"Strange Sanctuary" Fiction. *LIBERTY*, 16 (December 9, 1939), 15–20. Thirteen-year-old Dolly HAINES meets 15-year-old Clarke CRESSWELL while visiting the APPLETONS because her father, Morton HAINES, is ill. Her father tells her to call on her uncle Charlie CRAIG, who has just returned to town. When she goes to Uncle Charlie's house, she meets Major REDFERN and Miss Willie SHUGRUE, who tell her that her uncle is sick and they are taking care of him. Dolly becomes suspicious and discovers that her uncle is not even there. Redfern and Shugrue are discovered to be thieves, and Uncle Charlie and Dolly's father return home. "Strange Sanctuary" was originally written as "Make Yourself at Home," a story in the projected series about Gwen BOWERS; but after *The SATURDAY EVENING POST* declined it, Fitzgerald changed the characters' names in order to sell it elsewhere.

Strater, Henry H. (Mike) (1896–1987) PRINCETON sophomore who was one of the leaders of the anticlub movement in spring 1917 and who served as a partial model for Burne HOLIDAY in *TSOP*. In a June 3, 1920 letter responding to Princeton President John Grier HIBBEN's criticism of *TSOP*, Fitzgerald noted: "My view of life, President Hibben, is the view of Theodore Driesers and Joseph Conrads—that life is too strong and remorseless for the sons of men. My idealism flickered out with Henry Strater's anticlub movement at Princeton" (*Life in Letters*, p. 40). Strater became an artist and established an art museum in Ogonquit, Maine. See Michael Culver, "A Model for Fitzgerald," *Princeton Alumni Weekly*, 85 (June 19, 1985), 9–11.

Stromberg, Hunt (1894–1968) MGM producer for whom Fitzgerald worked on the screenplay for "Infidelity" from February to May 1938, when the project was dropped due to the taboo on a movie about adultery, and on the screenplay for *The Women* (1939) from May to October 1938, when he and collaborator Donald Ogden STEWART were replaced by Anita LOOS and Jane Murfin (1893–1955). Fitzgerald described Stromberg as "a sort of one-finger Thalberg, without Thalberg's scope, but with his intense power of work and his absorption in his job" (to Maxwell PERKINS, March 4, 1938; *Life in Letters*, p. 353; *Scott/Max*, p. 242).

Stuart, Charles David Character in "The Pusher-in-the-Face." Man who is arrested for pushing a woman in the face at the theater.

Stubbs, Jack Character in "Six of One—". Young man who plays high-school football despite the loss of an arm while hunting. Ed BARNES helps him through PRINCETON and hires him when he graduates.

Sturgis, Sam Childhood friend of Fitzgerald in ST. PAUL. On Saturdays they went together to vaudeville matinees at the Orpheum Theatre; and at parties they re-enacted what they had seen.

Sturtevant, Ruth Friend and correspondent in whom Fitzgerald confided about his off-again on-again courtship of Zelda Sayre [FITZGERALD] (see *Letters*, pp. 453–459, 461). See Roger Lewis, "Ruth Sturtevant and F. Scott Fitzgerald (1916–1921)," *Fitzgerald/Hemingway Annual* (1979), pp. 3–21.

Stutz-Mozart Character in *The Vegetable*. Italian leader of an orangutan band which DORIS hired to play jazz at her wedding reception.

Styles, Phyllis Character in *TSOP*. "An intercollegiate prom-trotter" (p. 137) who tricks Burne HOLIDAY into asking her to the PRINCETON-Harvard football game.

Summer, John Character mentioned in "Between Three and Four." Sarah SUMMER's deceased husband.

Summer, Sarah Belknap Character in "Between Three and Four." Woman who asks Howard BUTLER to rehire her and who he later mistakenly thinks commits suicide.

Summit Avenue ST. PAUL, Minnesota, neighborhood where Fitzgerald was born and where his family lived, in rented houses and apartments, when they returned to St. Paul in 1908. Summit—which was the best street in St. Paul—runs from the Cathedral of St. Paul at the intersection of Summit and Selby four and a half miles to the Mississippi River; it is considered the best-preserved Victorian residential boulevard in America. "Summit Avenue" referred to a 12-square block area at the eastern end of Summit above downtown St. Paul.

See Ernest R. Sandeen, *St. Paul's Historic Summit Avenue* (St. Paul: Living Historical Museum, Macalester College, 1978).

Swanson Character in *TITN*. Vice-consul in ROME who accompanies Dick DIVER to court after Dick is beaten and jailed.

Swanson, H. N. (1900–1991) Fitzgerald's HOLLYWOOD agent and Harold OBER's associate, who had published Scott and Zelda FITZGERALD's stories when he was editor of *COLLEGE HUMOR*. In early 1939 he found Fitzgerald an assignment on *Winter Carnival*. Fitzgerald left the Swanson agency in December 1939 because he was dissatisfied with Swanson's handling of his screenwriting career; and he hired Leland HAYWARD as his new agent. Swanson's memoir, *Sprinkled with Ruby Dust* (New York: Warner Books, 1989), is untrustworthy about Fitzgerald.

Swanson, Johnny Character in *LT/LOLT*. Has-been cowboy actor. Based on actor Harry Carey (1878?–

1947). Fitzgerald's plans for the unwritten episodes include a scene at Stahr's funeral, for which Swanson is mistakenly asked to be a pallbearer, with the result that his career is revived. This scene was based on an anecdote about Irving THALBERG's funeral, for which Harry Carey was mistakenly invited to be a pallbearer. Fitzgerald's notes read: "Harry Cary gets Cary Wilson's invite. A new career"; but both Harry Carey and writer Carey Wilson (1889–1962) were pallbearers at Thalberg's funeral.

"The Swimmers" Fiction. Written July–August 1929. *The SATURDAY EVENING POST*, 202 (October 19, 1929), 12–13, 150, 152, 154; *Bits of Paradise*. Henry Clay MARSTON, a Virginian living in PARIS, suffers a nervous collapse after discovering his French wife, Choupette MARSTON, in a compromising situation. While he is recovering he and his family go to the shore, where an American GIRL teaches him to swim. The Marstons return to America for three years, and Choupette becomes involved with Charles WIESE. Henry tells them that he wants a divorce but that Choupette cannot have custody of the children. Henry, Choupette, and Wiese go for a ride in a motorboat, and Wiese reveals that he has obtained a document from a mental special-

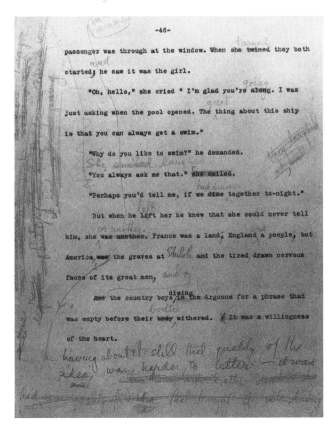

Fitzgerald's revised typescript for the eloquent ending of "The Swimmers" (Bruccoli Collection, University of South Carolina)

ist declaring Henry unfit to have custody of his children. When the motorboat stalls, Henry—the only one of the three who can swim—offers to swim for help only if they grant him custody of the children. After his divorce Henry returns to EUROPE and again encounters the American girl on his ship. As he looks back at his homeland, he reflects on his feelings about America: "France was a land, England was a people, but America, having about it still that quality of the idea, was harder to utter—it was the graves at Shiloh and the tired, drawn, nervous faces of its great men, and the country boys dying in the Argonne for a phrase that was empty before their bodies withered. It was a willingness of the heart" (*Bits of Paradise*, p. 210).

Fitzgerald described "The Swimmers" as "the hardest story I ever wrote" (c. August 1929; *As Ever*, p. 142). This patriotic story, in which Fitzgerald described "the best of America" as "the best of the world" (p. 209), appeared just before the Wall Street crash in October 1929.

Switzerland Zelda FITZGERALD entered VAL-MONT CLINIC at GLION on May 22, 1930 and was transferred to PRANGINS CLINIC at NYON on June 5. Wanting to be near Zelda, Fitzgerald spent summer 1930 commuting between PARIS and Switzerland, staying in hotels at Glion, Vevey, Caux, LAUSANNE, and Geneva. That fall he settled at the HOTEL DE LA PAIX in Lausanne, with excursions to Swiss resorts. To finance Zelda's treatment and his expenses, he wrote stories for *The SATURDAY EVENING POST*, including "Babylon Revisited" (written in December; published February 1931) and "One Trip Abroad" (written in August; published October 1930), in which he describes Switzerland as "a country where very few things begin, but many things end" (*AOAA*, p. 161). He traveled to America in January 1931 for his father's funeral, returning to EUROPE at the end of February; by April Zelda was allowed to travel with him to Montreux and Geneva. After Zelda's discharge from Prangins on September 15, 1931, they returned to America. Although the stay in Switzerland interrupted Fitzgerald's work on *TITN*, it provided him with material for the novel.

Swope, Herbert Bayard (1882–1958) Executive editor of the *New York World* who lived at GREAT NECK, where he hosted lavish parties. Fitzgerald listed the Swopes as a source for Chapter III of *GG*.

Syneforth, Clara Character in "Sentiment—and the Use of Rouge." Clay SYNEFORTH's younger sister, whom he rebukes for wearing too much makeup.

Syneforth, Lieutenant Clay Harrington Character in "Sentiment—and the Use of Rouge." Young man who is disturbed by the changes he encounters in moral

values when he returns to England during World War I. He is later killed in battle.

Syneforth, Lieutenant Richard Harrington (Dick) Character in "Sentiment—and the Use of Rouge." Clay SYNEFORTH's elder brother and Eleanor MARBROOKE's fiancé, who was killed in World War I.

Syracuse, New York Fitzgerald's father, Edward FITZGERALD, was transferred by Procter & Gamble from BUFFALO, New York, to Syracuse in January 1901. The family lived in apartments on James Street and on East Willow Street. Annabel FITZGERALD was born in Syracuse in July, and Scott attended Miss Goodyear's School. The company transferred Edward Fitzgerald back to Buffalo in September 1903.

Syrel, John Character in "The Mystery of the Raymond Mortgage." Twenty-three-year-old reporter for the *New York Daily News* who solves the murder of Agnes RAYMOND.

Talbot, Harry Character in "A Luckless Santa Claus." Young man whose fiancée, Dorothy HARMON, challenges him to give away $25 to strangers on Christmas Eve.

Tales of the Jazz Age Story collection. New York: Charles SCRIBNER's Sons, 1922; London: Collins, 1923. Dedication: "QUITE INAPPROPRIATELY TO MY MOTHER." Contents: *My Last Flappers*—"The Jelly-Bean," "The Camel's Back," "May Day," "Porcelain and Pink"; *Fantasies*—"The Diamond as Big as the Ritz," "The Curious Case of Benjamin Button," "Tarquin of Cheapside,"

" 'O Russet Witch!' "; *Unclassified Masterpieces*—"The Lees of Happiness," "Mr. Icky," "Jemina." Published on September 22, 1922 in a first printing of 8,000 copies at $1.75, with a dust jacket illustrated by John HELD, Jr. and an annotated table of contents with Fitzgerald's mostly tongue-in-cheek comments about each piece. The volume sold well and was widely reviewed but regarded as merely popular entertainment. Fitzgerald considered various titles for the collection before settling on *Tales of the Jazz Age.* When Maxwell PERKINS told him that the Scribners book salesmen had criticized the title because of the current reaction against all jazz,

John Held, Jr.'s dust jacket for Fitzgerald's second short-story collection, published in 1922 (Bruccoli Collection, University of South Carolina)

Fitzgerald responded on May 11, 1922 that he favored the "Jazz Age" title because "It will be bought by *my own personal public,* that is by the countless flappers and college kids who think I am a sort of oracle. . . . It is better to have a title + a title-connection that is a has-been than one that is a never-will-be. The splash of the flapper movement was too big to have quite died down—the outer rings are still moving. . . . I hate titles like *Sideshow* and *In One Reel + Happy End* They have begun to sound like viels and apologies for bringing out collections at all" (*Scott/Max,* p. 59).

Tana (Tanalahaka) Character in *B&D*. Anthony and Gloria PATCH's talkative Japanese servant at their house in MARIETTA. Maury NOBLE pretends that Tana is really a German agent named Tannenbaum and sends him mysterious letters; this episode was based on George Jean NATHAN's joke about the Fitzgeralds' Japanese servant, Tana.

Tantrum, Jemina Character in "Jemina . . ." Teen-aged girl who supports her parents by brewing whiskey and who dies in a fire caused by the feud with the DOLDRUMS.

Taps at Reveille Story collection. New York: Charles SCRIBNER's Sons, 1935. Dedication: "TO HAROLD OBER." Contents: *Basil*—"The Scandal Detectives," "The Freshest Boy," "He Thinks He's Wonderful," "The Captured Shadow," "The Perfect Life"; *Josephine*—"First Blood," "A Nice Quiet Place," "A Woman with a Past"; "Crazy Sunday," "Two Wrongs," "The Night of Chancellorsville," "The Last of the Belles," "Majesty," "Family in the Wind," "A Short Trip Home," "One Interne," "The Fiend," "Babylon Revisited." Published on March 20, 1935 in a single printing of 5,100 copies at $2.50, with a dust jacket illustrated by Doris SPIEGEL. Fitzgerald's last and largest collection, *TAR* was a Literary Guild alternate in June 1935 and received mostly favorable reviews. John Chamberlain of the *New York Times* defended Fitzgerald against the common charge that his material was futile, arguing that Fitzgerald's characters were no more futile than those of William Faulkner (1897–1962), Marcel Proust (1871–1922), Gustave Flaubert (1821–80), or Sinclair LEWIS, and asserting: "Mr. Fitzgerald knows the generation that grew up during the war as no one else does" ("Books of the Times," March 27, 1935, p. 19; *FSF: The Critical Reception,* p. 341). Fitzgerald considered many possible titles

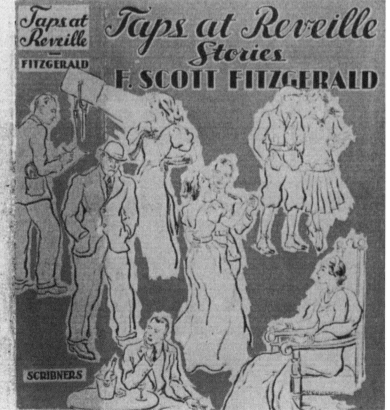

Doris Spiegel's dust jacket for the 1935 story collection, the last published during Fitzgerald's lifetime (Bruccoli Collection, University of South Carolina)

for this collection, including "More Tales of the Jazz Age," "Basil, Josephine and Others," "When Grandma Was a Boy," "Last Year's Steps," "The Salad Days," "Many Blues," "Just Play One More," "A Dance Card," "Last Night's Moon," "In the Last Quarter of the Moon," "Golden Spoons," and "Moonlight in My Eyes." When Fitzgerald expressed concern that "Reveille" would be a difficult word for readers to pronounce, Maxwell PERKINS assured him it was not and urged him to keep what he considered a good title. Fitzgerald wrote a short foreword for the volume but decided to omit it: "Before the last of these stories were written the world that they represented passed. In consequence the reviewer may be tempted to apply the title harshly to the fate of the collection. Yet almost all these stories, the winnowing of fifty odd, meant a great deal to the author at the time of the writing: all of them tried for an arduous precision in trying to catch one character or one emotion or one adventure—which is all that one can do in the length of a short story" (quoted in Matthew J. BRUCCOLI, *Some Sort of Epic Grandeur,* p. 464).

Tarbox, Horace Character in "Head and Shoulders." A precocious youth who sacrifices a promising intellectual career when he marries actress Marcia MEADOW and performs in gymnastic exhibitions to earn money.

Tarbox, Marcia Hume Character in "Head and Shoulders." Horace and Marcia [MEADOW] TARBOX's baby.

Tarbox, Marcia Meadow *See* Marcia MEADOW.

Tarkington, Booth (1869–1946) American author who won Pulitzer Prizes for *The Magnificent Ambersons* (1918) and *Alice Adams* (1921) and whose writing impressed young Fitzgerald. In 1922 Fitzgerald wrote to a fan that Tarkington and Compton MACKENZIE "together taught me all I know about the English language" (to Hazel McCormack, postmarked June 26, 1922; PRINCETON UNIVERSITY LIBRARY). An 1893 graduate of PRINCETON UNIVERSITY, Tarkington had founded the TRIANGLE CLUB. Fitzgerald reviewed Tarkington's *Penrod and Sam* (1916) for *The NASSAU LITERARY MAGAZINE*; and he included *Seventeen* (1916), which he called "the funniest book I've ever read," in his 1923 list of "10 Best Books I Have Read" (*FSF on Authorship,* p. 86). In his 1922 review of *Gentle Julia,* Fitzgerald noted: "It is a pity that the man who writes better prose than any other living American was brought up in a generation that considered it a crime to tell the truth" ("Tarkington's 'Gentle Julia' "; *In His Own Time,* pp. 131–132). He made a similar comment in a July 1, 1928 letter: "My contempt for Tarkington extends only to his character of being ashamed of his early sins and thus cutting out of his experience about one-half of life. He

woke up one morning sober and 40, and thought that no one had ever been lascivious or drunk or vain except himself, and turned deliberately back to the illusions of his boyhood" (to Julian Street; *Letters,* p. 494).

Fitzgerald believed that Tarkington had wasted his talent, observing in his *Notebooks:* "I have a horror of going into a personal debauch and coming out of it devitalized with no interest except an acute observation of the behavior of colored people, children, and dogs" (#1061). Fitzgerald's fear of following in Tarkington's footsteps influenced his decision not to publish the Basil Duke LEE and Josephine PERRY stories as a separate volume (to Maxwell PERKINS, May 21, 1934; *Scott/Max,* p. 199).

See James Woodress, *Booth Tarkington: Gentleman from Indiana* (Philadelphia: Lippincott, 1955).

"Tarkington's 'Gentle Julia' " Review of *Gentle Julia* by Booth TARKINGTON. *St. Paul Daily News,* May 7, 1922, feature section, p. 6; *In His Own Time.* Fitzgerald complains about the "lack of any unity of design" in this narrative composed of stories written over a period of 10 years but admits that "parts of the book . . . are as funny as anything [Tarkington] has ever done" (*In His Own Time,* pp. 130 & 131).

Tarleton, Georgia Fictional Southern city which was the setting of "The Ice Palace" (May 1920), "The Jelly-Bean" (October 1920), and "The Last of the Belles" (March 1929). "A little city of forty thousand that has dozed sleepily for forty thousand years in southern Georgia, occasionally stirring in its slumbers and muttering something about a war that took place sometime, somewhere, and that everyone else has forgotten long ago" (*TJA,* p. 3). Loosely based on MONTGOMERY, Alabama.

Tarleton, Mr. and Mrs. *See* Mr. and Mrs. MARQUAND.

Tarmes Fictional village in *TITN* where Dick and Nicole DIVER live in the VILLA DIANA. Probably based on Eze, a village in the hills east of Antibes, France.

"Tarquin of Cheepside" Fiction. *The NASSAU LITERARY MAGAZINE,* 73 (April 1917), 13–18; *Apprentice Fiction.* Revised and expanded as "Tarquin of Cheapside," *The SMART SET,* 64 (February 1921), 43–46; *TJA.* SOFT SHOES, who is being pursued by two men, seeks refuge in the home of Wessel CAXTER. The pursuers tell Caxter that the man they seek has done violence to a woman—one man's sister and the other's wife. When they leave, Caxter confronts Soft Shoes, who spends the night writing the story of his escapade. Its identification as "The Rape of Lucrece" indicates that Soft Shoes is William Shakespeare (1564–1616).

Taswell, Captain Character in "The End of Hate." Union officer whose marriage proposal Josie PILGRIM refuses.

Tate, Emily Character in "The Camel's Back." Mr. and Mrs. Howard TATE's young daughter, who announces that there is a camel on the stairs.

Tate, Mr. and Mrs. Howard Characters in "The Camel's Back." Couple who are hosting a dance for their daughter Millicent TATE. Perry PARKHURST mistakenly shows up at their party rather than at the TOWNSENDS' circus ball.

Tate, Millicent Character in "The Camel's Back." Daughter of Mr. and Mrs. Howard TATE, who are giving a dance for her on the night of the TOWNSENDS' circus ball.

taxi driver Character in "The Camel's Back." Man whom Perry PARKHURST bribes to wear the back part of the camel costume. His insistence that he is married to Betty MEDILL as much as Perry is persuades Betty to return to Perry.

Taylor, Cecilia Delihant Fitzgerald's "Cousin Ceci," the daughter of Eliza DELIHANT. Fitzgerald was a ribbon-holder at Ceci's wedding in Montgomery County, Maryland, in 1903; and he visited her in Norfolk, Virginia, at Easter in 1912. By the time Fitzgerald was at PRINCETON, she was a widow with four young daughters; and she served as the model for Amory BLAINE's widowed cousin, Clara PAGE, in *TSOP*. Fitzgerald remained close to Cousin Ceci all his life, and he named Cecelia BRADY in *LT/LOLT* for her.

Taylor, Mr. Character in "The Jelly-Bean." Man who shoots craps with Nancy LAMAR.

Taylor, Virginia Character in *Coward.* Romantic and foolish girl who becomes engaged to Lieutenant ALTWATER.

the Taylors Characters in "The Hotel Child." Europeanized Americans in the diplomatic service who look down on Fifi SCHWARTZ and who decline to present Miss HOWARD at court after she is caught running away with Count BOROWKI.

"Teamed with Genius" Fiction—Pat HOBBY story. Submitted October 2, 1939. *ESQUIRE*, 13 (April 1940), 44, 195–197; *AOAA*; *PH*. Producer Jack BERNERS assigns Pat Hobby to collaborate on a script with René WILCOX. When Pat discovers that Wilcox has completed a shooting script while working at night, he forges a note calling Wilcox back to England because of the death of his two brothers and sends secretary Katherine HODGE to borrow Wilcox's script secretly; Pat lightly revises the script and adds his own name to it. When he submits it to Berners, the producer informs Pat the script had been discarded a year ago. Wilcox had been in his office when Katherine, who has a relationship with him, arrived; and he had sent the old script to Pat.

Tearle, Betty Character in "The Smilers." Woman with whom Sylvester STOCKTON had once been in love and who leaves her husband and children.

Templeton, Brooks Fish Character in "Presumption." Noel GARNEAU's fiancé, whom she sends away after San Juan CHANDLER declares his love for her.

Templeton, Charles Martin Character in "The Rubber Check." Mercia TEMPLETON's father, who gives Val SCHUYLER a job on his farm.

Templeton, Mercia Character in "The Rubber Check." Ellen MORTMAIN's cousin, who dislikes Val SCHUYLER when she first meets him but later becomes interested in him.

Templeton, V. (Mrs. Charles Martin Templeton) Character in "The Rubber Check." Mercia TEMPLETON's mother, who spreads the rumor of Val SCHUYLER's bounced check.

"10 Best Books I Have Read" Article. *Jersey City Evening Journal*, April 24, 1923, p. 9; *FSF on Authorship*. Fitzgerald's list includes *The Note-Books of Samuel Butler* (1912; *see* BUTLER); *The Philosophy of Friedrich Nietzsche* (1908) by H. L. MENCKEN; *A Portrait of the Artist as a Young Man* (1916) by James JOYCE; *Zuleika Dobson* (1911) by Max Beerbohm (1872–1956); *The Mysterious Stranger* (1916) by Mark TWAIN; *Nostromo* (1904) by Joseph CONRAD; *Vanity Fair* (1848) by William Makepeace Thackeray (1811–63); *The Oxford Book of English Verse* (1921); *Thaïs* (1890) by Anatole FRANCE; and *Seventeen* (1916) by Booth TARKINGTON.

"Ten Years in the Advertising Business" Satirical article. *The Princeton Alumni Weekly*, 29 (February 22, 1929), 585; *AOAA*. Brief dialogue between Fitzgerald and advertising executive Mr. Cakebook, beginning with Fitzgerald's first job in advertising at $95.00 a month and jumping forward ten years to his service as a judge in an advertising contest for $1,500.

Tender Is the Night Novel. New York: Charles SCRIBNER'S Sons, 1934; London: Chatto & Windus, 1934. Dedication: "TO/GERALD AND SARA/MANY FÊTES." (*See* Gerald and Sara MURPHY.) Serialized in *SCRIBNER'S MAGAZINE*, 95 (January 1934), 1–8, 60–80;

Dust jacket for Fitzgerald's fourth novel, 1934 (Bruccoli Collection, University of South Carolina)

(February 1934), 88–95, 139–160; (March 1934), 168–174, 207, 229; (April 1934), 252–258, 292–310.

Three weeks after the publication of *GG*, Fitzgerald wrote to Scribners editor Maxwell PERKINS, "The happiest thought I have is of my new novel—it is something really NEW in form, idea, structure—the model for the age that Joyce and Stien are searching for, that Conrad didn't find" (May 1, 1925; *Life in Letters*, p. 108; *Scott/Max*, p. 104). The novel, variously called "Our Type," "The Boy Who Killed His Mother," "The Melarky Case,"

and "The World's Fair," was about Francis Melarky, a young American movie technician who murders his domineering mother while traveling with her in EUROPE. Fitzgerald worked on this version, with interruptions, from late 1925 to 1930, writing five drafts, none of which exceeded four chapters. A section of this version was posthumously published as "The World's Fair" in *The Kenyon Review* (Autumn 1948). The novel opens with the arrival of Francis and his mother on the RIVIERA, where he is taken up by Americans Seth and Dinah Piper (also called Roreback) and their friend, alcoholic composer Abe Grant (Herkimer). Francis visits a movie studio and acts as a second in a duel between Gabriel Brugerol and writer Albert McKisco. He then travels to PARIS with the Pipers to see Grant off to America; and he falls in love with Dinah, who does not reciprocate. In a flashback opening chapter Francis is beaten by the police in ROME. Many of these events adumbrate episodes in *TITN,* and the characters are connected: the Pipers become Dick and Nicole DIVER; Abe Grant becomes Abe NORTH; Gabriel Brugerol becomes Tommy BARBAN; and part

of Francis becomes Rosemary HOYT. Sources for the Melarky/matricide version include the Leopold-Loeb case; Dorothy Ellingson, a San Francisco girl who murdered her mother in 1925; Theodore DREISER's *An American Tragedy* (1925); Walker ELLIS; and Theodore CHANLER.

During the years he was working on the novel, Fitzgerald's short stories dealt with transatlantic travel and Europe's effects on EXPATRIATE Americans; and he transferred themes, descriptions, and phrases from stories to drafts of his novel and from the novel drafts to stories. Stories from which he borrowed passages for *TITN* include "The Popular Girl" (February 1922), "The Third Casket" (May 1924), "Love in the Night" (March 1925), "A Penny Spent" (October 1925), "Not in the Guidebook" (November 1925), "The Adolescent Marriage" (March 1926), "Jacob's Ladder" (August 1927), "The Love Boat" (October 1927), "A Short Trip Home" (December 1927), "The Bowl" (January 1928), "Magnetism" (March 1928), "The Scandal Detectives" (April 1928), "A Night at the Fair" (July 1928), "Basil and Cleopatra" (April 1929), "The Rough Crossing"

Chart for the composition of Tender Is the Night, *outlining parallels between Zelda Fitzgerald's and Nicole Diver's cases* (Princeton University Library)

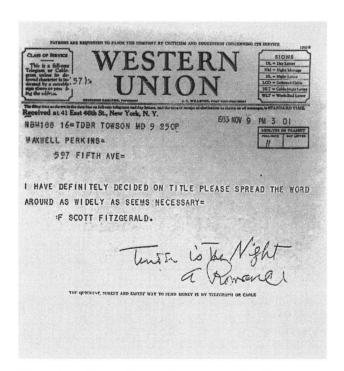

The working titles for Fitzgerald's fourth novel had been "Doctor Diver's Holiday," "The Drunkard's Holiday," and "Richard Diver." The final title is written in Maxwell Perkins's hand. (Princeton University Library)

(June 1929), "At Your Age" (August 1929), "The Swimmers" (October 1929), "Two Wrongs" (January 1930), "First Blood" (April 1930), "A Nice Quiet Place" (May 1930), "A Woman with a Past" (September 1930), "One Trip Abroad" (October 1930), "A Snobbish Story" (November 1930), "The Hotel Child" (January 1931), "Babylon Revisited" (February 1931), "Indecision" (May 1931), "Emotional Bankruptcy" (August 1931), "Diagnosis" (February 1932), "Flight and Pursuit" (May 1932), "The Rubber Check" (August 1932), "What a Handsome Pair!" (August 1932), "Crazy Sunday" (October 1932), "One Interne" (November 1932), "On Schedule" (March 1933), "More Than Just a House" (June 1933), "I Got Shoes" (September 1933), and "On Your Own" (unpublished until 1979). The most important borrowings were from "Jacob's Ladder," "Magnetism," "Indecision," and "One Trip Abroad." (See George Anderson, "F. Scott Fitzgerald's Use of Story Strippings in *Tender Is the Night*," Appendix D in Matthew J. BRUCCOLI's *Reader's Companion to F. Scott Fitzgerald's Tender Is the Night.*)

In June 1929 Fitzgerald told Perkins: "I am working night + day on novel from new angle that I think will solve previous difficulties" (*Scott/Max,* p. 156). Fitzgerald wrote two chapters, set on shipboard, about movie director Lew Kelly and his wife, Nicole, who are traveling to Europe. Also on the ship is a young actress

named Rosemary who hopes Kelly will help her start her movie career. In 1930 Fitzgerald returned to the Melarky material, salvaging material from previous drafts.

In April 1930 Zelda FITZGERALD's collapse and hospitalization in SWITZERLAND interrupted Fitzgerald's work on the novel and provided him with new material about which he had intense feelings. His new concerns are reflected in "One Trip Abroad" (1930), which depicts the gradual deterioration of Americans Nicole and Nelson KELLY as they travel in Europe and end up as patients in a Swiss clinic.

Zelda was released from PRANGINS CLINIC in September 1931, and the Fitzgeralds returned to America. In January 1932 Fitzgerald reported to Perkins that he was planning to spend five consecutive months on his novel and was replanning it. His work was again interrupted by Zelda's second breakdown in February and her hospitalization at the PHIPPS CLINIC of JOHNS HOPKINS UNIVERSITY HOSPITAL in BALTIMORE.

While in MONTGOMERY early in 1932 or at "LA PAIX," the house he rented near Baltimore in May, Fitzgerald prepared plot outlines, chronologies, and character

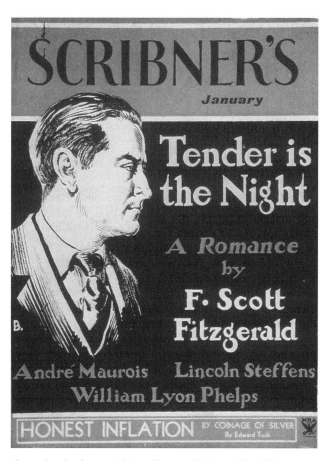

Cover for the first serial installment of Fitzgerald's 1934 novel (Bruccoli Collection, University of South Carolina)

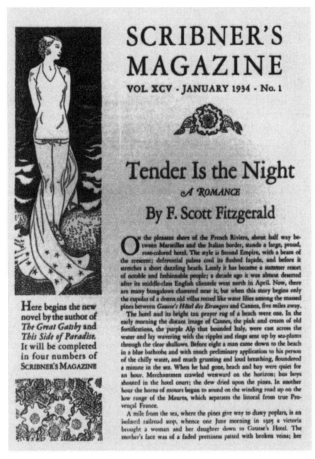

Opening page of the first installment, with decorations by Edward Shenton (Bruccoli Collection, University of South Carolina)

sketches for the novel. (See *F. Scott Fitzgerald Manuscripts IVb*, Part 1, pp. 3–23.) In August 1932 he noted in his *Ledger*: "The Novel now plotted + planned, never more to be permanently interrupted" (p. 186). His notes show that Zelda's illness, which supplied many of the details for Nicole Diver's illness, was the determining factor in his final approach to the novel, as well as providing the emotional focus for the work. The preliminary material also demonstrates that the published novel did not begin with Fitzgerald's 1932 work, but rather developed through the long process of composition, salvaging portions of the early Melarky drafts. Fitzgerald considered the titles "The Drunkard's Holiday," "Doctor Diver's Holiday," and "Richard Diver" before settling on *Tender Is the Night*, a phrase from John KEATS's ode "To a Nightingale."

Fitzgerald's 1932 notes for the novel also include a memo on the three-part structure which indicates that the shifts in point-of-view were planned from the beginning of the Diver version. Book I, "From outside mostly," opens on the Riviera in 1925 and depicts an idealized view of the Divers through the eyes of young

actress Rosemary Hoyt. Book II, "Nicole from Dick," goes back to 1917 when Dick met Nicole at a Swiss psychiatric clinic during World War I. Chapter 10 of Book II, Nicole's interior monologue, summarizes the Divers' marriage and provides a time bridge returning the action to the beginning of the novel in 1925. The rest of the novel is presented in chronological order, and Book III focuses on Dick and his decline. Although Fitzgerald later reconsidered the flashback structure after disappointing reviews, he did not alter his structural plan during the composition of the novel.

As early as 1925 *MCCALL'S* expressed interest in serializing Fitzgerald's fourth novel; in 1926 agent Harold OBER negotiated a first-refusal agreement with *LIBERTY*; and in 1933 *COSMOPOLITAN* expressed interest in the serial. However, Fitzgerald decided he preferred to have his most ambitious novel appear in *SCRIBNER'S MAGAZINE*, which carried four monthly installments (January–April 1934). Fitzgerald worked on the text for magazine and book publication at the same time, revising proof for the magazine and then revising the serial again for book publication.

Tender Is the Night was published on April 12, 1934, nine years after *GG*, in a first printing of 7,600 copies at $2.50, with decorations by Edward SHENTON. The first printing sold out quickly, and there were two more printings of 5,075 and 2,520 copies that spring. *TITN* was 10th on the best-seller lists in *Publishers Weekly* for April and May; but the sales, though respectable for a novel published during the Depression, did not meet Fitzgerald's expectations. *TITN* received mixed reviews, and Fitzgerald was disappointed by its reception. It is commonly thought that the novel failed because, due to the Depression, it was considered politically irrelevant; yet a list of the best-selling novels for 1934 demonstrates no reader preference for proletarian fiction. Some reviewers found Dick Diver's decline unconvincing, and others criticized the flashback structure and the disappearance of Rosemary Hoyt at the end of Book I. John Chamberlain defended the documentation of Diver's collapse in a *New York Times* review: "It seemed to us that Mr. Fitzgerald proceeded accurately, step by step, with just enough documentation to keep the drama from being misty, but without destroying the suggestiveness that added to the horror lurking behind the surface" ("Books of the Times," April 16, 1934, p. 15; *FSF: The Critical Reception*, pp. 311–312). (*See* also CRITICAL REPUTATION AND RECEPTION OF NOVELS.)

Fitzgerald came to believe that the structure was responsible for complaints that Diver was unconvincing. In 1936 he proposed a new edition for the Modern Library that would include headings to clarify the time scheme, but his proposed alterations made the project too expensive. On December 24, 1938 he wrote to Perkins that the novel's "great fault is that the <u>true</u>

beginning—the young psychiatrist in Switzerland—is tucked away in the middle of the book. If pages 151–212 were taken from their present place and put at the start the improvement in appeal would be enormous" (*Life in Letters,* p. 374; *Scott/Max,* p. 251; see also *Notebooks* #1075 for Fitzgerald's "Analysis of Tender"). Perkins did not pursue the project, and there is no record of further discussion of the revision.

When Fitzgerald died his books included a copy of *TITN* with his note on the front endpaper: "This is the <u>final version</u> of the book as I would like it." The volume was disbound and reassembled with the chapters in chronological order, beginning with Dick Diver's arrival in Switzerland in 1917; Fitzgerald had made some 40 corrections or revisions, ending about halfway through the book. Malcolm COWLEY used this volume as the basis for his 1951 edition of *TITN* "With the Author's Final Revisions," claiming that the chronological rearrangement improved the novel. Reviews of the revised edition were unenthusiastic; reader preference was clearly for the 1934 edition; and Scribners let the revised version go out of print after 1959.

Although chronological rearrangement of the entire novel was unnecessary and unsatisfactory, the time scheme of the novel is blurred and requires clarification. The novel opens "one June morning in 1925" (p. 7). Other major time signals specified in the novel are "this past year and a half on the Zugersee" (p. 188) and "For eighteen months now he had lived at the clinic" (p. 189). The eighteen-month interval following Christmas 1925 in the previous chapter indicates that Book II, Chapter 14 occurs during summer 1927, which fits the 1928 date specified in the Rome chapters (p. 219). Fitzgerald's statement that Dick's final departure from the Riviera occurs five years after Rosemary's first

visit to the Riviera (first edition, p. 364) places the end of the novel in summer 1930, after the October 1929 stock-market crash, which is not mentioned in the novel. A post-crash ending is unlikely: Tommy Barban specifies that he has "good stocks," and Nicole responds that "Dick's getting rich" (p. 280). Fitzgerald's use of "five years" probably resulted from his counting 1925 as a full year; he frequently made chronological errors due to confusing seasons with years. His preliminary notes for the Diver version indicate that the novel was to span June 1925 to July 1929—five summers, but only four years. See Matthew J. Bruccoli's discussion of the time scheme and chronology in *Reader's Companion to F. Scott Fitzgerald's Tender Is the Night,* pp. 190–195.

In addition to the chronological inconsistencies and contradictions, there are some 50 errors—particularly geography and foreign languages—that have the cumulative effect of undermining the reader's confidence in the author. See Bruccoli's *Reader's Companion* and his edition of *TITN* (London: Everyman, 1996).

In April and May 1934 Fitzgerald collaborated with Charles Marquis WARREN on a movie treatment for *TITN* (published in Bruccoli, *Some Sort of Epic Grandeur,* Appendix 1), but they were unable to sell it. In 1985 *TITN* was made into a movie for television from a script by Dennis Potter (Showtime, BBC; directed by Robert Knights).

BOOK I

Chapter 1

Eighteen-year-old American actress Rosemary Hoyt and her mother, Mrs. Elsie SPEERS, arrive at GAUSSE's Hôtel des Etrangers on the Riviera, five miles from CANNES. On the beach Rosemary meets Luis CAMPION, Mrs.

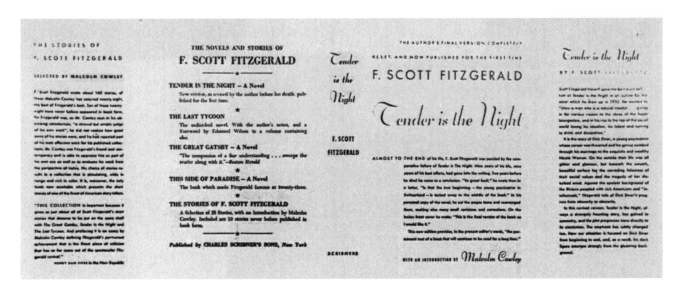

Dust jacket for Malcolm Cowley's 1951 edition of "the author's final version" (Bruccoli Collection, University of South Carolina)

ABRAMS, Albert and Violet MCKISCO, and Royal DUMPHRY, but she is more interested in a group of tanned people farther down the beach.

Chapter 2
Dick Diver, the leader of the tanned group, wakes Rosemary on the beach to keep her from getting more sunburned.

Chapter 3
Rosemary tells her mother that she fell in love on the beach and that wherever they go everyone has seen her movie, *Daddy's Girl*.

Chapter 4
On the beach two days later, Dick invites Rosemary to join his group, which includes his wife, Nicole; composer Abe North and his wife, Mary NORTH; and soldier-of-fortune Tommy Barban. Dick's voice seems to promise "an endless succession of magnificent possibilities" (p. 20). Rosemary tells her mother that she is desperately in love with Dick.

Chapter 5
Rosemary goes to Monte Carlo to see director Earl BRADY, who wants to work with her.

Chapter 6
The Divers host a party at their house, the VILLA DIANA, at TARMES. The guests include Rosemary, Mrs. Speers, Brady, Campion, Dumphry, Mrs. Abrams, the McKiscos, the Norths, and Barban. Rosemary tells Dick she fell in love with him the first time she saw him.

The Fitzgeralds on the Riviera, 1929

Chapter 7
At the Divers' party, Mrs. McKisco comes upon "a scene" when she goes upstairs to the bathroom.

Chapter 8
Dick invites Rosemary to go to Paris with him and Nicole to see Abe North off for America. The Divers' party ends.

Chapter 9
Mrs. Speers tells Rosemary to go ahead and pursue a relationship with Dick. Luis Campion tells Rosemary that there is going to be a duel between Tommy Barban and Albert McKisco.

Chapter 10
Abe North tells Rosemary that the cause of the duel is Tommy Barban's trying to make Violet McKisco shut up about the Divers and what she saw at the party.

Chapter 11
Rosemary goes with Campion to the duel on a golf course; both shots miss.

Chapter 12
The Divers, the Norths, and Rosemary are in Paris. Rosemary goes shopping with Nicole.

Chapter 13
The Divers, the Norths, and Rosemary visit the World War I battlefield of Beaumont Hamel. Dick says it was "the last love battle" (p. 62) and that it took "religion and years of plenty and tremendous sureties and the exact relations that existed between the classes" (p. 61). He mourns, "All my beautiful lovely safe world blew itself up here with a great gust of high explosive love" (p. 62).

Chapter 14
Back in Paris, Rosemary realizes that Abe North is always drinking. Dick says that he may abandon his scientific treatise.

Chapter 15
In the taxi on the way back to the hotel, where Nicole had returned earlier, Dick and Rosemary kiss. She asks him to come to her room, where she says "Take me." He is astonished and recites for her all the reasons why they shouldn't have an affair.

Chapter 16
The next day Rosemary sees that Dick is beginning to fall in love with her. The Divers and Norths attend a screening of *Daddy's Girl*; and Rosemary announces that she has arranged for Dick to have a screen test, which he refuses.

Chapter 17
Dick tells Rosemary, "I'm afraid I'm in love with you . . . and that's not the best thing that could happen" (p. 79). He explains that he and Nicole have to go on together and that their relationship is complicated.

Nevertheless, he kisses her as they go up the hotel stairs.

Chapter 18
The Divers host a party in Paris.

Chapter 19
At the train station Nicole rebukes Abe for giving up on everything and for his dissipation. Rosemary, Dick, and Mary North join them to see Abe off on his train. Maria WALLIS, whom the Divers know, shoots a man in the train station. Dick feels panic over his loss of control over his relationship with Rosemary.

Chapter 20
Collis CLAY, a Yale student with whom Rosemary attended the prom the preceding fall, tells Dick about Rosemary getting in trouble in a locked train compartment with a boy named Bill HILLIS. The thought of someone else with Rosemary makes Dick desire her more; he goes to the film studio to find her, realizing that this marks a turning point for him.

Chapter 21
Rosemary has already left the studio; Dick calls her at the hotel, telling her he'd like to be with her.

Chapter 22
The Divers learn that Abe North is still in Paris, and Nicole reflects that "so many smart men go to pieces nowadays" (p. 104).

Chapter 23
Abe spends the day in the RITZ BAR.

Chapter 24
Dick goes to Rosemary's hotel room, where they kiss. Abe comes to the door with Jules PETERSON, a black man who helped Abe identify another black man who reportedly stole some money from Abe. The police arrested the wrong man, and now several people are after Peterson for his betrayal. Dick, Rosemary, and Abe discuss the situation in Dick's room while Peterson waits in the corridor.

Chapter 25
When Abe leaves, Rosemary returns to her room, where she discovers Peterson's murdered body on her bed. To protect Rosemary from scandal, Dick moves the body to the hall, where he tells the hotel manager it was found. Dick takes Rosemary's bloody bedclothes for Nicole to wash, and Rosemary sees Nicole's hysteria in the bathroom.

BOOK II

Chapter 1
This chapter begins a flashback to spring 1917, when Dick Diver arrives in Zürich to study at the university after attending Yale, being a Rhodes Scholar, completing medical school at Johns Hopkins, and studying and writing medical articles in Vienna. After completing his degree in Zürich, he is commissioned in the United States army and returns to Zürich in spring 1919 after his discharge.

Chapter 2
In April Dick visits Franz GREGOROVIOUS at DOHMLER's clinic on the Zürichsee, where they discuss the letters Dick has received from wealthy mental patient Nicole Warren, whom he had met just after joining the army.

Chapter 3
Franz relates Nicole's history to Dick. About a year and a half before, her father, Devereux WARREN of Chicago, had brought her to the clinic because she was showing signs of mental illness. When Warren had failed to return for his promised visit, Doctor Dohmler had issued an ultimatum that he must come before he returned to America; and Warren had revealed an incestuous episode with Nicole.

Chapter 4
Dick tells Franz that he plans "to be a good psychologist—maybe to be the greatest one that ever lived" (p. 138). He reflects that "he wanted to be good, he wanted to be kind, he wanted to be brave and wise, but it was all pretty difficult. He wanted to be loved, too, if he could fit it in" (p. 140).

Chapter 5
Dick visits Nicole at the clinic, and she plays American records for him.

Chapter 6
Franz tells Dick that Nicole is apparently in love with him, and Doctor Dohmler expresses his concern over their relationship. Dick says that he has considered marrying her.

Chapter 7
Dick, Franz, and Dohmler decide that Dick should go away, and when he sees Nicole next he is cold and distant.

Chapter 8
Dick is dissatisfied with the end of the affair. He works on his forthcoming book and plans another. He encounters Nicole and her sister, Baby WARREN, on the GLION funicular.

Chapter 9
Dick joins Nicole and Baby after dinner. Baby discusses Nicole's situation with Dick and reveals her hope that Nicole will fall in love with a doctor back in Chicago. Dick and Nicole kiss. Baby asks Dick to escort Nicole back to the clinic, and he realizes "her problem was one they had together for good now" (p. 165).

Chapter 10
In September Dick has tea with Baby, who is displeased with his desire to marry Nicole. Nicole's free-associa-

tion reverie recounts their marriage, honeymoon, the births of their two children, her relapses, their travels, and Dick's growing dependence on the Warren money, and ends with meeting Rosemary on the beach, bringing the time back to the beginning of the novel.

Chapter 11

After Peterson's murder, Rosemary moves to another hotel and the Divers return to the Villa Diana, where Dick considers a new plan for the book he is writing. Dick tells Mrs. Speers that he is in love with Rosemary. He reflects on Nicole's two recent collapses: in the Paris hotel and earlier at their party.

Chapter 12

Dick reflects on Nicole's money and its rapid increase in recent years; nevertheless he has maintained "a qualified financial independence" (p. 178).

Chapter 13

While the Divers are in GSTAAD to ski, Franz Gregorovious proposes that he and Dick buy a clinic together, a plan which Baby Warren encourages. Dick senses that Baby's message is "We own you" (p. 185).

Chapter 14

Dick and Franz have had their clinic for 18 months. Dick becomes emotionally attached to a female patient with severe eczema.

Chapter 15

Nicole receives a letter from a former patient at the clinic who falsely claims Dick seduced her daughter. At the Ägeri Fair Nicole runs away because she sees a young girl looking at Dick. On the way home she grabs the steering wheel from Dick and runs their car off the road.

Chapter 16

After Nicole's recovery from her breakdown, Dick takes a leave of absence from the clinic, ostensibly to attend a psychiatric conference, but really just to get away.

Chapter 17

In Munich Dick encounters Tommy Barban and learns that Abe North was beaten to death in a NEW YORK speakeasy.

Chapter 18

In Innsbruck Dick reflects that he has "lost himself" (p. 209) between the time he met Nicole and the time he met Rosemary. He feels that the Warrens own him, and he is attracted to every pretty woman he sees. He receives a telegram that his father has died, and the news reinforces his growing awareness of his own lack of dedication to duty.

Chapter 19

Dick sails to America for his father's funeral; on his return voyage to Europe he encounters Albert McKisco,

now a successful novelist. In Rome he encounters Rosemary, "the person he had come to see" (p. 215).

Chapter 20

The year is specified as 1928. Dick goes to Rosemary's hotel room, where they kiss but she stops his further advances. The next day he accompanies her to the movie set; and when they return to the hotel, they consummate their relationship.

Chapter 21

Dick encounters Baby Warren, who suggests he and Nicole move to LONDON, an idea he rejects. Dick realizes he is not in love with Rosemary, a discovery which increases his passion for her. He asks about her sex life; and she tells him that NICOTERA, an Italian actor, wants to marry her. Dick reflects, "I guess I'm the Black Death. . . . I don't seem to bring people happiness any more" (p. 227).

Chapter 22

Dick goes out drinking with Collis Clay. After an altercation with a taxi driver, Dick is beaten by the Rome police and put in jail.

Chapter 23

Dick summons Baby Warren to rescue him from jail, and her persistence at the Consulate accomplishes his release.

BOOK III

Chapter 1

Franz's wife, Kaethe GREGOROVIOUS, complains to her husband about Nicole and plants in his mind the idea that "Dick is no longer a serious man" (p. 249).

Chapter 2

When Dick returns to the clinic, Franz sends him to LAUSANNE to interview a prospective patient, an alcoholic homosexual, whose case Dick refuses after the interview. While in Lausanne he learns that Nicole's father is there being treated for alcoholism and is dying. Kaethe Gregorovious unwisely tells Nicole of the situation; Nicole leaves for Lausanne, but by the time she arrives her father has departed.

Chapter 3

Back at the clinic a week later, patient Von Cohn MORRIS is being taken away by his parents, who claim he has twice smelled liquor on Dick's breath. Franz and Dick agree to break up their partnership.

Chapter 4

The Divers are back on the Riviera, where Dick writes a little; and they have more money than ever. They visit Mary North, who is now the Contessa di MINGHETTI. Dick mistakes the count's sister for a maid, insulting the family's honor; and the Divers and Mary part on bad terms.

Chapter 5
Back at the Villa Diana, the Divers' relationship grows more strained; and Nicole tells Dick, "I've ruined you" (p. 274). At a party on a yacht they encounter Tommy Barban; and Dick, who has been drinking too much, quarrels with Lady Caroline SIBLY-BIERS.

Chapter 6
The next morning Tommy, who drove the Divers home from the party, has a sore throat; against Dick's wishes Nicole gives Tommy a jar of camphor rub that has to be ordered from Paris.

Chapter 7
The Divers' relationship has been deteriorating for months, and Nicole fears that Dick is planning a "desperate solution" (p. 286). On the beach they encounter Rosemary, who had telegraphed them of her arrival; Nicole is irritated by Dick's attempts to show off for Rosemary in an aquaplane stunt. Rosemary tells Dick she had heard that he had changed, and he replies: "The change came a long way back—but at first it didn't show. The manner remains intact for some time after the morale cracks" (p. 291). Nicole reflects that she is nearly complete without Dick, and she writes a provocative letter to Tommy.

Chapter 8
While Dick is out of town, Tommy comes to see Nicole; and they go to a shore hotel, where they sleep together. Tommy brings Nicole home before daylight.

Chapter 9
The next afternoon Dick comes home, and he and Nicole quarrel. He tells her, "I can't do anything for you any more. I'm trying to save myself" (p. 306). She calls him a coward and a failure and completes her psychological break from him: "The case was finished. Doctor Diver was at liberty" (p. 307).

Chapter 10
In response to a phone call in the middle of the night, Dick goes to the police station to bail out Mary Minghetti and Caroline Sibly-Biers, who had dressed as French sailors and picked up two girls.

Chapter 11
Tommy confronts Dick and tells him that Nicole wants a divorce, and Dick concedes.

Chapter 12
Mary Minghetti asks Dick why he isn't always nice anymore and tells him she has spent her summer defending him. Dick blesses the beach as he leaves the Riviera.

Chapter 13
Nicole and Tommy are married. Dick is in America working on his uncompleted book and moving from one small town to another practicing general medicine with diminishing success. He writes to Nicole that he

is in Geneva, New York: "Perhaps, so she liked to think, his career was biding its time, again like Grant's in Galena; his latest note was post-marked from Hornell, New York, which is some distance from Geneva and a very small town; in any case he is almost certainly in that section of the country, in one town or another" (p. 321).

Fitzgerald's assessment of his novel is evident in his inscription in book reviewer Philip Lenhart's copy of *GG:* "This is an attempt at the 'tour de force.' . . . If you like my stuff I hope to God you'll read 'Tender Is the Night', which is a confession of faith" (c. April 1934; *Life in Letters,* pp. 251–252).

See *TITN,* the Centennial Edition, ed. Matthew J. Bruccoli (London: Everyman, 1996); *TITN* (facsimile of Bruccoli's emended copy of the first printing), ed. Bruccoli (London: Samuel Johnson, 1995); *F. Scott Fitzgerald Manuscripts IVa* (2 vols): "*TITN:* The Melarky and Kelly Versions"; *F. Scott Fitzgerald Manuscripts IVb* (5 vols): "*TITN:* The Diver Version"; Bruccoli and Judith S. Baughman, *Reader's Companion to F. Scott Fitzgerald's Tender Is the Night;* Bruccoli, *The Composition of Tender Is the Night: A Study of the Manuscripts;* Milton R. Stern, *Tender Is the Night: The Broken Universe;* Stern, ed., *Critical Essays on F. Scott Fitzgerald's Tender Is the Night;* and Marvin J. LaHood, ed., *Tender Is the Night: Essays in Criticism.*

Tepper, Saul (**b. 1899**) Illustrator of two PHILIPPE stories for *REDBOOK:* "In the Darkest Hour" (October 1934) and "The Count of Darkness" (June 1935). Like most illustrators of the 1920s and 1930s, Tepper illustrated equally for both fiction and advertisements.

Terhune, Miss Grace Character in "Strange Sanctuary." Assistant headmistress of Dolly HAINES's school; Clarke CRESSWELL's aunt, whom he is visiting.

Terrell, Elaine Character in "Babes in the Woods." Girl whom ISABELLE visits during Christmas vacation. This character is renamed Sally WEATHERBY in *TSOP.*

Thalberg, Irving Grant (1899–1936) Movie producer and model for *LT/LOLT* hero Monroe STAHR. Born in Brooklyn, New York, Thalberg was unable to finish high school because of rheumatic fever; but he completed a commercial course in night school. In 1918 Carl Laemmle (1867–1939) of Universal Studios employed him as a secretary-stenographer in the NEW YORK office; by age 20 Thalberg was manager of the California studio. In 1923 he became Vice-President of the Mayer Company; when Loew's, Inc. formed Metro-Goldwyn-Mayer in 1924 he became Second Vice-President and Supervisor of Production. Thalberg and Louis B. Mayer (1885–1957) quarrelled over the division of profits; and in 1933 while Thalberg was in EUROPE recuperating from a collapse caused by overwork, Mayer removed him as

Movie producer Irving Thalberg, the model for Monroe Stahr

production head and instituted an employee pay cut, which Thalberg had opposed. Thalberg's opposition to the Screen Writers Guild provided a plot element for *LT/LOLT.*

After Thalberg's death Fitzgerald wrote to Oscar KALMAN: "Talbert's final collapse is the death of an enemy for me, though I liked the guy enormously. He had an idea that his wife and I were playing around, which was absolute nonsense, but I think even so that he killed the idea of either Hopkins or Frederick Marsh doing 'Tender is the Night'" (September 19, 1936; *Correspondence,* pp. 451–452). There is no evidence that Thalberg blocked the movie sale of *TITN,* and neither Miriam Hopkins nor Fredric March was under contract to MGM at the time.

Fitzgerald's draft of an inscription for the copy of *LT/LOLT* which was to be presented to Thalberg's widow, actress Norma SHEARER, explains Thalberg's role as a model for Stahr: "though the story is purely imaginary," the book is "an attempt to preserve something of Irving. My own impression of him shortly recorded but very dazzling in its effect on me, inspired the best part of the character of Stahr" (*Life in Letters,* p. 468).

See Bob Thomas, *Thalberg: Life and Legend* (Garden City, NY: Doubleday, 1969).

"That Kind of Party" Fiction. *The Princeton University Library Chronicle,* 12 (Summer 1951), 167–180; *B&J.* Terrence R. TIPTON, who is in love with Dolly BARTLETT, persuades Joe SHOONOVER to host a party for the purpose of kissing games. Terrence and Joe send a forged telegram to Joe's mother to keep her away from the party, but the telegram is mistakenly delivered to Terrence's mother instead. Mrs. SHOONOVER arrives at the party and offers to play the piano for Clap-in-and-clap-out. Carpenter MOORE, whose younger brother, Albert

MOORE, had fought with Terrence earlier that day, enlists the other children in a plot against Terrence, who overhears the plan and locks Carpenter in a closet. Terrence later accidentally dumps him out of the wheelchair, and he stands and walks a few steps for the first time in five years. After the party Dolly Bartlett invites Terrence to supper.

Fitzgerald wrote this as a Basil Duke LEE story but changed the name to Terrence R. Tipton in an unsuccessful attempt to market the story separately from the Basil series. *Ladies' Home Journal* rejected it because the children "were both precocious and rather unpleasant"; the editor told Harold OBER that "parents do not like to think of children ten years old being so much interested in sex" (*As Ever,* p. 317).

Thayer, Lowell Character in "The Rich Boy." Paula LEGENDRE's first husband, a wealthy Bostonian. He and Paula have three children before their divorce.

"The Third Casket" Fiction. Written March 1924. *The SATURDAY EVENING POST,* 196, (May 31, 1924), 8–9, 78; *The Price Was High.* At age 60 Cyrus GIRARD sends for the sons of his three best friends to compete to take over his business and possibly marry his daughter, Lola GIRARD. George VAN BUREN, John Hardwick PARRISH, and Rip JONES prove equally satisfactory in business; so Girard gives them two weeks of leisure to spend as they will when they retire. He is furious to discover that Rip Jones is in Chicago on business when he is supposed to be relaxing; but when he realizes that Jones shares his passion for work, he decides to make him his partner and not to retire yet himself. Meanwhile, Jones has married Lola.

The title of "The Third Casket" is taken from William Shakespeare's *The Merchant of Venice,* in which a young woman's suitors must choose one of three caskets prepared by her father.

"This Is a Magazine" Humorous article. *Vanity Fair,* 15 (December 1920), 71; *In His Own Time.* Dramatic dialogue among various stories, articles, and poems in a magazine, including an "Edith Wharton Story," a "Baseball Yarn," a "Detective Story," a "British Serial," a "Robert Chambers Story," and two love poems.

This Side of Paradise Novel. New York: Charles SCRIBNER's Sons, 1920; London: Collins, 1921. Dedication: "TO SIGORNEY FAY." While in ARMY training camp at FORT LEAVENWORTH, Kansas, in November 1917, Fitzgerald began writing a novel titled "The Romantic Egotist" (which he sometimes spelled "Egoist") which he later described as "a somewhat edited history of me and my imagination" ("Who's Who—and Why," September 1920; *AOAA,* p. 84). He worked with a sense of urgency which he described in a note in the

manuscript: "I'm trying to set down the story part of my generation in America and put myself in the middle as a sort of observer and conscious factor. But I've got to write now, for when the war's over I won't be able to see these things as important—even now they are fading out against the back-ground of the map of Europe. I'll never be able to do it again; well done or poorly. So I'm writing almost desperately—and so futily" (PRINCETON UNIVERSITY LIBRARY, p. 19). On January 10, 1918 he wrote to Edmund WILSON that he had completed 18 of 23 chapters, noting: "Really if Scribner takes it I know I'll wake some morning and find that the debutantes have made me famous over night. I really believe that no one else could have written so searchingly the story of the youth of our generation" (*Life in Letters,* p. 17). The manuscript for this novel does not survive, but the five carbon-copy typescript chapters reveal that it was an early version of *TSOP.*

At the end of February 1918 Fitzgerald received leave from the army and finished his novel at the COTTAGE CLUB at PRINCETON in March. He sent the completed typescript to Shane LESLIE, who recommended it to his publisher, Charles SCRIBNER, on May 6 (*Correspondence,*

p. 29). Scribners rejected the novel on August 19 but suggested Fitzgerald submit a revised version (*The Romantic Egoists,* p. 34). Fitzgerald revised the novel while at CAMP SHERIDAN and resubmitted it. The revised novel was rejected in October, and Fitzgerald captioned the telegram in his scrapbook "the end of a dream" (*The Romantic Egoists,* p. 35). Thinking the material might have been too strong for the conservative Scribners firm, Fitzgerald asked Scribners editor Maxwell PERKINS to send the novel to another publisher, who also declined it.

In July 1918 Fitzgerald met Zelda Sayre [FITZGERALD], who eventually agreed to marry him when he succeeded in NEW YORK, where he moved in February 1919 and took a job with the Barron Collier advertising agency. That spring he wrote 19 stories and received 122 rejections, selling only a revision of his 1917 NASSAU LITERARY MAGAZINE story "Babes in the Woods" to *The SMART SET*—his first commercial story sale. Zelda broke their engagement in June, and Fitzgerald quit his job and returned to ST. PAUL in July to work on his novel.

On July 26, 1919 Fitzgerald wrote to Maxwell Perkins

W. E. Hill's dust jacket for Fitzgerald's first novel, published in 1920 (Bruccoli Collection, University of South Carolina)

that he had completed the first draft of a novel called "The Education of a Personage," explaining inaccurately that it was "in no sense a revision of the ill-fated <u>Romantic Egotist</u> but it contains some of the former material improved and worked over and bears a strong family resemblance besides" (*Life in Letters,* p. 28; *Scott/Max,* p. 17); his September 4 letter details the connections between the two versions of the novel (*Life in Letters,* pp. 31–32; *Scott/Max,* p. 20). On August 16 he informed Perkins of the new title, *This Side of Paradise,* taken from the last lines of Rupert BROOKE's "Tiare Tahiti"—"Well, this side of paradise/There's little comfort in the wise"—which appeared on the title page of Fitzgerald's novel. Fitzgerald sent the typescript to New York with a friend, Thomas Daniels, on September 4 (*Life in Letters,* pp. 29–31; *Scott/Max,* pp. 18–19); and Perkins accepted the novel on September 16 (*Scott/ Max,* p. 21).

Fitzgerald described his own response in "Early Success," published 17 years later: "Then the postman rang, and that day I quit work and ran along the streets, stopping automobiles to tell friends and acquaintances about it—my novel *This Side of Paradise* was accepted for publication. That week the postman rang and rang, and I paid off my terrible small debts, bought a suit, and woke up every morning with a world of ineffable toploftiness and promise" (October 1937; *CU,* p. 86).

Fitzgerald moved to NEW ORLEANS to write, and during visits to MONTGOMERY he persuaded Zelda to marry him. He returned to New York for a month but moved to the Cottage Club at the end of February 1920 so he would be in Princeton when his novel was published.

This Side of Paradise was published on March 26, 1920 at $1.75, with a dust jacket illustrated by W. E. HILL; the first printing of 3,000 copies sold out in three days. Fitzgerald's slogan "A NOVEL ABOUT FLAPPERS WRITTEN FOR PHILOSOPHERS" appeared in the first ads. As Fitzgerald had predicted, he became famous almost overnight. Most of the reviews of his novel were positive. H. L. MENCKEN called it "the best American novel that I have seen of late" (*The Smart Set,* 62 [August 1920], 140; *FSF: The Critical Reception,* p. 28). Burton Rascoe wrote in the *Chicago Tribune:* " 'This Side of Paradise' gives him, I think, a fair claim to membership in that small squad of contemporary American fictionists who are producing literature. . . . It bears the impress, it seems to me, of genius. It is the only adequate study that we have had of the contemporary American in adolescence and young manhood" ("A Youth in the Saddle," April 3, 1920, p. 11; *FSF: The Critical Reception,* p. 3). (*See* also CRITICAL REPUTATION AND RECEPTION OF NOVELS.)

One reviewer described *TSOP* as "the collected works of F. Scott Fitzgerald" (R.V.A.S., *The New Republic,* 22 [May 12, 1920], 362; *FSF: The Critical Reception,* p. 22);

and the novel does contain a variety of Fitzgerald's earlier work, notably several poems, the story "Babes in the Woods," and the play "The Debutante." Fitzgerald himself described the novel as "A Romance and a Reading List" (*Notebooks,* #1021), for he characterizes Amory BLAINE through his reading, mentioning 64 titles and 98 writers. (See Dorothy Ballweg Good, " 'A Romance and a Reading List': The Literary References in *This Side of Paradise,*" *Fitzgerald/Hemingway Annual* [1976], 35–64.) Like Amory, Fitzgerald was influenced by the "quest novels" of Compton MACKENZIE (*Sinister Street,* 1913–14), Robert Hugh BENSON (*None Other Gods,* 1910), and H. G. WELLS (*The Research Magnificent,* 1915): "In the 'quest' book the hero set off in life armed with the best weapons and avowedly intending to use them as such weapons are usually used, to push their possessors ahead as selfishly and blindly as possible, but the heroes of the 'quest' books discovered that there might be a more magnificent use for them" (*TSOP,* pp. 131–132). The first edition of *TSOP* was peppered with spelling and usage errors, and its sloppy text was responsible for starting Fitzgerald's reputation as a careless writer.

In "The Author's Apology," which was tipped into copies of the third printing of *TSOP* distributed at the American Booksellers Association convention in May 1920, Fitzgerald wrote: "I don't want to talk about myself because I'll admit I did that somewhat in this book. In fact, to write it took three months; to conceive it—three minutes; to collect the data in it—all my life. The idea of writing it came on the first of last July: it was a substitute form of dissipation" (*In His Own Time,* p. 164). In 1925 he wrote in his own copy of *TSOP:* "I like this book for the enormous emotion, mostly immature and bogus, that gives every incident a sort of silly 'life.' . . . But the faked references and intellectual reactions + cribs from MacKenzie, Johnston, Wells, Wilde, Tarkington give me the pip" (Princeton University Library, p. 305). Fitzgerald had previously written a preface for the novel which was not used; *see F. Scott Fitzgerald's Preface to This Side of Paradise.*

BOOK ONE: THE ROMANTIC EGOTIST

1. *Amory, Son of Beatrice*

Amory Blaine is indulged by his eccentric mother, Beatrice BLAINE, with whom he travels around the country during his boyhood. Amory feels a sense of superiority, that he is "a boy marked for glory"; and he formulates a code of "aristocratic egotism" (p. 19). He meets Monsignor Thayer DARCY, with whom his mother had once had a romance, and feels an immediate kinship with the priest, who becomes a major influence in his life. Amory is unpopular in his first year at ST. REGIS prep school, but over time he is accepted and becomes a star quarterback and editor of the school paper.

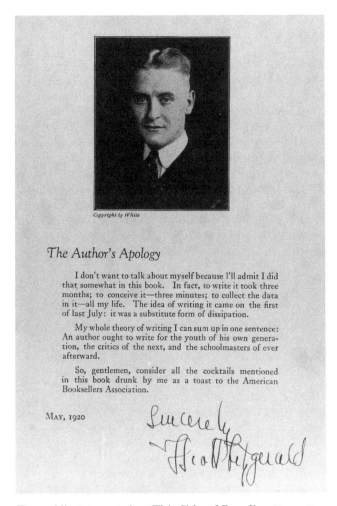

The Author's Apology

I don't want to talk about myself because I'll admit I did that somewhat in this book. In fact, to write it took three months; to conceive it—three minutes; to collect the data in it—all my life. The idea of writing it came on the first of last July: it was a substitute form of dissipation.

My whole theory of writing I can sum up in one sentence: An author ought to write for the youth of his own generation, the critics of the next, and the schoolmasters of ever afterward.

So, gentlemen, consider all the cocktails mentioned in this book drunk by me as a toast to the American Booksellers Association.

MAY, 1920

Sincerely,
F. Scott Fitzgerald

Fitzgerald's statement about This Side of Paradise *(Bruccoli Collection, University of South Carolina)*

2. *Spires and Gargoyles*

Amory enters Princeton, where he wants "to pull strings" and "to be admired" (p. 52). He joins the TRIANGLE CLUB and the board of the *Princetonian* and is elected to the Cottage Club. During Christmas vacation of his sophomore year he falls in love with Isabelle BORGÉ (an episode borrowed from Fitzgerald's 1917 story "Babes in the Woods").

3. *The Egotist Considers*

When Isabelle comes to Princeton for the prom, she and Amory quarrel and break up. Amory fails a crucial exam in conic sections and thus loses several opportunities for leadership in college. His father dies, and Amory learns of the dwindling of his family's fortune. Monsignor Darcy explains to Amory his distinction between a personality and a personage: "Personality is a physical matter almost entirely; it lowers the people it acts on—I've seen it vanish in a long sickness. But while a personality is active, it overrides 'the next

thing.' Now a personage, on the other hand, gathers. He is never thought of apart from what he's done. He's a bar on which a thousand things have been hung— glittering things sometimes, as ours are; but he uses those things with a cold mentality back of them" (pp. 113–114). Darcy classifies both Amory and himself as personages. While in the apartment of two New York showgirls Amory senses "a sort of infinite evil" (p. 126) and the presence of a devil figure.

4. *Narcissus Off Duty*

Amory's friend Burne HOLIDAY leads a revolt against the clubs at Princeton. Amory meets his widowed cousin, Clara PAGE, with whom he falls in love; but she refuses to marry him. Amory and his friends graduate from Princeton and join the armed services.

Interlude: May, 1917–February, 1919

Amory serves in the war (though his experiences are not detailed since Fitzgerald had no firsthand knowledge of battle). Beatrice Blaine dies, and Amory learns of the further dwindling of her estate. After the war he and two friends from Princeton, Alec CONNAGE and Thomas Parke D'INVILLIERS, plan to take an apartment together in New York.

BOOK TWO: THE EDUCATION OF A PERSONAGE

1. *The Débutante*

Amory, who has taken a job with an advertising agency, falls in love with Alec's sister Rosalind CONNAGE, and they talk of marriage; but she eventually breaks up with him to marry wealthy Dawson RYDER because she fears a life of boredom and responsibility while Amory struggles to make his way. This section is a revision of Fitzgerald's 1917 play "The Debutante."

2. *Experiments in Convalescence*

Amory quits his job and spends three weeks drinking to get over the loss of Rosalind, ending his spree when Prohibition begins. Alec Connage moves home. Amory is bored and restless, and he argues to Tom D'Invilliers that the war "sort of killed individualism out of our generation" (p. 228). Tom and Amory move out of their apartment when Tom's mother falls ill, and Amory travels to Maryland to visit an uncle.

3. *Young Irony*

In Maryland Amory meets Eleanor SAVAGE, a reckless, romantic atheist who chafes at the limitations of being a girl. His interest in her fades when, on their last night together before his return to New York, she nearly rides off a cliff to prove she won't call for God's help on her deathbed.

4. *The Supercilious Sacrifice*

In Atlantic City Amory encounters Alec Connage and agrees to share his hotel suite when Alec's friend who

occupies the other room has to leave town. When a hotel detective pounds on the door in the middle of the night because Alec was seen going upstairs with Jill WAYNE, Amory pretends Jill was with him so Alec won't get into trouble. Two days later he learns of Rosalind's engagement to Dawson Ryder, is informed of the further decline of his inheritance, and learns of Monsignor Darcy's death.

5. *The Egotist Becomes a Personage*
Reflecting bitterly on his life, Amory feels a sudden "overwhelming desire to let himself go to the devil" (p. 281). He thinks there are no more heroes, and he resents that people who have pretended to know something really knew nothing. He is disillusioned by the contradictions he sees in others, and he concludes: "Life was a damned muddle . . . a football game with every one off-side and the referee gotten rid of—every one claiming the referee would have been on his side. . . ." (p. 285). He attends Monsignor Darcy's funeral and decides that he wants to be indispensable and to give people a sense of security like Monsignor Darcy and Burne Holiday. Amory argues socialism with a man who offers him a ride as he is walking to Princeton and who turns out to be the father of one of his Princeton classmates. Princeton goes on "as an endless dream . . . the spirit of the past brooding over a new generation" for whom Amory feels sorry: "a new generation dedicated more than the last to the fear of poverty and the worship of success; grown up to find all God's dead, all wars fought, all faiths in man shaken" (p. 304). Without knowing why, Amory has decided to continue his struggle, to "use to the utmost himself and his heritage from the personalities he had passed" (p. 305). He cries, "I know myself . . . but that is all" (p. 305).

TSOP is significant in American fiction for its combination of realism and romanticism and for its serious treatment of college life and the liberated girl. It was the first serious American college novel since Owen Johnson's (1878–1952) *Stover at Yale* (1911), which was written for boys. Young people read *TSOP* as a guidebook to college, and John O'HARA later wrote that half a million men and women between 15 and 30 fell in love with the book (*The Portable F. Scott Fitzgerald*, p. vii).

See *F. Scott Fitzgerald Manuscripts I* (2 vols): "*TSOP*: The Manuscripts and Typescripts," and Matthew J. BRUCCOLI, "Fitzgerald's Marked Copy of *This Side of Paradise*," *Fitzgerald/Hemingway Annual* (1971), 64–70.

Thomas, Mrs. Character in "Between Three and Four." Illiterate cleaning woman whom Howard BUTLER asks to confirm what he thinks he has read in the newspaper about Sarah SUMMER's suicide.

Thorne, Vienna Character in "The Bowl." Dolly HARLAN's fiancée, whose brother was killed in a prep-

school football game and who temporarily convinces Dolly to give up football.

Thoughtbook of Francis Scott Key Fitzgerald Introduction by John R. Kuehl. Princeton, N.J.: PRINCETON UNIVERSITY LIBRARY, 1965. Reprinted from *The Princeton University Library Chronicle*, 26 (Winter 1965), 102–108 and unpaged plates. Facsimile of a journal which Fitzgerald kept in 1910 and 1911, recording his romances and his striving for popularity.

"Thousand-and-First Ship" Verse. *Notebooks*, #857; *CU*; *Poems*. This six-stanza poem, which THE NEW YORKER declined in 1935, includes six lines which originally appeared in "Sleeping and Waking," a 1934 ESQUIRE article; they became Fitzgerald's best-known verse:

> In the fall of '16 in the cool of the afternoon
> I met Caroline under a white moon
> There was an orchestra—Bingo-Bango
> Playing for us to dance the tango
> And the people all clapped as we arose
> For her sweet face and my new clothes—
> (*CU*, pp. 67–68)

"Three Acts of Music" Fiction. Written February 1936. ESQUIRE, 5 (May 1936), 39, 210; *The Price Was High*. A DOCTOR and a NURSE who have not yet completed their medical training discuss marriage, but don't follow through. Years later he returns from Vienna to find her supervising an operating room and proud of her success. Several years after that, when she is superintendent of a woman's hospital, he remarks that they'll never get married because it's too late. She concludes that all they had was the music they listened to together, composed by Vincent Youmans (1898–1946), Irving Berlin (1888–1989), and Jerome Kern (1885–1945).

"Three Cities" Essay. *Brentano's Book Chat*, 1 (September–October 1921), 15, 28; *In His Own Time*. Fitzgerald's impressions of PARIS, Florence, ROME, and Oxford.

Three Comrades In 1937 Fitzgerald was assigned to write the screenplay for *Three Comrades*, a 1929 novel about postwar Germany by Erich Maria Remarque (1898–1970), for MGM producer Joseph MANKIEWICZ. He submitted two-thirds of the screenplay on September 1 before flying east to visit Zelda FITZGERALD at HIGHLANDS HOSPITAL in ASHEVILLE, North Carolina. On September 4, Fitzgerald wrote to Mankiewicz requesting that he be allowed to work alone on the revisions. Mankiewicz wired on September 9 that what Fitzgerald had submitted was "simply swell" (PRINCETON UNIVERSITY LIBRARY) and that he could continue alone. However, when Fitzgerald returned to HOLLYWOOD he was assigned E. E. PARAMORE as a

Poster for the 1938 movie that earned Fitzgerald his only screen credit (Bruccoli Collection, University of South Carolina)

collaborator to help with construction. Fitzgerald and Paramore disagreed over the latter's role: Paramore regarded himself as an equal partner, but Fitzgerald wrote to him on October 24, "I *prefer to keep* the responsibility for the script as a whole" (*Letters*, p. 558).

Fitzgerald and Paramore submitted six revisions of the screenplay, dated November 5, 1937, December 7, December 13, December 21, January 21, 1938, and February 1. Mankiewicz heavily revised the final script, but screen credit was shared by Fitzgerald and Paramore. Fitzgerald resented Mankiewicz's interference, noting in his copy of the shooting script, "37 pages mine about 1/3, but all shadows + rythm removed." On January 20, 1938 he wrote Mankiewicz an emotional letter that he may not have sent:

> To say I'm disillusioned is putting it mildly. For nineteen years, with two years out for sickness, I've written best-selling entertainment, and my dialogue is suppos-

edly right up at the top. But I learn from the script that you've suddenly decided that it isn't good dialogue and you can take a few hours off and do much better. . . . You are simply tired of the best scenes because you've read them too much, and having dropped the pilot, you're having the aforesaid pleasure of a child with a box of chalk. You are <u>or have</u> been a good writer, but this is a job you will be ashamed of before it's over. The little fluttering life of what's left of my lines and situations won't save the picture. . . . Oh, Joe, can't producers ever be wrong? I'm a good writer— honest. I thought you were going to play fair (*Life in Letters*, pp. 343–345).

At a private screening the German consul in Los Angeles objected to the movie's anti-Nazi stance. Joseph Breen (1890–1987), censor for the movie industry, recommended to Mankiewicz that the movie be altered to make the villains communists rather than Nazis. Mankiewicz says that when he refused and threat-

ened to resign, Fitzgerald hugged him in the MGM commissary to congratulate him for standing firm.

Three Comrades, directed by Frank BORZAGE and starring Robert Taylor (1911–69), Margaret Sullavan (1911–60), Franchot Tone (1905–68), and Robert Young (b. 1907), was released in June 1938; a box-office success, it ranked as one of the 10 best movies of the year. Margaret Sullavan was nominated for an Academy Award and won both the New York Critics Award and the British National Award for best actress of the year. The movie brought Fitzgerald his only screen credit; and during his revisions with Paramore, MGM renewed his contract for a year at $1,250 per week.

Fitzgerald's original screenplay, without Paramore's and Mankiewicz's revisions, has been published as *F. Scott Fitzgerald's Screenplay for Erich Maria Remarque's Three Comrades*, edited with afterword by Matthew J. BRUCCOLI (Carbondale & Edwardsville: Southern Illinois University Press, 1978).

"Three Hours Between Planes" Fiction. Written c. 1940. ESQUIRE, 16 (July 1941), 41, 138–139; *Stories*; *Three Hours Between Planes* (Agincourt, Ontario: The Book Society of Canada Limited, 1970). During a three-hour wait between planes Donald PLANT visits Nancy GIFFORD, whom he had loved when he was 12. She welcomes him eagerly and they kiss; but while looking through old photographs she realizes that she has mistaken him for Donald BOWERS, with whom she used to go to a cave; and she sends him away.

Elihu Winer (b. 1914) wrote a one-act play based on Fitzgerald's story (New York: Samuel French, 1958).

"Three Soldiers" Review of *Three Soldiers* by John DOS PASSOS. *St. Paul Daily News*, September 25, 1921, feature section, p. 6; *In His Own Time*. Fitzgerald praises this novel as "the first war book by an American which is worthy of serious notice" (*In His Own Time*, p. 121). The review is also noteworthy for Fitzgerald's renunciation of the influence of H. G. WELLS.

Thurber, James (1894–1961) American author and artist whose works include *My Life and Hard Times* (1933), *The Middle-Aged Man on the Flying Trapeze* (1935) and *My World—And Welcome to It* (1942). His late review of *LT* may have contributed to the Fitzgerald REVIVAL. Thurber focused on the novel's unfinished state and warned against comparing it to "Fitzgerald's perfection of style and form," which in *GG* "has a way of making something that lies between your stomach and your heart quiver a little." Nonetheless, he stated, if Fitzgerald had lived long enough he would have accomplished his plan for his depiction of "Hollywood and its great and little men," adding, "I know of no one else who

could" ("Taps at Assembly," *The New Republic*, 106 [February 9, 1942], 211–212; *FSF: The Critical Reception*, pp. 381 & 382).

Thurber gives an account of what he describes as his only meeting with Fitzgerald in "Scott in Thorns" (*Reporter*, 4 [April 17, 1951], 35–38 and *Credos and Curios* [New York: Harper & Row, 1962], pp. 153–163). He recalls a night in 1934 just before the publication of *TITN* when he met Fitzgerald in a NEW YORK bar; when Fitzgerald learned that Thurber was a writer, he talked to Thurber for five hours.

See Harrison Kinney, *James Thurber: His Life and Times* (New York: Holt, 1995).

Ticknor, Evangeline Character in "A Nice Quiet Place." Girl with whom Ridgeway SAUNDERS falls in love while Josephine PERRY is away at Island Farms. When Josephine wins Ridgeway back at Ed BEMENT's house party, Miss Ticknor leaves suddenly.

Tighe, Katherine Childhood friend of Fitzgerald in ST. PAUL. When Fitzgerald returned to St. Paul in the summer of 1919 to work on *TSOP*, Tighe offered advice on his work-in-progress. In a June 1926 letter to Ernest HEMINGWAY, Fitzgerald noted: "I've taken what proved to be excellent advice . . . on T. S. of Paradise from Katherine Tighe (you don't know her) who had probably never read a novel before" (*Life in Letters*, p. 142). *The Vegetable* bears this dedication: "TO KATHERINE TIGHE AND EDMUND WILSON, JR. WHO DELETED MANY ABSURDITIES FROM MY FIRST TWO NOVELS I RECOMMEND THE ABSURDITIES SET DOWN HERE."

Tipton, Terrence R. Character in "That Kind of Party." Boy who is in love with Dolly BARTLETT and who persuades Joe SHOONOVER to host a party with kissing games. This character was originally named Basil Duke LEE, but Fitzgerald changed the name in an effort to sell the story separately from the Basil series.

"To a Beloved Infidel" Poem. Fair-copy manuscript, titled "For Shielah, a Beloved Infidel," facsimiled on the front endpapers of *Beloved Infidel* by Sheilah GRAHAM and Gerold Frank (New York: Holt, 1958); *Poems 1911–1940*. Fitzgerald submitted the poem to ESQUIRE under the pseudonym of "John Darcy," but it was declined (to Arnold GINGRICH, February 23, 1940; *Life in Letters*, p. 434).

"To My Unused Greek Book (*Acknowledgments to Keats*)" Verse. *The NASSAU LITERARY MAGAZINE*, 72 (June 1916), 137; *In His Own Time*; *Poems*. Imitation of "Ode on a Grecian Urn" by John KEATS.

Tolliver, Mary Character in "News of Paris—Fifteen Years Ago." Bessie WING's friend, who Bessie says will understand her decision to break her engagement.

Tom Character in "Image on the Heart." Old family friend who rescues TUDY from poverty after the death of her first husband and marries her after sending her to school for a year.

Tomlinson, Tommy Character in " 'I Didn't Get Over." One of three classmates to whom HIBBING tells the story of Abe DANZER.

Tompkins, George Character in "Gretchen's Forty Winks." Interior decorator with whom Gretchen HALSEY spends time while her husband is working long hours. Though Tompkins constantly holds up his own "balanced" life as an example to Roger HALSEY, it is he, not Roger, who suffers from a nervous breakdown.

"Too Cute for Words" Fiction—Gwen BOWERS story. Written December 1935. *The SATURDAY EVENING POST*, 208 (April 18, 1936), 16–18, 87, 90, 93; *The Price Was High*. Widower Bryan BOWERS reluctantly allows his 13-year-old daughter, Gwen BOWERS, to go with her friends Dizzy CAMPBELL and Clara HANNAMAN to a dance the night before the PRINCETON football game. When the girls arrive at Princeton, Dizzy's cousin, Esther RAY, informs them that the dance has been called off; but she lets them go with her and her date to the Harvard-Princeton concert. When Esther leaves for the Princeton prom, the three girls decide to go observe the prom from outdoors. When they overhear debutante Marion LAMB getting engaged to HARRY, Harry swears them to secrecy in return for letting them into the gymnasium where they can watch the prom unobserved. When Esther's little brother, Tommy RAY, shows up with a telegram for his sister, Gwen dances across the floor with him to deliver it and is unaware that her father sees her. The next day she is horrified by her father's description of her as "too cute for words."

Torrence, Elizabeth Character in "The Woman from Twenty-One." Raymond TORRENCE's half-Javanese wife.

Torrence, Margaret Character in the Basil Duke LEE stories. Based on Fitzgerald's ST. PAUL friend Marie HERSEY. In "The Scandal Detectives" she had been Basil's girl at dancing school; but he asks her to return his ring, which he wants to give to Imogene BISSEL. In "He Thinks He's Wonderful" she tells everyone that Basil is wonderful, which makes him suddenly popular. At Connie DAVIES' dance Margaret reveals to Basil that Joe GORMAN and Hubert BLAIR have told everyone that Basil thinks he's wonderful. In "The Captured Shadow"

Margaret has a part in Basil's play, but Basil doesn't want her for the leading lady.

Torrence, Raymond (Ray) Character in "The Woman from Twenty-One." Man who is offended by the loud conversation of the WOMAN from Twenty-One.

Townsend, Mr. and Mrs. Characters in "The Camel's Back." Hosts of the circus ball.

Towson, Maryland The Fitzgeralds rented "LA PAIX" on the Bayard TURNBULL estate at RODGERS FORGE, Towson, outside BALTIMORE, May 1932–November 1933.

"The Trail of the Duke" Fiction. *The NEWMAN NEWS*, 9 (June 1913), 5–9; *Apprentice Fiction*. Mirabel WALMSLEY sends her fiancé, Dodson GARLAND, in search of "the Duke." Dodson thinks she means the Duke of Matterlane, who is visiting her father. He searches NEW YORK CITY to no avail and returns to Mirabel to learn that "the Duke" is her poodle, which had returned shortly after he left. Mirabel invites Dodson to meet the Duke of Matterlane the next day, but he refuses.

tramp (unnamed) Character in "The Count of Darkness." Bearded musician who fascinates LETGARDE.

"Trans-Continental Kitty" In March 1922 David O. SELZNICK asked Fitzgerald to write a movie synopsis for actress Elaine Hammerstein (1897–1948); if the synopsis was accepted, Fitzgerald was to receive $2,500 for expanding it into an 8,000-word screenplay. The 1,500-word synopsis for "Trans-Continental Kitty" which Fitzgerald submitted in April was declined.

Treadway Character in "The Freshest Boy." Basil Duke LEE's roommate at ST. REGIS. He refuses to accompany Basil to NEW YORK and takes his things out of their room to move in with Brick WALES.

Tressiger, Eric Character in "New Types." Paula JORGENSEN's invalid husband, a British nobleman whom she married secretly at age 17.

Tressiger, Lady Paula *See* Paula JORGENSEN.

Triangle Club PRINCETON UNIVERSITY theatrical group, founded by Booth TARKINGTON (Class of 1893), which produced an original musical comedy every year and toured during Christmas vacation. Fitzgerald's book and lyrics for *Fie! Fie! Fi-Fi!* won the 1914–15 competition. He and club president Walker ELLIS revised the script; Ellis awarded himself credit for dia-

Fitzgerald in costume for the Princeton Triangle Club (Bruccoli Collection, University of South Carolina)

logue and characters, with Fitzgerald receiving credit for plot and lyrics. Fitzgerald's failure of a make-up exam in coordinate geometry made him ineligible to perform in the play. On February 26, 1915 Fitzgerald was elected secretary of the Triangle Club for 1915–16. He expected to be president the following year; but his failure of a make-up exam in qualitative analysis made him ineligible for extracurricular activities, and the presidency went to Paul NELSON. However, Fitzgerald and Edmund WILSON collaborated on the 1915–16 show, *The Evil Eye,* with Wilson writing the book and Fitzgerald the lyrics. Although Fitzgerald was ineligible to perform, a photograph of him in a showgirl costume was used in publicity for the play. Fitzgerald's book for the 1916–17 show was rejected; but he wrote the lyrics for *Safety First,* written by John BIGGS, Jr. and J. F. Bohmfalk. Fitzgerald's Triangle Club lyrics are collected in *Poems 1911–1940* and *F. Scott Fitzgerald In His Own Time.*

See Donald Marsden, *The Long Kickline: A History of Princeton's Triangle Club* (Princeton: Princeton University Press, 1968). The After-Dinner Opera Company of New York performs the songs from Fitzgerald's three Triangle Club shows on a commercial cassette recording, *F. Scott Fitzgerald: Triangle Club Songs* (Bloom-

field Hills, Mich. & Columbia, S.C.: Bruccoli Clark, 1979).

Trimble, Louis Character in "The Lost Decade." Architect who tries to recapture a sense of reality after being drunk for a decade.

Trombone Mose Character in "The Offshore Pirate." The biggest of the "Six Black Buddies" who accompany Curtis CARLYLE.

" 'Trouble' " Fiction. Written June 1936. *The SATURDAY EVENING POST,* 209 (March 6, 1937), 14–15, 81, 84, 86, 88–89; *The Price Was High.* Glenola McClurg, a pretty and capable nurse nicknamed TROUBLE, injures her ankle when she falls off a deck into the arms of Doctor Dick WHEELOCK at the hospital's annual turtle race. That evening she receives a visit from Mrs. WINSLOW, whose son, Frederic WINSLOW, is in love with Trouble, and who asks her to reconsider her rejection of Frederic's proposal. Several days later Doctor Wheelock is treating Trouble's ankle when Mrs. JOHNSTON, the new superintendent of nurses, comes in and rebukes them for being together. Because Trouble speaks insultingly to Mrs. Johnston, Doctor COMPSON dismisses her. After Trouble sees Doctor Wheelock, to whom she is attracted, leaving town with a beautiful girl, she accepts Frederic's invitations to go riding and to have dinner at his family's home. Several days later she agrees to marry Frederic; but he gets drunk and follows her into the hospital to confront Doctor Wheelock, who tells her he has been worried about her and has gotten her job back for her. Trouble sees in Wheelock's eyes that he is interested in her, too, and she cancels her engagement to Frederic.

" 'Trouble' " was the last story Fitzgerald sold to the *Post.*

Trouble (Glenola McClurg) Character in " 'Trouble.' " A pretty and efficient nurse who becomes involved with Doctor Dick WHEELOCK after she falls off a deck into his arms at the hospital's annual turtle race. Fitzgerald hoped to develop a series about Trouble; but *The SATURDAY EVENING POST* declined the first story ("Cyclone in Silent Land"; unpublished) and accepted the second, " 'Trouble,' " reluctantly, advising him to abandon the series and invent a new character (see *As Ever,* p. 276).

The True Story of Appomattox July 1934. Reprinted in *In His Own Time.* Thirty-eight-line newspaper clipping, headed "Columnist Discovers That It Was Grant Who Surrendered To Lee Instead Of Lee Surrendering To Grant: Circumstances Divulged For The First Time By Captain X." The article reveals that Lee handed his

sword to Grant not in surrender but rather so that Grant could sharpen his pencil to put his own surrender in writing.

Fitzgerald wrote *The True Story of Appomattox* after Maxwell PERKINS took him to visit his cousin, Elizabeth LEMMON, at her family home "Welbourne" in Middleburg, Virginia. On July 30, 1934 he wrote to Perkins: "I managed to have my joke about Grant and Lee taken down on paper. Then last night I had it faked up by the 'Sun' here in Baltimore" (*Scott/Max,* p. 203). See [Joan Crane], "The True 'True Story of Appomattox': A Fitzgerald Fable Verified," *American Book Collector,* 5 (September–October 1980), 8–11.

Trust Scottie FITZGERALD created the Frances Scott Fitzgerald Smith Trust in July 1975 to administer the F. Scott Fitzgerald literary properties after her death. The document appointed three trustees: R. Andrew Boose, at that time her lawyer; Matthew J. BRUCCOLI; and S. J. Lanahan, her first husband. Lanahan resigned and was replaced by Eleanor Lanahan, the older daughter of Scottie and Lanahan; Boose resigned and was replaced by S. J. Lanahan. The business matters are managed by the Harold OBER Associates Agency, 425 Madison Avenue, New York, N.Y. 10017.

Tryon, North Carolina Resort town where Fitzgerald stayed in the OAK HALL HOTEL in February 1935 and January–June 1937.

Tudy Character in "Image on the Heart." Nineteen-year-old girl whose first husband dies a week after their wedding and who later marries TOM.

Tulliver, Doctor William (Bill) Character in "One Interne" and "Zone of Accident." In "One Interne" he is a young man beginning his medical internship who falls in love with Thea SINGLETON. In "Zone of Accident" he is a doctor who falls in love with his patient, actress Loretta BROOKE.

"Turkey Remains and How to Inter Them with Numerous Scarce Recipes" *CU*; *Notebooks,* #1234. Humorous suggestions for using up turkey left over after the holidays. A limited edition of 2,000 copies was printed by Cooper & Beatty of Toronto as a Christmas keepsake in 1956.

Turnbull, Andrew (1921–1970) Bayard and Margaret TURNBULL'S 11-year-old son, whom Fitzgerald befriended while living at "LA PAIX" in 1932 and 1933. Fitzgerald took him to PRINCETON football games, tried to interest him in boxing and firearms, and encouraged his interest in words. Turnbull became Fitzgerald's second biographer (*Scott Fitzgerald*) and edited the first collection of his letters (*The Letters of F. Scott Fitzgerald*).

Turnbull, Bayard and Margaret Couple from whom Fitzgerald rented "LA PAIX," a house on their estate at RODGER'S FORGE, TOWSON, Maryland, outside BALTIMORE, from May 1932 to December 1933. Fitzgerald and Bayard Turnbull, an architect, were not close; but Fitzgerald and Margaret Turnbull developed a warm friendship—they discussed books, and he asked her advice about raising his daughter, Scottie FITZGERALD. Fitzgerald was friendly with the three Turnbull children—Eleanor, Frances, and Andrew.

Tutu *See* Prince Gabriel PETROCOBESCO.

Twain, Mark (Samuel Langhorne Clemens) (1835–1910) American novelist and humorist whom Fitzgerald admired but who had minimal direct influence on Fitzgerald's writing. Fitzgerald mentioned Twain as the source for "The Curious Case of Benjamin Button" (May 1922), and the mountain of coal in *The Gilded Age* (1873) may have suggested the idea for "The Diamond as Big as the Ritz" (June 1922). Fitzgerald was impressed by *The Ordeal of Mark Twain* (1920) by Van Wyck BROOKS and subsequently read Albert Bigelow Paine's biography of Twain. Fitzgerald invoked Twain in a c. December 10, 1921 letter to Maxwell PERKINS defending his inclusion of Maury NOBLE'S skeptical account of the Bible in *B&D:* "The idea, refusing homage to the Bible + it's God, runs thru many of Mark Twain's essays + all through Paine's biography" (*Scott/Max,* p. 46).

Fitzgerald admired *The Adventures of Tom Sawyer* (1876) and *The Adventures of Huckleberry Finn* (London, 1884; *Adventures of Huckleberry Finn,* New York, 1885), and he listed *The Mysterious Stranger* (1916) as one of the "10 Best Books I Have Read"; however, he did not list any of Twain's books on the reading lists he prepared for Sheilah GRAHAM during his last years. In 1935 he wrote a statement for the celebration of Clemens's 100th birthday: "Huckleberry Finn took the first journey *back.* He was the first to look *back* at the republic from the perspective of the west. His eyes were the first eyes that ever looked at us objectively that were not eyes from overseas. There were mountains at the frontier but he wanted more than mountains to look at with his restless eyes—he wanted to find out about men and how they lived together. And because he turned back we have him forever" (*Correspondence,* p. 424).

"Two for a Cent" Fiction. Written September 1921. *METROPOLITAN MAGAZINE,* 55 (April 1922), 23–26, 93–95; *The Price Was High.* Forty-five-year-old ABERCROMBIE, now wealthy and successful, visits his small Southern hometown and meets Henry W. HEMMICK, who has recently moved out of Abercrombie's old house. Abercrombie expresses his resentment that he went North

only by accident rather than through ambition, and Hemmick reveals the circumstances that prevented him from going North. The penny which Hemmick had lost while serving as a runner for a bank had been found by Abercrombie, who needed one more cent to pay his train fare to Atlanta, his first step in leaving town.

Although Fitzgerald was not fond of "Two for a Cent," it was one of his most popular stories and brought his first textbook appearance, in *Short Stories for Class Reading* (1925).

"Two Old-Timers" Fiction—Pat HOBBY story. Submitted December 19, 1939. *ESQUIRE*, 15 (March 1941), 53, 143; *Stories*; *PH*. Former movie star Phil MACEDON and Pat Hobby are in an automobile collision involving alcohol. Pat is offended because Macedon doesn't remember that they have met before. While they are waiting in the police station, Sergeant GASPAR tells Macedon how much his war picture, *The Final Push*, meant to veterans. Pat tells Macedon he had been at the first day of shooting for that movie and recalls how director Bill CORKER had shoved Macedon into the shell hole and filmed him scrambling wildly to get out. After a sobriety test, Pat is released and Macedon is held for bail.

Fitzgerald wrote to Arnold GINGRICH that this story "was the way 'The Big Parade' was really made King Vidor pushed John Gilbert in a hole—believe it or not" (December 25, 1939; *Correspondence*, p. 570).

"Two Wrongs" Fiction. Written October–November 1929. *The SATURDAY EVENING POST*, 202 (January 18, 1930), 8–9, 107, 109, 113; *TAR*. Producer Bill MCCHESNEY gives aspiring dancer Emmy PINKARD a small part in one of his plays, and they are married suddenly when his play closes. They move to LONDON after he produces two flops in NEW YORK and quarrels with his best friend while drinking. He is successful in London, where he associates with aristocracy. While he is crashing a party given by Lady Sybil COMBRINCK, who is no longer interested in him, Emmy goes alone to the hospital, where their second child is stillborn. As Emmy recuperates, she revives her dream of dancing and takes up ballet lessons. Just when she is ready for her debut, Bill is diagnosed with tuberculosis and ordered West. She offers to go with him, but really wants to stay in New York; and he tells her to stay, but really wants her to accompany him. In the end, she stays in New York, justifying herself by recalling that he had let her down in London.

"Two Wrongs" reflects problems in Fitzgerald's personal life—his alcoholism and Zelda FITZGERALD's unsuccessful effort to dance professionally. His attempt to understand Zelda's commitment to ballet is reflected in his depiction of Emmy's feelings about it: "It seemed to her that the dance was woman's interpretation of music; instead of strong fingers, one had limbs with which to render Tschaikowsky and Stravinski; and feet could be as eloquent in Chopiniana as voices in 'The Ring' " (*TAR*, p. 241).

U

Uncle Dun Character in "The Jelly-Bean." Jim POW-ELL's uncle, who wants Jim to come work at his farm.

Uncle Jim Character in "Fate in Her Hands." Carol KASTLER's uncle, a minister whom she persuades to perform her wedding to Ben KASTLER just minutes before she is scheduled to marry Billy RIGGS.

"Under Fire" Review of *Through the Wheat* by Thomas BOYD. *The Literary Review of the New York Evening Post,* May 26, 1923, p. 715; *In His Own Time.* Excerpts from this review were printed on the dust jackets of Boyd's *Shadow of the Long Knives* (1928) and *Mad Anthony Wayne* (1929). Fitzgerald praises the novel as "not only the best combatant story of the great war, but also the best war book since 'The Red Badge of Courage' " (*In His Own Time,* p. 144).

undergraduate (unnamed) Character in "The Spire and the Gargoyle." Young man who squanders his freshman year and flunks out of the university. Years later he visits the campus, which for him symbolizes aspiration, and is overwhelmed by his own failure.

Unger, John T. Character in "The Diamond as Big as the Ritz." Boy from a town called Hades who spends the summer with Percy WASHINGTON, his classmate at ST. MIDAS'.

Unger, Mr. and Mrs. Characters in "The Diamond as Big as the Ritz." John T. UNGER's parents, who send their son to ST. MIDAS', the world's most expensive and exclusive boys' school.

Unpublished Stories Fifteen unpublished stories by Fitzgerald are known through the records of his agent, Harold OBER; his correspondence with Ober; and some surviving manuscripts and typescripts.

"The I.O.U." (1920). Ober described this story as "almost a satire on publishing business." The manuscript and a typescript survive.

"Recklessness" (1922). Lost: mentioned in correspondence, but no synopsis in Ober files and no surviving manuscript or typescript.

"Nightmare" ("Fantasy in Black") (1932). Set in an institution for the insane. Typescript survives.

"What to Do About It" (1933). About a doctor. One of the medical stories which resulted from Fitzgerald's experiences at JOHNS HOPKINS UNIVERSITY HOSPITAL in BALTIMORE. Typescript survives.

"Daddy Was Perfect" (1934). About a playwright. Lost: no mention in correspondence, and no surviving manuscript or typescript; Ober files include a synopsis.

"Travel Together" (1935). About a movie scriptwriter. Typescript survives.

"I'd Die for You" ("The Legend of Lake Lure") (1935–36): About a movie star. Synopsis, considerable correspondence about the story, and a typescript survive.

"The Pearl and the Fur" (1936). Sold to *Pictorial Review* but never published. Part of the Gwen BOWERS series. Lost. Considerable correspondence with Ober's suggestions for revisions, but no surviving manuscript or typescript.

"Cyclone in Silent Land" (1936). Part of a projected series about a nurse nicknamed "TROUBLE." A typescript survives.

"Thank You for the Light" (1936). Vignette about a tired saleswoman. A synopsis and typescript survive.

"They Never Grow Older" (1937). About a cartoonist. Lost: synopsis in Ober files and mentioned in correspondence, but no surviving manuscript or typescript.

"Offside Play" ("Athletic Interview," "Athletic Interval") (1937). Football story. Revised carbon copy, Ober synopsis, and considerable correspondence survive.

"Temperature" ("The Women in the House") (1939). Lost: mentioned in correspondence, but no surviving manuscript or typescript.

"The Couple" (date of composition unknown). About a couple on the verge of divorce who are reunited. Not mentioned in correspondence, but a typescript and synopsis survive.

"Salute to Lucie and Elsie" (1939). About a businessman's shock at his son's sexual escapades. A typescript survives.

Jennifer McCabe Atkinson quotes the Ober synopses and details the correspondence about all but the last of these stories in "Lost and Unpublished Stories by F.

Scott Fitzgerald," *Fitzgerald/Hemingway Annual* (1971), pp. 32–63. See also Alan Margolies, "A Note on Fitzgerald's Lost and Unpublished Stories," *Fitzgerald/Hemingway Annual* (1972), pp. 335–336, and Ruth Prigozy, "The Unpublished Stories: Fitzgerald in His Final Stage," *Twentieth-Century Literature*, 20 (April 1974), 69–90.

"The Unspeakable Egg" Fiction. Written April 1924. *The SATURDAY EVENING POST*, 197 (July 12, 1924), 12–13, 125–126, 129; *The Price Was High*. Fifi MARSDEN breaks her engagement to George VAN TYNE on the eve of their wedding because she thinks he is too perfect—more so than herself. While visiting her aunts, Josephine and Cal MARSDEN, at their home on the beach at Montauk Point, Long Island, Fifi becomes interested in a disheveled tramp named Mr. HOPKINS;

and her aunts call in psychiatrist Roswell GALLUP to treat her. They discover that the tramp is really Van Tyne, who wants to prove to Fifi that he can be uncivilized, and that Fifi has known his true identity all along.

"The Usual Thing by Robert W. Shameless" Prose parody. *The NASSAU LITERARY MAGAZINE*, 72 (December 1916), 223–228; *In His Own Time*. Unsigned—credited to Fitzgerald in the index to volume 72. Parody of the writings of novelist Robert W. Chambers (1865–1933).

Utsonomia, Mr. Character in "Forging Ahead." Japanese student at the state university. Eddie PARMELEE, whom Basil Duke LEE has paid to take his place at Rhoda SINCLAIR's party, sends Mr. Utsonomia instead.

THE USUAL THING

BY ROBERT W. SHAMELESS

SYNOPSIS OF PRECEDING CHAPTERS.

John Brabant, adopted son of Jules Brabant, the South American Peccadillo Merchant, reaches New York penniless. He has, however, six letters of introduction, one of them unsigned, unsealed, and in fact unwritten. He presents all five of them, including the sixth, to John Brabant. John Brabant, a young South American, is in love with pretty Babette Lefleur, the daughter of Jules Lefleur, a merchant from South America. Upon Jules presenting four of the six letters of introduction which Babette Brabant has written to Jules Lefleur, John begins to realize that Jules, John, and Babette are in league against Brabant and Lefleur for some sinister purpose. Upon presenting the unwritten letter, he realizes that of the five letters Jules or possibly Babette has given Brabant, the only clue to the case of Lefleur and his connection with Babette. At this point Jules and Lefleur meet in Central Park, and Jules presenting the sixth or fifth letter, finds that Babette has given Brabant the letter that Jules presents to John. Confused by this, and in fact, not realizing the importance of the third or fourth letter, he takes tea in his boudoir one day with Brabant. Brabant believes that some sinister connection with Lefleur has driven Babette from South America, where John had been employed in Lefleur's peccadillo factory. He takes boat to South America and on board, sees Brabant also bound South on some secret mission. They decide to combine forces and destroy the second letter. Meanwhile, on the same ship, unknown to the other two, Brabant is disguised as a steward with the first, third and part of the fifth letters of introduction in his possession. As they pass through the Suez Canal a boat rows out from Cairo, and Brabant boards the ship. The other four notice his arrival, but fearful for the safety of the fourth and part of the sixth letter, decide among themselves not to mention peccadillo's or South America in general. Meanwhile, Babette and Lefleur, still in Newport, are falling more and more deeply in love. Lefleur hears of this, and unwilling that Babette should become involved in an affair with this man, leaves his peccadillo factory in the charge of an employee named Brabant and comes North. George meets him in Troy at the business firm of Dulong and Petit, and boarding the train, they rush to Tuxedo Park to join the others, and incidently to seize the sixth letter, if the Countess has not already written it. Arriving in New York, they take rooms at the Ritz, and begin the search for Brabant. Babette, in her boudoir, is sorting towels when the door suddenly bursts open and Genevieve comes in.

CHAPTER XXXI

Tea was being served at the VanTynes. On the long lawn, the pear trees cast their shadows over the parties of three and four scattered about. Babette and Lefleur had secured a table in a secluded nook, and as the sun glimmered and danced on the burnished silver tea set, she told him the whole story. When she had finished neither spoke for a minute, while he reached into the little mother-of-pearl satchel that hung at his side for cigarettes.

He selected one; he lit a match.

She held it for him.

The cigarette instantly lighted.

"Well?" She smiled up at him, her eyes ringed with those long eyelashes that had evoked Rembrant's enthusiastic praise in Holland the previous summer.

Fitzgerald's unsigned parody of Robert W. Chambers's popular society novels, written for The Nassau Literary Magazine

V

Vagabond Junior Players A little theater group in BALTIMORE which produced Zelda FITZGERALD's play, *Scandalabra,* in June 1933. Through the group Fitzgerald met Charles Marquis WARREN, with whom he collaborated on a screenplay for *TITN,* and newspaper writer Rita Swann, whose home was a gathering place for Baltimoreans interested in the theater.

Valescure, France RIVIERA town, 2.5 kilometers above ST. RAPHAËL, where the Fitzgeralds rented VILLA MARIE June–October 1924.

Valley of Ashes In *GG,* a fictional location based on the Corona dump in the New York borough of Queens. The dump, which was being filled with ashes, horse manure, and garbage, is the present site of Shea Stadium. George WILSON's garage is in the Valley of Ashes.

Val-Mont Clinic Clinic at GLION, SWITZERLAND, which Zelda FITZGERALD entered on May 22, 1930 after discharging herself from MALMAISON CLINIC on May 11. Dr. H. A. Trutmann's report at Val-Mont reads in part:

> At the beginning of the stay Mrs. F. declared that she had never been ill and had been brought by force to the clinic. Every day she repeated that she wanted to return to Paris to resume her ballet work in which she thought she found the only satisfaction of her life. . . . The visits of her husband often offered the occasion for violent arguments, always provoked by the husband's attempts to reason with the patient and to refute the patient's insinuations because the patient suspected the husband of homosexuality. [Translated from the French] (PRINCETON UNIVERSITY LIBRARY)

Val-Mont specialized in gastrointestinal illness rather than psychiatric problems; and after Dr. Oscar FOREL diagnosed Zelda as a schizophrenic when he was brought in for a consultation on June 3, she was transferred to his PRANGINS CLINIC on June 5.

Van Beck, Betty Character in "What a Handsome Pair!" Teddy VAN BECK's wife, a former waitress.

Van Beck, Helen Character in "What a Handsome Pair!" Athletic young woman whose marriage to Stuart OLDHORNE dissolves into rivalry.

Van Beck, Theodore (Teddy) Character in "What a Handsome Pair!" Musician who is in love with his cousin, Helen VAN BECK.

Van Buren, George Character in "The Third Casket." One of three young men competing to take over Cyrus GIRARD's business when he retires.

Van Camp, Max Character in "Your Way and Mine." Young man who works for Henry MCCOMAS and shows initiative in an effort to beat a competitor in expanding a chain of hardware stores. McComas urges his daughter, Honoria MCCOMAS, to accept Van Camp's repeated proposals.

Van Dyke, Mike Character in *LT/LOLT.* Gag man who demonstrates a slapstick routine for George BOXLEY. Based on gag writer Robert Hopkins.

Van Schaik, Paul B. Character in "One Interne." Patient with a hangover whom Doctor NORTON assigns Bill TULLIVER to diagnose at the beginning of his internship.

Van Schellinger, Gladys Character in the Basil Duke LEE stories; a sheltered rich girl. In "A Night at the Fair" she invites Basil to sit in her box to watch the fireworks. When she invites Basil to visit her at home the next day, she asks him to bring Hubert BLAIR with him. In "He Thinks He's Wonderful" she names Basil as her favorite boy in town. In "The Captured Shadow" she is supposed to have the part of a cook in Basil's play, but her mother doesn't want her to be in a play about criminals.

Van Tyne, George Character in "The Unspeakable Egg." Fifi MARSDEN's fiancé, who dresses as a tramp after she rejects him for being too perfect.

Van Vechten, Carl (1880–1964) American novelist and music and drama critic whose works include *Peter*

Francis Cugat's paintings of the Valley of the Ashes, preliminary art for The Great Gatsby *dust jacket* (Arlyn Bruccoli Collection)

Whiffle (1922), *The Blind Bow-Boy* (1923), *The Tattooed Countess* (1924), *Firecrackers* (1925), *Nigger Heaven* (1926), and *Spider Boy* (1928). Van Vechten became a friend of the Fitzgeralds in 1923 and wrote about them as David and Rilda Westlake in his novel *Parties:* "Rilda and David tortured each other because they loved one another devotedly" (New York: Knopf, 1930; p. 239). Van Vechten was one of the people with whom the Fitzgeralds shared a four-apartment bungalow on the grounds of the AMBASSADOR HOTEL in HOLLYWOOD in early 1927. Van Vechten praised *TITN* in an April 1934 letter to Fitzgerald: "It seems to me to be a very poignant book. I was swept almost at once into the undertow of meanings and feelings. It is by no means as clear as Gatsby, but very possibly it is even a greater performance. There are passages which are almost unbearable in their deflected intensity. But I didnt believe the end. Anyway, congratulations. . . . Perhaps best of all I like the way your gallant creatures carry on against time, against space, almost against history" (*Correspondence*, p. 346).

See Bruce Kellner, *Carl Van Vechten and the Irreverent Decades* (Norman: University of Oklahoma Press, 1968).

Van Vleck, Martin Character in "Dice, Brass Knuckles & Guitar." Young man who snubs Jim POWELL and is dismissed from Powell's school for drinking.

Vandervere, Gordon Character in "Six of One—". Young man whom Ed BARNES helps through college. He plans to marry Esther CROSBY and go into the diplomatic service.

"The Vanished Girl" *See* "A Full Life."

Varland, Joe Character in "A Short Trip Home." Sinister man who preyed on girls traveling alone on trains and whose ghost haunts Ellen BAKER.

The Vegetable: or from President to postman Play. New York: Charles SCRIBNER's Sons, 1923. Augmented edition with unpublished scenes and corrections, intro-

duction by Charles Scribner III (New York: Charles Scribner's Sons, 1976). Dedication: "TO KATHERINE TIGHE AND EDMUND WILSON, JR. WHO DELETED MANY ABSURDITIES FROM MY FIRST TWO NOVELS I RECOMMEND THE ABSURDITIES SET DOWN HERE." While waiting for the publication of his second novel, *The Beautiful and Damned*, Fitzgerald wrote to his agent, Harold OBER, "I am concieving a play which is to make my fortune" (c. November/December 1921; *As Ever*, p. 32). Originally titled "Gabriel's Trombone," the published play was titled *The Vegetable*, with a title page epigraph attributed to "a current magazine": "*Any man who doesn't want to get on in the world, to make a million dollars, and maybe even park his toothbrush in the White House, hasn't got as much to him as a good dog has—he's nothing more or less than a vegetable.*" On March 2, 1922 Fitzgerald sent the play to Ober for circulation to producers, claiming that "Acts I + III are probably the best pieces of dramatic comedy written in English in the last 5 years" (*As Ever*, p. 39). Ober was unable to find a producer, and Fitzgerald revised the play in the summer of 1922. In October the Fitzgeralds moved to GREAT NECK, New York, where Fitzgerald revised the play for at least the third time. (He later claimed it was revised six times.) Fitzgerald later listed "Vegetable days in N. Y." as a source for the fourth chapter of *GG*.

Fitzgerald decided to publish the play as a book in the hope that the exposure might result in a stage production. In January 1923 he wrote to editor Maxwell PERKINS about publication plans, and his advice for advertising illuminates the problem with the play: "To be advertised, it seems to me rather as a book of humor, like the Parody outline of History or Seventeen

than like a play—because of course it is written to be read" (*Scott/Max*, p. 66). *The Vegetable* was published on April 27, 1923 in a printing of 7,650 copies at $1.50, with a dust jacket illustrated by John HELD, Jr. It was widely reviewed but regarded as a minor effort, and there was only one printing.

In the summer of 1923 Sam H. Harris (1872–1941) agreed to produce the play, with Sam Forrest (1870–1944) directing and Ernest Truex (1890–1973) taking the leading role of Jerry FROST. Fitzgerald was involved in the rehearsals, and he and Zelda FITZGERALD went with Ring and Ellis LARDNER to Atlantic City for the tryout. The play began a one-week run at Nixon's Apollo Theatre on November 19, 1923; on the disastrous opening night people walked out during the second-act fantasy. Zelda wrote to Xandra KALMAN:

> In brief, the show flopped as flat as one of Aunt Jemimas famous pancakes. . . . The first act went fine but Ernest says he has *never* had an experience on the stage like the second. I *heard* one woman hit the roof when the bible was mentioned. They seemed to think it was sacreligious or something. People were so obviously bored! And it was all very well done, so there was no use trying to fix it up. The idea was what people didn't like—Just hopeless! Scott suggested fixing it up by having Ernests teeth fall out when he heard about the Buzzard Islands, but I don't think anybody liked the suggestion except us—It is too terrible to contemplate.
> (PRINCETON UNIVERSITY LIBRARY)

Fitzgerald tried to improve the play during the Atlantic City tryout, but when its out-of-town tryout ended it was dead. After this failure, which left Fitzgerald in

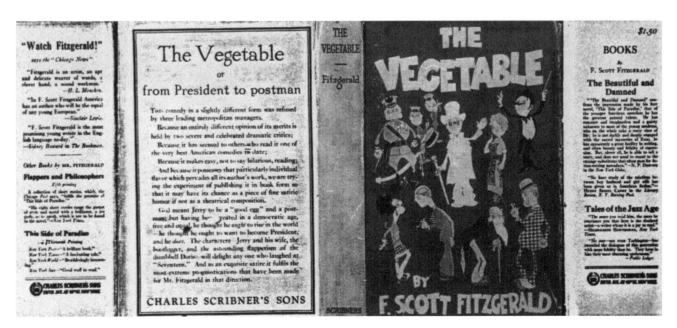

John Held, Jr.'s dust jacket for Fitzgerald's 1923 play (Bruccoli Collection, University of South Carolina)

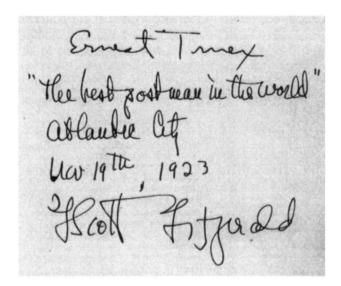

Inscription in The Vegetable *to Ernest Truex, who had appeared in the play's leading role* (Bruccoli Collection, University of South Carolina)

debt, he was no longer seriously interested in writing for the stage; and although he occasionally talked about writing another play, he never progressed beyond outlines.

ACT I

Railroad clerk Jerry Frost tells his wife, Charlotte FROST, that he got analyzed at work and that he told the analyzer that he didn't have any ambition left, although when he was a boy he had wanted to be a postman. When Charlotte mocks him, he tells her he "had an ambition to be President of the United States" (p. 16). They quarrel, but Charlotte "*knows that Jerry will always stay and slave for her*" (p. 17). Jerry asks his father, DADA, about the presidential convention. Charlotte's sister, DORIS, arrives and announces that she is engaged again to a man named FISH from Idaho. Bootlegger SNOOKS arrives and mixes some gin for Jerry. Jerry has several drinks, and he hears the noise of a cheering crowd outside. Mr. JONES, a "well-known politician," arrives and informs Jerry that he has unanimously been given the Republican nomination for President.

ACT II

On their wedding reception day, Doris's fiancé, Joseph Fish, senator from Idaho, arrives at the White House with a telegram from the people of Idaho demanding Jerry's immediate resignation as President because he made Dada Secretary of the Treasury. Major General PUSHING notifies Jerry that he and two other generals have voted to have a war against an enemy yet to be determined. The Honorable Snooks, Ambassador from Irish Poland, offers to sell the Buzzard Islands to the United States. Jerry agrees to buy the Islands on the

condition that he can include Idaho as a gift, and they settle on a price of $5 million. Doris tells Dada he should resign, and Dada reveals that he has destroyed all the money in the treasury in order to save the country because of the biblical saying that "It's easier for a camel to pass through a needle's eye than for a wealthy man to enter heaven" (p. 95). Snooks agrees to forfeit the $5 million and make a straight swap of the Buzzard Islands for Idaho. Chief Justice FOSSILE arrives to begin impeachment proceedings, and Charlotte tells Jerry, "Speak right up to them. Show them you're not just a vegetable" (p. 102). Jerry says that a state has to be part of the country to impeach anybody, and Idaho now belongs to Irish Poland. General Pushing arrives and announces that the enemy is Irish Poland, and Judge Fossile says that all treaties are off. Fossile pronounces the sentence of impeachment, and the Frosts leave the White House.

ACT III

Back at the Frosts' house, a week after Act I, Doris and Charlotte discuss the possible whereabouts of Jerry, who disappeared the morning after Snooks sold him the gin. Doris and Fish have been secretly married for three days. The new postman arrives with the mail, and neither Doris nor Fish recognizes that he is Jerry. Jerry tells them, "I'm new but I'm good. . . . I'm the best one they ever had" (p. 133). They tell him there's a woman in the house who really needs the right letter. Jerry, his face partially concealed by the hood of his rain cape, comes back later with a letter for Charlotte from himself, saying that he's doing what he wants and is happy. Charlotte asks the postman to find Jerry for her and says she will be proud of him even if he is a postman; and he promises to try to get Jerry there at six o'clock. Later, as she hears the postman's whistle approaching, she cries, "The best postman in the world!" (p. 145).

See *F. Scott Fitzgerald Manuscripts VI,* Part 1, for revised typescript of scenes deleted from *The Vegetable* before publication and holograph revisions for the play production.

Velance, Peppy　Character in "Inside the House." Actress whom Gwen BOWERS idolizes and whom she misses the opportunity to meet by sneaking out to a movie.

Venske, Gus　Character in "The Homes of the Stars." Man who gives tours of the homes of HOLLYWOOD stars.

Vidor, King (1894–1982)　Academy Award–winning MGM movie director whose movies include *The Big Parade* (1925), *The Crowd* (1928), *Street Scene* (1931), and *Our Daily Bread* (1934); friend of Fitzgerald. While Vidor was in PARIS in the summer of 1928, Fitzgerald introduced him to French novelist André CHAMSON;

Villa Marie, Valescure, where The Great Gatsby *was written*

and the three planned a movie collaboration that was abandoned when Chamson declined an invitation to HOLLYWOOD. Fitzgerald also introduced Vidor to Gerald MURPHY, who collected spirituals and who went to Hollywood as an advisor when Vidor made *Hallelujah!*, the first major all-black movie, in 1929. Vidor was the partial model for Miles CALMAN in "Crazy Sunday" (October 1932).

Viking (unnamed) Character in "In the Darkest Hour." Norwegian young man whom PHILIPPE encounters when he returns to France and with whom he shares a meal.

Villa America Home of Gerald and Sara MURPHY at CAP D'ANTIBES, France; a partial model for the VILLA DIANA in *TITN*.

Villa Diana In *TITN*, the fictional residence of Nicole and Dick DIVER in TARMES. Based on the VILLA AMERICA of Gerald and Sara MURPHY and the home of EXPATRIATE composer Samuel Barlow (1892–1982), whose villa was constructed from several houses in Eze, France.

Villa Fleur des Bois Villa on the Boulevard Eugène Gazagnaire in CANNES on the French RIVIERA which the Fitzgeralds rented July–September 1929.

Villa Marie Villa at VALESCURE, France, 2.5 kilometers above ST. RAPHAËL, on the RIVIERA, which the Fitzgeralds rented for $79 a month from June 1924 until they traveled to ROME in October. Fitzgerald wrote much of *The Great Gatsby* at the Villa Marie.

Villa Paquita Villa at JUAN-LES-PINS on the French RIVIERA which the Fitzgeralds rented from March to May or June 1926, when they turned it over to Ernest and Hadley HEMINGWAY.

Villa St. Louis Villa at JUAN-LES-PINS on the French RIVIERA which the Fitzgeralds rented from May or June to December 1926, when they returned to America.

Villefranche, Bertram de (*See* also COUNT CHARLES.) Character in "The Kingdom in the Dark." PHILIPPE's deceased father, who was put in charge of his property by King Charlemagne (742–814).

Vizier Character in "In the Darkest Hour." PHILIPPE's Spanish stepfather, who killed his father, COUNT CHARLES.

Wade, Marylyn Character in "The Ice Palace" and "The Jelly-Bean." Girl from TARLETON, Georgia. In "The Ice Palace" she goes swimming with Clark DARROW, Sally Carrol HAPPER, and Joe EWING. In "The Jelly-Bean" she attends a country club dance with Joe.

Waggoner, Dutch Character in "No Harm Trying." Movie director who is unreliable because of his drug use.

Wainwright, Ward Character in "Pat Hobby's Preview." Writer who is angry that Pat HOBBY will share the credit for a script written mostly by Wainwright.

" 'Wait Till You Have Children of Your Own!' " Essay. WOMAN'S HOME COMPANION, 51 (July 1924), 13, 105; *In His Own Time*. Fitzgerald discusses how parents "want their children not to follow blindly in their steps but rather to profit by their mistakes" (*In His Own Time*, p. 193). He says that he will teach his child to be less provincial and patriotic, to know about his body, to avoid overstimulation, to be suspicious of authority, and to form his own convictions.

Wales, Brick Character in the Basil Duke LEE stories. In "The Freshest Boy" he is Basil's enemy at the beginning of school. Basil's roommate, TREADWAY, leaves Basil to move in with him. Later in the year, while playing basketball, Wales calls Basil "Lee-y," a nickname that makes Basil happy. In "Basil and Cleopatra" he rooms with Basil and George DORSEY at Yale.

Wales, Charles J. (Charlie) Character in "Babylon Revisited." American businessman who lived a dissipated life in PARIS during the boom and returns as a recovering alcoholic to try to regain custody of his daughter.

Wales, Helen Character in "Babylon Revisited." Marion PETERS's sister and Charlie WALES's dead wife.

Wales, Honoria Character in "Babylon Revisited." Charlie and Helen WALES's daughter. Charlie unsuccessfully tries to regain custody of Honoria from his sister-in-law, Marion PETERS. Based on Scottie FITZGERALD.

Wales, Miss Character in "Zone of Accident." Head nurse in the hospital accident room.

Walker, Stella *See* Stella Walker CALMAN.

Wallis, Maria Character in *TITN*. Acquaintance of Dick and Nicole DIVER who shoots an Englishman at the PARIS train station where the Divers are seeing Abe NORTH off on the beginning of his trip to America. This shooting may be based on a March 1927 incident in the Gare du Nord, where Countess de Janze (formerly Alice Silverthorne of Chicago) shot Raymond Vincent de Trafford and then herself. (See James Fox, *White Mischief* [New York: Random House, 1982].)

Walmsley, Mirabel Character in "The Trail of the Duke." Wealthy young woman who sends her fiancé, Dodson GARLAND, in search of "the Duke."

Wanger, Walter (1894–1968) Producer of *Winter Carnival* (1939), on which Fitzgerald briefly collaborated with Budd SCHULBERG. When Wanger took the two writers to DARTMOUTH, the setting of the movie, Fitzgerald and Schulberg got drunk. Wanger fired both writers, but rehired Schulberg in California.

Warburton Character in "The Camel's Back." Interfering man who persuades Perry PARKHURST to force Betty MEDILL to make up her mind about marrying him. At the circus ball he tells Betty that he thinks part of the camel is Warren BUTTERFIELD, causing her to flirt with the camel.

Ward, Chauncey Character in "Last Kiss." Elderly Englishman with whom Pamela KNIGHTON resides.

Warner, Reuben Childhood friend and rival of Fitzgerald in ST. PAUL; he was the model for Hubert BLAIR in the Basil Duke LEE stories. Fitzgerald lost Margaret ARMSTRONG, a childhood sweetheart, to Warner. Fitzgerald noted in his *Ledger* for April 1911, "The Scandal detectives go after Reuben" (p. 165)—an incident he later used in his 1928 story "The Scandal Detectives."

Warren, Beth Evan (Baby) Character in *TITN*. Nicole DIVER's unmarried older sister. Although she hoped Nicole would marry a doctor, she is displeased with Nicole's engagement to Dick DIVER. She later urges Dick to use Nicole's money to buy the clinic with Franz GREGOROVIOUS, and Dick senses that her message is "We own you" (p. 185).

Warren, Charles *See* Devereux WARREN.

Warren, Charles Marquis (1868–1954) Writer whom Fitzgerald met in BALTIMORE in 1934 through the VAGABOND JUNIOR PLAYERS. Warren, whose statements about their friendship cannot be verified, claimed that he collaborated with Fitzgerald on *TITN*; however, the manuscripts for the novel provide no evidence of collaboration. Warren claimed that the change of Devereux WARREN's name to Charles Warren in Book III, Chapter 2 was Fitzgerald's acknowledgment of his help. Fitzgerald and Warren did collaborate in April and May 1934 on the movie treatment for *TITN* (published in Matthew J. BRUCCOLI, *Some Sort of Epic Grandeur*, Appendix 1), and Warren provided a musical score. When agent Harold OBER was unable to sell the treatment, Fitzgerald sent Warren to HOLLYWOOD to sell the treatment and look for a writing job, providing him with letters of introduction, including one to MGM story editor Samuel Marx (1902–92): Warren's "talents are amazingly varied—he writes, composes, draws and has this aforesaid general gift for the theatre—and I have a feeling that he should fit in there somewhere within a short time and should go close to the top, in fact I haven't believed in anybody so strongly since Ernest Hemingway" (May 21, 1934; *Correspondence*, p. 364). Although Warren didn't find a Hollywood job in 1934, he later became a producer-director for movies and television, creating the series *Gunsmoke* and *Rawhide*. Warren lived at Fitzgerald's MALIBU BEACH house for a brief time in 1938. Warren's untrustworthy account of his friendship with Fitzgerald is included in Aaron Latham's *Crazy Sundays* (New York: Viking, 1971).

Warren, Devereux (Charles) Character in *TITN*. Father of Baby and Nicole WARREN. When Nicole begins showing signs of mental illness, he takes her to DOHMLER's clinic, where he confesses an incestuous episode with her. Later he is treated for alcoholism. Charles Marquis WARREN, a BALTIMORE writer who collaborated with Fitzgerald on a movie treatment for *TITN*, claimed that Fitzgerald changed the character's name from "Devereux" to "Charles" (Book III, Chapter 2) to acknowledge his help on the novel; but there is no evidence of collaboration in the manuscripts.

Warren, Nicole *See* Nicole Warren DIVER.

Wash Character in "The End of Hate." Confederate soldier who is killed by Union cavalry.

Washington, Braddock Tarleton Character in "The Diamond as Big as the Ritz." Percy WASHINGTON's father, who owns the diamond mountain.

Washington, Mrs. Braddock T. Character in "The Diamond as Big as the Ritz." Mother of Percy, Jasmine, and Kismine WASHINGTON.

Washington, Fitz-Norman Culpepper Character in "The Diamond as Big as the Ritz." Percy WASHINGTON's grandfather, who went West after the Civil War and discovered a diamond mountain.

Washington, Jasmine Character in "The Diamond as Big as the Ritz." Percy WASHINGTON's sister, who invited friends to visit even though she knew they would be killed to keep the secret of the diamond.

Washington, Kismine Character in "The Diamond as Big as the Ritz." Percy WASHINGTON's beautiful sister, who falls in love with John UNGER.

Washington, Percy Character in "The Diamond as Big as the Ritz." Wealthy boy who invites John UNGER to spend the summer at his family's home even though he knows John will be murdered to keep the secret of the diamond.

Washington, Richard (Tubby) Childhood friend of Fitzgerald in ST. PAUL; a member of the ELIZABETHAN DRAMATIC CLUB. When Fitzgerald returned to St. Paul in summer 1919 to live with his parents while finishing *TSOP*, he renewed his friendship with Washington, who lived in the same row house on SUMMIT AVENUE. Washington treated Fitzgerald to Coca-Colas and cigarettes at nearby drugstores, since Fitzgerald's parents refused to finance his writing career.

watchman (unnamed) Character in "The Guest in Room Nineteen." Man who tells Mr. CASS about the GUEST in room nineteen and who dies while lifting a heavy log.

Watchman, Bill Character in " 'Send Me In, Coach.' " Boy at Camp Rahewawa who learns that his father, Cyrus K. Watchman, has committed suicide after being acquitted at a trial.

Waterbury, Ernest Character in "A Woman with a Past." Miss BRERETON's dull, priggish nephew whom Miss CHAMBERS enlists Josephine PERRY to entertain.

Waterbury, Judge Character in "The Swimmers." Virginian who tries to persuade Henry Clay MARSTON to return to Richmond from PARIS and for whom Marston later works for three years.

"The Way of Purgation" Verse. *Poet Lore* accepted this poem in September 1917 but did not publish it; this was Fitzgerald's first professional acceptance. Fitzgerald included the poem, untitled, at the beginning of the final chapter of *TSOP* (p. 273). It also appeared, in slightly different form, in an August 1917 letter to Edmund WILSON which was published in *CU* (p. 249; *Life in Letters,* p. 12).

Wayne, Jill Character in *TSOP.* Girl who is caught in an Atlantic City hotel room with Alec CONNAGE, but who Amory BLAINE tells the house detectives was with himself. She gives her name as "Stella Robbins" to the detective.

Weatherbee, Percy B. Character in *B&D.* An architect to whom Anthony PATCH unsuccessfully tries to sell stock in "Heart Talks" pamphlets.

Weatherby, Mrs. Character in *TSOP.* Sally WEATHERBY's mother.

Weatherby, Sally Character in *TSOP.* Isabelle BORGÉ's cousin, a Minneapolis girl who writes to Amory BLAINE at PRINCETON.

Weaver, Bette Character in "Her Last Case." Nurse who falls in love with her patient, Ben DRAGONET, and decides to break her engagement to Doctor Howard CARNEY.

Weicker, Mr. Character in "The Hotel Child." Assistant manager of the Hotel des Trois Mondes who objects to Fifi SCHWARTZ's presence in the hotel bar because she is too young and her behavior disturbs the other guests.

Wells, H. G. (1866–1946) English novelist now best known for his science-fiction romances, including *The Time Machine* (1895), *The Invisible Man* (1897), and *The War of the Worlds* (1898). Fitzgerald reviewed *God, the Invisible King* (1917) for the *The NASSAU LITERARY MAGAZINE* and in 1917 called *The New Machiavelli* (1911) "the greatest English novel of the century" (to Edmund WILSON, September 26, 1917; *Letters,* p. 318). Wells influenced *TSOP*: his novel *The Research Magnificent* (1915) was one of the "quest novels" that influenced Amory BLAINE, and Rosalind CONNAGE is partly based on Beatrice Normandy from *Tono-Bungay* (1909). (The influence of Wells's saturation techniques on

TSOP is examined by James E. Miller, Jr. in *F. Scott Fitzgerald: His Art and His Technique* [New York: New York University Press, 1964].) When Edmund Wilson read the typescript of *TSOP* in November 1919, he described it as "an exquisite burlesque of Compton Mackenzie with a pastiche of Wells thrown in at the end" (*Letters on Literature and Politics 1912–1972* [New York: Farrar, Straus & Giroux, 1977], p. 45). However, in a review of John DOS PASSOS's *Three Soldiers* (1921), Fitzgerald renounced Wells's influence: "Such a profound and gifted man as John Dos Passos should never enlist in Wells' faithful but aenemic platoon along with Walpole, Floyd Dell and Mencken's late victim, Ernest Poole. The only successful Wellsian is Wells. Let us slay Wells, James Joyce and Anatole France that the creation of literature may continue" (*In His Own Time,* p. 123). Wells's *Outline of History* (1920) was the foundation of Fitzgerald's "College of One" plan for educating Sheilah GRAHAM.

See Anthony West, *H. G. Wells: Aspects of a Life* (New York: Random House, 1984).

Wende, Hamilton Childhood friend of Fitzgerald in BUFFALO. On Saturdays they attended matinees at the Teck theater and later at home reenacted what they had seen.

Wendell, Peter Boyce Character in "Head and Shoulders." Newspaper columnist who wrote a poem about Marcia MEADOW, praised the style of her thank-you letter, and later sponsored and wrote an introduction for her book.

Wescott, Glenway (1901–1987) American author, an EXPATRIATE in the 1920s and early 1930s, whose works include *The Grandmothers* (1927) and *The Pilgrim Hawk* (1940). In 1925 or 1926 Fitzgerald urged Wescott to "help launch" Ernest HEMINGWAY. On February 6, 1934 Fitzgerald wrote to Wescott explaining that he hadn't read Wescott's story about sailors at Villefranche ("The Sailor," *Good-bye Wisconsin,* 1928) until after he had completed his own account in *TITN* (*Letters,* p. 507). Wescott responded with a friendly letter on February 20 (*Correspondence,* pp. 330–331). Wescott wrote an obituary essay on Fitzgerald for *The New Republic,* noting that to his contemporaries, Fitzgerald was "our darling, our genius, our fool" ("The Moral of Scott Fitzgerald," *CU,* p. 332).

West Egg In *GG,* a fictional community on the North Shore of Long Island, New York, corresponding to GREAT NECK, a popular residence for show business people; Fitzgerald lived there in 1922–24. Nick CARRAWAY and Jay GATSBY both reside in West Egg, which is less fashionable than neighboring EAST EGG.

West, Jebby Character in "The Bridal Party." Friend who hosts a tea for Caroline DANDY and Hamilton RUTHERFORD and with whom Michael CURLY dances at the wedding reception.

West, Nathanael (1903–1940) American novelist who impressed Fitzgerald by his willingness to finance the writing of his unpopular novels by screenwriting. In September 1934 Fitzgerald wrote a letter of recommendation for West's application for a Guggenheim Fellowship, calling West "a potential leader in the field of prose fiction" (*Correspondence*, p. 385). Fitzgerald and Sheilah GRAHAM enjoyed small parties in HOLLYWOOD with West and his brother-in-law, S. J. PERELMAN. Fitzgerald provided an endorsement for West's fourth novel, *The Day of the Locust* (1939); but the statement did not appear on the dust jacket until 1950: "The book, though it puts Gorki's 'The Lower Depths' in the class with 'The Tale of Benjamin Bunny,' certainly has scenes of extraordinary power—if that phrase is still in use. Especially I was impressed by the pathological crowd at the premiere, the character and handling of the aspirant actress and the uncanny almost medieval feeling of some of his Hollywood background set off by those vividly drawn grotesques" (*In His Own Time*, p. 160). West was killed in an automobile accident the day after Fitzgerald's death.

See Jay Martin, *Nathanael West: The Art of His Life* (New York: Farrar, Straus & Giroux, 1970).

Westgate Character in "The Passionate Eskimo." Edith CARY's suitor, whom she thinks sued for breach of promise, although it was actually his father who did so. When Westgate explains to Edith, they are reunited.

Westport, Connecticut Town where the newlywed Fitzgeralds rented the 18th-century Wakeman house on Compo Road near the Long Island Sound, about 50 miles from NEW YORK CITY, May–September 1920. They hosted alcoholic weekend parties and frequently visited New York. Fitzgerald began writing *B&D* in Westport, which served as the model for MARIETTA, New York, in the novel.

Wetherby, Cecile Character in *Assorted Spirits*. Peter WETHERBY's daughter, who is in love with Will CHAPMAN.

Wetherby, Dickie Character in *Assorted Spirits*. Peter WETHERBY's son, a "hypochondriac with hay fever" who unsuccessfully woos the visiting Clara KING.

Wetherby, Peter Character in *Assorted Spirits*. Man who is trying to sell his house to raise the $10,000 he needs to save his business.

Whaley, Marice Character in "First Blood." Girl whom Anthony HARKER could marry if he wanted to. She rebukes Anthony for his interest in Josephine PERRY and tells him that Josephine has a bad reputation.

Wharton, Edith (1862–1937) American novelist and short story writer whose works include *The House of Mirth* (1905), *Ethan Frome* (1911), and *The Age of Innocence* (1920; Pulitzer Prize). Fitzgerald admired Wharton; once when he learned that she was in the Scribner Building, he burst into Charles SCRIBNER's office and knelt at Wharton's feet. In a May 1924 letter Fitzgerald described her as "a very distinguished grande dame who fought the good fight with bronze age weapons when there were very few people in the line at all" (to Thomas BOYD; *Life in Letters*, p. 68). In 1923 Fitzgerald wrote the titles for the silent movie version of Wharton's *The Glimpses of the Moon* (1922); most of his titles were not used, but he earned $500 for the project.

Wharton's June 8, 1925 letter about *GG* was later published in *CU*; she praised the novel—"Let me say at once how much I like Gatsby, or rather His Book, & how great a leap I think you have taken this time—in advance upon your previous work"—but expressed her regret that Fitzgerald had not provided more information about Gatsby's early career: "That would have situated him, & made his final tragedy a tragedy instead of a 'fait divers' for the morning papers" (*CU*, p. 309).

In July 1925 Wharton invited the Fitzgeralds to tea at her home outside PARIS; Zelda FITZGERALD declined the invitation, and Fitzgerald went with American composer Theodore CHANLER. A widely published and repeated story about this visit reports that Fitzgerald was drunk and made a fool of himself; but Chanler, an eyewitness, provides a more accurate account. See "What Really Happened at the Pavillon Colombe," *Fitzgerald Newsletter*, pp. 25–26.

See R. W. B. Lewis, *Edith Wharton: A Biography* (New York: Harper & Row, 1975).

Wharton, Elsie Character in "The Adolescent Marriage." Lucy Wharton CLARK's mother, who is distressed by her daughter's elopement and separation.

Wharton, George Character in "The Adolescent Marriage." Lucy Wharton CLARK's father, who asks his friend Chauncey GARNETT to intervene to save Lucy's marriage.

Wharton, Lucy *See* Lucy Wharton CLARK.

"What Became of the Flappers?" Article by Zelda FITZGERALD. MCCALL's, 53 (October 1925), 12, 30, 66; *Zelda Fitzgerald: The Collected Writings*. Published with F. Scott Fitzgerald's "Our Young Rich Boys" under the joint title of "What Becomes of Our Flappers and

Sheiks?" Notes that the flapper "is growing old" and has "come to none of the predicted 'bad ends,' but has gone at last, where all good flappers go—into the young married set, into boredom and gathering conventions and the pleasure of having children, having lent a while a splendor and courageousness and brightness to life" (*Collected Writings,* p. 399).

"What Becomes of Our Flappers and Sheiks?" *See* "What Became of the Flappers?" and "Our Young Rich Boys."

"What a Handsome Pair!" Fiction. Written April 1932. *The SATURDAY EVENING POST,* 205 (August 27, 1932), 16–17, 61, 63–64; *Bits of Paradise.* Helen VAN BECK refuses to marry her cousin, musician Teddy VAN BECK, because they have nothing in common. She marries Stuart OLDHORNE, who shares her interest in sports; but when he is compelled to take sports-related jobs to support them, while she continues to play for enjoyment, their mutual interest turns to bitter rivalry. Teddy, who still loves Helen, is nonetheless happy with his wife, Betty VAN BECK, who shares none of his interests.

The depiction of a couple torn apart by their mutual interests in "What a Handsome Pair!" reflects the tension in the Fitzgeralds' marriage over the publication of Zelda's novel, *Save Me the Waltz* (1932).

"What I Think and Feel at Twenty-Five" Autobiographical article. *The American Magazine,* 94 (September 1922), 16, 17, 136–140; *In His Own Time.* Fitzgerald asserts that a man's vulnerability increases as he grows older because he can be hurt through attacks on his wife and children. He recalls that in preparatory school and in the ARMY he was overly concerned with what other people thought about him until he learned that "nobody knows half as much about your own interests as *you* know" (*In His Own Time,* p. 219). He complains that he dislikes old people because they always talk about their experience when they seldom have any; and he notes that "as old people run the world, an enormous camouflage has been built up to hide the fact that only young people are attractive or important" (p. 222).

"What I Was Advised to Do—And Didn't" Autobiographical note. *Philadelphia Public Ledger,* April 22, 1922, p. 11; *In His Own Time.* Fitzgerald's account of rejecting the advice of someone at the advertising agency where he worked to "give up writing and stay at your job" (*In His Own Time,* p. 166).

"What Kind of Husbands Do 'Jimmies' Make?" Article. *Baltimore American,* March 30, 1924, p. ME-7; *In His Own Time.* Fitzgerald deplores the lack of responsibility

on the part of the rich and the resulting waste of opportunity: "Here we come to something that sets the American 'leisure class' off from the leisure class of all other nations—and makes it probably the most shallow, most hollow, most pernicious leisure class in the world. It has frequently no consciousness that leisure is a privilege, not a right, and that a privilege always implies a responsibility" (*In His Own Time,* p. 188).

Wheeler, C.N.B. ST. PAUL ACADEMY headmaster, teacher, and coach who encouraged young Fitzgerald to write.

Wheelock, John Hall (1886–1978) American poet; assistant to Maxwell PERKINS at Charles SCRIBNER's Sons while Fitzgerald was working on *TITN,* and later senior editor at Scribners.

Wheelock, Mrs. Character in "Fate in Her Hands." University dean's wife who tells Carol KASTLER that Ben KASTLER is sitting in his office during nearby blasting.

Wheelock, Doctor R. H. (Dick) Character in " 'Trouble.' " Doctor who becomes involved with TROUBLE after she falls off a deck into his arms at the hospital's annual turtle race.

Whitby, Harry Character in "Indecision." A Cambridge University hockey player who is a guest at the same hotel as Tommy MCLANE.

White Bear Yacht Club Club in DELLWOOD on White Bear Lake outside ST. PAUL. Two of Fitzgerald's plays for the ELIZABETHAN DRAMATIC CLUB—*Coward* (1913) and *Assorted Spirits* (1914)—were performed there. Scott and Zelda Fitzgerald lived at the club June–August 1922 but were asked to leave because of their parties; they moved to the COMMODORE HOTEL.

See Carl B. Drake et al., *History of the White Bear Yacht Club, Dellwood, White Bear Lake, Minnesota* (St. Paul: Bruce Publishing Co., 1961).

White, Wylie Character in *LT/LOLT.* Screenwriter who demonstrates romantic interest in Cecelia BRADY in the hopes that she will influence her father to advance his career.

Whitney, Knowleton Character in "Myra Meets His Family." Wealthy young man who arranges an elaborate scheme to scare away his fiancée, Myra HARPER, who he thinks is only after his money.

"Who Can Fall in Love After Thirty?" Article by Zelda FITZGERALD. *COLLEGE HUMOR,* 15 (October 1928), 9, 92; *Zelda Fitzgerald: The Collected Writings.* Bylined "F. Scott and Zelda Fitzgerald" but credited to Zelda

in *Ledger*. Discussion of the differences between men who have never been romantic and those who have "the habit of being in love" (*Collected Writings*, p. 411).

"Who's Who—and Why" Autobiographical essay. *The SATURDAY EVENING POST*, 193 (September 18, 1920), 42, 61; *AOAA*. Fitzgerald characterizes his life as a "struggle between an overwhelming urge to write and a combination of circumstances bent on keeping me from it" (*AOAA*, p. 83). He describes the composition and publication of *TSOP*, which he calls "a somewhat edited history of me and my imagination" (p. 84).

" 'Why Blame It on the Poor Kiss if the Girl Veteran of Many Petting Parties Is Prone to Affairs After Marriage?' " Article. *New York American*, February 24, 1924, p. LII–3; *In His Own Time*. Fitzgerald asserts that marital unfaithfulness is much more widespread than commonly believed and suggests that two primary obstacles to monogamy are "a great disparity in age and a surrounding atmosphere of excessive alcoholic stimulation—two factors which occur chiefly among the well-to-do classes" (*In His Own Time*, p. 182). He argues that the "veteran of many petting parties" is prone to affairs not from experience but because of temperament.

Wiese, Charles Character in "The Swimmers." One of the richest men in the South. He has an affair with Choupette MARSTON.

Wiess, Miss Character in "Between Three and Four." Secretary at Howard BUTLER's office.

Wilcox, René Character in "Teamed with Genius." English playwright and inexperienced screenwriter who is assigned to collaborate on a script with Pat HOBBY.

Wilde, Oscar (1854–1900) Irish dramatist whose works include *Lady Windermere's Fan* (1892), *A Woman of No Importance* (1893), *An Ideal Husband* (1895), *The Importance of Being Earnest* (1895), and *The Ballad of Reading Gaol* (1898). *Fie! Fie! Fi-Fi!* imitates Wilde's epigrammatic style; and his work also influenced *TSOP*, which featured an epigraph adapted from Wilde's novel, *The Picture of Dorian Gray* (1891): "Experience is the name so many people give to their mistakes."

See Richard Ellmann, *Oscar Wilde* (New York: Knopf, 1987).

Wilder, Thornton (1897–1975) Pulitzer-Prize-winning American novelist and playwright, the first recipient of the National Medal for Literature (1965); his works include *The Cabala* (1926), *The Bridge of San Luis Rey* (1927), *Our Town* (1938), and *The Skin of Our Teeth* (1942). Wilder visited Fitzgerald at "ELLERSLIE" in February 1928; they corresponded but did not develop a close friendship.

See Gilbert Harrison, *The Enthusiast: A Life of Thornton Wilder* (New Haven, CT: Ticknor & Fields, 1983).

Wilkinson, Dr. Harvey Character in "A Full Life." Doctor who enlivens his boring life by following, through intermittent newspaper headlines, the career of a mysterious girl named Gwendolyn DAVIES whom he had once treated in the emergency room.

William Character in "More Than Just a House." The GUNTHERS' butler, who escapes uninjured when a tree falls on his room during a storm.

Williams, C. D. (Charles David) (1875–1954) Illustrator for "The Adjuster" (*REDBOOK*, September 1925) and "The Swimmers" (*The SATURDAY EVENING POST*, October 1929). He provided the line drawing illustrations for Booth TARKINGTON's *Monsieur Beaucaire* (1900).

Williams, Kitty Childhood sweetheart whom Fitzgerald met in dancing school in BUFFALO. He mentioned Kitty in his *Ledger* for October and December 1907 and January and February 1908 (p. 162), and recalled their relationship in a *Thoughtbook* entry on "My girls" dated August 1910 (pp. IX-X) and an "extract" from something he wrote after dancing school one night (p. XXII).

Willings, Private Character in *Coward*. Union soldier who attempts to plunder Judge DOUGLAS's house after the war. When he tries to steal Lindy DOUGLAS's necklace, Jim HOLWORTHY scares him away.

Wilmington, Delaware The Fitzgeralds resided at "ELLERSLIE" in EDGEMOOR near Wilmington, March 1927–March 1928 and September 1928–March 1929.

Wilson, Big Jack Character in " 'Boil Some Water—Lots of It.' " Director who is heading for Walter HERRICK, dressed as a Cossack, when Pat HOBBY assaults Herrick with a tray.

Wilson, Edmund ("Bunny") (1895–1972) Influential American literary and social critic whose friendship with Fitzgerald began at PRINCETON, where he was a member of the Class of 1916 and chairman of *The NASSAU LITERARY MAGAZINE*, to which Fitzgerald contributed. Fitzgerald and Wilson collaborated on the TRIANGLE CLUB's 1915 production, *The Evil Eye*, for which Wilson wrote the book and Fitzgerald wrote the lyrics. They remained lifelong friends; in 1936 Fitzgerald wrote: "For twenty years a certain man had

Edmund Wilson

been my intellectual conscience. That was Edmund Wilson" ("Pasting It Together," March 1936; *CU*, p. 79).

In November 1919 Fitzgerald sent Wilson a typescript of *TSOP*, which Wilson called "an exquisite burlesque of Compton Mackenzie with a pastiche of Wells at the end"; he warned Fitzgerald against becoming a "very popular trashy novelist" (*Letters on Literature and Politics 1912–1972* [New York: Farrar, Straus & Giroux, 1977], pp. 45 & 46).

At the time of the publication of *B&D* Wilson analyzed Fitzgerald's career in a long unsigned "Literary Spotlight" for the *The Bookman*, emphasizing the Midwest and his Irish background as important influences on Fitzgerald's work. At the request of Fitzgerald, to whom he had sent a pre-publication copy of the article, he deleted references to alcohol as a third influence (see Fitzgerald to Wilson, c. January 1922; *Life in Letters*, pp. 50–52). Wilson's article was condescending, open-

ing with a comment by "a celebrated person" (Edna St. Vincent Millay) that Fitzgerald was like "a stupid old woman with whom someone has left a diamond." Wilson explained: "For he has been given imagination without intellectual control of it; he has been given the desire for beauty without an aesthetic ideal; and he has been given a gift for expression without very many ideas to express" (*The Bookman*, 55 [March 1922], 20–25; Wilson, *The Shores of Light*, p. 27).

Wilson judged *TJA* better than *F&P* because Fitzgerald "lets his fancy, his humor and his taste for nonsense run wild" ("The Jazz King Again," *Vanity Fair*, 19 [November 1922], 24; *FSF: The Critical Reception*, p. 152). When Fitzgerald sent him a copy of his play, *The Vegetable*, Wilson responded: "As I say, I think that the play as a whole is marvelous—no doubt, the best American comedy ever written. I think you have a much better grasp on your subject than you usually have—you know what end and point you are working for, as isn't always the case with you. . . . I think you have a great gift for comic dialogue—even if you never can resist a stupid gag—and should go on writing plays" (May 26, 1922; *Letters on Literature and Politics 1912–1972*, p. 84). The published play (1923) bears this dedication: "TO KATHERINE TIGHE AND EDMUND WILSON, JR. WHO DELETED MANY ABSURDITIES FROM MY FIRST TWO NOVELS I RECOMMEND THE ABSURDITIES SET DOWN HERE."

When Fitzgerald died of a heart attack on December 21, 1940, he had written drafts of 17 of the projected 30 episodes for his novel-in-progress about HOLLYWOOD, *The Love of the Last Tycoon: A Western*. After editor Maxwell PERKINS decided against having another writer complete the novel, Wilson agreed to edit the work. The text he prepared conveys the impression of a more finished work than Fitzgerald's working drafts represent; extant documents show that he styled the punctuation, corrected spelling, altered names, replaced words, moved two scenes, and combined episodes into chapters in his attempt to prepare the novel for the general reader. He also provided a title—*The Last Tycoon*—without specifying a source.

In 1945, Wilson, who had wanted to include the "Crack-Up" essays in the *LT* volume—a proposal which was declined by Perkins—edited *The Crack-Up*, a collection of Fitzgerald's autobiographical essays, letters, and notebooks, as well as tributes from other writers. This volume contributed to the Fitzgerald REVIVAL.

See Jeffrey Meyers, *Edmund Wilson: A Biography* (Boston: Houghton Mifflin, 1995). Meyers also provides a list of Wilson's writings about Fitzgerald in *Scott Fitzgerald: A Biography*, pp. 390–391.

Wilson, George Character in *GG*. Myrtle WILSON's spiritless husband, the owner of a garage in the VALLEY OF ASHES. He determines to find Myrtle's killer; and

when Tom BUCHANAN reveals that Jay GATSBY owns the car which killed her, Wilson kills Gatsby and himself.

Wilson, Jim Character in *TSOP.* A Princetonian whom Amory BLAINE encounters at the Knickerbocker Bar after his breakup with Rosalind CONNAGE.

Wilson, Myrtle Character in *GG.* George WILSON's wife and Tom BUCHANAN's mistress. She is killed when Daisy BUCHANAN accidentally hits her while driving Jay GATSBY's car.

Winfield, George Character in "Six of One—". Young man who is finishing high school late because he had to drop out to support his family after his father's death. Ed BARNES helps send him to Yale, but he drops out after being suspended for his involvement in a drunk-driving accident. He ends up working for Jack SCHOFIELD.

Wing, Bessie Leighton Character in "News of Paris—Fifteen Years Ago." Girl with whom Henry Haven DELL has a one-afternoon fling in PARIS after she breaks her engagement to another man because her first marriage had been a failure.

Winlock, Bomar Character in "The Honor of the Goon." College student who is noted for his trick of falling down stairs and who is beaten up by FINGARSON for insulting fellow student Ella LEI CHAMORO, whom he dubbed "the Goon."

Winslow, Charlotte Character in "A Freeze-Out." Forrest WINSLOW's mother.

Winslow, Eleanor Character in "A Freeze-Out." Forrest WINSLOW's sister.

Winslow, Forrest Character in "A Freeze-Out." Young man who overcomes his family's prejudice to marry Alida RIKKER.

Winslow, Frederic Character in " 'Trouble.' " Young man who wants to marry TROUBLE but whom she doesn't love.

Winslow, Mr. Character in " 'Trouble.' " Frederic WINSLOW's father, who teases TROUBLE about the incident at the turtle race.

Winslow, Mrs. Character in " 'Trouble.' " Frederic WINSLOW's mother, who wants TROUBLE to marry her son.

Winslow, Pierce Character in "A Freeze-Out." Forrest WINSLOW's father, who objects to his son's relationship with Alida RIKKER. Forrest loses faith in his father when Mr. Winslow backs down from his plan to blackball Chauncey RIKKER because he is under obligation to Rikker's social sponsor, Walter HANNAN.

Winter Carnival (United Artists, 1939) In early 1939 Fitzgerald's HOLLYWOOD agent, H. N. SWANSON, found him an assignment for $1,250 a week collaborating with Budd SCHULBERG on *Winter Carnival,* which Walter WANGER was producing for United Artists. Schulberg's story featured a young woman fleeing to Canada with her child, whom she will lose if her husband catches her before she crosses the border; she is delayed at the DARTMOUTH winter carnival. Fitzgerald, Schulberg, and Wanger traveled to Dartmouth on February 10–12 to get fresh ideas. Fitzgerald and Schulberg got drunk during the trip, and Wanger fired both writers and ordered them out of town. They went to NEW YORK, where Schulberg and Sheilah GRAHAM got Fitzgerald admitted to Doctors Hospital with a fever of 103.8 and an upper respiratory infection. Wanger rehired Schulberg back in California, and Schulberg and Lester Cole (1904–85) shared credit for the screenplay. The movie was directed by Charles Riesner (1887–1962) and starred Ann Sheridan (1915–67). Schulberg's 1950 novel *The Disenchanted* is based largely on his trip to Dartmouth with Fitzgerald. (See John D. Hess, "Wanger Blends Abruptness with Charm in Personality," *The Dartmouth* [11 February 1939], 2, 13; *Fitzgerald/Hemingway Annual* [1979], pp. 35–36.)

"Winter Dreams" Fiction. Written September 1922. METROPOLITAN MAGAZINE, 56 (December 1922), 11–15, 98, 100–102, 104–107; *ASYM.* Young Dexter GREEN quits his caddy job at Black Bear Lake after encountering Judy JONES, a wealthy, imperious 11-year-old. Several years later he attends a famous university in the East and prospers in the laundry business. While visiting the golf club where he used to caddy, he again encounters Judy, who invites him to dinner the next night. Their relationship develops, and he asks her to marry him; but she continues to be interested in other men. Dexter becomes engaged to Irene SCHEERER, but abandons her when Judy again shows interest in him; but Judy breaks their own engagement after one month. Seven years later Dexter, who has moved to New York, hears that Judy is unhappily married and that her beauty has faded. Crushed by the loss of his dream of Judy, he grieves that he is no longer able to care. "Winter Dreams" is closely linked to *GG:* Fitzgerald described it to Maxwell PERKINS as "a sort of 1st draft of the Gatsby idea" (June 1, 1925; *Life in Letters,* p. 121; *Scott/Max,* p. 112), and he lifted Dexter's response to Judy's house from the magazine text of the story and wrote it into the novel as Jay GATSBY's reaction to Daisy Fay's [BUCHANAN's] house.

Wise, Bernie Character in "Last Kiss." Director or producer who gives Pamela KNIGHTON her first role but fires her for uncooperative conduct.

Wiskith, Samuel K. Character in "Pat Hobby's College Days." Dean of the student body at U.W.C.

Witchcraft, Sir Howard George Character in "Rags Martin-Jones and the Pr-nce of W-les." Captain of the *Majestic,* the ship on which Rags MARTIN-JONES returns to America.

Wolcott, Percy Character in *B&D.* Former beau whom Gloria Gilbert [PATCH] pushed off an embankment when he became too intimate.

Wolf, Captain Character in *B&D.* An army officer who spends the night with Rachael BARNES while her husband is away.

Wolfe, Thomas (1900–1938) American novelist whom Fitzgerald met during a trip to PARIS in June 1930. Wolfe believed that SCRIBNERS editor Maxwell PERKINS, who had recommended that Wolfe look up Fitzgerald, wanted to get Fitzgerald's opinion of him. After reading Wolfe's highly successful first novel, *Look Homeward, Angel* (1929), Fitzgerald wrote to Perkins: "You have a great find in him—what he'll do is incalculable. He has a deeper culture than Ernest and more vitality, if he is slightly less of a poet that goes with the immense surface he wants to cover. Also he lacks Ernests quality of a stick hardened in the fire. He is more susceptible to the world. John Bishop told me he needed advice about cutting ect, but after reading his book I thought that was nonsense. He strikes me as a man who should be let alone as to length, if he had to be published in five volumes. I liked him enormously" (c. September 1, 1930; *Life in Letters,* pp. 199–200; *Scott/Max,* p. 168).

In September 1930 Fitzgerald and Wolfe encountered one another several times in SWITZERLAND; but Wolfe tried to avoid Fitzgerald, who he thought was interfering with his work. Nevertheless, he wrote Fitzgerald a friendly letter after reading *TITN* in serial: "I thought you'd be interested to know that the people in the book are even more real and living now than they were at the time I read it. It seems to me you've gone deeper in this book than in anything you ever wrote. . . . I think it's the best work you've done so far, and I know you'll understand what I mean and won't mind if I get a kind of selfish hope and joy out of your own success" (March 1934; *Correspondence,* p. 332).

Despite Fitzgerald's early opinion that Wolfe should be allowed to make his books as long as he wanted, he wrote to him in July 1937 urging him to be less inclusive with his material: "The novel of selected incidents has this to be said that the great writer like Flaubert has consciously left out the stuff that Bill or Joe, (in his case Zola) will come along and say presently. He will say only the things that he alone see. So Mme Bovary becomes eternal while Zola already rocks with age" (*Life in Letters,* p. 332). Wolfe defended his method against the familiar criticism: "Well, don't forget, Scott, that a great writer is not only a leaver-outer but also a putter-inner, and that Shakespeare and Cervantes and Dostoevsky were great putter-inners—greater putter-inners, in fact, than taker-outers—and will be remembered for what they put in—remembered, I venture to say, as long as Monsieur Flaubert will be remembered for what he left out" (July 26, 1937; *CU,* p. 314).

Fitzgerald admired Wolfe's talent and wrote to Perkins that he, Wolfe, and Ernest HEMINGWAY had in common "the attempt that crops up in our fiction from time to time to recapture the exact feel of a moment in time and space exemplified by people rather than by things—that is, an attempt at what Wordsworth was trying to do rather than what Keats did with such magnificent ease, an attempt at a mature memory of a deep experience" (July 30, 1934; *Scott/Max,* pp. 203–204). However, he was critical about Wolfe's material, writing to his daughter, Scottie FITZGERALD, shortly before his death: "I started Tom Wolfe's book [*You Can't Go Home Again*] on your recommendation. It seems better than <u>Time and the River</u>. He has a fine inclusive mind, can write like a streak, has a great deal of emotion, though a lot of it is maudlin and inaccurate, but his awful secret transpires at every crevice—he did not have anything particular to say! The stuff about the GREAT VITAL HEART OF AMERICA is just simply corny. . . . However, the book doesn't commit the cardinal sin: it doesn't fail to live" (November 29, 1940; *Life in Letters,* p. 472). Fitzgerald was the model for Hunt Conroy in *You Can't Go Home Again.*

See David Herbert Donald, *Look Homeward: A Life of Thomas Wolfe* (Boston: Little, Brown, 1987).

Wolfshiem, Meyer Character in *GG.* Gambler who, according to Jay GATSBY, fixed the 1919 World's Series and who was involved with Gatsby in selling alcohol and in other illegal activities. Despite Nick CARRAWAY's attempts to persuade him to attend Gatsby's funeral, he protests that he can't get involved. Based on gambler and racketeer Arnold ROTHSTEIN, who had close connections with Edward M. Fuller, a stockbroker who, with his partner William F. McGee, was indicted for fraud. Fitzgerald had mentioned the Fuller-McGee case to Perkins during his revision of the novel (c. December 20, 1924; *Life in Letters,* p. 91; *Scott/Max,* p. 89). See Henry Dan Piper, "The Fuller-McGee Case," *Fitzgerald's "The Great Gatsby",* ed. Piper (New York: Scribners, 1970), pp. 171–184.

Woll, R. Parke Character in "Pat Hobby's Secret." Playwright who refuses to repeat his idea for a movie ending unless he is offered an 8-week contract. After being tricked into revealing the idea to Pat HOBBY, he is killed by a bouncer in a bar.

"The Woman from Twenty-One" Fiction. *ESQUIRE*, 15 (June 1941), 29, 164; *The Price Was High*. While watching a play, Raymond TORRENCE is offended by the loud conversation of the WOMAN from Twenty-One, who is sitting next to him and who keeps suggesting that her party return to Twenty-One, an expensive restaurant-bar in NEW YORK CITY. When he sees her face he recognizes her as a girl with whom he had played in Pittsburgh twenty years before. Because of the encounter, he decides to return to Java, the home of his wife, Elizabeth TORRENCE.

woman from Twenty-One (unnamed) Character in "The Woman from Twenty-One." Woman whose loud conversation at a play offends Raymond TORRENCE.

"A Woman with a Past" Fiction—Josephine PERRY story. Written June 1930. *The SATURDAY EVENING POST*, 203 (September 6, 1930), 8–9, 133–134, 137; *TAR*; *B&J*. Josephine Perry attends her first prom at Yale with Ridgeway SAUNDERS but falls in love with Dudley KNOWLETON, who is dating Adele CRAW. Josephine, who is beginning to be more serious, nevertheless gets in trouble unjustly at school. She is falsely suspected of leaning out her window talking to boys and is put on probation. While entertaining Ernest WATERBURY, headmistress Miss BRERETON's dull nephew, Josephine slips and lands in his arms; when Miss Brereton loses her head over the situation, Mr. PERRY removes Josephine from school. While visiting Hot Springs with her family, she sees Dudley again; but he tells her that he and Adele have plans and that Adele has always been his ideal. Josephine realizes that this is the first time she has failed to win a man in whom she is interested.

Woman's Home Companion Magazine which published "The Pusher-in-the-Face" (February 1925), "One of My Oldest Friends" (September 1925), "Not in the Guidebook" (November 1925), "Your Way and Mine" (May 1927), and " 'Wait Till You Have Children of Your Own!' " (July 1924). In October 1929 the magazine's interest in Fitzgerald was renewed by the appearance of "The Swimmers" in *The SATURDAY EVENING POST*, and an editor at *Woman's Home Companion* asked Har-

old OBER to submit Fitzgerald's work to her (*As Ever*, pp. 154–155). *Woman's Home Companion* declined a 1935 story, "I'd Die for You" (unpublished), and "Thumbs Up" (published as "The End of Hate," *Collier's*, June 1940). Although Ober mentioned the magazine to Fitzgerald as a potential market that would pay well for his stories (June 2, 1939; *As Ever*, p. 391), none of his work appeared in it after "Your Way and Mine."

The Women (MGM, 1939) Fitzgerald worked for MGM producer Hunt STROMBERG from May to October 1938 writing a screenplay based on the hit play *The Women* (1936) by Claire Booth Luce (1903–87). The cast included Norma SHEARER, Joan Crawford (1904–77), Paulette Goddard (1911–90), and Rosalind Russell (1908–76), all of whom Fitzgerald had to provide with equally good lines. The job was complicated by health problems which prevented Stromberg from giving adequate attention to the project. Toward the end of the assignment Donald Ogden STEWART was assigned to work with Fitzgerald, but they were replaced by Jane Murfin (1893–1955) and Anita LOOS when it was decided that female screenwriters were required. The 1939 movie was directed by George Cukor (1899–1983).

Woodley, Mr. Character in "Your Way and Mine." Henry MCCOMAS's early employer, who rebukes McComas for taking too long to make a perfect typed copy of a letter.

Wookey-Wookey Character in *TSOP*. Deaf housekeeper at ST. REGIS who tells Amory BLAINE that he is the best-looking boy she has ever seen.

workman (unnamed) Character in "The Four Fists." Horse-car passenger who is the second person to hit Samuel MEREDITH.

"The World's Fair" *Kenyon Review*, 10 (Autumn 1948), 567–578. A section of the Francis Melarky matricide version of *TITN*.

Wrackham, Percy Character in "The Rubber Check." Branch manager who fires Val SCHUYLER.

Wylie, Tanaduke Character in *TSOP*. A PRINCETON student whose poetry Amory BLAINE and Tom D'INVILLIERS admire until he takes to a Bohemian life.

Y

Yanci Bowman's aunt (unnamed) Character in "The Popular Girl." Relative with whom Yanci BOWMAN considers living after her father's death but who is traveling abroad for an indefinite period of time.

A Yank at Oxford (MGM, 1938) In July 1937 Metro-Goldwyn-Mayer hired Fitzgerald for six months at $1,000 a week with an option for another year at $1,250. His first assignment was to polish the dialogue in a screenplay by Frank Wead (1895?–1947) for *A Yank at Oxford,* based on an original story by John Monk Saunders (1897–1940). Fitzgerald's revision was rewritten by Malcolm Stewart Boylan and Walter Ferris (b. 1886), whose revision was polished by George Oppenheimer (1900–77). Fitzgerald was not one of the eight writers who received a screen credit. When the movie, directed by Jack Conway (1887–1952), was released, Fitzgerald wrote to Zelda FITZGERALD's mother, Minnie SAYRE, "Very few lines of mine are left in 'A Yank at Oxford.' I only worked on it for eight days, but the sequence in which Taylor and Maureen O'Sullivan go out in the punt in the morning, while the choir boys are singing on Magdalene Tower, is mine, and one line very typically so—where Taylor says, 'Don't rub the sleep out of your eyes. It's beautiful sleep.' I thought that line had my trade mark on it" (April 23, 1938; *Correspondence,* p. 498).

young man (unnamed) Character in "The Mystery of the Raymond Mortgage." Man whom GREGSON sees kneeling by the body of Agnes RAYMOND. He tells John SYREL that Agnes loved him, not STANDISH, providing a motive for the murder.

Young Seneca Character in "Lo, the Poor Peacock!" Man who works on Annie Lee DAVIS's family farm.

"Your Way and Mine" Fiction. Written February 1926. WOMAN'S HOME COMPANION, 54 (May 1927), 7–8, 61, 64, 67, 68; *The Price Was High.* Henry MCCOMAS, who likes to do things his own way, goes into business with Theodore DRINKWATER, who resents McComas's work habits, such as coming into the office at 11 o'clock every morning. Drinkwater urges Stella MCCOMAS to persuade her husband to change his ways. When she makes a down payment on a house they can't afford, McComas begins going to work earlier and forgoing his usual naps; but after a while the change takes a toll on him, and he is paralyzed for a year and a half. Drinkwater dissolves their partnership, and when McComas recovers he goes into business for himself. His daughter, Honoria MCCOMAS, wants to marry Russel

Fitzgerald's name on the cover sold magazines. (Bruccoli Collection, University of South Carolina)

CODMAN, his right-hand man. However, when Codman proposes to her he uses the same words her father had used with her mother. McComas urges Honoria to reject Codman because he is not his own man, and rather to marry Max VAN CAMP, who has proposed to her many times.

Fitzgerald told Harold OBER: "This is one of the lowsiest stories I've ever written. Just terrible! . . . It hasn't <u>one redeeming touch</u> of my usual spirit in it. I was desperate to begin a story + invented a business plot—the kind I can't handle" (received March 15, 1926; *As Ever,* p. 87).

Lobby card for Fitzgerald's first MGM assignment in 1937 (Courtesy of Fred Zenter, Cinema Bookshop)

Z

Zada, Madame (Amelia Wetherby Hendrix) Character in *Assorted Spirits*. Peter WETHERBY's sister, who earns her living as a fortune teller since her husband, Josephus HENDRIX, deserted her. She and Hendrix are reunited at the end of the play.

Zavras, Pete Character in *LT/LOLT*. Greek cameraman who is falsely rumored to have eye trouble and who breaks his arm when he jumps from the balcony of the Administration Building in a failed suicide attempt. When Monroe STAHR squelches the rumors about his eyesight, Zavras expresses his gratitude by offering to help if Stahr ever needs anyone's throat cut. Fitzgerald's notes for the unwritten episodes indicate that Zavras was to play an important role by warning Stahr of Pat BRADY's plot against him. This character's name is "Pedro Garcia" in Fitzgerald's manuscripts; but Fitzgerald's secretary Frances KROLL recalls that he used the name as a joke and intended to change it, as indicated by his note "Change Garcia to a Greek." Edmund WILSON emended the name to Pete Zavras when he edited the unfinished novel for publication.

Zelda Fitzgerald: The Collected Writings Edited by Matthew J. BRUCCOLI, with introduction by Mary Gordon. New York: Scribners, 1991. Contents: *Save Me the Waltz, Scandalabra*, "Our Own Movie Queen," "The Original Follies Girl," "Southern Girl," "The Girl the Prince Liked," "The Girl with Talent," "A Millionaire's Girl," "Poor Working Girl," "Miss Ella," "The Continental Angle," "A Couple of Nuts," "Other Names for Roses," "Friend Husband's Latest," "Eulogy on the Flapper," "Does a Moment of Revolt Come Sometime to Every Married Man?," "What Became of the Flappers?," "Breakfast," "The Changing Beauty of Park Avenue," "Looking Back Eight Years," "Who Can Fall in Love After Thirty?," "Paint and Powder," " 'Show Mr. and Mrs. F. to Number ——,' " "Auction—Model 1934," "On F. Scott Fitzgerald," Letters to F. Scott Fitzgerald.

"Zelda Fitzgerald's Tribute to F. Scott Fitzgerald" Article. *Fitzgerald/Hemingway Annual* (1974), pp. 2–7; in *Zelda Fitzgerald: The Collected Writings* as "On F. Scott Fitzgerald". Probably written for the group of tributes to Fitzgerald published in *The New Republic* in February and March 1941, but not used. Zelda notes: "Fitzgerald's books were the first of their kind and the most indicative. . . . His meter was bitter, and ironic and spectacular and inviting: so was life. There wasn't much other life during those times than to what his pen paid the tribute of poetic tragic glamour and offered the reconciliation of the familiarities of tragedy. Rest in peace" (*Collected Writings*, p. 441).

"Zone of Accident" Fiction. Written fall 1932, May 1935. *The SATURDAY EVENING POST*, 208 (July 13, 1935), 8–9, 47, 49, 51–52; *The Price Was High*. Doctor Bill TULLIVER treats actress Loretta BROOKE, who has been stabbed in the back by her former dancing partner, whose marriage proposal she rejected. Tulliver becomes attracted to her but is angry when he discovers that she has been faking her temperature to lengthen her stay in the hospital. Meanwhile, his fiancée, AMY, enters a contest sponsored by a film company; and he catches her kissing the HOLLYWOOD man who is running the contest. When Loretta Brooke, who is one of the contest judges, informs Tulliver that she will cast the deciding vote that can send Amy to Hollywood—perhaps to stay—he tells her to go ahead because Amy doesn't belong to him anymore; and it is understood that Loretta will take Amy's place in his life.

The *Post* rejected two earlier versions of this story, then titled "In the Safety Zone," in March 1931 and 1933.

CHRONOLOGY*

1853 Birth of Edward Fitzgerald at "Glenmary" farm near Rockville in Montgomery County, Maryland.

1858 Birth of Anthony D. Sayre in Tuskegee, Alabama.

1860 Birth of Mary ("Mollie") McQuillan in St. Paul, Minnesota. Birth of Minnie Buckner Machen in Eddyville, Kentucky.

June 1884 Marriage of Anthony Sayre and Minnie Machen at "Mineral Mount" near Eddyville, Kentucky.

February 12, 1890 Marriage of Edward Fitzgerald and Mollie McQuillan in Washington, D.C.

September 24, 1896 Birth of Francis Scott Key Fitzgerald at 481 Laurel Avenue, St. Paul.

April 1898 After failure of his St. Paul furniture factory, Edward Fitzgerald takes job as salesman with Procter & Gamble; moves with family to Buffalo, New York.

July 24, 1900 Birth of Zelda Sayre at South Street, Montgomery, Alabama.

January 1901 Fitzgerald family moves to Syracuse, New York, where Procter & Gamble transfers Edward Fitzgerald.

July 21, 1901 Birth of Annabel Fitzgerald.

September 1903 Fitzgerald family moves back to Buffalo, where Procter & Gamble transfers Edward Fitzgerald.

1907 Sayre family moves to 6 Pleasant Avenue, Zelda's home until her marriage.

March 1908 Edward Fitzgerald loses his job at Procter & Gamble.

July 1908 Fitzgerald family returns to St. Paul.

September 1908 F. Scott Fitzgerald enters St. Paul Academy.

1909 Judge Anthony Sayre of the City Court in Montgomery is appointed Associate Justice of the Supreme Court of Alabama.

October 1909 Publication of "The Mystery of the Raymond Mortgage" in *The St. Paul Academy Now and Then*—Fitzgerald's first appearance in print.

August 1911 Production of Fitzgerald's first play, *The Girl from Lazy J*, in St. Paul.

September 1911 Fitzgerald enters Newman School, Hackensack, New Jersey.

August 1912 Production of *The Captured Shadow* in St. Paul.

November 1912 Fitzgerald meets Father Sigourney Fay and Shane Leslie.

August 1913 Production of *Coward* in St. Paul.

September 1913 Fitzgerald enters Princeton University with Class of 1917; meets Edmund Wilson '16 and John Peale Bishop '17; contributes to *The Princeton Tiger*.

September 1914 Production of *Assorted Spirits* in St. Paul.

Fall 1914 Zelda enters Sidney Lanier High School.

December 1914 Production of *Fie! Fie! Fi-Fi!*, Fitzgerald's first Princeton Triangle Club show.

January 4, 1915 Fitzgerald meets Ginevra King in St. Paul.

April 1915 "Shadow Laurels," Fitzgerald's first publication in *The Nassau Literary Magazine*.

November 28, 1915 Fitzgerald attends his last class and drops out of Princeton for remainder of junior year.

December 1915 Production of *The Evil Eye* by Triangle Club.

September 1916 Fitzgerald returns to Princeton as member of Class of 1918.

December 1916 Production of *Safety First* by Triangle Club.

October 26, 1917 Fitzgerald receives commission as 2nd lieutenant in U.S. infantry.

November 20, 1917 Fitzgerald reports to Fort Leavenworth, Kansas; begins novel, "The Romantic Egotist."

End of February 1918 Fitzgerald receives leave from army; travels to Princeton, where he completes first draft of "The Romantic Egotist"; in March sends novel to Shane Leslie, who submits it to Scribners in May.

March 15, 1918 Fitzgerald reports to Camp Zachary Taylor, Louisville, Kentucky.

April 1918 Fitzgerald transferred to Camp Gordon, Georgia.

May 1918 Zelda Sayre graduates from Sidney Lanier High School.

June 1918 Fitzgerald reports to Camp Sheridan near Montgomery, Alabama.

*Adapted from Matthew J. Bruccoli's *Some Sort of Epic Grandeur*, revised edition (New York: Carroll & Graf, 1993).

July 1918 Fitzgerald and Zelda Sayre meet at country club dance in Montgomery.

August 1918 Scribners declines "The Romantic Egotist"; rejects revised typescript in October.

October 26, 1918 Fitzgerald's regiment shipped north to Camp Mills, Long Island, to await embarkation; war ends before unit sent overseas.

November 1918 Fitzgerald's unit is ordered back to Camp Sheridan, where he becomes aide-de-camp to Brigadier General J. A. Ryan.

February 1919 Fitzgerald discharged from army. Planning to marry Zelda Sayre, he goes to New York and works for the Barron Collier advertising agency; lives in room at 200 Claremont Avenue.

Spring 1919 Fitzgerald visits Montgomery in April, May, and June as Zelda Sayre remains reluctant to commit herself to marriage. *The Smart Set* takes "Babes in the Woods"—his first commercial story sale; published September 1919.

June 1919 Zelda Sayre breaks engagement.

July 1919 Fitzgerald quits advertising job and returns to St. Paul; rewrites novel while living with parents at 599 Summit Avenue.

September 16, 1919 Maxwell Perkins of Scribners accepts *This Side of Paradise*.

November 1919 Fitzgerald becomes client of Harold Ober at Reynolds agency. First sale to *The Saturday Evening Post:* "Head and Shoulders"; published February 1920.

November 1919–February 1920 *The Smart Set* publishes "The Debutante," "Porcelain and Pink," "Benediction," and "Dalyrimple Goes Wrong."

Mid-January 1920 Fitzgerald lives in boardinghouse at 2900 Prytania Street in New Orleans, where he stays less than a month before returning to New York. Engagement to Zelda Sayre resumes during his visits to Montgomery.

March–May 1920 "Myra Meets His Family," "The Camel's Back," "Bernice Bobs Her Hair," "The Ice Palace," and "The Offshore Pirate" appear in *The Saturday Evening Post.*

March 26, 1920 Publication of *This Side of Paradise.*

April 3, 1920 Marriage of Fitzgerald and Zelda Sayre at rectory of St. Patrick's Cathedral in New York. Honeymoon at Biltmore Hotel.

May 1920 Fitzgeralds rent house at Westport, Connecticut, where Fitzgerald begins writing *The Beautiful and Damned.*

July 1920 Publication of "May Day" in *The Smart Set.* Fitzgeralds drive to Montgomery; return to Westport by train.

September 10, 1920 Publication of *Flappers and Philosophers,* Fitzgerald's first collection of short stories.

October 1920 Fitzgeralds take apartment at 38 West 59th Street, New York City.

May 3, 1921 First trip to Europe: Fitzgeralds sail to England, then visit France and Italy. Return to America and visit Montgomery on July 27.

August 1921 Fitzgeralds rent cottage at White Bear Lake in Dellwood, outside St. Paul.

September 1921–March 1922 *The Beautiful and Damned* serialized in *Metropolitan Magazine.*

October 1921 Fitzgeralds move to Commodore Hotel in St. Paul.

October 26, 1921 Birth of daughter Scottie.

November 1921 Fitzgeralds rent house at 626 Goodrich Avenue, St. Paul.

March 4, 1922 Publication of *The Beautiful and Damned.*

June 1922 Publication of "The Diamond as Big as the Ritz" in *The Smart Set.*

June 1922 Fitzgeralds move to White Bear Yacht Club in Dellwood.

August 1922 Fitzgeralds move to Commodore Hotel in St. Paul.

September 22, 1922 Publication of *Tales of the Jazz Age:* Fitzgerald's second collection of short stories.

Mid–October 1922 Fitzgeralds rent house at 6 Gateway Drive in Great Neck, Long Island. Friendship with Ring Lardner.

December 1922 Publication of "Winter Dreams" in *Metropolitan Magazine.*

April 27, 1923 Publication of *The Vegetable.*

November 19, 1923 *The Vegetable* fails at tryout in Atlantic City, New Jersey.

May 1924 Second trip to Europe: Fitzgeralds sail for France; visit Paris, then leave for Riviera; stop at Grimm's Park Hotel in Hyères.

June 1924 Fitzgeralds settle at Villa Marie, Valescure, St. Raphaël. Publication of "Absolution" in *The American Mercury.*

Summer–Fall 1924 Fitzgerald completes and revises first draft of *The Great Gatsby.*

July 1924 Zelda Fitzgerald becomes involved with French aviator Edouard Jozan. Publication of " 'The Sensible Thing' " in *Liberty.*

Summer 1924 Fitzgeralds meet Gerald and Sara Murphy at Cap d'Antibes.

October 1924 Fitzgeralds stay at Hotel des Princes, Rome, where Fitzgerald revises *The Great Gatsby* galleys.

February 1925 Fitzgeralds travel to Capri; stay at Hotel Tiberio.

April 10, 1925 Publication of *The Great Gatsby.*

Late April 1925 Fitzgeralds move to Paris; rent apartment at 14 rue de Tilsitt.

May 1925 Fitzgerald meets Ernest Hemingway in Dingo bar.

Summer 1925 Fitzgerald begins planning novel that will become *Tender Is the Night.*

August 1925 Fitzgeralds leave Paris for month at Cap d'Antibes, then return to Paris.

January–February 1926 Zelda Fitzgerald takes "cure" at Salies de Béarn. Publication of "The Rich Boy" in *Redbook* magazine.

February 2, 1926 Play version of *The Great Gatsby*, by Owen Davis, opens on Broadway.

February 26, 1926 Publication of *All the Sad Young Men*: Fitzgerald's third collection of short stories.

Early March 1926 Fitzgeralds return to Riviera and rent Villa Paquita at Juan-les-Pins.

May or June 1926 Hemingways join Murphys and Fitzgeralds on Riviera. Fitzgeralds move to Villa St. Louis, Juan-les-Pins.

December 1926 Fitzgeralds return to America.

January 1927 First Hollywood trip: Fitzgeralds spend two months there, while Fitzgerald works on "Lipstick" (unproduced) for United Artists; they meet Lois Moran.

March 1927 Fitzgeralds rent "Ellerslie," near Wilmington, Delaware. Zelda Fitzgerald begins ballet lessons.

April 1928 Third trip to Europe: Fitzgeralds rent apartment at 58 rue de Vaugirard, Paris. Publication of "The Scandal Detectives" in *The Saturday Evening Post*: first of eight-story Basil Duke Lee series.

Summer 1928 Zelda Fitzgerald begins ballet training with Lubov Egorova in Paris.

October 7, 1928 Fitzgeralds return to America; live at "Ellerslie."

Early 1929 Zelda Fitzgerald begins writing series of short stories for *College Humor*; first in series, "The Original Follies Girl," published July 1929.

March 1929 Publication of "The Last of the Belles" in *The Saturday Evening Post*.

Fourth trip to Europe: Fitzgeralds travel from Genoa along Riviera, then to Paris in April; live in apartment on rue Mézières.

June 1929 Fitzgeralds leave Paris for Riviera; rent Villa Fleur des Bois, Cannes.

October 1929 Fitzgeralds return by car to Paris by way of Provence; take apartment at 10 rue Pergolèse.

February 1930 Fitzgeralds travel to North Africa.

April 1930 Publication of "First Blood" in *The Saturday Evening Post*: first of five-story Josephine Perry series.

April 23, 1930 After her first breakdown, Zelda Fitzgerald enters Malmaison Clinic outside Paris; discharges herself on May 11.

May 22, 1930 Zelda Fitzgerald enters Val-Mont Clinic in Glion, Switzerland.

June 5, 1930 Zelda Fitzgerald enters Prangins Clinic at Nyon, Switzerland.

Summer and Fall 1930 Fitzgerald commutes between Paris and Switzerland; in fall settles at Hotel de la Paix in Lausanne.

Christmas 1930 Fitzgerald takes Scottie skiing in Gstaad, Switzerland, after visit to Zelda Fitzgerald at Prangins.

January 26, 1931 Death of Edward Fitzgerald. Fitzgerald returns alone to America to attend burial; travels to Montgomery to report to Sayres about Zelda Fitzgerald.

February 1931 Fitzgerald returns to Europe; divides time between Paris and Switzerland. Publication of "Babylon Revisited" in *The Saturday Evening Post*.

July 1931 Fitzgeralds spend two weeks at Lake Annecy, France.

September 15, 1931 Zelda Fitzgerald released from Prangins. Fitzgeralds return to America; rent house at 819 Felder Avenue in Montgomery.

November–December 1931 Second Hollywood trip: Fitzgerald goes to Hollywood alone to work on *Red-Headed Woman* for Metro-Goldwyn-Mayer.

November 17, 1931 Death of Judge Sayre.

Early 1932 Fitzgerald plans Dick Diver version of *Tender Is the Night*.

January 1932 Fitzgeralds travel to St. Petersburg, Florida. Zelda Fitzgerald suffers second breakdown.

February 12, 1932 Zelda Fitzgerald enters Phipps Psychiatric Clinic of Johns Hopkins Hospital in Baltimore.

March 1932 Zelda Fitzgerald completes first draft of her novel, *Save Me the Waltz*, while at Phipps Clinic; Fitzgerald moves to Hotel Rennert in Baltimore.

May 20, 1932 Fitzgerald rents "La Paix" at Rodgers Forge, Towson outside Baltimore, where he writes most of *Tender Is the Night*.

June 26, 1932 Zelda Fitzgerald discharged from Phipps; joins family at "La Paix."

October 7, 1932 Publication of *Save Me the Waltz*.

October 1932 Publication of "Crazy Sunday" in *The American Mercury*.

June 26–July 1, 1933 Zelda Fitzgerald's play, *Scandalabra*, produced by Vagabond Junior Players in Baltimore.

December 1933 Fitzgerald rents house at 1307 Park Avenue, Baltimore.

January–April 1934 Serialization of *Tender Is the Night* in *Scribner's Magazine*.

February 12, 1934 After third breakdown, Zelda Fitzgerald returns to Phipps Clinic.

March 8, 1934 Zelda Fitzgerald transferred to Craig House, Beacon, New York.

March 29–April 30, 1934 Zelda Fitzgerald's art exhibition in New York at Cary Ross's gallery and Hotel Algonquin.

April 12, 1934 Publication of *Tender Is the Night*.

May 19, 1934 Zelda Fitzgerald transferred to Sheppard-Pratt Hospital in Towson, Maryland.

February 1935 Fitzgerald spends two weeks at Oak Hall Hotel in Tryon, North Carolina, then returns to Baltimore.

March 20, 1935 Publication of *Taps at Reveille.*

Summer 1935 Fitzgerald stays at Grove Park Inn, Asheville, North Carolina.

September 1935 Fitzgerald takes apartment at Cambridge Arms, Charles Street, Baltimore.

November–December 1935 Fitzgerald stays at Skyland Hotel in Hendersonville, North Carolina, where he begins writing "The Crack-Up" essays; returns to Cambridge Arms in Baltimore at end of December.

April 8, 1936 Zelda Fitzgerald transferred to Highland Hospital in Asheville.

July 1936 Fitzgerald returns to Grove Park Inn in Asheville.

September 1936 Death of Mollie McQuillan Fitzgerald in Washington. Scottie enters Ethel Walker School in Connecticut.

January 1937 Fitzgerald returns to Oak Hall in Tryon.

July 1937 Third Hollywood trip: Deeply in debt, Fitzgerald signs six-month contract with MGM at $1,000 a week; works on *A Yank at Oxford* script. Lives at Garden of Allah on Sunset Boulevard; meets Sheilah Graham on July 14.

July 1937–February 1938 Fitzgerald works on *Three Comrades* script, his only screen credit.

Early September 1937 Fitzgerald visits Zelda Fitzgerald in Asheville; they spend four days in Charleston and Myrtle Beach, South Carolina.

December 1937 MGM contract renewed for one year at $1,250 a week.

February 1938–January 1939 Fitzgerald works on MGM scripts for "Infidelity," *Marie Antoinette, The Women,* and *Madame Curie.*

End of March 1938 Fitzgeralds spend Easter at Virginia Beach and Norfolk, Virginia.

April 1938 Fitzgerald moves to bungalow at 114 Malibu Beach.

September 1938 Scottie enters Vassar College.

November 1938 Fitzgerald moves to cottage at "Belly Acres," the estate of actor Edward Everett Horton, 5521 Amestoy Avenue, Encino, California.

December 1938 MGM contract not renewed.

January 1939 Fitzgerald works briefly on *Gone With the Wind.*

February 10–12, 1939 Fitzgerald travels to Dartmouth College with Budd Schulberg to work on *Winter Carnival;* fired for drinking.

March 1939–October 1940 Fitzgerald takes freelance jobs at Paramount, Universal, Twentieth Century-Fox, and Goldwyn studios. Works on "Air Raid" (unproduced), *Open That Door, Everything Happens at Night, Raffles,* and *Life Begins at Eight–Thirty.*

April 1939 Fitzgeralds travel to Cuba. Fitzgerald goes on bender; is hospitalized on return to New York.

Summer 1939 Fitzgerald plans *The Love of the Last Tycoon: A Western;* attempts to sell serial rights to *Collier's* in September.

July 1939 Fitzgerald breaks with Harold Ober over the agent's refusal to resume making advance payments for unsold stories.

January 1940 Publication of "Pat Hobby's Christmas Wish" in *Esquire:* first of 17-story series.

March–August 1940 Fitzgerald works on "Cosmopolitan" ("Babylon Revisited") script for Lester Cowan.

Mid–April 1940 Zelda Fitzgerald discharged from Highland Hospital; lives with her mother at 322 Sayre Street in Montgomery.

May 1940 Fitzgerald moves to 1403 North Laurel Avenue, Hollywood.

December 21, 1940 Fitzgerald dies of heart attack at Sheilah Graham's apartment, 1443 North Hayworth Avenue, Hollywood.

December 27, 1940 Fitzgerald buried in Rockville Union Cemetery, Rockville, Maryland.

October 27, 1941 Publication of *The Last Tycoon,* ed. Edmund Wilson.

August 12, 1945 Publication of *The Crack-Up,* ed. Edmund Wilson.

September 1945 Publication of *The Portable F. Scott Fitzgerald,* ed. Dorothy Parker.

November 1947 Zelda Fitzgerald returns to Highland Hospital from Montgomery.

March 10, 1948 Zelda Fitzgerald dies in fire at Highland Hospital, Asheville, North Carolina.

March 17, 1948 Zelda Fitzgerald buried with Scott Fitzgerald.

November 7, 1975 Scott and Zelda Fitzgerald reinterred in Fitzgerald family plot at St. Mary's Church, Rockville, Maryland.

CATEGORICAL APPENDIX

Characters

the Abbot
Abbot, Charley
Abbot, Hamilton (Ham)
Abby
Abercrombie
Abercrombie, Bill
Abrams, Mrs.
Agge, Prince
Ahearn, Clarence
Ahearn, Mrs.
Alix
Allenby
Allerdyce, Mrs. Thomas
Allison, Parker
Altwater, Lieutenant Percy
Ambler, Joe
the American
Ames, Ellsworth (Ellie)
Amy
Andros, Ede
Andros, Edith
Andros, John
Andy
Appleton
Appleton, Lila
Appleton, Mrs.
Appleton, Warren
Aquilla's brother
Aquilla's sister
Aronstael
Ashton, Cecilia
Augustine
Aunt Georgie
Aunt Gladys
Aunt Mamie
Aunt Rose
Avery, Helen
Bach, Mr.
Bach, Mr.
Bacon, Doctor
Baedeker, Miss
Baer, Doctor Bill
Bailey, John Boynton
Baily
Baird, Tudor
Baker, Ellen
Baker, George
Baker, Jordan
Baker, Mrs.
Bangs, Angelina

Banizon, Mr.
Bannerman, Marie
Baptiste
Barban, Tommy
Barkis, Private
Barley
Barlotto
Barlow, Mr.
Barnes, Ed
Barnes, Rachael Jerryl
Barnes, Rodman
Barney, Charles
Barnfield, Teddy
Barrows, Colonel
Bartholomew
Bartlett, Dolly
Bartney, Walter Hamilton
 (William)
Barton, Mr.
Battles, Johanna
the Beard
Beauty Boy
Bebé
Becker, Gwen
Becker, Joe
Beebe, Evelyn
Beebe, Ham
Behrer, Doctor
Belknap, Sara
Bellamy, Gordon
Bellamy, Harry
Bellamy, Mr.
Bellamy, Mrs.
Bellamy, Myra
Beltzman
Bement, Ed
Bennett, Jim
Berl
Berners, Jack
Bernice
Berry, Ralph (Rafe)
Bibble, Ermine Gilberte
 Labouisse (Minnie)
Bibble, Mr. and Mrs.
Billings, Senator
Biloxi, "Blocks"
Bisby, Mrs. Caxton
Bishop
Bissel, Imogene
Black, Joseph

Blaine, Amory
Blaine, Beatrice O'Hara
Blaine, Stephen
Blair, Mr. and Mrs. George
 P.
Blair, Hubert
Blair, William Brevoort
Bliss, Doctor
Bloeckman, Joseph
Boldini, Jeff
Boone, Joe
Booth, Jacob
Booth, John Wilkes
Bopes
Bordon, Dolly
Borgé, Isabelle
Borgé, Mrs.
Borowki, Count Stanislas
 Karl Joseph
Bounds
Bourne, Mark H.
Bowers, Bryan
Bowers, Donald
Bowers, Gwen
Bowman, Tom
Bowman, Yanci
Boxley, George
Braden, Carty
Bradin, Edith
Bradin, Henry
Brady, Cecelia
Brady, Earl
Brady, Pat
the Brain
Brancusi, Mr.
Bray, Mrs.
Brereton, Miss
Brett, Mr.
Brimmer
Broaca, John
Bronson, Ed
Bronson, Edgar
Bronson, Will
Brooke, Loretta
Brother Brian
Brown, Ben
Brown, Bugs
Brown, Captain
Brown, Delia
Brown, Orrison

Brown, Satterly
Buchanan, Daisy Fay
Buchanan, Pammy
Buchanan, Tom
Buckner, Mrs.
Buckner, Riply, Jr.
Bugs (Trevellion)
Burke, Geraldine
Burne-Dennison, Martha
Burns, Phyllis
Busch, Arthur
Bushmill, Hallie
Bushmill, Jessie Pepper
Bushmill, Julius
Butler
Butler, Howard
Butterfield, Warren
Butterworth, Mr.
Button, Benjamin
Button, Mrs. Roger
Button, Roger
Button, Roscoe
Cable
Cable, Joe
Cale, Mr.
Calhoun, Ailie
Calkins, Mr.
Calman, Miles
Calman, Mrs.
Calman, Stella Walker
Cambell, Randy
Campbell, Dizzy
Campion, Luis
Canby, Carleton
Canby, Lieutenant Horace
Canisius, John
Cannel, John
Cannon, Mr.
Capps-Karr, Lady
Captain
Caramel, Richard (Dick)
Carhart, Peter
Carleton, Sammy
Carling
Carlyle, Curtis
Carmatle, Governor
Carney, Doctor Howard
Caroline
Carraway, Nick
Carroll, Peter

285

Carson
Carstairs, Bill
Carter, Eleanor
Carton, James
cartoonist
Carver
Cary, Colonel
Cary, Daisy
Cary, Edith
Cary, Esther
Cary, Jonquil
Cary, Mr. and Mrs.
Cary, Mrs.
Casasus
Case, Harold
Cass, Mr.
Cassius
Castle, Mr.
Castleton, Emily
Castleton, Harold, Jr.
Castleton, Harold, Sr.
Cathcart, Jim
Catherine
Catherine
Caxter, Wessel
Cedric
Chaffee, Book
Chambers, Miss
Chambers, Mr.
Chandelle, Jaques
Chandelle, Jean
Chandler, Cora
Chandler, San Juan
Chapman, William
Chase, Walter
Chauffeur
Cheever, Bessie Belle
Chestnut, John M.
Chevril, Mr.
Chillicheff, Prince
Choynski, Mrs.
Christopher
Civet, Doctor Webster
Clancy, Miss
Clark, Amanda Rawlins
Clark, Llewellyn
Clark, Lucy Wharton
Clark, Marjorie
Clay, Collis
Clayhorne, Ben
Clayhorne, Charlie
Clayhorne, Dicky
Clayhorne, Pete
Clothilde
Codman, Russel
Cody, Dan
Cohalan, Miss
Cola, Mr. ("Capone")
Cole, Miss
Coles, Joel
Collins, Captain
Collins, Marjorie
Collins, Miss
Colman, Ronald

Column, Phoebe
Combrinck, Lady Sybil
Combrinck, Lord
Compson, Doctor
Connage, Alec
Connage, Mr. and Mrs.
 Beverly
Connage, Cecelia
Connage, Dorothy
Connage, Hubert
Connage, Leland R.
Connage, Mrs. Leland R.
Connage, Rosalind
Cooley, Jim
Cooley, Milly
Coots, Mrs.
Corcoran
Corcoran, Caroline Martin
Corcoran, Dexter
Corcoran, George
Corcoran, Mrs.
Corker, Bill
Cortelyou, Henry
Costello, Bill
Count Charles
Cousin Jo
Craddock, Mr.
Craig, Charlie
Craker, Captain
Craw, Adele
Crawford, Jason
Crawford, Mr.
Cresswell, Clarke
Cromwell, George
Cromwell, Harry
Cromwell, Kitty Carr
Crosby, Esther
Crosby, Waldron
Crum, Hector
Crum, Lewis
Cupp, Walter
Curly, Michael
Curtain, Jeffrey
Curtain, Roxanne Mil-
 bank
Cushmael, T.
Dada
Daddy
Dale, Dick
Daley, Irene
Dalyrimple, Bryan
D'Amido, Elizabeth
 (Betsy)
Dandy, Caroline
Dandy, Mrs.
Dane, Oscar
Dangeu, Doctor
Danski, Mrs.
Danzer, Abe
Darcy, Jack
Darcy, Monsignor Thayer
Dare, Alicia
Darrow, Clark
Davey, George

Davies, Connie
Davies, Gwendolyn
Davis, Annie Lee
Davis, Jason
Davis, Jo
Davis, Katherine
Davis, Minna
Day, Helen
Dean, Philip
DeBec, Mayall
Debris, Percy B.
de Caros Moros, Count
Decker, Mary
de Coppet, Travis
Deems, Mr.
Deering, Humphrey
Deering, Jeff
Deglen, Joris
de la Guillet de la
 Guimpé, Marquis
 Eduard
de la Guillet de la
 Guimpé, Henri
de la Guillet de la
 Guimpé, Marquise
de la Guillet de la
 Guimpé, Miette
de la Guillet de la
 Guimpé, Noel
de la Guillet de la
 Guimpé, Comte Paul
de Lanclerc, Count
 Hennen
de Lanclerc, Countess
Delauney, Madame Noel
Delehanty, Jenny
Dell, Henry Haven
Demorest, Ethel
Dempster, Paul
Denzer, Catherine
Derocco, Doctor
Deshhacker, Mrs.
Destage
detective
DeTinc, Mr.
de Vinci, Leonard Edward
 Davies ("Skiddy")
Devlin
Devlin, Estelle (Mrs. John
 Devlin)
Dewitt, Marylyn
Deyo, Draycott
Deyo, Mrs.
Diamond Dick
Diamond, Margaret
Dicer, Christine
Dicer, Captain Edward
Dick
Dickey, Breck
Dickey, Diana
Dickey, Harry
Dickey, Mr. and Mrs.
Dignanni, Princess
Dillon, Jackson

Dillon, Mr. and Mrs.
 Warren
D'Invilliers, Thomas
 Parke
Diver, Dick
Diver, Lanier
Diver, Nicole Warren
Diver, the Reverend
Diver, Topsy
Divine, Babe
Divine, Rodney
Dixon, Leslie
doctor
doctor
Dodd, Martha
Dohmler, Doctor
Doldrum, Boscoe
Dollard, Professor
Dolores
Donald
Donilof
Donnelly, Pop
Donohue, Elsie
Donovan
Donovan, Margaret
Doolan, Catherine
Doolan, Kit
Doris
Dorrance, Sonny
Dorsey, George
Dorsey, Jobena
Dougall, Doctor
Douglas, Lieutenant
 Charles
Douglas, Clara
Douglas, Judge
Douglas, Lindy
Douglas, Mrs.
Douglas, Tommy
Dragonet, Amalie Eustace
 Bedford
Dragonet, Ben
Dragonet, Mrs. Ben
Drake, Fred
Drake, Jane
Drinkwater, Theodore
 (Ted)
Driscoll, William (Bill)
du Cary, Edith
du Cary, Noël
du Cary, René
Duckney, Angela
Dudley, Thorton Hart
Duke of Guyenne
Duke of Maine
Dulany, Tib
Dumphry, Royal
Dunn, Sir Humphrey
Dunning, Captain
Dureal, Officer Leon
Durfee, Doctor Howard
Earl
Earle, Helen
Early, General Jubal

Eckleburg, Doctor T. J.
Eddington, George
Edison, Edgar
Egan, Mr.
Elkins, Mrs. Arthur
 (Lilah)
Elkins, Ed
Ellinger, Mr.
Elliot, Emily
Emile
Emma
Emma Kate
Engels, Crenshaw
Engels, Mrs. Crenshaw
Engels, Mark
Eric
Este, Lord Charles
Estelle
Etherington, Sara
Evelyn
Everett, Tom
Ewing, Joe
Fairboalt, Mrs. Roger
Farnam, Ardita
Farnam, Mr.
Farrelly, Billy
fat man
Fay, Daisy
Fay, Ted
Fay, Teeny
Ferdie
Ferrenby, Jesse
Ferrenby, Mr.
Fiancé of Miss Hunter
Fielding, Cyrus
the Fiend
Filipino servant
Fingarson
the Finn
Finnegan
Fish, Joseph
fisherman
Fitzpatrick, Al
Flieshacker, Mort
Flint, Bill
Flowing Boots
Forney, Edward
Forrest, Mrs. Hugh
Forrester, Frank
fortune-teller
Fossile, Chief Justice
Fowler, John Jackson
Fowler, Mr.
Fragelle, Gen. Sir Evelyne
Fragelle, Lady
Fraser, Alfred J.
Freeman
Friar Brian
Frost, Charlotte
Frost, Horatio
Frost, Jerry (Jeremiah)
Frothington, Bill
Frothington, Mrs.
Frothington, Stella

Fulham, Mrs. Myra
Gallup, Doctor Roswell
Galt, Mr.
Garland, Dodson
Garneau, Mrs. Clifton
Garneau, Harold
Garneau, Noel
Garnett, Chauncey
Garovochi, Signor
Garrod, H. G.
Garvin
Gaspar, Sergeant
Gaspar, William ("Fat")
Gatsby, Jay
Gatz, Henry C.
Gatz, James (Jimmy)
Gausse
Gedney, Freddy
George
George
Gifford, Nancy Holmes
Gilbert, Catherine
Gilbert, Gloria
Gilbert, Russel
Gillespie, Howard
Girard, Cyrus
Girard, Lola
girl
girl
girl
Goebel, Eva
Golden, Mr.
Goldgreaves
Golding, T. F.
Golstein, Katie
Golstein, Thomas
Gonzoles, Tony
Gooddorf, Harry
the Goon
Gorman, Joe
Grady, Henry
Grainger, Arthur
Grainger, Merlin
Grainger, Olive Masters
Granby, Mr. and Mrs. Alec
Granby, John
Grandson
Grange, "Red"
Granny
Granville, Bonita
Green, Dexter
Gregorovious, Franz
Gregorovious, Kaethe
Gregory, Doctor
Gregory, Walter
Gregson
Gresham, John
Griebel, Louie
Griffin, Bob
Griffin, Mr.
Griselda
Guesculin
guest in room nineteen
Gunther, Amanda

Gunther, Bess
Gunther, Jean
Gunther, Mr.
Gunther, Mrs.
Gygsum
Haedge, Mr.
Hagerty, Peter
Haggin, Mr. and Mrs.
Haight, Marjorie
Haight, Mr.
Haines, Dolly
Haines, Morton
Halbird, June
Halbird, Mrs.
Halcyon, Cecilia
Halcyon, Helen
Halcyon, Mr.
Halcyon, Mrs.
Hale, Musidora
Halklite, Mr.
Hallam
Halliburton, Miss
Halloran
Halsey, Gretchen
Halsey, Maxy
Halsey, Roger
Hamil
Hamilton, John
Hammel, Lillian
Hammerton, Elsie
Hancock, Thornton
Hannaford, George
Hannaford, Kay Tompkins
Hannaman, Clara
Hannaman, Helen
Hannan, Carly
Hannan, Helen
Hannan, Walter
Hanson, Claud
Hanson, Mr.
Happer, Sally Carrol
Harker, Anthony
Harlan, Dolly
Harlan, Genevieve
Harlan, Madison
Harlan, Ronald
Harland, Alice
Harland, George
Harley, Ellen
Harman, Ned
Harmon, Dorothy
Harper, Billy
Harper, Myra
Harris, Ellen
Harris, Martin
Harris, Mary
Harris, Mike
Harrison, Doctor
Harrison, Edward
Harry
Hart, Charley
Hart, Mr.
Hart, Mr.
Harvey, Josephine

Harvey, Marjorie
Hatman, Mable
Hawkins, Mr. and Mrs.
Hazeldawn
Hearst
Hedrick, T. A.
Hélène
Hemmick, Henry W.
Hemple, Charles
Hemple, Chuck
Hemple, Luella
Henderson, Dick
Henderson, Ralph
Henderson, Mrs. T. R.
Henderson, T. R.
Hendrix, Amelia Weath-
 erby
Hendrix, Josephus
Herrick, Walter
Hesse, Mr.
Hibbing
Higgins, Sybil
Hilda
Hilliard, George
Hillis, Bill
Himmel, Peter
Hixson, Mrs.
Hobby, Pat
Hodge, Katherine
Hoffman, Phil
Holcome, Stuart
Holiday, Burne
Holiday, Kerry
Holliday, Mrs. Emily
Hollister, Dean
Holmes
Holt, Jerry
Holworthy, Jim
Hood, Gilly
Hopkins, Lieutenant
Hopkins, Mr.
Hopper, Joe
Hopper, Sally Carrol
Horton, George
Horton, Mrs.
Hosain
hotel manager
Howard
Howard
Howard
Howard, Miss
Howard, Mrs. Sigourney
Howland, Mr.
Hoyt, Rosemary
Hubbard, Spud
Hubbel, Mr.
Hubbel, Willard
Hudson, E. Brunswick
Hudson, Jewel
Hughes, Easton
Hugo
Hulda
Hull, Joe
Humbird, Dick

Hume, Charles
Hume, Dolores
Hunter, Anson
Hunter, Edna
Hunter, Miss
Hunter, Robert
"ickle durls"
Icky, Charles
Icky, Mr.
Icky, Ulsa
Indore, John Brown
 Hobby
Ireland, Louis
Irene
Irving, Gladys
Isabelle
Ives, George
Ives, Mrs.
Jaccy
Jackson, Ellery Hamil
Jackson, John
Jackson, Mary
Jackson, General Thomas
 Jonathan ("Stonewall")
Jacques (Jaques)
Jadwin, Philip
Jaggers, George
Janney, Butch
Janney, Forrest
Janney, Gene
Janney, Pinky
Janney, Rose
Jaques
Jaques, Leland
Jarvis
Jefferson (Jeff)
Jelke, Joe
Jerome, James
Jerry
Jerry
Jerryl, Rachael
Jesuit novice
Jewett, Doctor
Jimmy
Joe
Johns, William Delaney
 (Billy)
Johnson
Johnson, Earl
Johnson, Violet
Johnston, Hamilton T.
Johnston, Mrs.
Johnston, Mrs.
Jones, Catherine
Jones, Judy
Jones, Mr.
Jones, Mortimer
Jones, Rip (Oswald)
Jordan, Mr.
Jorgensen, Paula (Lady
 Paula Tressiger)
Jubal
Julia

Jumbo
Kagle, Miss Helen
Kahler
Kaluka
Kamp, Dr.
Kampf, William S. (Bill)
Kane, Muriel
Kapper, Lee
Karger, Dolly
Karr, Ede (Mrs. Alphonse
 Karr)
Kastler, Professor Benja-
 min (Ben)
Kastler, Carol
Kastler, Jean
Katie
Katzby, Martha
Katzby, Mrs. Poindexter
Kavenaugh
Kavenaugh, Howard
Kaye, Ella
Kearns, Doctor
Keatts, Lily
Keene, Doctor
Keith, Jean
Kelly
Kelly, Mr.
Kelly, Nelson
Kelly, Nicole
Kendall, George
Kendall, Mrs. George
Kenyon, Mary
Keogh, Nat
Key, Carrol
Key, George
Keyster, Doctor
Kieth
Killian, Cedric
Killian, Mrs. Cedric
Killian, Dorothy
Kilrain, Helen
Kimberly, Scott
Kincaid, Charley
King, Clara
King, George
King, Mrs. George
Kingsley, Mr.
Kinkallow, Marquis
 (Bopes)
Kinney, Joe
Klipspringer, Ewing
knight
Knighton, Pamela
Knowles, Bill
Knowleton, Dudley
Kresge, Jim
Kretching, Lieutenant
Kurman
La Borwits, Jaques
Lacy, Edward
Lacy, Mr. and Mrs.
Ladislau, Doctor
lady

Lafarge, Miss
Lahaye, Sidney
Lamar, Doctor
Lamar, Nancy
Lamarque
Lamb, Marion
Lamb, Nancy
Langueduc, "Slim"
Larned, Leticia
Larrabee, Ceci
Lascalles, Evylyn
Laurier, Anton
Lawrence, Mrs.
Leam, Max
Leaming, Elwood
Leanbaum
Lebaume, Beau
Lee, Alice Riley
Lee, Basil Duke
Lee, Margery
Lee, Lieutenant General
 Robert E.
Legendre, Mrs.
Legendre, Paula
Lei Chamoro, Ella
Lei Chamoro, Mister
Le Moyne, Littleboy
Leonard, James (Jim)
Le Poire
Le Poire, Becquette
Letgarde
Le Vigne, Carl
Libby, Malcolm
Lilymary
Lincoln, Sol
little girl
little girl
Livingstone, Warren
Llewellen, Frank
Lockhart, Andy
Lois
Long, Jimmy
Lorry, Annie
Lorry, Arthur
Lorry, Mabel Tollman
Louis II (Louis the Stam-
 merer)
Lovejoy, Evelyn
Lowrie, Jessie Piper
Lowrie, Lewis (Lew)
Lowrie, Tom
Lucienne
Lucille
Lucy
Luther
Lytell, Pete
MacDowell, Thomas J.
Macedon, Phil
Macy, Martin
Macy, Theron G.
Makova, Paul
Malone
man

the Man
Manfred, Jeff
Maplewood
Maranda, Mr.
Marbrooke, Eleanor
Marchbanks, Baron
Marcus, Harold
Marcus, Mr.
Margery, Nell
Margot
Margotson, Findle
Margotson, Mr.
Marion
Marjorie
Markey, Billy
Markey, Joe
Markey, Mrs. Joe
Marlowe, Axia
Marmora, Tino
Marquand, Mr. and Mrs.
Marsden, Cal
Marsden, Fifi
Marsden, Josephine
Marston, Choupette
Marston, Henry Clay
Martha
Martin, Caroline
Martin-Jones, Rags
Marvis, Julie
Marvis, Lois
Masters, Olive
Mather, Jaqueline
Mather, Jim
Matsko, James
Maude
Mavromichaelis
Mayburn, Helen
McBeth, Mr.
McCaffray
McCarthy, Gyp
McChesney, Bill
McChesney, Billy
McChesney, Emmy
 Pinkard
McClurg, Glenola
McComas, Henry
McComas, Honoria
McComas, Stella
McCracken, Miss
McCrary, Miss
McCutcheon, Mr.
McDowell
McGinniss, Officer
McGovern, Miss
McIlvaine, Bee
McIntyre
McIntyre, Warren
McKee, Chester
McKee, Lucille
McKenna, Mr.
McKibben, Mr.
McKisco, Albert
McKisco, Violet

McLane, Carter
McLane, Tommy
McRae, Mrs. Jenny
McTeague
McVitty, Mr.
Meadow, Marcia
Medill, Betty
Medill, Cyrus
Melon-Loper, Jan
Melon-Loper, Mrs. Jan
Melon-Loper, Jannekin
 (Janny)
Melon-Loper, Kaethe
Meloney, Jane
Meloney, Rose
Mercy, Olive
Meredith, Samuel
Meridien, Francois
Merriam, Constance Shaw
 and Eric
Merril, Mimi
Merritt, Ogden
Merriweather, Rosemary
Michael
Michaelis
Milbank, Hat
Milbank, Roxanne
Miles, Liddell and Cardine
Miller, Carl
Miller, Mrs. Carl
Miller, Rudolph
Minghetti, Conte di
 (Hosain)
Minghetti, Mary
Minghetti, Tony
Moncrief, General
Moncrief, Hildegarde
Monte
Moon, Charlie
Moon, Doctor
Moore, Albert
Moore, Carpenter
Moore, Charley
Moore, Doctor
Moore, Kathleen
Moreland, Colonel
Moreland, Toby
Morgan, Holly
Morris, Mr.
Morris, Von Cohn
Morrison, Hep J.
Mortmain, Ellen
Mortmain, Mrs.
Morton, Junie
Mother
Mother
Mridle
Muchhause
Mulkley, Oates
Muller, Mr.
Mulligan
Munn, Martin
Murdock, Evelyn

my friend
Myers, Gus
Nana
Napoleon, Prince
narrator
narrator
narrator
narrator
narrator
Narry
Nell
Nick
Nick
Nicotera
Noble, Maury
Nolak, Mr. and Mrs.
Nora
North, Abe
North, Mary
Norton, Doctor
Nosby, Claude
nurse
nurse
O'Connor, Helen
O'Flaherty, Sergeant
O'Flarity
O'Kane
O'Kelly, George
the Old Man
Old Wise One
Oldhorne, Helen Van
 Beck
Oldhorne, Stuart
Olive
Olson
Oral, Mrs.
Ormonde, Otis
Ormsby, Captain
O'Rourke, Jerry
O'Sullivan, Eddie
Otis
Owl Eyes
Packman, George
Page, Clara
Page, Howard
Palmer, Fats
Pan-e-troon
Paramore, Frederick E.
Parke
Parker, Froggy
Parkhurst, Perry
Parks, Allen
Parmelee, Eddie
Parrish, John Hardwick
Paskert
Patch, Adam J.
Patch, Adam Ulysses
Patch, Alicia Withers
Patch, Anthony Comstock
Patch, Gloria Gilbert
Patch, Henrietta Lebrune
Paterson, Director
Patt, Larry

Patton, Roger
Paul
Paul
Paulson, Charley
Paulson, Charlie
Paxton, Speed
Payson, Mr.
Pechard, Paul
Pepin, Mrs. George
Percy
Perrin
Perry, Constance
Perry, Mr. and Mrs.
 George (Herbert T.)
Perry, Josephine
Peter
Peters, Birdy
Peters, Elsie
Peters, Lincoln
Peters, Marion
Peters, Richard
Peterson, Jules
Petrocobesco, Prince
 Gabriel (Tutu)
Philippe
Pickman, Josephine
Pierce
Pierre
Pilgrim, Captain Doctor
Pilgrim, Josie
Pinkard, Emmy
Piper, Donald
Piper, Evylyn
Piper, Harold
Piper, Julie
Piper, Milton
Pirie, Dr.
Pitou
Plant, Donald
Poindexter, Mrs. Morton
 (Aunt Jo)
policeman
Popolous, Joe
Potter
Powell, Amanthis
Powell, Jim
Powell, Jim
Powers, Kenneth
preceptor
Preston, Kitty
Prince, Jenny
Pruit, Miss
Purley, Mae
Pushing, Mr.
Quarrles, Lorraine
Quill, Mr. Moonlight
Raffino
Ragland, Dick
Rahill
Raines, Marston
Raj, Sir Singram Dak
Ralston, Mrs.
Randall, Louie

Raudenbush, Miss
Ray, Mrs. Charles Wrot-
 ten
Ray, Esther
Ray, Tommy (Shorty)
Raycroft, Dorothy (Dot)
Raymond, Agnes
Raymond, Mr.
Raymond, Mrs.
Raymond, Robert Calvin
Reade
Real, Francisco
Real, Pardo Ciudad
Reardon, Mr.
Redfern, Major
Regan
Reilly, Benjamin
Reilly, Everett
Reilly, Grandfather
Reilly, Mrs.
Renaud
Rennard, Jules
Riccard, Lieutenant de
 Marine
Richard
Rickey
Ridingwood, Red
Rienmund, Joe
Riggs, Billy
Rikker, Alida
Rikker, Cathy Chase
Rikker, Chauncey
Rikker, Irene
Rikker, Teddy
Riply Buckner's aunt
Robbie, Martha
Robbins
Robbins, Stella
Robby
Robert the Frog
Robinson (Robby)
Robinson, Mr. and Mrs.
 Deering R.
Robinson, Mrs. George D.
Roderiguez, Mr.
Rogers, Alan
Rogers, Mrs. Orrin
Rombert
Rombert, George
Rombert, Mr. and Mrs.
 Thomas
Rooney, Mr.
Rooney, Mr.
Rose, Gus
Rosenthal, Rosy
Ross, Julia
Rostoff, Prince Paul Serge
 Boris
Rostoff, Princess
Rostoff, Prince Val
Rousseau, Miss
Rudd, Chinyman
Russel, Elaine

Ruth
Rutherford, Hamilton
Rutherford, Mr.
Ruthven, Mrs. Cassius
Ryder, Dawson
St. Claire, Mrs.
St. Claire, Myra
saleswoman
Sam
Sammy (Samuele Bendiri)
Sanderson, Carl
Sanderson, John (Jack)
Sandwood, Mr.
Sara (Marquise de la Guil-
 let de la Guìmpe) Mrs.
 Cedric Killian
Sarnemington, Blatchford
Sarolai, Count Chiki
Saunders, Miss
Saunders, Ridgeway
Savage, Eleanor
Savage, Phil
Savage, Ramilly
Schaeffer, Duncan
Schaeffer, Edna
Schaffer, May
Scharnhorst
Scheer, Gaston T.
Scheer, Minna
Scheerer, Irene
Scheerer, Mrs.
Schlach, Otto
Schmiel, Rosemary
Schoatze, George
Schoen, Lieutenant Earl
Schofield, Charley
Schofield, Jack
Schofield, Wister
Schroeder, Pete
Schuyler, Val
Schwartz, Father Adolphus
Schwartz, Fifi
Schwartz, John
Schwartz, Mrs.
Schwartze, Mannie
Second Story Salle
Sedgewick, Earl
"The Shadow"
Shaggy
Shalder, Howard
Shalder, Irene
Shaver, Harmon
the Shevlins
Shoonover, Joe
Shoonover, Mrs.
Shorty
Shugrue, Miss Willie
Shuttleworth, Edward
Sibly-Biers, Lady Caroline
Simmons, Rabbit
Simms, Lud
Sinclair, Rhoda
Singleton, Thea
Skiggs, Dr. Hepezia

Slagle
Sloane, Cary
Sloane, Fred
Sloane, Mr.
Slocum, Mr. and Mrs.
Smidy
Smith, Adrian
Smith, Edna
Smith, Eva
Smith, Mr.
Smith, Mr.
Smith, Mrs.
Smith, Priscilla
Snooks (Snukes)
Snyder, Becky
Soft Shoes
Speers, Mrs. Elsie
Spigot, Miss
Spillman, Mr.
Spirelli, Lieutenant
Squires, Tom
the squirt
Stacomb, Mr.
Stahr, Monroe
Standish, John
Stanley
Starheim, Lizzette
Stella
Sterrett, Gordon
Stinson, Eddie
Stirling, George
Stockton, Sylvester
Stoddard, G. Reese
Strain, Jim
Stuart, Charles David
Stubbs, Jack
Stutz-Mozart
Styles, Phyllis
Summer, John
Summer, Sarah Belknap
Swanson
Swanson, Johnny
Syneforth, Clara
Syneforth, Lieutenant Clay
 Harrington
Syneforth, Lieutenant
 Richard Harrington
 (Dick)
Syrel, John
Talbot, Harry
Tana (Tanalahaka)
Tantrum, Jemina
Tarbox, Horace
Tarbox, Marcia Hume
Tarbox, Marcia Meadow
Tarleton, Mr. and Mrs.
Taswell, Captain
Tate, Emily
Tate, Mr. and Mrs. Howard
Tate, Millicent
taxi driver
Taylor, Mr.
Taylor, Virginia
the Taylors

Tearle, Betty
Templeton, Brooks Fish
Templeton, Charles
 Martin
Templeton, Mercia
Templeton, V.
Terhune, Miss Grace
Terrell, Elaine
Thayer, Lowell
Thomas, Mrs.
Thorne, Vienna
Ticknor, Evangeline
Tipton, Terrence R.
Tolliver, Mary
Tom
Tomlinson, Tommy
Tompkins, George
Torrence, Elizabeth
Torrence, Margaret
Torrence, Raymond (Ray)
Townsend, Mr. and Mrs.
tramp
Treadway
Tressiger, Eric
Tressiger, Lady Paula
Trimble, Louis
Trombone Mose
Trouble (Glenola
 McClurg)
Tudy
Tulliver, Doctor William
 (Bill)
Tutu
Uncle Dun
Uncle Jim
undergraduate
Unger, John T.
Unger, Mr. and Mrs.
Utsonomia, Mr.
Van Beck, Betty
Van Beck, Helen
Van Beck, Theodore
 (Teddy)
Van Buren, George
Van Camp, Max
Van Dyke, Mike
Van Schaik, Paul B.
Van Schellinger, Gladys
Van Tyne, George
Van Vleck, Martin
Vandervere, Gordon
Varland, Joe
Velance, Peppy
Venske, Gus
Viking
Villefranche, Bertram de
Vizier
Wade, Marylyn
Waggoner, Dutch
Wainwright, Ward
Wales, Brick
Wales, Charles J. (Charlie)
Wales, Helen
Wales, Honoria

Wales, Miss
Walker, Stella
Wallis, Maria
Walmsley, Mirabel
Warburton
Ward, Chauncey
Warren, Beth Evan
 (Baby)
Warren, Charles
Warren, Devereux
 (Charles)
Warren, Nicole
Wash
Washington, Braddock
 Tarleton
Washington, Mrs. Brad-
 dock T.
Washington, Fitz-Norman
 Culpepper
Washington, Jasmine
Washington, Kismine
Washington, Percy
watchman
Watchman, Bill
Waterbury, Ernest
Waterbury, Judge
Wayne, Jill
Weatherbee, Percy B.
Weatherby, Mrs.
Weatherby, Sally
Weaver, Bette
Weicker, Mr.
Wendell, Peter Boyce
West, Jebby
Westgate
Wetherby, Cecile
Wetherby, Dickie
Wetherby, Peter
Whaley, Marice
Wharton, Elsie
Wharton, George
Wharton, Lucy
Wheelock, Mrs.
Wheelock, Doctor R. H.
 (Dick)
Whitby, Harry
White, Wylie
Whitney, Knowleton
Wiese, Charles
Wiess, Miss
Wilcox, René
Wilkinson, Dr. Harvey
William
Willings, Private
Wilson, Big Jack
Wilson, George
Wilson, Jim
Wilson, Myrtle
Winfield, George
Wing, Bessie Leighton
Winlock, Bomar
Winslow, Charlotte
Winslow, Eleanor
Winslow, Forrest

People

Ross, Cary
Rothstein, Arnold
Rumsey, Charles Cary
Ryan, Brigadier General
 J. A. (James Augustine)
Sayre, Anthony D., Jr.
Sayre, Anthony Dickinson
Sayre, Clothilde (Tilde)
 (Mrs. John Palmer)
Sayre, Daniel
Sayre, Marjorie (Mrs.
 Minor Williamson
 Brinson)
Sayre, Minnie Buckner
 Machen
Sayre, Musidora Morgan
Sayre, Rosalind ("Tootsie")
 (Mrs. Newman Smith)
Sayre, Zelda
Schulberg, Budd

Schulze, Katherine
Schurmeier, Gustave
 (Bobby)
Scribner II, Charles
Seldes, Gilbert Vivian
Selznick, David O.
Seymour, McNeil V.
Shank, Martha Marie
Shearer, Norma
Shenton, Edward
Shinn, Everett
Slocum, Dr. Clarence
Smith, Rosalind Sayre
Spengler, Oswald
Spiegel, Doris
Squires, Dr. Mildred Taylor
Starrett, Henrietta McCaig
Steele, Frederic Dorr
Stein, Gertrude
Stewart, Donald Ogden

Stivers, Harley Ennis
Stockton, Violet
Strater, Henry H. (Mike)
Stromberg, Hunt
Sturgis, Sam
Sturtevant, Ruth
Swanson, H. N.
Swope, Herbert Bayard
Tarkington, Booth
Taylor, Cecilia Delihant
Tepper, Saul
Thalberg, Irving Grant
Thurber, James
Tighe, Katherine
Turnbull, Andrew
Turnbull, Bayard and
 Margaret
Twain, Mark (Samuel
 Langhorne Clemens)
Van Vechten, Carl

Vidor, King
Wanger, Walter
Warner, Reuben
Warren, Charles Marquis
Washington, Richard
 (Tubby)
Wells, H. G.
Wende, Hamilton
Wescott, Glenway
West, Nathanael
Wharton, Edith
Wheeler, C. N. B.
Wheelock, John Hall
Wilde, Oscar
Wilder, Thornton
Williams, C. D. (Charles
 David)
Williams, Kitty
Wilson, Edmund ("Bunny")
Wolfe, Thomas

Places

Ambassador Hotel
Asheville, North
 Carolina
Astoria
Baltimore, Maryland
Beacon, New York
"Belly Acres"
Buffalo, New York
Cambridge Arms
Camp Boone
Camp Gordon
Camp Hooker
Camp Mills
Camp Sheridan
Camp Zachary Taylor
Cannes, France
Cap d'Antibes, France
Capri, Italy
Commodore Hotel
Craig House
Cuba
Dartmouth College
Dellwood, Minnesota
East Egg
Edgemoor, Delaware
"Ellerslie"

Encino, California
Europe
Fort Leavenworth, Kansas
Garden of Allah
Glion, Switzerland
Great Neck, Long Island,
 New York
Grove Park Inn
Gstaad, Switzerland
Hendersonville, North
 Carolina
Highland Hospital
Hollywood, California
Hotel de la Paix
Hotel des Princes
Hotel Rennert
Hotel Tiberio
Hyères, France
Italy
Johns Hopkins University
 Hospital
Juan-les-Pins, France
Lake Annecy, France
"La Paix"
Lausanne, Switzerland
London, England

Louisville, Kentucky
Malibu Beach, California
Malmaison Clinic
Marietta, New York
Montgomery, Alabama
New Orleans, Louisiana
New York City, New York
Newman School
North Africa
Nyon, Switzerland
Oak Hall Hotel
Paris, France
Phipps Clinic
Plage de la Garoupe
Plaza Hotel
Prangins Clinic
Princeton University
Ritz Bar
Riviera
Rockville, Maryland
Rodgers Forge, Maryland
Rome, Italy
St. Midas'
St. Paul Academy
St. Paul, Minnesota
St. Petersburg, Florida

St. Raphaël, France
St. Regis
Salies de Béarn
Sheppard-Pratt Hospital
Skyland Hotel
Summit Avenue
Switzerland
Syracuse, New York
Tarleton, Georgia
Tarmes
Towson, Maryland
Tryon, North Carolina
Valescure, France
Valley of Ashes
Val-Mont Clinic
Villa America
Villa Diana
Villa Fleur des Bois
Villa Marie
Villa Paquita
Villa St. Louis
West Egg
Westport, Connecticut
White Bear Yacht Club
Wilmington, Delaware

Publications and Organizations

A Book of Princeton Verse II
The American Mercury
College Humor
Collier's
Cosmopolitan
Cottage Club
Elizabethan Dramatic
 Club
Esquire

*F. Scott Fitzgerald Collection
 Notes*
F. Scott Fitzgerald
 Society
*Fitzgerald/Hemingway
 Annual*
Fitzgerald Newsletter
Hearst's International
Liberty

McCall's
Metropolitan Magazine
*The Nassau Literary
 Magazine*
The New Yorker
The Newman News
The Princeton Tiger
Redbook
The St. Paul Academy Now

and Then
*The Saturday Evening
 Post*
Scribner's Magazine
The Smart Set
Triangle Club
Vagabond Junior Players
Woman's Home Companion

Special Topics

Agents
Apprenticeship
Archives
Army
Bilphism
Biographical Studies
Bruccoli Collection
Centennial
Copyright
Correspondence
Critical Reputation

and Reception of
 Novels
Critical Studies
Critical Writings of Fitz-
 gerald
Earnings
Editing Fitzgerald's Texts
Elgin, Paul
Expatriates
Fitzgerald, Zelda—Writ-
 ings of

Home Page
Illustrations for Fitz-
 gerald's Magazine
 Stories
Jazz Age
Letters
Military Service of F. Scott
 Fitzgerald
Movies
Playwright, Fitzgerald as
Poetry

Princeton University
 Library
Revival of Fitzgerald's Liter-
 ary Reputation
Screenwriter, Fitzgerald as
Scribners
Short Story Writer, Fitzger-
 ald as
Trust, Frances Scott Fitzger-
 ald Smith
Unpublished Stories

Titles

"Absolution"
"The Adjuster"
"The Adolescent Marriage"
"Afternoon of an Author"
Afternoon of an Author
"Air Raid"
"An Alcoholic Case"
"Aldous Huxley's 'Crome
 Yellow' "
All the Sad Young Men
"The Ants at Princeton"
*The Apprentice Fiction of F.
 Scott Fitzgerald 1909–1917*
Assorted Spirits
"At Your Age"
"Auction—Model 1934"
"The Author's Apology"
"Author's House"
"An Author's Mother"
"Babes in Wonderland"
"Babes in the Woods"
"The Baby Party"
"Babylon Revisited"
"Ballet Shoes"
"The Baltimore Anti-
 Christ"
"Basil and Cleopatra"
*The Basil and Josephine
 Stories*
The Beautiful and Damned
"Benediction"
"Bernice Bobs Her Hair"
"Between Three and Four"
Bits of Paradise
*The Bodley Head Scott
 Fitzgerald*
" 'Boil Some Water—Lots
 of It' "
"A Book of One's Own"
"The Bowl"
"The Boy Who Killed His
 Mother"
"Breakfast"
"The Bridal Party"
"The Broadcast We Almost
 Heard Last September"
"Brooklyn Bridge"

*Cambridge Edition of the
 Works of F. Scott
 Fitzgerald*
"The Camel's Back"
"The Cameo Frame"
"The Captured Shadow"
The Captured Shadow
"Cedric the Stoker (The
 True Story of the Battle
 of the Baltic)"
"Censorship or Not"
"A Change of Class"
"The Changing Beauty of
 Park Avenue"
"A Cheer for Princeton"
"City Dusk"
"Confessions"
"The Continental Angle"
"Cosmopolitan"
"The Count of Darkness"
"A Couple of Nuts"
Coward
"The Crack-Up"
The Crack-Up
"Crazy Sunday"
"The Credo of F. Scott
 Fitzgerald"
"The Cruise of the Rolling
 Junk"
"The Curious Case of
 Benjamin Button"
"The Cut-Glass Bowl"
"Dalyrimple Goes Wrong"
"The Dance"
"Dearly Beloved"
"The Death of My Father"
"A Debt of Honor"
"The Debutante"
"The Defeat of Art"
"Design in Plaster"
"Diagnosis"
"The Diamond as Big as
 the Ritz"
"Diamond Dick and the
 First Law of Woman"
"The Diary of a Sopho-
 more"

"Dice, Brass Knuckles &
 Guitar"
"Director's Special"
"A Dirge (Apologies to
 Wordsworth)"
"Discard"
"Does a Moment of Revolt
 Come Sometime to
 Every Married Man?"
"Does a Moment of Revolt
 Come Sometime to
 Every Married Man?"
"Early Success"
"Echoes of the Jazz Age"
"Emotional Bankruptcy"
"The End of Hate"
"Eulogy on the Flapper"
The Evil Eye
*F. Scott Fitzgerald In His
 Own Time: A Miscellany*
*F. Scott Fitzgerald: Inscrip-
 tions*
"F. Scott Fitzgerald Is
 Bored by Efforts at
 Realism in 'Lit' "
*F. Scott Fitzgerald Manu-
 scripts*
*F. Scott Fitzgerald on Author-
 ship*
*F. Scott Fitzgerald's Ledger: A
 Facsimile*
*F. Scott Fitzgerald's Preface to
 This Side of Paradise*
*F. Scott Fitzgerald's St. Paul
 Plays, 1911–1914*
"The Family Bus"
"Family in the Wind"
"The Far-Seeing Skeptics"
"Fate in Her Hands"
"The Feather Fan"
Fie! Fie! Fi-Fi!
"The Fiend"
"Financing Finnegan"
"First Blood"
Flappers and Philosophers
"Flight and Pursuit"
" 'Football' "

"For Sheilah, a Beloved
 Infidel"
"Forging Ahead"
"The Four Fists"
"A Freeze-Out"
"The Freshest Boy"
"Friend Husband's Latest"
"A Full Life"
"Fun in an Artist's Studio"
The Girl from Lazy J
"The Girl the Prince
 Liked"
"The Girl With Talent"
"Girls Believe in Girls"
"Gods of Darkness"
Gone With the Wind
"Gracie at Sea"
The Great Gatsby
"Gretchen's Forty Winks"
Grit
"The Guest in Room
 Nineteen"
"Handle with Care"
"He Thinks He's
 Wonderful"
"Head and Shoulders"
"Her Last Case"
"The High Cost of Maca-
 roni"
"His Russet Witch"
"Homage to the
 Victorians"
"The Homes of the Stars"
"The Honor of the Goon"
"Hot & Cold Blood"
"The Hotel Child"
"How I Would Sell My
 Book If I Were a Book-
 seller"
"How to Live on Practi-
 cally Nothing a Year"
"How to Live on $36,000 a
 Year"
"How to Waste Material A
 Note on My Genera-
 tion"
" 'I Didn't Get Over' "

"I Got Shoes"
"The Ice Palace"
"Image on the Heart"
"Imagination—and a Few Mothers"
"In the Darkest Hour"
"In the Holidays"
"In Literary New York"
"Indecision"
"Infidelity"
"Inside the House"
"Institutional Humanitarianism"
"An Interview with F. Scott Fitzgerald"
"The Intimate Strangers"
"Jacob's Ladder"
"The Jelly-Bean"
"Jemina A Story of the Blue Ridge Mountains By John Phlox, Jr."
"John Jackson's Arcady"
John Jackson's Arcady
"The Kingdom in the Dark"
"Lamp in a Window"
"Last Kiss"
"The Last of the Belles"
The Last Tycoon
"The Lees of Happiness"
"Let's Go Out and Play"
Life Begins at Eight-Thirty
"Lipstick"
"Lives of the Dancers"
"Lo, the Poor Peacock!"
"The Long Way Out"
"Looking Back Eight Years"
"The Lost Decade"
"The Love Boat"
"Love in the Night"
The Love of the Last Tycoon: A Western
"A Luckless Santa Claus"
Madame Curie
"Magnetism"
"Majesty"
"Make Yourself at Home"
"A Man in the Way"
"Marching Streets"
" 'Margey Wins the Game' "
Marie Antoinette
"Martin's Thoughts"
"May Day"
"Mightier Than the Sword"
"A Millionaire's Girl"
"Minnesota's Capital in the Role of Main Street"
"Miss Ella"
"Mr. Icky The Quintessence of Quaintness in One Act"

"More Than Just a House"
"The Most Disgraceful Thing I Ever Did"
"My First Love"
"My Generation"
"My Lost City"
"My Old New England Homestead on the Erie"
"My Ten Favorite Plays"
"Myra Meets His Family"
"The Mystery of the Raymond Mortgage"
"A New Leaf"
"New Types"
"News of Paris—Fifteen Years Ago"
"A Nice Quiet Place"
"A Night at the Fair"
"The Night before Chancellorsville"
"No Flowers"
"No Harm Trying"
"Not in the Guidebook"
The Notebooks of F. Scott Fitzgerald
" 'O Russet Witch!' "
"Obit on Parnassus"
"The Offshore Pirate"
"On a Play Twice Seen"
"On an Ocean Wave"
"On Schedule"
"On the Trail of Pat Hobby"
"On Your Own"
"One Hundred False Starts"
"One Interne"
"One of My Oldest Friends"
"One Trip Abroad"
"Open That Door"
"The Ordeal"
"The Original Follies Girl"
"Other Names for Roses"
"Our American Poets"
"Our April Letter"
"Our Next Issue"
"Our Own Movie Queen"
"Our Young Rich Boys"
"Outside the Cabinet-Maker's"
"Pain and the Scientist"
"Paint and Powder"
"The Passionate Eskimo"
"Pasting It Together"
"Pat Hobby and Orson Welles"
"Pat Hobby Does His Bit"
"Pat Hobby, Putative Father"
The Pat Hobby Stories
"Pat Hobby's Christmas Wish"

"Pat Hobby's College Days"
"Pat Hobby's Preview"
"Pat Hobby's Secret"
"A Patriotic Short"
"A Penny Spent"
"The Perfect Life"
"The Pierian Springs and the Last Straw"
Poems 1911–1940
"Poor Old Marriage"
"Poor Working Girl"
"The Pope at Confession"
"The Popular Girl"
"Porcelain and Pink (A One-Act Play)"
The Portable F. Scott Fitzgerald
"Precaution Primarily"
"Presumption"
The Price Was High
"The Prince of Pests A Story of the War"
"Princeton"
"Princeton—The Last Day"
Public letter to Thomas Boyd
"The Pusher-in-the-Face"
Raffles
"Rags Martin-Jones and the Pr-nce of W-les"
"Rain before Dawn"
"Reade, Substitute Right Half"
Red-Headed Woman
"Reminiscences of Donald Stewart"
"Reunion at the Fair"
Review of *The Celt and the World* by Shane Leslie
Review of *David Blaize* by E. F. Benson
Review of *God, The Invisible King* by H. G. Wells
Review of *Penrod and Sam* by Booth Tarkington
Review of *Verses in Peace and War* by Shane Leslie
"The Rich Boy"
"Ring"
The Romantic Egoists
"The Room with the Green Blinds"
"The Rough Crossing"
"The Rubber Check"
"A Rugged Novel"
Safety First
The St. Paul Daily Dirge
"Salesmanship in the Champs-Élysées"
Save Me the Waltz
"The Scandal Detectives"

Scandalabra
"Self-Interview"
" 'Send Me In, Coach' "
" 'The Sensible Thing' "
"Sentiment—And the Use of Rouge"
"Shadow Laurels"
"Shaggy's Morning"
"Sherwood Anderson on the Marriage Question"
"A Short Autobiography (With Acknowledgments to Nathan)"
"A Short Trip Home"
" 'Show Mr. and Mrs. F. to Number——' "
"Six of One—"
"Sleep of a University"
"Sleeping and Waking"
"The Smilers"
"A Snobbish Story"
"Some Interrupted Lines to Sheilah"
"Southern Girl"
"The Spire and the Gargoyle"
"The Staying Up All Night"
The Stories of F. Scott Fitzgerald
"Strange Sanctuary"
"The Swimmers"
Tales of the Jazz Age
Taps at Reveille
"Tarkington's 'Gentle Julia' "
"Tarquin of Cheepside"
"Teamed with Genius"
"10 Best Books I Have Read"
"Ten Years in the Advertising Business"
Tender Is the Night
"That Kind of Party"
"The Third Casket"
"This Is a Magazine"
This Side of Paradise
Thoughtbook of Francis Scott Key Fitzgerald
"Thousand-and-First Ship"
"Three Acts of Music"
"Three Cities"
Three Comrades
"Three Hours Between Planes"
"Three Soldiers"
"To a Beloved Infidel"
"To My Unused Greek Book (*Acknowledgments to Keats*)"
"Too Cute for Words"
"The Trail of the Duke"

"Trans-Continental Kitty"
" 'Trouble' "
The True Story of Appo-mattox
"Turkey Remains"
"Two for a Cent"
"Two Old-Timers"
"Two Wrongs"
"Under Fire"
"The Unspeakable Egg"
"The Usual Thing by Robert W. Shameless"

"The Vanished Girl"
The Vegetable
" 'Wait Till You Have Children of Your Own!' "
"The Way of Purgation"
"What Became of the Flappers?"
"What Becomes of Our Flappers and Sheiks?"
"What a Handsome Pair!"
"What I Think and Feel at Twenty-Five"

"What I Was Advised To Do—And Didn't"
"What Kind of Husbands Do 'Jimmies' Make?"
"Who Can Fall in Love After Thirty?"
"Who's Who—and Why"
" 'Why Blame It on the Poor Kiss . . .' "
Winter Carnival
"Winter Dreams"

"The Woman from Twenty-One"
"A Woman with a Past"
The Women
"The World's Fair"
A Yank at Oxford
"Your Way and Mine"
Zelda Fitzgerald: The Collected Writings
"Zelda Fitzgerald's Tribute to F. Scott Fitzgerald"
"Zone of Accident"

F. SCOTT FITZGERALD'S PUBLICATIONS

Books

This chronological list omits privately printed pamphlets and keepsakes which were not for sale.

Fie! Fie! Fi-Fi! Cincinnati, New York & London: The John Church Co., 1914. Seventeen song lyrics.

The Evil Eye. Cincinnati, New York & London: The John Church Co., 1915. Seventeen song lyrics.

Safety First. Cincinnati, New York & London: The John Church Co., 1916. Twenty-one song lyrics.

This Side of Paradise. New York: Scribners, 1920; London: Collins, 1921. Novel.

Flappers and Philosophers. New York: Scribners, 1920; London: Collins, 1922. Stories.

The Beautiful and Damned. New York: Scribners, 1922; London: Collins, 1922. Novel.

Tales of the Jazz Age. New York: Scribners, 1922; London: Collins, 1923. Stories.

The Vegetable. New York: Scribners, 1923. Play.

The Great Gatsby. New York: Scribners, 1925; London: Chatto & Windus, 1926. Novel.

All the Sad Young Men. New York: Scribners, 1926. Stories.

John Jackson's Arcady, arranged for public reading by Lilian Holmes Strack. Boston: Baker, 1928. Story.

Tender Is the Night. New York: Scribners, 1934; London: Chatto & Windus, 1934. *Tender Is the Night,* "With the Author's Final Revisions." Ed. with intro. by Malcolm Cowley. New York: Scribners, 1951; London: Grey Walls, 1953. Novel.

Taps at Reveille. New York: Scribners, 1935. Stories.

The Last Tycoon. Ed. with intro by Edmund Wilson. New York: Scribners, 1941; London: Grey Walls, 1949. Unfinished novel. With *The Great Gatsby* and 5 stories.

The Crack-Up. Ed. with intro. by Edmund Wilson. New York: New Directions, 1945; Harmondsworth, U.K.: Penguin, 1965. Essays, selections from the Notebooks, and letters.

The Stories of F. Scott Fitzgerald. Ed. with intro. by Malcolm Cowley. New York: Scribners, 1951.

Afternoon of an Author. Ed. with intro. by Arthur Mizener. Princeton, N.J.: Princeton University Library, 1957; New York: Scribners, 1958; London: Bodley Head, 1958. Stories and essays.

The Pat Hobby Stories. Ed. with intro. by Arnold Gingrich. New York: Scribners, 1962; Harmondsworth, U.K.: Penguin, 1967.

The Apprentice Fiction of F. Scott Fitzgerald, 1909–1917. Ed. with intro. by John Kuehl. New Brunswick, N.J.: Rutgers University Press, 1965.

Dearly Beloved. Iowa City, Iowa: Windhover Press, 1970. Story.

F. Scott Fitzgerald In His Own Time: A Miscellany. Ed. with intro. by Matthew J. Bruccoli and Jackson R. Bryer. Kent, Ohio: Kent State University Press, 1971.

Three Hours Between Planes. Agincourt, Ontario: The Book Society of Canada Limited, 1970. Story.

The Basil and Josephine Stories. Ed. with intro. by Jackson R. Bryer and John Kuehl. New York: Scribners, 1973.

Bits of Paradise. Selected by Scottie Fitzgerald Smith and Matthew J. Bruccoli, with foreword by Smith and preface by Bruccoli. London: Bodley Head, 1973; New York: Scribners, 1974. Stories by Fitzgerald and 10 stories by Zelda Fitzgerald.

F. Scott Fitzgerald's Preface to This Side of Paradise. Ed. John R. Hopkins. Iowa City, Iowa: Windhover Press/Bruccoli Clark, 1975.

The Cruise of the Rolling Junk. Intro. by Matthew J. Bruccoli. Bloomfield Hills, Mich. & Columbia, S.C.: Bruccoli Clark, 1976. Three travel articles.

F. Scott Fitzgerald's Screenplay for Three Comrades by Erich Maria Remarque. Ed. with afterword by Matthew J. Bruccoli. Carbondale & Edwardsville, Ill.: Southern Illinois University Press, 1978.

F. Scott Fitzgerald's St. Paul Plays, 1911–1914. Ed. with intro. by Alan Margolies. Princeton, N.J.: Princeton University Library, 1978.

The Price Was High. Ed. with intro. by Matthew J. Bruccoli. New York & London: Harcourt Brace Jovanovich/Bruccoli Clark, 1979; London: Quartet, 1979. Stories.

Poems 1911–1940. Ed. Matthew J. Bruccoli; intro. by James Dickey. Bloomfield Hills, Mich. & Columbia, S.C.: Bruccoli Clark, 1981.

Babylon Revisited: The Screenplay. Intro. by Budd Schulberg. New York: Carroll & Graf, 1993.

Letters, Diaries, Notebooks

The Letters of F. Scott Fitzgerald. Ed. with intro. by Andrew Turnbull. New York: Scribners, 1963; London: Bodley Head, 1964.

Thoughtbook of Francis Scott Key Fitzgerald. Intro. by John Kuehl. Princeton, N.J.: Princeton University Library, 1965.

Dear Scott/Dear Max: The Fitzgerald-Perkins Correspondence. Ed. with intro. by John Kuehl and Jackson R. Bryer. New York: Scribners, 1971; London: Cassell, 1973.

As Ever, Scott Fitz—. Ed. with intro. by Matthew J. Bruccoli and Jennifer M. Atkinson, with foreword by Scottie Fitzgerald Smith. Philadelphia & New York: J. B. Lippincott, 1972; London: Woburn, 1973. The Fitzgerald/Harold Ober correspondence.

F. Scott Fitzgerald's Ledger: A Facsimile. Intro. by Matthew J. Bruccoli. Washington: NCR Microcard Books/ Bruccoli Clark, 1973.

The Notebooks of F. Scott Fitzgerald. Ed. with intro. by Matthew J. Bruccoli. New York & London: Harcourt Brace Jovanovich/Bruccoli Clark, 1978.

Correspondence of F. Scott Fitzgerald. Ed. with intro. by Matthew J. Bruccoli and Margaret M. Duggan, with Susan Walker. New York: Random House, 1980.

F. Scott Fitzgerald: A Life in Letters. Ed. with intro. by Matthew J. Bruccoli, with Judith S. Baughman. New York: Scribners, 1994.

Editions and Collections

The Portable F. Scott Fitzgerald. Ed. Dorothy Parker; intro. by John O'Hara. New York: Viking, 1945.

The Bodley Head Scott Fitzgerald, 6 vols. London: Bodley Head, 1958–1963.

The Stories of F. Scott Fitzgerald, 5 vols. Harmondsworth, U.K.: Penguin, 1962–1968.

F. Scott Fitzgerald on Writing. Ed. Larry W. Phillips. New York: Scribners, 1985.

The Short Stories of F. Scott Fitzgerald. Ed. with preface by Matthew J. Bruccoli. New York: Scribners, 1989; London: Scribners, 1991.

The Cambridge Edition of the Works of F. Scott Fitzgerald. Cambridge: Cambridge University Press, 1991– . *The Great Gatsby,* ed. with intro. by Matthew J. Bruccoli, 1991; *The Love of the Last Tycoon: A Western,* ed. with intro. by Bruccoli, 1993; *This Side of Paradise,* ed. with intro. by James L. W. West III, 1995.

Tender Is the Night. Ed. Matthew J. Bruccoli. London: Samuel Johnson, 1995. Facsimile of Bruccoli's emended copy of the first printing.

Tender Is the Night, Centennial Edition. Ed. with intro. and notes by Matthew J. Bruccoli. London: Everyman, 1996.

F. Scott Fitzgerald on Authorship. Ed. Matthew J. Bruccoli, with Judith S. Baughman. Columbia: University of South Carolina Press, 1996.

F. Scott Fitzgerald: The Jazz Age. Intro. by E. L. Doctorow. New York: New Directions, 1996.

Facsimiles

The Great Gatsby: A Facsimile of the Manuscript. Ed. with intro. by Matthew J. Bruccoli. Washington: Bruccoli Clark/NCR Microcard Books, 1973.

F. Scott Fitzgerald: Inscriptions. Columbia, S.C.: Matthew J. Bruccoli, 1988.

F. Scott Fitzgerald Manuscripts. Ed. Matthew J. Bruccoli. New York & London: Garland, 1990–1991. 18 vols: *This Side of Paradise, The Beautiful and Damned, The Great Gatsby* galleys, *Tender Is the Night, The Last Tycoon, The Vegetable,* Stories, and Articles.

Fie! Fie! Fi-Fi! Intro. by Matthew J. Bruccoli. Columbia: University of South Carolina Press for the Thomas Cooper Library, 1996. Music score and previously unpublished acting script.

Stories and Plays

Entries provide first periodical appearance and first publication in a Fitzgerald collection.

"The Mystery of the Raymond Mortgage," *The St. Paul Academy Now and Then,* 2 (October 1909), 4–8; *Apprentice Fiction.*

"Reade, Substitute Right Half," *The St. Paul Academy Now and Then,* 2 (February 1910), 10–11; *Apprentice Fiction.*

"A Debt of Honor," *The St. Paul Academy Now and Then,* 2 (March 1910), 9–11; *Apprentice Fiction.*

"The Room with the Green Blinds," *The St. Paul Academy Now and Then,* 3 (June 1911), 6–9; *Apprentice Fiction.*

"A Luckless Santa Claus," *The Newman News,* 9 (Christmas 1912), 1–7; *Apprentice Fiction.*

"Pain and the Scientist," *The Newman News* (1913), 5–10; *Apprentice Fiction.*

"The Trail of the Duke," *The Newman News,* 9 (June 1913), 5–9; *Apprentice Fiction.*

"Shadow Laurels," *The Nassau Literary Magazine,* 71 (April 1915), 1–10; *Apprentice Fiction.*

"The Ordeal," *The Nassau Literary Magazine,* 71 (June 1915), 153–159; *Apprentice Fiction.*

"The Debutante," *The Nassau Literary Magazine,* 72 (January 1917), 241–252; *The Smart Set,* 60 (November 1919), 85–96; *Apprentice Fiction.*

"The Spire and the Gargoyle," *The Nassau Literary Magazine,* 72 (February 1917), 297–307; *Apprentice Fiction.*

"Tarquin of Cheepside," *The Nassau Literary Magazine*, 73 (April 1917), 13–18; *Apprentice Fiction*. Revised and expanded as "Tarquin of Cheapside," *The Smart Set*, 64 (February 1921), 43–46; *TJA*.

"Babes in the Woods," *The Nassau Literary Magazine*, 73 (May 1917), 55–64; *The Smart Set*, 60 (September 1919), 67–71; *Apprentice Fiction*.

"Sentiment—And the Use of Rouge," *The Nassau Literary Magazine*, 73 (June 1917), 107–123; *Apprentice Fiction*.

"The Pierian Springs and the Last Straw," *The Nassau Literary Magazine*, 73 (October 1917), 173–185; *Apprentice Fiction*.

"Porcelain and Pink (A One-Act Play)," *The Smart Set*, 61 (January 1920), 77–85; *TJA*.

"Benediction," *The Smart Set*, 61 (February 1920), 35–44; *F&P*.

"Dalyrimple Goes Wrong," *The Smart Set*, 61 (February 1920), 107–116; *F&P*.

"Head and Shoulders," *The Saturday Evening Post*, 192 (February 21, 1920), 16–17, 81–82, 85–86; *F&P*.

"Mister Icky The Quintessence of Quaintness in One Act," *The Smart Set*, 61 (March 1920), 93–98; *TJA*.

"Myra Meets His Family," *The Saturday Evening Post*, 192 (March 20, 1920), 40, 42, 44, 46, 49–50, 53; *Price*.

"The Camel's Back," *The Saturday Evening Post*, 192 (April 24, 1920), 16–17, 157, 161, 165; *TJA*.

"The Cut-Glass Bowl," *Scribner's Magazine*, 67 (May 1920), 582–592; *F&P*.

"Bernice Bobs Her Hair," *The Saturday Evening Post*, 192 (May 1, 1920), 14–15, 159, 163, 167; *F&P*.

"The Ice Palace," *The Saturday Evening Post*, 192 (May 22, 1920), 18–19, 163, 167, 170; *F&P*.

"The Offshore Pirate," *The Saturday Evening Post*, 192 (May 29, 1920), 10–11, 99, 101–102, 106, 109; *F&P*.

"The Four Fists," *Scribner's Magazine*, 67 (June 1920), 669–680; *F&P*.

"The Smilers," *The Smart Set*, 62 (June 1920), 107–111; *Price*.

"May Day," *The Smart Set*, 62 (July 1920), 3–32; *TJA*.

"The Jelly-Bean," *Metropolitan Magazine*, 52 (October 1920), 15–16, 63–67; *TJA*.

"The Lees of Happiness," *Chicago Sunday Tribune* (December 12, 1920), Blue Ribbon Fiction Section, 1, 3, 7; *TJA*.

"His Russet Witch," *Metropolitan Magazine*, 53 (February 1921), 11–13, 46–51; in *TJA* as " 'O Russet Witch!' "

"The Far-seeing Skeptics," *The Smart Set*, 67 (February 1922), 48.

"The Popular Girl," *The Saturday Evening Post*, 194 (February 11 & 18, 1922), 3–5, 82, 84, 86, 89; 18–19, 105–106, 109–110; *Bits*.

"Two for a Cent," *Metropolitan Magazine*, 55 (April 1922), 23–26, 93–95; *Price*.

"The Curious Case of Benjamin Button," *Collier's*, 69 (May 27, 1922), 5–6, 22–28; *TJA*.

"The Diamond as Big as the Ritz," *The Smart Set*, 68 (June 1922), 5–29; *TJA*.

"Winter Dreams," *Metropolitan Magazine*, 56 (December 1922), 11–15, 98, 100–102, 104–107; *ASYM*.

"Dice, Brass Knuckles & Guitar," *Hearst's International*, 43 (May 1923), 8–13, 145–149; *Price*.

"Hot & Cold Blood," *Hearst's International*, 64 (August 1923), 80–84, 150–151; *ASYM*.

"Gretchen's Forty Winks," *The Saturday Evening Post*, 196 (March 15, 1924), 14–15, 128, 130, 132; *ASYM*.

"Diamond Dick and the First Law of Woman," *Hearst's International*, 45 (April 1924), 58–63, 134, 136; *Price*.

"The Third Casket," *The Saturday Evening Post*, 196 (May 31, 1924), 8–9, 78; *Price*.

"Absolution," *The American Mercury*, 2 (June 1924), 141–149; *ASYM*.

"Rags Martin-Jones and the Pr-nce of W-les," *McCall's*, 51 (July 1924), 6–7, 32, 48, 50; *ASYM*.

" 'The Sensible Thing,' " *Liberty*, 1 (July 5, 1924), 10–14; *ASYM*.

"The Unspeakable Egg," *The Saturday Evening Post*, 197 (July 12, 1924), 12–13, 125–126, 129; *Price*.

"John Jackson's Arcady," *The Saturday Evening Post*, 197 (July 26, 1924), 8–9, 100, 102, 105; *Price*.

"The Baby Party," *Hearst's International*, 47 (February 1925), 32–37; *ASYM*.

"The Pusher-in-the-Face," *Woman's Home Companion*, 52 (February 1925), 27–28, 143–144; *Price*.

"Love in the Night," *The Saturday Evening Post*, 197 (March 14, 1925), 18–19, 68, 70; *Bits*.

"One of My Oldest Friends," *Woman's Home Companion*, 52 (September 1925), 7–8, 120, 122; *Price*.

"The Adjuster," *Redbook*, 45 (September 1925), 47–51, 144–148; *ASYM*.

"A Penny Spent," *The Saturday Evening Post*, 198 (October 10, 1925), 8–9, 160, 164, 166; *Bits*.

"Not in the Guidebook," *Woman's Home Companion*, 52 (November 1925), 9–11, 135–136; *Price*.

"The Rich Boy," *Redbook*, 46 (January & February 1926), 27–32, 144, 146; 75–79, 122, 124–126; *ASYM*.

"Presumption," *The Saturday Evening Post*, 198 (January 9, 1926), 3–5, 226, 228–229, 233–234; *Price*.

"The Adolescent Marriage," *The Saturday Evening Post*, 198 (March 6, 1926), 6–7, 229–230, 233–234; *Price*.

"The Dance," *Redbook*, 47 (June 1926), 39–43, 134, 136, 138; *Bits*.

"Your Way and Mine," *Woman's Home Companion*, 54 (May 1927), 7–8, 61, 64, 67, 68; *Price*.

"Jacob's Ladder," *The Saturday Evening Post*, 200 (August 20, 1927), 3–5, 57–58, 63–64; *Bits*.

"The Love Boat," *The Saturday Evening Post*, 200 (October 8, 1927), 8–9, 134, 139, 141; *Price*.

"A Short Trip Home," *The Saturday Evening Post*, 200 (December 17, 1927), 6–7, 55, 57–58; *TAR*.

"The Bowl," *The Saturday Evening Post*, 200 (January 21, 1928), 6–7, 93–94, 97, 100; *Price*.

"Magnetism," *The Saturday Evening Post*, 200 (March 3, 1928), 5–7, 74, 76, 78; *Stories*.

"The Scandal Detectives," *The Saturday Evening Post*, 200 (April 28, 1928), 3–4, 178, 181–182, 185; *TAR; B&J*.

"A Night at the Fair," *The Saturday Evening Post*, 201 (July 21, 1928), 8–9, 129–130, 133; *B&J*.

"The Freshest Boy," *The Saturday Evening Post*, 201 (July 28, 1928), 6–7, 68, 70, 73; *TAR; B&J*.

"He Thinks He's Wonderful," *The Saturday Evening Post*, 201 (September 29, 1928), 6–7, 117–118, 121; *TAR; B&J*.

"Outside the Cabinet-Maker's," *Century Magazine*, 117 (December 1928), 241–244.

"The Captured Shadow," *The Saturday Evening Post*, 201 (December 29, 1928), 12–13, 48, 51; *TAR; B&J*.

"The Perfect Life," *The Saturday Evening Post*, 201 (January 5, 1929), 8–9, 113, 115, 118; *TAR; B&J*.

"The Last of the Belles," *The Saturday Evening Post*, 201 (March 2, 1929), 18–19, 75, 78; *TAR*.

"Forging Ahead," *The Saturday Evening Post*, 201 (March 30, 1929), 12–13, 101, 105; *B&J*.

"Basil and Cleopatra," *The Saturday Evening Post*, 201 (April 27, 1929), 14–15, 166, 170, 173; *AOAA; B&J*.

"The Rough Crossing," *The Saturday Evening Post*, 201 (June 8, 1929), 12–13, 66, 70, 75; *Stories*.

"Majesty," *The Saturday Evening Post*, 202 (July 13, 1929), 6–7, 57–58, 61–62; *TAR*.

"At Your Age," *The Saturday Evening Post*, 202 (August 17, 1929), 6–7, 79–80; *Price*.

"The Swimmers," *The Saturday Evening Post*, 202 (October 19, 1929), 12–13, 150, 152, 154; *Bits*.

"Two Wrongs," *The Saturday Evening Post*, 202 (January 18, 1930), 8–9, 107, 109, 113; *TAR*.

"First Blood," *The Saturday Evening Post*, 202 (April 5, 1930), 8–9, 81, 84; *TAR; B&J*.

"A Nice Quiet Place," *The Saturday Evening Post*, 202 (May 31, 1930), 8–9, 96, 101, 103; *TAR; B&J*.

"The Bridal Party," *The Saturday Evening Post*, 203 (August 9, 1930), 10–11, 109–110, 112, 114; *Stories*.

"A Woman with a Past," *The Saturday Evening Post*, 203 (September 6, 1930), 8–9, 133–134, 137; *TAR; B&J*.

"One Trip Abroad," *The Saturday Evening Post*, 203 (October 11, 1930), 6–7, 48, 51, 53–54, 56; *AOAA*.

"A Snobbish Story," *The Saturday Evening Post*, 203 (November 29, 1930), 6–7, 36, 38, 40, 42; *B&J*.

"The Hotel Child," *The Saturday Evening Post*, 203 (January 31, 1931), 8–9, 69, 72, 75; *Bits*.

"Babylon Revisited," *The Saturday Evening Post*, 203 (February 21, 1931), 3–5, 82–84; *TAR*.

"Indecision," *The Saturday Evening Post*, 203 (May 16, 1931), 12–13, 56, 59, 62; *Price*.

"A New Leaf," *The Saturday Evening Post*, 204 (July 4, 1931), 12–13, 90–91; *Bits*.

"Emotional Bankruptcy," *The Saturday Evening Post*, 204 (August 15, 1931), 8–9, 60, 65; *B&J*.

"Between Three and Four," *The Saturday Evening Post*, 204 (September 5, 1931), 8–9, 69, 72; *Price*.

"A Change of Class," *The Saturday Evening Post*, 204 (September 26, 1931), 6–7, 37–38, 41; *Price*.

"A Freeze-Out," *The Saturday Evening Post*, 204 (December 19, 1931), 6–7, 84–85, 88–89; *Price*.

"Six of One—," *Redbook*, 58 (February 1932), 22–25, 84, 86, 88; *Price*.

"Diagnosis," *The Saturday Evening Post*, 204 (February 20, 1932), 18–19, 90, 92; *Price*.

"Flight and Pursuit," *The Saturday Evening Post*, 204 (May 14, 1932), 16–17, 53, 57; *Price*.

"Family in the Wind," *The Saturday Evening Post*, 204 (June 4, 1932), 3–5, 71–73; *TAR*.

"The Rubber Check," *The Saturday Evening Post*, 205 (August 6, 1932), 6–7, 41–42, 44–45; *Price*.

"What a Handsome Pair!" *The Saturday Evening Post*, 205 (August 27, 1932), 16–17, 61, 63–64; *Price*.

"Crazy Sunday," *The American Mercury*, 27 (October 1932), 209–220; *TAR*.

"One Interne," *The Saturday Evening Post*, 205 (November 5, 1932), 6–7, 86, 88–90; *TAR*.

"On Schedule," *The Saturday Evening Post*, 205 (March 18, 1933), 16, 17, 71, 74, 77, 79; *Price*.

"More Than Just a House," *The Saturday Evening Post*, 205 (June 24, 1933), 8–9, 27, 30, 34; *Price*.

"I Got Shoes," *The Saturday Evening Post*, 206 (September 23, 1933), 14–15, 56, 58; *Price*.

"The Family Bus," *The Saturday Evening Post*, 206 (November 4, 1933), 8–9, 57, 61–62, 65–66; *Price*.

"No Flowers," *The Saturday Evening Post*, 207 (July 21, 1934), 10–11, 57–58, 60; *Price*.

"New Types," *The Saturday Evening Post*, 207 (September 22, 1934), 16–17, 74, 76, 78–79, 81; *Price*.

"In the Darkest Hour," *Redbook*, 63 (October 1934), 15–19, 94–98; *Price*.

"Her Last Case," *The Saturday Evening Post*, 207 (November 3, 1934), 10–11, 59, 61–62, 64; *Price*.

"The Fiend," *Esquire*, 3 (January 1935), 23, 173–174; *TAR*.

"The Night before Chancellorsville," *Esquire*, 3 (February 1935), 24, 165; *TAR*.

"Shaggy's Morning," *Esquire*, 3 (May 1935), 26, 160.

"The Count of Darkness," *Redbook*, 65 (June 1935), 20–23, 68, 70, 72.

"The Intimate Strangers," *McCall's*, 62 (June 1935), 12–14, 36, 38, 40, 42, 44; *Price*.

"The Passionate Eskimo," *Liberty*, 12 (June 8, 1935), 10–14, 17–18.

"Zone of Accident," *The Saturday Evening Post*, 208 (July 13, 1935), 8–9, 47, 49, 51–52; *Price*.

"The Kingdom in the Dark," *Redbook*, 65 (August 1935), 58–62, 64, 66–68.

"Fate in Her Hands," *American Magazine,* 121 (April 1936), 56–59, 168–172; *Price.*

"Image on the Heart," *McCall's,* 63 (April 1936), 7–9, 52, 54, 57–58, 62; *Price.*

"Too Cute for Words," *The Saturday Evening Post,* 208 (April 18, 1936), 16–18, 87, 90, 93; *Price.*

"Three Acts of Music," *Esquire,* 5 (May 1936), 39, 210; *Price.*

"The Ants at Princeton," *Esquire,* 5 (June 1936), 35, 201.

"Inside the House," *The Saturday Evening Post,* 208 (June 13, 1936), 18–19, 32, 34, 36; *Price.*

"An Author's Mother," *Esquire,* 6 (September 1936), 36; *Price.*

" 'I Didn't Get Over,' " *Esquire,* 6 (October 1936), 45, 194–195; *AOAA.*

" 'Send Me In, Coach,' " *Esquire,* 6 (November 1936), 55, 218–221.

"An Alcoholic Case," *Esquire,* 6 [7] (February 1937), 32, 109; *Stories.*

" 'Trouble,' " *The Saturday Evening Post,* 209 (March 6, 1937), 14–15, 81, 84, 86, 88–89; *Price.*

"The Honor of the Goon," *Esquire,* 7 (June 1937), 53, 216.

"The Long Way Out," *Esquire,* 8 (September 1937), 45, 193; *Stories.*

"The Guest in Room Nineteen," *Esquire,* 8 (October 1937), 56, 209; *Price.*

"In the Holidays," *Esquire,* 8 (December 1937), 82, 184, 186; *Price.*

"Financing Finnegan," *Esquire,* 9 (January 1938), 41, 180, 182, 184; *Stories.*

"Design in Plaster," *Esquire,* 12 (November 1939), 51, 169; *AOAA.*

"The Lost Decade," *Esquire,* 12 (December 1939), 113, 228; *Stories.*

"Strange Sanctuary," *Liberty,* 16 (December 9, 1939), 15–20.

"Pat Hobby's Christmas Wish," *Esquire,* 13 (January 1940), 45, 170–172; *PH.*

"A Man in the Way," *Esquire,* 13 (February 1940), 40, 109; *PH.*

" 'Boil Some Water—Lots of It,' " *Esquire,* 13 (March 1940), 30, 145, 147; *PH.*

"Teamed with Genius," *Esquire,* 13 (April 1940), 44, 195–197; *PH.*

"Pat Hobby and Orson Welles," *Esquire,* 13 (May 1940), 38, 198–199; *PH.*

"Pat Hobby's Secret," *Esquire,* 13 (June 1940), 30, 107; *PH.*

"The End of Hate," *Collier's,* 105 (June 22, 1940), 9–10, 63–64; *Price.*

"Pat Hobby, Putative Father," *Esquire,* 14 (July 1940), 36, 172–174; *PH.*

"The Homes of the Stars," *Esquire,* 14 (August 1940), 28, 120–121; *PH.*

"Pat Hobby Does His Bit," *Esquire,* 14 (September 1940), 41, 104; *PH.*

"Pat Hobby's Preview," *Esquire,* 14 (October 1940), 30, 118, 120; *PH.*

"No Harm Trying," *Esquire,* 14 (November 1940), 30, 151–153; *PH.*

"A Patriotic Short," *Esquire,* 14 (December 1940), 62, 269; *PH.*

"On the Trail of Pat Hobby," *Esquire,* 15 (January 1941), 35, 126; *PH.*

"Fun in an Artist's Studio," *Esquire,* 15 (February 1941), 64, 112; *PH.*

Elgin, Paul [pseud.]. "On an Ocean Wave," *Esquire,* 15 (February 1941), 59, 141; *Price.*

"Two Old-Timers," *Esquire,* 15 (March 1941), 53, 143; *PH.*

"Mightier Than the Sword," *Esquire,* 15 (April 1941), 36, 183; *PH.*

"Pat Hobby's College Days," *Esquire,* 15 (May 1941), 55, 168–169; *PH.*

"The Woman from Twenty-One," *Esquire,* 15 (June 1941), 29, 164; *Price.*

"Three Hours Between Planes," *Esquire,* 16 (July 1941), 41, 138–139; *Stories.*

"Gods of Darkness," *Redbook,* 78 (November 1941), 30–33, 88–91.

"The Broadcast We Almost Heard Last September," *Furioso,* 3 (Fall 1947), 8–10.

"News of Paris—Fifteen Years Ago," *Furioso,* 3 (Winter 1947), 5–10; *AOAA.*

"Discard," *Harper's Bazaar,* 82 (January 1948), 103, 143–144, 146, 148–149; *Price.*

"The World's Fair," *The Kenyon Review,* 10 (Autumn 1948), 567–568.

"Last Kiss," *Collier's,* 123 (April 16, 1949), 16–17, 34, 38, 41, 43–44; *Bits.*

"That Kind of Party," *The Princeton University Library Chronicle,* 12 (Summer 1951), 167–180; *B&J.*

"Dearly Beloved," *Fitzgerald/Hemingway Annual* (1969), pp. 1–3; *Bits.*

"Lo, the Poor Peacock!" *Esquire,* 76 (September 1971), 154–158; *Price.*

"On Your Own," *Esquire,* 91 (January 30, 1979), 55–67; *Price.*

"A Full Life," *The Princeton University Library Chronicle,* 49 (Winter 1988), 167–172.

Articles and Essays

Entries provide first periodical appearance and first publication in a Fitzgerald collection.

"S.P.A. Men in College Athletics," *The St. Paul Academy Now and Then,* 3 (December 1910), 7.

Untitled news feature about school election, *The New-man News* (1912), 18.

Untitled news feature about school dance, *The Newman News* (1913), 18.

"Who's Who—and Why," *The Saturday Evening Post*, 193 (September 18, 1920), 42, 61; *AOAA.*

"Three Cities," *Brentano's Book Chat*, 1 (September–October 1921), 15, 28; *In His Own Time.*

"What I Think and Feel at Twenty-Five," *American Magazine*, 94 (September 1922), 16, 17, 136–140; *In His Own Time.*

"How I Would Sell My Book If I Were a Bookseller," *Bookseller and Stationer*, 18 (January 15, 1923), 8; *In His Own Time.*

"10 Best Books I Have Read," *Jersey City Evening Journal* (April 24, 1923), 9.

"Imagination—and a Few Mothers," *Ladies' Home Journal*, 40 (June 1923), 21, 80–81.

"The Cruise of the Rolling Junk," *Motor*, 41 (February, March, April 1924), 24–25, 58, 62, 64, 66; 42–43, 58, 72, 74, 76; 40–41, 58, 66, 68, 70.

" 'Why Blame It on the Poor Kiss If the Girl Veteran of Many Petting Parties Is Prone to Affairs After Marriage?' " *New York American*, (February 24, 1924), LII-3; *In His Own Time.*

"Does a Moment of Revolt Come Sometime to Every Married Man?" *McCall's*, 51 (March 1924), 21, 36; *In His Own Time.*

"What Kind of Husbands Do 'Jimmies' Make?" *Baltimore American*, (March 30, 1924), ME-7; *In His Own Time.*

"How to Live on $36,000 a Year," *The Saturday Evening Post*, 196 (April 5, 1924), 22, 94, 97; *AOAA.*

" 'Wait Till You Have Children of Your Own!' " *Woman's Home Companion*, 51 (July 1924), 13, 105; *In His Own Time.*

"How to Live on Practically Nothing a Year," *The Saturday Evening Post*, 197 (September 20, 1924), 17, 165–166, 169–170; *AOAA.*

"Our Young Rich Boys," *McCall's*, 53 (October 1925), 12, 42, 69; *In His Own Time.*

"How to Waste Material A Note on My Generation," *The Bookman*, 63 (May 1926), 262–265; *AOAA.*

"Princeton," *College Humor*, 13 (December 1927), 28–29, 130–131; *AOAA.*

"Ten Years in the Advertising Business," *The Princeton Alumni Weekly*, 29 (February 22, 1929), 585; *AOAA.*

"A Short Autobiography (With Acknowledgments to Nathan)," *The New Yorker*, 5 (May 25, 1929), 22–23; *In His Own Time.*

"Girls Believe in Girls," *Liberty*, 7 (February 8, 1930), 22–24; *In His Own Time.*

"Echoes of the Jazz Age," *Scribner's Magazine*, 90 (November 1931), 459–465; *CU.*

"One Hundred False Starts," *The Saturday Evening Post*, 205 (March 4, 1933), 13, 65–66; *AOAA.*

"Ring," *The New Republic*, 76 (October 11, 1933), 254–255; *CU.*

"My Ten Favorite Plays," *New York Sun* (September 10, 1934), 19; *FSF on Authorship.*

"Introduction," *The Great Gatsby*. New York: Modern Library, 1934; *In His Own Time.*

"Sleeping and Waking," *Esquire*, 2 (December 1934), 34, 159–160; *CU.*

"The Crack-Up," *Esquire*, 5 (February 1936), 41, 164; *CU.*

"Pasting It Together," *Esquire*, 5 (March 1936), 35, 182–183; *CU.*

"Handle with Care," *Esquire*, 5 (April 1936), 39, 202; *CU.*

"Author's House," *Esquire*, 6 (July 1936), 40, 108; *AOAA.*

"Afternoon of an Author," *Esquire*, 6 (August 1936), 35, 170; *AOAA.*

"Early Success," *American Cavalcade*, 1 (October 1937), 74–79; *CU.*

"Foreword," *Colonial and Historical Homes of Maryland*, by Don Swann. Baltimore: Etchcrafters Art Guild, 1939; *In His Own Time.*

"The High Cost of Macaroni," *Interim*, 4, nos. 1–2, (1954), 6–15.

"My Generation," *Esquire*, 70 (October 1968), 119, 121, 123; *Profile of F. Scott Fitzgerald.*

Prose Parody and Humor

Entries provide first periodical appearance and first publication in a Fitzgerald collection. All items in this section, except those marked with a dagger, are collected in *FSF In His Own Time*. Items marked with an asterisk are not bylined and are attributed to Fitzgerald on the basis of other evidence.

*Untitled humor article, beginning "There was once a second group student . . . ," *The Princeton Tiger*, 25 (December 1914), 5.

*"How They Head the Chapters," *The Princeton Tiger*, 26 (September 1915), 10.

*"The Conquest of America (as some writers would have it)," *The Princeton Tiger*, 26 (Thanksgiving 1915), 6.

†*"Three Days at Yale," *The Princeton Tiger*, 26 (December 1915), 8–10.

*"Our Next Issue," *The Nassau Literary Magazine*, 72 (December 1916), unpaged.

*"Jemina A Story of the Blue Ridge Mountains by John Phlox, Jr.," *The Nassau Literary Magazine*, 72 (December 1916), 210–215; *Vanity Fair*, 15 (January 1921), 44; *TJA.*

*"The Usual Thing by Robert W. Shameless," *The Nassau Literary Magazine*, 72 (December 1916), 223–228.

*"Little Minnie McCloskey A Story for Girls," *The Princeton Tiger*, 27 (December 1, 1916), 6–7.

*"A Litany of Slang," *The Princeton Tiger*, 27 (December 18, 1916), 7.

*" 'Triangle Scenery by Bakst,' " *The Princeton Tiger*, 27 (December 18, 1916), 7.

*"Futuristic Impressions of the Editorial Boards," *The Princeton Tiger*, 27 (December 18, 1916), 7.

*" 'A glass of beer kills him,' " *The Princeton Tiger*, 27 (December 18, 1916), 7.

*Untitled joke, beginning " 'When you find a man doing a little more . . . ,' " *The Princeton Tiger*, 27 (December 18, 1916), 7.

*"Things That Never Change! Number 3333," *The Princeton Tiger*, 27 (December 18, 1916), 7.

*"The Old Frontiersman: A Story of the Frontier," *The Princeton Tiger*, 27 (December 18, 1916), 11.

*Untitled joke, beginning "Boy Kills Self Rather Than Pet . . . ," *The Princeton Tiger*, 27 (February 3, 1917), 12.

*"Things That Never Change. No. 3982," *The Princeton Tiger*, 27 (February 3, 1917), 12.

"Precaution Primarily," *The Princeton Tiger*, 27 (February 3, 1917), 13–14.

*"A Few Well-Known Club Types And Their Futures," *The Princeton Tiger*, 27 (March 17, 1917), 7.

*Untitled joke, beginning "McCaulay Mission—Water Street . . . ," *The Princeton Tiger*, 27 (March 17, 1917), 10.

"The Diary of a Sophomore," *The Princeton Tiger*, 27 (March 17, 1917), 11.

*"True Democracy," *The Princeton Tiger*, 27 (March 17, 1917), 18.

"Kenilworth Socialism," *The Princeton Tiger*, 27 (March 17, 1917), 22.

"The Prince of Pests A Story of the War," *The Princeton Tiger*, 27 (April 28, 1917), 7.

*Untitled joke, beginning " 'These rifles *** will probably not be used . . . ,' " *The Princeton Tiger*, 27 (April 28, 1917), 8.

*Untitled joke, beginning " 'It is assumed that the absence of submarines . . . ,' " *The Princeton Tiger*, 27 (April 28, 1917), 8.

*Untitled joke, beginning "Yale's swimming team will take its maiden plunge to-night," *The Princeton Tiger*, 27 (April 28, 1917), 8.

†"Somewhere in France," *The Princeton Tiger*, 28 (June 15, 1917), front cover.

†"The Dream and the Awakening," *The Princeton Tiger*, 28 (June 15, 1917), 16.

"The Staying Up All Night," *The Princeton Tiger*, 28 (November 10, 1917), 6.

*"Intercollegiate Petting-Cues," *The Princeton Tiger*, 28 (November 10, 1917), 8.

"Cedric the Stoker (The True Story of the Battle of the Baltic)," *The Princeton Tiger*, 28 (November 10, 1917), 12.

"This Is a Magazine," *Vanity Fair*, 15 (December 1920), 71.

"Reminiscences of Donald Stewart by F. Scott Fitzgerald (in the Manner of)," *St. Paul Daily News* (December 11, 1921), City Life Section, 6.

†"Some Stories They Like to Tell Again," *New York Herald* (April 8, 1923), magazine section, 11.

"The Most Disgraceful Thing I Ever Did: 2. The Invasion of the Sanctuary," *Vanity Fair*, 21 (October 1923), 53.

†"My Old New England Homestead on the Erie," *College Humor*, 6 (August 1925), 18–19.

"Salesmanship in the Champs-Élysées," *The New Yorker*, 5 (February 15, 1930), 20.

"The True Story of Appomattox," privately printed (1934).

"A Book of One's Own," *The New Yorker*, 13 (August 21, 1937), 19.

Verse

All verse listed here (except the last item) is collected in *Poems 1911–1940;* items for which no other publication is specified appeared for the first time in *Poems 1911–1914.* Items marked with an asterisk are not bylined and are attributed to Fitzgerald on the basis of other evidence.

" 'Football,' " *The Newman News*, 9 (Christmas 1911?), 19.

*"May Small Talk," *The Princeton Tiger*, 26 (June 1915), 10.

"A Cheer for Princeton," in "Mass Meeting To-Night To Practice New Song," *The Daily Princetonian* (October 28, 1915), 1.

*"Yais," *The Princeton Tiger*, 27 (June 1916), 13.

"To My Unused Greek Book (*Acknowledgments to Keats*)," *The Nassau Literary Magazine*, 72 (June 1916), 137.

*"One from Penn's Neck," *The Princeton Tiger*, 27 (December 18, 1916), 7.

*Untitled: "Oui, le backfield est from Paris . . . ," *The Princeton Tiger*, 27 (December 18, 1916), 7.

"Rain Before Dawn," *The Nassau Literary Magazine*, 72 (February 1917), 321.

*"Popular Parodies—No. 1," *The Princeton Tiger*, 27 (March 17, 1917), 10.

*"Undulations of an Undergraduate," *The Princeton Tiger*, 27 (March 17, 1917), 20.

*Untitled: "Ethel had her shot of brandy . . . ," *The Princeton Tiger*, 27 (April 28, 1917), 8.

"Princeton—The Last Day," *The Nassau Literary Magazine*, 73 (May 1917), 95.

"On a Play Twice Seen," *The Nassau Literary Magazine*, 73 (June 1917), 149.

"The Cameo Frame," *The Nassau Literary Magazine*, 73 (October 1917), 169–172.

"Our American Poets," *The Princeton Tiger*, 28 (November 10, 1917), 11.

"City Dusk," *The Nassau Literary Magazine*, 73 (April 1918), 315.

"My First Love," *The Nassau Literary Magazine*, 74 (February 1919), 102.

"Marching Streets," *The Nassau Literary Magazine*, 74 (February 1919), 103–104.

"The Pope at Confession," *The Nassau Literary Magazine*, 74 (February 1919), 105.

"We keep you clean in Muscatine," 1919, in Michel Mok, "The Other Side of Paradise," *New York Post* (September 25, 1936), p. 15.

"A Dirge (Apologies to Wordsworth)," *Judge*, 77 (December 20, 1919), 30.

Untitled: "Marylyn and Sall*ee* . . . ," *TSOP*.

Untitled: "So the gray car crept . . . ," *TSOP*.

"In a Lecture-Room," *TSOP*.

Untitled: "Victorians, Victorians, who never learned to weep . . . ," *TSOP*.

Untitled: "Songs in the time of order . . . ," *TSOP*.

Untitled: "We leave to-night . . . ," *TSOP*.

"Boston Bards and Hearst Reviewers," *TSOP*.

Untitled: "The February streets . . . ," *TSOP*.

Untitled: "When Vanity kissed Vanity . . . ," *TSOP*.

"A Poem That Eleanor Sent Amory Several Years Later," *TSOP*.

"A Poem Amory Sent to Eleanor and Which He Called 'Summer Storm,' " *TSOP*.

Untitled: "A fathom deep in sleep I lie . . . ," *TSOP*.

Untitled: "Carrots and peas . . . ," "The Offshore Pirate," *The Saturday Evening Post* (May 29, 1920).

Untitled: "Oh down— . . . ," "The Offshore Pirate," *The Saturday Evening Post* (May 29, 1920).

"Sleep of a University," *The Nassau Literary Magazine*, 76 (November 1920), 161.

"To Anne," in Peggy Mitchell, "Novelist Loved Atlanta Girl's Picture," *Atlanta Journal* (September 30, 1923), 5.

Untitled: "For the lands of the village triumph . . . ," in Peggy Mitchell, "Novelist Loved Atlanta Girl's Picture," *Atlanta Journal* (September 30, 1923), 5.

Untitled: "Then wear the gold hat, if that will move her . . . ," *GG*.

Untitled: "We sing not soft, we sing not loud . . . ," "The Captured Shadow," *The Saturday Evening Post* (December 29, 1928).

Untitled: "Oh—oh—oh—oh . . . ," *TITN*.

"Lamp in a Window," *The New Yorker*, 11 (March 23, 1935), 18.

"Obit on Parnassus," *The New Yorker*, 13 (June 5, 1937), 27.

"A Blues," *Notebooks*.

"Answer to a Poem," *Notebooks*.

"Apology to Ogden Nash," *Notebooks*.

Untitled: "The barber's too slick . . . ," *Notebooks*.

"Beg You to Listen," *Notebooks*.

"Clay Feet," *Notebooks*; early text included in June 10, 1917 letter to Cecelia Delihant Taylor, *Letters*, pp. 413–414.

Untitled: "Colors has she in her soul . . . ," *Notebooks*.

Untitled: "Come in! Come in! . . . ," *Notebooks*.

"Counter Song to the 'Undertaker,' " *Notebooks*.

Untitled: "Don't you worry I surrender . . . ," *Notebooks*.

"The Earth Calls," *Notebooks*.

Untitled: "Everytime I blow my nose I think of you . . . ," *Notebooks*.

Untitled: "First a hug and tease and a something on my knees . . . ," *Notebooks*.

"For a Long Illness," *Notebooks*.

Untitled: "For Song—Idea—," *Notebooks*.

Untitled: "For the time that our man spent in pressing your suit . . . ," *Notebooks*.

Untitled: "A god intoxicated fly . . . ," *Notebooks*.

"Half-and-Half Girl," *Notebooks*.

Untitled: "Hooray . . . ," *Notebooks*.

"Hortense—To a Cast-Off Lover," *Notebooks*; variant text titled "On a Certain Man" included with June 10, 1917 letter to Cecelia Delihant Taylor, *Letters*, p. 413.

Untitled: "I don't need a bit assistance . . . ," *Notebooks*.

Untitled: "If Hoover came out for the N.R.A. . . . ," *Notebooks*.

Untitled: "If you have a little Jew . . . ," *Notebooks*.

Untitled: "I hate their guts . . . ," *Notebooks*.

Untitled: "In a dear little vine-covered cottage . . . ," *Notebooks*; unauthorized publication as "The Boy Who Killed His Mother," *Neurotica*, 9 (Winter 1952), 38–39.

Untitled: "Keep the Watch! . . . ," *Notebooks*.

Untitled: "Life's too short to . . . ," *Notebooks*.

Untitled: "Listen to the hoop la . . . ," *Notebooks*.

Untitled: "Little by little . . . ," *Notebooks*.

Untitled: "Mr. Berlin wrote a song about forgetting to remember . . . ," *Notebooks*.

Untitled: "Mother taught me to—love things . . . ," *Notebooks*.

Untitled: "Now is the time for all good men to come to the aid of the party . . . ," *Notebooks*.

"Oh, Sister, Can You Spare Your Heart," *Notebooks*; *As Ever, Scott Fitz—*, pp. 196–198.

Untitled: "Oh where are the boys of the boom-boom-boom . . . ," *Notebooks*.

"One Southern Girl," *Notebooks*.

"Our April Letter," *Notebooks*.

"Pilgrimage," *Notebooks*.

Untitled: "Pretty Boy Floyd . . . ," *Notebooks*.

"Prizefighter's Wife," *Notebooks*.

"Refrain for a Poem. How to Get to So and So," *Notebooks.*

"Sad Catastrophe," *Notebooks.*

Untitled: "Scott Fitzgerald so they say . . . ," *Notebooks.*

Untitled: "She lay supine among her Pekinese . . . ," *Notebooks.*

"Song," *Notebooks.*

"Song—," *Notebooks.*

"A Song Number Idea," *Notebooks.*

Untitled: " 'Sticking along.' The voice so faint sometimes I could scarcely hear it . . . ," *Notebooks.*

"Thousand-and-First Ship," *Notebooks.*

"To Carter, a Friendly Finger," *Notebooks.*

Untitled: "Touchdown song based on . . . ," *Notebooks.*

Untitled: "Truth and—consequences . . . ," *Notebooks.*

Untitled: "You'll be reckless if you . . . ," *Notebooks.*

Untitled: "You'll never know . . . ," *Notebooks.*

Untitled: "You've driven me crazy . . . ," *Notebooks.*

"Martin's Thoughts," *Fitzgerald Newsletter* (Spring 1961), p. 53.

Untitled: "My mind is all a-tumble . . . ," from a letter to Elizabeth Clarkson, c. September 15, 1913. Facsimiled in Lloyd Hackl, "Fitzgerald in St. Paul," *Fitzgerald/Hemingway Annual* (1976), p. 119.

"On My Ragtime Family Tree."

Untitled: "My Very Very Dear Marie . . . ," letter to Marie Hersey. Facsimiled in *The Romantic Egoists,* p. 25.

"For Dolly."

"A Letter to Helen."

Untitled: "Ruth . . . ," letter to Ruth Sturtevant, c. February 1916. Roger Lewis, "Ruth Sturtevant and F. Scott Fitzgerald (1916–1921)," *Fitzgerald/Hemingway Annual* (1979), p. 9.

Untitled: "There was a young lady named Ruth . . . ," from a letter to Ruth Sturtevant, c. fall 1916. Roger Lewis, "Ruth Sturtevant and F. Scott Fitzgerald (1916–1921)," *Fitzgerald/Hemingway Annual* (1979), p. 9.

"When We Meet Again." Variant text included in June 10, 1917 letter to Cecelia Delihant Taylor, *Letters,* pp. 411–412; shorter version included in *TSOP.*

"Ellerslie," June 1917.

Untitled: "Ah May, Shall I splatter my thoughts in the air . . . ," c. 1918.

"1st Epistle of St. Scott to the Smithsonian," from a letter to Alida Bigelow, September 1919, *Letters,* p. 456.

"To the Ring Lardners," c. December 1927. *The Romantic Egoists,* p. 157.

"[Dog! Dog! Dog!]," c. 1924. Edmund Wilson, *The Twenties* (New York: Farrar, Straus & Giroux, 1975), pp. 222–223.

Untitled: "Of wonders is Silas M. Hanson the champ . . . ," postmarked June 26, 1925. Facsimiled in Paul C. Richards Catalogue 46.

Untitled: "There was a young man of Quebec . . . ," to Scottie Fitzgerald, January 25, 1928. Facsimiled in *The Romantic Egoists,* p. 159.

Untitled: "All the girls and mans. . . ." Herbert Gorman, "Glimpses of F. Scott Fitzgerald," *Fitzgerald/Hemingway Annual* (1973), p. 115.

Untitled: "Orange pajamas and heaven's guitars . . . ," to Carmel Myers, 1931.

Untitled: " 'Oh papa— . . . ,' " c. 1932. Helen Hayes and Lewis Funke, *A Gift of Joy* (New York: Evans, 1965), p. 193.

Untitled: "DON'T EXPECT ME . . . ," telegram to Mrs. Paul T. (Elizabeth Beckwith) Mackie, July 28, 1933.

"Momishness."

Untitled: "East of the sun, west of the moon . . . ," from January 16, 1935 letter to Brooks Bowman. *Fitzgerald/Hemingway Annual* (1974), p. 10.

"For 2nd Stanza Baoth Poem." Arthur Mizener, *The Far Side of Paradise,* p. 299.

"Because," 1935.

Untitled: "Oh Misseldine's, dear Misseldine's. . . ." Andrew Turnbull, *Scott Fitzgerald,* p. 284.

"Spring Song." Variant text in *Notebooks* as "To Carter and Marion."

"Lines on Reading Through an Autograph Album." Carmel Myers, "Scott and Zelda," *Park East* (May 1951), pp. 277–278.

Untitled: "Valentine was a Saint. . . ." R. L. Samsell, "Hollywood—It Wasn't All That Bad," *Fitzgerald/Hemingway Annual* (1969), p. 18.

Untitled: "SING HOTCH-CHA SING HEY-HI NINNY. . . ."

"Some Interrupted Lines to Sheilah." Facsimiled on the rear endpaper of Sheilah Graham and Gerold Frank, *Beloved Infidel* (New York: Holt, 1958).

Untitled: "This book tells that Anita Loos. . . ." Facsimiled in Anita Loos, *A Cast of Thousands* (New York: Grosset & Dunlap, 1977), p. 129.

"For Mary's Eighth Birthday," 1938. Helen Hayes and Lewis Funke, *A Gift of Joy* (New York: Evans, 1965), pp. 194–195.

"Les Absents Ont Toujours Tort." First five lines published in Sheilah Graham, *The Rest of the Story* (New York: Coward-McCann, 1964), p. 16.

"To a Beloved Infidel." Fair-copy manuscript titled "For Shielah, a Beloved Infidel" facsimiled on front endpapers of Sheilah Graham and Gerold Frank, *Beloved Infidel* (New York: Holt, 1958).

"The Big Academy Dinner." Sheilah Graham, *College of One* (New York: Viking, 1967), p. 139.

"Lest We Forget." Partial text published in Sheilah Graham and Gerold Frank, *Beloved Infidel* (New York: Holt, 1958), pp. 312–314.

Untitled: "From Scott Fitzgerald . . . ," inscription in *GG,* 1939. Lawrence D. Stewart, "Scott Fitzgerald D'Invilliers," *American Literature,* 29 (May 1957), 212.

Untitled: "Frances Kroll . . . ," inscription in *TAR*. Frances Kroll Ring and R. L. Samsell, "Sisyphus in Hollywood," *Fitzgerald/Hemingway Annual* (1973), p. 102.

"On Watching the Candidates in the Newsreels."

Untitled: "Now your heart is come so near. . . ."

"[Vowels]." Sheilah Graham, *College of One* (New York: Viking, 1967), pp. 108–109.

"Tribute."

"Choke down another Hic and Hail the king."

"Colds in the Head."

"Dopey Sal + Penthouse Jerry."

"The girls I met at the Chicago Fire."

Untitled: "Mr. McDonald was keen to lay eyes on his daughter. . . ."

Untitled: "Strombergs assorted pickels gather near. . . ."

Untitled: "There was no firelight. . . ."

"To My Grandfather."

Untitled: "Dear Mid . . . ," in Don C. Skemer, "Loveless in Louisville: F. Scott Fitzgerald's Verses to Mildred McNally, 1918," *Princeton University Library Chronicle*, 58 (Winter 1997), 322–324.

Book Reviews

These reviews, except for "The Defeat of Art," are collected in *F. Scott Fitzgerald In His Own Time*.

Untitled book review of *Penrod and Sam* by Booth Tarkington, *The Nassau Literary Magazine*, 72 (January 1917), 291–292.

Untitled book review of *David Blaize* by E. F. Benson, *The Nassau Literary Magazine*, 72 (February 1917), 343–344.

Untitled book review of *The Celt and the World* by Shane Leslie, *The Nassau Literary Magazine*, 73 (May 1917), 104–105.

Untitled book review of *Verses in Peace and War* by Shane Leslie, *The Nassau Literary Magazine*, 73 (June 1917), 152–153.

Untitled book review of *God, The Invisible King* by H. G. Wells, *The Nassau Literary Magazine*, 73 (June 1917), 153.

"The Baltimore Anti-Christ," *The Bookman*, 53 (March 1921), 79–81. H. L. Mencken's *Prejudices. Second Series*.

"Three Soldiers," *St. Paul Daily News* (September 25, 1921), feature section, 6. John Dos Passos's *Three Soldiers*.

"Poor Old Marriage," *The Bookman*, 54 (November 1921), 253–254. Charles Norris's *Brass*.

"Aldous Huxley's 'Crome Yellow,' " *St. Paul Daily News* (February 26, 1922), feature section, 6.

" 'Margey Wins the Game,' " *New York Tribune* (May 7, 1922), section 4, p. 7. John V. A. Weaver's *Margey Wins the Game*.

"Tarkington's 'Gentle Julia,' " *St. Paul Daily News* (May 7, 1922), feature section, 6.

"Homage to the Victorians," *New York Tribune* (May 14, 1922), section 4, p. 6. Shane Leslie's *The Oppidan*.

"A Rugged Novel," *The Literary Review of the New York Evening Post* (October 28, 1922), 143–144. Woodward Boyd's *The Love Legend*.

"The Defeat of Art," *St. Paul Daily News*, January 21, 1923, section 2, p. 6; *FSF on Authorship*. Heywood Broun's *The Boy Grew Older*.

"Minnesota's Capital in the Role of Main Street," *Literary Digest International Book Review*, 1 (March 1923), 35–36. Grace Flandrau's *Being Respectable*.

"Sherwood Anderson on the Marriage Question," *New York Herald* (March 4, 1923), section 9, p. 5. Sherwood Anderson's *Many Marriages*.

"Under Fire," *The Literary Review of the New York Evening Post* (May 26, 1923), 715. Thomas Boyd's *Through the Wheat*.

"F. Scott Fitzgerald Is Bored by Efforts at Realism In 'Lit,' " *The Daily Princetonian* (March 16, 1928), 1, 3. March issue of *The Nassau Literary Magazine*.

Public Letters and Statements

Entries provide first periodical appearance and first publication in a Fitzgerald collection.

"The Claims of the *Lit.*," *The Princeton Alumni Weekly*, 20 (March 10, 1920), 514.

"Contemporary Writers and Their Work: A Series of Autobiographical Letters—F. Scott Fitzgerald," *Editor*, 53 (Second July Number, 1920), 121–122.

Public letter to Thomas Boyd, *St. Paul Daily News* (February 20, 1921), feature section, 8; *In His Own Time*.

"The Author's Apology," tipped into copies of the third printing of *This Side of Paradise* (April 1920); *In His Own Time*.

"What I Was Advised to Do—And Didn't," *Philadelphia Public Ledger* (April 22, 1922), 11; *In His Own Time*.

"Confessions," *Chicago Daily Tribune* (May 19, 1923), 9; *In His Own Time*.

Letter to A. Philip Randolph (Great Neck, Long Island, May 25, 1923), *The Messenger*, 5 (June 1923), 749.

"Censorship or Not," *Literary Digest*, 77 (June 23, 1923), 31, 61; *In His Own Time*.

"In Literary New York," *St. Paul Daily News* (December 23, 1923), section 2, p. 5; *In His Own Time*.

"Who's Who in This Issue," *Woman's Home Companion*, 51 (July 1924), 110.

Letter to Class Secretary, *The Princeton Alumni Weekly*, 26 (April 14, 1926), 718.

"Fitzgerald Sets Things Right About His College," *Washington Herald* (June 28, 1929), section 2, p. 1; *In His Own Time.*

"False and Extremely Unwise Tradition," *The Daily Princetonian* (February 27, 1930), 2; *In His Own Time.*

Letter to H. N. Swanson, *College Humor,* no. 76 (April 1930), 134.

"Confused Romanticism," *The Princeton Alumni Weekly,* 32 (April 22, 1932), 647–648; *In His Own Time.*

"An Open Letter to Fritz Crisler," *Princeton Athletic News,* 2 (June 16, 1934), 3; *In His Own Time.*

"Anonymous '17," *The Nassau Literary Magazine,* 95 (June 1934), 9; *In His Own Time.*

Ad for *Appointment in Samarra* by John O'Hara. *New York Herald Tribune Books,* October 7, 1934, section 7, p. 17.

These Stories Went to Market, ed. Vernon McKenzie. New York: McBride, 1935, p. xviii. Comments on stories. *In His Own Time.*

Letter to Harvey H. Smith, *The Princeton Alumni Weekly,* 38 (January 28, 1938), 372.

Letter to Harvey H. Smith (MGM, January 3, 1939), *The Princeton Alumni Weekly,* 39 (February 3, 1939), 369–370.

Interviews

Entries provide first periodical appearance and first publication in a Fitzgerald collection.

Grey, Jane. "It's Great to Be a Girl—For Three Hours Only," *St. Paul Dispatch* (December 29, 1915), 5.

Broun, Heywood. "Books." *New York Tribune* (May 7, 1920), 14.

"More Than Hundred Notes of Rejection Failed to Halt Scott Fitzgerald's Pen," *St. Paul Pioneer Press* (September 12, 1920), section 2, p. 8.

H. H. ([Harry Hansen]). "Have Faith in Fitzgerald," *Chicago Daily News* (October 27, 1920), 12.

Smith, Frederick James. "Fitzgerald, Flappers and Fame," *Shadowland,* 3 (January 1921), 39, 75; *In His Own Time.*

Boyd, Thomas Alexander. "Scott Fitzgerald Here on Vacation; 'Rests' by Outlining New Novels," *St. Paul Daily News* (August 28, 1921), City Life Section, 6.

Boyd. "Scott Fitzgerald Speaks at Home," *St. Paul Daily News* (December 4, 1921), City Life Section, 6.

Boyd. "Literary Libels—Francis Scott Key Fitzgerald," *St. Paul Daily News* (March 5, 12, 19, 1922), City Life Section, 6; *In His Own Time.*

J.V.A.W. ([John V. A. Weaver]). "The Lion's Cage," *Brooklyn Daily Eagle* (March 25, 1922), 5.

Marshall, Marguerite Mooers. "F. Scott Fitzgerald, Novelist, Shocked by 'Younger Marrieds' and Prohibition," *New York Evening World* (April 1, 1922), 3; *In His Own Time.*

O'Donnell, John. "Fitzgerald Condemns St. Paul Flappers," *St. Paul Daily News* (April 16, 1922), section 1, pp. 1, 5.

"The Gossip Shop," *The Bookman,* 55 (May 1922), 333–334.

McCardell, Roy L. "F. Scott Fitzgerald—Juvenile Juvenal of the Jeunesse Jazz," *New York Morning Telegraph* (November 12, 1922), magazine section, 3.

"Novelist Flays Drys, Exalting Our Flappers," *New York Daily News* (January 24, 1923), 18.

"Prediction Is Made About James Novel: F. S. Fitzgerald Believes 'Ulysses' Is Great Book of Future," *Richmond Times-Dispatch* (June 24, 1923), section 2, p. 5.

"What a 'Flapper Novelist' Thinks of His Wife," *Detroit News* (September 30, 1923), Metropolitan Section, 3; *St. Paul Pioneer Press* (September 30, 1923), magazine section, 2; *In His Own Time.*

Wilson, B. F. "F. Scott Fitzgerald on 'Minnie McGluke,' " *Picture-Play,* 19 (October 1923), 83–84, 102.

Wilson. "F. Scott Fitzgerald Says: 'All Women Over Thirty-five Should Be Murdered,' " *Metropolitan Magazine,* 58 (November 1923), 34, 75–76; *In His Own Time.*

Wilson. "Notes on Personalities, IV—F. Scott Fitzgerald," *The Smart Set,* 73 (April 1924), 29–33.

Baldwin, Charles C. "F. Scott Fitzgerald," *The Men Who Make Our Novels* (New York: Dodd, Mead, 1924), 166–173; *In His Own Time.*

Wales, Henry. "N.Y. '400' Apes Chicago Manner; Fails; So Dull," *Chicago Daily Tribune* (December 7, 1925), 12.

"Ellin Mackay's Bored Debutantes Are Satirized By Scott Fitzgerald," *Chicago Daily Tribune,* Paris edition (December 7, 1925), 1.

"Novelist Admires French," *Baltimore Evening Sun* (December 21, 1926), 11.

Salpeter, Harry. "Fitzgerald, Spenglerian," *New York World* (April 3, 1927), 12M; *In His Own Time.*

Reid, Margaret. "Has the Flapper Changed?" *Motion Picture Magazine,* 33 (July 1927), 28–29, 104; *In His Own Time.*

Shaw, Charles G. "F. Scott Fitzgerald," *The Low-Down* (New York: Henry Holt, 1928), 163–169; *In His Own Time.*

"Fitzgerald Back from Riviera; Is Working on Novel," *Chicago Daily Tribune,* Paris edition (April 9, 1929), 8.

Whitman, William. "They Write Books—The Gin and Jazz Age," *Boston Globe* (April 13, 1929), 14.

Bald, Wambly. "La Vie de Bohème (As Lived on the Left Bank)," *Chicago Daily Tribune,* Paris edition (December 16, 1929), 5.

Walling, Keith. "Scott Fitzgeralds to Spend Winter Here Writing Books," *Montgomery Advertiser* (October 8, 1931), 1, 7; *In His Own Time.*

"Scott Fitzgerald Seeking Home Here," *Baltimore Sun* (May 8, 1932), 18, 12; *In His Own Time.*

"F. Scott Fitzgerald Is Hunting Trouble," *Baltimore Evening Sun* (June 29, 1932), 36.

"Fitzgeralds Felt Insecure in France; Now Live Here," *Baltimore Evening Sun* (October 25, 1932), 3.

" 'No, Not Cellar-Door!' Baltimore Writers Cry," *Baltimore Post* (December 13, 1932), 2.

"F. Scott Fitzgerald Is Visitor in City; New Book Appears Soon," *Charlottesville Daily Progress* (May 25, 1933), 1.

"Holds 'Flappers' Fail As Parents," *New York Times* (September 18, 1933), 17; "Kids of Ex-Flappers Have Pretty Sorry Treatment, F. Scott Fitzgerald Asserts," *St. Paul Pioneer Press* (September 18, 1933), 3.

Cowley, Malcolm. "Ivory Towers to Let," *The New Republic,* 78 (April 18, 1934), 260–263.

McBride, Mary Margaret. "Looking at Youth," *New York World-Telegram* (June 4, 1934), 21.

"F. Scott Fitzgerald Staying at Hotel Here," *Asheville Citizen-Times* (July 21, 1935), 1–2; *In His Own Time.*

Buttitta, Anthony. "Fitzgerald's Six Generations," *Raleigh News and Observer* (September 1, 1935), 3; *In His Own Time.*

Mok, Michel. "The Other Side of Paradise, Scott Fitzgerald, 40, Engulfed in Despair," *New York Post* (September 25, 1936), 1, 15; *In His Own Time.*

Hess, John D. "Wanger Blends Abruptness with Charm in Personality," *The Dartmouth* (February 11, 1939), 2, 13.

"An Interview with F. Scott Fitzgerald," *Saturday Review,* 63 (November 5, 1960), 26, 56.

Buttitta, Anthony. "An Encounter with Fitzgerald in a North Carolina Bookshop," *San Francisco Chronicle,* "*This World,*" (August 26, 1962), supplement, 38.

Unlocated Interviews

(Clippings in Fitzgerald's Scrapbooks)

"American Writer Finds a Home in Rome." Datelined Rome. Winter 1924–25.

"And whom did we see in New York? Well, there was F. Scott Fitzgerald, for one. . . ."

"Fitzgerald and Flappers."

"Fitzgerald Finds He Has Outgrown Jazz Age Novel," c. 1929.

Fulton, Bart. "Fitzgerald, Flapperdom's Fiction Ace, Qualifies as Most Brilliant Author, But Needs Press Agent, Says Scribe."

Babcock, Muriel. "Flaming Youth Called Feeble," Los Angeles, 1927; *In His Own Time.*

Rennels, Mary. "Frankness Often Wins a Husband!"

" 'Gatsby's' Author Boasts His Child, Not His Novel." Possibly in *New York Herald,* 1925.

"His Fame Arrived Early."

"Horace B. Liveright, Gelett Burgess, F. Scott Fitzgerald and Others of Authors' League Fellowship Help Along 'Friendly Discourse.' "

"Middle West Girl More at Home in Kitchen Than in Ballroom, Says F. Scott Fitzgerald," 1922–23.

"Painted St. Paul's Name on Literary Signboard."

"Popular Writer Leaves for Pau." Possibly in *Paris Herald* or *Paris Tribune,* c. January 1926.

Millen, Gilmore. "Scott Fitzgerald Lays Success to Reading," Los Angeles, c. 1927.

"There Are Super-Flappers in Addition to Flippant Ones, St. Paul Author Opines." Probably in St. Paul, Minn., paper, December 1921.

"The Virtue of Persistence."

Fulton, Bart. "Was This Author Merely Teasing at Woman's College or Did He Forget?" Probably in Montgomery, Ala., paper.

Interview with Fitzgerald about movie version of *TSOP, Grit,* and *The Vegetable.*

Interview with Fitzgerald and Cornelius Vanderbilt, Jr., about beauty contest, 1929.

Movie Projects

This list includes the produced and unproduced movies Fitzgerald is known to have worked on, some he may have worked on, and his proposals for movies.

"Trans-Continental Kitty" (unproduced). Movie synopsis which Fitzgerald submitted to David O. Selznick in April 1922; declined.

Titles for Edith Wharton's *Glimpses of the Moon* (adapted by L. Sheldon). Famous Players, 1923.

"This Side of Paradise." Notes for scenario, 1923? Probably for Famous Players—Lasky.

Grit. Film Guild, 1924. Original story by Fitzgerald.

"Lipstick" (unproduced). United Artists, January–February 1927. (*Fitzgerald/Hemingway Annual* [1978], pp. 3–35).

Red-Headed Woman. MGM, November-December 1931. Fitzgerald's screenplay was rejected.

"Gracie at Sea." With Robert Spafford. Treatment written on speculation for George Burns and Gracie Allen, 1934.

"Tender Is the Night." With Charles Warren. Treatment written on speculation, 1934. (Matthew J. Bruccoli, *Some Sort of Epic Grandeur,* Appendix 1).

"Ballet Shoes" (unproduced). Movie treatment which Fitzgerald wrote in 1936 for L. G. Braun, manager of ballerina Olga Spessivtzewa, who was arranging a movie contract with Samuel Goldwyn; nothing came of the project. (*Fitzgerald/Hemingway Annual* [1976], pp. 2–7).

A Yank at Oxford. With Frank Wead. MGM, July 1937. Fitzgerald polished the screenplay but did not receive screen credit.

Three Comrades. MGM, August 1937–February 1938. Fitzgerald shared screen credit with E. E. Paramore. (*F. Scott Fitzgerald's Screenplay for Three Comrades by Erich Maria Remarque.* Ed. with afterword by Matthew J. Bruccoli. Carbondale & Edwardsville, Ill.: Southern Illinois University Press, 1978).

"Infidelity" (unproduced). MGM, February–May 1938. (*Esquire,* 80 [December 1973], 193–200, 290–304).

Marie Antoinette. MGM, May 1938. Fitzgerald's screenplay was rejected.

The Women. MGM, May–October 1938. The screenplay by Fitzgerald and Donald Ogden Stewart was rejected.

Musical based on the Basil Duke Lee stories. Fitzgerald submitted a proposal to MGM in October 1938; the project was not developed.

Madame Curie. MGM, November 1938–January 1939. Fitzgerald's screenplay was rejected.

"Babes in Wonderland" (unproduced). Idea for a musical which Fitzgerald submitted to MGM producer John Considine (January 6, 1939; *Correspondence,* pp. 524–526); the project was not developed.

Gone With the Wind. Selznick International, January 1939. Fitzgerald polished the screenplay but did not receive screen credit.

Winter Carnival. With Budd Schulberg. United Artists (Walter Wanger), February 1939. Fitzgerald was fired.

"Air Raid" (unproduced). With Donald Ogden Stewart. Paramount, March 1939.

"Open That Door" (unproduced). Based on the novel *Bull by the Horns* by Charles Bonner. Universal, July or August 1939. Fitzgerald worked on the screenplay for one week.

Everything Happens at Night. Twentieth Century-Fox, September 1939. Fitzgerald was involved in a story conference for one day; he did not receive screen credit.

Raffles. Goldwyn, September 1939. Fitzgerald worked on the screenplay for one week; he did not receive screen credit.

"The Feather Fan" (unproduced). Movie treatment which Fitzgerald submitted to MGM, probably in 1939; proposal declined. (*Fitzgerald/Hemingway Annual* [1977], pp. 3–8).

"Cosmopolitan"/"Honoria" (unproduced). From "Babylon Revisited." Columbia (Lester Cowan), March–August 1940. (*Babylon Revisited: The Screenplay,* intro. by Budd Schulberg. New York: Carroll & Graf, 1993).

"Brooklyn Bridge" (unproduced). Twentieth Century-Fox. Fitzgerald wrote a memo and may have worked briefly on this proposed movie in August 1940.

Life Begins at Eight-Thirty. Based on the play *The Light of Heart* by Emlyn Williams. Twentieth Century-Fox, August–October 1940. Fitzgerald's screenplay was rejected.

Manuscripts and Archives

Princeton University Library, Princeton University, Princeton, N.J.

Matthew J. and Arlyn Bruccoli Collection, Thomas Cooper Library, University of South Carolina, Columbia, S.C.

ZELDA FITZGERALD'S PUBLICATIONS

Books

Save Me the Waltz. New York: Scribners, 1932; London: Grey Walls, 1953. Corrected edition, ed. Matthew J. Bruccoli. Carbondale & Edwardsville, Ill.: Southern Illinois University Press, 1967. Novel.

Bits of Paradise. Ed. Matthew J. Bruccoli. London: Bodley Head, 1973; New York: Scribners, 1974. Includes 10 stories by Zelda Fitzgerald.

Scandalabra. Foreword by Meredith Walker. Bloomfield Hills, Mich. & Columbia, S.C.: Bruccoli Clark, 1980. Play.

Zelda Fitzgerald: The Collected Writings. Ed. Matthew J. Bruccoli, with intro. by Mary Gordon. New York: Scribners, 1991.

Stories

All of these stories are in *Zelda Fitzgerald: The Collected Writings*.

"Our Own Movie Queen," *Chicago Sunday Tribune* (June 7, 1925), magazine section, pp. 1–4. Partly by Fitzgerald; but published under his name only. *Bits*.

"The Original Follies Girl," *College Humor*, 17 (July 1929), 40–41, 110. Bylined "Zelda and F. Scott Fitzgerald," but credited to Zelda in *Ledger*. *Bits*.

"Southern Girl," *College Humor*, 18 (October 1929), 27–28, 94, 96. Bylined "F. Scott and Zelda Fitzgerald," but credited to Zelda in *Ledger*. *Bits*.

"The Girl the Prince Liked," *College Humor*, no. 74 (February 1930), 46–48, 121–122. Bylined "F. Scott and Zelda Fitzgerald," but credited to Zelda in *Ledger*. *Bits*.

"The Girl with Talent," *College Humor*, no. 76 (April 1930), 50–52, 125–127. Bylined "F. Scott and Zelda Fitzgerald," but credited to Zelda in *Ledger*. *Bits*.

"A Millionaire's Girl," *The Saturday Evening Post*, 202 (May 17, 1930), 8–9, 118, 121. Bylined "F. Scott Fitzgerald" only, but credited to Zelda in *Ledger*. *Bits*.

"Poor Working Girl," *College Humor*, no. 85 (January 1931), 72–73, 122. Bylined "F. Scott and Zelda Fitzgerald," but credited to Zelda in *Ledger*. *Bits*.

"Miss Ella," *Scribner's Magazine*, 90 (December 1931), 661–665; *Bits*.

"The Continental Angle," *The New Yorker*, 8 (June 4, 1932), 25; *Bits*.

"A Couple of Nuts," *Scribner's Magazine*, 92 (August 1932), 80–84; *Bits*.

"Other Names for Roses," *Collected Writings*.

Articles

All of these articles are in *Zelda Fitzgerald: The Collected Writings*.

"Friend Husband's Latest," *New York Tribune* (April 2, 1922), magazine section, p. 11. Review of *B&D*.

"Eulogy on the Flapper," *Metropolitan Magazine*, 55 (June 1922), 38–39.

"Does a Moment of Revolt Come Sometime to Every Married Man?" *McCall's*, 51 (March 1924), 82. Published with companion article by Fitzgerald.

"Breakfast," *Favorite Recipes of Famous Women*, ed. Florence Stratton. New York & London: Harper & Brothers, 1925.

"What Became of the Flappers?" *McCall's*, 53 (October 1925), 12, 30, 66. Published with Fitzgerald's "Our Young Rich Boys" under the joint title "What Becomes of Our Flappers and Sheiks?"

"The Changing Beauty of Park Avenue," *Harper's Bazaar*, 62 (January 1928), 61–63. By-lined "Zelda and F. Scott Fitzgerald, but credited to Zelda in *Ledger*.

"Looking Back Eight Years," *College Humor*, 14 (June 1928), 36–37. Bylined "F. Scott and Zelda Fitzgerald," but credited to Zelda in *Ledger*.

"Who Can Fall in Love After Thirty?" *College Humor*, 15 (October 1928), 9, 92. Bylined "F. Scott and Zelda Fitzgerald," but credited to Zelda in *Ledger*.

"Paint and Powder." Written as "Editorial on Youth" for *Photoplay* in 1927. *The Smart Set*, 84 (May 1929), 68. Bylined "F. Scott Fitzgerald" only, but credited to Zelda in *Ledger*.

" 'Show Mr. and Mrs. F. to Number ——,' " *Esquire*, 1–2 (May & June 1934), 19, 154B; 23, 120. Bylined "F. Scott and Zelda Fitzgerald," but credited to Zelda in *Ledger*. *CU*.

"Auction—Model 1934," *Esquire,* 2 (July 1934), 20, 153, 155. By-lined "F. Scott and Zelda Fitzgerald," but credited to Zelda in *Ledger. CU.*

"Zelda Fitzgerald's Tribute to F. Scott Fitzgerald," *Fitzgerald/Hemingway Annual* (1974), pp. 2–7; in *Collected Writings* as "On F. Scott Fitzgerald."

WORKS ABOUT FITZGERALD

Bibliographies and Catalogues

American Literary Scholarship: An Annual, 1963– . Durham, N.C.: Duke University Press, 1965– . Includes chapters on Fitzgerald.

Bruccoli, Matthew J. *The Merrill Checklist of F. Scott Fitzgerald.* Columbus, Ohio: Merrill, 1970. Primary and secondary.

Bruccoli. *F. Scott Fitzgerald: A Descriptive Bibliography.* Pittsburgh: University of Pittsburgh Press, 1972. Primary.

Bruccoli. *Supplement to F. Scott Fitzgerald: A Descriptive Bibliography.* Pittsburgh: University of Pittsburgh Press, 1980. Primary.

Bruccoli. *F. Scott Fitzgerald: A Descriptive Bibliography.* Revised and augmented edition. Pittsburgh: University of Pittsburgh Press, 1987. Primary.

Bryer, Jackson R. *The Critical Reputation of F. Scott Fitzgerald.* Hamden, Conn.: Archon, 1967. Secondary.

Bryer. *The Critical Reputation of F. Scott Fitzgerald: Supplement One Through 1981.* Hamden, Conn.: Archon, 1984. Secondary.

Bucker, Park S., ed. *Catalogue of the Matthew J. and Arlyn Bruccoli F. Scott Fitzgerald Collection at the Thomas Cooper Library, The University of South Carolina.* Columbia, S.C.: MJB, 1997.

F. Scott Fitzgerald and Ernest M. Hemingway in Paris— An Exhibition at the Bibliothèque Benjamin Franklin. Bloomfield Hills, Mich. & Columbia, S.C.: Bruccoli Clark, 1972.

F. Scott Fitzgerald Centenary Exhibition. Columbia, S.C.: University of South Carolina for the Thomas Cooper Library, 1996. Exhibit catalogue.

F. Scott Fitzgerald 21 December 1940–21 December 1990. Columbia, S.C.: Thomas Cooper Society, 1991. Exhibit catalogue.

Fiestas, Moveable Feasts and "Many Fetes": in their time/ 1920–1940: An Exhibition at the University of Virginia Library December 1977–March 1978. Bloomfield Hills, Mich. & Columbia, S.C.: Bruccoli Clark, 1977. Exhibit catalogue.

Stanley, Linda C. *The Foreign Critical Reputation of F. Scott Fitzgerald.* Westport, Conn.: Greenwood, 1980. Secondary.

Biographies and Memoirs

Books

Bruccoli, Matthew J. *Scott and Ernest: The Authority of Failure and the Authority of Success.* New York: Random House, 1978. Revised as *Fitzgerald and Hemingway: A Dangerous Friendship.* New York: Carroll & Graf, 1994; London: André Deutsch, 1995.

Bruccoli. *Some Sort of Epic Grandeur.* San Diego: Harcourt Brace Jovanovich, 1981; London: Hodder & Stoughton. Revised edition, London: Cardinal, 1991; New York: Carroll & Graf, 1993.

Buttitta, Tony. *After the Good Gay Times.* New York: Viking, 1974; *The Lost Summer.* London: Robson, 1987.

Donaldson, Scott. *Fool for Love.* New York: Congdon & Weed, 1983.

Graham, Sheilah, and Gerold Frank. *Beloved Infidel.* New York: Holt, Rinehart & Winston, 1958.

Graham. *College of One.* New York: Viking, 1967.

Graham. *The Real F. Scott Fitzgerald: Thirty-Five Years Later.* New York: Grosset & Dunlap, 1976; London: W. H. Allen, 1976.

Hackl, Lloyd C. *F. Scott Fitzgerald and St. Paul: "Still Home to Me."* (Cambridge, Minn.: Adventure Publications, 1996).

Koblas, John J. *F. Scott Fitzgerald in Minnesota: His Homes and Haunts.* St. Paul: Minnesota Historical Society Press, 1978.

Lanahan, Eleanor, ed. *Zelda, An Illustrated Life: The Private World of Zelda Fitzgerald.* New York: Harry N. Abrams, Inc., 1996.

Latham, Aaron. *Crazy Sundays: F. Scott Fitzgerald in Hollywood.* New York: Viking, 1971.

LeVot, André. *F. Scott Fitzgerald.* Paris: Julliard, 1979; Garden City, N.Y.: Doubleday, 1983; London: Allen Lane, 1984.

Mayfield, Sara. *Exiles from Paradise.* New York: Delacorte Press, 1971.

Mellow, James R. *Invented Lives.* Boston: Houghton Mifflin, 1984.

Meyers, Jeffrey. *Scott Fitzgerald: A Biography.* New York: HarperCollins, 1994.

Milford, Nancy. *Zelda.* New York: Harper & Row, 1970.

Mizener, Arthur. *The Far Side of Paradise.* Boston: Houghton Mifflin, 1951. Revised edition, 1965.

Mizener. *Scott Fitzgerald and His World.* New York: Putnam, 1972.

Page, David and John Koblas. *F. Scott Fitzgerald in Minnesota: Toward the Summit.* St. Cloud: North Star Press, 1996.

Ring, Frances Kroll. *Against the Current: As I Remember F. Scott Fitzgerald.* San Francisco: Ellis/Creative Arts, 1985.

Smith, Scottie Fitzgerald, Matthew J. Bruccoli, and Joan P. Kerr, eds. *The Romantic Egoists: A Pictorial Autobiography from the Scrapbooks and Albums of F. Scott and Zelda Fitzgerald.* New York: Scribners, 1974.

Turnbull, Andrew. *Scott Fitzgerald.* New York: Scribners, 1962; London: Bodley Head, 1962.

Book Sections & Articles

Callaghan, Morley. *That Summer in Paris* (New York: Coward-McCann, 1963), passim.

Dardis, Tom. "F. Scott Fitzgerald: What Do You Do When There's Nothing to Do?" *Some Time in the Sun* (New York: Scribners, 1976), 17–78.

Donaldson, Scott. "F. Scott Fitzgerald, Princeton '17." *The Princeton University Library Chronicle,* 40 (Winter 1979), 119–154.

Fitzgerald, Frances Scott. "A Short Retort," *Mademoiselle* (July 1939), 41.

Fitzgerald. "Princeton and F. Scott Fitzgerald." *The Nassau Literary Magazine,* 100 (1942), 45; reprinted as "Princeton & My Father," *Princeton Alumni Weekly,* 56 (March 9, 1956), 8–9.

Gingrich, Arnold. "Publisher's Page—Will the Real Scott Fitzgerald Please Stand Up and Be Counted?" *Esquire,* 62 (December 1964), 8, 10, 12, 16.

Gingrich. "Scott, Ernest and Whoever," *Esquire,* 66 (December 1966), 186–189, 322–325.

Hearne, Laura Guthrie. "A Summer with F. Scott Fitzgerald." *Esquire,* 62 (December 1964), 160–165, 232, 236–237, 240, 242, 246, 250, 252, 254–258, 260.

Hemingway, Ernest. "Scott Fitzgerald," "Hawks Do Not Share," "A Matter of Measurements." *A Moveable Feast* (New York: Scribners, 1964), 147–163.

Lanahan, Frances Scott. "Fitzgerald as He Really Was." *Washington Post & Times-Herald,* April 27, 1958, p. E7.

Lanahan, Frances Fitzgerald. Introduction. *Six Tales of the Jazz Age and Other Stories* by F. Scott Fitzgerald (New York: Scribners, 1960), 5–11.

Lanahan, Frances. "My Father's Letters: Advice Without Consent." *Esquire,* 64 (October 1965), 95–97. Reprinted as Introduction to *Letters to His Daughter* by F. Scott Fitzgerald, ed. Andrew Turnbull (New York: Scribners, 1965), ix–xvi.

Lanahan, Scottie Fitzgerald. "Scott, Ernest, Arnold and Whoever." *Esquire,* 67 (March 1967), 159.

Lanahan, Frances Scott Fitzgerald. *When I Was 16.* Ed. Mary Brannum (New York: Platt & Munk, 1967), 200–216. Reprinted as "When I Was Sixteen," *Good Housekeeping,* 167 (October 1968), 100–101.

Meyers, Jeffrey. "Scott Fitzgerald and Edmund Wilson: A Troubled Friendship." *American Scholar,* 61 (Summer 1992), 375–388.

Miller, Linda Patterson. " 'As a Friend You Have Never Failed Me': The Fitzgerald-Murphy Correspondence," *Journal of Modern Literature,* 5 (September 1976), 357–382.

Ring, Frances and R. L. Samsell. "Sisyphus in Hollywood: Refocusing F. Scott Fitzgerald." *Fitzgerald/Hemingway Annual* (1973), 93–104.

Schulberg, Budd. "Old Scott: The Mask, the Myth, and the Man." *Esquire,* 55 (January 1961), 97–101. Reprinted in *The Four Seasons of Success* by Schulberg (Garden City, N.Y.: Doubleday, 1972).

Smith, Frances Fitzgerald. "Où Sont les Soleils d'Antan? par Francoise Fijeralde." *F. Scott Fitzgerald and Ernest M. Hemingway in Paris—An Exhibition at the Bibliotheque Benjamin Franklin* (Bloomfield Hills, Mich. & Columbia, S.C.: Bruccoli Clark, 1972).

Smith, Scottie Fitzgerald. "Christmas as Big as the Ritz," *Washington Post* (December 23, 1973), *Potomac* Magazine, pp. 7–8.

Smith. "The Maryland Ancestors of Zelda Sayre Fitzgerald," *Maryland Historical Magazine,* 78 (Fall 1983), 217–228.

Smith, Frances Scott Fitzgerald. "Mia Is the Daisy Father Had in Mind," *People,* 1 (March 4, 1974), 34.

Smith. "Notes about My Now-Famous Father," *Family Circle,* 84 (May 1974), 118, 120.

Smith, Scottie Fitzgerald. Foreword to *Zelda,* exhibition catalogue (Montgomery: Museum of Fine Arts, 1974). Reprinted as foreword to *Zelda Fitzgerald: The Collected Writings,* ed. Matthew J. Bruccoli (New York: Scribners, 1991), ix–x.

Smith. "The Colonial Ancestors of Francis Scott Key Fitzgerald." In Matthew J. Bruccoli, *Some Sort of Epic Grandeur* (San Diego: Harcourt Brace Jovanovich, 1981), 496–509.

Television Productions

"F. Scott Fitzgerald and 'The Last of the Belles.' " ABC, 1974. Script by James Costigan; directed by George Schaefer.

"F. Scott Fitzgerald in Hollywood." 1976. Directed by Anthony Page.

"Marked for Glory." 1963. Written and produced by Gwinn Owens.

Critical Studies

Books

Allen, Joan M. *Candles and Carnival Lights: The Catholic Sensibility of F. Scott Fitzgerald.* New York: New York University Press, 1978.

Anderson, George Parker. "A Writer Wastes Nothing:

F. Scott Fitzgerald's Stories and the Achievement of *Tender Is the Night.*" Dissertation: University of South Carolina, 1995.

Anderson, W. R. "The Fitzgerald Revival, 1940–1974." Dissertation: University of South Carolina, 1974.

Berman, Ronald. *The Great Gatsby and Modern Times.* Urbana, Ill.: University of Illinois Press, 1994.

Bruccoli, Matthew J. *The Composition of Tender Is the Night.* Pittsburgh, Pa.: University of Pittsburgh Press, 1963.

Bruccoli. *Apparatus for F. Scott Fitzgerald's The Great Gatsby [Under the Red, White and Blue].* Columbia, S.C.: University of South Carolina Press, 1974.

Bruccoli. *"The Last of the Novelists": F. Scott Fitzgerald and The Last Tycoon.* Carbondale & Edwardsville, Ill.: Southern Illinois University Press, 1977.

Bruccoli, with Judith S. Baughman. *Reader's Companion to F. Scott Fitzgerald's Tender Is the Night.* Columbia, S.C.: University of South Carolina Press, 1996.

Callahan, John. *The Illusions of a Nation.* Urbana, Ill.: University of Illinois Press, 1972.

Chambers, John B. *The Novels of F. Scott Fitzgerald.* London: Macmillan/New York: St. Martin's Press, 1989.

Crosland, Andrew T. *A Concordance to F. Scott Fitzgerald's The Great Gatsby.* Detroit, Mich.: Bruccoli Clark/Gale Research, 1975.

Cross, K. G. W. *Scott Fitzgerald.* New York: Grove, 1964.

Dixon, Wheeler W. *The Cinematic Vision of F. Scott Fitzgerald.* Ann Arbor, Mich.: UMI, 1986.

Eble, Kenneth. *F. Scott Fitzgerald.* New York: Twayne, 1963. Revised edition, 1977.

Fahey, William A. *F. Scott Fitzgerald and the American Dream.* New York: Crowell, 1973.

Fryer, Sarah Beebe. *Fitzgerald's New Women: Harbingers of Change.* Ann Arbor, Mich.: UMI, 1988.

Gallo, Rose A. *F. Scott Fitzgerald.* New York: Ungar, 1978.

Goldhurst, William. *F. Scott Fitzgerald and His Contemporaries.* Cleveland & New York: World, 1963.

Higgins, John A. *F. Scott Fitzgerald: A Study of the Stories.* New York: St. John's University Press, 1971.

Hook, Andrew. *F. Scott Fitzgerald.* London & New York: E. Arnold, 1992.

Kuehl, John. "Scott Fitzgerald: Romantic and Realist." Dissertation: Columbia University, 1958.

Kuehl. *F. Scott Fitzgerald: A Study of the Short Fiction.* Boston: Twayne, 1991.

Lehan, Richard D. *F. Scott Fitzgerald and the Craft of Fiction.* Carbondale, Ill.: Southern Illinois University Press, 1966.

Lehan. *The Great Gatsby: The Limits of Wonder.* Boston: Twayne, 1990.

Long, Robert Emmet. *The Achieving of The Great Gatsby.* Lewisburg, Pa.: Bucknell University Press, 1979.

Lowry, Malcolm and Margerie. *Notes on a Screenplay for F. Scott Fitzgerald's Tender Is the Night.* Bloomfield Hills, Mich.: Bruccoli Clark, 1976.

Mangum, Bryant. *A Fortune Yet: Money in the Art of F. Scott Fitzgerald's Short Stories.* New York: Garland, 1991.

Matterson, Stephen. *The Great Gatsby and the Critics.* London: Macmillan, 1990.

Miller, James E., Jr. *F. Scott Fitzgerald: His Art and His Technique.* New York: New York University Press, 1964. Revised as *The Fictional Technique of Scott Fitzgerald.* Folcroft, Pa.: Folcroft Press, 1974.

Moseley, Edwin. *F. Scott Fitzgerald.* Grand Rapids, Mich.: Eerdmans, 1967.

Moyer, Kermit. "The Historical Perspective of F. Scott Fitzgerald." Dissertation: Northwestern University, 1972.

Parkinson, Kathleen. *F. Scott Fitzgerald: Tender Is the Night.* Harmondsworth, U.K.: Penguin, 1986.

Parkinson. *F. Scott Fitzgerald: The Great Gatsby.* Harmondsworth, U.K.: Penguin, 1987.

Pendleton, Thomas A. *I'm Sorry about the Clock: Chronology, Composition, and Narrative Technique in The Great Gatsby.* Selinsgrove, Pa.: Susquehanna University Press, 1993.

Perosa, Sergio. *The Art of F. Scott Fitzgerald.* Ann Arbor, Mich.: University of Michigan Press, 1965.

Petry, Alice Hall. *Fitzgerald's Craft of Short Fiction: The Collected Stories.* Ann Arbor, Mich.: UMI, 1989.

Piper, Henry Dan. *F. Scott Fitzgerald: A Critical Portrait.* New York: Holt, Rinehart & Winston, 1965.

Potts, Stephen W. *The Price of Paradise: The Magazine Career of F. Scott Fitzgerald.* San Bernardino, Calif.: Borgo, 1993.

Roulston, Robert and Helen H. Roulston. *The Winding Road to West Egg: The Artistic Development of F. Scott Fitzgerald.* Lewisburg, Pa.: Bucknell University Press/ London: Associated University Presses, 1995.

Seiters, Dan. *Image Patterns in the Novels of F. Scott Fitzgerald.* Ann Arbor, Mich.: UMI, 1986.

Shain, Charles E. *F. Scott Fitzgerald.* Minneapolis, Minn.: University of Minnesota Press, 1961.

Sklar, Robert. *F. Scott Fitzgerald: The Last Laocoön.* New York: Oxford University Press, 1967.

Stavola, Thomas J. *Scott Fitzgerald: Crisis in an American Identity.* New York: Barnes & Noble, 1979.

Stebbins, Todd. *"Tender Is the Night:* The Last Love Battle, with a Newly Generated Concordance (Volumes I–IV)." Dissertation: University of South Carolina, 1993.

Stern, Milton R. *The Golden Moment: The Novels of F. Scott Fitzgerald.* Urbana, Ill.: University of Illinois Press, 1970.

Stern. *Tender Is the Night: The Broken Universe.* New York: Twayne, 1994.

Way, Brian. *F. Scott Fitzgerald and the Art of Social Fiction.* London: Arnold, 1980; New York: St. Martin, 1980.

West, James L. W., III. *The Making of This Side of Paradise.* Philadelphia: University of Pennsylvania Press, 1983.

Whitley, John S. *F. Scott Fitzgerald: The Great Gatsby.* London: Arnold, 1976.

Collections of Essays

Bloom, Harold, ed. with intro. *F. Scott Fitzgerald.* New York: Chelsea House, 1985. Contents: "FSF" by Edmund Wilson; "FSF" by Lionel Trilling; "SF and the Collapse of the American Dream" by Marius Bewley; "F: The Romance of Money" by Malcolm Cowley; "SF's Fable of East and West" by Robert Ornstein; "SF as Social Novelist: Statement and Technique in *LT*" by Michael Millgate; " 'Babylon Revisited': A Story of the Exile's Return" by Roy R. Male; "*TITN*" by Arthur Mizener; "Gods and Fathers in FSF's Novels" by James Gindin; "The Counter-Transference of Dr. Diver" by Mary E. Burton; "*GG:* Two Versions of the Hero" by David Parker; "Whistling 'Dixie' in Encino: *LT* and F's Two Souths" by Robert Roulston; "The Socialist and the Silk Stockings: F's Double Allegiance" by Ronald J. Gervais; "*TITN* and 'Ode to a Nightingale' " by William E. Doherty.

Bloom, ed. with intro. *F. Scott Fitzgerald's The Great Gatsby.* New York: Chelsea House, 1986. Contents: "The Structure of *GG*" by Kenneth Eble; "SF's Criticism of America" by Marius Bewley; "Two Versions of the Hero" by David Parker; "Gatsby and the Failure of the Omniscient 'I' " by Ron Neuhaus; "Another Reading of *GG*" by Keath Fraser; "Oral Aggression and Splitting" by A. B. Paulson; "*GG*" by Brian Way; "The *Waste Land* Myth and Symbols in *GG*" by Letha Audhuy.

Bloom, ed. with intro. *Gatsby.* New York: Chelsea House, 1991. Contents: 25 critical extracts; "Gatsby and the Hole in Time" by R. W. Stallman; "*GG* as Pastoral" by David Stouck; "The Promised Land" by Hugh Kenner; "Entropy vs. Ecology in *GG*" by Robert Ian Scott; "*GG:* Apogee of F's Mythopoeia" by Neila Seshachari; "*GG:* F's *Droit de Seigneur*" by Judith Fetterley; "Pecuniary Emulation of the Mediator in *GG*" by Patricia Bizzell; "Glamor on the Turn" by Richard Godden; "Fiction as Greatness: The Case of Gatsby" by Arnold Weinstein; "The Mystery of Ungodliness" by Bryce J. Christensen; "Gatsby and Emerson" by Emily Miller Budick; "Within and Without: Nick Carraway" by David H. Lynn; "Inventing Gatsby" by Richard Lehan.

Bruccoli, Matthew J., ed. *Profile of F. Scott Fitzgerald.* Columbus, Ohio: Merrill, 1971. Contents: "My Generation" by FSF; Introduction to *The Portable F. Scott Fitzgerald* by John O'Hara; "SF's Critical Opinions" by John Kuehl; "SF's Reading" by John Kuehl; "*GG*— A Study in Literary Reputation" by G. Thomas Tanselle and Jackson R. Bryer; "*TITN*—Reception and Reputation" by Matthew J. Bruccoli; "F Attends My F Seminar" by Vance Bourjaily.

Bruccoli, ed. with intro. *New Essays on The Great Gatsby.* Cambridge: Cambridge University Press, 1985. Contents: "Gatsby's Long Shadow" by Richard Anderson; "Money, Love, and Aspiration in *GG*" by Roger Lewis; "The Idea of Order at West Egg" by Susan Resneck Parr; "*GG* and the Great American Novel" by Kenneth E. Eble; "Fire and Freshness: A Matter of Style in *GG*" by George Garrett.

Bryer, Jackson R., ed. *F. Scott Fitzgerald: The Critical Reception.* New York: Burt Franklin, 1978. Contents: contemporary reviews of Fitzgerald's novels and short-story collections.

Bryer, ed. *The Short Stories of F. Scott Fitzgerald: New Approaches in Criticism.* Madison: University of Wisconsin Press, 1982. Contents: "The Romantic Self and the Uses of Place in the Stories of FSF" by Richard Lehan; "The Significance of Fantasy in F's Short Fiction" by Lawrence Buell; "Touches of Disaster: Alcoholism and Mental Illness in F's Short Stories" by Kenneth E. Eble; "F's Changes on the Southern Belle: The Tarleton Trilogy" by C. Hugh Holman; " 'Kissing, Shooting, and Sacrificing': FSF and the Hollywood Market" by Alan Margolies; "Money and Marriage in F's Stories" by Scott Donaldson; "To Be Both Light and Dark: The Jungian Process of Individuation in F's Basil Duke Lee Stories" by Joseph Mancini, Jr.; "F's Short Stories and the Depression: An Artistic Crisis" by Ruth Prigozy; "Hollywood in Fitzgerald: After Paradise" by Robert A. Martin; "Fitzgerald and *Esquire*" by James L. W. West III; "Psychic Geography in 'The Ice Palace' " by John Kuehl; "Seeing Slightly Red: F's 'May Day' " by James W. Tuttleton; " 'Winter Dreams' and Summer Sports" by Neil D. Isaacs; " 'Absolution': Absolving Lies" by Irving Malin; " 'No Americans Have Any Imagination': 'Rags Martin-Jones and the Pr-nce of W-les' " by Victor Doyno; "Freedom, Contingency, and Ethics in 'The Adjuster' " by Christiane Johnson; "Faces in a Dream: Innocence Perpetuated in 'The Rich Boy' " by Peter Wolfe; " 'The Swimmers': Paris and Virginia Reconciled" by Melvin J. Friedman; "Rich Boys and Rich Men: 'The Bridal Party' " by James J. Martine; "When the Story Ends: 'Babylon Revisited' " by Carlos Baker; "The Sane Method of 'Crazy Sunday' " by Sheldon Grebstein; "Two Sets of Books, One Balance Sheet: 'Financing Finnegan' " by George Monteiro; Appendix: "The Short Stories of FSF: A Checklist of Criticism" by Jackson R. Bryer.

Bryer, ed. *New Essays on F. Scott Fitzgerald's Neglected Stories.* Columbia: University of Missouri Press, 1996. Contents: "A Style Is Born: The Rhetoric of Loss in 'The Spire and the Gargoyle' " by Gerald Pike; " 'Dalyrimple Goes Wrong': The Best of the Neglected Early Stories" by Robert Merrill; "The Grace of 'Benediction' " by Edward Gillin; "Fitzgerald's

Christmas Carol, or the Burden of 'The Camel's Back' " by Alan Cheuse; " 'Bernice Bobs Her Hair': Fitzgerald's Jazz Elegy for *Little Women*" by Susan F. Beegel; " 'John Jackson's Arcardy': The Lamentable F. Scott Fitzgerald" by James J. Martine; "Climbing 'Jacob's Ladder' " by Alan Margolies; "Distant Idols: Fate and the Work Ethic in 'The Bowl' " by Bryant Mangum; " 'Outside the Cabinet-Maker's': Fitzgerald's 'Ode to a Nightingale' " by Bruce L. Grenberg; "The Southern and the Satirical in 'The Last of the Belles' " by Heidi Kunz Bullock; "Fitzgerald's Very 'Rough Crossing' " by William H. Loos and Victor A. Doyno; " 'The Swimmers': Strokes against the Current" by Robert Roulston; " 'Two Wrongs,' or One Wrong Too Many" by Scott Donaldson; "Flakes of Black Snow: 'One Trip Abroad' Reconsidered" by John Kuehl; "What Fitzgerald Thought of the Jews: Resisting Type in 'The Hotel Child' " by Barry Gross and Eric Fretz; "An Unsentimental Education: 'The Rubber Check' " by Ruth Prigozy; " 'What a Handsome Pair!' and the Institution of Marriage" by James L. W. West III; "Bette Weaver, R.N.: 'Her Last Case' " by George Monteiro; "The Cartoonist, the Nurse, and the Writer: 'An Alcoholic Case' " by Arthur Waldhorn; "Recovering 'The Lost Decade' " by Alice Hall Petry; "Initiation and Intertextuality in *The Basil and Josephine Stories*" by James Nagel; "Philippe, 'Count of Darkness,' and F. Scott Fitzgerald, Feminist?" by Peter L. Hays; "Will the Real Pat Hobby Please Stand Up?" by Milton R. Stern.

Claridge, Henry, ed. *F. Scott Fitzgerald: Critical Assessments.* 4 vols. Near Robertsbridge, East Sussex, U.K.: Helm Information, 1991. Contents: 226 essays. Volume I: Fitzgerald in Context, Memories and Reminiscences, Contemporary Critical Opinion; Volume II: Early Writings, *TSOP, B&D, The Vegetable,* and *GG;* Volume III: *TITN, LT, The Crack-Up,* and the Short Stories; Volume IV: General Perspectives, Fitzgerald and Other Writers.

Donaldson, Scott, ed. with intro. *Critical Essays on F. Scott Fitzgerald's The Great Gatsby.* Boston: Hall, 1984. Contents: "FSF" by Lionel Trilling; "Reading a Novel—*GG*" by Norman Holmes Pearson; "Style and Shape in *GG*" by F. H. Langman; "Something Borrowed, Something New: A Discussion of Literary Influences on *GG*" by Robert Roulston; "*GG* and Its Sources" by Richard D. Lehan; "Theme and Texture in *GG*" by W. J. Harvey; "The Craft of Revision: *GG*" by Kenneth E. Eble; "Patterns in *GG*" by Victor A. Doyno; "*GG*—The Intricate Art" by Robert Emmet Long; "*GG:* The Final Vision" by Christiane Johnson; "Style as Meaning in *GG:* Notes Toward a New Approach" by Jackson R. Bryer; "The Trouble with Nick" by Scott Donaldson; "Another Reading of *GG*" by Keath Fraser; "Beneath the Mask: The Plight of Daisy Buchanan" by Sarah Beebe Fryer; "The Essential

Houses of *GG*" by W. T. Lhamon, Jr.; "Photography and *GG*" by Lawrence Jay Dessner; "Novel to Play to Film: Four Versions of *GG*" by Alan Margolies; " 'A New World, Material Without Being Real': F's Critique of Capitalism in *GG*" by Ross Posnock; "*GG:* F's Meditation on American History" by Kermit W. Moyer; "FSF's *Gatsby* and the Imagination of Wonder" by Giles Gunn; "F's *Gatsby:* The World as Ash Heap" by James E. Miller, Jr.; 19 letters about *GG;* "Spring Flight" by Gilbert Seldes.

Eble, Kenneth, ed. with intro. *F. Scott Fitzgerald: A Collection of Criticism.* New York: McGraw-Hill, 1973. Contents: "My Friend SF" by Elizabeth Beckwith MacKie; "The Road to 'Paradise': F's Literary Apprenticeship" by Donald A. Yates; "*TSOP:* The Pageantry of Disillusion" by Sy Kahn; "*B&D*" by Sergio Perosa; "SF's Fable of East and West" by Robert Ornstein; "The Waste Land of FSF" by John W. Bicknell; "The Craft of Revision: *GG*" by Kenneth E. Eble; "F and the Simple, Inarticulate Farmer" by J. Albert Robbins; "SF and the 1920's" by Arthur Mizener; "*TITN* and the 'Ode to a Nightingale' " by William E. Doherty; "*LT*" by Michael Millgate; "F at the End" by Midge Decter.

Hoffman, Frederick J., ed. with intro. *The Great Gatsby: A Study.* New York: Scribners, 1962. Contents: "FSF" by Edmund Wilson; "FSF" by Paul Rosenfeld; Selected Quotations from *TSOP;* Fitzgerald Chronology 1920–1925; Selection from "The National Letters" by H. L. Mencken; Preface to *The Nigger of the Narcissus* by Joseph Conrad; Selections from *Joseph Conrad: A Personal Remembrance* by Ford Madox Ford; "Winter Dreams" by FSF; "The Delegate from Great Neck" by Edmund Wilson; "How to Live on $36,000 a Year" by FSF; "The Man Who Fixed the Series" by Leo Katcher; Excerpts from "Descriptions of Girls" by FSF; "An Introduction to *GG*" by FSF; Letters about *GG* from FSF; Letters to F about *GG* and Related Matters; "Scenic Narration: Selected Quotations"; "The Narrator and the Narrated: Selected Quotations"; "Beyond West Egg: The End of *GG*"; "The Moral of SF" by Glenway Wescott; "SF—the Authority of Failure" by William Troy; "FSF" by Lionel Trilling; "F's Brave New World" by Edwin Fussell; "SF's Criticism of America" by Marius Bewley; "The Theme and the Narrator of *GG*" by Thomas Hanzo; "*GG*" by Richard Chase; "F's Triumph" by Gale H. Carrithers, Jr.; "The Untrimmed Christmas Tree: The Religious Background of *GG*" by Henry Dan Piper.

Kazin, Alfred, ed. with intro. *F. Scott Fitzgerald: The Man and His Work.* Cleveland: World, 1951. Contents: "FSF" by Gertrude Stein; "FSF 1896–1940" by Arthur Mizener; "F at Princeton" by John Peale Bishop; "*TSOP*" by R.V.A.S.; "Paradise and Princeton" by Heywood Broun; "The Delegate from Great Neck" by

Edmund Wilson; "That Sad Young Man" by John Mosher; "F before *GG*" by Paul Rosenfeld; "F before *GG*" by Edmund Wilson; A Letter on *GG* by Maxwell E. Perkins; *"GG"* by H. L. Mencken; A Letter on *GG* by T. S. Eliot; *"TITN"* by John Chamberlain; "Mechanisms of Misery" by D. W. Harding; *"TITN"* by C. Hartley Grattan; *"Taps at Reveille"* by T. S. Matthews; "F in Hollywood" by Budd Schulberg; "On Rereading F" by Margaret Marshall; "The Moral of FSF" by Glenway Wescott; *"LT"* by Stephen Vincent Benét; " 'An Invite with Gilded Edges' " by Charles Weir, Jr.; "Third Act and Epilogue" by Malcolm Cowley; "A Note on FSF" by John Dos Passos; "F and His Brethren" by Andrews Wanning; "F's Tragic Sense" by Mark Schorer; "An American Confession" by Alfred Kazin; "Dealer in Diamonds and Rhinestones" by J. F. Powers; "SF—the Authority of Failure" by William Troy; "FSF" by Lionel Trilling; "Power without Glory" from *The Times Literary Supplement;* "FSF and the Future" by Weller Embler.

LaHood, Marvin J., ed. with intro. *Tender Is the Night: Essays in Criticism.* Bloomington, Ind.: Indiana University Press, 1969. Contents: "SF: Romantic and Realist" by John Kuehl; "FSF: *GG, TITN, LT*" by G. C. Millard; "The Moralism of the Later F" by Kent and Gretchen Kreuter; *"TITN"* by Richard D. Lehan; *"TITN"* by James E. Miller, Jr.; *"TITN"* by Arthur Mizener; "The 'Intricate Destiny' of Dick Diver" by Eugene White; "F's Fragmented Hero: Dick Diver" by James Ellis; "F's Portrait of a Psychiatrist" by Abraham H. Steinberg; "Dialogue and Theme in *TITN*" by William F. Hall; "Sensuality and Asceticism in *TITN*" by Marvin J. LaHood; " 'Daddy's Girl': Symbol and Theme in *TITN*" by Robert Stanton; *"TITN* and George Herbert Mead: An 'Actor's' Tragedy" by Lee M. Whitehead; *"TITN:* Keats and SF" by John Grube; *"TITN* and The 'Ode to a Nightingale' " by William E. Doherty.

Lee, A. Robert, ed. with intro. *Scott Fitzgerald: The Promises of Life.* London: Vision/New York: St. Martin's, 1989. Contents: "Cases for Reconsideration: F's *TSOP* and *B&D*" by Andrew Hook; " 'A quality of distortion': Imagining *GG*" by A. Robert Lee; *"TITN:* F's Portrait of a Gentleman" by Harold Beaver; *"LT:* F as Projectionist" by Robert Giddings; " 'All Very Rich and Sad': A Decade of F Short Stories" by Herbie Butterfield; " 'Made for—or against—the Trade': The Radicalism of F's *Saturday Evening Post* Love Stories" by Brian Harding; " 'The most poetical topic in the world': Women in the Novels of FSF" by Elizabeth Kaspar Aldrich; " 'A Touch of Disaster': F, Spengler, and the Decline of the West" by John S. Whitley; "The Lost Teigueen: FSF's Ethics and Ethnicity" by Owen Dudley Edwards.

Lockridge, Ernest, ed. with intro. *Twentieth Century*

Interpretations of The Great Gatsby. Englewood Cliffs, N.J.: Prentice-Hall, 1968. Contents: "Boats Against the Current" by James E. Miller, Jr.; "SF's Criticism of America" by Marius Bewley; "SF's Fable of East and West" by Robert Ornstein; "The Theme and Narrator of *GG*" by Thomas A. Hanzo; "Against *GG*" by Gary J. Scrimgeour; "Dream, Design, and Interpretation in *GG*" by David L. Minter; "Theme and Texture in *GG*" by W. J. Harvey; Letter to FSF by Maxwell Perkins; "FSF" by Conrad Aiken; *"GG"* by Peter Quennell; Letter to Edmund Wilson by FSF; Letter to FSF by Edith Wharton; From "Three Novels of Manners" by Richard Chase; "Introduction to *GG*" by FSF; "FSF" by Lionel Trilling; Letter to His Daughter by FSF.

Mizener, Arthur, ed. with intro. *F. Scott Fitzgerald: A Collection of Critical Essays.* Englewood Cliffs, N.J.: Prentice-Hall, 1963. Contents: "FSF" by Lionel Trilling; "SF—The Authority of Failure" by William Troy; "The Function of Nostalgia: FSF" by Wright Morris; "F: The Horror and the Vision of Paradise" by John Aldridge; "F's Brave New World" by Edwin Fussell; "F and His Brethren" by Andrews Wanning; "Third Act and Epilogue" by Malcolm Cowley; "Some Notes on FSF" by Leslie Fiedler; *"TSOP"* by Charles E. Shain; "FSF" by Edmund Wilson; "A Gesture of Indefinite Revolt" by James E. Miller, Jr.; "The Courtship of Miles Standish" by Donald Ogden Stewart; "FSF's *GG*" by John Henry Raleigh; "The Eyes of Dr. Eckleburg: A Re-Examination of *GG*" by Tom Burnam; *"GG:* Thirty-Six Years After" by A. E. Dyson; "SF's Criticism of America" by Marius Bewley; "The Mechanisms of Failure" by D. W. Harding; "The Significance of FSF" by D. S. Savage; "The Maturity of SF" by Arthur Mizener.

Piper, Henry Dan, ed. with intro. *Fitzgerald's The Great Gatsby: The Novel, The Critics, The Background.* New York: Scribners, 1970. Contents: *GG* by FSF; "Absolution" by FSF; "The Untrimmed Christmas Tree: The Religious Background of *GG*" by Henry Dan Piper; 6 letters about *GG;* [An Introduction to *GG*] by FSF; "The Craft of Revision: *GG*" by Kenneth Eble; *"GG"* by H. L. Mencken; *"GG"* by John M. Kenny, Jr.; "New York Chronicle" by Gilbert Seldes; [*GG*] by Arthur Mizener; "The Romance of Money" by Malcolm Cowley; "FSF's *GG:* Legendary Bases and Allegorical Significances" by John Henry Raleigh; "Color-Symbolism in *GG*" by Daniel J. Schneider; "The Greatness of 'Gatsby' " by Charles Thomas Samuels; "Patterns in *GG*" by Victor A. Doyno; [The Fuller-McGee Case] by Henry Dan Piper; 3 New York *Times* reports about the Fuller-McGee Case; [New York in the 1920's: Arnold Rothstein and His Circle] by Lloyd Morris; "Jay Gatsby's Hidden Source of Wealth" by John H. Randall III; "Fitzgerald's Jay

Gatz and Young Ben Franklin" by Floyd C. Watkins; [Rules for Self-Improvement] by Benjamin Franklin; "The Self-Made Man in America" by Irvin G. Wyllie; [The End of the American Dream] by David F. Trask.

Stern, Milton R., ed. with intro. *Critical Essays on F. Scott Fitzgerald's Tender Is the Night*. Boston: Hall, 1986. "*TITN*: The Text Itself" by Stern; "Material for a Centenary Edition of *TITN*" by Matthew J. Bruccoli; "The Psychopathic Novel" by Mary M. Colum; "Page after Page" by Michael March; "SF Re-enters, Leading Bewildered Giant" by James Gray; "True to Type—F Writes Superb Tragic Novel" by Gilbert Seldes; "Books of the Times" by John Chamberlain; "Stale; Unprofitable" by Edith H. Walton; "Decadence: F Again Tells a Sinful, Ginful Tale," Anonymous; "A Generation Riding to Romantic Death" by Horace Gregory; "F's Novel a Masterpiece" by Cameron Rogers; "Books of the Times" by John Chamberlain; "Mr. F Displays His Little White Mice" by H. A. MacMillan; "You Can't Duck Hurricane Under a Beach Umbrella" by Philip Rahv; "SF a Modern Orpheus" by Mabel Dodge Luhan; "The Worm i' the Bud" by William Troy; "Breakdown" by Malcolm Cowley; [Untitled Review] by C. Hartley Grattan; "Mechanisms of Misery" by D. W. Harding; "The Talk of the Town," Anonymous; "FSF, 1896–1940: The Poet of Borrowed Time" by Arthur Mizener; "FSF and the Image of His Father" by Henry Dan Piper; [Introduction to the Revised Edition] by Malcolm Cowley; "F's Brave New World" by Edwin Fussell; " 'Daddy's Girl': Symbol and Theme in *TITN*" by Robert Stanton; "The 'Intricate Destiny' of Dick Diver" by Eugene White; "Political Conscience in the Novels of FSF" by James F. Light; "The Strange Case of FSF and A. Hyd-(Hid)ell: A Note on the Displaced Person in American Life and Literature" by William Wasserstrom; "*TITN* and the 'Ode to a Nightingale' " by William E. Doherty; "*TITN*" by Arthur Mizener; "The Journey Back: Myth and History in *TITN*" by Alan Trachtenberg; "The Way Home: 'But Here There Is No Light' " by John F. Callahan; "F's 'Figured Curtain': Personality and History in *TITN*" by Bruce L. Grenberg; "Vitality and Vampirism in *TITN*" by James W. Tuttleton; "*TITN*: A Cross-Referenced Bibliography of Criticism" by Joseph Wenke.

Tributes. Columbia: Thomas Cooper Society, 1996. Contents: Statements on Fitzgerald by Jeffrey Archer, Margaret Atwood, Paul Auster, Richard Bausch, Robert Bausch, Thomas Berger, Sydney Blair, Vance Bourjaily, Frederick Busch, Nicholas Delbanco, Don DeLillo, James Dickey, Annie Dillard, Irvin Faust, Leslie A. Fiedler, George Garrett, George V. Higgins, John Iggulden, John Jakes, John le Carré, Norman Mailer, William Maxwell, Budd Schulberg, Charles

M. Schulz, Mary Lee Settle, Tony Tanner, and Arnold Wesker.

University of Minnesota Conference on F. Scott Fitzgerald . . . Proceedings. Minneapolis, Minn.: University of Minnesota, 1982. Contents: "Nick Carraway as an Unreliable Narrator" by Kent Cartwright; "FSF's 'Universe of Ineffable Gaudiness' " by Lawrence Thornton; "F in St. Paul: People Who Knew Him Reminisce" by Margot Kreil; "St. Paul's Wayward Son: F's Image in St. Paul Press, 1912–1945" by Diane Isaacs; "Fitzgerald and Howells: An Unremarked Resemblance" by Kenneth Eble; "Zelda: An Artist Without a Medium" by Shirley Garner; "On Generational Responses to FSF: The Case for Appreciation" by Howard Wolf; "*TITN*: A Survey of the Criticism in the Seventies" by Gary McIlroy; "Gold Star Mothers and Emergent Amazons: Depiction of Women in *TITN*" by Laura Haigwood; "Daddy's Girls: Father and Daughter Relationships in *TITN*" by Maureen Ryan; "All the (Un)Happy Endings: F and the Saturday Evening Post" by Stephen W. Potts; "F's Divided Sensibility in Two Short Story Heroines" by Dawn Cottle; "Sinclair Lewis and FSF: Fellow Minnesotans and Rival Novelists" by Robert L. Coard; "Frank Norris's Influence on FSF: An Assessment" by S. S. Moorty; "Beneath the Mask: The Plight of Daisy Buchanan" by Sarah Fryer; "Daddy's Girls: F's Victorian Sensibility in Mid-Career" by Shirley Mylan; "F and the Jews" by Barry Gross; "F's 'Dark Maw of Violence': Culture and Identity in the Roaring Twenties" by Norman H. Hostetler.

Wilson, Edmund, ed. *The Crack-Up*, 308–347. Contents: Three Letters about *GG:* from Gertrude Stein, Edith Wharton, and T. S. Eliot; "A Letter from John Dos Passos"; "A Letter from Thomas Wolfe"; "FSF" by Paul Rosenfeld; "The Moral of SF" by Glenway Wescott; "A Note on F" by John Dos Passos; "The Hours" by John Peale Bishop.

Journals

Fitzgerald Newsletter (quarterly, 1958–68). Reprinted Washington, D.C.: NCR Microcard Books, 1969. Includes checklists.

Fitzgerald/Hemingway Annual (1969–79). Washington, D.C.: NCR Microcard Books, 1969–73; Englewood, Colo.: Information Handling Services, 1974–76; Detroit: Gale Research, 1977–79. Includes checklists.

F. Scott Fitzgerald Collection Notes. Columbia, S.C.: Thomas Cooper Library, University of South Carolina, 1995– .

Book Sections & Articles

Aldridge, John W. "Fitzgerald—The Horror and the Vision of Paradise." *After the Lost Generation* (New York: McGraw-Hill, 1941), 44–58.

Alpert, Hollis. "Fitzgerald, Hollywood, and *The Last Tycoon:* The Spiegelian Theory of Filmmaking." *American Film,* 1 (March 1976), 8–14.

Anderson, W. R. "Fitzgerald After *Tender Is the Night.*" *Fitzgerald/Hemingway Annual* (1979), 39–63.

Arnold, Edwin T. "The Motion Picture as Metaphor in the Works of Fitzgerald." *Fitzgerald/Hemingway Annual* (1977), 43–60.

Atkinson, Jennifer. "Fitzgerald's Marked Copy of *The Great Gatsby.*" *Fitzgerald/Hemingway Annual* (1970), 28–33.

Atkinson. "The Lost and Unpublished Stories of F. Scott Fitzgerald." *Fitzgerald/Hemingway Annual* (1971), 32–63.

Berryman, John. "F. Scott Fitzgerald." *The Kenyon Review,* 8 (Winter 1946), 103–112.

Bewley, Marius. "Scott Fitzgerald's Criticism of America." *Sewanee Review,* 62 (Spring 1954), 223–246. Expanded as "Scott Fitzgerald and the Collapse of the American Dream." *The Eccentric Design* by Bewley (New York: Columbia University Press, 1959).

Bicknell, John W. "The Waste Land of FSF." *Virginia Quarterly Review,* 30 (Autumn 1954), 556–572.

Bigsby, C. W. E. "The Two Identities of F. Scott Fitzgerald." *The American Novel and the Nineteen Twenties,* ed. Malcolm Bradbury and David Palmer (London: Arnold, 1971), 129–149.

Bishop, John Peale. "The Missing All." *Virginia Quarterly Review,* 13 (Winter 1937), 106–121.

Bruccoli, Matthew J. "Bibliographical Notes on F. Scott Fitzgerald's *The Beautiful and Damned.*" *Studies in Bibliography,* 13 (1960), 258–261.

Bruccoli. "Fitzgerald's Marked Copy of *This Side of Paradise.*" *Fitzgerald/Hemingway Annual* (1971), 64–70.

Bruccoli. " 'A Might Collation': Animadversions on the Text of F. Scott Fitzgerald." *Editing Twentieth Century Texts: Papers Given at the Editorial Conference, University of Toronto, November 1969,* ed. Francess G. Halpenny (Toronto: University of Toronto Press, 1972), 28–50.

Bruccoli. "The Perkins/Wilson Correspondence about Publication of *The Last Tycoon.*" *Fitzgerald/Hemingway Annual* (1978), pp. 63–66.

Bruccoli. "Zelda Fitzgerald's Lost Stories." *Fitzgerald/Hemingway Annual* (1979), pp. 123–126.

Bruccoli. "Getting It Right: The Publishing Process and the Correction of Factual Errors—with Reference to *The Great Gatsby,*" *Essays in Honor of William B. Todd,* comp. Warner Barnes and Larry Carver (Austin: Harry Ransom Humanities Research Center, The University of Texas, 1991), 40–59; revised edition separately published (Columbia, S.C.: privately printed, 1994).

Bryer, Jackson R. "Four Decades of Fitzgerald Studies: The Best and the Brightest." *Twentieth Century Literature,* 26 (Summer 1980), 247–267.

Burhans, Clinton S. "Structure and Theme in *This Side of Paradise.*" *Journal of English and Germanic Philology,* 68 (October 1969), 605–624.

Carrithers, Gale H. "Fitzgerald's Triumph." Hoffman, 303–320.

Chase, Richard. "*The Great Gatsby.*" *The American Novel and Its Traditions* (Garden City, N.Y.: Doubleday, 1957), 162–167.

Corso, Joseph. "One Not-Forgotten Summer Night: Sources for Fictional Symbols of American Character in *The Great Gatsby.*" *Fitzgerald/Hemingway Annual* (1976), 9–34.

Cowley, Malcolm. "Third Act and Epilogue." *The New Yorker,* 21 (June 30, 1945), 53–54, 57–58.

Cowley. "The Scott Fitzgerald Story." *The New Republic,* 124 (February 12, 1951), 17–20.

Cowley. "Fitzgerald: The Double Man." *Saturday Review of Literature,* 34 (February 24, 1951), 9–10, 42–44.

Cowley. "F. Scott Fitzgerald: The Romance of Money." *Western Review,* 17 (Summer 1953), 245–255.

Doherty, William E. "*Tender Is the Night* and the 'Ode to a Nightingale.' " *Explorations of Literature,* ed. Rima D. Reck (Baton Rouge: Louisiana State University Press, 1966), 100–114.

Donaldson, Scott. "Scott Fitzgerald's Romance with the South." *Southern Literary Journal,* 5 (Spring 1973), 3–17.

Donaldson. "The Crisis of Fitzgerald's 'Crack-Up.' " *Twentieth Century Literature,* 26 (Summer 1980), 171–188.

Donaldson. "The Political Development of F. Scott Fitzgerald." *Prospects,* 6 (1981), 313–355.

Dos Passos, John. "Fitzgerald and the Press." *The New Republic,* 104 (February 17, 1941), 213.

Doyno, Victor A. "Patterns in *The Great Gatsby.*" *Modern Fiction Studies,* 12 (Winter 1966–67), 415–426.

Eble, Kenneth. "The Craft of Revision: *The Great Gatsby.*" *American Literature,* 36 (Autumn 1964), 315–326.

Elias, Amy J. "The Composition and Revision of Fitzgerald's *The Beautiful and Damned.*" *The Princeton University Library Chronicle,* 51 (Spring 1990), 245–266.

Emmitt, Robert J. "Love, Death and Resurrection in *The Great Gatsby.*" *Aeolian Harps,* ed. Donna G. and Douglas C. Fricke (Bowling Green, Ohio: Bowling Green University Press, 1976), 273–289.

Friedrich, Otto. "Reappraisals—F. Scott Fitzgerald: Money, Money, Money." *American Scholar,* 29 (Summer 1960), 392–405.

Fussell, Edwin S. "Fitzgerald's Brave New World." *ELH,* 19 (December 1952), 291–306.

Geismar, Maxwell. "F. Scott Fitzgerald: Orestes at the Ritz." *The Last of the Provincials* (Boston: Houghton Mifflin, 1943), 287–352.

Gervais, Ronald J. "The Socialist and the Silk Stockings:

Fitzgerald's Double Allegiance." *Mosaic,* 15 (June 1982), 79–92.

Good, Dorothy Ballweg. " 'A Romance and a Reading List': The Literary References in *This Side of Paradise,*" *Fitzgerald/Hemingway Annual* (1976), 35–64.

Goodwin, Donald W. "The Alcoholism of Fitzgerald." *Journal of the American Medical Association,* 212 (April 6, 1970), 86–90.

Grenberg, Bruce L. "Fitzgerald's 'Figured Curtain': Personality and History in *Tender Is the Night.*" *Fitzgerald/Hemingway Annual* (1978), 105–136.

Hanzo, Thomas A. "The Theme and the Narrator of *The Great Gatsby.*" *Modern Fiction Studies,* 2 (Winter 1956–57), 183–190.

Harding, D. W. "Scott Fitzgerald." *Scrutiny,* 18 (Winter 1951–52), 166–174.

Harvey, W. J. "Theme and Texture in *The Great Gatsby.*" *English Studies,* 38, no. 1 (1957), 12–20.

Haywood, Lynn. "Historical Notes for *This Side of Paradise.*" *Resources for American Literary Study,* 10 (Autumn 1980), 191–208.

Holman, C. Hugh. "Fitzgerald's Changes on the Southern Belle: The Tarleton Trilogy." Bryer (1982), 53–64.

Irish, Carol. "The Myth of Success in Fitzgerald's Boyhood." *Studies in American Fiction,* 1 (Autumn 1973), 176–187.

Kenner, Hugh. "The Promised Land." *A Homemade World* (New York: Knopf, 1975), 20–49.

Kuehl, John. "Scott Fitzgerald: Romantic and Realist." *Texas Studies in Literature and Language,* 1 (Autumn 1959), 412–426.

Kuehl. "Scott Fitzgerald's Reading." *The Princeton University Library Chronicle,* 22 (Winter 1961), 58–89.

Kuehl. "Scott Fitzgerald's Critical Opinions." *Modern Fiction Studies,* 7 (Spring 1961), 3–18.

Kuhnle, John H. "*The Great Gatsby* as Pastoral Elegy." *Fitzgerald/Hemingway Annual* (1978), 141–154.

Larsen, Erling. "The Geography of Fitzgerald's Saint Paul." *Carleton Miscellany,* 13 (Spring-Summer 1973), 3–30.

Lehan, Richard D. "F. Scott Fitzgerald and Romantic Destiny." *Twentieth Century Literature,* 26 (Summer 1980), 137–156.

LeVot, André. "Fitzgerald in Paris." *Fitzgerald/Hemingway Annual* (1973), 49–68.

Lewis, Janet. "Fitzgerald's 'Philippe, Count of Darkness.' " *Fitzgerald/Hemingway Annual* (1975), 7–32.

MacKendrick, Paul L. "The Great Gatsby and Trimalchio." *Classical Journal,* 45 (April 1950), 307–314.

Mann, Charles. "F. Scott Fitzgerald's Critique of *A Farewell to Arms.*" *Fitzgerald/Hemingway Annual* (1976), 140–153.

Margolies, Alan. "Fitzgerald's Work in the Film Studios." *The Princeton University Library Chronicle,* 32 (Winter 1971), 81–110.

Mizener, Arthur. "The Maturity of Scott Fitzgerald." *Sewanee Review,* 67 (Autumn 1959), 658–675.

Mizener. "Scott Fitzgerald and the 1920's." *Minnesota Review,* 1 (Winter 1961), 161–174.

Mizener. "The Voice of Scott Fitzgerald's Prose." *Essays and Studies,* 16 (1963), 56–67.

Morris, Wright. "The Ability to Function: A Reappraisal of Fitzgerald and Hemingway." *New World Writing,* no. 13 (June 1958), 34–51. Reprinted in *The Territory Ahead* by Morris (New York: Harcourt, Brace, 1958).

Moyer, Kermit W. "*The Great Gatsby:* Fitzgerald's Meditation on American History." *Fitzgerald/Hemingway Annual* (1972), 43–58.

Moyer. "Fitzgerald's Two Unfinished Novels: The Count and the Tycoon in Spenglerian Perspective." *Contemporary Literature,* 15 (Spring 1974), 238–356.

O'Hara, John. "On F. Scott Fitzgerald." *"An Artist Is His Own Fault": John O'Hara on Writers and Writing,* ed. Matthew J. Bruccoli (Carbondale, Ill.: Southern Illinois University Press, 1977), 135–154.

Ornstein, Robert. "Scott Fitzgerald's Fable of East and West." *College English,* 18 (December 1956), 139–143.

Piper, Henry Dan. "Scott Fitzgerald's Prep-School Writings," *The Princeton University Library Chronicle,* 17 (Autumn 1955), 1–10.

Podis, Leonard A. "The Unreality of Reality: Metaphor in *The Great Gatsby.*" *Style,* 11 (Winter 1977), 56–72.

Prigozy, Ruth. "Poor Butterfly: F. Scott Fitzgerald and Popular Music." *Prospects,* 2 (1976), 41–67.

Raleigh, John Henry. "F. Scott Fitzgerald's *The Great Gatsby:* Legendary Bases and Allegorical Significance." *University of Kansas City Review,* 24 (Autumn 1957), 55–58.

Rosenfeld, Paul. "F. Scott Fitzgerald." *Men Seen* (New York: Dial, 1925), 215–224.

Samuels, Charles T. "The Greatness of 'Gatsby.' " *Massachusetts Review,* 7 (Autumn 1966), 783–794.

Sanders, Barbara G. "Structural Imagery in *The Great Gatsby:* Metaphor and Matrix." *Linguistics in Literature,* 1, no. 1 (1975), 53–75.

Savage, D. S. "The Significance of F. Scott Fitzgerald." *Arizona Quarterly,* 8 (Autumn 1952), 197–210.

Schoenwald, Richard L. "F. Scott Fitzgerald as John Keats." *Boston University Studies in English,* 3 (Spring 1957), 12–21.

Schwartz, Delmore. "The Dark Night of F. Scott Fitzgerald." *The Nation,* 172 (February 24, 1951), 180–182.

Scribner, Charles, III. "Celestial Eyes: From Metamorphosis to Masterpiece." *The Princeton University Library Chronicle,* 53 (Winter 1992), 140–155.

Scrimgeour, Gary J. "Against *The Great Gatsby.*" *Criticism,* 8 (Winter 1966), 75–86.

Stallman, R. W. "Conrad and *The Great Gatsby.*" *Twentieth Century Literature,* 1 (April 1955), 5–12.

Stark, Bruce R. "The Intricate Pattern in *The Great*

Gatsby." *Fitzgerald/Hemingway Annual* (1974), 51–61.

Steinbrink, Jeffrey. " 'Boats Against the Current': Mortality and the Myth of Renewal in *The Great Gatsby.*" *Twentieth Century Literature,* 26 (Summer 1980), 157–170.

Tanselle, G. Thomas and Jackson R. Bryer. "*The Great Gatsby:* A Study in Literary Reputation." *New Mexico Quarterly,* 33 (Winter 1963–64), 409–425.

Thurber, James. "Scott in Thorns." *Reporter,* 4 (April 17, 1951), 35–38. Reprinted in *Credos and Curios* by Thurber (New York: Harper & Row, 1962).

Trilling, Lionel. "F. Scott Fitzgerald." *The Liberal Imagination* (New York: Viking, 1950), 243–254.

Trilling. "Fitzgerald Plain." *The New Yorker,* 26 (February 3, 1951), 90–92.

Troy, William. "Scott Fitzgerald—The Authority of Failure." *Accent,* 6 (Autumn 1945), 56–60.

Turnbull, Andrew W. "Scott Fitzgerald at La Paix." *The New Yorker,* 32 (April 7, 1956), 98–109.

Turnbull. "Further Notes on Fitzgerald at La Paix." *The New Yorker,* 32 (November 17, 1956), 153–165.

Van Antwerp, Margaret A., ed. "F. Scott Fitzgerald." *Dictionary of Literary Biography Documentary Series,* Vol. 1 (Detroit, Mich.: Bruccoli Clark/Gale, 1982), 239–290.

Watkins, Floyd C. "Fitzgerald's Jay Gatz and Young Ben Franklin." *New England Quarterly,* 27 (June 1954), 249–252.

Weir, Charles, Jr. " 'An Invite With Gilded Edges.' " *Virginia Quarterly Review,* 20 (Winter 1944), 100–113.

Wescott, Glenway. "The Moral of Scott Fitzgerald." *The New Republic,* 104 (February 17, 1941), 213–217.

Wilson, Edmund. "The Literary Spotlight—VI: F. Scott Fitzgerald." *The Bookman,* 55 (March 1922), 20–25.

Young, Philip and Charles W. Mann. "Fitzgerald's *Sun Also Rises.*" *Fitzgerald/Hemingway Annual* (1970), 1–9.

Study Guides

Altena, I. *Notes on Scott Fitzgerald's The Great Gatsby.* London: Methuen Educational, 1976.

Cooperman, Stanley. *F. Scott Fitzgerald's Tender Is the Night (A Critical Commentary).* New York: Monarch, 1965.

Cooperman. *F. Scott Fitzgerald's The Great Gatsby (A Critical Commentary).* New York: Monarch, 1965.

F. Scott Fitzgerald: The Great Gatsby Notes. Toronto: Coles, 1983.

Fowler, Austin. *F. Scott Fitzgerald's The Great Gatsby: A Critical Analysis in Depth.* New York: Barrister, 1966.

Goethals, Thomas R. *A Critical Commentary: The Great Gatsby.* Study Master. New York: American R.D.M. Corporation, 1963.

Goethals. *A Critical Commentary: Tender Is the Night.* Study Master. New York: American R.D.M. Corporation, 1964.

Handley, Graham. *Brodie's Notes on F. Scott Fitzgerald's The Great Gatsby.* London: Pan, 1978.

Northman, Phillip. *The Great Gatsby Notes.* Lincoln, Neb.: Cliffs Notes, 1966.

Ping, Tang Soo. *Notes on The Great Gatsby: F. Scott Fitzgerald.* London & Beirut: Longman/York Press, 1980.

Poston, Carol H. *Tender Is the Night Notes.* Lincoln, Neb.: Cliffs Notes, 1974.

Schwenker, Gretchen L. *Notes on Tender is the Night: Scott Fitzgerald.* London & Beirut: Longman/York Press, 1980.

Taylor, Douglas. *The Great Gatsby: Review Notes.* Boston: Ivy Notes, 1966.

White, Sidney Howard. *Barron's Simplified Approach to Fitzgerald: The Great Gatsby.* Woodbury, N.Y.: Barron's Educational Series, 1968.

Videorecordings

Bruccoli, Matthew J. *An Introduction to F. Scott Fitzgerald's Fiction.* Modern American Literature—Eminent Scholar/Teachers Series. Detroit: Omnigraphics, 1988. Videorecording with lecture guide by Thomas Jackson Rice.

Bruccoli. *Reading F. Scott Fitzgerald's The Great Gatsby.* Modern American Literature—Eminent Scholar/Teachers Series. Detroit: Omnigraphics, 1988. Videorecording with lecture guide by Thomas Jackson Rice.

BACKGROUND

Baker, Carlos. *Ernest Hemingway: A Life Story*. New York: Scribners, 1969.

Baker, ed. *Ernest Hemingway: Selected Letters, 1917–1961*. New York: Scribners, 1981.

Baughman, Judith S., ed. *American Decades: 1920–1929*. Detroit: Manly/Gale, 1995.

Baxter, John. *Hollywood in the Thirties*. London: Tantivy Press, 1968.

Beach, Sylvia. *Shakespeare & Company*. New York: Harcourt, Brace, 1959.

Berg, Scott. *Max Perkins: Editor of Genius*. New York: Congdon/Dutton, 1978.

Bondi, Victor, ed. *American Decades: 1930–1939*. Detroit: Manly/Gale, 1995.

Bruccoli, Matthew J., ed., with Robert W. Trogdon. *The Only Thing That Counts: The Ernest Hemingway/ Maxwell Perkins Correspondence*. New York: Scribners, 1996.

Bruccoli, Matthew J., and Robert W. Trodgon, eds. *American Expatriate Writers: Paris in the Twenties* (Detroit: Bruccoli Clark Layman/Gale Research, 1997). Dictionary of Literary Biography Documentary Series 15.

Cowley, Malcolm. *Exile's Return: A Literary Odyssey of the 1920s*. New York: Norton, 1934. Revised edition, New York: Viking, 1951.

Cowley. *A Second Flowering: Works and Days of the Lost Generation*. New York: Viking, 1973.

Cowley. *Unshaken Friend: A Profile of Maxwell Perkins*. Boulder, Colo.: Roberts Rinehart, 1985.

Cowley, Malcolm, and Robert Cowley, eds. *Fitzgerald and the Jazz Age*. New York: Scribners, 1966.

Delaney, John, ed. *The House of Scribner, 1905–1930* (Detroit: Bruccoli Clark Layman/Gale Research, 1997). Dictionary of Literary Biography Documentary Series 16.

Donnelly, Honoria M., with Richard N. Billings. *Sara and Gerald: Villa America and After*. New York: Times Books, 1982.

Hoffman, Frederick J. *The Twenties: American Writing in the Postwar Decade*. Revised edition, New York: Collier, 1962.

Kruse, Horst. *Die Romane der "flaming youth"; ein Beitrag zur Interpretation des amerikanischen Romans von 1920 bis 1930*. Heidelberg: C. Winter, 1962.

Lanahan, Eleanor. *Scottie, the Daughter of . . . : The Life of Frances Scott Fitzgerald Lanahan Smith*. New York: HarperCollins, 1995.

Meyers, Jeffrey. *Edmund Wilson: A Biography*. Boston: Houghton Mifflin, 1995.

Miller, Linda Patterson, ed. *Letters from the Lost Generation: Gerald and Sara Murphy and Friends*. New Brunswick, N.J.: Rutgers University Press, 1991.

Reynolds, Michael. *Hemingway: The Paris Years*. Oxford & New York: Basil Blackwell, 1989.

Rood, Karen Lane, ed., with foreword by Malcolm Cowley. *American Writers in Paris, 1920–1939; Dictionary of Literary Biography*, vol. 4. Detroit: Bruccoli Clark/Gale, 1980.

Spindler, Elizabeth Carroll. *John Peale Bishop: A Biography*. Morgantown, W.Va.: West Virginia University Library, 1980.

Toll, Seymour I. *A Judge Uncommon: A Life of John Biggs, Jr.* Philadelphia, Pa.: Legal Communications, 1993.

Tomkins, Calvin. *Living Well Is the Best Revenge*. New York: Viking, 1971.

Westbrook, Robert. *Intimate Lies: F. Scott Fitzgerald and Sheilah Graham*. New York: HarperCollins, 1995.

Wheelock, John Hall, ed. *Editor to Author: The Letters of Maxwell Perkins*. New York: Scribners, 1979.

Wilson, Edmund. *The Shores of Light*. New York: Farrar, Straus and Young, 1952.

Wilson. *The Twenties*, ed. Leon Edel. New York: Farrar, Straus and Giroux, 1975.

Wilson. *The Thirties: From Notebooks and Diaries of the Period*. New York: Farrar, Straus and Giroux, 1980.

Yardley, Jonathan. *Ring: A Biography of Ring Lardner*. New York: Random House, 1977.

ADAPTATIONS OF FITZGERALD'S WORK

Movies

"Head and Shoulders" (retitled *The Chorus Girl's Romance*). Metro, 1920. Scenario by Percy Heath; directed by William P. Dowlan. Photoplay adapted by Ethel Rosemon in "The Chorus Girl's Romance," *Moving Picture Stories,* 16 (October 1, 1920), 6–9.

"Myra Meets His Family" (retitled *The Husband Hunter*). Fox, 1920. Scenario by Joseph F. Poland; directed by Howard M. Mitchell.

"The Offshore Pirate." Metro, 1921. Directed by Dallas M. Fitzgerald.

The Beautiful and Damned. Warner Brothers, 1922. Adapted by Olga Printzlau; directed by William Seiter.

"The Camel's Back" (retitled *Conductor 1492*). Warner Brothers, 1924. Story by Johnny Hines; directed by Charles and Frank Hines.

The Great Gatsby (from the Owen Davis play). Famous Players, 1926. Script by Becky Gardiner; adaptation by Elizabeth Mechan; directed by Herbert Brenon.

"The Pusher-in-the-Face." Paramount-Famous-Lasky, 1928.

The Great Gatsby. Paramount, 1949. Screenplay by Cyril Hume and Richard Maibaum; directed by Elliott Nugent.

"Babylon Revisited" (retitled *The Last Time I Saw Paris*). MGM, 1954. Screenplay by Philip G. Epstein, Julius J. Epstein, and Richard Brooks; directed by Richard Brooks.

Tender Is the Night. Twentieth Century-Fox, 1962. Screenplay by Ivan Moffat; directed by Henry King.

The Great Gatsby. Paramount, 1974. Screenplay by Francis Ford Coppola; directed by Jack Clayton.

The Last Tycoon. Paramount, 1976. Screenplay by Harold Pinter; directed by Elia Kazan.

Plays

The Young and Beautiful by Sally Benson. Based on the Josephine Perry stories. New York: Samuel French, 1956. The play opened at the Longacre Theatre in New York, October 1, 1955.

Three Hours Between Planes by Elihu Winer. New York: Samuel French, 1958.

Bernice Bobs Her Hair by D. D. Brooke. Chicago: The Dramatic Publishing Company, 1982.

Television Productions

"Bernice Bobs Her Hair." Learning in Focus, 1977. Written and directed by Joan Micklin Silver.

"Tender Is the Night." Showtime/BBC, 1985. Script by Dennis Potter; directed by Robert Knights.

"The Last of the Belles." A Herbert Brodkin production, written for television by James Costigan. North Hollywood: Hollywood Select Video, 1994. Distributed by Timeless Video.

INDEX

NOTE: **Boldface** numbers indicate primary discussion of a topic. <u>Underlined</u> numbers indicate illustrations. The following abbreviations are used: FSF = F. Scott Fitzgerald; ZF = Zelda Fitzgerald; B&D = *The Beautiful and Damned*; GG = *The Great Gatsby*; LT or LOLT = *The Last Tycoon* or *The Love of the Last Tycoon*; TITN = *Tender Is the Night*; TSOP = *This Side of Paradise*.

A

Abbot **1**, 21, 97
Abbot, Charley **1**, 57, 215
Abbot, Hamilton (Ham) **1**, 150
Abby **1**
Abercrombie **1**, 259–260
Abercrombie, Bill **1**
Abrams, Mrs. **1**, 245–246
"Absolution" **1**, 2, 4, 100, 152, 166, 197, 223, 228, 233
"The Adjuster" **1–2**, 23, 53, 117, 137, 168, 208, 273
"The Adolescent Marriage" **2**, 38, 94, 198, 233, 242, 271
"Afternoon of an Author" **2**, 48–49, 68, 74, 227, 228
Afternoon of an Author (Mizener, ed.) **2**, 167
Agge, Prince **2**, 154, 155
Ahearn, Mr. and Mrs. Clarence **2**, 51, 156, 194
"Air Raid" **2**, 121, 233
"A La Carte" 90
"An Alcoholic Case" **2**, 23, 34, 119, 177, 233
"Aldous Huxley's 'Crome Yellow'" **2**, 72, 74
Alix **2**
Allenby **3**
Allerdyce, Mrs. Thomas *see* Caroline; Dare, Alicia
Allison, Parker **3**
All the Sad Young Men **2–3**, <u>3</u>, 9, 52, 92, 123, 132, 143, 214, 228, 275
Altwater, Percy **3**, 240
Ambassador Hotel (Los Angeles) **3**, 120, 148, 172, 264
Ambler, Joe **3**
American **3**, 155, 168, 232
The American Mercury 1, **4**, 44–45, 128, 134, 164, 173, 228

Ames, Betty **4**, 130
Ames, Ellsworth (Ellie) **4**, 150
Ames, Ted **4**
Amy **4**, 124, 222, 280
Anderson, Sherwood **4**, 35, 74, 113, 227, <u>227</u>
Andros, Ede **4**, 9, 160
Andros, Edith **4**, 9, 160
Andros, John **4**, 9, 160, 184
Andy **4**, 109
"The Ants of Princeton" **4**
Appleton **4**, 45, 234
Appleton, Lila **4**, 45, 234
Appleton, Mrs. **4**, 45, 111, 234
Appleton, Warren **4**, 45, 172, 234
apprenticeship **4–6**
Aquilla's brother **6**
Aquilla's sister **6**
Armstrong, Margaret **6**, 19, 22, 117, 268
Aronstael **6**
Asheville, North Carolina *see also* Highland Hospital; Park Grove Inn, **6**
 FSF in **6**, 11, 20, 30, 52, 76, 80, 84, 106, 207, 211, 226
Ashton, Cecilia **6**
Assorted Spirits **6–7**
 characters in 37–38, 117, 124–125, 139, 170, 180, 225, 231, 271, 280
 in collected works 75
 for Elizabethan Club 5, 6, 55, 67, 195, 272
 at White Bear Yacht Club 6, 55, 272
Astoria (New York City) **7**, 65
"At Your Age" **7**, 31, 63, 131, 137, 150, 198, 219, 228, 231, 243
"Auction—Model 1934" (FSF-ZF) **7**, 44, 68, 88, 280

Augustine **7**
Aunt Georgie **7**
Aunt Gladys **7**
Aunt Jo **197**
Aunt Mamie **7**
Aunt Rose **7**
"The Author's Apology" **7–8**, 72, 129, 252,
"Author's House" 2, **8**, 68, 74, 90, 207
"An Author's Mother" **8**, 85, 133–134, 199

B

"Babes in Wonderland" **9**, 121
"Babes in the Woods" **9**
 characters in 34, 129, 139, 198, 249
 in collected works 4, 9
 manuscripts of 74
 in *Nassau Literary Magazine* 6, 9, 173, 230
 recycling of 6, 9, 173, 249, 252, 253
 in *Smart Set* 9, 230, 251
 sources for 139
"Babylon Revisited" **9**
 characters in 2, 170, 190, 193, 205, 212, 221–222, 268
 in collected works 9, 23, 197, 228, 233, 238
 and *Colliers* 39
 critical analysis of 9
 earnings from 41, 42, 43
 film rights for 41, 42, 43, 121–122
 and FSF as short story writer 228
 FSF's views about 39
 FSF's writing of 69, 151, 235

illustrations in 127
manuscripts of 74
in *Post* 9, 127, 218, 228, 232, 235
recycling of 243
screenplay for 9, 42
setting for 70
sources for 170, 221
"The Baby Party" 2, 4, **9**, 111, 160, 184, 197, 233
Bach, Mr. ("A Man in the Way") **9**
Bach, Mr. ("Zone of Accident") **9**
Bacon, Doctor **10**
Baedeker, Miss **10**
Baer, Doctor Bill **10**, 155
Bailey, John Boynton **10**, 70, 109, 138, 186, 230
Baily **10**, 158
Baird, Tudor **10**
Baker, Benjamin May **10**, 133, 165
Baker, Ellen **10**, 228, 233, 264
Baker, George **10**, 58, 161
Baker, Jordan **10**, 19, 29, 100, 101, 102, 103, 104, 131, 150, 185, 191
Baker, Mrs. **10**
Baker, William H. **10**
 dancing class of 4, 6, 10, 19, 23, 106, 117, 130, 207, 223, 226
"Ballet Shoes" **10**
Ballion, Paul **10**, 137
Baltimore, Maryland **10–11**
 FSF in 10–11, 20, 31, 76, 80, 98, 124, 143, 165, 169, 233, 269
 FSF's views about 11
 in FSF writings 50, 169
"The Baltimore Anti-Christ" **10**, 74, 164
Bangs, Angelina **11**
Banizon, Mr. **11**, 189

Bannerman, Marie 1, **11**, 31, 52, 98, 134, 139
Baptiste **11**
Barban, Tommy **11**, 38, 98, 109, 163, 245
 McKisco duel with 32, 163, 246
 Nicole Diver's affair and marriage to 11, 58, 59, 249
 sources for 11, 26, 115, 119, 136, 242
 and TITN storyline 246–249
Barkis, Private **11**
Barley **11**
Barlotto **11**
Barlow, Mr. **11**
Barnes, Ed **11**, 129, 161, 222, 229, 234, 264, 275
Barnes, Rachael Jerryl **11**, 15, 16, 40, 276
Barnes, Rodman **11**
Barney, Charles **11**
Barnfield, Teddy **11**, 17
Barr, Bert (Bertha Weinberg Goldstein) **11–12**, 156, 203
Barron, Joseph **12**
Barrows, Colonel **12**, 130
Bartholomew **12**
Bartlett, Dolly **12**, 250, 256
Bartney, Walter Hamilton (William) **12**, 186, 229
Barton, Mr. **12**
"Basil and Cleopatra" **12**
 characters in 4, 19, 34, 38, 60, 94, 136, 145, 146, 268
 in collected works 2, 12
 in *Post* 12, 91, 111, 175, 186, 221, 232
 recycling of 12, 19, 242
 sources for 10, 139
Basil Duke Lee stories
 see also specific story